Explorations in LITERATURE

for Christian Schools®

Second Edition

Raymond A. St. John

Bob Jones University Press, Greenville, South Carolina 29614

NOTE:
The fact that materials produced by other publishers may be referred to in this volume does not constitute an endorsement of the content or theological position of materials produced by such publishers. Any references and ancillary materials are listed as an aid to the student or the teacher and in an attempt to maintain the accepted academic standards of the publishing industry.

EXPLORATIONS IN LITERATURE for Christian Schools®
Second Edition

Raymond A. St. John, Ph.D.
William L. Yost, Ph.D., contributing author

Produced in cooperation with the Bob Jones University Division of English Language and Literature of the College of Arts and Science, the School of Religion, and Bob Jones Junior High School.

for Christian Schools is a registered trademark of Bob Jones University Press.

© 1998 Bob Jones University Press
Greenville, South Carolina 29614
First Edition © 1984 Bob Jones University Press

ISBN 1-59166-648-1

15 14 13 12 11 10 9 8 7 6 5 4 3 2 1

Acknowledgments

A careful effort has been made to trace the ownership of selections included in this textbook in order to secure permission to reprint copyright material and to make full acknowledgment of their use. If any error or omission has occurred, it is purely inadvertent and will be corrected in subsequent editions, provided written notification is made to the publisher.

Alfred A. Knopf, Inc.: "Godolphin Horne" by Hilaire Belloc. From *Cautionary Verses* by Hilaire Belloc. Published in 1941 by Alfred A. Knopf, Inc.

Ann Elmo Agency, Inc.: "Most Valuable Player" by W. L. Heath from *Adventures for Readers,* Book II, 1963. Reprinted by permission of the Ann Elmo Agency, Inc.

Arkham House Publishers, Inc.: "Midnight Storm" from *Rendezvous in a Landscape* by August Derleth, 1952. Reprinted by permission of Arkham House Publishers, Inc.

Augsburg Publishing House: "Love Story, Sort Of" by Phyllis Reynolds Naylor. "Love Story, Sort Of" reprinted by permission from *Change in the Wind* by Phyllis Reynolds Naylor, copyright Augsburg Publishing House.

Bantam Doubleday Dell: "Being a Public Character" by Don Marquis copyright 1917 by the Crowell Publishing Company from *The Revolt of the Oyster* by Don Marquis.

Barthold Fles Literary Agency: "The Life and Death of a Western Gladiator" by Charles Finney, first published in *Harper's Magazine,* 1958. Used by permission.

Brandt and Brandt: "A Kind of Murder" by Hugh Pentecost. First published in *Ellery Queen Mystery Magazine* © 1962 by Davis Publications, Inc. Reprinted by permission of Brandt & Brandt Literary Agents, Inc.

"Nancy Hanks" by Rosemary & Stephen Vincent Benét. Holt Rhinehart & Winston, Inc. Copyright, 1933, by Rosemary & Stephen Vincent Benét. Copyright renewed © 1961 by Rosemary Carr Benét. Reprinted by permission of Brandt & Brandt Literary Agents, Inc.

Childrens Press: "Martin and Abraham Lincoln" by Catherine Cate Coblentz. Reprinted by permission of Childrens Press.

Christian Life Missions: "Sioux Trouble" by Bernard Palmer. Reprinted by permission from *The Gift of His Heart and Other Short Stories,* Christian Life Missions, 396 E. St. Charles Rd. Wheaton, IL 60188.

Christian Reformed Church in North America: "Death" by Verna K. Peterson. Copyright © 1973, Board of Publications, Christian Reformed Church in North America. Reprinted from *The Banner* (June 22, 1973) with permission.

John Ciardi: "Speed Adjustments" by John Ciardi. From *The Monster Den* by John Ciardi. Copyright 1963 by John Ciardi. Reprinted by permission of the author.

Concordia Publishing House: "The Friend Inside" by T. Morris Longstreth. From *Treasury of Christian Literature.* © 1949 Concordia Publishing House. Used by permission.

Curtis Brown, Ltd.: "All Yankees Are Liars" by Eric Knight. Reprinted by permission of Curtis Brown Ltd. Copyright © 1938 by the Curtis Publishing Co. Copyright renewed © 1966 by Jere Knight, Betty Noyes Knight, Winifred Knight Mewborn, and Jennie Knight Moore. First appeared in *The Saturday Evening Post.* Published by the Curtis Publishing Company.

"Gold-Mounted Guns" by F. R. Buckley. Reprinted by permission of Curtis Brown Associates, Inc. Copyright © 1922, 1949 by F. R. Buckley.

"Slurvian Self-Taught" by John Davenport. Reprinted by permission of Curtis Brown Associates, Inc. Copyright © 1949 by John Davenport, originally appeared in *The New Yorker.*

Dodd, Mead & Company: "How We Kept Mother's Day" by Stephen Leacock. Reprinted by permission of Dodd, Mead & Company, Inc. from *Laugh with Leacock* by Stephen Leacock. Copyright 1930 by Dodd, Mead & Company, Inc. Copyright renewed 1958 by George Leacock.

Edna St. Vincent Millay Society: "The Courage That My Mother Had" by Edna St. Vincent Millay. From *Collected Poems,* HarperCollins. Copyright © 1954, 1982 by Norma Millay Ellis. All rights reserved. Reprinted by permission of Elizabeth Barnett, literary executor.

Edward B. Marks Music Company: "Lift Ev'ry Voice and Sing" by James Weldon Johnson. © Copyright Edward B. Marks Music Corporation. Used by permission.

EPM Publications, Inc.: "Our Blessed Land" by James J. Kilpatrick. © 1977 Op Ed, Inc., from *The Foxes' Union,* EPM Publications, Inc., McLean, Virginia 22101.

Esquire Associates: "Uncle Randolph's Buried Treasure" by Dan Wickenden. Reprinted with permission from *Esquire* (January 1939). Copyright © 1938 by Esquire Associates.

Lewis Gardner: "How to Avoid Contact" by Lewis Gardner. Copyright © 1973 by Lewis Gardner. Reprinted by permission.

Girl Scouts of the U.S.A.: "Betsy Dowdy's Ride" from *The American Girl* July 1938. Reprinted by permission of the Girl Scouts of the U.S.A.

"One of Us" from *The American Girl* May 1941. Reprinted by permission of the Girl Scouts of the U.S.A.

Granada Publishing Limited: "The Attack" and "Castaways" from *Survive the Savage Sea* by Dougal Robertson. Reprinted with permission of Granada Publishing Limited.

Harcourt Brace Jovanovich: "Mr. K*A*P*L*A*N, the Comparative and Superlative" by Leonard Q. Ross. From *The Education of H*Y*M*A*N K*A*P*L*A*N* by Leonard Q. Ross, copyright 1937 by Harcourt Brace Jovanovich, Inc.; renewed 1965 by Leo Rosten. Reprinted by permission of the publisher.

"Primer Lesson" by Carl Sandburg. From *Slabs of the Sunburnt West* by Carl Sandburg, copyright 1922 by Harcourt Brace Jovanovich, Inc.; renewed 1950 by Carl Sandburg. Reprinted by permission of the publisher.

Harold Ober Associates: "Mother's Hallowe'en Trick" by Sherwood Anderson. Reprinted by permission of Harold Ober Associates Incorporated. Copyright © 1924 by W. B. Huebsch, Inc. Renewed 1951 by Eleanor Copenhaver Anderson.

3 GENEROSITY

4 OUR LAND

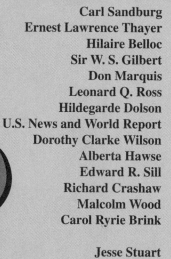

1

Courage

Courage is not just the force behind spectacular public acts but is also the motivation to carry out deeds hardly noticeable to others.

Courage

In Los Angeles a short time ago, a citizen reacted with what we often call true courage. While driving beside a roadside park, he saw a blind man being mugged. As he rushed to the rescue, the attacker fled. The good citizen did not give up, though. Risking his life, he gave chase, first in his car and then on foot. Finally he caught the mugger and then held him until police arrived.

An eighteen-year-old Canadian nearly paid the ultimate price for his courage—his life. While he was hiking in British Columbia's Glacier National Park with his girlfriend, a mother grizzly attacked them. With one blow it knocked the boy unconscious. Then it began to bite and tear at the girl. When the boy regained his senses, he leaped onto the bear and stabbed it in the neck with his hunting knife. At this the enraged animal turned its full fury on him, grabbing him like a toy between its front paws and squeezing him. Then with a violent swat at his head, the grizzly peeled off a large section of the boy's hair and scalp. Next it wrapped its front legs around him and rolled to the bottom of a gully. There it repeatedly slashed at the boy's face with its claws. When the boy became still, the bear scraped dirt and leaves over him and shuffled away. It took over a thousand stitches—and later, more than forty operations—to repair the damage to the boy's face and head. Surprised at the public recognition he received, the boy said that he had done nothing heroic. He had not even considered running away and leaving his friend at the mercy of the bear.

Heroes like these often receive public honor. In fact, since its founding in 1904, the Carnegie Hero Fund Commission has awarded more than eight thousand medals to deserving persons in the United States, Canada, and Europe. To qualify for the award, a person must have performed an act of unusual courage in saving human life.

Even though dramatic, a public act of courage is not any more outstanding than many a private act. Those who fight against severe physical disabilities, for instance, display courage as glorious as those who risk their lives. Although Glenn Cunningham was crippled by injuries resulting from a schoolhouse fire, he courageously overcame his disabilities to become a record holder in the mile run. Helen Keller, both blind and deaf, has inspired thousands with her courageous triumph over her disabilities.

Those who stand for right, especially in the face of opposition, are also truly courageous. This type of courage requires us to deny ourselves—our own wishes, fears, and embarrassment—and to stand up for our convictions, sometimes even against our friends. Perhaps of all types of courage this type is the most difficult to practice consistently.

The Bible states important principles about Christians and courage. It commands us to be of good courage and to be strong. It also makes clear that our strength lies in the confidence that comes from God's presence with us. Although the world recognizes the relationship between strength and courage, it ignores God, the source of our strength. The psalmist says, "Wait on the Lord: be of good courage, and he shall strengthen thine heart: wait, I say, on the Lord" (Ps. 27:14).

Heroes of the Bible reflect different types of courage in the midst of crisis. David dared to challenge the Philistine giant Goliath. The young shepherd's boldness in the Lord's strength encouraged the frightened army of Israel and led to a great victory. Facing a life of captivity by his nation's enemies, Daniel quietly decided to obey God when the pagan king made a law that conflicted with God's commands. Josiah, who had the Scriptures read to his people for the first time in several generations, bravely turned the Jews back toward God. His determination to seek God helped bring revival to Israel.

The Bible also gives us examples of men who lacked courage. Although not much is said about Demas, the Bible does tell us that he forsook the faith after he had served for a time with Paul (II Tim. 4:10). At Jesus' trial Peter lacked the courage to admit his association with his Lord. But unlike Demas, Peter confessed his sin and ever after spoke boldly for Christ, even dying for Him. The ten spies who returned with Caleb and Joshua after their mission into Canaan lacked the courage to trust God's promises for victory in the Promised Land. Their cowardice was contagious, for all the people supported them.

To live courageously demands wholehearted commitment. Some Christians profess to have the courage to die for Christ, but they lack the courage to live daily for Him. In the excerpt from *John and Betty Stam: A Story of Triumph,* you will see the calm resolve of two twentieth-century martyrs whose courageous deaths for Christ came from the confidence they had gained through living for Him. Not all who make courageous decisions to do right, however, carry through their decisions. Like Demas, they begin well, but they falter. Have you ever made a resolution for a new beginning but then found yourself wavering after a short while? Do you know someone who failed to overcome a problem because his friends influenced him to make wrong choices? This weakness appears in "A Kind of Murder," the story of a student who lacks the courage to continue doing right.

Courage is not just the force behind spectacular public acts. It is also the motivation to carry out private deeds hardly noticeable to others. For Christians, courage in our own strength is false courage (I Cor. 10:12), a guarantee of failure. "Fight the good fight with all thy might," declares the hymn writer; "Christ is thy strength, and Christ thy right." Real courage comes from our desire to do what is right, from our confidence in God's working through us, and from our doing what God wants regardless of the circumstances.

'Twas a Dark and Dreary Night

Patrick F. McManus

Laughter, doctors tell us, is good medicine. It is also an effective way to expose human weaknesses without giving undue offense. In the following selection, the author uses humor to expose his own youthful fear. In doing so he also shows us the dangers in pretending to be courageous when we are not.

Back during my single-digit ages, I often thought about running away and joining the French Foreign Legion.* The uniform was nice, and I liked the idea of riding horses and camels across the desert. Only one thing bothered me. I wondered if the Legionnaires were issued night lights. My love of adventure had its limits. I could easily imagine a battle-hardened Legionnaire sergeant reporting to his company commander, "Looks grim, sir. We've run out of food and water and the ammunition's nearly gone. Worse yet, we're

short on fuel for the men's night lights." With my luck, I'd be the one whose night light ran out of fuel first.

French Foreign Legion: an elite branch of the French military that performs special operations in foreign countries

---

I realized, of course, that fear of darkness was a serious flaw in my character. Since my character was riddled with flaws anyway, I didn't worry much about one more. Nevertheless, I didn't want my friends to find out I was afraid of the dark, and I went to great lengths to keep my secret from them. Take, for instance, the time Ronnie Ditmire came out to our farm to spend the night with me.

Ronnie had no sooner set foot in the house than he came up with the suggestion that he and I sleep out in the backyard. He said he'd had a lot of experience sleeping out in backyards in town, but this was his first opportunity to do so in the country.

"Yeah, well," I said. "Sure. In the dark, you mean? Sleep out. That would be fun. You don't mind a lot of black widow spiders crawling all over you, do you, Ronnie?"

"You got black widow spiders in your yard?"

Patting my hair back down, I retracted a few premature goosebumps. Unfortunately, my evil sister, the Troll, overheard our conversation and rushed to put in her oar and roil*the waters. "What are you telling Ronnie? There are no black widow spiders in our yard, you silly!"

---

roil: to make muddy; to stir up

"There are too," I said nervously.

"Ma!" the Troll roared. "Are there any black widow spiders in the yard?"

Mom, ever ready to rush to my defense, stuck her head out of the kitchen. "No, of course not. Where did you ever get a dumb idea like that?"

"See?" the Troll said.

"I thought there were," I said, smiling weakly at Ronnie.

"Good," he said. "Then we can sleep out in the yard tonight, after all."

"I can't think of any reason why not," I said. "Unless you happen to be bothered by poisonous snakes. Ever seen anybody get snakebit? First they swell up into a great big horrible ball, and then they turn blue and green and yellow and then it starts to get real bad."

"My dad says there ain't any poisonous snakes around here," Ronnie said. "So we don't have to worry about snakes."

"I thought we did," I said.

"Of course not," the Troll put in. "There aren't any poisonous snakes around here—not even when it's *dark*!" She cackled trollishly.

"Ma!" I yelled. "The Troll is bothering us. Tell her to leave us alone!"

"Don't refer to your sister as the Troll," my mother said. "Now, Trudy, get out of there and leave the boys alone."

The Troll backed slowly out of the room, grinning evilly. "Hope you have a good time sleeping out—in—the—dark. The weather report in the paper says there's going to be heavy darkness all night tonight *cackle cackle*!"

Just my luck—heavy darkness. And here was Ronnie, pressing ahead with his plan for sleeping out. This was getting out of hand. We were actually getting some old blankets and quilts down out of the attic to make a bed in the yard. What madness! I considered asking Ronnie to take an oath of secrecy and then confessing to him my disgusting fear of darkness. He would probably understand.

"I'll tell you something weird," Ronnie said. "I tried to get Fred Phelps to sleep out with me one night, and he said he couldn't, he was afraid of the dark. A big guy like Fred, you wouldn't expect him to be a yellow-bellied chicken, would ya? He even made me take a secret oath not to tell anybody."

"Fred's dumb, too," I said. So much for that idea . . .

Darkness was already coming down off the mountain, crawling out of the woods, and oozing up from the creek bottom. Down in the swamp, a chorus of frogs welcomed the coming of night. Stupid frogs.

Several times in my young life, through some monumental miscalculation, I had been surprised by darkness while playing with friends at a neighboring farm. Galloping along at the head of a column of French Legionnaires, I would yell over my shoulder, "Watch out for an ambush, men. It's getting dark and . . ."

Woah, hoss.

I take a look around Hannnnnhhh! My deadly enemy, darkness, has slipped in between me and my house! "Uh-oh," I tell the other Legionnaires. "I'm late for supper." And then I fire myself into the darkness. I can feel its long, bony fingers clutching at me, its grisly jaws nipping at my heels, and I streak, *streak* I say, through the silent, creepy blackness until, at last, I burst into the benevolent, life-saving light of my kitchen. Startled by the bang and whoosh of my sudden arrival, the womenfolk emit small shrieks and bound about in a mist of hairpins. Ah! Once again I have defeated the enemy! I slide into my chair and ask, "What's for supper?"

The Troll detected my fear of darkness early on, and used it for her own amusement. Once, walking home with her through the woods in winter, I noticed that the shadows of the trees had lengthened and were now blending together into great patches of—darkness. The last of the daylight slid up the barren birches as if being sucked through giant straws into the gaping maw* of night.

gaping maw: mouth or jaws of a vicious, hungry animal

"It's getting dark!" I warned.

"So what?" the Troll said, crunching on ahead through the snow.

"We'd better run," I said. "We don't want to get caught out here after dark."

The Troll stopped, turned around, and studied me thoughtfully.

"We can't run," she said. "If we run, the wolves will attack."

I looked around, as one is wont to do after such an announcement. "What wolves?"

"The wolves that have been following us," she said. "Don't tell me you haven't seen them!"

Well, now that she mentioned it, I did indeed see the wolves, slipping along through the shadows to the left and right of us.

The Troll calmly studied my reaction. "Why are you twisting yourself all up like that, you silly?"

Apparently she had never before seen anybody wind up the mainspring. Not run! I would have laughed if I'd had the time and the inclination, but I had neither. *Sprannnnnnngg!* And I was gone.

At the time I knew nothing about the infectious nature of panic. Otherwise I wouldn't have been so surprised when, upon reaching my top cruising speed, I noticed the Troll passing me on the left and still accelerating, her braids snapping like bullwhips as she cut in front of me. Maybe she thought there actually were some wolves following us, I don't know. More than likely it was simply that panic loves company. For my part, I couldn't have cared less about a mere pack of wolves. A pack of wolves wasn't even in the same league as a pack of darkness.

But now here were Ronnie and I, engaged in the insanity of actually spreading quilts and blankets on top of an old hay tarp in preparation for spending the night outdoors. If I even relaxed my feigned enthusiasm for the undertaking—good word that, undertaking—Ronnie would become suspicious. Then *both* Fred Phelps and I would become outcasts at school next fall, when Ronnie spread the word that we two yellow-bellied chickens were scared of the dark. Poor ol' Fred's reputation was already shot; mine hung in precarious* balance.

---

precarious: dangerously unstable

Of course, all I needed was a tiny little night light. Something the size of a birthday-cake candle would do—a fifteen-foot birthday-cake candle. Any obvious night light, though, would cause Ronnie to put some tough questions to me, like, "What you doing with that flashlight and the big stack of batteries?" Even if I'd had a big stack of batteries, I couldn't have risked it.

"What say we turn in?" Ronnie asked. "It's already dark."

"I noticed," I said.

I glanced longingly up at our house, the lights of which were being flicked off one by one as my mother made her final rounds. She opened the back door and called out, "I'm going to bed now. You boys all right?"

"Yep," Ronnie said.

"Yaup," I said.

Mom went back inside, and minutes later the last light on our side of the house flicked off. Ronnie and I were in *TOTAL DARKNESS!* Not just the well-defined cube of darkness that filled a bedroom, but a great shapeless ocean of night!

"You ever hear the story about the stranger who got himself hung for claim-jumping, and his ghost still wanders these parts looking for revenge?" Ronnie said.

"Yeah, I heard it."

"Well, my pa seen that ghost crossing a field right out this way one night. Foggy it was, he said, and . . ."

Idea! Why hadn't I thought of it before! I leaped out of the covers and told Ronnie I'd be right back. "I forgot to brush my teeth," I said, rushing toward the house. In the bathroom, I jerked the string on the overhead light, waited an appropriate length of time, and then sauntered back outside. Perfect! The light from the bathroom window cast a nice rectangular patch of light right next to my side of the hay tarp.

"You left the bathroom light on," Ronnie said.

"If that doesn't beat all! Oh, well, a little light won't hurt anything."

"This ghost story is better if it's plumb dark," Ronnie said. "But anyway, this ghost . . ." He droned on about the ghost and its horrible doings. I smiled sleepily, starting to drift off as I secretly stroked the grassy patch of protective light, occasionally turning to admire it in all its loveliness.

Without warning, an ominous shadow suddenly appeared in my patch of light. Wha? I turned and looked up at the bathroom window. No! There, framed in the window, stood the Troll! She was a silhouette, so I couldn't see her face, but I knew she was grinning her evil grin as she stared down in my direction. Slowly her hand reached for the light string. NO! DON'T DO IT! She made several teasing motions with the light string, then—Zap! The light was gone. Faintly, off in the darkness, I could hear the hollow sound of trollish laughter. She would have already locked all the doors to the house. Trolls are nothing if not thorough.

So now there was nothing to do but suffer the night away. For me, the Troll had murdered any hope of sleep. Under my breath I put a curse on her: May a garter snake turn up in your underwear drawer! (And a garter snake would, which shows you can't discount the power of curses.)

A friendly wind swept back the clouds and a few stars appeared. Starlight was better than

nothing. I noticed several little black shapes flitting about among the stars.

"And after the ghost got done with the two boys . . ." Ronnie was saying. "Hey, what are those black shapes flitting about among the stars?"

"Just some bats," I said.

"Bats!" cried Ronnie. "I can't stand bats! Quick, let's go inside!"

"Too late," I said. "The Troll has locked all the doors."

"Aaaaiiiiigh!" Ronnie said. "What'll we do?"

"I don't mind bats, myself," I said. "But if they scare you, maybe you can hide under the covers. Sometimes bats like to crawl under the covers, but if I see any try it, I'll drive them off." I studied the quivering lump under the blanket. "I'm going to be awake anyway."

About the Essay

1. In the first two paragraphs the author confesses that he is afraid of the dark. What is he even more afraid of than the dark?
2. How is Ronnie Ditmire like the narrator? How are they different?
3. In the narrator's relationship with his sister, does he display courage? Why do you think he calls her "the Troll"? What is a troll?
4. What dangers does the narrator create for himself through his pretending to be courageous?
5. Adam Lindsay Gordon wrote that in life "Two things stand like a stone, / Kindness in another's trouble, / Courage in your own." How do the narrator's attitudes in this essay stand up against this quotation? Are they like stone or something else?

About the Author

Patrick McManus (b. 1933) was born in Sandpoint, Idaho, and spent much of his youth moving with his family to various places throughout the mountains of Idaho, where his mother taught in one-room schoolhouses. The anecdotes contained in his many books of humor are based on actual experiences, although McManus admits to fictionalizing them a bit. His father died when Patrick was only six years old, so his formative years were spent in the company of his mother, his grandmother, and his sister, Patricia, the "Troll," who was six years older than he. The family also owned a dog, called Strange, short for Stranger.

McManus recounts having loved the outdoors from the time he was very young. Hence, many of his stories relate adventures that take place during a camping, hunting, or fishing trip. A number of his book titles reflect this love as well: *Never Sniff a Gift Fish, Kid Camping from Aaaaiiii! to Zip,* and *They Shoot Canoes, Don't They?* being a few of them.

Although the majority of McManus's books were published in the 1980s and 1990s, his writing career began long before. In 1956 McManus worked as a news reporter for the *Daily Olympian,* and then he moved on to working as an editor and professor at Washington State University for several decades. Currently McManus lives once again in the mountains of Idaho with his wife, Darlene.

Run, Boy, Run!

William Herman

Have you ever dreamed of becoming a famous athlete? But what if you had been badly burned and now walk with a limp? Would your mind be stronger than your body? This selection shows how Glenn Cunningham courageously overcame physical limitations to become a world-class miler.

Racing across the frozen Kansas earth, thirteen-year-old Floyd Cunningham lowered his head and called upon his young muscles for more speed.

Behind him, far to the rear, came little Glenn, his eight-year-old brother. At each step of their pounding feet, the distance between them grew greater. The little fellow panted heavily and tried to keep up.

Floyd approached the wooden fence which barred their path, he thrust his hands forward, pressed them against the fence top, and swung himself over. A moment later Glenn followed, going through the same gestures. But the fence was much too formidable* an obstacle for an

eight-year- old. Glenn tumbled roughly on the hard ground.

---

formidable: difficult

Floyd started to laugh. Then he saw the hurt look and humiliation* on the face of his little brother. Instead, he smiled, reached over the fence, and helped him to the other side.

---

humiliation: shame

"You have a lot of nerve, Glenn," he said admiringly. "Why, I wouldn't even have tried to jump that fence when I was eight. You sure have a lot of nerve."

A big grin of embarrassment and gratitude replaced the humiliated look on Glenn's face. As he looked into the sympathetic, strong eyes of his older brother, he realized all over again how fortunate he was to have someone like Floyd in the family.

But there was little time for reflection on that bitterly cold winter morning of 1918. The boys were already late for their regular chore.

"Let's go, Glenn," Floyd said. "The teacher and the kids will be getting there soon. We'd better have that fire roaring by then."

Glenn needed no further urging. The job meant a few pennies of extra income, and pennies were important in the Cunningham household. Some of them, too, were set aside for their college fund. He and Floyd often talked about what important doctors they were going to be when they grew up.

Minutes later the two puffing youngsters arrived at the small, one-room frame building. They immediately began selecting bits of kindling and paper which they stuffed into the potbelly stove in the center of the classroom.

"Get me the kerosene!" Floyd cried as he filled the stove and opened the draft. Glenn came running with the can.

Floyd poured some kerosene into the stove. Now he turned to Glenn. "We'll need

some more wood for the fire and some to stock the bin, too."

Glenn dashed toward the door. A sudden blast sent him sprawling to the floor. He heard a tremendous crash. A moment later great flames were feeding on the dry wood. Fiery fingers reached out for him where he lay in the doorway.

Glenn bounced to his feet and leaped out of range. Except for a smoldering* patch on his heavy woolen jacket, he had escaped injury.

---

smoldering: slowly burning

However, once outside, cold air clearing his head, he abruptly remembered. Where was Floyd? Had he escaped or was he trapped inside?

The answer was not long in coming. From the building came piercing cries.

"Floyd!" Glenn raced up the wooden stairs and back into the fire. He coughed violently, and his lungs filled with smoke.

"Floyd! Floyd!"

It was fully five hours later when he regained consciousness in his own bed. With it came a combination of pains the eight-year-old farm boy never before had experienced. His gauze-covered legs were a mass of agony. Sharp twinges spiraled* up his spine.

---

spiraled: rose

He raised his head as he dimly made out the faces around him. "Where's Floyd?" he asked hoarsely.

There was no answer. And Glenn knew. Never again would he play or romp with Floyd.

As the days passed after the accident, the farm boy was faced with a need for all his courage.

The tiny legs, swathed* in layers of white, became numb. The fire had eaten deeply into the flesh. Now the legs lay limp and nerveless on the white-sheeted bed.

---

swathed: bandaged

The wise old country doctor, called in to attend him, could do nothing. He called in specialists. They, too, shook their heads helplessly.

"We can do nothing," they told his grieving parents. "The best thing to do is to amputate. Remove these worthless legs now," they counseled. "Now is the best time. If this is done while Glenn is a child, he will have time and heart to adjust himself. And it will be easier for him to get used to artificial legs."

Glenn, tears streaming down his cheeks, cried: "No! Please, no!"

Clint Cunningham and his wife drew closer together in the face of their tragic dilemma.* The specialist stood firm for immediate amputation. Glenn pleaded, "No! Please, no!"

---

dilemma: choice

What should they do?

Their answer, when it came, was decisive.* Glenn should have his way. He might not have full use of his legs. Perhaps, as the doctors warned, he would never again be able to walk. But Glenn Cunningham would be a whole man.

---

decisive: firm

There would be no amputation.

The doctors tried one last vain warning, shrugged, and turned away, expressing sorrow for the Cunninghams.

As the young invalid lay in bed, he prayed. He would walk again. He was certain of it.

His legs were twisted sticks, his knees and shins bare of flesh. The toes of his left foot were completely gone. The transverse arch* was practically destroyed.

---

transverse arch: bone extending across the ball of the foot, necessary for walking and running

---

Glenn, of course, knew only that his legs were numb and useless. But he had faith that he would walk again.

The faith was sorely tested as he heard the voices of other children in the distance who, he knew, were playing leapfrog and running races.

Weeks passed. In the middle of spring the bandages were removed.

Clint Cunningham and his wife took turns rubbing the skinny, red bones covered with scar tissue. They massaged* until their own arms ached and their eyes were red from lack of sleep.

---

massaged: rubbed

But they detected no signs of life in the dead limbs.

Maybe crutches would help. Perhaps a good, solid brace.

Glenn shook his head. "Next week," he said, "I'm going to get out of bed. I'm going to walk."

Clint and his wife exchanged a brief glance and withdrew to hide their tears.

The following week, early in the summer of 1919, Glenn announced he wanted to try to leave his bed. As he was being helped by his parents, his legs dropped limply to the side and hung there numb and lifeless.

Slowly, slowly, he was steadied until his feet came in contact with the floor.

"I—I can feel the floor!" he cried excitedly.

Poor Glenn! What he felt, in his unaccustomed vertical position, was pressure. As he lifted his body and tried to stand, the legs buckled and he collapsed to the floor.

Clint Cunningham picked up a sobbing heap and restored it to the bed.

That was but the first attempt. Daily, doggedly,* the routine was repeated with no change in results. As the weeks wore on, the prayers became more fervent.*

---
doggedly: stubbornly
fervent: passionate

At last, one day, the grim little invalid slid off the bed and waited for the strong arms of his father to draw away. Gradually Clint Cunningham relaxed his grip. Glenn's body trembled, then swayed uncertainly.

The small body stiffened. The knee twitched. There was a sharp, wonderful pain as blood spurted through the small veins.

Tears of happiness crawled slowly down his cheeks. His face was alight with a radiant smile. And in the Cunningham household the flood of joy burst. Glenn was standing on his own two feet.

It was only for a few seconds. The two parents were hugging each other, weeping without shame and thanking God for the miracle. They did not notice that Glenn, exhausted, meanwhile had sunk to the floor, a puzzled but happy look on his face.

It was just a matter of days now before he took tiny, halting steps across the bedroom floor.

Glenn Cunningham, the boy who would "never walk again," was walking.

Soon he could negotiate* the distance to the kitchen and back to the bedroom. Soon he was able to limp out to the yard; but to return to the house, he partly walked, partly crawled.

---
negotiate: manage

The rubbings continued. When his parents were not available, he rubbed his legs himself. He began reading extensively* about physical culture.* He studied his diet and chose foods which would help give him strength. Sweets he shunned;* he avoided coffee. Milk, however, he consumed by the quart.

---
extensively: widely
physical culture: behavior of the body
shunned: avoided

As the months passed, walking became easy, but the awkward limp persisted.* More strenuous* exercise, he told himself, might enable him, the boy who was not expected to walk at all, to stand straight among his fellow men, perhaps even to run.

---
persisted: continued
strenuous: vigorous

Glenn tried to run at every opportunity. He ran while doing chores, he ran in the fields, he ran after wood and returned, running, with arms loaded. He could be seen often in the little community of Elkhart, running through the streets, a loaf of bread or a quart of milk under his arm.

Later on he would run while thousands of people stood in the stadiums and cheered him

to the tape. But never would the cheers contain more wholehearted enthusiasm than was shown in the faces of the citizens of Elkhart as they saw him racing with his clumsy limp through the streets. They knew of his iron determination, and they talked about his faith.

Run, boy!

He never walked when he could run. To school, to help his father around the farm, to the store.

Run, boy!

To the barn, to the tool shed, to the granary.

Run, boy, run!

Years passed and the ugly scar tissue hardened over a developing layer of strong muscle. The toeless left foot grew graceful and strong. By the time he was thirteen, his chest and arms were the envy of his friends. Constant running, planned exercise, hard work on the farm—all combined to make him an enviable* physical specimen.

enviable: desirable

He still had a slight limp, but there was no one among the young fellows in the county who could overtake him in a foot race.

Glenn loved to run. He never got over that love. People around Elkhart used to say he could run a mile without stopping and without apparently slowing up.

One spring day in 1923 he was attracted by a trophy in a local store window. A sign announced that the trophy would be given to the winner of the mile race at the Morton County Fair.

Glenn studied the silver-plated cup. It had shining handles and neat engraving. He had never, he thought, seen anything quite so beautiful.

Impulsively, the thirteen-year-old lad signed up to run.

That race, over the uneven track at the county fairground, gave Glenn one of the greatest thrills of his life. Later, when he smashed world records and etched* his name high among the greatest athletes of all time, he would still look back upon his first running contest wistfully.*

etched: printed
wistfully: wishfully

Glenn Cunningham's time for his first competitive mile was 5 minutes, 18 seconds.

The rest of the field had trailed far behind. The crowd gasped when it learned that the youngster with the limp had traveled a mile with speed enough to qualify for a good high school team.

The joy of winning was dampened when Glenn showed up to claim his trophy. "I don't know what happened to it," the storekeeper shrugged. Nor was it ever found.

Today, Glenn Cunningham will survey his trophies, hundreds of them piled shelf on shelf, and he will tell you: "They're nice, all right, but I'd give the lot of them to get my hands on that one little silver cup that was promised me for winning the mile race at the Morton County Fair."

The fairground victory fired him with a new kind of enthusiasm. As he performed his man's work in the Elkhart granary, he frequently let his mind dwell on the accomplishments of the great milers of his day.

He thrilled to the exploits* of Paavo Nurmi, Joey Ray, and Ray Conger. No one was more stirred than Cunningham when the newspapers announced that Conger had flashed across a mile of cinders in 4 minutes and 13 seconds. He gave the race and the running time considerable thought.

---

exploits: heroic actions

"The day may come," Glenn said dreamily, "when a human being will run that distance in 4 minutes flat."

Those who heard the remark laughed. A 4-minute mile! Fantastic!

Glenn gave the matter more thought. Only a year before, in 1928, he had won the mile event at the Kansas Relay Carnival. Wearing the colors of Elkhart High School, he had cleared the distance in exactly 4½ minutes, establishing a new relay record only seconds shy of the state record.

In 1929, the year Conger startled the world with his record-shattering mile, Elkhart decided to have an entry in the National Scholastic Relays in Chicago. Glenn Cunningham was the unanimous choice.

The town had begun to feel effects of the depression but everyone, it seemed, wanted to contribute to defray* fare expense.

---

defray: pay

Glenn felt keenly the responsibility entrusted to him. More than anything else in the world he wanted to win that race.

It was not to be. He took his first long train ride. He was nervous, tired. It was the first time he had been out of his native state. The tension mounted for the inexperienced youth. He ran a poor race and lost.

He crept back to his railroad berth. The people of Elkhart would feel he had let them down. How would he face them?

His misgivings were promptly dispelled* when the train pulled into the station. A waiting crowd cheered him as mightily as though he had returned victorious.

---

dispelled: driven away; scattered

If he ever had another chance, Glenn resolved, he would not fail them again.

He went to Chicago the next year. He did not fail them. This time the boy rested on the train. He dismissed from his mind thoughts of the crowds in the stands. He forgot to be nervous. He centered his thoughts on one goal—Victory.

And what a victory! Truly, Elkhart was now on the map. The lad who "would never walk" ran a mile in the fastest time in the history of world interscholastic competition—4 minutes, 24.7 seconds!

Even more astonishing was the fact that this scarred streak from Kansas had run the second half mile faster than the first!

"That's interesting," Coach Roy Varney of Elkhart High School said thoughtfully. He weighed Nurmi's principle of the "even pace" in running a mile against the prevalent* belief that such a distance could not be run in good time without the advantage of initial speed. The approved pattern had been: Get a good start, run a fairly swift first half mile, taper off into a second wind, then make the final burst of speed about a hundred yards from the tape.

---

prevalent: widespread

Paavo Nurmi had introduced a radical departure from the pattern. He said: "Just strike an even pace. Try to determine what your best possible time will be, the fastest you can run for the entire mile distance, then keep it up."

Which method was best?

Coach Varney had seen Cunningham, and he had his own ideas. In the remaining months of Glenn's high school career, Varney assigned himself the task of measured, scientific training for a runner, who, he became certain, someday would sweep the old records from the recordbooks.

His high school days ended, Glenn had been a long time deciding to enter Kansas University. He now could command a man's pay at the granary. His foreman asked him to stay on. He was popular in Elkhart.

As for running, many of his friends were openly skeptical.* Sure, he had been a star in high school. In the tough college field he would need his toes and his transverse arch. The grinding stretch drives* would require that he get up on his toes to overtake his competitors. Glenn, they shook their heads, didn't have it.

---

skeptical: disbelieving
stretch drives: last length of a race

A memory, long dim, recurred vividly to Glenn. In his mind's eye rose the scene of the specialists grouped about the bed of a boy with numb legs. "They should be amputated. He'll never walk again." Glenn Cunningham enrolled in Kansas University.

All during Glenn's freshman year at Kansas, he was put through routine training paces. He seldom ran a full race, although Brutus Hamilton, his coach, was aware that the young freshman could defeat any of his varsity competitors.

Reports of his increasing fleetness spread. The folks back home, even the skeptical ones,

now began to predict that Glenn would be one of the great runners of all time.

One who said so, loudly and often, was charming Margaret Speir. The pretty sorority girl frequently came out to watch him. They had occasional dates. Margaret soon was wearing his fraternity pin.

Meanwhile, Glenn went through his daily paces under the watchful eye of Brutus Hamilton. The genial* coach was besieged* by sports writers alert for news.

---

genial: friendly
besieged: surrounded

"Will this kid with the burned legs make the grade in the big time?"

"Will this fellow Cunningham measure up to his advance high school notices?"

Hamilton waved his hand and said, "Wait and see."

No artist ever attended the unveiling of his own creation with more pride than did Hamilton when he presented Glenn Cunningham to the world in the Big Six Championship Competition in 1932.

Glenn Cunningham, the lad who "would never walk," literally ran away with all laurels.* He won the half-mile event with ease. He showed his heels to the entire field in the mile run. When it was over, press tickers all over the country flashed the name of a new champion.

---

laurels: honors

A fellow named Cunningham had run the mile in 4 minutes, 14.3 seconds!

What was even more astounding, he had run the second half of that distance in 1 minute, 53.5 seconds. Cunningham not only was maintaining the "even pace" but was running his second half mile with considerably more speed than the first.

Glenn, recognized for his exploit from coast to coast, now heard from all sides one word, repeated over and over again—Olympics!

One obstacle stood in his path. He would have to defeat Henry Brocksmith of Indiana in the National College eliminations. Brocksmith was considered by the nation's sports authorities to be the outstanding miler in the country.

Glenn Cunningham not only defeated Brocksmith but established a new United States record when he was clocked at 4 minutes, 11.1 seconds.

Misfortune dogged Cunningham in the Los Angeles Olympic competition. He was seized with a severe attack of tonsillitis which left him weak. He finished fourth and had the thin consolation* that he had been the first United States runner to cross the tape.

consolation: comfort

In 1933, Glenn was invited East to compete on the fast board tracks.* In the spring and summer of that year he ran twenty-seven races. He won twenty-five. The board track soon blistered under his flying feet. He faced the brightest stars of his day and matched their skill, speed, and stamina. Though defeated, they sang the praises of this amazing man from Kansas.

board tracks: wooden indoor tracks

One matter puzzled Glenn. Why did the people in the East act so coldly toward him? He sought the answer.

He was a show-off, they said. He tossed his head up and down like a race horse. He was the last to remove the conspicuous warm-up suit. He overworked in warming up.

Glenn, troubled more than he would publicly admit, remained silent. His coach did not. "Glenn's chilled leg muscles worry him," he explained. "His legs, having been so badly burned when he was a child, are extremely sensitive to the cold. That's why he keeps his suit on until just before he goes onto the track. As for tossing his head in warm-up, he's got to do it. He suffers very often from a strain in his neck. That's got to be worked out if he's to run up to par. And it helps his breathing. Glenn has very small nostrils."

After that there was no question as to who was the most popular as well as the greatest miler of his time.

Glenn kept on racing and winning. One afternoon, after setting a new mile record of 4 minutes, 9.8 seconds, he returned to the track and forced Indiana's Charles Hornbostel to break a world record of his own in the half mile to defeat him by inches.

He traveled to Europe and Asia, meeting and conquering champions wherever he ran. He was overseas when he heard that his world record for the mile had been broken by Jack Lovelock of New Zealand.

Glenn, proud of his hard-fought laurels, promptly returned to America where he set a new cinder-track record of 4 minutes, 6.7 seconds. Shortly afterwards, running on a board track, in the Dartmouth Handicap, he shaved more seconds from his own previous record to make the new world's record 4 minutes, 4.4 seconds.

In his early thirties, Glenn Cunningham, "The Grand Old Man of Track," finally retired. He settled down with the former Margaret Speir.

For a decade, he had met and vanquished* the greatest runners of his day. At the end he was competing only against time.

---

vanquished: defeated

The skeptics were finally silenced. Glenn Cunningham, he of the seared* legs, toeless foot, and small nostrils, was universally acknowledged the fastest man in the world.* . . .

---

seared: burned
acknowledged the fastest man in the world: in 1949

The style for running the mile prior to his revolutionary departure from it was as simple as it was long-established. Milers broke from the starting tape at top speed, maintained the grueling* pace as long as possible, then stumbled and staggered to the finish line. Sprint records were established for the first half mile while the second half became a torturous endurance contest.

---

grueling: exhausting

Cunningham's method was almost the direct opposite. Starting at the top comfortable pace which he could maintain, he sustained* it for the first half mile. The third-quarter pace was stepped up and then, as he phrased it, "When my heart and lungs and glands are built up to maximum efficiency, that is the time for applying the pressure." So well did he "apply the pressure" that his sprint finishes shattered records wherever he ran.

---

sustained: kept up

And this was Glenn Cunningham, the racing immortal who overcame the handicap of lameness to become a world's champion!

About the Story

1. What disaster alters Glenn's life when he is a young boy?
2. Why are Glenn's legs not amputated?
3. How do Glenn's parents contribute to his success?
4. What contributions does Glenn make to the world of running?
5. Is Glenn Cunningham a *victim* or a *victor?* Why?

The Most Important Day

Helen Keller

Can you imagine trying to learn without being able to hear your teacher or read your assignments? Helen Keller had both problems because she was deaf and blind. Many people know the story of her courage in overcoming these difficulties. But few know of the less obvious courage portrayed in her repentance and sorrow for a stubborn will.

The most important day I remember in all my life is the one on which my teacher, Anne Mansfield Sullivan, came to me. I am filled with wonder when I consider the immeasurable contrasts between the two lives which it connects. It was the third of March, 1887, three months before I was seven years old.

On the afternoon of that eventful day I stood on the porch—dumb,* expectant.* I guessed vaguely* from my mother's signs and from the hurrying to and fro in the house that something unusual was about to happen, so I went to the door and waited on the steps. The afternoon sun penetrated* the mass of honeysuckle that covered the porch, and fell on my upturned face. My fingers lingered almost unconsciously on the familiar leaves and blossoms which had just come forth to greet the sweet Southern spring. I did not know what the future held of marvel or surprise for me. Anger and bitterness had preyed upon* me continually for weeks, and a deep languor* had succeeded* this passionate struggle.

dumb: incapable of speaking
expectant: waiting
vaguely: uncertainly
penetrated: shone through
preyed upon: eaten away at
languor: lack of energy
succeeded: followed

Have you ever been at sea in a dense fog when it seemed as if a tangible,* white darkness shut you in, and the great ship, tense and anxious, groped her way toward the shore with plummet and sounding line,* and you waited with beating heart for something to happen? I was like that ship before my education began, only I was without compass or sounding line and had no way of knowing how near the harbor was. "Light! Give me light!" was the wordless cry of my soul, and the light of love shone on me in that very hour.

tangible: capable of being felt
plummet and sounding line: weight and line used for measuring ocean depth

I felt approaching footsteps. I stretched out my hand, as I supposed, to my mother. Someone took it, and I was caught up and held close in the arms of her who had come to reveal all things to me and, more than all things else, to love me.

The morning after my teacher came she led me into her room and gave me a doll. The little blind children at the Perkins Institution had sent it. . . . When I had played with it a little while, Miss Sullivan slowly spelled into my hand the word "d-o-l-l." I was at once interested in this finger play and tried to imitate it. When I finally succeeded in making the letters correctly, I was flushed with childish pleasure and pride. Running downstairs to my mother, I held up my hand and made the letters for *doll*. I did not know that I was spelling a word or even that words existed; I was simply making my fingers go in monkey-like imitation. In the days that followed I learned to spell in this uncomprehending way a great many words, among them, *pin, hat, cup* and a few verbs like *sit, stand,* and *walk*. But my teacher had been with me several weeks before I understood that everything has a name.

One day while I was playing with my new doll, Miss Sullivan put my big rag doll into my lap also, spelled "d-o-l-l," and tried to make me understand that "d-o-l-l" applied to both. Earlier in the day we had had a tussle* over the words "m-u-g" and "w-a-t-e-r." Miss Sullivan had tried to impress it upon me that "m-u-g" is *mug* and that "w-a-t-e-r" is *water,* but I persisted in confounding* the two. In despair, she had dropped the subject for the time, only to renew it at the first opportunity. I became impatient at her repeated attempts, and seizing the new doll, I dashed it upon the floor. I was keenly delighted when I felt the fragments of the broken doll at my feet. Neither sorrow nor regret followed my passionate outburst. I had not loved the doll. In the still,

dark world in which I lived, there was no strong sentiment* or tenderness. I felt my teacher sweep the fragments to one side of the hearth, and I had a sense of satisfaction that the cause of my discomfort was removed. She brought me my hat, and I knew I was going out into the warm sunshine. This thought, if a wordless sensation* may be called a thought, made me hop and skip with pleasure.

---

tussle: struggle
confounding: confusing
sentiment: emotion
sensation: feeling

We walked down the path to the well house, attracted by the fragrance of the honeysuckle with which it was covered. Someone was drawing water, and my teacher placed my hand under the spout. As the cool stream gushed over one hand, she spelled into the other the word *water,* first slowly, then rapidly. I stood still, my whole attention fixed upon the motions of her fingers. Suddenly I felt a misty consciousness as of something forgotten—a thrill of returning thought—and somehow the mystery of language was revealed to me. I knew then that "w-a-t-e-r" meant that wonderful cool something that was flowing over my hand. That living word awakened my soul, gave it light, hope, joy, set it free! There were

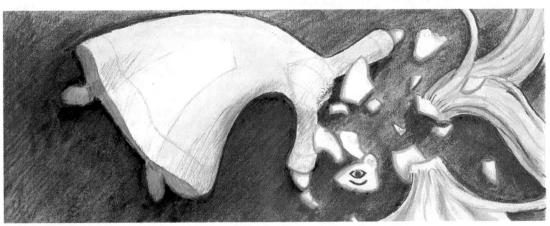

barriers still, it is true, but barriers that could in time be swept away.

I left the house eager to learn. Everything had a name, and each name gave birth to a new thought. As we returned to the house, every object which I touched seemed to quiver with life. That was because I saw everything with the strange, new sight that had come to me. On entering the door, I remembered the doll I had broken. I felt my way to the hearth and picked up the pieces. I tried vainly to put them together. Then my eyes filled with tears, for I realized what I had done, and for the first time I felt repentance and sorrow.

About the Essay

1. Why is the day that Anne Sullivan comes to Helen Keller considered by the author to be the most important day?
2. What does Keller consider Sullivan's most important function?
3. What elements of nature does Helen Keller use to describe her journey toward understanding?
4. Why is Helen Keller's use of nature in this piece amazing?
5. Why is Helen Keller repentant for destroying the doll?

About the Author

The life of Helen Keller (1880-1968) is a remarkable one. The journey from angry, ignorant child to college graduate cum laude to worldwide speaker on behalf of the blind is due in large part to the determination of Anne Sullivan Macy, called "Teacher" by Helen all of her life. Helen Keller had remarkable family connections, from the first teacher of the deaf in Switzerland to Robert E. Lee. The list of her distinguished friends reads like a "Who's Who" in every area of life: presidents such as Calvin Coolidge and Woodrow Wilson, writers such as Mark Twain, and inventors such as Alexander Graham Bell, whose lifelong interest in teaching the deaf brought about the invention of the telephone as a byproduct. It is no wonder that under Anne Sullivan's teaching and the influence of these friends, Helen Keller assured herself a position in history. Though blind, deaf, and mute, Helen Keller acquired not only a full knowledge of the world through hands-on experiences like petting circus lions but also a thorough education; learning to read French, German, Greek, and Latin, as well as English gave her access to the world's mind. However, without her "Teacher" and the teachable spirit cultivated by Anne Sullivan, Helen could have accomplished nothing as shown by the doll episode of this selection. How appropriate that water, crucial to physical life, was the key to Helen's mental life through which she enriched those who knew her, bettered those who were like her, and inspires those who read about her today.

Columbus

Joaquin Miller

Columbus faces two problems: the criticism and fear of his shipmates and the physical dangers of the unknown ocean. How does he overcome both? What inspiration for daily living does this poem reveal to us?

Behind him lay the gray Azores,*
    Behind the Gates of Hercules;*
Before him not the ghost of shores;
    Before him only shoreless seas.
The good mate* said: "Now must we pray,   5
    For lo! the very stars are gone,
Brave Adm'r'l,* speak, what shall I say?"
    "Why, say: 'Sail on! sail on! and on!' "

"My men grow mutinous* day by day;
    My men grow ghastly wan* and weak."   10
The stout* mate thought of home; a spray
    Of salt wave washed his swarthy* cheek.
"What shall I say, brave Adm'r'l, say,
    If we sight naught* but seas at dawn?"
"Why, you shall say at break of day: 15
    'Sail on! sail on! sail on! and on!' "

They sailed and sailed, as winds might blow,
    Until at last the blanched* mate said:
"Why, now not even God would know
    Should I and all my men fall dead.   20
These very winds forget their way,
    For God from these dread seas is gone.
Now speak, brave Adm'r'l, speak and say—"
    He said: "Sail on! sail on! and on!"

They sailed. They sailed. Then spake the mate: 25
    "This mad sea shows his teeth tonight.
He curls his lip, he lies in wait,
    With lifted teeth, as if to bite!

Glossary:
Azores: islands in the mid-Atlantic
Gates of Hercules: Straits of Gibraltar: waterway between Spain and Northern Africa
mate: officer on a ship
Adm'r'l: Admiral
mutinous: rebellious
wan: horribly pale
stout: brave
swarthy: sunburned
naught: nothing
blanched: pale

Brave Adm'r'l, say but one good word:
    What shall we do when hope is gone?"   30
The words leapt like a leaping sword:
    "Sail on! sail on! sail on! and on!"

Then, pale and worn, he kept* his deck,   kept: stayed on
    And peered through darkness, Ah, that night
Of all dark nights! And then a speck—   35
    A light! A light! At last a light!
It grew, a starlit flag unfurled!*   unfurled: unrolled
    It grew to be Time's burst of dawn.
He gained a world; he gave that world
    Its grandest lesson: "On! sail on!"   40

About the Poem

1. Identify the lines in the poem that relate specific problems Columbus met on his voyage.
2. What was Columbus's answer to each of the problems he met?
3. Would turning back toward home have guaranteed the men's safety?
4. Which difficulty do you think concerned Columbus more—the dangers of the sea or the complaining disbelief of his men?
5. What does the poem teach us about daily living?

About the Author

Cincinnatus Hiner Miller (1839-1913) lived part of his early life in the West as a cook in a mining camp, a participant in skirmishes with the Indians, and a horse thief. During the Civil War, he taught school and studied law. Later, during his journalistic years as editor of a newspaper, he received his nickname "Joaquin" (wo ken) after having printed a letter in defense of a Mexican outlaw named Joaquin Murietta. After leading a successful raid against unfriendly Indians near Canyon City, Oregon, Miller was enthusiastically elected as a county court judge. About this same time his poetry began to receive favorable attention from Bret Harte and other regional literary figures. Encouraged by his local acceptance as a poet, Miller traveled to England, where he succeeded in publishing a private volume of verse. With the attention gained from this book and his western garb, complete with chaps and sombrero, Miller became a celebrity of sorts. His popularity, however, was largely confined to Britain, for his fellow Americans began to criticize his imitative style, his literary blunders, and his romantic presentation of the West.

Betsy Dowdy's Ride

Ellis Credle

Nearly everyone has heard of the famous ride of Paul Revere, but perhaps Betsy Dowdy's ride took just as much courage. Paul Revere was a well-known New England silversmith, but Betsy Dowdy was only a sixteen-year-old girl. She showed self-sacrificial courage in her daring ride to help alert her countrymen of a surprise attack by the British.

Along the highway which leads into Manteo, North Carolina, where the first English settlement in the New World was attempted, are several historical markers. One tells briefly of a sixteen-year-old girl, Betsy Dowdy, who, in the winter of 1776, swam her pony across Currituck Sound and rode fifty miles through the wilderness to warn General Skinner of the coming of the enemy.

Thousands of people on the way to see the famous historical pageant,* *The Lost Colony*, at Manteo have passed that sign and wondered at the bravery of the young girl who took a ride vastly more difficult and dangerous than that of the better-known Paul Revere. No doubt they have wished to know more of Betsy Dowdy and how she came to make her perilous* journey.

---

pageant: drama
perilous: dangerous

The story begins in the year 1774 when Betsy Dowdy was only fourteen years old. In that year most of our vast land was uncharted wilderness. Only thirteen colonies, the ones along the eastern coast of North America, were populated and those only thinly. The few roads which traversed* this new country were hardly more than trails through the wilderness.

---

traversed: crossed

Betsy Dowdy lived in a wild and lonely spot. The roar of the ocean was always in her ears, for her father's small cottage huddled in the shelter of a great dune on a desolate sand bar called Currituck Beach. It was one of a chain of long, narrow islands. In front of her door the Atlantic tossed endlessly, and in every other direction a waste of sandy hillocks* and dunes reared and tumbled and sprawled out over the landscape.

hillocks: small hills

The sandbanks of North Carolina, on which Betsy lived, have been the dread of all mariners* since the first settlement of the land. Here long fingers of sand stretch out into treacherous* currents to pull down any ship which comes within reach. In the early days, when all commerce was done by water, hundreds of vessels went down in that death grip, and the white sand of Currituck Beach was strewn with the bleaching skeletons of wrecked ships.

mariners: sailors
treacherous: dangerous

Joe Dowdy, Betsy's father, made his living from these wrecks. As their valuable merchandise was washed ashore he recovered it, stored it as best he could, and later shipped it away to be sold for whatever it would bring. This was a legitimate business in those days, and Joe Dowdy was an upright and God-fearing man. Every night before going to bed, he prayed devoutly* for the souls of all sailors at sea, asking God to take care of them and preserve them from shipwreck. But he always closed with a silent petition that if there should be a wreck, it might be on Currituck Beach.

devoutly: sincerely

Perhaps Joe Dowdy's prayers were answered, for many times had young Betsy Dowdy stood upon the beach, braced against the gale, and watched some proud vessel founder* in the thunderous surf. Joe Dowdy always did his utmost to save the unfortunate passengers and crew, and often Betsy peered through blinding rain and salt spray to watch her father and their only neighbor, Sammy Jarvis, struggling to get a life line to some doomed ship.

founder: sink

After a wreck, Joe Dowdy's humble cottage was often crowded with exhausted, water-soaked survivors. Some of them lingered for weeks recovering from exposure and shock. Joe gave them every care his small home afforded, and Betsy was glad to do her part in nursing them back to health.

From these castaways came her only word of the great world beyond the sandbanks. A fine gentleman, who sat sipping daintily at a bowl of clam chowder which she had prepared for him, told young Betsy about England and the magnificent affairs of the court of King George III, but these grand doings across three thousand miles of ocean seemed remote and unreal to the little girl of the sandbanks. The stories of places nearer home interested her more. She listened, entranced,* when a shipwrecked planter told her of Edenton. This important town of the growing colony was less than fifty miles from her own home—not too far away to dream of going there some day. She was all ears as the planter described the grand houses there, the high paneled rooms and tall carved mantels, the beautiful ladies dressed in silks and brocades* who played so very sweetly on the harpsichord.* He pictured for her the white plantation houses along Albemarle Sound, their green lawns sloping down to the water front and blowing with flowers planted from English seeds and cuttings.

entranced: carried away with wonder
brocades: heavy, ornamental fabric
harpsichord: piano-like instrument

COURAGE

Around his leaping driftwood fire, Joe Dowdy often discussed the questions of the day with his shipwrecked guests. Sometimes their neighbor, Sammy Jarvis, took part. Betsy, sitting on the edge of the group, gathered from the talk that the colonies were not always on the best of terms with the mother country. The words "taxation without representation" meant little to her, but she disliked it when the conversation drifted around to them, for these words always brought the men to the pitch of shouting and brandishing* fists. It was only after a castaway had told of the Edenton tea party that Betsy began to understand their meaning.

brandishing: shaking

Fifty-one Edenton ladies, related the shipwrecked citizen, had gathered one afternoon at the home of Mrs. Elizabeth King. They had drunk a beverage made of the leaves of dried raspberries, and had drawn up a resolution* declaring that they would drink no more tea until England removed the hateful tax on tea.

resolution: declaration

It was quite understandable to young Betsy that the ladies should be annoyed at having to pay more for their tea, but why her father should work himself into a fury over it she could not understand. The only tea that was ever served in the Dowdy home was made of yaupon,* the kind which the Indians had taught them to use. There was no tax on that, no cost of any kind, for the leaves were gathered from low glistening green bushes which grew wild in the lee* of the dunes.

yaupon: holly
lee: shelter

"I'd be mad if they put a tax on sand crabs!" cried Joe Dowdy when his daughter asked him to explain. "It's takin' away our freedom! England ain't got no right to lay taxes on us unless we consent to it. And she ain't even asked our consent. We ain't got nobody over there to represent us in the parliament, and it's the right of every Englishman to have a say-so in the government. They shan't take that right away from us! Englishmen always will be free—that they will!"

"Yes! That they will!" shouted his guests.

Betsy came to understand that freedom was a very precious thing, something for which men were willing to fight and, if need be, to die.

The little girl of the sand dunes had no companions of her own age, but she was never lonely. There was much to be done around the house, and she spent many a happy hour, galloping over the dunes on her small mare, Nellie. Nellie belonged to a breed of horse peculiar to the sandbanks. For this reason they were called banker ponies. Larger than ponies, yet smaller than proper horses, hundreds of them grazed wild among the marshes and low myrtle bushes.* When a banker pony was thirsty, he pawed a hole in the sand and waited for the brackish* water to seep* into it.

myrtle bushes: evergreen bushes with white and pink flowers
brackish: salty
seep: ooze

No one knows how these wild ponies came to be upon the sandy islands of the Carolina coast. It is one of the many mysteries of the region, but it is known that early settlers found them there. And up to this day they may still be seen, cropping the rushes along the sandbanks.

In those colonial days, Joe Dowdy herded hundreds of the wild ponies, broke them to the saddle, and sold them to the settlers along the Albemarle. His daughter Betsy had taken one for her own. The young girl galloped many a mile over the dunes, and through the tall pines and the live oak trees, to fill great baskets with

wild grapes or bright wild flowers. With flying hooves, Nellie took her young mistress wherever she wished to go and brought her safely back again.

On these long rides, Betsy turned over in her mind the things which she had heard at her father's hearth fire. She began to understand why the men always grew angry at the thought of taxes laid by England. What right had those Englishmen, far across the sea, to lay taxes on this new land? *They* had not built the houses, nor chopped down the trees, nor plowed the ground, nor fought off the Indians. Betsy's young and independent mind told her that this land should belong to those who settled it. They should be the ones to govern it. They should decide the taxes.

In 1775, the violent gales of the fall equinoxes* sent a Massachusetts schooner aground upon Currituck Beach. Those saved from the wreck were full of a battle fought at Lexington. The words tumbled over each other, so eager were they to tell of the happenings of that early morning of April nineteenth, 1775.

---
fall equinoxes: late September

The British Regulars had set out secretly, they related, under cover of night, to arrest the great Massachusetts leaders, Samuel Adams and John Hancock. But their secret had been found out. Paul Revere, artist and silversmith of Boston, had ridden madly through the countryside, ahead of the advancing army, and had given the alarm. On the village green of Lexington, the British had found fifty stern-faced farmers, muskets in hand, blocking their way.

"Disperse,* ye villains!" the British leader, Pitcairn, had shouted. But the minutemen had not dispersed.

Disperse: scatter

The British had opened fire, and eighteen embattled* farmers had fallen, eight dead, ten wounded.

---
embattled: prepared for battle

"Then it's war!" said Joe Dowdy, shaking his head.

Yes, war with England had come at last. Young Betsy's mind was prepared for it, but it still seemed unreal, like another tale told around her father's fireside. All summer, while the ocean lay rolling lazily and blinking at the sun, the opening battles of the Revolutionary War had been fought. To Betsy Dowdy, living on Currituck Sound, the war seemed far away and unconnected with the pleasant autumn days along the sandbanks.

It was not until the winter, when the tail end of tropical hurricanes set the clouds flying and the ocean churning,* that the war came

near to Betsy. A fishing schooner from Norfolk, Virginia, having fared badly in one of these gales, anchored off the Currituck coast to repair her shredded sails and cracked masts. Joe Dowdy, with young Betsy, rowed out to inquire the news of the day.

---

churning: swirling

"Hey-oh, up there!" shouted Joe Dowdy through cupped hands. "What news on the mainland?"

"News a-plenty!" shouted back a gnarled old seaman.

A swaying rope ladder was let over the side, and father and daughter climbed on board. The word was that Lord Dunmore, the Royal Governor of Virginia, had been driven from his palace in Williamsburg by the indignant* settlers. Taking his army with him, he

had marched upon Norfolk, the most important city in the state.

---

indignant: angry

When they heard this, Betsy and her father pricked up their ears, for Norfolk was scarcely more than fifty miles from their home.

The fishermen interrupted each other to tell of the outrages of Dunmore. He had destroyed the hard-won crops of the settlers round about Norfolk, they related indignantly. He had burned houses, and slaughtered cattle, hogs, and poultry. Planters had seen their life work destroyed in the space of an hour. And it was rumored, declared they, that Dunmore was planning to march upon North Carolina and destroy the settlement along the Albemarle.

That night, sitting around the driftwood fire, Joe Dowdy retold the news to his neighbor, Sammy Jarvis. "The British swine!" he shouted, red in the face with indignation. "There's a report that he's plannin' to march into the Albemarle settlement, a-burnin', and a-killin', and a-plunderin' as he goes."

Across the hearth, Betsy sat quietly, but her eyes were wide and her small face pale.

"I'm a-goin' crost the sound to the mainland tomorrow and find out all about it!" declared Sammy Jarvis, and the next morning his neighbors watched him set off in a small boat, his back bending valiantly to the oars.

It was late afternoon when he returned. Betsy was making preparations for supper when there came a knocking at the door.

"Come in!" bawled Joe Dowdy, and Sammy Jarvis burst into the room. Betsy stared up at the sight of his staring eyes and perspiring face.

"It's a fact!" shouted Sammy at the top of his lungs, without waiting for a word of greeting.

". . . What's a fact, Sammy? You mean Dunmore's marching into Carolina?"

"He's on his way!" panted Sammy Jarvis. "Got as far as Great Bridge, right this side o' Norfolk!"

Betsy Dowdy said nothing, but she put aside the bluefish she was about to fry.

"Ain't there nobody tryin' to stop him?" asked Joe Dowdy, half out of his chair.

"Well, they say some Virginia troops are marchin' toward Great Bridge—John Marshall is with 'em. But there's only a handful of 'em, and them as green as grass!" Sammy Jarvis ran his hand through his hair until it stood up wildly. "Why, it's just like opposin' a lion with a swarm o' gnats!"

"Why don't they get word to General Skinner up on Yeopim Creek?" asked Joe Dowdy. "He's got the militia up there, a whole passel* of 'em. He'd stop old Dunmore, if anybody could."

---

passel: large number

"There was talk o' that," said Sammy Jarvis, "but hit's so . . . far to Yeopim Creek, they don't figger they could make it before dark—and t'would be too late to wait till tomorrow to set off to Yeopim. If he didn't get the word by daybreak tomorrow, he couldn't get to Great Bridge in time."

"If a man rode all night, seems to me like he'd be able to make it to Yeopim Creek by daybreak," said Betsy's father.

"Take that ride all night!" cried Sammy Jarvis. "Man alive, are you crazy? There's fifty miles o' swamp and woods and water atween here and Yeopim Creek. It's as much as a man can do to get through in the daytime. There ain't a chance in a hundred he could do it at night. And there's Currituck Sound atween here and the mainland, how'd you get your horse acrost it? It's safe enough to swim him acrost in the daylight—but in the night, with the tide runnin' strong, well—I'd ruther commit suicide some other way!"

Joe Dowdy looked down at the floor. "Reckon you're right, Sammy," he agreed slowly. "Reckon there ain't nothin' we can do about gettin' word to General Skinner."

Sixteen-year-old Betsy Dowdy still stood by the table. Already she could see the British putting torches to the fine homes along the Albemarle. She could hear the lowing* of cattle led to the slaughter, the whinnying of horses driven off with the hateful British army. Like a sword thrust came the thought that her own home might be one of those laid waste, her own beloved Nellie taken away for some detested British soldier to ride. A wave of devotion for her own wild home-place surged upon Betsy and half choked her. She loved the tumbling hills, the lonely stretches of marsh-land, and the gnarled live oaks. Her eyes caressed the humble and familiar things in her father's home. The fish nets hanging from the rafters—during long hours her father had worked at them, twisting the threads and knotting them by hand—and in the corner her own little bed with its patchwork quilt—what labor had gone into the making of that! Pots and kettles simmering over the blazing fire; upon the window sill a row of treasures gathered along the beach—a conch shell lined with pink, a starfish, and a branch of rose coral washed up from who knows what tropical shore. This was home!

---

lowing: mooing

Betsy's young face set into firm lines. The British should not lay waste the plantations along the Albemarle, not if she could help it! They should not put the torch to her own small home! Silently she brought out a small pouch and filled it with coins; into another pouch she put some slices of meat and a piece of corn-bread. The two men, engrossed in the impending* disaster, spread their hands to the fire and croaked on and on. They did not even look up as the girl, a heavy cape across her shoulders, opened the cottage door and slipped outside.

---

impending: about to occur

The sun was sinking and chill mists were winding about the dunes as she stepped from the cottage door and made her way to the herding pen.

"Nellie! Nellie!" she called softly. The banker pony came whickering* out of the fog. Dear, faithful Nellie, companion of many a happy gallop across the dunes! She was to have a longer, grimmer ride tonight, and before it was over, she was to prove her worth. With sure hands Betsy cinched* the saddle upon the pony's back and flung herself into it. Her long cape flew out with the wind as they set off at a gallop across the sands.

---

whickering: whinnying
cinched: tightened

The pony's hoofs fell with muffled beat as they sped on and on. Well-known mounds and hillocks seemed strange and unfamiliar in their misty winding sheets. The wind was cold and, before five miles had been passed, Betsy began to think wistfully of her father and his old friend sitting cozily in front of the fire. But she did not consider turning back. Along the sandbank she flew, the ocean beating upon one side, Currituck Sound lapping gently at the other.

Betsy knew that in order to reach the mainland she must cross the sound* which seemed to stretch so shorelessly to the right of her. Its narrowest stretch was at a point opposite Church Island and she rode her pony slowly now, peering anxiously across the water, she saw a dark smudge which might be the pines and live oaks on Church Island. The moon was up now, but shining so faintly through the mist that she could not be sure, though she knew that she must chance it.

---

sound: a wide ocean inlet

Tucking up her skirts, she urged her pony into the murky* water. The sturdy animal waded until her feet could no longer touch bottom, then she swam. The tide was running strong as the brave animal struck out through the deep water for the distant shore line. Three long miles she swam through chill dark water and, when at last her hoofs touched solid ground, the young girl on her back breathed a prayer of thankfulness. They had reached the shore of Church Island.

---

murky: dark

Nellie shook herself and threaded her way among the somber* pines and fragrant myrtles toward the opposite shore. The whole of Currituck Sound was not yet crossed: a still longer stretch lay between the island and the mainland. Betsy did not pause as she reached the far beach.

---

somber: dark and gloomy

"Come on, Nellie! One more stretch to cross! On! On!" The little mare dashed again into the cold waters of the Currituck. Wide silver ripples streamed out behind the two in the water as the pony swam strongly against the tide. Betsy clung to the saddle and kept her eyes wishfully upon the dark line which was the mainland. It grew steadily larger as Nellie swam confidently on.

Dripping with cold water, the pony climbed at last upon the marshy shore of the mainland. With a thankful heart Betsy turned and looked back at the water just passed. Her cottage home with its hearth fire seemed far away in some other, secure existence. There could be no turning back now, and she set her mind resolutely* ahead.

---

resolutely: determinedly

This territory was new and strange to the girl. She had heard her father describe the trails that ran through this country, but the things did not look as she had pictured them. The marsh stretched out for miles and there did not seem to be a path anywhere. Perhaps the pony's eyes were keener than her own. Betsy gave her free rein, and Nellie stepped out confidently. Sometimes she sank into the mire* and floundered* almost to her belly in mud. The dry rushes swirled around her rider's legs. They struggled on and on, and at last the ground grew firmer under foot.

mire: soggy ground
floundered: sank

A dark wall of forest stood up in front of them now, grimly forbidding. Betsy tried not to think of the stories she had heard of the Currituck wilderness: the lurking Indians always ready with their tomahawks, the bears, the poisonous moccasins, the panther-cats ready to leap from overhead branches upon the unwary* traveler. At the edge of the forest, the banker pony snorted and pranced unwillingly. Betsy trembled, but she urged Nellie into the blackness.

unwary: not alert

Trying to close her mind to the terror of the forest, Betsy kept her thoughts steadfastly upon the fine house on Yeopim Creek, the militia, and General Skinner, but she could not help shivering at each rustling in the underbrush, each unexpected snapping of a twig. Perhaps the beasts and the reptiles and the savages declared a truce* that night, for Betsy Dowdy passed through the forest unharmed. The rude trail led her at last to the shores of the Pasquotank River. She knew that a ferry was run here by an old man called Gid Lamb, and she thudded up to his cabin and knocked upon the door.

truce: temporary stop

"Hello!" called Betsy. "Hello! Hello!"
There was no answer, and the girl leaned over and pounded loudly on the door.

Gid Lamb at last put his head out of the door. "Eh—eh—what's up? Who's disturbin' the peace so late at night?" he inquired crossly.

"It's me—me, Betsy Dowdy," a young voice piped out of the dark. "Please hurry up! Take me across the river—I'm riding to warn General Skinner that the British are coming!"

"Eh! What! The British are comin'?" Betsy could hear the old man stumbling hurriedly about inside. Soon he appeared, half dressed. Betsy guided her mount upon the ferryboat and Gid Lamb loosed it upon the current.

As the old man started to pole his flatboat across the river, Betsy dismounted. The pony stood quietly, grateful for the short rest. The moon sailed high now and Betsy's spirits rose. Half the journey was behind her—she would get there in time, she knew she would!

As the ferry bumped the shore, she took a coin from her bag and offered it to the ferryman, but he waved it aside.

"No charge for you tonight, child," he said, "and Godspeed to you!"

Betsy leaped into the saddle. "Thank you, sir!" she cried, and went pounding away into the darkness. On and on she rode, through the swamps of Pasquotank, threading a perilous way among cypress and juniper trees.

In the cold darkness just before the dawn, she clattered wearily into the town of Hertford. Her pony's hoof beats echoed among the silent houses. That house with the grand double porches must be the Eagle Tavern. Betsy knew it by description from castaway guests. She drew up, knocked upon the door and shouted for directions to General Skinner's place on Yeopim Creek. The innkeeper, roused from his bed, set her on the right road and on she thudded.

A flush of pink, like the lining of her treasured conch shell, was spreading over the sky as Betsy rode up the highlands of Perquimans County, through which ran Yeopim Creek. Soon she would be at the end of her journey. She thought, almost with unbelief, of the dark and dangerous miles between her and her home.

The sun was rising as she rode in through the gate of General Skinner's home on Yeopim Creek. Life on the busy plantation was just beginning for the day. Slaves and indentured servants* were going about their tasks, and the General himself was at hand to see that all began smoothly. When he saw the mud-splattered girl on her tired pony, he came forward and greeted her with amazement. His eyes snapped as she poured out her story of Lord Dunmore and the impending battle at Great Bridge.

---

indentured servants: those working to repay money borrowed for passage to America

---

Hardly waiting for her to finish, the hardy* soldier began shouting for his horse, his sword, his boots and spurs. Young Betsy was handed over to the care of his three daughters, Dolly, Penelope, and Lavinia, and the General rode swiftly away to assist the Virginians at Great Bridge.

---

hardy: strong

Resting upon a huge bed in an upstairs room of the comfortable plantation house, Betsy could hardly believe that this was she. She glanced upward at the snowy valance* of the tall four-poster bed and aside at the three beautiful and daintily dressed young ladies fluttering about, one carrying washbasin and towels, another a tray with rolls, slices of venison and wild turkey, and still another a pot of yaupon tea. They plied her with a hundred questions.

---

valance: canopy

The little girl of the sandbanks lingered in the plantation house of the Yeopim only until noon. Her father, she felt sure, would be anxious about her. She mounted her pony after the midday meal, and set off on the homeward journey.

Lord Dunmore and his British soldiers did not destroy the humble home on the sandbanks. He did not lay waste the fine plantations on the Albemarle. He got no farther toward North Carolina than Great Bridge across the Virginia line. There he was met by the Virginia sharpshooters and the troops from North Carolina, and he was defeated utterly. The patriots sent him flying back to Norfolk where he took refuge on the "Liverpool," a British battleship, which had just sailed into the harbor.

The humble cottage where Betsy Dowdy lived has long since fallen into ruin, and even the site of it has been forgotten. But the brave young girl and her banker pony are still remembered. Around the hearth fires which glow in the homes along the sandbanks, and through the lush* farm country which she once saved from the British, they still tell the story of Betsy Dowdy's ride to save her homeland.

lush: fertile

About the Story

1. How does Betsy's father earn a living?
2. What unusual opportunities does Betsy have as a result of this?
3. How is Betsy's response to the news of Lord Dunmore's planned attack different from Sammy's or her father's?
4. What does Betsy have to ride through in order to reach General Skinner?
5. Who helps Betsy in her all-night ride?
6. What happens as a result of Betsy's ride?

About the Author

Ellis Credle (pronounced *cradle*) was born in the swamp region of North Carolina in 1902. After college she became a schoolteacher in the Blue Ridge Mountains but found teaching an unsuitable occupation. Interested and talented in art, she was hired in 1933 to draw illustrations for two different art museums. On her day off each week, she worked on an original picture book entitled *Down, Down the Mountain*, which, after numerous rejections, was published in 1934. She married Charles Townsend in 1935 and continued writing and illustrating picture books, sometimes collaborating with her husband, a skilled photographer.

The Friend Inside

T. Morris Longstreth

How would you react if you were asked to be a special messenger for the president of the United States? In this story Jim Kaley gets such an opportunity. The job sorely tests his courage to do right. What does he do in order to get victory over temptation? What does the title mean?

Jim Kaley descended the winding stairway in the deepest gloom of his seventeen years. He should have stayed at home on the farm.

"You've got to have pull," Uncle Joe had warned him.

"The army's pulling me. That's pull enough," Jim had told him.

But apparently it wasn't. The recruiters weren't taking minors. The sour-jawed man whom he had just seen, declined his services. And now he had spent so much time in his vain search that he hadn't money enough to get home.

As he emerged on Pennsylvania Avenue, Jim was aware that he had left his hat in the War Department office. "Calf brain!" he ejaculated* in disgust. He hated to reveal his absent-minded carelessness to the sour-jawed man, but he couldn't afford to leave his hat. So he turned back up the winding stairs, angrily taking two at a stride. Suddenly his head butted into a man descending—forcibly, blindly into the man's middle.

---

ejaculated: exclaimed

"Hold on there!" gasped a voice.

"Mr. President, are you hurt?" sounded another.

Then an indignant army officer shouted at Jim, "Do you realize you've hurt the President of the United States?"

"Not hurt, General—a bit winded. I only wish that our army could charge like this boy."

Jim, blushing and breathless, looked up at the man who headed the nation, the man he

admired most in the world. "Excuse me, Mr. Lincoln. I'm mortified* something terrible. I just left my hat upstairs."

mortified: ashamed

"Are you one of our messengers?" Lincoln asked kindly.

"No, sir. I wanted to get into the army, but they won't let me."

"I think that's a mistake," Lincoln chuckled. "I can vouch for* your hitting power."

vouch for: give witness of

The general was impatient. "If I may venture to suggest, Mr. President . . ."

"One moment, General. Perhaps I can help this young man. Come upstairs with me," Lincoln said to Jim. "Tell me your name and a little about yourself."

Jim passed the angry general and followed the President. He had never dreamt of speaking to his hero. And now a general was cooling his heels while the commander in chief was doing Jim a service. Whatever happened, he would remember this all his life.

The sour-jawed man rose respectfully. Lincoln laid a hand on Jim's shoulder. "Ambrose, this hard-headed young man wants to serve his country in some way. I wish you could find him some suitable employment at a good remuneration."*

remuneration: payment

"Certainly, Your Excellency," Mr. Ambrose replied. "It occurs to me that Benner will be leaving the messenger line tomorrow. Perhaps . . ."

"Just the thing!" Lincoln exclaimed. He lifted his hand from Jim's shoulder. "Mr. Ambrose will instruct you. We shall meet again; but not on a dark stairway, I hope."

Before Jim could express his thanks, Lincoln strode away.

Three days later Jim Kaley woke in the dark from the first nightmare of his healthy young life. He had been given a confidential dispatch* by the President and had lost it. Jim struggled awake as from an underground cell in Libby Prison.* The collar of his nightshirt was wet with perspiration of fright.

dispatch: an official written message
Libby Prison: a Confederate prison at Richmond, Virginia

The three days had been confusing, difficult, and glorious. How could he make his mother and Uncle Joe and the rest understand the glory? Or the difficulties! He must know where to find the members of Mr. Lincoln's cabinet. He must know the most direct route to the generals, naval commanders, the Senators and Representatives. He must carry his dispatches safely, swiftly. Jim shuddered at his nightmare. If this horror of carelessness happened in real life, he would die of shame, to say nothing of being deprived of his glory.

For it was glory to walk into the White House as if it were his own. He tried not to feel superior to the crowds of the curious and of office seekers who had to wait whole days, sometimes, to see the President; and he, Jim Kaley of Rabbit Hill, Maryland, could take precedence over* Vice-President Hamlin.

take precedence over: go before

Then one day he was alone with the President, who was writing a letter, and Jim had a glowing feeling that he was really working with Mr. Lincoln, even though he was the smallest kind of partner in the firm.

The President wrote a sentence, then read it over and laid down his pen and thought. Presently he took up the paper and read the last sentence aloud. "I desire so to conduct the affairs of this administration that if, at the end, when I come to lay down the reins of power, I have lost every other friend on earth, I shall

have at least one friend left, and that friend shall be down inside of me."

Jim thrilled to hear the words that he was sure came from the very center of Mr. Lincoln's being; you could tell it by his voice. Lincoln looked up at Jim and said: "You will hear lots in this room you must not pass on, my boy."

"Yes, sir," Jim replied. "But I wish I could pass on that—about keeping the friend inside. I intend never to forget that, sir."

Lincoln's calm, piercing eyes searched Jim's face for a moment. "Someday you'll find that the Bible and Shakespeare have said the same thing, Jim—and said it better."

"Yes, sir. But you make it mighty plain."

It was on the day after the nightmare that Jim was given his first really important errand. John Hay, Lincoln's secretary, had just brought some disturbing message to the President. Lincoln wrote a few lines hastily and beckoned Jim to him. "You know your way to the Capitol now, Jim?" and at Jim's "Yes, sir," Lincoln handed him the paper. "Take that to Senator Sherman. Give it to no one else. Do

not cease searching till you find him. Wait and bring his answer to me. This is urgent and confidential."

Jim Kaley left the White House elated.* The dispatch was in an inner pocket, although he carried his dispatch bag. He would find the Senator and amaze Lincoln by his promptness. Life was very good.

---

elated: in high spirits

Jim had hardly left the White House grounds before he was accosted* by a man of thirty or so who had apparently run after him. "You are Jim Kaley, the messenger?" the man asked.

---

accosted: approached

Jim was startled, but he remembered the rules laid down by Mr. Ambrose. "It makes no difference who I am," Jim said without a tone of offense.

"Don't be a fool," the stranger broke out. "Mr. Hay sent me out to catch you. The President wishes to make some changes in the dispatch you are carrying."

Jim was troubled. He had his instruction, and he had Mr. Ambrose's rules, the chief of which was to carry out instructions at the risk of his life, and he had sworn to obey. "How do I know what Mr. Hay wants?" Jim demanded. "I have only your word for it."

"Come, come, you greenhorn," the man exclaimed, and he held out a paper on which Jim saw the official seal. "Give me your paper, and take this one, and don't make a scene in the street. If you hand Senator Sherman the wrong paper, you will get Mr. Lincoln into a peck of trouble and be out of a job."

The fact that this stranger spoke of Senator Sherman when the dispatch was confidential, wrung* Jim's fortitude.* But the sour-jawed man had made a deep impression. "My business is urgent, or I might return with you," Jim

told the stranger. "I'm sorry, but I shall have to go on."

wrung: twisted: i.e., shook
fortitude: strength of mind

"What a stubborn idiot!" As he snarled this, the stranger reached for the dispatch case and wrenched it almost loose from Jim's hand. Jim, half through the clenched fist of anger and half through wariness, was prepared. He not only held on to the case, but with his other hand grabbed the man by his coat collar and started to drag him toward the policeman seated astride a horse at the corner. The stranger wrenched loose. "You fool, you'll hear of this later!" he shouted as he ran.

Jim, worried and shaken, continued to the Capitol. He found Senator Sherman and returned with his response to Lincoln's note. As he approached the White House, Jim felt ill. After boasting in his letters home, he might be serving his last hour as the President's messenger. He strode past the waiting office seekers without gloating* now. He entered Mr. Lincoln's office. Secretary of War Stanton was haranguing* the President. Jim handed Mr. Lincoln the dispatch from the Senator and stood like a condemned man on the hangman's trap.*

gloating: feeling self-satisfied
haranguing: speaking with strong feeling to
hangman's trap: trap door

"Thank you, Jim," Lincoln said and glanced at his messenger. "You look pale. I'm afraid you've been hurrying too fast."

Jim wanted to blurt out what had happened, but he restrained himself. He sought his seat and listened.

"There is no use in trying to talk me over, Stanton," Lincoln said. "We don't override* the law. Get the law changed first. You remind me of the kindhearted gentleman who was in here yesterday. He was pleading for a private locked up because he had knocked down his captain. I couldn't send him away empty-handed. 'I'll tell you what I'll do,' I said to console* him. 'You go to the Capitol and get Congress to make it legal for a private to knock down his captain, and I'll pardon your man.' "

override: set aside
console: comfort

Lincoln chuckled, and even the grim Stanton laughed in his beard and turned away. And suddenly Jim knew that he would not burden Mr. Lincoln with his adventure. The friend down inside approved.

A week later Jim strolled down [a Washington street] after dusk. He had stopped in front of Ford's Theater to watch the people enter, when a large man with very solid-looking shoulders came up to him. Jim had grown somewhat accustomed to sizing up people. This hulking fellow with the fancy waistcoat had a tight line for a mouth, and dark eyes that looked as if they were used to having their way.

The Friend Inside 37

"I know you. You're Jim Kaley," the man said quietly. "I've been watching you, and you're smart."

Jim was already on his guard. A compliment from this man affected him like an insult. Jim said nothing.

"I like that, too," the man went on. "You've learned to keep your trap shut. I pay high for that, Bud."

Jim flared inside. He hated familiarity from a stranger.

"Drink?" the man asked suddenly.

"No," Jim said.

"That's dandy. Can't do my work if you drink. Let's go somewhere and have a little talk."

"No, thank you. I have a job." Jim started to move away. A hand restrained him.

"Didn't I say I knew all about you?" the stranger continued. "I know you've got a job. But if I could tell you how to make five dollars in gold every day, maybe several times a day, for five minutes' work, wouldn't that be a nice present to send home to your mother?"

"No job pays that," Jim said.

"Now wait. I said you was smart. But you ain't so smart if you can't listen, Bud. I stand to pay five dollars in gold for five minutes of your time. And if I get what I want, I make it a hundred dollars in gold."

Jim could not help being curious. "What is it you want that bad?"

"There's a tobacco shop on the avenue across from the War Building. The man who runs it is a buddy of mine. All I want is for you to go in there, lay your dispatch case down while you're having a soft drink, and when it's hot like this you need one."

Jim saw what was coming, and an anger such as he had never felt before began to burst in him.

The stranger went on. "My buddy in there will pay you five dollars in gold for every time you stop, and if he finds the dispatch he wants, it's a hundred doll—"

Jim could not help it. He was sorry an instant later. But in between, his closed fist met the face of the bigger man. The stranger crumpled and fell, and his head struck the cobblestone pavement.

Jim was too proud to run. Instead, he bent down to help his victim up. A crowd had already encircled them. The fallen man lay unconscious. A policeman shouldered the onlookers aside. "You'd better come with me," he said to Jim.

"He's dead," announced a bystander.

"Call a doctor, quick," shouted another.

"You'd better hold that fellow," advised another. "He's dangerous."

Jim Kaley sat on the hard cot in his cell. Locked up like a criminal!

Jim figured that it was after eleven o'clock. He had followed Mr. Ambrose's instructions: if in trouble, show your badge and demand that your message be immediately delivered to this office. Yet he had sent his message three hours ago.

Jim leaned his face in his hands. The President's voice came back to him, ". . . if I have lost every other friend on earth, I shall have at least one friend left, and that friend shall be down inside of me." That earnest, low voice, so telling in its sincerity! Jim took heart a little from the memory. At least he was still friends with himself.

Voices sounded at the end of the darkened cell block. He recognized the jailer's sour and sleepy "It's very irregular, sir."

"It is irregular, you must admit, for a boy to be held up in the streets of Washington. Bring him to me."

"I have to have a writ* sir."

writ: a written order from a court

"I tell you the President assumes responsibility. He has notified your chief. Bring me Mr. Kaley at once."

Jim had heard that voice. It was forceful, impatient. Inmates of adjoining cells were waking, grumbling. A yellow light appeared. Keys turned. The jailer, looking sleepy, called into Jim's cell. "Come out. You're wanted."

And then sarcastically, "I didn't know you was the pers'nal friend of the President."

Jim followed the light. By the door stood the stranger who had tried to grab Jim's dispatch case. "You're a nice one," this man said curtly,* but he smiled at the same time. "Come, you're keeping the President out of bed."

curtly: rudely abrupt

"But you?" Jim gasped. The mysteries were too thick.

"I'll tell you in the hack."

They left the jail, entered the vehicle, and Jim's rescuer said: "I'm a secret service operator, Kaley. I happened to be with Mr. Lincoln over in the War Office when your message came. In spite of your having sent our best operative to the hospital, the President insisted upon your being liberated. You're fortunate. He seems to be interested in you."

"Then you didn't mean to snatch my case?" said Jim.

"You were being tested, Kaley. You didn't suppose we could allow somebody we weren't sure of to carry dispatches that might rock the nation if disclosed,* did you? I test a new messenger for presence of mind, alertness, courage. And then we let Harvey, the man you wouldn't have much to do with . . ." the stranger laughed once and continued, "then we let him try your morals. He tries to get you to drink, tries to bribe, and if there's the slightest inclination* to waver, then you're not for us. But it was a little excessive of you, Kaley, to . . ."

disclosed: made known
inclination: tendency

"Then he's not dead?" Jim asked. This man couldn't laugh if he were.

"Dead? Of course not. How did you get that impression? He was stunned, but the surgeon says there's no concussion, and he'll be around tomorrow."

Jim felt relieved. The hack was stopping in front of the War Department. "The President's in the telegraph office. You know, at the head of the first stairway. I've got another duty."

"Oh, thanks! Thanks so much!" Jim said.

Jim climbed the winding stairs, thinking many things. He entered the dim office. A telegraph instrument was clicking away. An operator in shirt sleeves was decoding a message. President Lincoln was reading a yellow sheet and the furrows* across his brow were deep. But as he saw the country boy, his face lit noticeably. "Glad you're back, Jim," he said as if nothing had happened. "I was asking for you, just as your message arrived. I've an errand for you, and I think you can do it."

---
furrows: wrinkles

"I'll try, sir. I'm sorry for all the bother I've caused, Mr. Lincoln. But I didn't know that Mr. Harvey wasn't . . . real."

"Harvey's a little like myself—well paid for getting into trouble," Lincoln said with a chuckle. "Don't you worry about him. You were keeping friends with yourself, and that always costs somebody something. I would say this, however"—Lincoln paused and smiled broadly—"if in the future you have to discipline somebody, hit him with a club, or a crowbar, and not with your fist—or head!"

About the Story

1. What lesson does Jim "intend never to forget"?
2. Why does Jim put the important dispatch in his pocket, not in the dispatch case?
3. Jim Kaley is the main character in the story, but what does the reader discover about President Lincoln?
4. With what positive character qualities does Jim meet and pass his test?
5. What does Lincoln mean by stating that he is "well paid for getting into trouble"?

About the Author

Being "born a Philadelphia Quaker in the midst of a February blizzard" accounts for T. Morris Longstreth's (1886-1975) interest in weather. Being a traveling tutor accounts for his interest in boys and for the time spent "viewing boyhood from different angles." Being the historian of the Royal Canadian Mounted Police accounts for his interest in history. Believing that "history gives sound footing to interest," Longstreth often used boys as main characters in historical selections as he does in this one.

Yes, Your Honesty

George and Helen W. Papashvily

It takes courage to swim against the world's currents. In this story an immigrant who understands little of his adopted land's language and customs is consistently given the wrong advice by those who should know better. His friends tell him that he should plead guilty in court to breaking a city ordinance. If he does so, they explain, he will solve his problem. What does he decide to do? Does his decision cost him?

Six months in America and already I was a jailbird. Happened this way. The weeks seemed extra long that first half year I was in New York. No holidays, no feast days, no celebrations to break up the time and then when Saturday came around I had only twelve dollars—at most fourteen dollars—in my pay envelope.

The man I met in Central Park on my first day in America gave me a job in his garage like he promised. But after I was there about two months his wife's mother got sick and they closed up and moved to the country. With my poor language, wasn't easy to find another place.

I tried silk mill and after that factory where they made statues—ugly ones—from plaster. I stayed there until head artist gave me camel to cast, only looked like a cow, this camel. I was ashamed to make such a monstrosity animal so I changed shape little bit here and there to give some camel personality to it.

But when artist saw he got mad and told me how many schools he was in—London, Paris, Dresden—(just my point, no camels living in any of those places, certainly) and I'm fired again.

Then I went for house painter but somehow the boss and me didn't suit each other. Finally I met a Russian, who worked in a cleaning factory, and he took me for his assistant. It was awful place. I dipped the clothes to take away spots. The gas we used came up in my head and through my throat and out my ears. My every piece of meat whole week long was spiced with that gas.

But no matter how the week went the Sundays were good because then we made all day the holiday and took ourselves in Van Cortlandt Park where there was country and trees and flowers. We could make fires and roast cubed lamb *shashliks** and walk on the grass and forget the factory. For one day anyway we could enjoy to live like human beings.

shashliks: shish kebab

From six o'clock on, every Sunday morning, subway was packed full. Russians, Syrians, Greeks, Armenians, all kinds of peoples, carrying their grampas and babies and gallon jugs and folding chairs and charcoal sacks and hammocks and samovars* and lunch baskets and rugs. Everyone hurrying to their regular place in the park so they could start tea and lay out the lunch, to make the day last a long, long time.

samovars: metal urns used for boiling tea (Russian)

Well, this particular Sunday when all my trouble began was in the late spring. Bright blue day with a high sky and white lamb clouds. The kind of day that's for adventures. I had my first American-bought suit on and a purple-striped tie with a handkerchief to match and a real Yankee-Doodle hat from straw. I felt happy and full of prance.*

full of prance: lively

Five or six other fellows and me were visiting around the park. We went from family to family we knew—and drank a glass of wine here, tried a piece of cake there, met an uncle just came from Buffalo, saw a new baby first time out, and so on.

While we were making short cut down a quiet path to get on other side of the park we came to a beautiful tree foaming over with white blossoms, how they call in English—dogswood.

"Flowers, Flowers," one Russian fellow, name of Cyrille, said. "I gonna pick. Take bouquet to my lady friend." I don't know who he was, this fellow he joined us some place we stopped.

"Pick! Pick!" Everybody got the idea. "Pick flowers, take a bouquet to all the lady friends."

"Why spoil a tree?" I said. "Use your brains better. If you want to make friends with a nice young lady, ask her to take a walk. Tell her you gonna show her a bouquet bigger than a house, and bouquet growing right out of the ground. Something interesting. That way you get a chance to be acquainted while you're walking. Maybe you know so good on the way back you can invite for ice cream."

No, no—won't listen. They have to break the tree down. Tear his arms and legs off like wolves. Jumping. Jumping. Who's gonna get the biggest branch? Makes me sick.

"Personally," I said, "I would be ashamed to give a lady flowers that I got for nothing. That I stold. I prefer better to buy. Shows more respect. Or else don't give."

All of a sudden that fellow Cyrille, who had now the biggest bunch, climbed down from the top branches and said to me, "I have to tie my shoelace. Hold my bouquet for a minute. I'll be back." So I held. In that minute a policeman was there.

"Awright, awright," he said. "Defacing public property. Awright." He asked us our names and started writing them down on a piece of paper.

"What he does?" I asked Sergei.

"Gives us a summons."

"Summons?"

"We have to go in court."

"We're arrested?"

"Something like that. If we pay the fine, everything be okay. But if we ignore, throw away the summons, they chase us—lock us up."

"What's your name, buddy?" policeman asked me.

I explained the best I can I'm not picking, I'm only holding for the other fellow.

But he doesn't believe me. "Don't argue," he said. "Don't argue or I'll run you in right now."

I explained again. "Boys will tell you," I said. "I wasn't picking."

No, he doesn't believe them neither. "Don't alibi him," he said.

I'd be sorry to be a man like that policeman, suspicious that everybody is a liar. What's the use for a person to live if he can't trust nobody?

So he wrote a ticket for me, too, and went away. And still tying his shoe, that fellow Cyrille wasn't back yet.

"This is an awful, awful thing," I said.

"It's nothing." Sergei could laugh.

"Nothing! I lived my whole life at home and I was never in trouble. Now I'm six months in America and I'm a crook. Nothing, you think? How my father likes to hear such kind of news? Arrested. What will our village say? The first man from Kobiankari ever comes in U.S.A.—for what? To go in prison!"

"Look," Sergei said. "You don't even have to go in court. Send the money. Plead guilty."

"But I'm not."

"You only say you are. Saves time."

"Then the policeman's right never to believe anybody. Say first, I didn't. Then next time, change around, say I did."

"If you won't plead guilty, you'll have to go in court and have a trial."

"Then I'll go."

"Lose a day's pay."

"I lose."

"How about we find the policeman," Arkady suggested, "and try once more?"

"No use," Sergei said. "For myself I'm gonna plead guilty, but the best thing we can do for Giorgi Ivanitch, let's we go back in New York and see a fixer."

"What means vixer?" I said. "Vixer? Kind of a fox, isn't it?"

"*Ef.* Fixer. It's a man. People pays him for fixing things. He knows how to manage all kinds of permits; he fills out income tax blanks, tears up traffic tickets. Suppose you're refused a license for something, you give the fixer money, he finds some way around to get it anyway for you."

"Still sounds like a fox."

"That's vixen," Sergei said. "Keep straight the words in your head. You get everybody mixed up. Fixers has big connections. Influences."

So we went and fixer had big rooms to show up he's a somebody, but the floor was imitation marble; the stand lamps some kind of cast metal golded over to look real—and on a veneer* table sets a big plated vase full with paper roses. Is plank mahogany, the panels in the wall? I felt them. Nope. Plyboard.

veneer: a thin layer of fine wood

"If he matches his office," I told the boys, "he's not even gonna be a real man. Gonna be a dummy stuffed with straw and a Victrola* in his mouth."

Victrola: record player

"Shut up or you'll be twice in jail."

Fixer came in. "So what can I do for you, my boys? In trouble?"

I showed the summons.

"Trouble with the police?" The fixer shook his head very sad. "Trouble with the police is serious business. No doubt you're a foreigner?"

"In the U.S.A. I am, yes," I said.

"Well, give me a retaining fee.* Ten dollars is customary, but I'll take you for five and we see what we can do."

retaining fee: fee for hiring a lawyer

I paid him the money over.

"Now let's hear."

My committee explained the whole story.

Fixer thought. Look through his papers. Made a few notes on a pad. Thought again. "I tell you," he said finally, "only one solution. You go in court tomorrow, plead guilty, is about a two-dollar fine and it's all over. I use my connections on the side to fix everything for you."

"Look," I told him, "I didn't pick flowers. So I'm not gonna say I did. Hang me in chains but nobody can make me say I did do what I didn't do."

So that ends that. No more help from the fixer. He's mad. Sergei suggested how about we go to see old Mr. Cohen; he was years and years in the U.S.A. Maybe he can think of something.

"Listen," Mr. Cohen said, when we told him everything. "Fixer mixer leave alone all. Take my advices. I been a citizen for forty-seven years with full papers. President Hayes signed me in personal. Go in court. When they ask you the first question say, 'Not guilty, Your Honor.'"

"Not guilty, Your Honor. What means 'Your Honor'?"

"Means the judge. All judges in U.S.A. named Your Honor."

"Not guilty, Your Honor. Then?"

"Just tell your story nice way."

"With my broken words?"

"Say the best way you can. Probably judge gonna listen and try to understand you. Of course it can happen you get a mean judge, one that's too tired to pay attention, that don't like foreigners to bother him. But very few those kind. If you get such a one, pay your fine, don't argue. But don't be disgusted with the U.S.A. Just come and tell me."

"What you gonna do?"

"Why next time, I vote against him, naturally. We don't keep him in office no more, if he don't act nice."

So next morning I went in court. Called the other names Igor, Arkady, Sergei, Phillip. Guilty. Guilty. Guilty. All sent money to pay their fines.

Now my name. I couldn't understand a word they asked me. I was nervous. My English was running out of my head like sand through a sieve. How they told me to call a judge? Your Honorable? No. Your Highness? No, that's Russian. Your? —They were asking me something. I had to answer. I took my courage in my two hands and spoke out.

"Not guilty, Your Honesty."

Courtroom went wild. Laughing and laughing. Laughing like hyenas. The judge pounded with hammer. Bang. Bang. Bang! His face was red like a turkey's. What I done? I was sure I was going in Sing Sing* and be thrown in the deepest-down dungeon.

Sing Sing: state prison in New York

But the judge was bombasting* the audience first. "Word honesty—applied by this—cause such mirth—contempt of court."

---

bombasting: lecturing

"Young man"—now he was through with them, it be my turn—"address the Court as Sir."

"Yes, sir."

"Did I understand you to plead not guilty?"

"Yes, sir. Not guilty."

"This officer says you and your friends were violating an ordinance* destroying a tree. Breaking the limbs."

---

ordinance: city regulation

"Yes, sir. Some was picking. I wasn't."

"Have you any proof of this?"

"No, sir. Friends were with me, but they can't come today. They all pleaded guilty, sent you a fine. Cheaper than to lose a day's pay."

"Why didn't you do that?"

"Because if I'm guilty I admit it, but if I'm not guilty, no man gonna make me say I am. Just as much a lie to say you guilty when you not as to say you innocent if you did wrong."

"Yes, that's correct. How long are you in the United States?"

"Six months."

"In court here before?"

"No, sir."

"Ever in trouble at home? Assault or kill a man?"

"Yes, sir."

"How many?"

"Hundreds. After the first year, I never counted them any more."

"Where was this?"

"In the war. I'm a sniper. It's my job to shoot all the Germans I see. Sometimes Bulgarians, too, but mostly they didn't have much interest to show themselves, poor fellows."

"I see. I mean in civil life. When you were not a soldier, not in the army. Ever hurt or strike anybody?"

"Yes, sir. Once."

"What?"

"Knocked a man's teeths out. Few."

"Why?"

"Catched him giving poisoned meat to my dog to eat."

"Understandable. Only time?"

"Yes, sir."

"Sure?"

"Yes, sir."

"Did you actually see this man," His Honesty asked the policeman, "breaking the tree?"

"No, sir. Not exactly, but all the others admitted guilt and he was with them, holding a bunch of flowers."

"I believe he's a truthful man, Officer, and this time you were probably mistaken. Case dismissed."

And then His Honesty, big American judge, leaned over. And what do you think he said to me—ignorant, no speaking language, six months off a boat, greenhorn foreigner? "Young man, I like to shake hands with you."

And in front of that whole courtroom, he did.

About the Story

1. Why does Cyrille ask the speaker to hold the flowers?
2. Why is the speaker's title for the judge important?
3. The speaker continually remarks upon his language difficulties, which are amusing both to characters in the story and to the reader, but how do they also reveal the perception of the speaker?
4. How does the reader know that Giorgi Ivanitch is an honest man?
5. Does the speaker's honesty cost him anything?

About the Author

"A tale of tribulation and bewilderment"—so one critic labels *Anything Can Happen* from which this story was taken. Giorgi Ivanitch is George Papashvily (1898-1978) who emigrated to America in 1923 to get training in aviation. Instead he got an education in culture, a wife, and a new country. Born in Kobiankari, Georgia (Russia), Papashvily had little formal education. His "father paid a prince a bag of grain to teach [George] the letters of the alphabet and how to write [his] name." As a child he learned the leather-making trade and later became a sword maker. His interest in aviation arose from his service in the Russian army during World War I. His wife, Helen, an established writer in her own right, wrote down the stories of his immigrant years, and soon they were published as *Anything Can Happen*, and it does, in America the "land of opportunity."

Rikki-Tikki-Tavi

Rudyard Kipling

In this story the central figure is a mongoose. This small, extremely quick animal is known for killing poisonous snakes, especially cobras. Rikki-tikki-tavi fights an all-out war to save the lives of his adopted human family from the dangerous fangs of the evil Nag and Nagaina. While doing so, he displays traits very much like those that mark the highest level of courage—wisdom and persistence.

This is the story of the great war that Rikki-tikki-tavi fought single-handed, through the bathrooms of the big bungalow in Segowlee cantonment.* Darzee the Tailorbird helped him, and Chuchundra the Muskrat, who never comes out into the middle of the floor, but always creeps round by the wall, gave him advice, but Rikki-tikki did the real fighting.

Segowlee cantonment: British military station in India

He was a mongoose, rather like a little cat in his fur and his tail, but quite like a weasel in his head and his habits. His eyes and the end of his restless nose were pink. He could scratch himself anywhere he pleased with any leg, front or back, that he chose to use. He could fluff up his tail till it looked like a bottle brush, and his war cry as he scuttled* through the long grass was: *Rikk-tikk-tikki-tikki-tchk!*

---
scuttled: scurried

One day, a high summer flood washed him out of the burrow where he lived with his father and mother, and carried him, kicking and clucking, down a roadside ditch. He found a little wisp of grass floating there, and clung to it till he lost his senses. When he revived, he was lying in the hot sun in the middle of a garden path, very draggled* indeed, and a small boy was saying, "Here's a dead mongoose. Let's have a funeral."

---
draggled: wet and dirty

"No," said his mother, "let's take him in and dry him. Perhaps he isn't really dead."

They took him into the house, and a big man picked him up between his finger and thumb and said he was not dead but half choked. So they wrapped him in cotton wool, and warmed him over a little fire, and he opened his eyes and sneezed.

"Now," said the big man (he was an Englishman who had just moved into the bungalow,)* "don't frighten him, and we'll see what he'll do."

---
bungalow: a one-story house with a low-pitched roof

It is the hardest thing in the world to frighten a mongoose, because he is eaten up from nose to tail with curiosity. The motto of all the mongoose family is "Run and find out," and Rikki-tikki was a true mongoose. He looked at the cotton wool, decided that it was not good to eat, ran all around the table, sat up and put his fur in order, scratched himself, and jumped on the small boy's shoulder.

"Don't be frightened, Teddy," said his father. "That's his way of making friends."

"Ouch! He's tickling under my chin," said Teddy.

Rikki-tikki looked down between the boy's collar and neck, snuffed at his ear, and climbed down to the floor, where he sat rubbing his nose.

"Good gracious," said Teddy's mother, "and that's a wild creature! I suppose he's so tame because we've been kind to him."

"All mongooses are like that," said her husband. "If Teddy doesn't pick him up by the tail, or try to put him in a cage, he'll run in and out of the house all day long. Let's give him something to eat."

They gave him a little piece of raw meat. Rikki-tikki liked it immensely, and when it was finished he went out into the veranda* and sat in the sunshine and fluffed up his fur to make it dry to the roots. Then he felt better.

---

veranda: porch

"There are more things to find out about in this house," he said to himself, "than all my family could find out in all their lives. I shall certainly stay and find out."

He spent all that day roaming over the house. He nearly drowned himself in the bathtubs, put his nose into the ink on a writing table, and burned it on the end of the big man's cigar, for he climbed up in the big man's lap to see how writing was done. At nightfall he ran into Teddy's nursery to watch how kerosene lamps were lighted, and when Teddy went to bed Rikki-tikki climbed up too. But he was a restless companion, because he had to get up and attend to every noise all through the night, and find out what made it. Teddy's mother and father came in, the last thing, to look at their boy, and Rikki-tikki was awake on the pillow.

"I don't like that," said Teddy's mother. "He may bite the child."

"He'll do no such thing," said the father. "Teddy is safer with that little beast than if he had a bloodhound to watch him. If a snake came into the nursery now—"

But Teddy's mother wouldn't think of anything so awful.

Early in the morning Rikki-tikki came to early breakfast in the veranda riding on Teddy's shoulder, and they gave him banana and some boiled egg. He sat on all their laps one after the other, because every well brought up mongoose always hopes to be a house mongoose some day and have rooms to run about in; and Rikki-tikki's mother (she used to live in the general's house at Segowlee) had carefully told Rikki what to do if ever he came across white men.

Then Rikki-tikki went out into the garden to see what was to be seen. It was a large garden, only half cultivated, with bushes, as big as summer houses, of Marshal Niel roses, lime and orange trees, clumps of bamboos, and thickets of high grass. Rikki-tikki licked his lips. "This is a splendid hunting ground," he said, and his tail grew bottle-brushy at the thought of it, and he scuttled up and down the garden, snuffing here and there till he heard very sorrowful voices in a thornbush. It was Darzee the Tailorbird and his wife. They had made a beautiful nest by pulling two big leaves together and stitching them up the edges with fibers, and had filled the hollow with cotton and downy fluff. The nest swayed to and fro, as they sat on the rim and cried.

"What is the matter?" asked Rikki-tikki.

"We are very miserable," said Darzee.

"One of our babies fell out of the nest yesterday and Nag ate him."

"H'm," said Rikki-tikki, "that is very sad—but I am a stranger here. Who is Nag?"

Darzee and his wife only cowered* down in the nest without answering, for from the thick grass at the foot of the bush there came a low hiss—a horrid cold sound that made Rikki-tikki jump back two clear feet. Then inch by inch out of the grass rose up the head and spread hood of Nag, the big black cobra, and he was five feet long from tongue to tail. When he had lifted one-third of himself clear of the ground, he stayed balancing to and fro exactly as a dandelion tuft balances in the wind, and he looked at Rikki-tikki with the wicked snake's eyes that never change their expression, whatever the snake may be thinking of.

---

cowered: shrank

"Who is Nag?" said he. "*I* am Nag. The great God Brahm* put his mark upon all our people, when the first cobra spread his hood to keep the sun off Brahm as he slept. Look, and be afraid!"

Brahm: the supreme god of the Hindus

He spread out his hood more than ever, and Rikki-tikki saw the spectacle mark on the back of it that looks exactly like the eye part of a hook-and-eye fastening. He was afraid for the minute, but it is impossible for a mongoose to stay frightened for any length of time, and though Rikki-tikki had never met a live cobra before, his mother had fed him on dead ones, and he knew that all a grown mongoose's business in life was to fight and eat snakes. Nag knew that too and, at the bottom of his cold heart, he was afraid.

"Well," said Rikki-tikki, and his tail began to fluff up again, "marks or no marks, do you think it is right for you to eat fledglings out of a nest?"

Nag was thinking to himself, and watching the least little movement in the grass behind Rikki-tikki. He knew that mongooses in the garden meant death sooner or later for him and his family, but he wanted to get Rikki-tikki off his guard. So he dropped his head a little, and put it on one side.

"Let us talk," he said. "You eat eggs. Why should not I eat birds?"

"Behind you! Look behind you!" sang Darzee.

Rikki-tikki knew better than to waste time in staring. He jumped up in the air as high as he could go, and just under him whizzed by the head of Nagaina, Nag's wicked wife. She had crept up behind him as he was talking, to make an end of him. He heard her savage hiss as the stroke missed. He came down almost across her back, and if he had been an old mongoose he would have known that then was

the time to break her back with one bite; but he was afraid of the terrible lashing return stroke of the cobra. He bit, indeed, but did not bite long enough, and he jumped clear of the whisking tail, leaving Nagaina torn and angry.

"Wicked, wicked Darzee!" said Nag, lashing up as high as he could reach toward the nest in the thornbush. But Darzee had built it out of reach of snakes, and it only swayed to and fro.

Rikki-tikki felt his eyes growing red and hot (when a mongoose's eyes grow red, he is angry), and he sat back on his tail and hind legs like a little kangaroo, and looked all round him, and chattered with rage. But Nag and Nagaina had disappeared into the grass. When a snake misses its stroke, it never says anything or gives any sign of what it means to do next. Rikki-tikki did not care to follow them, for he did not feel sure that he could manage two snakes at once. So he trotted off to the gravel path near the house, and sat down to think. It was a serious matter to him.

If you read the old books of natural history, you will find they say that when the mongoose fights the snake and happens to get bitten, he runs off and eats some herb that cures him. That is not true. The victory is only a matter of quickness of eye and quickness of foot—snake's blow against mongoose's jump—and as no eye can follow the motion of a snake's head when it strikes, this makes things much more wonderful than any magic herb. Rikki-tikki knew he was a young mongoose, and it made him all the more pleased to think that he had managed to escape a blow from behind.

It gave him confidence in himself, and when Teddy came running down the path, Rikki-tikki was ready to be petted. But just as Teddy was stooping, something wriggled a little in the dust, and a tiny voice said: "Be careful. I am Death!" It was Karait, the dusty brown snakeling* that lies for choice on the dusty earth; and his bite is as dangerous as the cobra's. But he is so small that nobody thinks of him, and so he does the more harm to people.

snakeling: small snake

Rikki-tikki's eyes grew red again, and he danced up to Karait with the peculiar rocking, swaying motion that he had inherited from his family. It looks very funny, but it is so perfectly balanced a gait* that you can fly off from it at any angle you please, and in dealing with snakes this is an advantage.

gait: manner of movement

If Rikki-tikki had only known, he was doing a much more dangerous thing than fighting Nag, for Karait is so small, and can turn so quickly, that unless Rikki bit him close to the back of the head, he would get the return stroke in his eye or his lip. But Rikki did not know. His eyes were all red, and he rocked back and forth, looking for a good place to hold. Karait struck out. Rikki jumped sideways and tried to run in, but the wicked little dusty gray head lashed within a fraction of his shoulder, and he had to jump over the body, and the head followed his heels close.

Teddy shouted to the house: "Oh, look here! Our mongoose is killing a snake." And Rikki-tikki heard a scream from Teddy's mother. His father ran out with a stick, but by the time he came up, Karait had lunged out once too far, and Rikki-tikki had sprung, jumped on the snake's back, dropped his head far between his forelegs, bitten as high up the back as he could get hold, and rolled away.

That bite paralyzed Karait, and Rikki-tikki was just going to eat him up from the tail, after the custom of his family at dinner, when he remembered that a full meal makes a slow mongoose, and if he wanted all his strength and quickness ready, he must keep himself thin. He went away for a dust bath under the castor-oil bushes, while Teddy's father beat the dead Karait.

"What is the use of that?" thought Rikki-tikki. "I have settled it all."

And then Teddy's mother picked him up from the dust and hugged him, crying that he had saved Teddy from death, and Teddy's father said that he was a providence,* and Teddy looked on with big scared eyes. Rikki-tikki was rather amused at all the fuss, which, of course, he did not understand. Teddy's mother might just as well have petted Teddy for playing in the dust. Rikki was thoroughly enjoying himself.

providence: a God-sent gift

That night at dinner, walking to and fro among the wineglasses on the table, he might have stuffed himself three times over with nice things. But he remembered Nag and Nagaina, and though it was very pleasant to be patted and petted by Teddy's mother, and to sit on Teddy's shoulder, his eyes would get red from time to time, and he would go off into his long war cry of "*Rikk-tikk-tikki-tikki-tchk!*"

Teddy carried him off to bed and insisted on Rikki-tikki sleeping under his chin. Rikki-tikki was too well bred to bite or scratch, but as soon as Teddy was asleep he went off for his nightly walk round the house, and in the dark he ran up against Chuchundra the Musk-rat creeping around by the wall. Chuchundra is a broken-hearted little beast. He whimpers and cheeps all the night, trying to make up his mind to run into the middle of the room. But he never gets there.

"Don't kill me," said Chuchundra, almost weeping. "Rikki-tikki, don't kill me!"

"Do you think a snake-killer kills musk-rats?" said Rikki-tikki scornfully.

"Those who kill snakes get killed by snakes," said Chuchundra, more sorrowfully than ever. "And how am I to be sure that Nag won't mistake me for you some dark night?"

"There's not the least danger," said Rikki-tikki. "But Nag is in the garden, and I know you don't go there."

"My cousin Chua the Rat told me," said Chuchundra, and then he stopped.

"Told you what?"

"H'sh! Nag is everywhere, Rikki-tikki. You should have talked to Chua in the garden."

"I didn't—so you must tell me. Quick, Chuchundra, or I'll bite you!"

Chuchundra sat down and cried till the tears rolled off his whiskers. "I am a very poor man," he sobbed. "I never had spirit enough to run out into the middle of the room. H'sh! I mustn't tell you anything. Can't you *hear,* Rikki-tikki?"

Rikki-tikki listened. The house was as still as still, but he thought he could just catch the faintest *scratch-scratch* in the world—a noise as faint as that of a wasp walking on a windowpane—the dry scratch of a snake's scales on brick work.

"That's Nag or Nagaina," he said to himself, "and he is crawling into the bathroom sluice.* You're right, Chuchundra; I should have talked to Chua."

sluice: drain

He stole off to Teddy's bathroom, but there was nothing there, and then to Teddy's

mother's bathroom. At the bottom of the smooth plaster wall there was a brick pulled out to make a sluice for the bath water, and as Rikki-tikki stole in by the masonry curb where the bath is put, he heard Nag and Nagaina whispering together outside in the moonlight.

"When the house is emptied of people," said Nagaina to her husband, "*he* will have to go away, and then the garden will be our own again. Go in quietly, and remember that the big man who killed Karait is the first one to bite. Then come out and tell me, and we will hunt for Rikki-tikki together."

"But are you sure that there is anything to be gained by killing the people?" said Nag.

"Everything. When there were no people in the bungalow, did we have any mongoose in the garden? So long as the bungalow is empty, we are king and queen of the garden; and remember that as soon as our eggs in the melon bed hatch (as they may tomorrow), our children will need room and quiet."

"I had not thought of that," said Nag. "I will go, but there is no need that we should hunt for Rikki-tikki afterwards. I will kill the big man and his wife, and the child if I can, and come away quietly. Then the bungalow will be empty, and Rikki-tikki will go."

Rikki-tikki tingled all over with rage and hatred at this, and then Nag's head came through the sluice, and his five feet of cold body followed it. Angry as he was, Rikki-tikki was very frightened as he saw the size of the big cobra. Nag coiled himself up, raised his head, and looked into the bathroom in the dark, and Rikki could see his eyes glitter.

"Now, if I kill him here, Nagaina will know; and if I fight him on the open floor, the odds are in his favor. What am I to do?" said Rikki-tikki-tavi.

Nag waved to and fro, and then Rikki-tikki heard him drinking from the biggest water jar that was used to fill the bath. "That is good," said the snake. "Now, when Karait was killed, the big man had a stick. He may have that stick still, but when he comes in to bathe in the morning he will not have a stick. I shall wait here till he comes. Nagaina—do you hear me?—I shall wait here in the cool till daytime."

There was no answer from outside, so Rikki-tikki knew Nagaina had gone away. Nag coiled himself down, coil by coil, round the bulge at the bottom of the water jar, and Rikki-tikki stayed still as death. After an hour he began to move, muscle by muscle, toward the jar. Nag was asleep, and Rikki-tikki looked at his big back, wondering which would be the best place for a good hold. "If I don't break his back at the first jump," said Rikki, "he can still fight. And if he fights—O Rikki!" He looked at the thickness of the neck below the hood, but that was too much for him; and a bite near the tail would only make Nag savage.

"It must be the head," he said at last; "the head above the hood. And, when I am once there, I must not let go."

Then he jumped. The head was lying a little clear of the water jar, under the curve of it; and, as his teeth met, Rikki braced his back against the bulge of the red earthenware to hold down the head. This gave him just one second's purchase,* and he made the most of it. Then he was battered to and fro as a rat is shaken by a dog—to and fro on the floor, up and down, and around in great circles, but his eyes were red and he held on as the body cart-whipped over the floor, upsetting the tin dipper and the soap dish and the flesh brush* and banged against the tin side of the bath.

---

purchase: advantage
flesh brush: for bathing

As he held he closed his jaws tighter and tighter, for he made sure he would be banged to death, and, for the honor of his family, he

preferred to be found with his teeth locked. He was dizzy, aching, and felt shaken to pieces when something went off like a thunderclap just behind him. A hot wind knocked him senseless and red fire singed* his fur. The big man had been wakened by the noise, and had fired both barrels of a shotgun into Nag just behind the hood.

---

singed: burned

Rikki-tikki held on with his eyes shut, for now he was quite sure he was dead. But the head did not move, and the big man picked him up and said, "It's the mongoose again, Alice. The little chap has saved *our* lives now."

Then Teddy's mother came in with a very white face, and saw what was left of Nag, and Rikki-tikki dragged himself to Teddy's bedroom and spent half the rest of the night shaking himself tenderly to find out whether he really was broken into forty pieces, as he fancied.

When morning came he was very stiff, but well pleased with his doings. "Now I have Nagaina to settle with, and she will be worse than five Nags, and there's no knowing when the eggs she spoke of will hatch. Goodness! I must go and see Darzee," he said.

Without waiting for breakfast, Rikki-tikki ran to the thornbush where Darzee was singing a song of triumph at the top of his voice. The news of Nag's death was all over the garden, for the sweeper had thrown the body on the rubbish heap.

"Oh, you stupid tuft of feathers!" said Rikki-tikki angrily. "Is this the time to sing?"

"Nag is dead—is dead—is dead!" sang Darzee. "The valiant* Rikki-tikki caught him by the head and held fast. The big man brought the bang stick, and Nag fell in two pieces! He will never eat my babies again."

---

valiant: courageous

"All that's true enough. But where's Nagaina?" said Rikki-tikki, looking carefully around him.

"Nagaina came to the bathroom sluice and called for Nag," Darzee went on, "and Nag came out on the end of a stick—the sweeper picked him up on the end of a stick and threw

him upon the rubbish heap. Let us sing about the great, the red-eyed Rikki-tikki!" And Darzee filled his throat and sang.

"If I could get up to your nest, I'd roll your babies out!" said Rikki-tikki. "You don't know when to do the right thing at the right time. You're safe enough in your nest there, but it's war for me, down here. Stop singing a minute, Darzee."

"For the great, the beautiful Rikki-tikki's sake I will stop," said Darzee. "What is it, O Killer of the terrible Nag?"

"Where is Nagaina, for the third time?"

"On the rubbish heap by the stables, mourning for Nag. Great is Rikki-tikki with the white teeth."

"Bother my white teeth! Have you ever heard where she keeps her eggs?"

"In the melon bed, on the end nearest the wall, where the sun strikes nearly all day. She hid them there weeks ago."

"And you never thought it worthwhile to tell me? The end nearest the wall, you said?"

"Rikki-tikki, you are not going to eat her eggs?"

"Not eat exactly, no. Darzee, if you have a grain of sense you will fly off to the stables and pretend that your wing is broken, and let Nagaina chase you away to this bush. I must get to the melon bed, and if I went there now she'd see me."

Darzee was a feather-brained little fellow who could never hold more than one idea at a time in his head. And just because he knew that Nagaina's children were born in eggs like his own, he didn't think at first that it was fair to kill them. But his wife was a sensible bird, and she knew that cobra's eggs meant young cobras later on. So she flew off from the nest, and left Darzee to keep the babies warm, and continue his song about the death of Nag. Darzee was very like a man in some ways.

She fluttered in front of Nagaina by the rubbish heap and cried out, "Oh, my wing is broken! The boy in the house threw a stone at me and broke it." Then she fluttered more desperately than ever.

Nagaina lifted up her head and hissed. "You warned Rikki-tikki when I would have killed him. Indeed and truly, you've chosen a bad place to be lame in." And she moved toward Darzee's wife, slipping along over the dust.

"The boy broke it with a stone!" shrieked Darzee's wife.

"Well! It may be some consolation* to you when you're dead to know that I shall settle accounts with the boy. My husband lies on the rubbish heap this morning, but before night the boy in the house will lie very still. What is the use of running away? I am sure to catch you. Little fool, look at me!"

consolation: comfort

Darzee's wife knew better than to do *that,* for a bird who looks at a snake's eyes gets so frightened that she cannot move. Darzee's wife fluttered on, piping* sorrowfully, and

never leaving the ground, and Nagaina quickened her pace.

---

piping: chirping

Rikki-tikki heard them going up the path from the stables, and he raced for the end of the melon patch near the wall. There, in the warm litter above the melons, very cunningly hidden, he found twenty-five eggs, about the size of a bantam's eggs, but with whitish skins instead of shells.

"I was not a day too soon," he said, for he could see the baby cobras curled up inside the skin, and he knew that the minute they were hatched they could each kill a man or a mongoose. He bit off the tops of the eggs as fast as he could, taking care to crush the young cobras, and turned over the litter from time to time to see whether he had missed any. At last there were only three eggs left, and Rikki-tikki began to chuckle to himself, when he heard Darzee's wife screaming:

"Rikki-tikki, I led Nagaina toward the house, and she has gone into the veranda and—oh, come quickly—she means killing!"

Rikki-tikki smashed two eggs, and tumbled backward down the melon bed with the third egg in his mouth, and scuttled to the veranda as hard as he could put foot to the ground. Teddy and his mother and father were there at early breakfast, but Rikki-tikki saw that they were not eating anything. They sat stone-still, and their faces were white. Nagaina was coiled up on the matting by Teddy's chair, within easy striking distance of Teddy's bare leg, and she was swaying to and fro, singing a song of triumph.

"Son of the big man that killed Nag," she hissed, "stay still. I am not ready yet. Wait a little. Keep very still, all you three! If you move I strike, and if you do not move I strike. Oh, foolish people, who killed my Nag!"

Teddy's eyes were fixed on his father, and all his father could do was to whisper, "Sit still, Teddy. You mustn't move. Teddy, keep still."

Then Rikki-tikki came up and cried, "Turn round, Nagaina. Turn and fight!"

"All in good time," said she, without moving her eyes. "I will settle my account with you presently. Look at your friends, Rikki-tikki. They are still and white. They are afraid. They dare not move, and if you come a step nearer I strike."

"Look at your eggs," said Rikki-tikki "in the melon bed near the wall. Go and look, Nagaina!"

The big snake turned half around, and saw the egg on the veranda. "Ah-h! Give it to me," she said.

Rikki-tikki put his paws one on each side of the egg, and his eyes were blood-red.

"What price for a snake's egg? For a young cobra? For a young king cobra? For the last—the very last of the brood? The ants are eating all the others by the melon bed."

Nagaina spun clear round, forgetting everything for the sake of the one egg. Rikki-tikki saw Teddy's father shoot out a big hand, catch Teddy by the shoulder, and drag him across the little table with the teacups, safe and out of reach of Nagaina.

"Tricked! Tricked! Tricked! *Rikk-tck-tck!*" chuckled Rikki-tikki. "The boy is safe, and it was I—I—I that caught Nag by the hood last night in the bathroom." Then he began to jump up and down, all four feet together, his head close to the floor. "He threw me to and fro, but he could not shake me off. He was dead before the big man blew him in two. I did it! *Rikki-tikki-tck-tck!* Come then, Nagaina. Come and fight with me. You shall not be a widow long."

Nagaina saw that she had lost her chance of killing Teddy, and the egg lay between Rikki-tikki's paws. "Give me the egg, Rikki-tikki. Give me the last of my eggs, and I will go away and never come back," she said, lowering her hood.

"Yes, you will go away, and you will never come back. For you will go to the rubbish heap with Nag. Fight, widow! The big man has gone for his gun. Fight!"

Rikki-tikki was bounding all round Nagaina, keeping just out of reach of her stroke, his little eyes like hot coals. Nagaina gathered herself together and flung out at him. Rikki-tikki jumped up and backward. Again and again and again she struck, and each time her head came with a whack on the matting of the veranda and she gathered herself together like a watch spring. Then Rikki-tikki danced in a circle to get behind her, and Nagaina spun round to keep her head to his head, so that the rustle of her tail on the matting sounded like dry leaves blown along by the wind.

He had forgotten the egg. It still lay on the veranda, and Nagaina came nearer and nearer to it, till at last, while Rikki-tikki was drawing breath, she caught it in her mouth, turned to the veranda steps, and flew like an arrow down the path, with Rikki-tikki behind her. When the cobra runs for her life, she goes like a whiplash flicked across a horse's neck. Rikki-tikki knew that he must catch her, or all the trouble would begin again.

She headed straight for the long grass by the thornbush, and as he was running Rikki-tikki heard Darzee still singing his foolish little song of triumph. But Darzee's wife was wiser. She flew off her nest as Nagaina came along, and flapped her wings about Nagaina's head. If Darzee had helped her they might have turned her, but Nagaina only lowered her hood and went on. Still, the instant's delay brought Rikki-tikki up to her, and as she plunged into the rathole where she and Nag used to live, his little white teeth were clenched on her tail, and he went down with her—and very few mongooses, however wise and old they may be, care to follow a cobra into its hole.

It was dark in the hole; and Rikki-tikki never knew when it might open out and give Nagaina room to turn and strike at him. He held on savagely, and stuck out his feet to act as brakes on the dark slope of the hot, moist earth.

Then grass by the mouth of the hole stopped waving, and Darzee said, "It is all over with Rikki-tikki! We must sing his death song. Valiant Rikki-tikki is dead! For Nagaina will surely kill him underground."

So he sang a very mournful song that he made up on the spur of the minute, and just as he got to the most touching part, the grass quivered again, and Rikki-tikki, covered with dirt, dragged himself out of the hole leg by leg, licking his whiskers. Darzee stopped with a little shout. Rikki-tikki shook some of the dust out of his fur and sneezed. "It is all over," he said. "The widow will never come out again." And the red ants that live between the grass stems heard him, and began to troop down one after another to see if he had spoken the truth.

Rikki-tikki curled himself up in the grass and slept where he was—slept and slept till it was late in the afternoon, for he had done a hard day's work.

"Now," he said, when he awoke, "I will go back to the house. Tell the Coppersmith, Darzee, and he will tell the garden that Nagaina is dead."

The Coppersmith is a bird who makes a noise exactly like the beating of a little hammer on a copper pot. The reason he is always making it is because he is the town crier* to every Indian garden, and tells all the news to everybody who cares to listen. As Rikki-tikki went up the path, he heard his "attention" notes like a tiny dinner gong, and then the steady "*Ding-dong-tock! Nag is dead—dong! Nagaina is dead! Ding-dong-tock!*" That set all the birds in the garden singing, and the frogs croaking, for Nag and Nagaina used to eat frogs as well as little birds.

<hr>

town crier: one who shouts public announcements

<hr>

When Rikki got to the house, Teddy and Teddy's mother (she looked very white still, for she had been fainting) and Teddy's father came out and almost cried over him; and that night he ate all that was given him till he could eat no more, and went to bed on Teddy's shoulder, where Teddy's mother saw him when she came to look late at night.

"He saved our lives and Teddy's life," she said to her husband. "Just think, he saved all our lives."

Rikki-tikki woke up with a jump, for the mongooses are light sleepers.

"Oh, it's you," said he. "What are you bothering for? All the cobras are dead. And if they weren't, I'm here."

Rikki-tikki had a right to be proud of himself. But he did not grow too proud, and he kept that garden as a mongoose should keep it, with tooth and jump and spring and bite, till never a cobra dared show its head inside the walls.

About the Story

1. What characteristic makes it hard to frighten a mongoose and accounts for his motto "Run and find out"?
2. What is a mongoose's job in life?
3. How does the mongoose show wisdom in fighting Nag? Nagaina?
4. How does the mongoose show persistence?
5. Rikki-tikki-tavi accuses Darzee of not knowing "when to do the right thing at the right time." What are some examples in the story of doing the right thing at the right time?
6. Who other than the mongoose demonstrates courage?

About the Author

The best-known British writer since Charles Dickens, Rudyard Kipling (1865-1936) was born in India and loved her ever afterward. Many of his stories such as "Rikki-Tikki-Tavi" are set in India and detail the lives of ordinary British citizens there to promote the British Empire through trade or military service. Kipling wrote in several genres including news writing, poetry, novels, and history, but he excelled at the short story. Associated mainly with the age of Queen Victoria and British imperialism, Kipling's works both inspired the exploits of Britain's empire builders and gloried in their efforts. Kipling was offered the poet laureatship after Alfred, Lord Tennyson but refused it as he also refused the Order of Merit. He did receive the Nobel Prize for literature in 1907 and was buried in Westminster Abbey's Poet's Corner. Kipling used dialect and reality to communicate his view of the world and to evaluate Britain's role in it.

A Kind of Murder

Hugh Pentecost

When a fifteen-year-old student goes against his classmates, he will pay the price. In this story the central character, at first, has the courage to do the right thing. But later, under pressure from his friends, he wavers. Is his cowardice revealed in something he actually does to Mr. Warren or in something he fails to do? Does James 4:17 have any bearing on his problem? Does he ever regret his cowardice?

You might say this is the story of a murder—although nobody was killed. I don't know what has become of Mr. Silas Warren, but I have lived for many years with the burden on my conscience of having been responsible for the existence of a walking dead man.

I was fifteen years old during the brief span of days that I knew Mr. Silas Warren. It was toward the end of the winter term at Morgan Military Academy. Mr. Etsweiler, the chemistry and physics teacher at Morgan, had died of a heart attack one afternoon while he was helping to coach the hockey team on the lake. Mr. Henry Huntingdon Hadley, the headmaster, had gone to New York to find a replacement. That replacement was Mr. Silas Warren.

I may have been one of the first people to see Mr. Warren at the Academy. I had been excused from the afternoon study period

because of a heavy cold, and allowed to take my books to my room to work there. I saw Mr. Warren come walking across the quadrangle toward Mr. Hadley's office, which was located on the ground floor under the hall where my room was.

Mr. Warren didn't look like a man who was coming to stay long. He carried one small, flimsy suitcase spattered with travel labels. Although it was a bitter March day, he wore a thin summer-weight topcoat. He stopped beside a kind of brown lump in the snow. That brown lump was Teddy, the school dog.

Teddy was an ancient collie. They said that in the old days you could throw a stick for Teddy to retrieve until you, not he, dropped from exhaustion. Now the old, gray-muzzled dog was pretty much ignored by everyone except the chef, who fed him scraps from the dining room after the noon meal.

Mr. Warren stopped by Teddy, bent down, and scratched the dog's head. The old, burr-clotted tail thumped wearily in the snow. Mr. Warren straightened up and looked around. He had narrow, stooped shoulders. His eyes were pale blue, and they had a kind of frightened look in them. *He's scared,* I thought; *coming to a new place in the middle of a term, he's scared.*

I guess most of the other fellows didn't see Mr. Warren until he turned up at supper time at the head of one of the tables in the dining room. We marched into the dining room and stood behind our chairs waiting for the cadet major to give the order to be seated. The order was delayed. Mr. Henry Huntingdon Hadley, known as Old Beaver because of his snowy white head, made an announcement.

"Mr. Warren has joined our teaching staff to fill the vacancy created by the unfortunate demise* of Mr. Etsweiler." Old Beaver had false teeth and his *s*'s whistled musically. "I trust you will give him a cordial welcome."

demise: death

"Be seated," the cadet major snapped.

We sat. Old Beaver said grace. Then we all began to talk. I was at Mr. Warren's right. He had a genial,* want-to-be-liked smile.

genial: friendly

"And your name is?" he asked me in a pleasant but flat voice.

"Pentecost, sir."

He leaned toward me. "How's that?" he asked.

"Pentecost, sir."

Sammy Callahan sat across from me on Mr. Warren's left. Sammy was a fine athlete and a terrible practical joker. I saw a gleam of interest in his eyes. As Mr. Warren turned toward him, Sammy spoke in an ordinary conversational tone.

"Why don't you go take a jump in the lake, sir?"

Mr. Warren smiled. "Yes, I guess you're right," he said.

Sammy grinned at me. There was no doubt about it—Mr. Warren was quite deaf!

It was a strange kind of secret Sammy and I had. We didn't really know what to do with it, but we found out that night. Old Beaver was not a man to start anyone in gradually. It would have been Mr. Etsweiler's turn to take the night study hour, so that hour was passed on to Mr. Warren.

He sat on the little platform at the head of the study hall—smiling and smiling. I think there must have been terror in his heart then. I think he may even have been praying.

Everyone seemed unusually busy studying, but we were all waiting for the test. The test always came for a new master the first time he had night study hour. There would be a minor disturbance and we'd find out promptly whether this man could maintain discipline, or not. It came after about five minutes—a loud, artificial belch.

Mr. Warren smiled and smiled. He hadn't heard it.

Belches sprang up all over the room. Then somebody threw a handful of torn paper in the air. Mr. Warren's smile froze.

"Now, now, boys," he said.

More belches. More torn paper.

"Boys!" Mr. Warren cried out, like someone in pain.

Then Old Beaver appeared, his eyes glittering behind rimless spectacles. There was something I never understood about Old Beaver. Ordinarily his shoes squeaked. You could hear him coming from quite a distance away—squeak-squeak, squeak-squeak. But somehow, when he chose, he could approach as noiselessly as a cat, without any squeak at all. And there he was.

The study hall was quiet as a tomb. But the silence was frighteningly loud, and the place was littered with paper.

"There will be ten demerit marks against every student in this room," Old Beaver said in his icy voice. "I want every scrap of paper picked up instantly."

Several of us scrambled down on our hands and knees. Mr. Warren smiled at the headmaster.

"Consider the lilies of the field," Mr. Warren said. "They toil not, neither do they spin. Yet I tell you that Solomon in all his glory—"

"Silence!" Old Beaver hissed, with all the menace* of a poised cobra.* He turned to Mr. Warren. "I'll take the balance of this period, Mr. Warren. I suggest you go to your room and prepare yourself for tomorrow's curriculum."*

---

menace: threat
poised cobra: one ready to strike
curriculum: courses

I didn't have any classes with Mr. Warren the next day, but all you heard as you passed in the corridors from one class period to the next were tales of the jokes and disorders in the physics and chemistry courses. Somehow nobody thought it was wrong to take advantage of Mr. Warren.

The climax came very quickly. In the winter, if you weren't out for the hockey or winter sports team, you had to exercise in the gym. There were the parallel bars, and the rings, and the tumbling mats. And there was boxing.

The boxing teacher was Major Durand, the military commandant. I know now that he was a sadist.* Major Durand was filled with contempt for everyone but Major Durand. I saw the look on his face when Mr. Warren appeared.

---

sadist: one who delights in cruelty

Mr. Warren had been assigned to help in the gym. He was something to see—just skin and bones. He had on a pair of ordinary black socks and, I suspect, the only pair of shoes he owned—black oxfords. He'd borrowed a pair of shorts that could have been wrapped twice around his skinny waist. Above that was a much-mended shortsleeved undershirt. He looked around, hopeless, amiable.*

---

amiable: friendly

"Mr. Warren!" Major Durand said. "I'd like you to help me demonstrate. Put on these gloves, if you will." He tossed a pair of boxing gloves at Mr. Warren, who stared at them stupidly. One of the boys helped him tie the laces.

"Now, Mr. Warren," Durand said. The Major danced and bobbed* and weaved, and shot out his gloves in short, vicious jabs at the air. "You will hold your gloves up to your face, sir. When you're ready you'll say, 'Hit!'—and I shall hit you."

---

bobbed: moved up and down

I'd seen Major Durand do this with a boy he didn't like. You held up the gloves and you covered your face and then, with your throat dry and aching, you said, "Hit!"—and Major Durand's left or right would smash through your guard and pulverize* your nose or mouth. It was sheer strength, I know now, not skill.

pulverize: pound

Mr. Warren held up his gloves, and he looked like an actor in an old Mack Sennett comedy—the absurd* clothes, the sickly smile.

absurd: silly

Durand danced in front of him. "Whenever you say, Mr. Warren. Now watch this, boys. The feint*—and the jab."*

feint: fake
jab: punch

"Hit!" said Mr. Warren, his voice suddenly falsetto.*

falsetto: high

Pow! Major Durand's left jab smashed through the guard of Mr. Warren's nose. There was a sudden geyser* of blood.

geyser: spray

"Again, Mr. Warren!" the Major commanded, his eyes glittering.

"I think I'd better retire to repair the damage," Mr. Warren said. His undershirt was spattered with blood and he produced a soiled handkerchief which he held to his nose. He hurried out of the gym at a sort of shambling* gallop.

shambling: shuffling

That night the payoff came in study hall. Mr. Warren was called on this time to substitute for Old Beaver, who had taken over for him the night before. Sammy Callahan staged it. Suddenly handkerchiefs were waved from all parts of the room—handkerchiefs stained red. Red ink, of course.

"Hit!" somebody shouted. "Hit, hit!" Nearly all the boys were bobbing, weaving, jabbing.

Mr. Warren, pale as a ghost, cotton visibly stuffed in one nostril, stared at us like a dead man.

Then there was Old Beaver again.

Somehow the word was out at breakfast the next morning. Mr. Warren was leaving. He didn't show at the breakfast table. I felt a little squeamish* about it. He hadn't been given a chance. Maybe he wasn't such a bad guy.

squeamish: sickened

It was during the morning classroom period that we heard it. It was a warm day for March and the ice was breaking up on the lake. The scream was piercing and terrified. Somebody went to the window. The scream came again.

"Somebody's fallen through the ice!"

The whole school—a hundred and fifty boys and masters—hurried down to the shore of the lake. The sun was so bright that all we could see was a dark shape flopping out there, pulling itself up on the ice and then disappearing under water as the ice broke. Each time the figure rose there was a wailing scream.

Then the identification. "It's Teddy!" someone shouted.

The school dog. He'd walked out there and the ice had caved in under him. The screams were growing weaker. A couple of us made for the edge of the ice. Old Beaver and Major Durand confronted us.

"I'm sorry, boys," Old Beaver said. "It's a tragic thing to have to stand here and watch the old dog drown. But no one—no one connected with the school—is to try to get to him. I'm responsible for your safety. That's an order."

We stood there, sick with it. Old Teddy must have seen us, because for a moment there seemed to be new hope in his strangled wailing.

Then I saw Mr. Warren. He was by the boathouse, his old suitcase in his hand. He looked out at the dog, and, so help me, there were tears in Mr. Warren's eyes. Then, very calmly, he put down his bag, took off his thin topcoat and suit jacket. He righted one of the overturned boats on the shore and pulled it to the edge of the lake.

"Mr. Warren! You heard my order!" Old Beaver shouted at him.

Mr. Warren turned to the headmaster, smiling. "You seem to forget, sir, I am no longer connected with Morgan Military Academy, and therefore not subject to your orders."

"Stop him!" Major Durand ordered.

But before anyone could reach him, Mr. Warren had slid the flat-bottomed rowboat out onto the ice. He crept along on the ice himself, clinging to the boat, pushing it across the shiny surface toward Teddy. I heard Mr. Warren's thin, flat voice.

"Hold on, old man! I'm coming."

The ice gave way under him, but he clung to the boat and scrambled up and on.

"Hold on, old man!"

It seemed to take forever. Just before what must have been the last, despairing shriek from the half-frozen dog, Mr. Warren reached him. How he found the strength to lift the water-soaked collie into the boat, I don't know; but he managed, and then he came back toward us, creeping along the cracking ice, pushing the boat to shore.

The chef wrapped Teddy in blankets, put him behind the stove in the kitchen, and gave him a dose of warm milk and cooking brandy. Mr. Warren was hustled to the infirmary. Did I say that when he reached the shore with Teddy the whole school cheered him?

Old Beaver, for all his tyranny, must have been a pretty decent guy. He announced that night that Mr. Warren was not leaving after all. He trusted that, after Mr. Warren's display of valor,* the boys would show him the respect he deserved.

---

valor: courage

I went to see Mr. Warren in the infirmary that first evening. He looked happier than I'd ever seen him.

"What you did took an awful lot of courage," I told him. "Everybody thinks it was really a swell thing to do."

Mr. Warren smiled at me—a thoughtful kind of smile. "Courage is a matter of definition," he said. "It doesn't take courage to stand up and let yourself get punched in the nose. It takes courage to walk away. As for Teddy— somebody had to go after him. There wasn't anyone who could but me, so courage or not, I went. You'd have gone if Mr. Hadley hadn't issued orders." He sighed. "I'm glad to get a second chance here. Very glad."

It was a week before Mr. Warren had the night study hall again. It was a kind of test. For perhaps fifteen minutes nothing happened, and then I heard Sammy give his fine artificial belch. I looked up at Mr. Warren. He was smiling happily. He hadn't heard. A delighted giggle ran around the room.

I was on my feet. "If there's one more sound in this room I'm going after Old Beaver," I said. "And after that I'll personally take on every guy in this school, if necessary, to knock sense into him!"

The room quieted. I was on the student council and I was also captain of the boxing team. The rest of the study period was continued in an orderly fashion. When it was over and we were headed for our rooms, Mr. Warren flagged me down.

"I don't know quite what was going on, Pentecost," he said, "but I gather you saved the day for me. Thank you. Thank you very much. Perhaps when the boys get to know me a little better they'll come to realize—" He made a helpless little gesture with his bony hands.

"I'm sure they will, sir," I said.

"They're not cruel," Mr. Warren said. "It's just high spirits, I know."

Sammy Callahan was waiting for me in my room. "What are you, some kind of a do-gooder?" he said.

"Give the guy a chance," I said. "He proved he has guts when it's needed. But he's helpless there in the study hall."

Sammy gave me a sour grin. "You and he should get along fine," he said. "And you'll need to. The guys aren't going to be chummy with a do-gooder like you."

It was a week before Mr. Warren's turn to run the study hour came around again. In that time I'd found that Sammy was right. I was being given the cold shoulder. Major Durand, who must have hated Mr. Warren for stealing the heroic spotlight from him, was giving me a hard time. One of the guys I knew well came to me.

"You're making a mistake," he told me. "He's a grown man and you're just a kid. If he can't take care of himself, it's not your head-ache."

I don't like telling the next part of it, but it happened.

When Mr. Warren's night came again, the study hall was quiet enough for a while. Then came a belch. I looked up at Mr. Warren. He was smiling. Then someone waved one of those fake bloody handkerchiefs. Then, so help me, somebody let out a bawling howl—like Teddy in the lake.

Mr. Warren knew what was happening now. He looked down at me, and there was an agonizing, wordless plea for help in his eyes. I—well, I looked away. I was fifteen. I didn't want to be called a do-gooder. I didn't want to be snubbed. Mr. Warren was a grown man and he should have been able to take care of himself. The boys weren't cruel; they were just high-spirited—hadn't Mr. Warren himself said so?

I looked up from behind a book. Mr. Warren was standing, looking out over the room. His stooped, skinny shoulders were squared away. Two great tears ran down his pale cheeks. His last chance was played out.

Then he turned and walked out of the study hall.

No one ever saw him again. He must have gone straight to his room, thrown his meager* belongings into the battered old suitcase, and taken off on foot into the night.

---

meager: few

You see what I mean when I say it was a kind of murder?

And I was the murderer.

About the Story

1. If "nobody was killed," what is murdered in the story?
2. How does Mr. Warren demonstrate his courage?
3. How are Teddy and Mr. Warren similar?
4. Why does the speaker consider himself, not the rest of the boys, the murderer?
5. Is Mr. Warren's excuse that the boys were just "high-spirited" a valid one?

About the Author

Hugh Pentecost, known by his real name of Judson Pentecost Philips (b. 1903), was a well-known writer of detective stories. Although he always aspired to be an actor, acting was not for him. He, in fact, had a part in a silent film when he was eighteen and liked the experience so well that he "wrote a script that had a part for an eighteen-year-old boy; [he] sold the script but . . . didn't get the part!" As a writer, Philips has tried almost every genre—writing radio scripts such as "Father Brown," television scripts for "Hallmark Hall of Fame," detective novels, short stories, and dramas as well. Asked what he hadn't done that he'd like to do, he said, "Play centerfield for the Yankees." After a lifetime of writing best-selling hits, he solved the mystery of where his talent lies.

Edith Cavell

Hermann Hagedorn

Julius Caesar in Shakespeare's drama speaks the following memorable lines: "Cowards die many times before their deaths, / The valiant never taste of death but once." How might Caesar's lines apply to the heroine of this story?

She sits before her judges, a tall, slender woman, with the beauty of a noble spirit on the calm, high forehead, in the gray, unperturbed eyes. Behind her sits her attorney, but she may not speak to him. Behind her testify her accusers, but she may not turn to see who they are. She scarcely knows why she is in this great Hall of Deputies where the German authorities who rule in Brussels are holding their military court; but she hears herself called a "spy."

A spy! She, Edith Cavell! A smile comes to her sensitive, humorous lips at the thought. The idea that she who is direct and frank to a fault should be thought a spy would be superbly* comical, if the Germans apparently did not take it seriously. She is nothing so clever or so heroic, she would tell you if you asked her. She is just a nurse and head of a training school for nurses in Brussels, which, since the outbreak of war, had been turned into a Red Cross hospital; a very unimportant person, she will tell you.

---

superbly: exceptionally

She is not alone, facing the judges. At her right and at her left sit her friends, the Princess of Croy, the Countess of Belleville, and some

two dozen others. No definite, formal indictment* is brought against any of them, but it appears in the course of the proceedings that they are all accused of the same crime.

indictment: a legal document charging a person with a specific offense

There is something very appealing in the story as it unfolds. After the swift German advance in the summer of 1914, a year before, especially after the battle of Mons in which the British troops were heavily engaged, English soldiers, cut off from their army, have hidden in the forests and fields of Hainaut and Brabant seeking to avoid discovery by the German patrols, which have a way of shooting on sight, and taking no prisoners.

The Princess of Croy, an elderly spinster, has turned her chateau* near Mons into a Red Cross hospital, and from wounded soldiers, whom she helps to nurse, hears of the forsaken fugitives, living for months like hunted animals, knowing that to be found means to die. It seems to her and her neighbor and friend, the Countess of Belleville, no great crime to help these poor boys to make their way to Brussels where they stand a better chance with the German authorities than in the open where the patrols go.

chateau: French manor house

They draw a number of others into their confidence and before long have organized an "underground railway" similar to the system once in operation in the United States for aiding fugitive slaves to escape into Canada. They send them to Brussels; what happens to them after they get there is a matter into which they do not inquire. The fact is that in Brussels, directly under the noses of the German authorities, others take the young men and send them on toward the Dutch border. At the border the "railway" has its terminus.* If Holland, in defiance of international law, shuts one eye and lets them go on to England or France, that is Holland's business, not the business of the devoted little company which starts the fugitives on their journey.

terminus: end

Edith Cavell's hospital is a station on this "underground railway." She whose life work is to alleviate* suffering has it not in her, in the face of such pain and trouble, to pass by on the other side. She procures money for the fugitives, and guides, does it naturally as a part of the day's work. She nurses the German wounded as tenderly as she nurses the English, the French, or the Belgian, but she feels under no obligation to respect the authority of the German invaders.

alleviate: to make more bearable

Somehow the Germans hear of what she is doing; how, no one, perhaps, will ever know. A nurse gossiping, perhaps. "It is no small prudence to keep silence in an evil time," Edith Cavell remarks a little wistfully as the net closes upon her.

It is August. The Germans put her in prison. They are not unkind to her and she bears them no resentment. She finds herself, in fact, almost grateful to them. Her life has been filled with work from morning till night, from one year's end to the other; but here in prison she cannot work. She has time to meditate, to examine the record of her experience, to think quietly of life and death and love and duty. She is deeply religious, with a Puritan conscience. She reproaches herself that she has been too stern with others, not stern enough with herself. The days pass into weeks; a month passes, two months. For her it is a period of purification.

She has not yet been told what specific law she has broken. She has not been brought to trial. Quietly she waits for the ponderous military machinery of Germany to reach her case and decide it. She is not nervous, nor afraid. Hitherto life has been "so hurried"; now she is at peace. She can afford to be patient.

Meanwhile, she has not been forgotten. She has friends. Everyone who knows her in Brussels admires her, loves her. Word of her imprisonment reaches the American Minister, Brand Whitlock, who is in charge of British interests, and he instantly writes Baron von der Lancken, head of the Political Department of the German military government in Brussels, asking for particulars.

He receives no reply.

A month later he writes again. Two days later he has his answer. "Miss Cavell," writes His Excellency, "is in the prison of St. Gilles. She has admitted having hidden English and French soldiers in her home, admitted giving them money and guides. She is in solitary confinement. No one may see her."

A month thereafter she is in the Chamber of Deputies, facing the German court. It is a military court, not a law court. Here there are no safeguards to protect the accused from injustice. As far as those hard-faced judges in their field-gray uniforms are concerned, everything "goes." They are not brutal men in their personal relations, those judges, no harder, no more selfish probably than other men. But they are not individuals where they sit, behind the long table on the platform. They are parts of a machine, a machine that knows no human feeling, that is conscious of its power and uses it blindly according to certain printed rules. It has crushed and beaten Germans for years, crushed them mercilessly, crushed the fine flower of their freedom, their wisdom, their pure light-heartedness, made them stupid little cogs* in its great machine. Now it has gone forth to crush Germany's neighbors. The machine is in the Chamber of Deputies not to see justice done, but to protect the German army. Let the accused protect themselves.

---
cogs: the teeth in a wheel or gear

Edith Cavell has no instinct for self-protection. She denies nothing, evades nothing; if anything, she takes a certain modest pride in what she has done. She is entirely calm and self-possessed.

"You admit aiding English soldiers left behind after the battle of Mons?"

"Yes. They were English, and I am English, and I will help my own."

The judges become a little human; they are clearly impressed by her fearless words. One of them leans forward. "You admit that you helped as many as twenty?"

"Yes," she answers. "More than twenty. Two hundred."

"English?"

"No, not all English. French and Belgians too."

"But the French and Belgians are not of your nationality," one judge points out.

"You were foolish to help the English," interposes another. "The English are ungrateful."

"No," she answers. "The English are not ungrateful."

"How do you know?"

"Because some of them have written to me from England to thank me."

It was a fatal admission. She has been charged hitherto merely with aiding men to reach a neutral country, but now she has admitted that she has helped them to reach England, and the English army. The officers of the court look solemn. Her friends are horrified. But that is Edith Cavell, honest, frank, direct, unafraid.

The trial begins on Thursday, and lasts two days. What is the judgment. No one knows.

The court is weighing the evidence, but the American Minister hears rumors which disquiet him. He communicates with Baron von der Lancken's office, and is told that no decision has been reached. "Will the Baron please inform Mr. Whitlock when the sentence has been pronounced?"

"Of course, Your Excellency," is the reply. "At once. Without question."

Sunday. There is no news except a rumor that the judges are not in agreement.

Monday. Baron von der Lancken's office, in answer to repeated inquiries, states that the judgment has not been pronounced, and will not be pronounced until the following day. But the American Legation* is anxious, and restless. A sense of foreboding hangs over it.

Legation: the minister and staff who represent the interests of a specific government in a foreign country

---

The weather is wet and chill. Leaves are falling; autumn is here. And Imperial Germany is stronger than ever, with all Belgium under her heel, and power of life and death in the hands of her servants.

Tomorrow, judgment is to be pronounced. Tomorrow?

At nine o'clock that night, two nurses, frightened and in tears come to the Legation. The court-martial, they declare, has given its decision. Miss Cavell has been condemned to death and is to be executed at six o'clock the next morning. They have it on the best authority.

Whitlock is horror-stricken. He is ill; he cannot leave the house. He sends his aide and the legal adviser of the Legation, a Belgian, to find von der Lancken. The Spanish Minister, Villalabar, joins him. The Baron is at the theater. He is annoyed at being disturbed, and refuses to come to them until the play is over. When he meets them at last he declares that he has heard of no judgment. The story is absurd, impossible. The German Governor-General would not think of executing a woman on such short notice. He is angry at the thought that the Americans should imagine such a thing of the German authorities.

"All right," says Whitlock's aide. "Suppose you call up the prison?"

The Baron goes to the telephone and comes back flushed and a little embarrassed. The story is true.

The American and the Spaniard argue with him, plead, beg for time, ask him to see the Governor-General, point out what the world will say. Von der Lancken is impressed, and goes to the Governor of the city. But the Governor is obdurate.* He will not listen. He will not even receive the appeal for mercy. The machine never admits a mistake. The judgment stands.

---

obdurate: hardhearted; stubborn

And Edith Cavell? She is in her cell writing letters, quite calm. She has not expected a sentence of death, certainly not expected execution to follow so swiftly on the heels of the judgment, but she is wasting no time in lamentation. She has letters to write to her mother and to some friends in England, advice to five of the nurses in her training school, a last word to send to a poor girl who is struggling with a drug habit.

The British chaplain comes to her cell. They are old friends.

"I am glad you came," she says quietly. "I want my friends to know that I gladly give my life for my country. I have no fear nor shrinking. I have seen death so often that it is not strange or fearful to me. They have been very kind to me here, and this period of rest before the end has been a great mercy. I have had a chance to meditate on many things. And I have learned this: standing as I do in view of God and eternity, I realize that patriotism is not enough. I must have no hatred or bitterness toward anyone."

They partake of Holy Communion together, and when he repeats the verses of "Abide with Me," she joins softly in the end.

It is time for the chaplain to go. "Goodbye," he says.

She smiles gently as she clasps his hand. "We shall meet again."

And now she is alone, waiting. And now the German chaplain, gentle and courteous, is with her. And now the officer comes to lead her to her execution.

The corridors of the prison are dark and silent. Here and there they pass a guard in the shadows. There is something appallingly* furtive* about this thing that is about to happen, that even now is happening, this slipping down dark halls, dark stairs, in the dim light of an October dawn. Why this blind haste? Is the Military Machine afraid that mercy might somehow get her hand through the iron ring? She is a woman, a frail, slender woman, and the great Machine is so afraid of her that she must be done away with before reason shall have time to discomfit the judges, or an indignant world shall have an opportunity to voice its protest.

---

appallingly: frightfully
furtive: hidden motives or purposes

The very walls seem to cry, "Look at her, gentlemen, you with your spiked helmets! Can this woman plot? Can this woman deceive? And would your own wives and daughters not do what she has done for their countrymen if the occasion came? And would you not be proud of them if they did? Keep this woman in prison if you must, but execute her in cold blood? What can she do to you? Living, what can she do? And *dead*, what can she *not* do?"

The footsteps ring hard and metallic on the cement floor. Now she is in the black van rushing to the place of execution. Now she is in the yard with the firing squad before her. She speaks a word to the German chaplain. Her voice is unwavering, her face is bright. She is tied loosely to a pillar.

"The grace of our Lord Jesus Christ, and the love of God and the fellowship of the Holy Ghost be with thee now and forever."

It is the chaplain who is trembling. She herself is quite calm. But the soldier who places the bandage over her eyes notes that they are full of tears.

Seconds pass. They seem endless. Then the sharp word of command cuts the appalling silence. Twelve rifles ring out in one clap of thunder. She sinks to the ground. She is dead.

The rain ceases, the air is soft and warm, the sunlight shines through an autumn haze. Edith Cavell is dead, Edith Cavell, the unknown nurse, the head of an unimportant training school is dead; her work is done. But another Edith Cavell has risen from her grave to do a work so vastly more important that the other fades into insignificance beside it. The world has her name, the world has her story. Was the Military Machine afraid of the living woman? What will they say of her now that they have struck her down? Dead? Yes. Buried, too. And yet all over the world, she speaks! What are orators, with all their eloquence beside her? What are flaring posters? What are books, cartoons, pamphlets? Just the repetition of her name tells more than any fiery words could. She is a cry in every heart, a picture burned into every brain in England, France, Belgium, America. Recruiting in England instantly jumps ten thousand a day; British soldiers shout *For Edith Cavell!* as they climb out of the trenches and charge. Through America runs a shudder, and those who were neither hot nor cold toward the forces fighting in Europe awake with sudden comprehension to what it is which has made itself strong in

Belgium and northern France. The Kaiser, himself, they say, is displeased, and hastens to commute* the sentences of the Princess of Croy and the Countess of Belleville and their friends. Even he recognizes that the Great Machine he has built up may be too ruthless, too stupid, too blind. It is not the German people which has done this thing. It is not even the ruler of the German people which has done it. A Machine acted. It has struck in hysterical fury at the enemy, but it has inflicted a deeper wound upon the German people and the German cause.

---

commute: change the penalty to a lower one

For Edith Cavell, living, could help a few wounded or starving boys into Holland, that is all. But Edith Cavell, dead, is an angel with a flaming sword sweeping through the conscience of mankind, and calling the world to battle.

About the Story

1. Who is on trial for spying?
2. Why would the Germans choose to prosecute Cavell actively but not the others?
3. Paragraphs 5 and 6 give an account of the logic behind the efforts to help the soldiers. Do you think Edith Cavell is as unaware of the dangers as the princess and the countess seem to be?
4. The judges of the German court "are parts of a machine." Why do you think Hagedorn chose to make this comparison?

About the Author

Known primarily as a poet, Hermann Hagedorn (1882-1964) nonetheless excelled at prose. He began his poetry career while an English instructor at Harvard. World War I had a profound influence on him, however. He and friends established a group called the Vigilantes to train boys in citizenship and also to recruit for the war effort. He later became "ashamed of 'silly chants and little hymns of hate.' " He was also "somewhat guiltily conscious of his Germanic blood," not surprising, considering the actions of the Axis powers. He does manage in this account, however, to present a balanced treatment of Germany's activities, separating the government from the people. He also met Theodore Roosevelt during the war and became captivated by the man's spirit. Researching the man, compiling documents about his presidency, and establishing the Theodore Roosevelt Memorial Association were the fruits of that meeting. From Roosevelt's Rough Riders to an English nurse, Hagedorn has recognized heroism and seen to it that his readers do so as well.

Whether by Life or by Death

Mary Geraldine Taylor

John and Betty Stam could have chosen an easier occupation and an easier location. Instead, they traveled halfway around the world to serve God in China, which was in the process of falling to the Communists. Knowing that they might die, as had other missionaries to China, they boldly continued to serve the Savior. Their courage rested on God's unfailing strength. Who else in these two chapters from John and Betty Stam: A Story of Triumph *imitates the Stams' courageous self-sacrifice?*

It was not unprepared that John and Betty met the sudden, unexpected attack of the Red forces that captured the city of Tsingteh on the sixth day of December. Crossing the mountains by unfrequented paths, they came in behind the government army, sixty miles to the south. With scarcely any warning, their advance guard scaled* the city wall and threw open the gates. It was early morning. Betty was bathing little Helen when the first messenger came, telling them of danger. Another and another quickly followed. The District Magistrate, after a short, ineffectual* resistance, had fled. Chairs* and coolies* were obtained as quickly as possible, but before an escape could be made, firing was heard on the streets—the looting* of the city had begun.

---

scaled: climbed
ineffectual: powerless
Chairs: portable chairs on which a rider sits while being
 carried by two porters
coolies: porters
looting: violent robbing on a large scale

Then John and Betty knelt with their faithful servants in prayer. They were perfectly composed,* and even when the Reds thundered at the door they opened to them with quiet courtesy. While John was talking with

COURAGE

the leaders, trying to satisfy their demands for goods and money, Betty actually served them with tea and cakes. But courtesy was as useless as resistance would have been. John was bound and carried off to the Communist headquarters, and before long they returned for Betty and the baby. The cook and maid pleaded to go with them, and were only deterred* when the Reds would have shot them down.

composed: calm
deterred: prevented

"It is better that you stay here," whispered Betty. "If anything happens to us, look out for the baby."

Through the terrible hours that followed, the young missionaries showed no fear. All the testimony of eye-witnesses goes to prove that, spiritually, they were masters of the situation. When John was allowed to return, under guard, to their pillaged* home, to seek clothing and food for the baby, he was glad to be able to comfort the servants who were still there.

pillaged: thoroughly robbed

"Do not be afraid," he said to the weeping woman who was telling him how everything had been taken. "God is on the throne. These little things do not matter:—our Heavenly Father knows. You go and sleep with old Mrs. Li tonight, and the cook will look after you."

That same day, amid* all the carnage* and horror, he managed to write one brief, revealing letter:

> Tsingteh An[hwei]
> Dec. 6, 1934
> China Inland Mission, Shanghai.
>
> Dear Brethren,
>
> My wife, baby and myself are today in the hands of the Communists, in the city of Tsingteh. Their demand is twenty thousand dollars for our release.
>
> All our possessions and stores are in their hands, but we praise God for peace in our hearts and a meal tonight. God grant you wisdom in what you do, and us fortitude,* courage and peace of heart. He is able—and a wonderful Friend in such a time.
>
> Things happened so quickly this a.m. They were in the city just a few hours after the ever-persistent rumors really became alarming, so that we could not prepare to leave in time. We were just too late.
>
> The Lord bless and guide you, and as for us, may God be glorified whether by life or by death.
>
> In Him,
> John Stam

amid: during
carnage: great slaughter
fortitude: strength to bear pain with courage

Spikenard Very Precious

An army of two thousand Communists, soon increased to six thousand, was now in possession of the district, and the people, already suffering from semi-famine conditions, had to see their meager* supplies disappear as before hungry locusts. But that was a minor misery. For when the Reds abandoned Tsingteh the next morning, they left many dead behind them and carried away many captives. Their next

destination was Miaosheo, the little town twelve miles across the mountains. . . .

meager: few

Over the familiar road John walked, a prisoner, carrying his precious little one, not yet three months old. Betty was on horseback part of the way, and they both smiled at the few people who saw them as they passed. That little Helen was there at all seems to have been the first miracle in her deliverance, for her life was to have been taken even before they left Tsingteh. Part of the torture of her parents, it is stated, was that their captors discussed before them whether or not they should kill the infant out of hand,* to save trouble. And this would have been done, but that an unexpected protest was raised by one who was looking on. Who he was or where he came from does not appear [in the records used by the author]. He had been released from prison by the Communists when they sacked* the town, and now dared to come forward and urge that the baby at any rate had done nothing worthy of death.

out of hand: immediately
sacked: stripped of valuables

"Then it's your life for hers!" was the angry retort.*

retort: reply

"I am willing," replied the old farmer. And it is stated that he was killed on the spot.

At any rate, the little life was spared, and John and Betty had their treasure with them as they traveled wearily over the mountains to Miaosheo.

Arriving in the town, how they must have longed to go to the home of their friends the Wangs! But, of course, terror reigned supreme. All who could had fled, before the looting of the place began. Betty and John were hurried into the postmaster's shop and left there under guard, thankful to be out of sight of all that was taking place.

"Where are you going?" asked the postmaster, when he recognized the prisoners.

"We do not know where they are going," John answered simply, "but we are going to heaven."

The postmaster offered them fruit to eat. Betty took some—she had the baby to nurse—but John made the most of the opportunity for writing again to Shanghai. This note he entrusted to the postmaster to forward.

Miaosheo, An.
December 7, 1934

China Inland Mission

Dear Brethren,

We are in the hands of the Communists here, being taken from Tsingteh when they passed through yesterday. I tried to persuade them to let my wife and baby go back from Tsingteh with a letter to you, but they wouldn't let her, and so we both made the trip to Miaosheo today, my wife traveling part of the way on a horse.

They want $20,000 before they will free us, which we have told them we are sure will not *be paid. Famine relief money and our personal money and effects are all in their hands.*

God give you wisdom in what you do and give us grace and fortitude. He is able.

Yours in Him,
John C. Stam

. . . Little remains to be told, for thank God, their sufferings were not prolonged. When the Communists again turned their attention to them, they were taken to a house belonging to some wealthy man who had fled. There they were put in a room in an inner courtyard, closely guarded by soldiers, and though Betty seems to have been left free to care for the baby, John was tightly bound with ropes to a post of the heavy bed.

No one knows what passed between John and Betty [during the long night], or what fears assailed* those young hearts. . . . Betty was not overwhelmed, but was enabled to plan with all a mother's tenderness for the infant they might have to leave behind, alone and orphaned, amid such perils.* Could that little life survive? And if it did, what then? But had they not given her to God in that so recent dedication service? Would not He care for His own?

---

assailed: violently attacked
perils: dangers

Never was that little one more precious than when they looked their last on her baby sweetness, as they were roughly summoned* the next morning and led out to die. Yet there was no weakening. Those who witnessed the tragedy marveled, as they testify, at the calmness with which both John and Betty faced the worst their misguided enemies could do. Theirs was the moral, spiritual triumph, in that hour when the very forces of hell seemed to be let loose. Painfully bound with ropes, their hands behind them, stripped of their outer garments and John barefooted (he had given Betty his socks to wear) they passed down the street where he was known to many, while the Reds shouted their ridicule and called the people to come and see the execution.

---

summoned: sent for

Like their Master, they were led up a little hill outside the town. There, in a clump of pine trees, the Communists harangued* the unwilling onlookers, too terror-stricken to utter protest—But no, one man broke the ranks! The doctor of the place and a Christian, he expressed the feelings of many when he fell on his knees and pleaded for the life of his friends. Angrily repulsed* by the Reds, he still persisted,* until he was dragged away as a prisoner, to suffer death when it appeared that he too was a follower of Christ.

---

harangued: delivered long speeches to
repulsed: pushed away
persisted: firmly continued

John had turned to the leader of the band, asking mercy for this man, when he was sharply ordered to kneel—and the look of joy on his face, afterwards, told of the unseen Presence with them as his spirit was released. Betty was seen to quiver* but only for a moment. Bound as she was, she fell on her knees beside him. A quick command, the flash of a sword which mercifully she did not see—and they were reunited. . . .

---

quiver: tremble

Darkness had fallen upon the streets of Miaosheo. Behind closed doors, people spoke in whispers of the tragedy of the morning. In a deserted home a little baby cried and slept alone.

All that night and on into the second day, no one crossed the threshold. On the hillside where they had fallen, lay the two who loved her best, silent and still. Could there have been a more helpless little life, a more hopeless situation? No one dared approach the house, for the Reds were only three miles away. They might at any time return, and their spies seemed to be everywhere. Yet, as an old Bible-woman in Ningpo said through her tears: "The angels themselves took care of her!"

Hiding in the hills near-by were refugees who had fled from the Communists, hungry and homeless. And among them, strange to say, were the Evangelist Lo and his wife, who were to have come weeks before to settle in Miaosheo. Had they done so, they would have been occupying the Mission premises, and would undoubtedly have been killed by the Reds or taken prisoners. Detained* in unexpected ways, they reached the town only a few hours before its capture and looting. Had they been a little later they would have met refugees on the road, and would not have come at all. As it was, they had arrived and were staying the night with Mrs. Wang and her family when the trouble came.

Detained: delayed

With the first appearance of soldiers, the younger women fled to the mountains, but Evangelist Lo and Mrs. Wang's son lingered to see what was happening. The advance guard of the Reds were seeking the headmen of the town, and some one pointed out these two. Wang immediately ran for his life, but Lo, not being a headman, stood his ground. He was of course taken prisoner, but Chang the medicine seller (who gave his life next day in a vain effort to save his missionary friends) was able to identify him.

"This man is a stranger here," he said. "I know him. He distributed tracts and treats diseases, as I do. He only came last night to Miaosheo."

Not realizing that "tracts" were Christian publications, the Reds gave Lo his freedom. Marveling at his deliverance, he quietly walked away, and as quickly as possible joined the refugees. For two days and two nights they suffered cold and hunger in the mountain refuge, not daring to make a fire. Happily there were wild chestnuts for food, and one man had a sickle,* and cut enough grass to protect them a little, in place of bedding.

---

sickle: tool with a curved blade and short handle

A rumor reached them on the second day that the Reds had a foreigner captive. Could it be the Roman Catholic priest from Tsingteh, Lo questioned. His own missionaries had doubtless been warned in time to make their escape. But later arrivals said that two foreigners had been brought by the Reds to Miaosheo, a husband and wife, and that they had been publicly executed. Harrowing details were given, and in great distress Lo set out to learn more about what had transpired.* It was Sunday morning, the 9th of December. From their hiding place the refugees had seen government troops come into the valley, in pursuit of the Reds. There was desultory* fighting, which had drawn the Communists away from the town. So the Wangs returned to their home,

COURAGE

and with them Mr. Lo's wife and child, the latter very ill from cold and exposure.

transpired: happened
desultory: random

The place was strangely quiet, and even from people who were about, Lo could learn very little. No one dared speak out, for fear of Communist spies, and his good friend the medicine seller could not be found. Just as he was leaving the street, however, to explore the hill, an old woman ventured to whisper that there was a baby, a foreign baby, still alive. Urged to say more, she only pointed furtively* in the direction of an empty house. Wondering what he should find, Lo entered it. Room after room showed traces of the bandit army. The place was silent. . . . It seemed deserted. But—what was that? A little cry! Lo hastened to the inner chamber, and soon the baby, left alone for almost thirty hours, was in his kindly arms.

furtively: secretly

He found her lying on the bed, just as her mother's hands and heart had planned. Safe in her sleeping bag with its zipper fastening, little Helen was warm and snug, and seemingly none the worse for her long fast. Taking her with him Lo went on up the hill, for the saddest part of his task was yet before him.

The finding of his missionary friends was, as he wrote, "an unspeakable tragedy." Grief and horror almost overwhelmed him. But immediate action was necessary, for the Reds might be returning at any time. Happily Mrs. Lo was at hand to take charge of the baby. With the help of Mrs. Wang and her son, coffins were procured* and the bodies wrapped in white cotton material, the only thing to be had in the town. Meanwhile a crowd had gathered on Eagle Hill, as Mr. Birch wrote a few days later.

procured: obtained

Nothing but sorrow and regret were expressed for the death of this fine young couple. Some even dared to curse the Reds for the crime. When they had done all they could, the three Christians bowed in prayer. Then straightening himself, Lo addressed the people.

"You have seen," he said, "these wounded bodies, and you pity our friends for their suffering and death. But you should know that they are children of God. Their spirits are unharmed, and they are at this moment in the presence of their Heavenly Father. They came to China and to Miaosheo, not for themselves but for you, to tell you about the great love of God, that you might believe in the Lord Jesus and be eternally saved. You have heard their message. Remember, it is true. Their death proves it so. Do not forget what they told you—repent, and believe the Gospel."

Lo tells me that many of the listeners wept. Personally, I have not seen tears in China, in response to our message. Why the change? Why the melted hearts? They had a demonstration of the love and power of God and the truth of the Gospel. We expect much fruit from the triumphant death and faithful testimony of these two Shining Ones.

But the urgent matter was to save little Helen; so leaving the coffins to the care of Mrs. Wang and her son, Lo hastened back to his family. And what distresses, what alarms lay before them! Their money and few possessions, left in Mrs. Wang's home, had all been stolen. Their little boy of four, their only son, was desperately ill. A journey of about a hundred miles had to be taken, through mountainous country infested* with bandits, to say nothing of Communist soldiers. And most serious of all, they had a little foreign baby to hide and to protect.

infested: overrun

On foot and as secretly as possible they made their escape from Miaosheo, the children hidden in two large rice baskets, hanging from the ends of a bamboo carrying pole. They would have had no money to pay the brave man who undertook to carry the baskets, had they not found the provision Betty had made that last night for her baby. Inside the sleeping bag she had tucked away a clean nightdress and some diapers, all she had been able to bring with her, and among them she had pinned two five-dollar bills. It was enough, just enough to provide for the little party, with the help of young Chinese mothers along the way, who gladly fed the orphan baby, at Mrs. Lo's request.

It was no small cheer on this desperate journey when Mr. and Mrs. Lo, in spite of all their fears, saw their sick child come to himself again. After many hours of semi-consciousness he sat up and began to sing a hymn, and from that time steadily recovered.

Passing through Kinghsien, they were able to buy a tin of Lactogen.* Mrs. Lo had been in the Wuhu Methodist hospital for Uenseng's birth, and had learned the foreign way of caring for infants. She even had with her the feeding bottle used for her own baby, and was able to put little Helen on a proper three hours' schedule for the rest of the way. Was it by chance that a woman thus equipped was at hand in that hour of need, in a remote corner of inland China?

Lactogen: prepared baby formula

On the 14th of December Mr. Birch was alone in Süancheng, his wife being at Wuhu with the children. Just as lunch was served he heard sounds as of some unexpected arrival, followed by a knock at the door. A travel-stained woman came in, carrying a bundle. To his thankfulness, it was Mrs. Lo.

"This is all we have left," she said brokenly.

Fearing that her husband had been killed and that she only had escaped with the child, he took the bundle she held out to him, and uncovered the sleeping face of—little Helen Priscilla! Then Mr. Lo came in, having settled with the chair coolies, and the wonderful story was told which has given this little one the name of the "Miracle Baby."

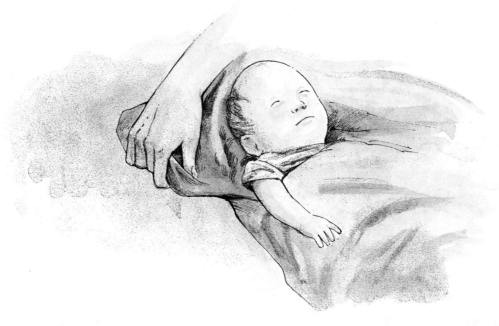

And a miracle indeed it seemed when it was found that the infant was so well that not even her mother could have wished to see her happier or better. The doctors in the Wuhu hospital pronounced her to be in perfect health and all hearts were won by her appealing sweetness. To the grandparents in Tsinan, Mrs. Walton wrote while in charge of her:

I am so anxious for you to see little Helen, for she is simply perfect! She is a beautiful baby, so well and strong and as good as gold. She scarcely ever cries. And she is such a dear combination of Betty and John. Her eyes are just like Betty's. She smiles most of her waking moments, and coos and talks so sweetly!

To Dr. and Mrs. Scott, the coming of this little one to their loving care in Tsinan seemed like a resurrection from the dead.

Everything about her deliverance [they wrote] tells of God's love and power. And we know that if He could bring a tiny, helpless infant, not three months old, through such dangers in perfect safety, He could no less surely have saved the lives of her precious parents, had that been in His divine plan for them.

About the Story

1. In what ways are John and Betty Stam "not unprepared" to meet the Chinese Communist forces?
2. What Bible verses does John Stam's first letter remind you of?
3. Why is baby Helen allowed to stay with her parents?
4. Who in this story other than John and Betty Stam demonstrates courage in the face of death?
5. List the three deliverances of baby Helen.
6. List God's provisions for the Stams even in their martyrdom.
7. What is the Bible verse referred to in the title of the second chapter, and what is its significance?

About the Author

The Triumph of John and Betty Stam was written by Mary Geraldine Taylor, the daughter-in-law of Hudson Taylor and herself a missionary under the China Inland Mission founded by Mr. Taylor. Though little is known of Mary Taylor, much information is known about her father-in-law. Hudson Taylor was a remarkable man whose full surrender to God made the opening of China to the gospel a reality. In 1853 after years spent in medical training and, more importantly, learning to trust God fully, he left for China. For, as he said, "When I get out to China, . . . I shall have no claim on anyone for anything. My only claim will be on God. How important to learn, before leaving England, to move man, through God, by prayer alone." And learn to do this effectively he did. In 1865 he was moved by God to begin the China Inland Mission by asking God for twenty-four workers and their necessary support. Within a year they were in China. In 1875 he asked God for eighteen men to pioneer the nine yet-unreached districts of China. In 1881 he asked for seventy more workers, and in 1886 he asked God for one hundred workers. By the time Hudson Taylor resigned the leadership of the Mission in 1900, there were 750 missionaries, 700 Chinese workers, and 13,000 baptized converts. The mission had never been in debt, supported by God's children moved by God alone. George Mueller, himself a prayer warrior for the needs of his orphans, took on the support of several of the mission members. Hudson Taylor's desire was to reach the Chinese people as effectively as possible. To do so, he created no little stir among the European community when, after a year or so in China, he adopted Chinese dress and wore his hair in a queue in order to travel and minister more easily among the Chinese. The history of the China Inland Mission reveals the dedication of its founder and its members, like John and Betty Stam, who glorified God "by life and by death."

Stand Up for Jesus

George Duffield

Stand up, stand up for Jesus,
Ye soldiers of the cross,
Lift high His royal banner,
It must not suffer loss;
From victory unto victory,
His army shall He lead,
Till every foe is vanquished
And Christ is Lord indeed.

Stand up, stand up for Jesus,
The trumpet call obey;
Forth to the mighty conflict,
In this His glorious day.
"Ye that are men, now serve Him,"
Against unnumbered foes;
Let courage rise with danger,
And strength to strength oppose.

Stand up, stand up for Jesus,
Stand in His strength alone;
The arm of flesh will fail you—
Ye dare not trust your own;
Put on the gospel armor,
Each piece put on with prayer;
Where duty calls, or danger,
Be never wanting there.

Stand up, stand up for Jesus,
The strife will not be long;
This day the noise of battle,
The next, the victor's song;
To him that overcometh,
A crown of life shall be;
He with the King of glory
Shall reign eternally.

The Bible and Courage

Then Nebuchadnezzar in his rage and fury commanded to bring Shadrach, Meshach, and Abed-nego. . . . Nebuchadnezzar spake and said unto them, Is it true, O Shadrach, Meshach, and Abed-nego, do not ye serve my gods, nor worship the golden image which I have set up?

Shadrach, Meshach, and Abed-nego, answered and said to the king, O Nebuchadnezzar, we are not careful to answer thee in this matter. If it be so, our God whom we serve is able to deliver us from the burning fiery furnace, and he will deliver us out of thine hand, O king. But if not, be it known unto thee, O king, that we will not serve thy gods, nor worship the golden image which thou hast set up.

Then was Nebuchadnezzar full of fury, and the form of his visage was changed against Shadrach, Meshach, and Abed-nego: therefore he spake, and commanded that they should heat the furnace one seven times more than it was wont to be heated. And he commanded the most mighty men that were in his army to bind Shadrach, Meshach, and Abed-nego, and to cast them into the burning fiery furnace.

Then these men were bound in their coats, their hosen, and their hats, and their other garments, and were cast into the midst of the burning fiery furnace. Therefore because the king's commandment was urgent, and the furnace exceeding hot, the flame of the fire slew those men that took up Shadrach, Meshach, and Abed-nego.

And these three men, Shadrach, Meshach, and Abed-nego, fell down bound into the midst of the burning fiery furnace.

Then Nebuchadnezzar the king was astonied, and rose up in haste, and spake, and said unto his counsellors, Did not we cast three men bound into the midst of the fire? They answered and said unto the king, True, O king. He answered and said, Lo, I see four men loose, walking in the midst of the fire, and they have no hurt; and the form of the fourth is like the Son of God. (Daniel 3:13-14, 16-25)

According to my earnest expectation and my hope, that in nothing I shall be ashamed, but that with all boldness, as always, so now also Christ shall be magnified in my body, whether it be by life, or by death. For to me to live is Christ, and to die is gain.

Only let your conversation be as it becometh the gospel of Christ: that whether I come and see you, or else be absent, I may hear of your affairs, that ye stand fast in one spirit, with one mind striving together for the faith of the gospel; And in nothing terrified by your adversaries: which is to them an evident token of perdition, but to you of salvation, and that of God.

For unto you it is given in the behalf of Christ, not only to believe on him, but also to suffer for his sake; Having the same conflict which ye saw in me, and now hear to be in me. (Philippians 1:20-21, 27-30)

2

Nature & Man

The heavens declare the glory of God; and the firmament sheweth his handywork.

Nature and Man

Have you ever stood outside at night gazing at the stars? Did you wonder how God made them? how far away they really are? what causes them to shine? whether astronauts will ever travel to them or beyond?

Perhaps David wondered about the stars too. In Psalm 19 he wrote, "The heavens declare the glory of God; and the firmament showeth his handywork." In other words, David expresses what we too can see—that the stars, like the rest of what we call "nature," point us to the Creator of heaven and earth. As a Christian experiences what God has created, he can truthfully say, "This is my Father's world."

God created us with the ability to receive pleasure from nature. As a result, we enjoy seeing fleecy white clouds lazily float across a light blue sky, hearing the rhythmic slapping of waves against a beach, feeling the spring sun gently warm our faces, smelling the fragrance of the early lilacs, tasting the juicy sweetness of a red-ripe apple.

Adam and Eve must have delighted in every part of the world God created. But when they sinned, they brought God's curse upon the earth. As a consequence, nature shows us another aspect, one from which we retreat, often in fear: the lightning bolts savagely splitting blackened skies, wind-whipped waves crashing heavily against a beach, the fierce rays of a blistering summer sun, the smell of death from a stagnant pond or rotting animal carcass, the bitterness of apples too green to eat.

Although nature is cursed, we have a close relationship with it. It supplies us with food and clothing. It offers us rest from the hectic pace of life. When the twelve disciples returned from a time of preaching and working miracles, Christ told them to "come . . . apart into a desert place, and rest a while" (Mark 6:31). Nature helps reveal God to us. Because the created world shows to all people that God truly exists (Rom. 1:20), no one can truthfully say at the day of judgment that he did not know that there is a God. Nature also displays the greatness of the Creator. The psalmist expresses in Psalm 8 his wonder that the Creator of this world should be interested in mankind.

At times nature has also served as the instrument of God's judgment. When the earth became so wicked that God would no longer endure its wickedness, He sent the Flood to destroy everyone but Noah and his family. When the Egyptian army defied God by pursuing the Israelites, He caused the Red Sea to swallow up the whole army, including horses and chariots.

In His Word God often uses nature to teach principles to mankind. Solomon, for instance, tells us to be industrious, like the ant (Prov. 6:6-8). "Whatsoever a man soweth," declares Paul, "that shall he also reap" (Gal.

6:7). Just as we do not plant cucumber seeds and reap tomatoes, so do we not sow fleshly desires and reap spiritual fruit. In His earthly ministry Christ illustrated many spiritual principles by comparing them to creatures and events in nature. "Consider the lilies of the field, how they grow," He told His disciples. "They toil not, neither do they spin: and yet I say unto you, that even Solomon in all his glory was not arrayed like one of these. Wherefore, if God so clothe the grass of the field, which to day is, and to morrow is cast into the oven, shall he not much more clothe you, O ye of little faith?" (Matt. 6:28-30).

Yet despite the fact that God made nature to serve His purposes, many have "changed the truth of God into a lie, and worshipped and served the creature more than the Creator" (Rom. 1:25). Some have bowed themselves before the sun or a tree or a river or some other part of creation. Others have falsely believed that they will find God's truth through nature only, and not in the Bible.

Still others have thought that the closer they are to unspoiled nature, the nearer they can come to God. Yet in the Garden of Eden, the most unspoiled place ever to exist on earth, Adam and Eve sinned. In fact, throughout history, whenever people have gone into nature to worship God, they have ended up worshiping the devil. The "groves" of the Old Testament were places of great natural beauty, but they became sites of idol worship and immorality (Deut. 16:21; I Kings 14:22-23; II Chron. 14:2-4). It is a mistake for a person to believe that he can best serve God by being alone in nature and away from others. God calls us to serve Him by ministering to others (Matt. 28:19-20; II Tim. 2:2), not by isolating ourselves.

Numerous writers have explored the relationship between nature and man. Some, like James Thurber in "Snapshot of a Dog," focus on the special bond between people and a pet. Others show man at war with an animal, as in Russell Cordon Garter's "Old Sly Eye." Still others show man at war with nature in general. In the excerpts from *Survive the Savage Sea* we see six shipwrecked people courageously struggling for thirty-eight days against a harsh and merciless ocean.

Many a writer has turned to nature to help show his readers how they may better understand themselves and their world. The Puritan poet Anne Bradstreet, the first important woman writer in America, used nature to clarify an important fact about death. Four centuries later Robert Frost used nature to mock the foolish pride of modern scientists. The fables of the ancient Greek writer Aesop teach readers principles for right living. The words of the hymn writer, though, point us to the most important fact in our experience with the world around us:

> This is my Father's world:
> I rest me in the thought
> Of rocks and trees, of skies and seas—
> His hand the wonders wrought.

Swift Things Are Beautiful

Elizabeth Coatsworth

This poem about things in nature is organized by two lists. What do you think the poet could—or should—have added to her poem?

Swift things are beautiful:
Swallows and deer,
And lightning that falls
Bright veined and clear,
Rivers and meteors,   5
Wind in the wheat,
The strong-withered* horse,   withers: the ridge
The runner's sure feet.   between the shoulder
                                                   bones

And slow things are beautiful:
The closing of day,   10
The pause of the wave
That curves downward to spray,
The ember* that crumbles,   ember: a glowing coal of
The opening flower,   a fire
And the ox that moves on   15
In the quiet of power.

About the Author

Elizabeth Coatsworth, born on May 31, 1893, in Buffalo, New York, used her traveling experiences in North Africa, Europe, Mexico, and the Orient to inspire her numerous poems and stories written for children and older readers. Her awards include the Newbery Medal for a Japanese tale, *The Cat Who Went to Heaven*.

The Panther

Ogden Nash

Ogden Nash plays with words—and with us—as he describes two dangerous animals.

The panther is like a leopard,
Except it hasn't been peppered.
Should you behold a panther crouch,
Prepare to say OUCH.
Better yet, if called by a panther,
Don't anther.

The Rhinoceros

The rhino is a homely beast,
For human eyes he's not a feast.
Farewell, farewell, you old rhinoceros,
I'll stare at something
   less prepoceros!

About the Author

"I've been in love with words all my life." So says Ogden Nash (1902-71) of himself. And he turned his love of words into a lifelong occupation. Writing was not the only occupation he had, however. During World War II he patrolled the streets of Baltimore as an air raid warden on guard against potential Nazi bombers. He also traveled on the lecture circuit and helped to sell war bonds. He came from a prominent Southern family; one of his ancestors "gave his name to Nashville, Tennessee." At Harvard, he played football. Or did he? As he relates, "You can get an idea of how good I was from the fact that although we lost The Game 49-0, I didn't get to play a minute of it." So his love of words stood him in good stead as he wrote verse after verse and children's story after children's story, which were often illustrated by his daughter. He also wrote lyrics to several classical pieces of music such as "The Carnival of the Animals," "Peter and the Wolf," and "The Sorcerer's Apprentice." Nash chose to communicate through the disarming medium of what often seems to be nonsense verse, but usually is not.

Catalogue

Rosalie Moore

The word catalogue *means "a systematized list." Is it an appropriate title for this poem? What does the dictionary give as the standard abbreviation of* catalogue?

Cats sleep fat and walk thin.
Cats, when they sleep, slump;
When they wake, stretch and begin
Over, pulling their ribs in.
Cats walk thin.   5

Cats wait in a lump,
Jump in a streak.
Cats, when they jump, are sleek
As a grape slipping its skin—
They have technique.   10
Oh, cats don't creak.
They sneak.

Cats sleep fat.
They spread out comfort underneath them
Like a good mat,   15
As if they picked the place
And then sat;
You walk around one
As if he were the City Hall
After that.   20

If male,
A cat is apt to sing on a major scale;
This concert is for everybody, this
Is wholesale.
For a baton, he wields a tail.   25
(He is also found,
When happy, to resound
With an enclosed and private sound.)

A cat condenses.
He pulls in his tail to go under bridges,   30
And himself to go under fences.
Cats fit
In any size box or kit,
And if a large pumpkin grew under one,
He could arch over it.   35

When everyone else is just ready to go out,
The cat is just ready to come in.
He's not where he's been.
Cats sleep fat and walk thin.

. . . About the Author . . . .

Rosalie Moore, born October 8, 1910, in Oakland, California, wrote most of her children's books and stories along with her husband under the names Bill and Rosalie Brown. She claimed that her husband's expertise in finding good stories and her ability as a poet to tell the stories in clear sensory language combined to create the exciting, funny stories her children's reading books lacked. Her poetry, often resulting from her own experiences, includes poems both for children and about children. One of her poems was inspired by the antics of her own pet cat, Jay Bird. Whenever she would try to write something, he would sit on her paper or typewriter. After having been moved, the cat would climb up again to look at his master. Frustrated, the poet finally decided to write about the cat and penned the first line of her most frequently reprinted poem, "Catalogue."

About the Poems

1. Other than beauty, what do the "swift things" and "slow things" that Coatsworth describes have in common?
2. In "The Panther" what does Nash compare the panther to? What word makes the comparison clear?
3. Skilled poets use all the tools at their disposal to communicate their ideas; how does Nash use capitalization?

4. In both of these poems, Nash's play on words involves what common poetic expectation?
5. Identify some unusual descriptions of the cat in Moore's poem.

The Mahogany Fox

Samuel Scoville Jr.

This story pits three hunters and their packs of hounds against the mahogany fox. Do you expect to sympathize with the fox or with the hounds and the hunters? Does your sympathy change as you read the story? Is the fox at a disadvantage?

He began life as a red cub. As he grew older, his coat became darker until it was the exact shade of a well-polished mahogany table and gained him his name. By the time Old Mahogany had reached his full growth, he was the largest, the handsomest, and the wiliest* fox in all that hill country of Litchfield County.

wiliest: cleverest

In his fifth year the three best fox hunters of Cornwall conspired* against him. Myron Dean, off the Barrack, Rashe Howe, down from the Cobble, and Mark Hurlburt, out of the Hollow, agreed to pool their packs and hunt him down.

conspired: plotted

"Let Mark start off tomorrow morning with his young dogs," said Myron, when they met at the village store. " 'Bout the middle o' the morning Rashe here can spell* him. In the afternoon, if he's still goin', I'll turn my old dogs loose."

spell: relieve

"He'll be goin' all right," returned Rashe. "I don't believe there's a dog livin' that can run [him] down. . . ."

"Well, that's right," returned Myron, "but perhaps fifteen of 'em can."

The next day, early in the morning, the great fox left his den in the side of Rattlesnake Mountain. The deep mahogany of his back showed glints of gold, his long, slim legs were coal black, and his flanks and thighs a blending of tawny* pinks, russets,* and ebony,* while his brush seemed tipped with snow.

tawny: brownish
russets: reddish browns
ebony: black

On the hillside, where the pale-rose sedges* waved in the wind, he suddenly stopped and the next moment pounced* upon a tuft of grass that had moved ever so slightly. Thrusting his slim muzzle down between his forepaws, the great fox gripped and swallowed in a couple of gulps a round-bodied, short-tailed meadow mouse. Before he left the hill, he had caught and eaten six more and finished his breakfast by drinking sparingly from a little brook whose shadowed surface showed like a twisted strip of watered silk against the snow.

sedges: grasses
pounced: jumped

A little later and Old Mahogany was well satisfied that he had not eaten more heavily, as he heard from the bare crest of the Cobble the bell-like notes of Rashe Howe's dappled* black-and-yellow fox hounds.

dappled: spotted

For an instant the trim figure stood tense, like a statue of speed. Then he was gone—and only a flash of red against the melting drifts at the far end of the valley showed where.

As the hounds quartered* the valley, they came upon the fresh tracks of the great fox, and the hillsides echoed with their baying.

quartered: crisscrossed

A mile ahead, circling Rattlesnake Mountain, the fox moved with a long, easy stride that ate up the ground like fire. Through thickets and second growth timber he ran straight and true, with the clamor* of the pack sounding louder behind him, until he reached the middle of a great sandbank that stretched for some distance along the mountainside. The loose, dry sand completely covered both his tracks and his scent.

clamor: confused barking

For two hundred yards he made his way along the slanting sand until he came to where a white ash grew horizontally from the side of the hill about six feet above his head. For an instant the fox stopped and eyed the tree above him. Then, with a tremendous bound, he hooked his forepaws over it, scrambled up on the trunk, and the next moment had disappeared in a thicket on the slope of the mountain.

A little later the pack burst out of the valley in full cry. At the sandbank they lost the scent, separated, ran along both edges of the bank, and circled each end without finding any sign of the fox's tracks. Again and again the well-trained dogs hunted back and forth, trying vainly to locate the spot where the fox had left the bank. At last their leader, a crafty veteran, happened to run out a few feet on the ash tree. Instantly he caught the lost scent, and the next second his loud bay brought the other hounds to the spot.

For half the length of the trunk the fox tracks showed in the snow. Then they disappeared. It was plain to the pack what had happened. The fox had leaped from the tree trunk and landed somewhere in the surrounding thickets. Instantly every hound was nosing and sniffing his way through masses of close-set bushes until suddenly one of them gave tongue—and the chase was on again.

All this delay, however, had given the fugitive a long start; and by the time his pursuers were on his trail, he had crossed the mountain. On its farther side he came out upon a cement state road that connected two of the larger towns of that northern country. Down its long stretch the fox moved leisurely, his wise face wrinkled deeply as if he were planning some new stratagem.* Then, as he heard again the baying of the pack from the crest of the mountain behind him, he increased his pace, only to leave the road with a bound and crouch in a thicket as he saw a car approaching.

stratagem: trick

It was only the battered sedan in which Bunker Rogers was bringing back a load of groceries from Cornwall Bridge, but to the hunted animal it was refuge and escape. With a quick spring he landed on the spare tire at the rear of the car and, crouching there, doubled back on his trail without leaving track or trace of his going.

Undoubtedly the Red One had expected to be far away in an opposite direction to the trail that the hounds were following long before

they reached the road. If so, he had miscalculated their speed, for the car met them racing along hot on the fresh scent. Old Bunker sounded his horn, and the pack reluctantly divided to allow the car to pass. If but one of them had looked back, he would have seen, not six feet away, Old Mahogany clinging to the spare tire.

As he whirled past his enemies, unseen, the Red One's tongue lolled* out, and if ever a fox grinned, that one did.

lolled: hung loosely

It was Mark Hurlburt who prevented Old Mahogany from making a clean getaway. Mark was a great believer in Irish terriers, and in a flivver* of ancient vintage* overflowing with tawny little dogs, he had been patrolling the road a few miles farther on, convinced that sooner or later the fox would follow the highway.

flivver: car
vintage: year of origin

When at last he met and passed Bunker's car, his terriers began to yelp frantically. Looking back, Mark saw a mass of dark-red fur at the rear of the speeding sedan; but, by the time he had stopped and turned around, the other car was nearly out of sight.

Then began an unusual fox chase. Rattling along in his old flivver, Mark tooted his horn incessantly,* while beside him the terriers barked and howled at the top of their shrill voices. For a time the fox gained on the pack. Gradually, however, running at full speed, the flivver began to overtake the sedan, and before long Mark could plainly see the fox clinging to the spare tire and grinning defiance* at him.

incessantly: constantly
defiance: a challenge

At last the tumult* of toots and barks penetrated even Bunker's deaf ears, and he stopped his car, while the fox leaped down from his perch and disappeared in the brush. With some difficulty Mark managed to unleash his tugging terriers, and in another moment they were hot on Old Mahogany's trail as he headed toward the Hollow, the largest valley in Cornwell Township.

---

tumult: uproar

All that morning the fox had run without stop or pause, save for the short ride, and the pace had begun to tell—otherwise the terriers could never have kept so close to him. They were in sight as he reached the slow, deep brook that wound its way through the Hollow, and they were still nearer when directly ahead of him sounded the baying of the Howe hounds, that had raced back along the road and crossed the Hollow when they heard the yelps of the terriers.

Then it was that the Red One, with a pack behind him and a pack before, and his strength half gone, fell back upon the craft that had saved his life so many times before.

Hollow Brook was a good thirty feet wide and filled with floating ice. At one point a broken tree trunk spanned about a third of its width and along that the fox made his way until he reached the end of the stub. From there it might have been possible for him to reach the farther bank, but with such a slippery take-off the chances were all against him.

Old Mahogany, however, had not the least intention of risking that jump. Turning in his tracks, he went back along the slanting trunk until he reached the bank and then broke his trail by a tremendous bound into a near-by thicket, whence he made his way up the mountainside to the highway again. Hardly was he out of sight when both packs came into view from either end of the valley and met at the brook. The terriers reached the tree trunk first. Following the hot scent along the stub, the staunch little dogs made their way to its end

and from there plunged into the icy water and swam to the farther shore.

The hounds were hard on their heels. By a tremendous jump the leader just managed to make the opposite bank, but the force of his spring broke the decayed trunk and plunged the rest of the pack into the brook. The next minute they had joined the dripping terriers on the farther bank and were casting back and forth trying to find some trace of the vanished fox.

The leader of the hounds, after he had quartered the whole bank without picking up a scent, decided that both packs had been deceived by the unscrupulous* fox. With a melancholy* bay he plunged into the freezing water and swam back to the other bank, followed by hounds and terriers alike. There they soon picked up the trail again, but the time lost had given the hunted animal a long lead.

---

unscrupulous: crafty
melancholy: sad; dejected

In the meantime, Old Mahogany was trotting along the state road, perhaps hoping for another ride such as had almost baffled* his pursuers a few hours before. No such good luck was his this time, for the highway stretched away before him, deserted and untraveled, nor was it long before he heard again down the wind the baying of the hounds.

baffled: bewildered

At the sound the fox turned into an abandoned road that crossed the tracks of a little branch railway leading to some quarries.* The long chase since early morning had begun to wear down even his iron endurance. The brush,* which had flaunted* high all day like a dark-red plume, drooped; and the long, easy bounds that had taken him so far and fast had shortened by the time the trestle* spanning Deep River like a vast cobweb was in sight.

quarries: open pits for mining stone
brush: tail
flaunted: waved
trestle: framework supporting a railroad

The baying of the packs sounded much nearer. All at once around a bend in the road appeared the

hounds in front and the terriers strung out behind. As they came in sight, from far down the track came the whistle of an approaching train. At the sound the red fox ran more and more slowly until, by the time he had reached the path that spiraled* up to the trestle, he was

The Mahogany Fox 97

he was leading his pursuers by a scant* hundred yards.

---

spiraled: circled
scant: skimpy

As the packs rushed up the path and reached the trestle, to find the fox plodding along the ties with dropping brush and lowered head, every dog gave tongue and dashed after him.

Suddenly there was another whistle, and around the bend came the train. Before the pack even realized their danger, the engine had reached the trestle and was rushing toward them. At the sight the mahogany fox came to life and with a quick bound sprang from the middle of the track to a series of beams not six inches wide that joined the end of the ties at the edge of the trestle.

Fifty feet below was the black river; yet he ran unconcernedly at full speed toward the approaching train. Then, when it seemed as though he had but a few seconds to live—the fox disappeared. Long ago Old Mahogany had learned that in the middle of that great span a tie had been taken out, leaving an entrance to a winding set of steps for workmen on the bridge.

As the engineer saw the dogs just ahead, he set his brakes, while the pack turned and fled for their lives. Even so, the engine would have run them down if it had not been for the leader of Rashe Howe's pack. Seeing that he was about to be overtaken, he instantly leaped out into space, to land in a great snowdrift by the edge of the river, immediately followed by the rest of the pack until the air was full of leaping, yelping dogs. All escaped with their lives but were too shaken to do any more fox hunting that day.

As the train came to a full stop at the far side of the trestle, Mark's car rattled up the steep grade to the track.

" 'Twarn't your fault," the old man bellowed to the engineer. " 'Twas that red ... who blame nigh killed off two o' the best packs of huntin' dogs in this county. There he goes now," he shrieked a second later.

Sure enough, loping leisurely across the railway bridge was the fox, who had popped up as soon as the train passed above him.

"You ain't got away yet," muttered Mark. "Myron Dean's on the river road with his pack, an' he'll give you the run o' your life."

As he spoke, he fired both barrels of the shotgun that he carried, the agreed signal of the approach of the fox. So as Old Mahogany trotted along the narrow road that followed the farther side of the river, he heard a car approaching; and even as he plunged into the nearest thicket, Myron Dean pulled up beside the trestle and unloaded his pack.

For generations the black packs of the Barrack had been celebrated throughout Litchfield County. Other hunters might experiment with brown and yellow and white, but for a hundred years the Deans had bred their hounds black. The six that tugged at their leashes as Myron stopped his car had not a white spot on their ebony bodies; only their ears and a patch of their flanks were marked with tan.

Released, the pack at once caught the fresh scent, and for an instant their blended voices rose in one high, vibrant* note; then they settled down to the grim silence in which the dogs of the Barracks always hunted.

---

vibrant: thrilling

The spent day was all rose red and pearl, while tiny ponds scattered among the trees gleamed like pools of blurred silver in the wistful light* as the mahogany fox sped through the slowly darkening woods.

---

wistful light: twilight

There was little time to try any more of his wiles.* Once, indeed, he ran along the top rail of a fence in an old pasture, hoping to break his trail by springing to some overhanging bough, but he fell off from sheer weakness before he had gone many feet.

wiles: tricks

For a brief moment he rested and saw far below him the wide curve of the stream. Then, as he squeezed the snow water out of his brush, he heard an ominous* pad, pad behind him, and six black shadows flashed out of a thicket not fifty yards away.

ominous: threatening

Calling upon the last of his speed, the Red One raced toward the river, through the umber* patches of withered fern, with the dark hounds at his heels. Even as he reached the bank, a great cake of rough ice floated past, a good twenty feet away. Without a pause the hunted animal leaped far out. If he missed, or if he failed to keep his footing, he was lost, for no land animal could have lived for a moment in the rush of that swollen stream.

umber: brownish

As his body arched high above the black water, it seemed as though he would fall short; but like the crack jumper that he was, the fox shot forward and landed full and fair* on the floating slab of ice. It swayed and sank for a moment beneath his weight; but clamping his blunt claws deep into the rough surface of the ice pan, he clung to it, and the next moment he was whirling down the stream.

fair: cleanly

For a time the black hounds ran along beside him. Then, as a crosscurrent swept the mass of ice toward the farther shore, they turned and raced back across the railroad trestle to take up the hunt again on the other side of the river.

As the floe* grounded, Old Mahogany sprang ashore and dashed away with a great show of speed. As soon, however, as the pack was out of sight, he hurried back to the bank, leaped aboard the ice cake as it floated off, and started once more on another voyage.

floe: floating ice

By the time the pack had crossed on the trestle and raced down to where the fox had landed, he was out of sight downstream; and while the dogs tried in vain to puzzle out his trail, he leaped to an overhanging willow tree on the opposite bank, a mile away, and made his way ashore.

Convinced at last that he had tangled his trail past all unraveling,* the Red One moved like a shadow through the thickets. There was a smoky red flare in the east, and a crimson rim showed among the black-violet shadows of the horizon as he loped up the slope of Coltsfoot Mountain. Slowly the moon climbed the sky and became a great shield of raw gold, which turned the dark to silver. In the still light the fox made his way to the edge of a little clearing where stood an abandoned haystack, one of his many hunting lodges.

unraveling: solving

Beneath it he had dug a long, winding burrow, connected with a maze* of tunnels driven here and there and everywhere through the soft, dry hay. In the very center of the stack he had hollowed out a room in which was cached* a brace* of partridges, part of a covey* dug out from under the snow a few weeks before. On these Old Mahogany feasted full, and then, curled up in a round ball with his soft nose and tired paws buried in his warm brush, he slept soundly, as a fox should sleep who has outrun, outlasted, and outwitted in one day the three best packs of hunting dogs in the State of Connecticut.

maze: confusing network
cached: stored
brace: pair
covey: small flock

About the Story

1. What is the probable cause of the fox hunt?
2. The title as well as the opening paragraph of the story focuses on the color of the fox as being unusual. For what other element in the story does the author focus on color?
3. Why does the author refer to the fox as "Old Mahogany"?
4. What characteristic is most often associated with a fox, and how is that characteristic demonstrated in this story?

About the Author

Samuel Scoville Jr. was born June 9, 1872, in Norwich, New York. His father was a Congregational minister and his mother the niece of Harriet Beecher Stowe (author of *Uncle Tom's Cabin*). Samuel graduated from Yale in 1893 and later from the University of the State of New York with a degree in law. Although he won no scholastic honors at these schools, he did distinguish himself by contributing a great deal of writing to the literary publications at both universities as well as publishing nearly twenty books during his lifetime. Scoville's favorite pastime and hobby was nature study. Although warned by doctors to avoid strenuous activity—fifty years before he died—Scoville continued to enjoy the outdoors until his death at the age of seventy-eight on December 4, 1950.

Wild Blackberries

Frances McConnel

A poet often forces us to look at familiar objects and events in a totally new way. In this description of a family outing, does Frances McConnel tell us what we expect? Or does she surprise us?

We dressed for December then,
When the heat crawled on our skin:
Not an inch open to the thorns
Except our mouths, necessary to tongue
The berries from our bruised fingers.   5
My father put socks on our hands
And with old strong hat pulled to his ears
He led us into the thickest thorns.

That bright July heart above us
Beat its anguish to our heavy bones.   10
Our juices fermented from the pores
Became blood with the berries' smears.
Yet we plucked the fruit lightly;
Stifled* in our protection while   Stifled: smothered
Thorns clawed at our hair   15
But fell away. Gladly the hot berries,
July berries, melted our quick tongues.

There were creatures at odds with us.
Chiggers so sly and small
The pungent oil* filtered none away.   20   pungent oil: smelly lotion
If there were a way to revoke them*   used for protection
My father would have known it.   revoke them: call them
Even fat ticks are known   back
To bury in the picker's skin:
Our harehound pup came home   25
Dalmatiated* with the black bulbs.

                                              Dalmatiated: spotted

Also the yellow-banded bees,
The ones that bumble into your legs,
Attack your sneakered feet,
Defied* our protection.   30   Defied: challenged
Those bees nest near the briars,
Under the lame* grass we trampled,   lame: limp
Are easily shaken to erupt
From the earth in lava bubbles.

And so then, run home   35
To the scrubbed kitchen; wash
The green spiders* from the harvest;   green spiders: stems
Husk your hot bodies;   and bristles that
Shower away the afternoon;   resemble spiders
And in white dress and shirt   40
Taste the blackberry, absorbed
Summer in fragrant cream, black suns
Dancing in the white, white summer sky.

About the Poem

1. How did the berry pickers protect themselves from "the thickest thorns"?
2. What are some of the discomforts the berry pickers endured to get the fruit? Identify the lines illustrating specific annoyances.
3. What is the "July heart" of line 9? How do you know?
4. What are the "juices fermented from the pores"? What does the poet mean when she says that these juices "became blood"?
5. What does the poet mean when she says in line 38, "husk your hot bodies"?
6. What is the reward described in the last stanza for all of the discomforts described in the first four stanzas?

The Life and Death of a Western Gladiator

Charles G. Finney

A gladiator is a fighter, originally someone trained to entertain crowds by fighting to the death in the ancient Roman arena. The gladiator of this essay, however, needs no training. His actions are purely instinctive. Because he follows his instincts, he brings himself into conflict with mankind—with disastrous results.

He was born on a summer morning in the shady mouth of a cave. Three others were born with him, another male and two females. Each was about five inches long and slimmer than a lead pencil.

Their mother left them a few hours after they were born. A day after that his brother and sisters left him also. He was all alone. Nobody cared whether he lived or died. His tiny brain was very dull. He had no arms or legs. His skin was delicate. Nearly every thing that walked on the ground or burrowed in it, that flew in the air or swam in the water or climbed trees was his enemy. But he didn't know that. He knew nothing at all. He was aware of his own existence, and that was the sum of his knowledge.

The direct rays of the sun could, in a short time, kill him. If the temperature dropped too low, he would freeze. Without food he would starve. Without moisture he would die of dehydration.* If a man or a horse stepped on him, he would be crushed. If anything chased him, he could run neither very far nor very fast.

dehydration: excessive loss of water from the body

Thus it was at the hour of his birth. Thus it would be, with changes, all his life.

But against these drawbacks he had certain abilities that fitted him for this world and its warfare. He could exist a long time without food or water. His very smallness at birth protected him when he most needed protection. Instinct provided him with what he lacked in experience. In order to eat, he first had to kill; and he was well suited for killing. In sacs* in his jaws, he secreted* a deadly poison. To inject that poison, he had two fangs, hollow and pointed. Without that poison and those fangs he would have been among the most helpless creatures on earth. With them he was among the deadliest.

sacs: pouches
secreted: produced

He was, of course, a baby rattlesnake, a desert diamondback, named Crotalus. He was grayish brown in color with a series of large, dark, diamond-shaped blotches on his back. His tail was white with five black crossbands. It had a button on the end of it.

Little Crotalus lay in the dust in the mouth of his cave. Some of his kinfolk lay there too. It was their home. That particular tribe of rattlers had lived there for scores of years.

The cave had never been seen by a white man.

Sometimes as many as two hundred rattlers occupied the den. Sometimes the numbers shrank to as few as forty or fifty.

The tribe members did nothing at all for each other except breed. They hunted singly; they never shared their food. They derived some degree of safety from their numbers, but their actions were never directed toward using their numbers to any end. If an enemy attacked one of them, the others did nothing about it.

Young Crotalus' brother was the first of the litter to go out into the world and the first to die. He achieved a distance of fifty feet from the den when a Sonoran racer* four feet long and hungry, came upon him. The little rattler, despite his poison fangs, was a tidbit. The racer snatched him up by the head and swallowed him down. Powerful digestive juices in the racer's stomach did the rest. Then the racer, appetite sharpened, prowled around until it found one of Crotalus' little sisters. She went the way of the brother.

Sonoran racer: a fast-moving snake

The downfall of the second sister was a chaparral cock.* This cuckoo, or road runner as it is called, found the baby amid some rocks, uttered a cry of delight, scissored it by the neck, shook it until it was almost lifeless, banged and pounded it upon a rock until life had indeed left it, and then gulped it down.

chaparral cock: a fast-moving Southwestern bird

Crotalus, sleeping in a cranny* of the cave's mouth, neither knew nor cared. Even if he had, there was nothing he could have done about it.

cranny: small opening

On the fourth day of his life he decided to go out into the world himself. He rippled forth uncertainly, the transverse* plates on his belly serving him as legs.

transverse: crosswise

He could see things well enough within his limited range, but a five-inch-long snake can command no great field of vision. He had an excellent sense of smell. But, having no ears, he was stone deaf. On the other hand, he had a pit, a deep pockmark between eye and nostril. Unique, this organ was sensitive to animal heat. In pitch blackness Crotalus, by means of the heat messages recorded in his pit, could tell whether another animal was near and could also judge its size. That was better than an ear.

The single button on his tail could not, of course, yet rattle until that button had grown into three segments. Then he would be able to buzz.

He had a wonderful tongue. It looked like an exposed nerve and was probably exactly that. It was forked, and Crotalus thrust it in and out as he traveled. It told him things that neither his nose nor his pit told him.

Snake fashion, Crotalus went forth, not knowing where he was going, for he had never been anywhere before. Hunger was probably his prime mover.* In order to satisfy that hunger, he had to find something smaller than himself and kill it.

prime mover: the first cause for movement

He came upon a baby lizard sitting in the sand. Eyes, nose, pit, and tongue told Crotalus it was there. Instinct told him what it was and what to do. Crotalus gave a tiny one-inch strike and bit the lizard. His poison killed it. He took it by the head and swallowed it. This was his first meal.

During his first two years Crotalus grew rapidly. He attained* a length of two feet; his tail had five rattlers on it and its button. He rarely bothered with lizards any more, prefer-

ring baby rabbits, chipmunks, and round-tailed ground squirrels. Because of his slow motion he could not run down these agile* little things. He had to plan instead to be where they were when they would pass. Then he struck swiftly, injected his poison, and ate them after they died.

attained: reached
agile: quick-moving

At two he was formidable.* He had grown past the stage where a racer or a road runner could safely tackle him. He had grown to the size where other desert dwellers—coyotes, foxes, coatis,* wildcats—knew it was better to leave him alone.

formidable: difficult to defeat
coatis: animals similar to raccoons

And, at two, Crotalus became a father. Thus Crotalus, at two, had carried out his major primary function: he had reproduced his kind. In two years he had experienced everything that was reasonably possible for desert diamondback rattlesnakes to experience except death.

He had not experienced death for the simple reason that there had never been an opportunity for anything bigger and stronger than himself to kill him. Now at two, because he was so formidable, that opportunity became more and more unlikely.

He grew more slowly in the years following his initial spurt. At the age of twelve he was five feet long. Few of the other rattlers in his den were older or larger than he.

He had a castanet* of fourteen segments. It had been broken off occasionally in the past, but with each new molting* a new segment appeared.

castanet: an instrument made of two small shells tied to the thumb and used in Spanish dances to beat a tempo (here, the snake's rattle)
molting: shedding of skin

The Life and Death of a Western Gladiator   105

His first skin-shedding back in his baby-hood had been a bewildering experience. He did not know what was happening. His eyes clouded over until he could not see. His skin thickened and dried until it cracked in places. His pit and his nostrils ceased to function. There was only one thing to do and that was to get out of that skin.

Crotalus managed it by nosing against the bark of a shrub until he forced the old skin down over his head, bunching it like the rolled top of a stocking around his neck. Then he pushed around among rocks and sticks and branches, literally crawling out of his skin by slow degrees. Wriggling free at last, he looked like a brand-new snake. His skin was bright and satiny, his eyes and nostrils were clear, his pit sang with sensation.

For the rest of his life, he was to molt three or four times a year. Each time he did it, he felt as if he had been born again.

At twelve he was a magnificent reptile. Not a single scar defaced his rippling symmetry.* He was diabolically* beautiful and deadly poisonous.

---

symmetry: the balanced design on his skin
diabolically: wickedly

His venom was his only weapon, for he had no power to crush. Yellowish in color, his poison was odorless and tasteless. . . . His venom worked on the blood. The more poison he injected with a bite, the more dangerous the wound. The pain rendered by his bite was instantaneous, and the shock accompanying it was profound. Swelling began immediately, to be followed by a ghastly oozing. Injected directly into a large vein, his poison brought death quickly, for the victim died when it reached his heart.

At the age of twenty, Crotalus was the oldest and largest rattler in his den. He was six feet long and weighed thirteen pounds.

His whole world was only about a mile in radius. He had fixed places where he avoided the sun when it was hot and he was away from his cave. He knew his hunting grounds thoroughly, every game trail, every animal burrow.

He was a fine old machine, perfectly adapted to his surroundings, accustomed to a life of leisure and comfort. He ruled his little world.

The mighty seasonal rhythms of the desert controlled the lives of the rattlesnakes too. Spring sun beat down, spring rains fell, and, as the plants of the desert ended their winter hibernations, so did the vipers in their lair.* The plants opened forth and budded; the den "opened" too, and the snakes crawled forth. The plants fertilized each other, and new plants were born. The snakes bred, and new snakes were produced. The desert was repopulated.

---

lair: den

In the autumn the plants began to close; in the same fashion the snake den began to close. The reptiles returned to it, lay like lingering blossoms about its entrance for a while, then disappeared within it when winter came.

There they slept until summoned forth by a new spring.

Crotalus was twenty years old. He was in the golden age of his viperhood.

But men were approaching. Spilling out of their cities, men were settling in that part of the desert where Crotalus lived. They built roads and houses, set up fences, dug for water, planted crops.

They homesteaded the land. They brought new animals with them—cows, horses, dogs, cats, barnyard fowl.

The roads they built were death traps for the desert dwellers. Every morning new dead bodies lay on the roads, the bodies of the things

the men had run over and crushed in their vehicles.

That summer Crotalus met his first dog. It was a German shepherd which had been reared on a farm in the Midwest and there had gained the reputation of being a snake-killer. Black snakes, garter snakes, pilots, water snakes; it delighted in killing them all. It would seize them by the middle, heedless of their tiny teeth, and shake them violently until they died.

This dog met Crotalus face to face in the desert at dusk. Crotalus had seen coyotes aplenty and feared them not. Neither did the dog fear Crotalus, although Crotalus then was six feet long, as thick in the middle as a motorcycle tire, and had a head the size of a man's clenched fist. Also this snake buzzed and buzzed and buzzed.

The dog was brave, and a snake was a snake. The German shepherd snarled and attacked. Crotalus struck him in the underjaw; his fangs sank in almost half an inch and squirted big blobs of poison into the tissues of the dog's flesh.

The shepherd bellowed with pain, backed off, groveled* with his jaws in the desert sand, and attacked again. He seized Crotalus somewhere by the middle of his body and tried to flip him in the air and shake him as, in the past, he had shaken slender black snakes to their death. In return, he received another poison-blurting stab in his flank and a third in the belly and a fourth in the eye, as the terrible, writhing snake bit wherever it could sink its fangs.

---

groveled: wallowed

The German shepherd had enough. He dropped the big snake and in sick, agonizing bewilderment* crawled somehow back to his master's homestead and died.

---

bewilderment: confusion

The homesteader looked at his dead dog and became alarmed. If there was a snake around big enough to kill a dog that size, it could also kill a child and probably a man. It was something that had to be eliminated.

The homesteader told his fellow farmers, and they agreed to initiate* a war of extermination* against the snakes.

---

initiate: begin
extermination: complete destruction

The campaign during the summer was sporadic.* The snakes were scattered over the desert, and it was only by chance that the men came upon them. Even so, at summer's end, twenty-six of the vipers had been killed.

---

sporadic: unorganized

When autumn came, the men decided to look for the rattlers' den and execute mass slaughter. The homesteader had become desert-wise and knew what to look for.

They found Crotalus' lair without too much trouble—a rock outcropping on a slope that faced the south. Castoff skins were in evidence in the bushes. Bees flew idly in and out of the den's mouth. Convenient benches and shelves of rock were at hand where the snakes might lie for a final sunning in the autumn air.

They killed the three rattlers they found at the den when they first discovered it. They made plans to return in a few more days when more of the snakes had congregated.* They decided to bring along dynamite with them and blow up the mouth of the den so that the snakes within would be sealed there forever and the snakes without would have no place to find refuge.

---

congregated: gathered

On the day the men chose to return, nearly fifty desert diamondbacks were gathered at the entrance of the cave. The men shot them, clubbed them, smashed them with rocks. Some of the rattlers escaped the attack and crawled into the den.

Crotalus had not yet arrived. He came that night. The den's mouth was a shattered mass of rock, for the men had done their dynamiting well. Dead members of his tribe lay everywhere. Crotalus nosed among them, tongue flicking as he slid slowly along.

There was no access to the cave any more. He spent the night outside among the dead. The morning sun warmed him and awakened him. He lay there at full length. He had no place to go.

The sun grew hotter upon him, and instinctively he began to slide toward some dark shade. Then his senses warned him of some animal presence nearby; he stopped, half coiled, raised his head, and began to rattle. He saw two upright figures. He did not know what they were because he had never seen men before.

"That's the granddaddy of them all," said one of the homesteaders. "It's a good thing we came back." He raised his shotgun.

About the Story

1. Name the various stages of Crotalus' life that are recorded and tell how big he is at each.
2. Why do the homesteaders view the snakes as enemies?
3. For what reasons does Crotalus kill?
4. Based on these reasons, are the homesteaders right to view the snakes as enemies and to kill them? Why or why not?

About the Author

Charles Grandison Finney was an American novelist and newspaperman and should not be confused with the famous nineteenth-century evangelist by the same name. Finney was born on December 1, 1905, and began his writing career when stationed in China for three years during a term in the army. Later he chose Tuscon, Arizona, as his home, where he worked for the *Arizona Daily Star.* The author has drawn from these locales to write a variety of works, ranging from his best-known and prize-winning fantasy novel, *The Circus of Dr. Lao,* to the more realistic type of essay found here. Finney's knowledge of rattlesnakes is evidenced by one biographical sketch that identifies the author's hobbies as "pistol-shooting and snake-catching" and further reports that he is "permanently attached" to his Tuscon home and nearby desert because "there are plenty of snakes to catch."

The King's Provider

Jean George

In the novel My Side of the Mountain, *Sam Gribley fulfills a teenage fantasy. He leaves his home in New York City to live alone off the land on his ancestors' home place in the Catskill Mountains.*

By the time this chapter begins, Sam has established a comfortable home for himself in a hollow tree. But he is lonely at times in spite of the excitement of his adventure. In the selection below he captures a hawk, which he calls Frightful. The hawk becomes his constant companion. Later, after he trains it, the bird catches rabbits and pheasants for him to eat just as a king's falcons did in bygone days.

Miss Turner* was glad to see me. I told her I wanted some books on hawks and falcons, and she located a few, although there was not much to be had on the subject. We worked all afternoon, and I learned enough. I departed when the library closed. . . .

Miss Turner: the helpful, friendly librarian in the village
  to which Sam hitchhikes

I didn't get back to my tree that night. The May apples were ripe, and I stuffed on those as I went through the woods. They taste like a very sweet banana, are earthy and a little slippery. But I liked them.

At the stream I caught a trout. Everybody thinks a trout is hard to catch because of all the fancy gear and flies and lines sold for trout fishing, but honestly, they are easier to catch than any other fish. They have big mouths, and snatch and swallow whole anything they see when they are hungry. With my wooden hook in its mouth, the trout was mine. The trouble is that trout are not hungry when most people have time to fish. I knew they were hungry that evening because the creek was swirling, and minnows and everything else were jumping out of the water. When you see that, go fish. You'll get them.

I made a fire on a flat boulder in the stream and cooked the trout. I did this so I could watch the sky. I wanted to see the falcon again. I also put the trout head on the hook and dropped it in the pool. A snapping turtle would view a trout head with relish.

I waited for the falcon patiently. I didn't have to go anywhere. After an hour or so, I was rewarded. A slender speck came from the valley and glided up the stream. It was still far away when it folded its wings and bombed the earth. I watched. It arose, clumsy and big—carrying food—and winged back to the valley.

I sprinted down the stream and made myself a lean-to near some cliffs where I thought the bird had disappeared. Having learned that day [at the library] that duck hawks prefer to nest on cliffs, I settled for this site.

Early the next morning, I got up and dug the tubers* of the arrow-leaf that grew along the stream bank. I baked these and boiled mussels* for breakfast; then I curled up behind a willow and watched the cliff.

---

tubers: swollen underground stems
mussels: shellfish

The hawks came in from behind me and circled the stream. They had apparently been out hunting before I had gotten up, as they were returning with food. This was exciting news. They were feeding young, and I was somewhere near the nest.

I watched one of them swing in to the cliff and disappear. A few minutes later it winged out empty-footed. I marked the spot mentally and said, "Ha!"

After splashing across the stream in the shallows, I stood at the bottom of the cliff and wondered how on earth I was going to climb the sheer wall.

I wanted a falcon so badly, however, that I dug in with my toes and hands and started up. The first part was easy; it was not too steep. When I thought I was stuck, I found a little ledge and shinnied up to it.

I was high, and when I looked down, the stream spun. I decided not to look down any more. I edged up to another ledge, and lay down on it to catch my breath. I was shaking from exertion and I was tired.

I looked up to see how much higher I had to go when my hand touched something moist. I pulled it back and saw that it was white—bird droppings. Then I saw them. Almost where my hand had been sat three fuzzy whitish-gray birds. Their wide-open mouths gave them a startled look.

"Oh hello, hello," I said. "You are cute."

When I spoke, all three blinked at once. All three heads turned and followed my hand as I swung it up and toward them. All three watched my hand with opened mouths. They were marvelous. I chuckled. But I couldn't reach them.

I wormed forward, and *wham!*—something hit my shoulder. It pained. I turned my head to see the big female. She had bit me. She winged out, banked, and started back for another strike.

Now I was scared, for I was sure she would cut me wide open. With sudden nerve, I stood up, stepped forward, and picked up the biggest of the nestlings. The females are bigger than the males. They are the "falcons." They are the pride of kings. I tucked her in my sweater and leaned against the cliff, facing the bulletlike dive of the falcon. I threw out my foot as she struck, and the sole of my tennis shoe took the blow.

The female was now gathering speed for another attack, and when I say speed, I mean fifty to sixty miles an hour. I could see myself battered and torn, lying in the valley below, and I said to myself, "Sam Gribley, you had better get down from here like a rabbit."

I jumped to the ledge below, found it was really quite wide, slid on the seat of my pants to the next ledge, and stopped. The hawk apparently couldn't count. She did not know I had a youngster, for she checked her nest, saw the open mouths, and then she forgot me.

I scrambled to the riverbed somehow, being very careful not to hurt the hot, fuzzy body that was against my own. However, Frightful, as I called her right then and there because of the difficulties we had had in getting together, did not think so gently of me. She dug her talons* into my skin to brace herself during the bumpy ride to the ground.

---

talons: claws

I stumbled to the stream, placed her in a nest of buttercups, and dropped beside her. I fell asleep.

When I awoke, my eyes opened on two gray eyes in a white . . . head. Small pinfeathers were sticking out of the . . . down, like feathers in an Indian quiver. The big blue beak curled down in a snarl and up in a smile.

"Oh, Frightful," I said, "you are a raving beauty."

Frightful fluffed her nubby feathers and shook. I picked her up in the cup of my hands and held her under my chin. I stuck my nose in the deep warm fuzz. It smelled dusty and sweet.

I liked that bird. Oh, how I liked that bird from that smelly minute. It was so pleasant to feel the beating life and see the funny little awkward movements of a young thing.

The legs pushed out between my fingers, I gathered them up, together with the thrashing wings, and tucked the bird in one piece under my chin. I rocked.

"Frightful," I said, "you will enjoy what we are going to do."

I washed my bleeding shoulder in the creek, tucked the torn threads of my sweater back into the hole they had come out of, and set out for my tree.

About the Story

1. The author, in the guise of storytelling, includes several facts about falcons. List as many as you can from the story.
2. Why does Sam choose the name "Frightful" for his hawk?
3. The author uses very descriptive language, especially verbs, to communicate her ideas. List some of these vibrant verbs from the story.
4. Man is to be master of nature and yet is often in conflict with it. Find examples from the story to support both of these ideas.

About the Author

Known as America's "premier naturalist novelist," Jean George (b. 1919) brings to her writing a thorough knowledge of the nature she writes about and a meticulous attention to detail. Jean and her brothers spent their summer holidays at the family farm in Pennsylvania reveling in nature and came to know firsthand the material they would write about. In fact, Jean George writes convincingly about the hawk Frightful in this excerpt because her brothers "were responsible for beginning the sport of falconry in the United States," encouraging its popularity by writing for *National Geographic* during their high school years. The interest in nature permeated the author's family as well as professional life: when her daughter was born, she was renamed "Twig" because "she's so small she's not even a branch on the family tree." Jean George's skill has been rewarded, for in 1969 her book *My Side of the Mountain* was made into a film, and in 1973 her book *Julie of the Wolves* was a Newbery Medal winner.

Snapshot of a Dog

James Thurber

Sometimes snapshots are blurred, and sometimes they are sharply focused. Is this "snapshot" of a bull terrier out of focus or clear? Which of Rex's qualities do you most admire?

I ran across a dim photograph of him the other day, going through some old things. He's been dead twenty-five years. His name was Rex (my two brothers and I named him when

we were in our early teens), and he was a bull terrier. "An American bull terrier," we used to say proudly; none of your English bulls. He had one brindle* eye that sometimes made him look like a clown and sometimes reminded you of a politician with derby hat and cigar. The rest of him was white except for a brindle saddle that always seemed to be slipping off and a brindle stocking on a hind leg.

Nevertheless, there was a nobility about him. He was big and muscular and beautifully made. He never lost his dignity even when trying to accomplish the extravagant* tasks my brothers and myself used to set for him. One of these was the bringing of a ten-foot wooden rail into the yard through the back gate. We would throw it out into the alley and tell him to go get it. Rex was as powerful as a wrestler, and there were not many things that he couldn't manage somehow to get hold of with his great jaws and lift or drag to wherever he wanted to put them, or wherever we wanted them put. He would catch the rail at the balance and lift it clear of the ground and trot with great confidence toward the gate. Of course, since the gate was only four feet wide or so, he couldn't bring the rail in broadside. He found that out when he got a few terrific jolts, but he wouldn't give up. He finally figured out how to do it, by dragging the rail, holding onto one end, growling. He got a great wagging satisfaction out of his work. We used to bet kids who had never seen Rex in action that he could catch a baseball thrown as high as they could throw it. He almost never let us down. Rex could hold a baseball with ease in his mouth, in one cheek, as if it were a chew of tobacco.

brindle: darkly spotted
extravagant: extreme

He was a tremendous fighter, but he never started fights. I don't believe he liked to get into them, despite the fact that he came from a line of fighters. He never went for another dog's throat but for one of its ears (that teaches a dog a lesson), and he would get his grip, close his eyes, and hold on. He could hold on for hours. His longest fight lasted from dusk until almost pitch-dark, one Sunday. It was fought in East Main Street in Columbus with a large, snarly nondescript* that belonged to a big colored man. When Rex finally got his ear grip, the brief whirlwind of snarling turned to screeching. It was frightening to watch and to listen to. The Negro boldly picked the dogs up somehow and began swinging them around his head, and finally let them fly like a hammer in a hammer throw, but although they landed ten feet away with a great plump, Rex still held on.

nondescript: mixed breed

The two dogs eventually worked their way to the middle of the car tracks, and after a while two or three streetcars were held up by the fight. A motorman tried to pry Rex's jaws open with a switch rod; somebody started a fire and made a torch of a stick and held that to Rex's tail, but he paid no attention. In the end, all the residents and storekeepers in the neighborhood were on hand, shouting this, suggesting that. Rex's joy of battle, when battle was joined, was almost tranquil.* He had a kind of pleasant expression during fights, not a vicious one, his eyes closed in what would have seemed to be sleep had it not been for the turmoil of the struggle. The Oak Street Fire Department finally had to be sent for—I don't know why nobody thought of it sooner. Five or six pieces of apparatus* arrived, followed by a battalion chief. A hose was attached and a powerful stream of water was turned on the dogs. Rex held on for several moments more while the torrent buffeted* him about like a log in a freshet.* He was a hundred yards away from where the fight started when he finally let go.

tranquil: peaceful
apparatus: equipment
buffeted: struck forcefully
freshet: flooded stream

The story of that Homeric fight* got all around town, and some of our relatives looked upon the incident as a blot on the family name. They insisted that we get rid of Rex, but we were very happy with him, and nobody could have made us give him up. We would have left town with him first, along any road there was to go. It would have been different, perhaps, if he had ever started fights or looked for trouble. But he had a gentle disposition. He never bit a person in the ten strenuous* years that he lived, nor ever growled at anyone except prowlers. He killed cats, that is true, but quickly and neatly and without especial malice,* the way men kill certain animals. It was the only thing he did that we could never cure him of doing. He never killed, nor even chased, a squirrel. I don't know why. He had his own philosophy about such things. He never ran barking after wagons or automobiles. He didn't seem to see the idea of pursuing something you couldn't catch, or something you couldn't do anything with even if you did catch it. A wagon was one of the things he couldn't tug along with his mighty jaws, and he knew it. Wagons, therefore, were not a part of his world.

Homeric fight: a great battle
strenuous: vigorously active
malice: desire to see others suffer

Swimming was his favorite recreation. The first time he ever saw a body of water (Alum Creek) he trotted nervously along the steep bank for a while, fell to barking wildly, and finally plunged in from a height of eight feet or more. I shall always remember that shining, virgin* dive. Then he swam upstream and back just for the pleasure of it, like a man. It was fun to see him battle upstream against a stiff current, struggling and growling every foot of the way. He had as much fun in the water as any person I have known. You didn't have to throw a stick in the water to get him to go in. Of course he would bring back a stick to you if you did throw one in. He would even have brought back a piano if you had thrown one in.

virgin: first

That reminds me of the night, way after midnight, when he went a-roving in the light of the moon and brought back a small chest of drawers that he found somewhere—how far from the house nobody ever knew; since it was Rex, it could easily have been half a mile. There were no drawers in the chest when he got it home, and it wasn't a good one—he hadn't taken it out of anybody's house; it was just an old, cheap piece that somebody had abandoned on a trash heap. Still, it was something he wanted, probably because it presented a nice problem in transportation. It tested his mettle.* We first knew about his achievement when, deep in the night, we heard him trying to get the chest up onto the porch. It sounded as if two or three people were trying to tear the house down. We came downstairs and turned on the porch light. Rex was on the top step, trying to pull the thing up, but it had caught somehow and he was just holding his own. I suppose he would have held his own till dawn if we hadn't helped him. The next day we carted the chest miles away and threw it out. If we had thrown it out in a nearby alley, he would have brought it home again, as a small token of his integrity* in such matters. After all, he had been taught to carry heavy wooden objects about, and he was proud of his prowess.*

mettle: spirit and courage
integrity: remaining true to one's values
prowess: superior skill and strength

I am glad Rex never saw a trained police dog jump. He was just an amateur jumper himself, but the most daring and tenacious* I have ever seen. He would take on any fence we pointed out to him. Six feet was easy for him, and he could do eight by making a tremendous leap and hauling himself over finally by his paws, grunting and straining; but he lived and died without knowing that twelve- and sixteen-foot walls were too much for him. Frequently, after letting him try to go over one for a while, we would have to carry him home. He would never have given up trying.

tenacious: stubborn

There was in his world no such thing as the impossible. Even death couldn't beat him down. He died, it is true, but only, as one of his admirers said, after "straight-arming the death angel" for more than an hour. Late one afternoon he wandered home, too slowly and too uncertainly to be the Rex that had trotted briskly homeward up our avenue for nearly ten years. I think we all knew when he came through the gate that he was dying. He had apparently taken a terrible beating, probably from the owner of some dog that he had got into a fight with. His head and body were scarred. His heavy collar with the teethmarks of many a battle on it was awry; some of the big brass studs in it were sprung loose from the leather. He licked at our hands and, staggering, fell, but got up again. We could see that he was looking for someone. One of his three masters was not home. He did not get home for an hour. During that hour the bull terrier fought against death as he had fought against the cold, strong current of Alum Creek, as he had fought to climb twelve-foot walls. When the person he was waiting for did come through the gate, whistling, ceasing to whistle, Rex walked a few wobbly paces toward him, touched his hand with his muzzle, and fell down again. This time he didn't get up.

About the Story

1. What primary characteristic associated with bulldogs does Rex exhibit? List examples of this characteristic from the story.
2. What are the two meanings of the title?
3. Does Thurber's story give a focused or an unfocused picture of Rex? What aspects of Rex are clearly in focus?
4. One of the strengths of Thurber's writing is his ability to make his subjects almost as real as people we know. Man can learn many lessons from nature; what are the lessons that can be learned from Rex?

About the Author

Legend has it that James Thurber's childhood escapades included dropping light bulbs on legislators at the capitol in Columbus, Ohio. Whether or not that legend is true, James Thurber (1894-1961) suffered one childhood incident of lasting consequence: his brother's shooting him with an arrow resulted in the loss of sight in his left eye. Deteriorating sight in his right eye left Thurber dictating his stories by the end of his writing career. He was an American humorist well known for his short stories, fables, and amusing cartoons of dogs and men. Thurber's seemingly effortless prose resulted from serious revision, sometimes as many as twenty-five times on a piece! A significant contributor to the *New Yorker,* Thurber began his employment there as managing editor and worked his way down the ladder to a columnist, a position that left him time for his own writing. Satire was Thurber's game, and it is a tribute to his skill that he often amused the very people he was criticizing.

The Attack

Dougal Robertson

Dougal Robertson was taking his family on a cruise around the world. For years he had thought about the educational value of such a voyage. Little did he realize, however, that he, four members of his family, and Robin Williams were in for the education of their lives.

Survive the Savage Sea opens with the six people calmly carrying out their morning duties aboard their yacht. The next minute their hull is split open and water is pouring in. With electrifying speed they are plunged into a battle for survival against the Pacific Ocean.

We were on the eve of our departure for the Marquesas Islands,* three thousand miles to the west, and now, as the wind swung to the east under a gray mantle* of rain cloud, I felt anxious to be gone, for if we left now we would be out from under the lee of the island by morning. Lyn protested vehemently* at the thought of starting our journey on June the thirteenth, even when I pointed out that the most superstitious of seafarers didn't mind so long as it wasn't a Friday as well, but Douglas and Robin both now joined with my feelings of anxiety to be gone, and after a short spell of intense activity, we stowed* and lashed* the dinghy and secured all movables on deck and below.

Marquesas Islands: eleven volcanic islands in the
  South Pacific northeast of Tahiti
mantle: covering
vehemently: emphatically
stowed: packed tightly
lashed: secured with rope

By five o'clock in the afternoon we were ready for sea, and with mainsail and jibs set we heaved* the anchor home,* reached past the headland into the strait, then altering course to the west ran free toward the Pacific, a thousand square feet of sail billowing above *Lucette* as she moved easily along the ragged black coastline of Fernandina* toward the largest stretch of ocean in the world. . . .

---

heaved: lifted
home: toward the vessel
Fernandina: one of the Galapagos Islands

The wind moderated* a little during the following night and breaks in the clouds enabled us to catch glimpses of stars in the pre-dawn sky; on the morning of the fifteenth we had our first glimpse of the sun since leaving the Galapagos and with the slackening of wind and speed *Lucette* settled to a more comfortable movement in the diminishing* seas.

---

moderated: lessened
diminishing: decreasing in force

The morning sun shone fitfully from the thinning cloud, and as I balanced myself against the surge* of *Lucette's* deck, sextant glued to my eye, I watched for the right moment when the image of the sun's rim would tip the true horizon, no easy combination when both deck and horizon are in constant motion.

Douglas and Sandy were in the cockpit, one steering and the other tending the fishing line, while Robin, finding it difficult to sleep in his own bunk on the port side of the main cabin, had nipped* quietly into Sandy's bunk on the starboard side of the fo'c'sle to rest after his spell* on the four to eight morning watch. Neil was reading a book in his own bunk on the port side of the fo'c'sle, and Lyn had just started to clean up the usual chaos* which results from a rough stretch of sailing. At last the sun, the horizon and the deck cooperated to give me a fairly accurate reading, and noting the local time by my watch at $9^h54^m5^s$,* I . . . retired below to the relative comfort of the after cabin to work out our longitude. . . .

surge: rise
nipped: stolen; sneaked
spell: turn
chaos: disorder
$9^h54^m5^s$: 9:54 A.M.

With my sextant carefully replaced in its box I had turned to my books to work up a reasonably accurate dead-reckoning position when sledgehammer blows of incredible* force struck the hull beneath my feet, hurling me against the bunk, the noise of the impact almost deafening my ears to the roar of inrushing water. I heard Lyn call out, and almost at the same time heard the cry of "Whales!" from the cockpit. My senses still reeled* as I dropped to my knees and tore up the floorboards to gaze in horror at the blue Pacific through the large splintered hole punched up through the hull planking between two of the grown* oak frames. Water was pouring up through the hole with torrential* force and although Lyn called out that it was no use, that the water was pouring in from another hole under the w.c.* flooring as well, I jammed my foot on the broken strakes and shouted to her to give me large cloths, anything to stem* the

flood. She threw me a pillow and I jammed it down on top of the broken planking, rammed the floorboard on top and stood on it; the roar of the incoming water scarcely diminished, it was already above the level of the floorboards as I heard Douglas cry from the deck "Are we sinking, Dad?" "Yes! Abandon ship!"; my voice felt remote as numbly I watched the water rise rapidly up the engine casing;* it was lapping my knees as I turned to follow Lyn, already urging Neil and Robin on deck.

incredible: unbelievable
reeled: whirled
grown: fully mature
torrential: violent
w.c.: water closet: bathroom
stem: reduce
casing: cover

Wading past the galley stove, . . . [I] glimpsed the sharp vegetable knife, and grabbing it in passing I leaped for the companionway; the water, now up to my thighs, was already lapping the top of the batteries in the engine room; it was my last glimpse of *Lucette's* interior, our home for nearly eighteen months. Lyn was tying the twins' lifejackets on with rapid efficiency as I slashed at the lashings holding the bow of the dinghy to the mainmast; Douglas struggled to free the self-inflatable raft from under the dinghy and I ran forward to cut the remaining lashings holding the stern of the dinghy to the foremast, lifting the dinghy and freeing the raft at the same time. Lyn shouted for the knife to free the water containers and I threw it toward her; Douglas again shouted to me if he should throw the raft over, disbelieving that we were really sinking. "Yes, get on with it!" I yelled, indicating to Robin, who now had his lifejacket on, to help him. Grasping the handles at the stern of the dinghy, I twisted it over from its inverted* stowed position and slid it toward the rail, noting that the water was now nearly

level with *Lucette's* deck as she wallowed* sluggishly* in the seaway. Douglas ran from the afterdeck with the oars and thrust them under the thwarts as I slid the dinghy seawards across the coach roof, then he took hold of the stern from me and slid the dinghy the rest of the way into the sea, Robin holding on to the painter to keep it from floating away. The raft, to our relief, our great and lasting relief, had gone off with a bang* and was already half-inflated, and Lyn, having severed the lashings on the water containers and flares, was carrying them to the dinghy. I caught up the knife and again shouted "Abandon ship!" for I feared *Lucette's* rigging might catch one of us as she went down, then cut the lashings on a bag of onions, which I gave to Sandy, instructing him to make for the raft, a bag of oranges which I threw into the dinghy and a small bag of lemons to follow. It was now too dangerous to stay aboard, and noting that Douglas, Robin and Sandy had already gone and that Neil was

still sitting in the dinghy which was three-quarters full of water, I shouted that he also should make for the raft. He jumped back on *Lucette,* clutching his teddy bears, then plunged into the sea, swimming strongly for the raft. Lyn struggled through the rails into the water, still without a lifejacket, and I walked into the sea, first throwing the knife into the dinghy, the water closing over *Lucette's* scuppers as we left her.

inverted: upside down
wallowed: rolled
sluggishly: lazily
bang: had begun inflating properly

I feared that the whales would now attack us and urged everyone into the raft, which was fully inflated and exhausting surplus gas noisily. After helping Lyn into the raft I swam back to the dinghy, now completely swamped,* with oranges floating around it from the bag which had burst, and standing inside it to protect myself from attack, threw all the or-

anges and lemons within reach into the raft. The water containers had already floated away or had sunk as had the box of flares, and since the dinghy was now three feet under the water, having only enough flotation to support itself, I made my way back to the raft again, grabbing a floating tin of gas as I went. On leaving the dinghy I caught a last glimpse of *Lucette,* the water level with her spreaders and only the tops of her sails showing. Slowly she curtsied below the waves, a lady to the last; she was gone when I looked again.

swamped: filled with water

I climbed wearily into the yellow inflatable, a sense of unreality flooding through me, feeling sure that soon I would waken and find the dream gone. I looked at my watch; it was one minute to ten. "Killer whales," said Douglas. "All sizes, about twenty of them. Sandy saw one with a big V in its head. I think three of them hit us at once." My mind refused to take in the implications of the attack; I gazed at the huge Genoa sail lying on the raft floor where Lyn was sitting with the twins. "How . . . did that get there?" I asked stupidly. Douglas grinned. "I saw the fishing-line spool floating on the surface unwinding itself," he said, "so I grabbed it and pulled it in; the sail was hooked in the other end!"

Three killer whales; I remembered the ones in captivity in the Miami Seaquarium weighed three tons and that they swam at about thirty knots* into an attack; no wonder the holes in *Lucette!* The others had probably

eaten the injured one with the V in its head, which must have split its skull when it hit *Lucette's* three-ton lead keel. She had served us well to the very end, and now she was gone.

---

knots: thirty-five land miles per hour

Lyn gazed numbly at me, quietly reassuring the twins who had started crying, and, apart from the noise of the sea around us, we gazed in silent disbelief at our strange surroundings.

Castaways

Although the savage sea has swallowed up their boat, it does not conquer their spirit. With courage and resourcefulness, they fight back for thirty-eight long days. What special desire underlies their determination? Who consistently turns to God for help?

First day

We sat on the salvaged pieces of flotsam* lying on the raft floor, our faces a pale bilious* color under the bright yellow canopy, and stared at each other, the shock of the last few minutes gradually seeping* through to our consciousness. Neil, his teddy bears gone, sobbed in accompaniment to Sandy's hiccup cry, while Lyn repeated the Lord's Prayer, then, comforting them, sang the hymn "For Those in Peril on the Sea." Douglas and Robin watched at the doors of the canopy to retrieve* any useful pieces of debris which might float within reach and gazed with dumb* longing at the distant five-gallon water container, bobbing its polystyrene lightness ever further away from us in the steady trade wind. The dinghy *Ednamair* wallowed, swamped, nearby with a line attached to it from the raft, and our eyes traveled over and beyond to the heaving undulations* of the horizon, already searching

for a rescue ship even while knowing there would not be one. . . .

---

flotsam: cargo still afloat after a ship sinks
bilious: brownish yellow
seeping: oozing
retrieve: recover
dumb: silent
undulations: waves

We cleared a space on the floor and opened the survival kit, which was part of the raft's equipment, and was contained in a three-foot-long polythene* cylinder; slowly we took stock:

---

polythene: plastic

Vitamin fortified bread and glucose* for ten men for two days.

---

glucose: sugar

Eighteen pints of water, eight flares (two parachute, six hand).

One bailer, two large fish hooks, two small, one spinner and trace, and a twenty-five-pound breaking strain fishing line.

A patent* knife which would not puncture the raft (or anything else for that matter), a signal mirror, torch, first-aid box, two sea anchors, instruction book, bellows,* and three paddles.

patent: recently invented
bellows: for blowing; inflating

In addition to this there was the bag of a dozen onions which I had given to Sandy, to which Lyn had added a one-pound tin of biscuits* and a bottle containing about half a pound of glucose sweets, ten oranges, and six lemons. How long would this have to last us? As I looked around our meager* stores my heart sank and it must have shown on my face for Lyn put her hand on mine. "We must get these boys to land," she said quietly. "If we do nothing else with our lives, we must get them to land!" I looked at her and nodded, "Of course, we'll make it!" The answer came from my heart but my head was telling me a different story. We were over two hundred miles downwind and -current from the Galapagos Islands. To try to row the small dinghy into two hundred miles of rough ocean weather was an impossible journey even if it was tried by only two of us in an attempt to seek help for the others left behind in the raft. The fact that the current was against us as well only put the seal of hopelessness on the idea. There was no way back.

biscuits: crackers
meager: few

The Marquesas Islands lay 2,800 miles to the west but we had no compass or means of finding our position; if, by some miraculous feat of endurance, one of us made the distance the chances of striking an island were remote.

The coast of Central America, more than a thousand miles to the northeast, lay on the other side of the windless Doldrums, . . . [a] dread area of calms and squalls.* . . .

squalls: brief, violent rainstorms

What were our chances if we followed the textbook answer, "Stay put and wait for rescue"? In the first place we wouldn't be missed for at least five weeks and if a search was made, where would they start looking in three thousand miles of ocean? In the second place the chance of seeing a passing vessel in this area was extremely remote and could be discounted completely, for of the two possible shipping routes from Panama to Tahiti and New Zealand, one lay four hundred miles to the south and the other three hundred miles to the north. Looking at the food, I estimated that six of us might live for ten days and since we could expect no rain in this area for at least six months, apart from an odd shower, our chances of survival beyond ten days were doubtful indeed. . . .

My struggle to reach a decision, gloomy whichever way I looked at it, showed on my face, and Lyn leaned forward. "Tell us how we stand," she said, looking around. "We want to know the truth." They all nodded. "What chance have we?" I could not tell them I thought they were going to die so I slowly spelled out the alternatives, and then suddenly I knew there was only one course open to us; we must sail with the trade winds to the Doldrums four hundred miles to the north. We stood a thin chance of reaching land but the only possible shipping route lay in that direction, our only possible chance of rain water in any quantity lay in that direction even if it was four hundred miles away, and our only possible chance of reaching land lay in that direction, however small that chance might be. We would work and fight for our lives at least;

better than dying in idleness! "We must get these boys to land," Lyn had said. I felt the reality of the decision lifting the hopelessness from my shoulders and looked around; five pairs of eyes watched me as I spoke, Lyn once again with her arms around the twins. "We have no alternative," I said. "We'll stay here for twenty-four hours to see if any other wreckage appears, then we must head north and hope to find rain in the Doldrums." I looked around, "We might also find an easterly current there which will help us to the coast of Central America, if we've not been picked up by then." The lifting of my depression communicated and as I talked of the problems and privations* which confronted us, I saw the resolve* harden on Douglas's face. Robin nodded and fired a question about shipping lanes,* Lyn smiled at me, not caring that I was offering her torture from thirst, starvation, and probably death if we were not rescued, just as long as we had a working chance. The twins dried their tears and eyed the sweets; we were in business again. . . . We were all clad in swimming shorts and shirts with the exception of Lyn, who was wearing a nylon housecoat. . . . As evening drew in we had one biscuit and a sip of water, one orange for six, and a glucose sweet each, generally speaking a pretty sumptuous* banquet in the light of things to come, but meager enough rations for us at that time.

---

privations: lack of necessities
resolve: determination
shipping lanes: ocean routes
sumptuous: luxurious

Lyn sang "The Lord Is My Shepherd," and then prayed most earnestly for our safety. As the sun set, the wind grew suddenly colder and we shivered as we drew our terylene sailcloth sheets about us. Lyn suddenly laughed. "Well, tell us," we urged. "When I was swimming to the raft," she said, "and it was making that funny noise with the extra gas, Douglas thought the raft was leaking and blocked the pipes with his fingers; he shouted to me to give him a patch; in the middle of the Pacific!" She chuckled again. "He kept on so I gave him an orange and said, 'Will this do?' "

Second day

The long night paled into the beautiful dawn sky of the South Pacific; slowly we collected our scattered wits for already our dreams of being elsewhere than on the raft had taken on the vivid reality of hallucination.* Wretched with cramp and discomfort it had been such a simple solution to go next door and there I would find my childhood bed, so clear in every forgotten detail, waiting for me. . . .

---

hallucination: a compelling but false sense of events

I looked across at Lyn, rubbing the cramp out of the twins' legs. "We'll see to the *Ednamair* after breakfast"; I looked hopefully at the water jar, but it was nearly empty. We had emptied the glucose sweets out of their glass jar so that it could be used to hold drinking water as it was decanted* from the tin, for although we had discussed the issue of equal rations of water (there wasn't enough to do that) we had decided simply to pass the jar around, each person limiting him- or herself to the minimum needed to carry on; at the same time, the visible water level in the jar enabled everyone to see there was no cheating. Breakfast consisted of one quarter-ounce biscuit, a piece of onion, and a sip of water, except for Robin and Neil who could not eat and were with difficulty persuaded to take some extra water with a seasickness pill. We had used two pints of water in one day among six, hardly a maintenance ration* under a tropic sun, which

I remembered had been placed as high as two pints per person per day! We ate slowly, savoring* each taste of onion and biscuit with a new appreciation and, although we hardly felt as if we had breakfasted on bacon and eggs, we were still sufficiently shocked at our altered circumstances not to feel hunger.

decanted: poured
maintenance ration: survival portions
savoring: delighting in

. . . As dusk drew in, Lyn settled the twins to sleep after playing "I spy," and singing to them. Robin was more cheerful and chatted about his travels across the continent of America by bus, working casually for his keep, and as we listened, we wondered if we would ever see land again. During the day Lyn had cut pieces of sail for the twins and Douglas to write letters, telling their friends in England and America what had happened, while she had written a loving farewell letter to our nineteen-year-old daughter, Anne. Robin had written to his mother, and I added a footnote to Anne's letter sending her my best wishes for her happiness in life with my love. In the footnote to Robin's I apologized for having been instrumental in* bringing his life to such an untimely end. These farewell notes were placed in a waterproof wrapping and tucked in one of the pockets of the raft, for we knew that when the time came to write such farewell

letters, we would be unable, both in mind and body, to cope with the effort.

instrumental in: responsible for

Third day

. . . The patter of raindrops on the canopy warned us that we were about to get rain. A pipe led down from the center of the rain catchment area on the roof and, pulling this to form a depression in the roof, we prepared to gather our first rainwater. With fascinated eyes we gazed at the mouth of the pipe, at the liquid that dribbled from the end, bright yellow, and saltier than the sea. As soon as the salt had been washed off the roof, we managed to collect half a pint of yellowish rubbery-tasting liquid before the shower passed over. I looked at the jar of fluid (one could hardly call it water) sadly; we would need to do a lot better than that if we were to survive.

The raft, now pitching heavily, required blowing up every hour to keep it rigid, and the undulations and jerks did nothing to ease the spasms* of seasickness which Neil and Robin were suffering; they both looked drawn and pale, refusing even water in spite of Lyn's pleading. As the raft slid up the twenty-foot swells to the breaking combers at the top, Lyn prayed desperately for calm weather and for rain. . . . Then quietly she sang "The Lord Is My Shepherd" to the twins as I put away the still empty cans and the jar containing the foul-tasting yellow stuff; it was better than sea water. . . .

spasms: convulsions

Fourth day

. . . I climbed . . . into *Ednamair* to try my hand at catching a dorado.* Since they are game fish and feed mostly on flying fish, I would either have to use live bait or a spinner, and since I had a spinner I decided to try that.

dorado: dolphin

Three small female dorado suddenly swam near, and excited, I cast the spinner well out and ahead of them. To my utter dismay I watched the spool curve outward in a gentle arc after the spinner, land in the water, and sink quietly into the depths. The line had gone. I was tempted to go after it but a lively deterrent* in the shape of a large triangular fin belonging to a white-tipped shark appeared on the other side of the raft and I cursed my stupidity in frustrated anguish.* How could I have been so careless as to leave the line unfastened to the mast? Our only spinner and our only wire trace, chucked over the side as if I were a kid at a Sunday school picnic. My knuckles beat at my brow; if I was going to make stupid mistakes like this now, what would it be like later? This was the sort of carelessness that cost lives at sea and if I was making these mistakes now what could I reasonably expect from newcomers to the sea like Robin, or youngsters like Neil and Sandy? I resolved to examine every move before I made it, and every decision before we acted upon it, for sooner or later, because I had overlooked something, someone would die. . . .

deterrent: hindrance
anguish: distress

Fifth day

. . . I rarely slept at all now, listening all the time to the sounds of the raft, the sea, the fish, the dinghy, and thinking of ways of catching fish, of the possibility of straining plankton* from the sea, and of covering the raft canopy with sailcloth to exclude the filthy yellow dye from the water; of what would happen to us when the raft became untenable* as it would do in time to come. I knew that Lyn too lay awake at night, and that her thoughts were never far away from methods of getting food and water into the twins' bodies, and of helping them and us to survive in this alien* environment. We now welcomed our call to go on watch, if only to relieve the burden of our minds in action, and to stop having to pretend to rest. . . .

plankton: tiny animals and plants
untenable: unsuitable for use
alien: hostile

Sixth day

This day started, apart from watch-keeping, at the early hour of two in the morning when a noise like a sail in a gale, flapping and a-slapping, from *Ednamair* announced that a large fish had miscalculated its flight path and was trying to put the error to rights.

Quickly pulling the dinghy alongside the raft I jumped aboard and fell on top of the huge dorado struggling in the bottom of the boat, its body arching violently in its attempts to escape. Hanging on with one hand to the part just forward of the tail, I pulled the knife from the thwart where it was kept, plunged it into the head just behind the eye, and sawed desperately, finally severing the head altogether; then just to make sure that no reflex action would reactivate it, I cut its tail off as well. It was a beautiful thirty-five-pounder and I quickly informed everyone within hearing distance of the joyful news, and washing the blood from my hands, chest, and legs as best I could in the darkness, returned to the raft to wait for daylight. At four in the morning we were dozing quietly when a flying fish flew straight through the door of the raft, striking Lyn in the face. Now Lyn is a very steady and reliable person in a crisis; she seems to be able to do the right thing at the right time automatically while less able people like myself are floundering* around wondering what to do, but her reaction to being slapped in the face by a wet fish at four in the morning, after all our previous excitement, had us all scrambling around the raft looking for something like the Loch Ness monster until the eight-inch leviathan* was finally secured and made safe for breakfast. . . .

floundering: moving clumsily
leviathan: sea monster

As the sun crept around to the port side of the raft, and we lay gasping in the torrid* heat, sucking at pieces of rubber trying to create saliva to ease the burden of our thirst, Lyn quietly arranged the bedding so that we should at least start the night with dry sheets, and then passed the water around for sips. . . .

torrid: scorching

As the evening shadows darkened the inside of the raft, I opened another tin of water and decanted it into the jar; Lyn prayed quietly for rain and Robin stared dully at the jar for a moment. . . .

Douglas, sponge in hand, mopped up the sea water in the bottom of the raft while the twins brought out the food boxes ready for the last meal of the day. The breeze blowing gently from the south now died away, leaving the sea almost calm except for the marching swells of the southeast trades, and *Ednamair's* sail hung limp for the first time since we had started our voyage north. We still had about a hundred and fifty miles of northing* to make before we would come under the influence of Doldrums weather, and with the six pints of water left (including the brackish* stuff) I wondered if we had come to the end of the road. . . .

northing: progress to the north
brackish: somewhat salty

Seventh day

The windless night filled our ears with unaccustomed silence, and in the quiet of the calm swell the phosphorescent* gleam of the large dorado, streaking from under the raft and leaping high into the air, to land in bursting showers of green glowing fire, was a display not often seen by men.

phosphorescent: shining

The foul dryness of our mouths aggravated* the discomfort of our sleepless bodies as we tried to ease the agony of our thirst, twisting this way and that, then breathlessly we watched the gathering clouds obscure the stars and as dawn paled the eastern horizon, it began to rain, a heavy shower this time, with a steady downpour. Slowly the water in the pipe from the canopy ran clear and we filled our empty cans and spare plastic bags, our bellies and our mouths until we could not force down another drop. We lay with our faces turned to the sky and let the pure fresh water cleanse the salt from our beards and hair; suddenly everything had changed from the shadow of the specter* of death to the joyful prospect of life, and all by a shower of rain. We would make the Doldrums now! We lay uncaring, chewing strips of dorado and reveling* in the absence of thirst, talking excitedly of good food and watching the bulging plastic bags swing lazily from the roof of the canopy. We had water!

aggravated: worsened
specter: ghost
reveling: delighting

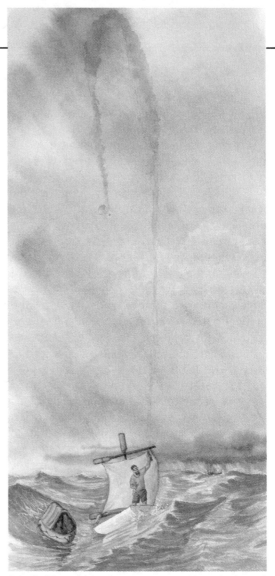

Douglas, lazily watching the dispersing* clouds, suddenly sat up with a start, pointing excitedly. "A ship! A ship! It's a ship!" We all crowded to the door of the raft, staring in the direction of his pointing finger; a cargo vessel of about six thousand tons was approaching us on a course that would bring her within three miles of us. I felt my heart pound against my ribs. "Get out the flares," I said hoarsely, "and pass them to me in the dinghy, they'll see us better from there."

dispersing: scattering

Three miles was a fair distance, but on a dull day like this, against a background of rain they should see us easily. I clambered* into the dinghy and Douglas passed me the rockets and hand flares; my hands trembled as I ripped open a parachute rocket flare and, with a mute* appeal to the thing to fire, struck the igniter on the fuse. It spluttered and hissed, then roared off on a trajectory* high above the raft, its pinkish magnesium* flare slowly spiraling downward leaving a trail of smoke in the sky. They couldn't fail to see it. I waited a moment or two watching for the ship to alter course, then struck a hand flare, holding it high above my head. The blinding red light was hot to hold and I pointed it away from the wind to ease my hand, the red embers of the flare dropping into the dinghy; as it went out I struck another, smoke from the first now a rising plume* in the sky; surely they must see that. I waited a little, my hands trembling. "This chance might not come again," I said, anxious faces crowding the door of the raft. "I'm going to use our last rocket flare and one more hand flare." We watched tensely as the second rocket flare soared and spiraled its gleaming distress message high above us; desperately I struck the third hand flare and held it high, standing on the thwart and holding on to the mast. "Look, look, you [fools]!" I shouted. "Set fire to the sail!" Lyn's voice. I stuck the flare to the sail but it only melted. The ship sailed on, slowly disappearing behind a rain shower, and when she reappeared her hull was half obscured by the horizon, five miles distant and disappearing fast. The time was eleven o'clock. My shoulders drooped. "We daren't use another," I said. "They won't see it now and we have to keep something for the next one." We had three hand flares left. Lyn smiled cheerfully. "It says in the instruction book that the first one probably wouldn't see us," she said slowly, "and I'd already told the twins not to expect anything." She gathered the twins to her, comfortingly. We stared at the dwindling speck on the horizon and felt so lonely that it hurt. "I'm sorry, lads." I felt very tired. "We used to consider that one of the most important tenets* of good seamanship was 'Keep a good lookout.' That lot seemed to be pretty poor seamen!"

clambered: scrambled
mute: silent
trajectory: path of a moving object
magnesium: light, silvery chemical that burns
plume: feather
tenets: rules

I surveyed the empty flare cartons bitterly, and the one smoke flare which was damp and wouldn't work, and something happened to me in that instant that for me changed the whole aspect of our predicament. . . . We would survive . . . ; that was the word from now on, "survival" not "rescue" or "help" or dependence of any kind, just survival. I felt the strength flooding through me, lifting me from the depression of disappointment to a state of almost cheerful abandon.*

abandon: unrestrained emotion

. . . We had brains and some tools. We would live for three months or six months from the sea if necessary, but "We would get these boys to land" as Lyn had said, and we would do it ourselves if there was no other way. . . .

Toward late afternoon we felt an unusually hard bump on the raft floor, unlike the quick thrust of the striking dorado, and poking our heads out of the stern door of the raft we found ourselves gazing at the large scaly head of a turtle, protruding eyes set above a nasty-looking beak, surveying us with a dispassionate* unblinking scrutiny.* The day before I would have said, "Leave it, we can't manage that," but now things were different. "We'll have this one," I said. "Let's get it aboard the dinghy." . . .

dispassionate: calm
scrutiny: close examination

Eighth day

As dawn broke and we awoke again to the realization that the ship had not seen us, Lyn called from her watch-keeping at the doorway:

"What's the password for the day?" The answer "Survival" came with surprising vigor from us all and we set about the morning chores of mopping up and drying bedding with a cheerfulness scarcely appropriate to our desperate situation. I went over to *Ednamair* to dress the turtle. It took me an hour and a half to remove the belly shell, sawing and hacking with the knife blade which grew blunter as the shell seemed to grow thicker; finally with a bit of undercutting, I managed to lift the shell off and set about extracting* the meat. The turtle has a low yield in ratio* to its weight, about twenty-five percent to thirty percent, and it has its joints in the most inaccessible* places. It took me another hour to hack out the shoulder meat and that surrounding the back flipper bones. I opened the stomach and found, to my delight, a golden cascade* of a hundred or so yellow egg yolks awaiting collection. I cut some meat from the shoulder piece and then with a couple of dozen eggs in a dish returned to the raft for breakfast where all waited curiously for their first taste of turtle meat.

---

extracting: removing
ratio: relation
inaccessible: unreachable
cascade: quantity

As we all eyed the raw meat with some distaste, a grace by Robert Burns came to my mind and I quoted:

Some hae* meat and canna* eat,
Some hae nane* and want it,
But we hae meat and we can eat,
So let the Lord be thanked.

---

hae: have
canna: cannot
nane: none

Neil grinned and sank his teeth into a piece of steak. "Good" was all he said, and we all fell to with a will. We swallowed the egg yolks, bursting them like yellow plums inside our mouths and allowing their creamy richness to permeate* our taste buds, enjoying the flavor of the raw food as only starving people can. Robin declined the eggs—too rich for him— but chewed vigorously at the tender meat declaring that he enjoyed his steaks done "rare." Douglas, Lyn, and Sandy, after some initial distaste, chewed at the pieces of meat with increasing interest as rejection of the idea of raw meat gave way to acceptance of the taste of it. We washed it down with a drink of water and lay back and reflected on our good fortune. If we could catch turtles, and rain, we would survive all right; I thought of the fish spear; with turtles and dorado, we'd be wealthy! . . .

---

permeate: penetrate

Twelfth day

. . . I was on watch between nine and eleven that night and as I finished my bailing for a few minutes, a fish splashed noisily beside the raft. I looked down and dropped my arm into the water, hand taut* like a claw, and hoped that coincidence would bring my hand in contact with the right part of the dorado to let me pull it aboard. I had touched their backs a time or two but always in the wrong place, but I'm an optimist when it comes to catching food and I felt sure that sooner or later it had to happen. I picked up the bailer and was about to start

bailing again when there was a loud splash and again the raft trembled under a blow from a large fish. I was tensed ready when the fish jumped a third time; it landed against the side of the raft just under my right arm. I hooked my right arm under it and grabbed quickly with my left hand, then feeling the unslippery skin looked down at the white belly and U-shaped mouth of a five-foot shark lying docile* in my arms like a baby. Realizing that one slash of that mouth would finish the raft completely, I dropped it as if it was a red hot poker;

it snapped its savage jaws, struck the raft a blow with its tail, and was gone. Thankfully I resumed bailing. We didn't want to evacuate* just yet!

taut: stiff
docile: quiet
evacuate: withdraw

Fifteenth day

It rained at dawn, beautiful, gorgeous rain. We saved three and a half gallons and drank our fill besides; the wind, from the south, freshened a little and as the weather cleared we lay back and enjoyed the sensation of being without thirst, bailing and blowing* unheeded* for the moment. We talked of the ship that didn't see us, for that had happened after the last rain, and argued whether it would have seen us better if it had been night time. The twins were talking when Douglas, on watch, his voice desperate with dismay, called, "Dad, the dinghy's gone!" I was across the raft in an instant. I looked at the broken end of wire trailing in the water, the broken line beside it. The dinghy was sixty yards away, sailing still and our lives were sailing away with it; I was the fastest swimmer, no time for good-bys, . . . [forget the] sharks; the thoughts ran through my head as I was diving through the door, my arms flailing* into a racing crawl even as I hit the water. I heard Lyn cry out but there was no time for talk. Could I swim faster than the dinghy could sail, that was the point; I glanced at it as I lifted my head to breathe, the sail had collapsed as the dinghy yawed, I moved my arms faster, kicked harder, would the sharks let me, that was another point; my belly crawled as I thought of the sharks, my arms moved faster still; I glanced again, only thirty yards to go but she was sailing again, I felt no fatigue, no cramped muscles, my body felt like a machine as I thrashed* my way through the sea only one thought now in mind, the dinghy or us. Then I was there; with a quick heave* I flipped over the stern of the dinghy to safety, reached up and tore down the sail before my knees buckled* and I lay across the thwart trembling and gasping for breath, my heart pounding like a hammer. I lifted my arm and waved to the raft, now two hundred yards away, then slowly I untied the paddle from the sail and paddled back to the raft; it took nearly half an hour. The long shapes of two sharks circled curiously twenty feet down; they must have had breakfast.

blowing: to keep the raft inflated
unheeded: ignored
flailing: beating
thrashed: beat
heave: pull
buckled: collapsed

Lyn had been sitting against the central thwart trying to rest after her watch and the following is her account of what happened in the raft after Douglas shouted, "Dad, the dinghy's gone."

> I saw Dougal's body hurtle past me as he dived into the sea. The silence was broken by the cry of "Shark" from Douglas, followed by a despairing shriek from Neil, "Daddy! Daddy!" We all crowded to see past Douglas blocking the doorway. Dougal was cutting through the water faster than *Ednamair* was sailing and could not have kept up such a speed for more than a few minutes. The shark was close behind him to his right and his feet were threshing the water in a racing crawl. "I can't see him," I said, "he's gone." The raft had slewed* around in the swell and we had lost sight of him. "Don't panic! Don't panic!" Robin shouted. Then Douglas cried, "He's done it! He's made it!" "Good old Dad,"

this from Sandy. Only Douglas could see him now and he gave us a running commentary. "He's taking the sail down now, it's down, he's getting the paddle off the sail." Douglas craned* his neck to see as the raft slewed around more, and we scrambled over the thwart to the aft compartment to look through the back door. There, miraculously, we saw him, the dinghy like a cockleshell* on the crest of a wave with Dougal paddling furiously, first one side then the other with such a look of concentration and determination on his haggard* face. Relief flooded through me and I heard myself singing "Somewhere My Love," that wonderful song from *Dr. Zhivago*. It was a long time before he reached us and as he fell through the doorway into the bottom of the raft, his face gray with exhaustion, I

pressed the sipper jar to his lips. He shook his head but I made him drink, then I put a piece of glucose in his mouth, cradling* his head in my arms until his strength returned, and shuddering as I thought of how lonely and desperate we had felt cut off from our only hope for survival, *Ednamair* and my beloved Dougal.

slewed: turned
craned: stretched
cockleshell: small, light boat
haggard: exhausted
cradling: rocking

On my return to the raft we tested the wire and found it frayed under the plastic in two places, broke it, rejoined it and in doing so, made it short enough to fasten a large nylon rope between the raft and the dinghy as a reserve, after which we rigged up a sea anchor

namair broke away from the raft again, and stop her from sailing away. We had not only closed the stable door this time, we'd hobbled the horse* as well! I didn't relish a repeat performance of that swim; not ever. . . .

---

hobbled the horse: fastened the legs together

Sixteenth day

. . . That night will live in our memories as one of utter misery. Our mouths were raw with the rough surface of the bellows tube, our lungs and cheeks ached with the effort of keeping the raft inflated. Because of the sea water on the floor of the raft we tried to lie with our bodies on top of the flotation chambers, and because we lay on the flotation chambers we squeezed the air out of them more quickly. . . . I estimated that we could probably keep the raft afloat for a few days more, but the effort involved was depriving us of all bodily stamina, our limbs, almost hourly, suffered extensions* of boil-infested* areas, and we were pouring our lives away in this struggle to keep afloat. Our evacuation to the dinghy had to come, and soon; death in the dinghy would come as a result of an error of judgment, a capsize* perhaps, or through being swamped in heavy weather; either of these in my estimate was preferable to the deterioration* of our physical and mental state, through sheer* exhaustion, into submission and death.

---

extensions: enlargements
infested: covered
capsize: overturning
deterioration: worsening
sheer: utter

Seventeenth day

. . . I announced that I hoped to transfer to the dinghy today. . . .

Nineteenth day

. . . The rain cleared after midday and toward two o'clock another blue-footed booby (a young one this time) circled the dinghy and landed in the water, inspecting our strange appearance, then deciding we were harmless enough it flew around us again, and swooped down, folding its five-foot wingspan to land on Douglas' shoulder as he sat in the stern of the dinghy. Douglas, looking a bit like Long John Silver, glanced sideways at the four-inch razor-sharp beak two inches from his right eye and hastily averted* his eye in case it pecked at him. The bird seemed quite unafraid and while we admired its beautiful plumage and streamlined appearance we could not help our thoughts turning to this alternative source of food. I told what I knew about seabirds, that they were salty, stringy, and full of lice. Having agreed that only in an extreme emergency would we consider these birds as a source of food a small voice piped* up from the bow, "Pluck it, I'll eat it!" We turned in astonishment to Neil, the source of this comment and assured him that he could have some turtle meat if he was hungry. It seemed that we adults were slower to adjust after all! . . .

---

averted: turned away
piped: spoke

Twenty-fifth day

. . . We were all improving steadily in condition now, our sores and boils had started to heal and although the storm had taken heavy toll of our energy we generally felt much more rested than during our frantic bailing and blowing marathons* in the raft. . . .

marathons: long, strenuous periods

The evening brought quiet seas and calm weather, a glorious sunset and peacefulness of spirit. We sang the old songs of Scotland which the children loved to hear, for they carried a story with them. We sang Welsh songs for Robin whose Welsh inheritance did not, alas, extend to the musical traditions of the Welsh people (he was tone deaf); Lyn sang Brahms' Lullaby . . . for the twins, and as twilight deepened and watches were set, I felt

that we had already gone beyond thinking in terms of survival. We had started living from the sea as an adapted* way of life, for not only were we surviving, we were improving our physical condition. . . .

adapted: suitable

We no longer thought of rescue as one of the main objectives of our existence; we were no longer subject to the daily disappointment of a lonely vigil,* to the idea that help might be at hand or was necessary. We no longer had that helpless feeling of dependence on others for our continued existence. We were alone, and stood alone, inhabitants of the savage sea.

vigil: watch

Thirty-eighth day

. . . I chopped up some dried turtle meat for tea, and Lyn put it with a little wet fish to soak in meat juice. She spread the dry sheets for the twins under the canopy, then prepared their "little supper." . . . My eye, looking past the sail, caught sight of something that wasn't sea. I stopped talking and stared; the others all looked at me. "A ship," I said. "There's a ship and it's coming toward us!" I could hardly believe it but it seemed solid enough. "Keep

still now!" In the sudden surge* of excitement, everyone wanted to see. "Trim her! We mustn't capsize now!" All sank back to their places.

surge: rise

I felt my voice tremble as I told them that I was going to stand on the thwart and hold a flare above the sail. They trimmed the dinghy as I stood on the thwart. "Right, hand me a

flare, and remember what happened with the last ship we saw!" They suddenly fell silent in memory of that terrible despondency* when our signals had been unnoticed. "O God!" prayed Lyn, "please let them see us." I could see the ship quite clearly now, a Japanese tuna fisher. Her gray and white paint stood out clearly against the dark cross swell. "Like a great white bird," Lyn said to the twins, and she would pass within about a mile of us at her nearest approach. I relayed the information as they listened excitedly, the tension of not knowing, of imminent* rescue, building like a tangible, touchable, unbearable unreality around me. My eye caught the outlines of two large sharks, a hundred yards to starboard. "Watch the trim," I warned. "We have two maneating sharks waiting if we capsize!" Then, "I'm going to light the flare now, have the torch ready in case it doesn't work."

despondency: despair
imminent: ready to take place

striker: device used for lighting
primer: tube containing an explosive
searing: burning
radiating: spreading
apprehension: fear
cork-screwing: twisting

I ripped the caps off, pulled out the striker* and struck the primer.* The flare smoked then sparked into life, the red glare illuminating *Ednamair* and the sea around us in the twilight. I could feel my index finger roasting under the heat of the flare and waved it to and fro to escape the searing* heat radiating* outward in the calm air; then unable to bear the heat any longer, I dropped my arm, nearly scorching Lyn's face, and threw the flare high in the air. It curved in a brilliant arc and dropped into the sea. "Hand me another, I think she's altered course!" My voice was hoarse with pain and excitement and I felt sick with apprehension* that it might only be the ship cork-screwing* in the swell, for she had made no signal that she had seen us. The second flare didn't work. . . . "The torch!" I shouted, but it wasn't needed, she had seen us, and was coming toward us.

I flopped down on the thwart. "Our ordeal is over," I said quietly. Lyn and the twins were crying with happiness; Douglas, with tears of joy in his eyes, hugged his mother. Robin laughed and cried at the same time, slapped me on the back and shouted "Wonderful! We've done it. Oh! Wonderful!" I put my arms about Lyn feeling the tears stinging my own eyes: "We'll get these boys to land after all." As we shared our happiness and watched the fishing boat close with us, death could have taken me quite easily just then, for I knew that I would never experience another such pinnacle* of contentment.

pinnacle: peak

About the Story

1. Does the account in "The Attack" hint at the possibility of the tragedy in any way?
2. What fact about the activities of the family members heightens the tragedy?
3. Why would the bags of onions, lemons, and oranges be important enough to take with the family to the raft?
4. In "The Castaways" excerpt, what character quality is illustrated by the primary goal of the adults in the raft?
5. Who depends on God's help, and what evidence is there of this fact?
6. Why does the attitude of the castaways change from getting help to surviving?
7. How does the rescue of the castaways illustrate the truth that there must be a balance between man's efforts and his reliance on God?

About the Author

As one might gather from the selection itself, this account is autobiographical. The skills Dougal Robertson (1924-91) used and the attitude with which he met this experience were gathered from twelve years spent in the British Merchant Navy. Mr. Robertson ended his naval career with the rank of master mariner, and that degree of skill contributed to the survival of those in his care. After retiring from the sea, Mr. Robertson married and in 1971 decided to take his family on the round-the-world trip that this account relates. He also wrote a book titled *Sea Survival: A Manual*, which discusses in depth the skills needed to survive an ordeal such as this one.

Sailing and Nautical Terms

aft—toward the back of a boat

bow—the front of a boat

dead reckoning—estimation of position from course steered and distance traveled

dinghy—small rowboat

fo'c'sle—forecastle, i.e., the cabin nearest the bow

free—to sail with the wind near the rear of the boat

freeboard—distance from the water to the top of the side of a boat

Genoa sail—large sail used in light winds

gunwale—top of the side of a boat

headland—point of land extending into the water

jibs—triangular sails

keel—the structural backbone of a vessel, extending from bow to stern

lee—the side sheltered by the wind

mainsail—the primary (or principal) sail

mast—vertical pole supporting the sails

painter—a rope attached to the bow of a boat, used for tying up

port—the left side

reef—to reduce the sail area

rigging—gear used to control the sails and masts of a ship

sea anchor—device used to limit the drifting of a boat, a water parachute

scuppers—openings on the sides of a boat to allow water to run off the deck

sextant—navigational instrument used to measure altitude of celestial bodies

spreaders—bars keeping the sails apart

squall—storm

starboard—the right side

strakes—planks extending the entire length of the boat

swells—waves caused by distant winds

thwart—a seat across a boat in which the oarsman sits

trim—distribution of the center of gravity so as to maintain balance

trip—to raise an anchor

yaw—to turn sideways

Old Sly Eye

Russell Gordon Carter

Like the Robertsons, Alben Hastings is courageous and resourceful in his battle against nature. Unlike them, though, he faces a specific enemy, a one-eyed panther that will show him no mercy. And if Alben loses, other members of his family will die.

It was a May evening in the [late 1600s]. Alone in his father's log house on the northern edge of Dover township in the province of New Hampshire, Alben Hastings lit the lantern and opened his worn copy of *The Pilgrim's Progress*. Suddenly a loud commotion sounded in the direction of the barn—mad squeals and frightened bellowings and the hollow thudding of hoofs. Leaping erect, he seized his musket and, lantern in hand, went racing outside.

He was within a dozen yards of the barn, the wind singing in his ears, when the moon rolled from beneath a formation of ragged clouds, and he checked himself abruptly. There beside the shed lay the recently born calf, and over it crouched a big catlike creature, its solitary eye gleaming, its great round tufted tail weaving savagely to and fro—a panther.

Dropping the lantern, Alben raised the musket and fired, only to see the creature leap sidewise, apparently unhurt. The next instant it swept past him and vanished in the deep shadows between the house and woods.

The boy clenched* his teeth. "Old Sly Eye!" he muttered angrily, and his thoughts went swiftly back to the morning, two weeks earlier, when his father had set forth with Mr.

Stephen Wainright on a prolonged trapping expedition beyond the Piscataqua.

clenched: gritted

"Yes, my lad," John Hastings had said then, "I know how much you would like to come along, but 'tis your duty to stay behind and look after your mother and sister. And mind ye keep a good watch over the livestock! I wouldn't want to come home and find Old Sly Eye had done to us what he's done to others."

Alben strode to where the calf was lying. It wasn't his fault that Old Sly Eye had managed somehow to break into the barn, for his father himself had said the barn was reasonably secure against varmints.* The calf lay motionless—there was no question that it was dead. Within the barn the cow and the two oxen were still stamping about and letting out occasional bellows, but the boy was not so much concerned with them; they were safe and unhurt.

varmints: harmful animals

As Alben continued to stare at the calf, he thought of other plunderings within the township—cattle and swine slain by the big one-eyed panther that often killed for the mere sake of killing. Ever since the previous autumn Old Sly Eye had eluded* the bullets and traps of

the angry settlers—and tonight he, Alben Hastings, had had an easy shot at it and had failed to bring it down!

eluded: cunningly escaped

Well, regrets wouldn't help. Since the calf was dead, it would serve as food, and therefore the thing for him to do was to hang it on a tree or against the barn, high enough so that nothing could get at it. At the cabin—up in the loft, where he and his father were accustomed to sleep—there was a coil of rope he could use. Returning to the lantern, which had gone out, he picked it up and started for the house.

In the south, silver-edged clouds were racing past the moon. He wondered what the hour might be. Perhaps his mother and Rebecca would soon be coming home from the Wainright cabin, a mile or so to the west. They had gone over to help care for old Mrs. Wainright, who had fallen and broken a leg.

The door to the log house was swinging and creaking on its hinges, and as he shouldered his way inside, the wind caught it and thrust it shut behind him. Striding to the fireplace, he groped* for the powder horn and bag of shot on the high mantel and reloaded the musket.

groped: searched with his hands

On the frontier a loaded musket sometimes meant the difference between life and death. After he had set it down, resting the muzzle against the wall, he crossed the hardpacked earthen floor to the ladder leading to the loft. It would be as black as midnight up there, but there was no need to bother with flint and steel. He knew exactly where the rope was hanging.

With quick, sure steps he started up the ladder, but as his hands closed on the top rung he felt his heart tighten and his throat go suddenly dry. Something was in the loft—something heavy enough to cause the boards to creak! He was about to back downward when there was a snarl and a rush of padded feet, and the next instant a heavy body thudded against his shoulder and then hurtled past him, knocking the ladder violently sidewise. With a desperate lunge, Alben clutched at the edge of the loft, and for several seconds after the ladder had crashed to the floor, he clung there, his legs dangling. Then he succeeded in swinging himself upward.

Old Sly Eye! Crouching on the edge of the high platform, Alben felt the tumultuous* pounding of his heart as he stared downward into blackness. The panther was over near the door; he could hear it crooning* and snarling. He could hear the occasional thump and swish of its long heavy tail against the wall. Presently it moved, and he had a partial glimpse of it in a narrow band of moonlight slanting through an opening in the shutter across the south window. He saw its solitary gleaming eye, the other lost perhaps in an encounter with another panther.

---

tumultuous: violent
crooning: growling

Then it vanished again in the blackness, and now he could hear it going round and round the room, hissing and muttering and making other catlike sounds deep within its throat.

Why had Old Sly Eye entered the house? Alben asked himself the question while he was groping about for something with which to defend himself. Was it in hope of finding another victim? Panthers as a rule kept away from humans, yet Old Sly Eye was no ordinary panther. Or was it, perhaps, curiosity that had

prompted the creature to enter the partly open door? The boy could not be sure. He knew only that the panther was down there, unable to get out, and that he himself was in danger.

The loft held no weapon or heavy object that could be used as a weapon. In his two hands he held the rope. It was a stout, new, half-inch Portsmouth rope, more than a score of* feet long—but what good was it? As he finally tossed it aside, he thought longingly of his loaded musket down near the fireplace.

---

score of: twenty

The panther continued to move here and there, now and again passing through the band of moonlight. Every little while it would snarl in a way that made Alben shiver, and once he thought he heard it sharpening its claws on one of the logs. Or was it trying to reach the loft? The logs that formed the walls were unevenly placed—it might come slithering upward. And he was utterly defenseless, lacking even a knife.

Suddenly, with a feeling of icy water cascading* down his spine, he remembered his mother and sister. Why had he not thought of them before? They, perhaps more than himself, were the ones who were in danger! Even at that moment they might be approaching the house. They would open the door and then—

---

cascading: rushing

Perspiration bathed his face and neck and armpits. With cold hands clutching one of the posts, he stared downward, lips drawn tight across his teeth. What could he do to warn them? Of course, if he should hear them coming he could shout; yet, even so, Rebecca might think he was joking. He remembered with regret some of the jokes he had played in the past. But it was possible that they might reach the door before he heard them. The thought of the two of them unsuspectingly entering the cabin sent a chill through him. "I must do something!" he said to himself.

Yes, but what? He was a virtual* prisoner in the loft. There were no windows, and the only way to get down was either to jump or to slide down the rope secured to a post. In either case the panther would be waiting for him. Again he thought of his musket. Was there any way he could reach it, perhaps with the aid of the rope? No, the weapon was too far away.

---

virtual: actual

The more he pondered, the more he became convinced that the only thing to do would be to go down the rope and then make a rush for the door. It would take perhaps three seconds to go down the rope, and another three to reach the door—but during that time Old Sly Eye was not likely to be sitting quietly on his haunches! Alben drew his sleeve across his moist forehead. He was strong and active, but what chance would he have in a barehanded struggle with a powerful panther? Nevertheless there seemed no other way.

Knotting an end of the rope securely round a post, he gathered up the rest of it, ready to toss it downward. His eyes had by now grown more accustomed to the darkness, and he thought he could make out the panther directly below him. He let the rope drop, and an instant later the house resounded to a frightful scream that set his teeth to chattering. He saw the creature bound through the band of moonlight, and then heard it snarling over near the door.

While he waited, listening, he fancied he heard distant voices, as if his mother and sister, coming through the forest, might be talking to each other—or was it merely the sound of the wind? Raising his own voice, he shouted, "Mother! Rebecca! Keep away, there's a panther in the house!" There was no response. He waited a minute or two and then shouted again. Still there was no response. He had the sudden unhappy feeling that perhaps no one could hear him outside the stout log house—that no matter how much he might shout, it would do no good.

The night was silent now, save for occasional gusts of wind and the snarling of the panther and the thumping of its tail against the door. Supposing the door should suddenly open and Rebecca should call, "Alben, are you asleep?" Then the panther would leap and strike—and then . . .

It was more than he could endure! He must risk his life. He mustn't remain idle another moment. But if only he had a weapon of some sort—anything, even a short stick with which he could thrust! Maybe he could find a stick. He would make another search. It would take only a few seconds.

As he was feeling about in the darkness, his hands encountered the blankets that on cold nights he and his father used for sleeping. There they were, neatly folded against the wall. With a quick exclamation he seized one and shook it out. Here was something perhaps better than a stick! The blanket was thick and heavy—at least it would protect his face.

Holding it loosely over his left arm, he seated himself on the edge of the loft, ready to descend. The panther was still over by the door, and he imagined it waiting for him, teeth bared, claws prepared to strike and to rip. Again he thought of the musket. If only he could get his hands on it!

Still holding the blanket loosely over his left arm, he started downward. His feet had hardly touched the floor when a nerveshattering scream filled the house and a glistening body flashed toward him through the band of moonlight. Crouching, he flung the blanket out protectingly almost at the instant the panther was upon him.

For perhaps half a minute it seemed that he and the panther and the blanket were all

hopelessly entangled. He could feel the rough wool against his face. He could feel the weight of the creature upon him and smell the strong unpleasant odor of it. Then needlelike claws, caught in the folds of wool, were raking his back and shoulders. Lashing out with hands and feet, Alben tried desperately to free himself. A corner of the blanket covered his head. He reached upward, tore it loose, then rolled sidewise, all the while kicking and struggling.

Suddenly he was free! Rolling twice over, he sprang to his feet. The musket over there by the fireplace! Darting across the room, he snatched it up.

At that moment, above the snarls of the panther, still with claws entangled in the blanket, he heard voices outside. It was not the wind, it was not his fancy—the voices were real. With musket raised, he hesitated. Should he risk a shot in the darkness? If he were to miss, it might be fatal, not merely to himself, but also to his mother and sister. No, he must not miss! Racing to the door, he flung it wide and leaped outside.

His mother and Rebecca were crossing the clearing from the western edge of the woods. Catching sight of him in the moonlight, the girl shouted, "Alben, what are you doing?"

He paid no heed to her. He was half a score of yards now from the open door of the cabin, musket raised, jaws set. The seconds passed while he waited, listening to the thumping of his heart.

"Alben!" This time it was his mother. "What is wrong?"

At that moment a great tawny, glistening shape appeared in the doorway, its solitary eye gleaming. It swung its head first to the right and then to the left. It raised its voice in a prolonged scream. Then spying the boy, it came bounding forward.

A tongue of flame flashed from the musket, and the crash sent the echoes flying. They continued to tremble across the moonlit clearing while the panther lay twitching on the grass.

Alben strode to where it was lying. "Dead," he said to himself. "As dead as the calf!" But there were two bullet marks on the panther, one on the throat and the other on the side of the small narrow head, close to one of the rounded ears! Suddenly he understood. His first shot had not missed, after all! Probably it was that first bullet, momentarily bewildering the creature, which had caused it to seek shelter in the house.

"Alben, Alben! Oh, Alben!"

He turned to confront the others. Both were talking to him at once. "Your shirt, 'tis torn to shreds! And you are bleeding! Oh, Alben, are you badly hurt? Tell us what happened!"

He took a deep breath and then smiled. It was easy enough to smile now!

About the Story

1. Alben first feels anger and then fear regarding the panther. What causes this change in emotions?

2. What physical descriptions tell us that Alben is afraid? Give at least three.

3. Name a few characteristics that Alben exhibits in this story.

About the Author

Born on January 1, 1892, in Trenton, New Jersey, Russell Gordon Carter was a reporter and editor for several newspapers in addition to serving with the publicity department of the Democratic National Committee. He wrote more than thirty junior books of historical, adventure, and animal stories. Before his death on May 7, 1957, he had won several awards including first prize in the Julia Ellsworth Ford Foundation Contest for best juvenile literature in 1935 as well as the Junior Book Award Certificate from the Boys Clubs of America in 1950.

Each of the following poems uses nature to teach an important truth. What are these truths? What passages most clearly state the poet's lessons for us?

The Rainy Day

Henry Wadsworth Longfellow

The day is cold, and dark, and dreary;
It rains, and the wind is never weary;
The vine still clings to the moldering* wall,   moldering: decaying
But at every gust the dead leaves fall,
   And the day is dark and dreary.   5

My life is cold, and dark, and dreary;
It rains, and the wind is never weary;
My thoughts still cling to the moldering past,
But hopes of youth fall thick in the blast,
   And the days are dark and dreary.   10

Be still, sad heart! and cease repining;*   repining: complaining
Behind the clouds is the sun still shining;
Thy fate is the common fate of all,
Into each life some rain must fall,
   Some days must be dark and dreary.   15

About the Author

Popular in both the United States and England, Henry Wadsworth Long-fellow (1807-82) was America's first influential professor-poet, serving at both Bowdoin College in Maine and at Harvard. He is most highly regarded for his Americanization of European themes and forms. The poems most praised in his day were the epic-length works drawn heavily from the American past: *Evangeline, The Song of Hiawatha,* and *The Courtship of Miles Standish.*

Midnight Storm

August Derleth

He stood in the open and looked to where
tall clouds towered in the windy air
to cover moon and stars. On one side,
an old barn, a willow tree, a hill; and wide
upon the other, thunderheads* banked high
into that midnight, moonlit sky.

5   thunderheads:
    thunderclouds

On the dark, now brooding* hill,
the whippoorwills were still.

brooding: gloomy

The sudden thunder muttered and the lightning flared.
He stood there watching as long as he dared;

10

beauty and terror were there
alike in windy moonlit air.
It was enough to make him realize
the limitations of his size.

About the Author

August Derleth was born February 24, 1909, in Sauk City, Wisconsin. A writer from the age of thirteen, he worked as an editor, freelance writer, publisher, and weekly columnist. In addition, he wrote over one hundred books, including both prose and poetry, before his death on July 4, 1971.

In Memory of My Dear Grandchild
Elizabeth Bradstreet
Who Deceased August, 1665,
Being a Year and Half Old

Anne Bradstreet

Farewell dear babe, my heart's too much content,*
Farewell sweet babe, the pleasure of mine eye,
Farewell fair flower that for a space* was lent,
Then ta'en* away unto eternity.
Blest babe, why should I once bewail* thy fate,   5
Or sigh thy days so soon were terminate,*
Sith* thou art settled in an everlasting state.*

By nature trees do rot when they are grown,
And plums and apples thoroughly ripe do fall,
And corn and grass are in their season mown,   10
And time brings down what is both strong and tall.
But plants new set to be eradicate,*
And buds new blown to have so short a date,*
Is by His hand alone that guides nature and fate.

my heart's . . . content: The writer has thought too much of her grandchild.

space: time

ta'en: taken

bewail: cry over

terminate: ended

Sith: since

everlasting state: heaven or hell

eradicate: literally pulled out by the roots

date: life

About the Author

One of the two major poets from the heritage of Puritan America, Anne Bradstreet (1612-72) left England to come to America with her husband. The distinct change in circumstances between her comfortable home in England and the rigors of the settlement in Boston revealed a sturdy woman prepared to meet the challenges of life. And meet them she did. Mother of eight children, daughter of the second governor of the Massachusetts Bay Colony, and wife of another (who governed after her death), Anne Bradstreet somehow found the necessary strength to meet all the obligations of being a wife, mother, and leader in the colony as well as a writer of poetry. It was quite by accident that her work was published. Her brother-in-law gathered up her poems and sent them to England without her approval! Nonetheless, her work was well received, and she again found the time to make revisions and even to write new poems. In reality it is not the how but the what that makes Anne Bradstreet's poetry admirable. She chose to write about the concerns of her life: her husband, her children, the house fire that destroyed all her earthly

NATURE AND MAN

possessions, but not her heavenly treasure. In Bradstreet's writings can be seen the Puritan beliefs not only preached in the pulpits of early America but also lived in the actions and attitudes of this founding mother.

The Windmill

Robert Bridges

The green corn* waving in the dale,*
The ripe grass waving on the hill:
I lean across the paddock pale*
And gaze upon the giddy* mill.

Its hurtling* sails a mighty sweep   5
Cut through the air: with rushing sound
Each strikes in fury down the steep,
Rattles, and whirls in chase around.

Besides his sacks the miller stands
On high within the open door: 10
A book and pencil in his hands,
His grists* and meal he reckoneth o'er.

corn: wheat
dale: valley
paddock pale: pasture
  fence
giddy: whirling rapidly
hurtling: moving with
  great speed
grists: the grain before it
  is ground

His tireless merry slave the wind
Is busy with his work today:
From whencesoe'er, he* comes to grind;   15   he: the wind
He hath a will and knows the way.

He gives the creaking sails a spin,
The circling millstones faster flee,
The shuddering timbers groan within,
And down the shoot the meal runs free.   20

The miller giveth him no thanks,
And doth not much his work o'erlook:
He stands beside the sacks, and ranks*   ranks: arranges
The figures in his dusty book.

About the Author

Robert Bridges (1844-1930) had one ambition in life: to be a poet. He knew, however, that being a poet was a full-time job, and he had to find a way to support his ambition. He, therefore, decided to become a doctor and practice medicine until age forty, then retire and concentrate on writing. And his ambition became a reality. Due to illness he had to retire from medicine a bit early, but he recovered and spent his remaining life writing. He also had "a lifelong interest in words for music" and wrote lyrics for several musical pieces. Critics have said that there is little truly remarkable in his verses, yet taken as a whole, they are full of elegant expression. This criticism did not hinder his appointment as poet laureate in 1913.

About the Poems

1. What two things are being compared in Longfellow's poem?
2. In the third stanza of "The Rainy Day" the author rebukes himself for feeling sorry for himself. What is his conclusion regarding life?
3. What two seemingly opposite elements of nature exist at the same time in Derleth's poem?
4. What conclusion does the observer in "Midnight Storm" come to?
5. What images from nature does Bradstreet use to express her ideas about death?
6. Who does Bradstreet say governs all aspects of life?
7. What are the three main characters in "The Windmill"?
8. What major character flaw does the miller exhibit?

A Hillside Thaw

Robert Frost

In this poem nature is a backdrop to reveal man's pride. Notice the poet's striking metaphors.

To think to know the country and not know
The hillside on the day the sun lets go
Ten million silver lizards out of snow!
As often as I've seen it done before
I can't pretend to tell the way it's done.   5
It looks as if some magic of the sun
Lifted the rug that bred them on the floor
And the light breaking on them made them run.
But if I thought to stop the wet stampede,
And caught one silver lizard by the tail,   10
And put my foot on one without avail,
And threw myself wet-elbowed and wet-kneed
In front of twenty others' wriggling speed,—
In the confusion of them all aglitter,
And birds that joined in the excited fun   15
By doubling and redoubling song and twitter,
I have no doubt I'd end by holding none.

It takes the moon for this. The sun's a wizard
By all I tell; but so's the moon a witch.
From the high west she makes a gentle cast   20
And suddenly, without a jerk or twitch,
She has her spell on every single lizard.
I fancied when I looked at six o'clock
The swarm still ran and scuttled just as fast.
The moon was waiting for her chill effect.   25
I looked at nine: the swarm was turned to rock
In every lifelike posture of the swarm,
Transfixed on mountain slopes almost erect.
Across each other and side by side they lay.
The spell that so could hold them as they were   30
Was wrought through trees without a breath of storm
To make a leaf, if there had been one, stir.
It was the moon's: she held them until day,
One lizard at the end of every ray.
The thought of my attempting such a stay!   35

...About the Author

Robert Frost was born on March 26, 1875, in San Francisco, California, more than three thousand miles from the New England region he used as the background for the majority of his poems. After the death of his father in 1885, young Robert and his family moved to the home of Robert's paternal grandfather in Massachusetts. He married his childhood sweetheart in 1895 and later attended Harvard for two years, during which time his poetry began to appear in magazines. He struggled for several years as a farmer in New Hampshire but finally moved his family to England in 1912 in hopes of finding an audience for his poetry. In just one year he published *A Boy's Will* and achieved recognition as an important poet. Receiving numerous honors and several academic positions in a variety of colleges and universities, he published ten more volumes of poetry during his lifetime. He was even invited to read his poetry at the inauguration of President John F. Kennedy in 1961. A temptation exists to describe much of his work as delightfully simple nature poetry. However, Frost claims that a poem "begins in delight and ends in wisdom." Although the poet describes quite vividly the New England countryside, he uses nature only as a means of teaching a lesson about man. Frost's death on January 29, 1963, ended a career that spanned over fifty years.

These three animal fables are modern translations of stories told twenty-five hundred years ago by a Greek slave named Aesop. Although about animals, they illustrate specific and valuable truths about life. Did you know that in Judges 9:6-15 the Bible records a fable of the trees and bramble?

The Raven and the Swan

The raven, who earned a comfortable livelihood picking up scraps, became dissatisfied with his lot.* He would be especially unhappy whenever he saw the swan floating gracefully about a nearby pool.

lot: condition of life

"What makes that swan so white and beautiful?" he would say. "Could it be that the water has magic qualities to turn one's feathers from black to white?"

So the raven left his comfortable home and betook himself to the pools and streams. There he washed and plumed* his feathers, but all to no purpose. His plumage* remained as black as ever, and before long he perished for want* of his usual food.

plumed: smoothed
plumage: feathers
want: lack

Moral: A change of scene does not change one's character.

The Swallow's Advice

A farmer was sowing his field with hemp seeds while a swallow and some other birds sat on the fence watching him.

"Beware of that man," said the swallow solemnly.*

solemnly: seriously

"Why should we be afraid of him?" asked the other birds.

"That farmer is sowing hemp seed," replied the swallow. "It is most important that you pick up every seed that he drops. You will live to regret it if you don't."

But, of course, the silly birds paid no heed* to the swallow's advice. So, with the coming of the spring rains, the hemp grew up. And one day the hemp was made into cord, and of the cord nets were made. And many of the birds that had despised* the swallow's advice were caught in the nets made of the very hemp that was grown from the seeds they had failed to pick up.

heed: attention
despised: looked down on

Moral: Unless the seed of evil is destroyed, it will grow up to destroy us.

The Farmer and the Stork

A farmer, who was tired of having his newly planted corn stolen by the cranes, set a net in his field. When he went to examine his snare he found that he had caught several of them, and included in their number was a stork.

"Please, sir," begged the stork, "don't kill me. I am not one of these greedy cranes who eat all your corn. I am a good and pious* bird. I take care of my aged parents. I—"

pious: dutiful

But the farmer cut him short. "All that you say about yourself may be true. All I know, however, is that I have caught you with those who were destroying my crops, and I'm afraid that you will have to suffer the same fate as those in whose company you were captured."

Moral: You are judged by the company you keep.

. . . **A**bout the Author . . . .

Originally told orally, Aesop's fables were first written down in the sixth century B.C. Two thousand years later a Byzantine monk published a collection of them. Little historical information about Aesop exists. Supposedly, he was a Greek slave who traveled widely and, according to legend, earned his freedom by telling his stories to King Croesus of Lydia. First translated into Latin verse, the fables have lasted throughout centuries and have been translated into many different languages.

About the Poem and Fables

1. What are the "silver lizards" (line 3) and the "spell" (line 30)?
2. What does the speaker conclude would be the result if he attempted to "stop the wet stampede"?
3. What lesson does this poem teach us?
4. What character flaw(s) does the raven exhibit?

5. What are some Bible verses that come to mind when you read the fable of the raven?
6. What is ironic about the swallow's advice to the birds?
7. What other well-known saying could serve as the farmer's reply to the stork?

Koyo, the Singer

Kenneth Gilbert

This story portrays a sympathetic bond between a boy and the blue foxes that he and his father care for on an island in Puget Sound. Koyo, the leader of the foxes, tries unsuccessfully to communicate a message to the boy. What kind of song does the fox sing? Does the boy ever understand the message?

Midnight! As the moon lifted clear of the hills, it was greeted by a quavering, sobbing cry that was neither squawl nor bark, yet both. This was a cry quite unlike any other sound—the clan call of the blue foxes; the one which signifies danger, help urgently needed.

The moon was very large and pale, of the hue of fireweed honey. Such a moon can be seen only on a glamorous May night when all nature seems a-tiptoe with the expectancy of summer. Over the inland sea of Puget Sound* the moon searched out and defined the wooded islands of the San Juan group.

Puget Sound: an inlet in northwestern Washington State

At the shoreline, where the ebbing* tide still licked at the foot of cliffs, the phosphorus*-charged water left a white edge. To a belated* black duck, who moved here and there on whistling wings, looking for his flock, the shape of each body of land was marked in cold fire. Like balls of the same cold fire, the big stars hung low. The night air which lay over these timbered islets* was filled with fragrance—the tang of new needles on the fir trees, new spring flowers in the silent forest glades, and the pleasing smell of moist earth freshly turned by countless growing shoots pushed upward through the soil.

ebbing: falling back
phosphorus: a glowing, nonmetallic element
belated: tardy
islets: small islands

There was magic in the night. Yet the spell of enchantment was shattered by that weird cry which seemed to sharpen the senses of every living thing that heard it. The moon, rising higher, outlined dimly the maker of it—a blue fox who sat on the lip of a little cliff overlooking a placid cove. Bulky he appeared to be in the half light. His thick, fluffy tail was curled neatly about his feet. The long fur was brushed smartly back from his chops. His sharp ears were pricked forward expectantly, while his topaz-jade eyes glowed as he turned his head.

For a moment he stared down in the waters of the cove. On the beach lay the offering of the sea, brought in by the flood tide: young crabs in thin, soft shells, pulpy varieties of the starfish family, and drumfish, who like to crawl into the lee* of a sunken log at high tide to lay eggs. Such sea creatures have been food for foxes since the beginning of time. Yet Koyo, the ruler of his clan of this island, saw them only with passing interest. Something else, which a casual glance did not reveal, was down there. At thought of it, Koyo pointed his nose once more toward the low-hung stars and voiced his cry. Then his jaws parted, and his

tongue lolled,* as if he were grinning. His command was being obeyed.

lee: shelter
lolled: hung out

From near-by clumps of alder, from the lee of wild blackberry thickets, from behind windfalls,* other topaz-jade eyes glowed suddenly. Perhaps there were a hundred of them from which the moonlight struck fire. They stared at Koyo, who, by right of strength and wisdom, was the chief of their clan. Never was that peculiar clan call of the blue foxes uttered unless there was reason for it. Hearing it, they had come from all parts of the island, expecting to find Koyo at death grips with some foe.

windfalls: objects blown down by the wind

Yet there he sat, apparently grinning, unharmed. They stared at him for a full minute. To a beholder it would have seemed that he was trying to communicate some command to them, some warning which they failed to understand because no danger was in sight, nor did their keen noses detect any. Then, one by one, they vanished silently as they had come. The clear space at the lip of the cliff was empty, save for Koyo, who still sat there, staring down in the depths of the cove.

Once more he voiced his command, but this time it was unheeded. Like those who had gone to help the boy who had cried "Wolf!" when there was no wolf, the blue clansmen would not be fooled again. As if seeming to understand this, Koyo himself vanished at last, and the glades were silent.

Down in the cove, in a deep hole among the rocks, at the mouth of a small cave seen only at extreme low tide, the water was agitated* in strange fashion. A school of sea perch which had come in with the flood tide, suddenly vanished seaward in alarm. Presently, however, the water was quiet again. The moon climbed higher until the whole place was nearly as bright as in daytime. The spell of silence settled over the island once more.

agitated: stirred up

Yet down in the cabin by the beach at the opposite side of the island, young Dan Scott, strangely wakeful that night, heard the song of Koyo and stirred uneasily on his couch. There was something of dire portent* in the weird cry that had come faintly across the island. He felt that something had happened or was about to happen.

portent: sign of coming evil

As the boy lay there listening, the cry came again. This time he got up softly and stole to the window and peered out. The matchless beauty of the night held him entranced* for a moment. The white beach, damp from the receding tide, was defined with that line of white fire. A moon path lay across the water. The island itself was washed with a mystic* light. The world seemed changed to a fairy-land. Over all was silence, for the clan call was not repeated again.

entranced: motionless with delight
mystic: mysterious

In the next room Dan's father was sleeping. For a time the boy debated waking him. Dan had been born on this fox-farm island. He had come to understand these sly little half-wild creatures better, perhaps, than did the man who owned them. The boy knew that the clan call was uttered by Koyo. He knew, too, that Koyo was mighty in wisdom, and that as clearly as possible he was trying to tell the blue clansmen, perhaps Dan and his father also, that something was wrong on the island despite the fact that all seemed peaceful.

Surely there was something wrong on the island. Dan and his father had known it for weeks. Foxes were disappearing in mysterious fashion. Particularly were the pups, just old enough to play around outside the dens and take occasional trips to the beach, yielding to the menace, whatever it was. These same fox pups were worth five hundred dollars a pair, and losses were mounting rapidly. Dan's father went around more silent than usual. A worried frown was creasing his brow. Each night, almost from the same spot on the island, the big fox uttered his summons.* The cry was unusual, since it came at a time of the year when the foxes were seldom heard. Silence is the rule when the crooked tunnels are inhabited with puppies. The parents seem to understand that nothing must be done to attract the attention of a possible enemy at this season.

summons: call to come

The foxes continued to disappear. Koyo nightly sang dolefully* of it. Dan worried even more than his father did. It was not the value of the little fur bearers that made their loss so hard to bear. They were all shy friends of Dan's. They watched him as he made his rounds of the feed houses late each afternoon, bringing delicious mashes of ground meat and cereal. These same friends were now in trouble. Dan felt that upon him, who understood them so well, rested the burden of their safety.

dolefully: sadly

It was this desire to help them that impelled* him now to return to his room, dress hurriedly, and slip out of the house, without waking his father. He set off briskly on a trail that led across the island, in the direction whence the doleful cry of Koyo had come.

impelled: caused

Once in the depth of the woods, the world seemed to undergo a change. Here, the darkness was almost complete, save where breaks in the

For a moment they stared at each other. It seemed as if the big blue fox were trying to convey some message to the boy. Presently, however, he turned and trotted away up the path in the direction Dan was going. The latter followed, glad of his company.

Now Dan knew that he was being watched by other foxes. From almost every thicket a pair of glowing eyes was fixed upon him. No more warning barks were uttered, for they understood that he was their friend. These intelligent foxes seemed merely curious to know why he was abroad at this time of night.

He became aware that Koyo had stopped and was waiting for him. At this point the trail swung away from the beach, and headed more inland. Koyo waited until Dan was quite close and then he did a curious thing. He seemed of a sudden to be stricken with some ailment. He partly collapsed and then sought to drag himself into the brush, in the direction of the beach, uttering piteous cries.

Dan stared, puzzled for a moment; then he grinned. Somewhere near by was Koyo's den, with a fine litter of pups guarded by the mother. The big fox, no doubt, was seeking to distract the boy's attention. Dan merely shrugged his shoulders and started on.

Now the cries of Koyo became more insistent. Indeed they were so real that Dan wondered if the animal were not really in pain. As clearly as if he were using human speech, the fox seemed to be trying to tell him to come toward the beach. Dan paused, wondering. Koyo knew him very well, knew that he had no designs upon the pups back there in the woods. It was strange that he would trouble with such a trick to draw Dan away from the den. There came to Dan once more the realization that something unexplained was menacing the island. Into his mind leaped the wild thought that Koyo might be trying to tell him

foliage overhead permitted the moonlight to be in pools upon the path. There was silence in the woods; a silence that seemed beaded with some hint of danger. Dan broke into a cheery whistle to lift his fears. Yet he could not forget that there was something wrong on the island.

He had not gone a hundred yards before his whistle ended abruptly. Almost beside him in the brush something rustled suddenly. There was a short, muffled bark, and Dan jumped. The next moment he grinned to himself, ashamed of his taut* nerves, for he knew that it was merely one of the blue foxes whom he had disturbed. A pair of glowing eyes showed, and the boy stood quite still. Then Koyo, leader of the clan, came into the path and stood there eyeing Dan, quite unafraid.

taut: tightly drawn

of it. With a shrug he turned back and followed the fox.

Through the thick brush they went. At last they stopped at the edge of the cliff where Koyo was wont* to sing his doleful song. Ten feet distant from him Koyo stopped, squatted on haunches, and allowed his tongue to loll in a grin. Dan, grinning back in spite of himself, nevertheless felt sheepish* and vexed.* Plainly the fox merely wanted to lead him away from the den. Now having brought him to this cliff, he was good-naturedly asking Dan what he was going to do about it. This was a reasonable explanation; yet somehow it did not seem enough to satisfy the boy.

---

wont: accustomed
sheepish: embarrassed
vexed: irritated

Dan stepped to the edge of the cliff and looked downward. As he did so the sharp-pointed ears of the fox pricked forward expectantly. However, there was no menace to be seen down there in the dark water. The tide was nearly at full ebb. A strip of sand showed, except at one corner of the cove, where the water was deep. For a full minute, Dan stared down into those depths. Once it seemed that he saw something moving there, but he did not see it again. He finally decided that his imagination was playing a trick on him.

Scattered along the beach were stranded shellfish, which had been brought up by the tide—the most delightful food for foxes—yet for some unexplained reason there were no foxes there gathering a meal. That in itself was a strange thing. Dan turned to look at Koyo, but the fox had gone. Shaking his head and feeling a little foolish at having been twice tricked by the cunning old clan leader, Dan turned homeward and crept into bed without waking his father.

The nightly song of Koyo was still heard but went unnoticed, although the disappearance of young foxes continued. Always the song of the fox came from one direction. Dan guessed that Koyo had taken regularly to sitting on the cliff and pouring out the woe in his soul. It went on until the moon, eaten away by the demon in the sky, as the old Indian said, was but little more than rind of its former self. It no longer flooded the island with its pale, unearthly light. When this happened, Dan knew that the time for fire fishing had come.

Usually he went with his father on these trips, for the task is easier with two. However, late that afternoon his father had gone to the mainland in the motorboat planning to return the following morning. So, with a net in the skiff,* Dan set out alone. He was planning to make a haul of the many schools of sea perch that came close inshore with the flood tide. Some two hours after sundown, and with the night a moonless black pall,* the boy found himself in the skiff opposite the cove where Koyo was wont to come and voice his plaint.*

---

skiff: flat-bottomed boat
pall: gloom
plaint: utterance of grief

For weeks there had been no rain. The sea was a vast pool of hidden fire which needed only to be stirred to make itself visible. Standing up in the skiff, he rowed by facing ahead. As his eyes searched the water near shore for signs of perch, it seemed to Dan that he could detect the movement of every living thing in acres of water. Big jellyfishes were outlined in pale silver. Indeed, they possessed a gleam of their own, a cold light. In one spot the water seemed to burn, stirred by the movements of millions of tiny shrimp. A run of smelt* shimmered near the surface, only to break apart as a single streak of fire shot toward them—a king salmon. The smelt scattered wildly, but the salmon took toll of the laggards.* Presently, too, he vanished swiftly, pursued by an even broader streak of pale flame, a hungry seal abroad in his night hunting. At last Dan saw that which he sought—a patch of water close inshore at the cove, which was stirred by thousands of fish. Noiseless as possible, Dan made his way toward it.

---

smelt: small, silvery fish
laggards: ones that lag behind

Now he was in the midst of the strangely illuminated* patch but so quietly had he approached that the perch had not taken alarm. His eyes glowed with anticipation. There were several hundred pounds of them, enough to make food for foxes for several days.

---

illuminated: lighted up

They saw him now, but they did not vanish in deep water. Rather their curiosity was aroused at sight of the boat, for they swam around it in a vast swarm. Their eyes were glowing in the light which the passage of their bodies stirred in the water. Still cautiously, careful to make no splash, Dan eased the skiff to shore. He dropped on the beach an anchor that was secured to one end of the net. Then he rowed seaward again, with the net paying* off the stern of the skiff. In a half-circle he proceeded. The fish followed him, but moved a little closer inshore as they saw the net. At the lower edge of this were slugs* of lead that carried it to the shallow, sandy bottom.

---

paying: running
slugs: lumps

At last the operation was complete. The fish were within the net and Dan drove his skiff ashore. Then began the task of hauling the net. Frightened, the perch made a sudden bolt seaward and struck the net with such force that the corks which floated its upper edge sagged under for a moment. Not finding es-

cape at that point, the now frantic fish charged at another spot, but again they met that same mysterious mesh. Knowing that he had them safe, Dan threw himself into the task of hauling in the net.

He became aware, too, that he had a watcher. As the fish surged back and forth, the phosphorescent* water bathed the beach there in a dim light. That light found response in two glowing balls of fire at the top of the cliff. Dan knew that Koyo was in his usual spot, watching his operation: yet the fox made no sound. He seemed intensely interested, for he sat perfectly quiet at the lip of the cliff and stared downward. Yet he made no attempt to descend. Indeed, he seemed to avoid the water's edge at this spot. This was strange, Dan thought, for whenever a haul of fish was made, usually the entire fox population of the island was on hand to await an opportunity to snatch a finny prize.

---

phosphorescent: glowing

The net came in slowly, only inch by inch, for the strength of the fish surging against it almost equaled the pull of the boy. Never had he made a haul for fish at this spot before. So he did not know the condition of the bottom. A sunken snag might either tear the net or else hang it up in such fashion that the fish could escape beneath it and make all his labor fruitless. As he hauled, he hoped that this might not happen.

Yet it did. As he neared the edge of the rock, the heavy net stuck fast, and all his strength could not budge it. He knew then that his only course was to wade out and lift the net over the snag, at the same time frightening the fish away from the opening thus created. The water would be ice cold. The temperature of Puget Sound is nearly the same in summer as in winter. Yet there was no help for it. Dan plunged in.

The snag was not more than thirty feet from shore, yet the beach shelved off rather steeply. Dan found the water nearly to his waist before he reached the place. Meanwhile, the fish had surged away from him, frightened, to another point in the net. This was well, for he had but to lift the mesh over the thing which was holding it back and then let it drop to bottom again on the shoreward side, to bring the haul of fish in as before. His arms groped deeply as he sought to locate the sunken branch or log.

Then he became aware that the net was moving in a strange fashion; seaward, it seemed. At the same instant, he felt his ankles entangled in what he guessed to be the net. Suddenly the water was stirred violently. His fingers touched something which attempted to seize his hand as he jerked it away. He screamed in horror at the thought of what had happened. His net had snagged on an octopus, numerous in those waters, and sometimes growing to giant size!

Only one advantage lay with him, and that a slim one. The sea beast was snarled in the meshes of the net. That prevented its using its eight arms and at the same time kept it from getting an anchor-hold on a rock or sunken log that would enable it to bring its tremendous strength into play. The tip of one tentacle had him by an ankle. He had managed to jerk the other foot free before the gristly arm could coil. Another tentacle was groping in search of his body. The monster was seeking to draw him into deep water, where it could dispatch* him with ease.

---

dispatch: put to death quickly

How large it was he had no way of knowing then, but that it was a big one there could be no question. The phosphorescent water was stirred violently by the struggles of the devilfish, or octopus, to free itself of the entangling net. It was stirred until Dan could see his foe as plainly as if it were daylight. The sight made him cry out again, a futile* call for help, where there was no one to hear him. At the same time he threw his weight and strength into the task of drawing himself into shallow water, where the octopus would be at a greater disadvantage. He would have torn loose from the grip of that single tentacle, but it held him like a vise. Yet he gained a few inches before the weight of the octopus told. Dan felt a second arm tighten around his ankle.

---

futile: useless

In his pocket was a heavy clasp knife, which he often used in work about the island. He knew that he must depend upon it as his only weapon. Quickly he got it out and opened the blade with trembling fingers, while he braced himself against that pull seaward. The octopus renewed its efforts to draw Dan into deep water. The monster was fully aroused now. Although its struggles had hopelessly entangled it in the net it was not finished. It was still a foe with which to be reckoned. Gripping the knife in his right hand, Dan put every ounce into another pull toward shore. Seemingly the octopus was caught unaware, for Dan gained several feet before his strength gave out. Again came that tension, with neither battler giving an inch.

Then Dan took a daring chance. At risk of being seized by a tentacle that had become freed of the net, he thrust his right arm under water, located one of the gristly, steel-like ribbons about his ankle, and slashed. The knife was sharp, and he felt the blade take hold, although the tentacle was too tough to be severed* in a single stroke. He saw the round saucerlike eyes of the beast half hidden under the meshes of the nets; saw them cloud suddenly in new fury at the pain of the wound. Then came a sudden heave that all but threw

Dan off his feet. In panic, he struck again with the knife, and the tentacle loosened. Whether it was severed, or whether the octopus, in pain, had merely unfastened it, Dan could not know. Quick to seize advantage of the situation, he lurched closer to shore, drawing the octopus with him.

---
severed: cut apart

He saw that the thing was all of sixteen feet from tip to tip of its longest arms. He made another desperate effort and came closer to shore. Then he stared up at the cliff at sight of a curious thing. The rim of it was packed almost solid with blue foxes, staring at this tremendous battle going on in the cove below. In the center of them, Dan fancied that he could see Koyo, the clan leader, himself.

Dan remembered now that when he had uttered that first cry of fear, it had been echoed by the big fox. However, Dan had paid no attention, having been occupied with the octopus. Yet that eerie* summons had gone echoing over the island. As usual it had been answered by the blue clan, but instead of finding their leader sitting quietly by the edge of the cliff, with no harm in sight, the foxes had come on this struggle. Somehow the word seemed to be passed to the others of the blue legion, back in the woods, for the number of them on the cliff grew magically. Desperately, Dan struggled closer to shore, dragging that tremendous weight. Soon his strength would give out. Then what? He fell, got up in sudden fear of what that meant if it happened again, and attacked the remaining arm with the knife.

---
eerie: mysterious

The boy's struggles were growing weaker, and the tentacles seemed to have the strength of whalebone. After that, Dan did not remember clearly what was happening, save that he sensed, dimly, that a tremendous commotion was going on up there on the cliff. There were sharp yappings and squallings, as the foxes, tremendously excited, surged back and forth. Then he saw that he had drawn the devilfish into water so shallow that the upper half of the beast was exposed.

Still slashing away at the remaining arm, Dan felt himself knocked aside, just as his knife blade cut through the last strand and his foot came free. He seemed to be in the center of a furry, milling* mass that surged over him. The foxes rushed upon the octopus madly! Rolling, crawling, he managed to get clear at last, almost deafened by a chorus of cries as the foxes swarmed upon the hated thing in the net. He succeeded in getting to the beach. Then he did something he had never done before—fainted. As blackness engulfed him, that mighty chorus of cries—sent forth while the blue clansmen took vengeance for many a slaughtered friend—was the last thing he heard.

milling: churning

Dan regained consciousness with the feeling that he was alone. Quickly his mind caught up the thread of events where it had put it down. Dizzily he got to his feet and stumbled over to the skiff, where he always carried a flashlight. He turned its white beam on the now darkened water, which was unstreaked by fire from a moving fish. At the left, a short distance from where he had fought with the octopus, he saw a half-submerged cave in the rocks. He guessed that this was where the monster had lurked while it took toll of young foxes who were foolhardy* enough to visit the beach at low tide in search of prize bits of sea food. So long as the fox remained on the beach itself, it was safe. Let it wade in the water past that cave in an endeavor to fish a clam or young crab from between the rocks, and the demon of the cavern exacted* tribute.*

foolhardy: unwisely bold
exacted: demanded
tribute: payment

This Dan saw, and then the flashlight turned to the net. It was now merely shredded mesh, for the sharp teeth of the blue foxes had slashed its strands in an effort to get at the enemy inside. Of the octopus itself nothing remained. The foxes themselves had gone back to their dens. Dan told himself that he had lost a fine haul of perch, and that he would need a new net, but the price paid for victory with the sea beast was cheap enough.

Back to their caves had the blue clansmen gone, and all was silent in the cove. Yet Dan's flashlight, groping through the gloom along the top of the cliff, paused as its fire struck response there. Koyo, the singer, who need sing no more of the menace of the cove, had tarried and his yellowish-green eyes shone like twin balls of fire in the white light. Then he, too, was gone; and somehow Dan felt that all was well.

About the Story

1. What is the message that Koyo tries to communicate to the clan and to the boy?
2. What hints does the author give the reader about the danger?
3. How does the author create the eerie atmosphere in the story?
4. Why does the author develop the sympathetic relationship between Dan and the foxes, and Koyo in particular?

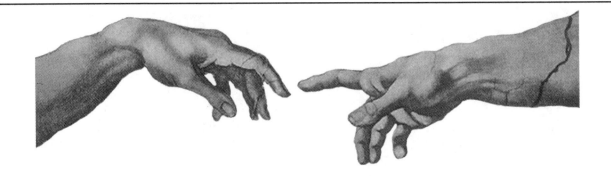

This Is My Father's World

Maltbie D. Babcock

This is my Father's world,
And to my listening ears
All nature sings, and round me rings
The music of the spheres.*

spheres: heavens

This is my Father's world:
I rest me in the thought
Of rocks and trees, of skies and seas—
His hand the wonders wrought.*

wrought: fashioned
artistically

This is my Father's world,
The birds their carols raise,
The morning light, the lily white,
Declare their Maker's praise.

This is my Father's world:
He shines in all that's fair;
In the rustling grass I hear Him pass,
He speaks to me everywhere.

This is my Father's world,
O let me ne'er forget
That though the wrong seems oft so strong,
God is the Ruler yet.

This is my Father's world:
The battle is not done;
Jesus who died shall be satisfied,
And earth and heaven be one.

The Bible and Nature

By the word of the Lord were the heavens made; and all the host of them by the breath of his mouth. He gathereth the waters of the sea together as an heap: he layeth up the depth in storehouses. Let all the earth fear the Lord: let all the inhabitants of the world stand in awe of him. For he spake, and it was done; he commanded, and it stood fast.

Let us come before his presence with thanksgiving, and make a joyful noise unto him with psalms. For the Lord is a great God, and a great King above all gods. In his hand are the deep places of the earth: the strength of the hills is his also. The sea is his, and he made it: and his hands formed the dry land. O come, let us worship and bow down: let us kneel before the Lord our maker. For he is our God; and we are the people of his pasture, and the sheep of his hand.

When I consider thy heavens, the work of thy fingers, the moon and the stars, which thou hast ordained; What is man, that thou art mindful of him? and the son of man, that thou visitest him? For thou hast made him a little lower than the angels, and hast crowned him with glory and honour. Thou madest him to have dominion over the works of thy hands; thou hast put all things under his feet: All sheep and oxen, yea, and the beasts of the field; The fowl of the air, and the fish of the sea, and whatsoever passeth through the paths of the seas. O Lord our Lord, how excellent is thy name in all the earth! (Psalms 33:6-9; 95:2-7; 8:3-9)

3

Gener·os·i·ty

Generosity begins not in outward
actions but in inner attitude.

Generosity

On January 13, 1982, an Air Florida jet taking off from Washington, D.C., crashed into the icy Potomac River. Several passengers managed to struggle out of the submerged plane to the surface. A Coast Guard helicopter, alerted to the disaster, hovered anxiously overhead.

Bystanders noticed that rescue activity particularly centered upon a group of six passengers. These were trying to stay afloat in the freezing water by clinging to pieces of wreckage. One man of the six, reported eyewitnesses, repeatedly caught the lifeline dropped from the helicopter. But each time, they also noticed, he handed it to someone else. Rescuers airlifted one after another to safety. But when they returned for the last, he was nowhere to be found in the debris-choked, icy water.

Later, after all the dead had been recovered, authorities discovered that seventy-seven had died from crash-related injuries. Only one victim, the seventy-eighth, had drowned. The evidence revealed that this was the man who had sacrificed his life so that five others might live.

Probably none of us will have an opportunity for so dramatic an act of generosity. Yet the possibility for generous actions lies within the grasp of any one of us. Generosity begins not in outward actions but in an inner attitude. It gives to others without expectation of reward. It regards others as more important than self. For us it may take many forms, from caring for an injured stray animal to welcoming and befriending a new student at school.

The Bible gives numerous examples of generosity. The greatest, of course, is the example of Christ, who died for us when we were not righteous or even friendly toward Him. Instead, we were outright enemies (Rom. 5:8). David gives us another stirring example. Even though King Saul believed him to be an enemy and tried repeatedly to kill him, David showed mercy to Saul in sparing his life (I Sam. 24:1-22). After Saul and Jonathan were dead and David had become king, he searched for Saul's crippled grandson Mephibosheth. When he found him, David brought him to the palace and restored to him all of Saul's possessions (II Sam. 9).

Perhaps the most illuminating passage on generosity appears in Christ's parable of the good Samaritan (Luke 10:30-37). This parable reveals that generosity includes a genuine concern for others, a willingness to give one's possessions to help others, and action to carry out one's concern. In this unit many of the selections, although not Christian in subject matter or theme, illustrate at least one of these qualities.

First, generous people give of what they are. Although inner strengths cannot always be felt or seen, they nevertheless become significant when placed in God's hands to be used for others. In "Stopover in Querétaro," the citizens of a small Mexican town do not have much of this world's goods, but their understanding and compassion make the American visitor's tragedy more bearable. The sheriff in "Gold-Mounted Guns" also shows his generosity by guiding a young man into making the right choice.

Second, generous people give liberally of their abundance. The Christian knows that his possessions have come from God. He is therefore willing to let God use them. In "The Two Strangers" a one-armed war veteran gives his most prized possession to make a retired couple happy. In "The Buffalo Dance" two young Indians from enemy tribes exchange treasured gifts as symbols of the respect they have gained for one another.

Finally, generous people perform generous acts. In "The Last Leaf," a little-known artist paints a work that helps a young friend live. In the poem "Country Doctor," a doctor sacrificially serves his patients in ways few people see. Sometimes actions that have little monetary worth turn out to be invaluable to the recipient.

What we are, what we have, and what we do are essential traits of the generosity shown by the good Samaritan. He displayed interest even though others, who should have known better, were unconcerned. It would have been of little value, though, if the good Samaritan had been only interested. When he translated his interest into caring for the victim and paying the bill, he demonstrated his sincerity. He showed, in other words, that a genuine neighbor is also generous.

Not all of the selections in this unit, however, present examples of true generosity. In "The Strangers That Came to Town," two brothers thoughtlessly ruin a day's catch of fish for a family needing the food. In "Preacher's Kid," a story you will need to read with discernment, a mother yields to her daughter's pleas to buy a dress that the family cannot afford. As a result of her generosity, the mother becomes entangled in a web of trouble. You will need to decide whether her generous act is also a wise act.

To cultivate generosity is to nurture a character trait that God wants us to possess (II Cor. 8:9-15). We should be willing to share with others not only our goods and money but also our time and energy. We willingly share with others only when we realize that everything we are and everything we have is God's and is merely lent for a time to us.

Mr. Payne's Investment

Mark Hager

In this story you will see a striking contrast. One man wants to be generous but does not have the resources. Another has the resources but does not have a generous spirit. Which character do you admire? Does your attitude toward these two change during the story?

Though now grown and scattered, we who were children on the farm still remember with affection Mr. Delhart Payne. As far back as the oldest of us can recall, Mr. Payne lived at our house.

When Father had hired him, the old man, though crippled in one leg, could get around enough to help out on the place. He was good about feeding the stock and taking care of odd jobs—"jimwhacking around," Father called it.

The old man used to tell us how he came to have a crippled leg. He didn't mind if we eased up his breeches leg to see that he didn't have any calf on his leg where the minnie ball* had hit him.

---

minnie ball: rifle bullet

The old man's eyes always twinkled with a kind of delight when we would bring up the subject. He liked a chance to tell us about a day in July, '63,* when he had climbed the hill with Gen. Pickett's men at Gettysburg; in fact, old Mr. Payne always seemed a little prouder of that wounded leg than he did his good one. It always seemed to give the old man a proud spirit.

'63: 1863

And, speaking of his proud spirit, that is why it hurt the old man when our father would scold him for giving away the apples, cherries, and things around the place.

The old man liked children, and always managed to get out on his cane and down by the road fence at the time he knew the school children would be coming along. In our cherry orchard, there was a row of trees by the fence, the first row in the orchard. Mr. Payne would be down there, and the long limbs would be swinging out across the fence. The old man would reach up with the crook of his cane and pull the limbs down to the kids.

Then Father would yell at him, and the kids would break out running, holding a bunch of red cherries. The old man wouldn't say anything, but just quit when Father yelled.

On days when Father was away on more important business, old Mr. Payne would dig a hole by the fence, and fill it with red autumn apples. We children used to climb and help him get the fruit and fill the hole with apples, cover them with straw, and then throw the dirt on the straw. He would leave a hole on the side near the fence with a wad of straw in it, and in the winter the old man would slip out down by the road.

I can see him now, his big old coonskin cap pulled over his ears, the bushy tail swinging behind. Our mother always knitted the old man a pair of yarn mittens and a couple of pairs of socks for wintertime. He would put on a big old gray coat he had brought back from the

War Between the States, polish the brass buttons by rubbing them with the yarn mittens, and then slip out. When the children came by, the old man would get out the cold, ripe-red apples and pass them across the fence until Father saw and stopped him.

Father could never seem to see any sense in the way Mr. Payne carried on like that, and said it was no wonder the man had come to his old days penniless and a subject for charity. Mother would never agree on that, and when Father would discuss the old man and bring out that he was now too old to be worth his keep, Mother would say:

"But in days gone by the old man has been a lot of help. He helps me with the children and the housework more than you think. And, besides, he's made us a lot of friends. I think every kid within five miles likes him."

But Father was a more stern and practical man. Even when he fell off the hayrack* and hurt his back, he could see no help in having the old man around.

hayrack: a wagon for carrying hay

"Amy," Father said to our mother, "I've been telling you for years we should have somebody on the place who can work. See, now? The way my back feels, and according to the doctor, I may not be able to hit a lick* for a month or two; and here it is with the cherry orchard ripe, and the hay all ready to be put up."

hit a lick: work at all

Mother raked her graying hair behind her ears, and said, "It did happen at a bad time, Joe. Maybe the old man and I can get some work done somehow."

Old Mr. Payne did not seem alarmed at all when she mentioned the matter to him out by the springhouse one morning when Father wouldn't hear. He actually grinned, and there

was a twinkle in his blue eyes when Mother explained that with the man of the house flat on an injured back, the whole burden of taking care of the cherry orchard and the hay crop fell on the rest of us.

When Mr. Payne spoke, he said, "Well, Amy, I reckon the cherries come first. I want you to gather up every bucket on the place and have them ready in the morning. I will dilly-dally* down by the road today and see if I can get somebody lined up to help us."

dilly-dally: linger

Mother replied, "But you see, Mr. Payne, we are not in any shape to begin hiring help, not with this doctor bill and all, and Joe laid up."

The old man just grinned and moseyed off* down by the road. He spent most of the day down there, and several times he pulled down cherry tree limbs with his cane for the children, for now he wasn't afraid Father would see and scold him.

moseyed off: moved along

The next morning, when our father looked out the window, he shouted to Mother, "Oh, Amy! Amy!" And Mother ran to him from the kitchen.

"Who are all the people climbing the cherry trees with buckets?" Father yelled. "Has the old man hired people with nothing to pay?"

Mother answered calmly, "No, Joe, he didn't hire them. They are just young folks who have grown up around here. I reckon they are the ones old Mr. Payne has given cherries and apples to."

The sick man turned and groaned. He still could not seem to understand what was happening, but old Mr. Payne knew. He stood down by the fence and beckoned the folks across when they came. He handed them buckets and explained that Father was down on his

back. He told them that if he didn't have that war leg, and could crawl back a few years, he wouldn't need this help.

A few days later there was the clatter of machinery out around the barnyard. When we looked out, the neighbor men had come— strong and brawny* men, they were, hitching up the mowing machine and the hayrake. When Father pulled back the curtain and looked out, there was amazement in his eyes. Old Mr. Payne was standing proud as the crowing roosters in the barnyard, and by the time we could wheel our father out on the front porch, the meadow was dotted with haystacks. The cherries were gone from the trees and on their way to the market.

brawny: muscular

"Amy," our father observed, "I sometimes wonder whether a person ever gives. Don't you think, Amy, it is more of an investment?"

Mother answered, "Joe, you have a good thought there," and she continued her sweeping.

But during the next March, old Mr. Payne took a cold and a cough, and a few weeks later he died. At that time the grown-ups said it was so unfortunate quite elderly men seem to die during that time of year before any blossoms came. But we children, and the neighboring children, knew that the first blossoms that come in our section are the whitest, and we ran to the woods.

Two dozen of us came with our arms full of the twigs of dogwood with the tender white flowers. We covered old Mr. Delhart Payne with the white dogwood blossoms, and we knew if he could open his eyes, they would twinkle and sparkle at the sight of the blossoms we had brought him. We knew how the old man's heart would have leaped could he have seen the biggest crowd of school children ever to attend a funeral in our neighborhood, for old Mr. Payne had made an investment in the hearts of the boys and the girls who came along the road.

About the Story

1. What might account for Mr. Payne's "proud spirit"?
2. Is Mr. Payne really a "subject for charity" as Father thinks?
3. When Mother tells Mr. Payne that they will have to be responsible for the cherries and the hay crop, why does he grin?
4. Does Father develop a different attitude toward Mr. Payne's practices by the end of the story? Why or why not?
5. How does Mr. Payne profit from the investment he made?

. . . About the Author . . . .

Unlike many writers, Mark Hager did not grow up with the dream of becoming an author. After marrying his childhood sweetheart, he seemed content to work for the railroad in his hometown of Williamson, West Virginia. One day, however, in an effort to aid his children in their schoolwork, he bought them a typewriter. Though this purchase did little to spark a creative imagination in his offspring, Hagar himself became enamored with the idea of writing stories. When his first story was accepted, Hagar said, "I thought the earth shook!" Since that time, he has published over a hundred stories, many of which "reflect his deep interest in young people and their problems."

Stopover in Querétaro

Jerrold Beim

An automobile accident is a terrible thing, especially when someone dies. When the accident happens in a foreign country where there is a language barrier, the tragedy is almost unbearable. Jerrold Beim tells us more than the facts surrounding this terrible automobile accident in Mexico. What does he want us to notice about the people of Querétaro? What lessons about life are portrayed here?

Two years ago my family and I were driving to Mexico City on the Juarez highway.* We had a blowout and the car turned over. My wife, who was driving, and my daughter were killed instantly. One of my twin sons, Andy, suffered a severe concussion and had to be hospitalized in a town called Querétaro,* about ninety kilometers* from Mexico City. My other son, Seth, was uninjured but stunned by what had happened; and I had minor injuries and was in a state of shock.

Juarez highway: highway south of Juarez, a Mexican border town
Querétaro: a state capital of Mexico
ninety kilometers: about fifty-four miles

Many people have said to me since: "Wasn't it awful that it had to happen in a strange country?" And I'll confess that at the time, staying at the hospital in Querétaro, I felt that I was at the end of the world, far from family or friends who could have been of help or comfort to me. But let me tell it as it happened.

Immediately after the accident we were surrounded by Mexicans, mostly country people in sombreros and *rebozos,** and all, naturally, total strangers. But one man, in a business suit, was leading Seth and me to his car. In excellent English he explained that he had been behind us and had seen our car turn over. It was he who had summoned the police and ambulance from Querétaro, and now he was driving Seth and me to the hospital. The ambulance had sped ahead with Andy. The man told me his name was Juan Martinez. He asked if I knew any Spanish, and when I told him I spoke only a little he assured me that he would stay with me until he saw we were getting proper care.

---

rebozos: shawls

Querétaro was a sizable town, but it seemed primitive, and I doubted that we could get adequate medical attention. The sight of the hospital did not ease my anxiety. It was run by a Dr. Francisco Alcozer Pozo, and did not even look like a hospital. The nurse who greeted us explained that the doctor lived on one side of the patio,* and his mother lived on the opposite side. To the rear was the hospital itself, a row of little rooms opening off the patio. Seth and I were taken into one of these rooms. The nurse explained too rapidly for me to understand (Juan Martinez interpreted) that the doctor was busy with Andy.

---

patio: roofless courtyard

Juan took Seth out to the patio while the nurse cleaned and bandaged the cut on my head. I glanced about the room and noticed that the paint on the walls was scaling,* the furnishings were antiquated.* I was overwhelmed by what had happened to my wife and daughter, and certain that in this . . . place Andy would not receive the medical care he would need to survive.

---

scaling: flaking
antiquated: old

Soon Juan returned with Seth and a man in a white coat.

"This is the doctor," Juan said. "Doctor Pozo."

My spirit rallied* slightly when I saw the doctor. He was tall and thin, and he had an intelligent face. In slow and not very good English he expressed his deep sympathy for all that had happened. He said he doubted that any of Andy's bones were broken—he'd have to wait for the X rays—but he was sure Andy had a severe concussion. The boy was still unconscious.

---

rallied: revived

I wanted to send to Mexico City for a specialist at once. Doctor Pozo said he would do whatever I desired but he thought we should see the X rays first. He looked at the cut on my head, my finger, and then he examined Seth, who was sitting on the foot of the bed.

Suddenly from outside I heard voices that made my heart leap. They were definitely American!

"It must be *Señor* and *Señora** MacKenzie," Doctor Pozo explained. "They are Americans who live here."

Señor and Señora: Mr. and Mrs.

Americans here! They came in, an attractive man and woman, who apparently knew the doctor well. Doctor Pozo left me alone with them.

The MacKenzies had heard of the accident and had come at once to offer help. They said they were the only Americans in Querétaro, Mr. MacKenzie being the manager of a local gabardine* factory. They assured me that Doctor Pozo was a very competent* physician; but I felt that they would have to say that, under the circumstances.

---

gabardine: cotton fabric
competent: well qualified

Seth, apparently still stunned, sat silent on the bed.

"Let us take Seth home for the time being," Mrs. MacKenzie suggested. "We have a five-year-old boy who would love his company. At least, you won't have to worry about him."

Even though these people were complete strangers, Seth readily went with them. I think he was glad to get away from all the horrors of the past few hours.

There were scores of things I had to do. My family and my wife's family had to be notified, and the MacKenzies helped get them on the telephone which was just outside the room. My wife and I had always approved of cremation,* and the MacKenzies offered to make all the arrangements. When they finally left they promised to bring Seth back for a visit the next day.

---

cremation: burning the body

It wasn't until they were gone that I realized Juan Martinez had disappeared. I rang for the nurse and made her understand that I was looking for the man who had brought me here. She said he had left the hospital. And I hadn't even had a chance to thank him for all he had done.

Later Doctor Pozo returned. Andy was still unconscious, and it was clearly evident that he had a severe concussion. I repeated that I wanted to call in a brain specialist from Mexico City, and Doctor Pozo put in the call. The specialist said that Andy could not be moved for weeks, and he didn't feel there was any point in his coming to Querétaro. It was obvious to him that Andy's progress depended on time and he said that Doctor Pozo could handle the situation as well as he. He suggested, however, that we keep him informed by telephone. I still wasn't satisfied. If Andy pulled through, I felt it would be only a matter of luck.

Doctor Pozo now turned to setting my dislocated finger. I remember fading from consciousness while it was being done and dreaming we were in the car again, on our way to Mexico City. Then I would come to and realize what had happened. Only heavy sedatives* put me to sleep that night.

---

sedatives: drugs having a quieting, soothing effect

Another nurse was on duty in the morning. This one spoke a bit of English, and told me there was no change in Andy, but that a man was waiting to see me.

It was Juan Martinez. I greeted him like an old friend. Where had he disappeared to yesterday?

He had seen me with the Americans, and knew they would take care of me. But he had stayed overnight in Querétaro wanting to be of further help and hoping that maybe the little boy would be better. Now he had to get on to Mexico City.

I didn't know how to express my gratitude for all he had done. We exchanged addresses. I would look him up in Nogales.* We would be sure to see each other again.

Nogales: a Mexican border town

I was lonelier than ever after Juan Martinez left. Only the telephone kept me bolstered* through the day. Family and friends called, offering all kinds of help. It was decided that I should send Seth to his grandmother's while I remained with Andy.

---

bolstered: supported

Mrs. MacKenzie visited me during the day, too, bringing Seth, along with her own boy. The children had had a wonderful time together. Arrangements were made for Seth to be driven to Mexico City, then to go on to the United States by plane.

When Mrs. MacKenzie was there Doctor Pozo summoned me. Andy had regained consciousness. He stared at me with recognition, though not a sound came from his lips. Doctor Pozo said it might be weeks before he spoke.

Bidding good-by to Seth was hard. Though I knew the separation was only temporary, it emphasized how broken my family had become.

Late in the afternoon an unexpected call came through from my brother. He lived in San Francisco, but he had flown to Mexico City and was leaving for Querétaro in a few minutes.

His first words as he came in were, "We must have you removed to Mexico City at once!"

I explained why that couldn't be done. But it was wonderful having him with me. He spent the night in the hospital, and we sat up talking for hours.

For the next few days Andy's condition scarcely changed. Doctor Pozo drained fluid from the boy's spine and hinted that an operation might be necessary if he didn't begin to talk soon.

Doctor Pozo had suggested to my brother that I should leave Andy's bedside for a while, and explore the town. So one sunny morning we ventured outdoors. The hospital was located on a narrow, cobblestoned street and at the very next corner was a small-town Mexican market place, swarming with flies and filled with unappetizing food. My brother had come through this market on his arrival in Querétaro—that was why he had been so shocked. We walked until we reached the plaza,* with its inevitable* bandstand, and we sat on one of the benches under large shade trees. I felt myself being eyed by everyone who walked past.

---

plaza: public square
inevitable: unavoidable

"This town is off the usual tourist beat," I told my brother. "They're not accustomed to seeing Americans."

An old woman in a dark-blue shawl approached us.

"I guess she wants money," my brother said, digging into his pocket. But her hand wasn't out, and she was speaking to me. After she had repeated her words, I understood, and I fought to keep back the tears.

"She knows that I am the American who was in the accident," I told my brother, "and that my little boy is very sick. She is praying—for the souls of my wife and daughter—and for the recovery of my boy."

One afternoon just before my brother had to leave, I was sunning in the patio while he sat with Andy. Suddenly he came running toward me.

"I showed him a book and asked if he'd like me to read it to him—and he spoke. Just one word—'Yes'—but he spoke!"

We found the doctor and went to Andy's bedside. Yes—he spoke—just a word at a time, slowly, with effort, and only when asked something—but he spoke!

As I returned to the hospital after seeing my brother off, a cluster of ragged urchins* was around the door. They looked at me and grinned.

---

urchins: small, mischievous children

"El niño está hablando!"* one of them said. They had heard the good news already. And one of the children held out a toy, a little horse carved of balsa wood and painted colorfully. "Por el niño!"*

El niño está hablando!: The boy is talking!
Por el niño!: For the boy!

One afternoon I ventured into a local hotel for lunch; I had waited until Andy had fallen asleep, and had left word where I would be. Soon after I was seated the waiter told me I was wanted on the telephone. I became alarmed, and as I lifted the phone it was a vast relief to hear the voice of an American—a man:

"You don't know me, sir, but I'm here with a group of American doctors visiting hospitals and clinics all over Mexico. I met Doctor Pozo this morning and he told me about your accident. I saw him perform an operation this morning, and I thought you would be interested in knowing that I consider him a very fine doctor and an excellent surgeon. Your son is in very good hands."

I apologized to Doctor Pozo for my lack of confidence. He said that it was only natural for a father to be anxious, especially one who had gone through all I had.

As the days went by Andy got constantly better. He was talking more and soon he was able to sit up in the sunny patio.

One afternoon Doctor Pozo said Andy could travel at the end of the week, if we would like to move to Mexico City. Andy would have to be hospitalized for a while longer, but Doctor Pozo thought we would be more comfortable there.

I had a job to do before I left, one that I had put off for days. I had to decide what to do with my wife's and daughter's clothes. I spoke to Doctor Pozo and he suggested that I give the adult clothes to the clinic where they would be distributed to needy people, and the child's things to the orphanage. Doctor Pozo would take the things for the clinic, but he thought it would be nice if I went to the orphanage myself. It was in a building that once had been a private residence, and Doctor Pozo said it was an example of pure colonial architecture that I ought to see.

It wasn't an easy mission, sorting my little girl's clothes and then carrying them to the orphanage. All the buildings along the street looked very much alike, with crumbling pink, blue or white walls; but the convent* was easily distinguishable by its sturdy architecture and by the cross over the doorway. I rang the bell and managed to say to the old man who let me in, "Clothes for the children."

convent: building occupied by nuns

He led me into the most beautiful patio I have ever seen. A fountain played in an expanse of green lawn, and arches curved on the three walls of the house that enclosed it. The Mother Superior* in her long black robes came toward me. We conversed for a few moments, and then I started to leave.

Mother Superior: woman in charge of the convent

"The children wish to thank you," she said, and motioned me into one of the interior rooms.

It was an immense, beautiful room, with shiny tile floors and a high, carved ceiling. It was sparsely furnished, but what there was

looked like precious Spanish antiques. The Mother Superior disappeared for a moment, then returned leading a line of small girls in neat blue pinafores.*

pinafores: dresses

My daughter had been blue-eyed and flaxen-haired. These little girls were black-haired, with dark, shining eyes. I had been deprived of my daughter and these were children without fathers or mothers. I wanted to take every one in my arms. They thanked me for the clothes, in clear, piping* voices, and then I left.

piping: high-pitched

I remember being unable to go right back to the hospital. I sat in the plaza, getting control of myself, so that I could return to Andy. Then I noticed a tall, nice-looking man about my age, walking hesitantly toward me.

He sat down beside me. Was I the gentleman staying at the hospital with the little boy who had been hurt?

Yes, I was.

He owned that dry-goods store on the corner, he told me, nodding proudly toward it. I tried to convey that I thought it a fine-looking store. I couldn't bring myself to say that I wanted to be alone.

And then he explained why he had ventured to intrude on my privacy. He had seen me sitting here in the plaza and had wanted to talk to me many times. Because he felt a deep sympathy for me. A few years ago he and his family had started for Mexico City. His wife's parents lived there, and he used to take his wife and their three children to visit them once or twice a year. On that last trip, his car had been in an accident, too—a speeder had crashed into it. His wife and two of his children had been killed. And since then life for him had been an agony.

"Only now it is a little better. It is such an old proverb and it must sound foolish to you now, but time does help things. And time will help you, even though you still have much pain to live through."

I couldn't answer him. But suddenly I wasn't alone and I knew that really I had never been a stranger in Querétaro, nor was this such a foreign land. I was sitting beside someone who had been through the same ordeal. There were benches like this and people like us in every country of the world.

It was about two days later that I left by hired car for Mexico City. Andy was settled comfortably in the back seat and I was beside the driver.

Doctor Pozo, the MacKenzies, the nurses, the servants—all had said good-by to us from the hospital door. Word had got around that we were leaving, and people of the town—men in

sombreros, women in shawls, a man in the doorway of a dry-goods store—waved to us as we left Querétaro.

About the Story

1. Why does the author feel that he is "being eyed by everyone who walked past"? Is he right?

2. What lessons about life does the author illustrate in his account?
3. Who displays generosity in the story?
4. What truth does the narrator learn?

About the Author

Jerrold Beim (b. 1910) determined at a young age to be a writer. His first writing effort, a fourth-grade essay on "The Life of a Christmas Seal," won his teacher's approval and the remark "Jerry, you ought to be a writer." His first story sold was about Cinderella's stepsisters, from their point of view! He tried several careers such as banking and advertising, but he always wished to write. After finally selling a big story, he and his wife bought a car and traveled to Mexico. During their two-year stay there, they collaborated on a children's book. That success kept them writing even after they returned to New York. They adopted children, bought an old farm, fixed up the place, and kept writing. This story obviously came out of their time in Mexico and reveals their skill at using realism as the basis for their stories.

Martin and Abraham Lincoln

Catherine Cate Coblentz

This story illustrates at least three acts of generosity. Can you identify them?

"Flour and sugar and butter and eggs. Flour and sugar and butter and eggs." Martin Emery kept saying the words over to himself as he went slowly up the lane.

He had heard his mother whispering them again and again these past days. The words reminded him of the songs which his friend, Snowden, sang. Only Martin felt sure Mother's words were not a song but a prayer. For Mother needed so many things for Martin, for Maria, and Amanda, and Anna, the baby.

Martin gulped. When Father was at the fort nearby he had seen to it that Mother had these things. But he was gone. He would be gone for a long time. Somehow or other Martin felt he must take his place and help. After all he wore a new uniform now with shiny buttons. It was just like the one Father was wearing the last time Martin had seen him.

By this time Martin had come to the end of the lane. So he climbed up on the big rock by the roadside. Then he turned about and waved at the little gray house. Maria and Amanda and Anna, the baby, were standing in the doorway. They all waved back. Though Maria had to start Anna's hand going.

Then Martin looked up the road. It was Saturday and time for Snowden and Nellie to appear around the curve. Pretty soon he saw Nellie's long white ears. He heard the bell on Nellie's neck, and the jingle of her harness. He heard the creaking wheels on Nellie's cart. He saw the baskets of fresh vegetables in the back.

He saw Snowden, but Snowden didn't see Martin. Snowden was bent over on the front seat. In his hand was a stub of a pencil; on his knee a piece of paper. "I sure got to make a lot of money today," he said loud enough for Martin to hear him. "I sure got to. There's flour to get for Rosebell, and sugar and butter and eggs."

But if Snowden didn't see Martin, Nellie did. As soon as she came to the rock, Nellie stopped still. She looked at Martin. Then she turned her head and looked at Snowden. Then she flicked her ears.

When Nellie flicked her ears it was a sign. As soon as Martin saw it, he began scrambling over the wheel. He climbed up on the seat beside Snowden. Snowden blinked with surprise.

"May I go to Washington with you?" Martin asked.

Snowden started to nod. Then he stopped and asked, "Does your mother know?"

"She knows," said Martin. "That's why she let me wear my new suit." He stood up so Snowden could see the suit better. He stretched his shoulders as high as he could.

Snowden looked him up and down. He didn't miss a quirk* of the soldier-like cap or a single shiny button. "Hmm," he said. "Nice, Martin. Just like your father's."

---

quirk: i.e., any part

"Father's regiment brought Mother the cloth," said Martin, "and the buttons."

"Snowden," began Martin, as the cart moved on toward Washington, "how do you get flour and sugar and butter and eggs?"

Snowden sighed, "Sometimes I declare I don't know myself, Martin. Rosebell and the children need so many things." He took up the pencil once more. When he put it down again, Martin asked another question.

"When the war is over, will my father come home, Snowden?"

Snowden drew a deep breath. "All the war prisoners will come home then, Martin. All those that the northern army has taken will go back south to their homes. And all those that the southern army has taken will go back to their homes."

"I wish the war was over now," burst out Martin.

Snowden looked at him. "So do I," he said. "Abraham Lincoln does, too, I reckon."

Martin knew who Abraham Lincoln was. His picture was in the little gray house at the end of the lane. He never could decide which picture he liked better, that of his father or of Abraham Lincoln. His mother said they are both very important people. "Mr. Lincoln is the best President this country ever had, Martin," she said. "And your father is the best cobbler."*

---

cobbler: shoemaker

Best cobbler, best cobbler went Nellie's iron shoes, as they thumped, thumped across the bridge that led from Alexandria into Washington. Martin kicked his feet back to feel whether the empty basket was under the seat. It was. Martin knew why it was there. He knew, too, what would happen to that basket.

At the very first house, Snowden began his morning song. Martin waited to hear what the song was. It was a different one every week. This week it was a good song. Martin joined in after the first time. He sang as loud as he could:

Squash and beans and 'taters,
Garden fresh, garden fresh,
Beans and squash and 'taters.

After every sale, Snowden would put a scoop of beans or 'taters, or maybe a big squash into the basket under the seat.

The faster Snowden sold what he had, the bigger the gifts to the basket. And when everything else was sold that basket would be quite full. When Snowden and Martin and Nellie went home, Snowden would stop at the little gray house at the end of the lane.

"Got some leftovers, Mrs. Emery," Snowden would say. "Thought maybe you'd help me out by using them." Then he always added, "Martin was a big help to me today, Mrs. Emery."

Had it not been for Snowden's leftovers, Martin knew that he and Maria and Amanda and Anna would be hungry oftener than they were. Now, if they only had flour and sugar and butter and eggs, Mother wouldn't need to worry.

So on this Saturday Martin tried harder than ever to help Snowden as much as he could. He called:

Squash and beans and 'taters,
at the top of his lungs. Earlier in the season it had been:

Rhubarb and radishes, ripe and red.
Later there would be cabbages and parsnips and turnips, and Snowden would make up new songs for them to call.

"You are good at making up songs," said Martin as the cart rattled along the wide streets.

"And you are good at singing them," replied Snowden. "Words said over and over make a good song."

Words said over and over! That made Martin think of his mother, and the words she made into a prayer. He drew a long, quivering sigh.

"Wars, which put fathers in prison when they are needed at home, are a bad thing," Snowden said. He had been watching Martin closely.

Martin nodded. He swallowed the lump in his throat and called:

Squash and beans and 'taters,
Garden fresh, garden fresh,
Beans and squash and 'taters.

However, his voice didn't sound nearly as cheerful as it usually did. Toward the end of the morning it began trailing after Snowden's like a small echo.

Squash and beans and 'taters,
Snowden would sing.

Beans and 'taters,
would come Martin's echo.

Snowden glanced at Martin several times. It was very hot. Martin looked pale. Snowden made up his mind he would take him to a cool spot, while he went off to buy the groceries which Rosebell needed.

So a little before noon, Snowden turned Nellie about. And when they came to a big parklike place filled with shade trees, Snowden pulled the reins.

"Whoa, Nellie," he said.

"Now, Martin," he went on, "you just stay here in the shade and rest until Nellie and I come back. It's a good place for anyone in a uniform like yours. There's been lots of soldiers on this lawn, I can tell you. I've seen them sleeping here at night sometimes. And all over the place in the day. And I've seen them jump up and stand just as proud and straight when Abraham Lincoln came along."

"Came along here, Snowden? Abraham Lincoln?"

"Of course, Martin. See that building there? That's the Capitol, Martin—our Capitol."

Martin stood on the ground and stared. Snowden and Nellie started to leave. Then

Nellie stopped and flicked her ears. That made Snowden remember something. He reached in his pocket.

"I most forgot," he said. "Rosebell gave me a sandwich for you, Martin. And an apple."

"I have a sandwich." Martin pointed to his pocket. He did not take it out, for he did not want Snowden to see how small and thin that sandwich was. There was no butter on the bread, only a smear of molasses.

"You'd better take this," urged Snowden. "Rosebell made it special."

"Thank you," said Martin, reaching for the thick sandwich and the apple. He would just take a bite or two out of the sandwich and save the rest for Maria and Amanda and Anna. He would save the apple, too, most of it.

When Snowden and Nellie were gone, and when the last sound of Nellie's bell, the jingle of her harness, and the creaking of the cart wheels faded in the distance, Martin wandered about for a little. Then he climbed on a bench. He ate his thin sandwich. He ate a little of Snowden's thick one. It was so good. Half of it was gone before he knew it. He re-wrapped it in the paper Rosebell had put about it, and laid it on the bench. When Martin wasn't looking a fat squirrel slipped up on the bench and grabbed at it. Martin felt the squirrel touch his hand. He jumped. The squirrel jumped. The sandwich fell and landed in a puddle.

Martin could have cried when he saw that. But he didn't. He would save all the apple, he decided, for Maria and Amanda and Anna. He would not take even a bite.

The sun was hot. Martin went over and sat down on the stone steps of the Capitol. The steps were clean and cool. His eyes closed a little as he leaned back, his head resting against the stone at one side.

Then, as always when he was alone and it was still, Martin began thinking about his father. The lump in his throat began to grow.

He heard someone coming down the steps in back of him. But there was plenty of room so Martin didn't move. He just sat there and watched dreamily as a long shadow moved over the step he was on, and went slither-sliding* down the step ahead. And the next. And the next. And the next.

---
slither-sliding: gliding

Then the shadow stopped still and stayed in one place. A voice just in back of Martin said, "Well, well! How's my little soldier?"

Soldier! When his father's friends said that, Martin had always done as his father had taught him, jumped to his feet and saluted. So, forgetting how tired and sad he had been, he sprang to his feet, flinging his head back and his hand up at the same time.

As his fingers touched the visor of his little blue cap, Martin's heart began to thud like a drum. For Abraham Lincoln was standing there looking down at him, his sad face losing its look of worry, and breaking slowly into a smile. Abraham Lincoln, himself!

"What is your name, soldier?" the great man asked, gravely returning the salute.

Martin told him.

"Where were you born, Martin?"

"In Vermont. In a log cabin."

The man nodded. "I was born in a log cabin, too."

"I know, Mother told me. She said some day I might get to be President like you."

"All mothers say that, Martin. What does your father say?"

"I don't know." Martin's voice slowed. "You see, he is away. He used to be a cobbler, but now he is your soldier."

"What regiment? And where is he now?"

The lump in Martin's throat was growing worse. It was difficult to make the words come. "The First Vermont—" he managed.

And then the sobs had him. "He's in Andersonville Prison,"* he jerked.

But the great man was bending over. Strong arms were lifting Martin. In another moment the man had taken Martin's place on the steps. Martin was folded into his lap.

The boy's face was hidden now, in Abraham Lincoln's vest.

Abraham Lincoln just sat there, holding the little boy whose sobbing had been so long kept back. A great hand patted him gently and understandingly between the shoulders. When Martin grew quieter the man began to talk.

"So your father is a cobbler. Is he a good cobbler, Martin?"

Martin nodded his head so hard that his nose went up and down against Abraham Lincoln's ribs.

"Good cobblers are mighty important," said the man. "Never made a pair of shoes myself. But I saw a boy once that needed some mighty bad." The President settled his back a little more comfortably into the corner of the step and the wall.

"It happened when I was postmaster back in Illinois," he went on. "People didn't write many letters in those days, so I carried them in my hat. One cold day as I was going along with the letters in my hat, I saw Ab Trout. He was barefoot as the day he was born and chopping a pile of logs from an old barn that had been torn down. The logs were gnarled* and tough. And Ab's ax kept going slower and slower.

gnarled: knotty

" 'What do you get for this job, Ab?' I asked him.

" 'A dollar.'

" 'What do you aim to do with it?'

" 'Buy a pair of shoes,' he said.

" 'You'll never get one shoe at this rate, Ab,' I told him. 'Better go in and warm yourself and you'll work faster.' So he did. Funniest thing, Martin. When Ab came out, that wood was all chopped! Now, what do you think of that?"

Martin sat up and looked straight at Abraham Lincoln. "I think you chopped that wood," he said.

"Maybe you're right," smiled Lincoln. "After all, folks must help each other."

Martin nodded. "I help my mother all I can," he said. "I fix the rough places when they come in the shoes of Maria and Amanda and Anna. I can do it most as well as Father did. Mother says it helps a lot."

"I am sure it does." The President nodded.

"Vermont is a long way off," he went on. "Tell me, how do you happen to be here, Martin?"

Martin wiped his last tear from his cheek with the handkerchief Mr. Lincoln handed him. He could talk now. He wanted to.

"Father went to war," he began. "He was stationed at a fort near Alexandria. So, after a time he found a house near the fort, and sent for Mother and me and Maria and Amanda and Anna. We came on the train. At first we saw Father often. Then one night when some of the soldiers were sent out to take a railroad bridge, Father was captured. He was sent to prison."

"How does your mother manage to take care of you?" asked Abraham Lincoln.

"Well, it's like you said. Folks help. The soldiers—Father's friends—bring their mending to her. They ask her to cook for them. And sometimes they bring their washing for her to do. They pay as much as they can. The soldiers give us cloth for our clothes, too.

"And Snowden helps. Snowden is my friend. He sells vegetables and I help him call. Snowden fills the basket under the seat with vegetables and calls them leftovers. He gives the basket to Mother. But the vegetables aren't leftovers. Not really."

Martin didn't tell about his mother's prayer for flour and sugar and butter and eggs. He didn't need to. For Abraham Lincoln seemed to know all about that prayer.

"Hmm!" he began. "It seems to me, Martin, that part of this job of helping belongs to the army—your father's army, and mine. I will speak to somebody, and I'm pretty sure there will be food from the army stores every week for your mother. Things that Snowden and the soldiers can't supply, like butter and bacon and other things."

There wasn't any lump in Martin's throat now. He felt wonderful. But for some reason the tears began to pour down his face.

The man pretended not to see. Instead, he raised himself to his feet, and a sudden frown grew deep between his eyes. "It's my shoe, Martin," he explained. "There's a nail sticking right into my foot. And I keep forgetting to have it fixed."

"Oh, wait," cried Martin. "I can help you." He darted off to a pile of stones by the steps. Luckily he found the kind he wanted right away. When he came back Abraham Lincoln sat on the steps with his shoe off, waiting to be helped.

Martin sat down beside him. He slipped one stone inside the great shoe. With the other he pounded hard on the sole.

"My father showed me how," he boasted between pounds. "He is a good cobbler."

Abraham Lincoln smiled. "I'd like to be a cobbler myself, Martin. A good cobbler."

"That's what I am going to be," nodded Martin.

Down the street he could hear the sound of Nellie's bell, the jingle of her harness and the creaking of the wheels on Nellie's cart. But he finished the shoe and gave it to Abraham Lincoln.

The man put on the shoe. He stood up and set the foot, where the nail had been, down carefully. He pressed harder, while Martin watched his face. There was no frown between Abraham Lincoln's eyes.

"It's a good job, Martin," he praised. "It feels just fine." He paused and looked over Martin's head far into the distance. The worry had gone now from the President's face. "You have helped me, Martin," he said, "more than you know!"

Martin said nothing. He only slipped his hand inside Abraham's Lincoln's. They came down the steps together.

They were waiting when Snowden and Nellie arrived.

Snowden's mouth popped wide open. Nellie stopped. She flicked her ears and Snowden swept off his hat.

The man beside Martin lifted his gravely in return. Then he bent and raised Martin high in the air and put him on the seat beside Snowden.

"Good-by, soldier," he said.

Martin saluted. Snowden saluted. Abraham Lincoln saluted. Nellie started toward home.

About the Story

1. What are several acts of generosity illustrated in the story?
2. Which character states the main point of the story and why is that fact important?
3. What does Lincoln mean when he says, "You have helped me, Martin, . . . more than you know"?
4. Why does Martin cry when Lincoln says that the army will bring food every week for the Emerys?

. . . About the Author . . . .

Catherine Coblentz wanted to write from an early age. When she was an eight-year-old, eager reader, she read a book whose writer apparently had forgotten what it was like to be eight years old. Then and there Catherine decided she would remember what it was like to be eight so that she could write for other eight year olds someday. In the summer of her ninth grade year, she became librarian for her small town in Vermont. In high school she became a newspaper reporter for the weekly paper and began her writing career. She built on the storytelling skills she had developed teaching Sunday school, incorporated her love of American history, and began writing for those eight year olds (and others) just as she had promised herself she would.

The Buffalo Dance

Cornelia Meigs

It may seem strange to think that enemies can treat one another with generosity. What generous acts do Neosho and Chanuka show to each other? Are they forced to be generous?

In the cool silence and in the level light of the late afternoon, Chanuka's canoe seemed to be the only moving thing in the wide expanse of marshy lake country. There was so little breeze that the tall reeds stood motionless, knee-deep in the still water. The Indian boy was not hunting today, nor was he watching for any enemy, that he moved so silently. It was only his unwillingness to break that spell of utter quiet that made him guide his light craft so noiselessly across the narrow stretches of open water, over the shallows, where the water grasses brushed softly along the birch-bark bottom and between those tufts of green where rocks, brush, and poplars or pines rose from the water here and there in a myriad* of tiny green islands. Everywhere the tall rushes* stood stiffly erect, so that he could not see, in any direction, more than a few yards beyond the high painted bow of his boat. Yet he moved forward steadily, threading his way without hesitation through that maze of concealing reeds and winding water lanes.

myriad: large number
rushes: grasslike plants

He liked to feel that he was the only human being within twenty, fifty, or perhaps a hundred miles, that he and the fish and the waterfowl had all to themselves this stretch of lake and marsh and river, which lay to the southward of the hunting grounds of his tribe.

Somewhere beyond that watery domain* lay the grassy open country where dwelt the Dakotas,* the unforgotten enemies of his tribe.

domain: region
Dakotas: also called Sioux

The older warriors still talked beside the campfire of the long wars which had raged intermittently* and furiously between nation and nation for a hundred years. Neither tribe could ever call itself actually victorious, but fighting would cease at times from sheer exhaustion on both sides. For some years now there had been uneasy truce with the smoldering hatred ready to break out into fierce flame again at any moment.

---

intermittently: periodically

Once Chanuka had said to one of the old braves, "The Dakotas live on the prairies and hunt the buffalo, and we dwell in the forest and get our meat from the deer and the moose. We do not need to quarrel over hunting grounds. Why should we be always at war with the prairie men?"

To which the scarred and wrinkled fighter had replied, "We hate them; so did our fathers, so will our sons. That is cause enough. And you will understand when you grow older, that when spring comes, then the young warriors are ever restless and eager to be on the warpath. And for us the warpath must always lead southward."

Chanuka could understand the second explanation better than the first; for he knew that stirring of the spirit and the body in the spring, which might lead one anywhere.

Through those last years when there had been no fighting between Ojibway* and Dakota, both sides had avoided this special stretch of lake and swamp which lay between their two domains, so that it had long been left empty even of hunters. Now, moved by that same restlessness, which comes with the bursting loose of ice-imprisoned streams and the stir of life in the vast green wood, Chanuka had turned aside from his hunting to explore this unknown land and these unfamiliar waters. In spite of the knowledge that such journeying was forbidden by his chief, he could not forbear* going farther and farther southward into the empty waste.

Ojibway: also called Chippewa
forbear: hold back from

The last lake through which he had passed was wooded only on three sides, while the grassy prairie swept all the way up to its southern banks. This was proof indeed that he was coming close to the lands of the enemy. But the dense forest was still massed behind and immediately about him, and the sharp hoofprints of deer and the big splayfooted* tracks of moose had trampled the grass and mud of the shores where the wild creatures had come down to the water to drink or to feed on the lily pads.

---

splayfooted: with flat, turned-out feet

A blot of dense green, showing through the pale stems of the rushes, told him finally that he was approaching an island, solid ground in this empty wilderness of ripples and swaying reeds. He came near, dipping his blade easily and lightly, and then suddenly paused, with his paddle half lifted, frozen into an immovable statue of wary listening. He had heard a voice issuing from the dense undergrowth of the island, a voice which muttered, dropped into silence, then fell to muttering again or rose to a curious half-choked cry.

With a motion as soundless as that of a fish's quivering fin, Chanuka paddled nearer, yard by yard, until he was stealing under the drooping boughs of overhanging trees, until he was peering out at a bit of gravel beach and a narrow grassy clearing.

That which he saw first was a canoe, or rather had once been a canoe. It was not a trim birch-bark vessel such as was bearing Chanuka on his voyaging, but the clumsier dugout craft of the sort that the Indians dwelling on the southern rivers fashioned from tree trunks. It was battered and trampled now into hopeless ruin, stamped halfway into the soft ground, with the snapped blade of the paddle lying beside it along with a broken bow and a spilled quiver of arrows. After one long, silent survey Chanuka stepped ashore and walked, without attempt at concealment, across the slope where the turf was plowed and torn by the stamping hoofs of some great animal.

The master of that broken vessel was extended at full length, half hidden below a thicket of brambles. One arm was crumpled under him; the other was flung before his face. Long, lean, and red-skinned, he lay inert* and helpless, muttering and whispering to himself, taking no notice even when Chanuka finally knelt down beside him on the grass. The arm under him was undoubtedly broken; his whole body was bruised and torn with a dozen jagged gashes, while the hot fever of untended wounds was evidently running like fire through his whole being. Chanuka laid his firm brown fingers against that burning skin and nodded.

---

inert: unable to move

"No one but a plains-dwelling Dakota," he

commented within himself, "would know so little as to stand against the charge of a wounded moose."

All up and down upon the grass was written the record of that encounter when the great ugly-tempered beast, wounded and furious, had turned upon the unwary* hunter. Here were wounds of lashing, goring* horns; here was the broken bow from which the arrow had sped too late.

---

unwary: not cautious
goring: piercing

"He thought he was hunting a creature like one of his stupid buffalo," the Ojibway boy reflected in scorn.

The Dakota had evidently followed the animal through the marsh, not knowing that the moment it felt firm ground under its feet the moose would turn upon him in deadly attack. Canoe, weapons, the limp, helpless body under its feet—all alike were objects of the huge beast's blind onslaught.* One final charge had carried it clean over the fallen quarry,* and it had gone, plunging and splashing across the marsh, leaving the silent glade* far behind. The keen eyes of the Indian boy could read plainly the whole tale.

---

onslaught: attack
quarry: prey
glade: open space in a forest

Chanuka's eye glinted with a sudden spark as he stooped over the wounded stranger. He had thought, more than once, as he paddled through the reeds and the rapids, of the black disfavor with which the chief of his village would greet him upon his return. The year before in the same foolhardy curiosity he had journeyed down into the prairies region and on his return had been met with severe reprimand* and punishment as well.

---

reprimand: rebuke; show of disapproval

"If a warrior seeks out the enemy's country, he must not come home empty-handed," the hardfaced old Indian had said, and had set the boy to do squaw's work for the waxing and waning* of the first snow-moon. The memory of that penalty had often burned hotly in Chanuka's heart, but it had not kept him back when the spring unrest set him once more to roving. And this time he would not come home empty-handed; he would bring a captive from the tribe of their foes, a Dakota warrior, helpless in the bottom of his canoe.

waxing and waning: becoming full and then decreasing to the new moon

He stooped and half lifted, half dragged the limp figure out from among the brambles to lie upon the open grass. As he did so the glittering light in his eyes died suddenly. For a long minute he stood frowning down upon that truth which a better view had revealed. Long of limb though the Dakota might be, he was evidently not yet a grown warrior. His age must be much the same as Chanuka's own.

A boy, a boy taken with the same sudden impulse to wander into hostile country for no better reason than that it was forbidden! It would have been glorious triumph to carry home a captured brave. But would the triumph be quite the same, when the captive was a head-long* blundering* lad who had dared the same dangers as himself and had fallen into unexpected misfortune?

head-long: reckless
blundering: clumsy

Hardly admitting, even in his own mind, just what was his final purpose, Chanuka stooped once more and began, as best he could, to tend the other's hurts. Every warrior knew a little of how bleeding wounds would be bound up with leaves and bark. Darkness fell while he was still at work; he kindled a fire, brought from his canoe a wild duck,

which he had shot earlier in the day, and set it to broiling before the coals.

When the savory* fowl was ready he attempted to feed the wounded Dakota, but that burning throat would swallow nothing but water. After the first long cool drought from the bark cup, which Chanuka set to his lips, the long lad's tossing and mumbling eased a little. He kept repeating a single word thereafter, which Chanuka began to understand stood for water—ever more water. In the end, the Ojibway boy forgot to eat and bent all his absorbed effort upon bringing sufficient water, and moving the sufferer from time to time when one position became unbearable and he stirred and struggled feebly to shift to another.

savory: appetizing

The moon rose and stood high above the trees; the dark ripples lapped softly on the shore, and that muttering voice went on and on. There was never a querulous* note of complaint. Even with his mind and spirit wandering somewhere in that land of shadows which borders upon death, the young Dakota's instinct held true. Not once did he cry out with the pain which was consuming him.

querulous: grumbling

All night Chanuka toiled over him. It was only when the moon was dropping and the sky growing white to the eastward that the fever seemed to abate* and the Dakota lay more quietly. When the morning broke over the silent marsh, the two Indian boys lay together upon the grass, side by side, both fast asleep.

abate: decrease

There followed some days of strange comradeship. On the second morning the Dakota tried to stand, but could not; on the third he made determined effort to walk and by the fourth could move about, although but slowly and painfully. His wounds would give him pain for a long time still, and the scars would be with him throughout his life; but the iron strength of an Indian would not yield to weakness and fever for more than the briefest stretch of days.

The two could not talk together; nor did they make any real effort to communicate by that language of signs with which all red men are familiar. That they were enemies, brought together in surprising and accidental truce, was a thing which neither of them seemed able to forget. Yet they caught fish and cooked them together, snared rabbits and ate them in company, and, as on that first night, slept side by side upon the grass.

It was the Dakota who made the only effort at further acquaintance. His name, it seemed, was Neosho. He offered this information and once or twice seemed to be trying, further, to give his rescuer some knowledge of the country in which he dwelt and the life of his people in their buffalo-skin lodges beside the big southward-flowing river. But Chanuka did not offer much attention to what the other was attempting to tell, and after a little the Dakota ceased any efforts at a semblance* of talk. Had not Chanuka, on that foolhardy journey of seven moons ago, seen those same lodges of Neosho's people in the open country near that same river? He had stolen so close, under cover of the darkness, that he had actually lain hidden on one side of a small creek while, upon the flat open ground of the opposite bank, the people of that Dakota village had built their circle of fires and had danced the Buffalo Dance. He could see and hear them still, the red flames, the strangely moving dancers, the chanting voices, and the thumping of the drums coming out of the darkness.

semblance: appearance

The Buffalo Dance celebrates the festival when the Dakota braves have come home from their summer hunting, laden with the meat which is to be their provision* against the winter. Only three dancers take part in it. First comes the warrior who represents the buffalo, wrapped in a brown, hairy robe and bearing the shaggy horned head pulled down over his own like a mask. He crouches and dances forward, tossing the head from side to side, imitating the lumbering gait* of the buffalo. Next comes the horse, a man wrapped in a pony's hide and covering his face with the rude effigy* of the animal's head. He moves it up and down, imitating the jogging motion of a horse loping* along the buffalo trail. Last comes the hunter with his bow and arrows, rehearsing in pantomime* all the adventures of the summer's chase.

provision: supply
gait: movement
effigy: figure
loping: running
pantomime: with bodily movements only

Much as Chanuka would have liked to know more of the Dakotas and their ways, he fought against paying heed to what Neosho was trying to tell him. He would sit beside the fire moody* and brooding,* or would go silently about his work of bringing food and caring for his comrade's wounds. There had been some idea in his mind, at first, of letting the Dakota boy recover somewhat and then of challenging him to mortal combat, as was fitting between enemies. But as he watched the other limping back and forth across the glade, slowly coming again to his former strength, the Ojibway's determination failed. The days passed, and no challenge came.

moody: gloomy
brooding: pondering

Even through their long silences there was something growing up between them. Could it be called friendship between two mortal enemies? One had fallen into dire* misfortune; the other had scorned to take advantage of his helplessness. Does such a thing make friends? Neither would betray by word or sign whether such were possible.

dire: disastrous

It was on the fifth day that they finally parted. The sun was rising red above the marsh when Chanuka signed to the other to take his place in the bow of the bark canoe. Neosho could not have known whether he was to be carried to freedom or back into the forest to fall into the hands of his deadly foes. He cast one glance at his broken bow still lying upon the ground and then with unchallenging face stepped into the light craft which was already lifting to the ripples. Chanuka dipped his paddle and they slipped away through the rushes.

The unseen hand of a slight current bore them away southwestward; carried them at gathering speed through a narrow stream, then out upon the broad silver of a quiet lake. The forest was behind them; from the opposite shore the prairie lands, dotted with groves of trees, stretched away in green and rolling ridges. Chanuka brought the bow of the boat to land, and sat waiting without a word while his companion stepped out upon the grassy bank and strode away up the green rise. As he crossed the shoulder of the ridge, Neosho looked back and raised his hand. Chanuka lifted his paddle. That was the whole of their leave-taking before the Dakota disappeared beyond the grassy summit. The Ojibway pushed off his vessel into deep water, swung the bow, and set himself to paddling steadily northward.

If Chanuka wondered, on his homeward journey, what was to be the end of that forbidden adventure, he wondered still more when he arrived at his journey's end. He had been made to do sharp penance* for that earlier expedition into the plains country, but this time, when he returned after an unexplained absence of eleven days and with nothing to show but a few wild ducks and a string of fish, no word was said. He was conscious that the eyes of the wrinkled old chief followed him as he went to and fro in the village. But if there was to be punishment for his disobeying, it was slow in coming.

penance: punishment

The months of the summer passed with all the braves occupied by the season's hunting. Then the autumn began to draw on. The wild rice was ripening along the edge of the marshes, the swamp maples were turning red, and the dry rustle of the wind in the poplars foretold the coming of the winter tempests.

It was after a long day of hunting in the rice swamps that Chanuka was summoned at evening to the lodge of his chief. The great man sat alone before the smoldering fire and looked at the young brave with hard, narrow

eyes. The moment of reckoning* for that stolen expedition* had come.

reckoning: accounting
expedition: journey

"You, who have a heart so set upon voyages to the southward, are now to take a new journey," the chief said at last.

As a proper brave should, Chanuka waited in silence for the whole substance* of his leader's commands.

whole substance: complete statement

"It may be that the time is coming for us to do battle once more against our agelong enemies, the Dakotas," the other went on. "The signs of sky and forest point to a hard winter; but our hunting has been good, so that our tribe will not have lost strength before the spring. We must discover whether our foes are to fare* as well through the season of the snows. That is to be your task."

fare: get along

He paused, seeming to search the boy's face for any sign of dismay.* Yet Chanuka's countenance* was as unmoved as his own as the chief continued, "You are to seek out the largest village of the Dakotas, which lies in a great grove of walnut trees where one big river forks into three, and you are to go in haste so that you may see their braves come home from the buffalo hunt. If their store of dried meat for the winter is scanty,* they will hunger and weaken when the snows begin and sickness will go from lodge to lodge. And then when spring comes the Ojibway will fall upon them. It is of this matter that you are to bring news, whether the Dakota hunters come home heavily or lightly laden. By the word which you carry we will determine whether there is to be war again, or longer peace."

dismay: alarm or fear
countenance: facial expression
scanty: small

The Buffalo Dance   193

A journey is apt to seem shorter each time it is repeated. Chanuka, traveling over the now familiar waterways, seemed to approach his journey's end more swiftly than either time before. It almost seemed that his paddle lagged,* but brisk autumn winds and streams brimming from autumn rains carried him relentlessly* onward. It was not until he had passed over half the distance that a strange question began to form itself within his mind. Was it possible that he did not wish to go so quickly? Was he a reluctant messenger; had those days upon the island marsh so weakened the resolution* of a proper warrior that he, the first one chosen for the warpath, was going forward unwillingly? The thought stung him as though it were one of the wild black bees who were gathering their final store of honey in the sheets of yellow flowers which bordered all the streams. He dipped his blade and sped southward with all the haste which his paddle could add to the breezes and currents behind him. Yet as he journeyed his face darkened, for, ply* his paddle as he would, he could not seem to leave that haunting* question behind. He did not know that he was offering vain* battle against a natural force far stronger than even the relentless will of an Indian warrior. Wars may last a hundred years, or a thousand; but the spirit of friendship which can grow up between one growing youth and another is older and more powerful than tribal hatreds.

---

lagged: fell behind
relentlessly: persistently
resolution: determination
ply: use diligently
haunting: unforgettable
vain: unsuccessful

He came to that green shore where he had left Neosho, and from there hastened forward on foot until he came in sight of the forks of the big river and saw the Dakota lodges scattered through the grove of walnut trees. From daybreak until evening he lay in hiding on the opposite side of the stream, watching all those who went back and forth among the lodges or came down to the bank for water. At first it was plain that only squaws and children and old men inhabited the place, that all the young and able-bodied braves were still away hunting the buffalo. Chanuka's chief had timed well the sending of his messenger, for the boy had waited only a night and a day before he witnessed the return of the hunters.

They advanced across the plain in a cloud of dust, a long line of laden ponies and weary huntsmen. From the shouts and from the delight with which they were greeted by those who ran out to meet them and escort them to their own lodges, it seemed that the chase had been crowned with success. Of that, however, Chanuka could not be certain until he stole nearer. This it was his plan to do on the night when the Dakotas lit their ceremonial fires on the flat bank just across from him and made ready to dance the Buffalo Dance.

Another warrior, so Chanuka reflected, might be content to watch and spy and carry home his news gathered only by observing from a distance. But he was determined to steal through the whole village, to peer into every lodge, and to carry away, perhaps from the dwelling of the chief, some token of actual proof that he had walked among the very campfires of the enemy. A beaded pouch, a bow, or a carved pipe—something he must surely have to bear away. Had not his chief said that he who seeks out the country of the enemy must not come home empty-handed? The darkness of the chosen night had fallen and the women were preparing the heaps of wood for the circle of fire when he slipped into the river to swim silently across.

He came out dripping, and crouched under the low bank to listen. All the voices and movements were on the flat ground to the right of him, where the whole village seemed to be gathering. He found his way to a break in the slope of the shore and, under the scanty cover of wild blackberries and hickory brush, he crept unnoticed to the very edge of the camp. The lodges stood tenantless* with the embers* of spent fires dying before every door. He peered into one empty dwelling, then another and another. It was even as he had guessed from afar, the stores were plenty; the hunt had been successful. The Dakotas were rich indeed this season with dried meat and buffalo robes; there would be no starving when the winter came.

tenantless: empty
embers: ashes

He had reached the very center of the camp and was looking about him to determine which was the chief's lodge, the most worthy dwelling to be plundered.* It would be easy to bear away anything that he wished, for every living soul, it seemed, was on the open ground beside the river. A sudden tumult of voices almost at his elbow startled him into the knowledge that he was mistaken.

plundered: robbed

From the Medicine Lodge below the biggest walnut tree there came forth a group of laughing, shouting warriors. The dull fire behind them and the light of the stars above showed him that here was the Medicine Man himself, with an escort of young braves, walking down through the lodges, to appear the last of all beside the river and to give the signal for the dance to begin.

The young men spread their line out through the camp, perhaps to see whether every person had gone. There was nothing for Chanuka to do but to give way before them, slipping from one shadow to another, taking advantage of any possible cover, but still being driven steadily down toward that space of light and tumult where the whole village was gathered. In absolute desperation he took refuge at last under the edge of a great pile of firewood.

The shouting warriors passed close beside him. One of them even stopped, seemed to hesitate a moment, and then went on with the others. An old brave came hobbling up to the opposite side of the heap of fuel and gathered an armful to fling upon the fire just kindled not ten yards away. The flare of red light showed the crowding women and children, the warriors in their feathered headdresses, and the fringed branches of the walnut trees moving softly in the rush of hot air. It would be impossible now to slip from that hiding place and reach the river unseen. From time to time more wood was thrown upon the fire, keeping the light ablaze and steadily lessening Chanuka's only cover. The drums thumped under the trees; the Medicine Man's voice rose in slow chant. The dance was about to begin.

Of a sudden Chanuka, tense as a whipcord, felt a touch upon his arm. He started; in the presence of his excitement he might have cried out. Someone was stooping over him, a queer misshapen* figure quite unrecognizable in the firelight. But the voice which spoke Chanuka's name in a whisper was Neosho's.

misshapen: deformed

At such highly wrought* moments minds move quickly, and understanding comes without need of words. Neosho, it seemed, was to take the part of the horse, in the coming dance. Crouching low at the edge of the heap of wood, he wrapped about his former comrade the sheltering garment of horsehide and thrust into his hands the wooden, skin-covered likeness of a horse's head. Already the brave who was to take the part of the buffalo was dancing and stamping his slow way around the circle inside the ring of fires. Every eye was upon that

moving figure with its tossing horns and lashing tail. One round the buffalo was to make alone; then was to be followed by the horse, then by the hunter. So intent were all the spectators about the fires that no one noted the brief pause before the horse came out from the shadows and the second dancer joined the first.

---

wrought: excited

As has been said, Chanuka had seen the dance before, watching from afar across the stream. It was well for him that an Indian's mind is trained to notice and to store up every detail which his eye had once seen. With his heart hammering against his ribs, and with his eyes peering desperately through the holes in the clumsy head, Chanuka set himself to imitate the stamping dance step of the man before him, while he moved the horse's head, up and down, up and down, just as he had seen the dancer, a year ago, imitate the jogging motion of a loping pony. In that breathless moment during which Dakota and Ojibway had changed places, Neosho's quick eye had noted one detail which might have betrayed them both. He had kicked off his beaded moccasins and had pointed to Chanuka's, cut and embroidered* in a different fashion and proclaiming his tribe to any watchful eye. The long-limbed plainsman was larger than the lad of the forest, so that now Chanuka, dancing for his life, found the moccasins awkwardly big as he jerked and shuffled forward in the wake of the

shuffling buffalo. He had circled the ring of flickering red light and now, from a shout behind him, knew that the hunter had joined the other two and that all interest and every glance were centered upon the final dancer alone. Once more they made the circuit, the three together. It seemed to the panting boy wrapped in the heavy horsehide that the round of firelit grass had stretched to the compass of a mile. But at last he saw the buffalo stop, look backward over his shoulder, and then step aside to mingle with the crowd. A few more steps he danced; then, where the spectators had dwindled to a broken line on the rough footing just above the riverbank, the horse also slipped out of the circle and disappeared beyond the curtain of darkness that hung beyond the fire.

---

embroidered: sewn

There was a soft splash in the water, as though a great fish had jumped. It attracted the attention of a single lean young warrior who alone turned to listen and who, presently, edged his way to the brink of the river and there gathered up an abandoned horsehide and the rudely fashioned model of a horse's head. Although he stood silent and hearkening, for long minutes, there was no sound to be heard above the drums, no hint of a wet, supple* figure clambering out of the stream on the opposite bank and setting forth to bear a message northward.

---

supple: limber

It was three days later that Chanuka stood before his chief again and gave the news that the Dakota tribe had had good hunting and that this was no time to prepare for the renewing of war. The other heard him, frowning.

"And how do I know that you really traveled so far, that you speak the truth when you say that you actually peered into the Dakota lodges beside the river?" he asked.

"By these," returned Chanuka briefly. He held up a pair of buffalo-hide moccasins, beaded and ornamented after a pattern never used by an Ojibway.

And from the lodgepole* of a certain dwelling of the Dakotas there swung, at that same moment, a pair of smaller moccasins, embroidered with bright porcupine quills, such as are worn by the forest hunters. For long years they hung there, the silent witness of a friendship of which no word had ever been spoken aloud.

---

lodgepole: center support pole

About the Story

1. How is Chanuka not an average Indian?
2. How do the Indian boys demonstrate generosity?
3. Why is it significant that it is Chanuka who fulfills the old saying that to truly understand a man one must walk a mile in his moccasins?
4. Chanuka is told that he must not return empty-handed from the land of his enemy. Which trip is his most profitable and why?
5. How does Chanuka stand against the peer pressure of his tribe?

About the Author

Cornelia Meigs (1884-1973) began writing children's works at the time when children began to be the focus of writers, librarians, and publishers. But her popularity was not dependent on her being interested in the right thing at the right time. She has been recognized for her considerable skill in writing by receiving the Newbery Medal for *Invincible Louisa,* her biography of Louisa May Alcott, another famous children's writer. She developed her storytelling skills as a teacher and was able to turn those oral skills into written ones. She found, as seen in this selection, that "the American history that [she] was interested in gave [her] endless material for stories."

The Two Strangers

Havilah Babcock

Have you ever found something valuable that someone else has lost? Did you think "Finders keepers, losers weepers," or did you realize that you should return the article? How did you feel about finding the owner? How does Mr. Junes feel in this story? What makes the veteran's generosity special?

"It's been three weeks, hasn't it, Mr. Junes?" After forty years she still called her husband "mister." There are people like that. "Have you made any effort to find the owner? There may be someone in the neighborhood or over at Pittfield—"

"Why, yes—of course. But he's probably not a neighborhood dog. Wouldn't have stayed here so contentedly."

"Not so sure about that!" she chided* gently, laying aside the Grimes Golden apples she had been peeling. "The way you've been pampering the big rascal, and stuffing him with our best crackling bread."

chided: scolded

Mr. Junes didn't answer. His chair tilted against the trunk of a gnarled mulberry, he contemplated the rank and untended fields in the little valley below, over which an Indian-summer haze was now settling, and the knoll beyond, where the hickories were already mellowing under the impact of the first frost.

"Aren't you supposed to put an ad in the paper?" She brought him back to reality. "Doesn't the law require—"

"Yes. Three times in the lost-and-found. I asked the magistrate in Pittfield this morning."

"But you didn't insert the ad?"

"Been sort of busy here lately," he defended lamely.*

lamely: weakly

"Mr. Junes," she said with mock severity, "are you an honest man?"

"Why, certainly. Of course!" He looked up with a start. Odd, he had often reflected, how a good woman could fathom a man's innermost thoughts. "I'll look after it tomorrow. One thing bothers me: if we advertise him, how can we be sure a claimant is the rightful owner? I'd hate to see a fine dog like that—"

"Make any claimant describe his dog before seeing ours," she said practically. "And make him call our dog by a name he will respond to. That way we can tell. By the way, have you hit on his name yet?"

"No. I've tried every name a dog could be called by, especially a bird dog. Can you give me some more to try?"

"Here's another list," she said, reaching into the pocket of her apron.

Henry Junes had spent most of his life enamored of* a dream. Until fourteen he had lived in the country, where he had spent many enchanted afternoons hunting squirrels with his fox terrier and his beloved single-shot .22, which didn't shoot very straight maybe, but if a fellow allowed for its friendly eccentricities . . .

enamored of: in love with

But when he was fourteen his father had died, the farm had been foreclosed, and his mother had moved to the city and found employment as a seamstress. As a boy he had worked at various jobs while going to school, helping his mother eke out* a meager* livelihood for the family. Later he attended night classes at the university and got a job as assistant bookkeeper at a downtown bank, where he saw a lot of money but didn't get much of it. Thirty-five years in one office, over one desk, doing the same thing through endless days.

eke out: make
meager: small

However, don't you go feeling sorry for him, because Mr. Junes was enamored of a dream: he would someday go back to the country and pick up the shining thread of his boyhood days. Nor did hope deferred* make his heart sick. Now, at sixty-six, he had achieved his dream, at least in part. He had acquired a farm, an abandoned homestead in an outlying district where land was not too high, but still a farm. It was not good squirrel country, he soon discovered, but in his rambles* he had walked into populous coveys of bobwhite quail, and the clamor of their takeoff upset him and filled him with a tremulous thrill.

deferred: postponed
rambles: wanderings

He had acquired a beautiful 20-gauge double against this very day; but a dog? He had none, and the kind he wanted would have been hard to come by, even if he had the money. Now, by one of those interpositions* of Providence that, however unaccountable and improbable, do sometimes happen, a dog had come from nowhere and attached himself to the Junes household a few weeks before the hunting season.

interpositions: acts

That he would have to advertise the dog, Mr. Junes had known from the outset, but from day to day he had postponed doing so. Now he felt honor-bound to do it, and somewhat ashamed and surprised at himself for not having done it sooner. Such a fine-looking dog would hardly go unclaimed, he reasoned uneasily. Ultimately he must relinquish him to the rightful owner.

Right was right, he told himself as he drove back from Pittfield the next day, and he felt better for having discharged his legal and moral duty. A vague consciousness of guilt still persisted, however, for the strong are only so strong, and the honest only so honest.

A few days later an advertisement appeared in the lost-and-found column of the Pittfield paper: "Found: one dog. Owner may recover by identifying same and reimbursing* finder." He had compressed the ad into the smallest possible compass,* hoping it would be overlooked. He had no intention, of course, of accepting payment for the dog's keep. That was put in to deter false claimants, he told himself.

reimbursing: repaying the expense of
compass: space

The first day his concern was somewhat abated* when the ad appeared at the bottom of the column. The second day it had moved halfway up but was still inconspicuously buried among sundry* lost-and-founds. But in the third and final issue Mr. Junes fearfully discovered that the ad had been graduated to the top of the column. It brought him a feeling of panic. Surely someone would appear within the very hour to claim the dog. But nobody did, and after a few days his anxiety began to subside.

abated: lessened
sundry: various

It was a week later that a car pulled up in front of the house, a big car bearing an out-of-state license, Mr. Junes absently noted. Under the shade of the friendly old mulberry Mr. Junes had been making apple cider, and his wife was just coming from the orchard with an apronful of purple plums for another kettle of damson preserves. "Mercy me!" she said. "We are such sights! Ask him around to the front door."

But the stranger strode toward them. They noticed that he was tall, that a boyish grin lit up his features, and that one coat sleeve hung limp by his side.

"I hope you folks will forgive my intrusion,"* he said. "I saw you were busy and didn't want to trouble you. What I've come to see you about—apple cider!" he interrupted himself with a delightful whistle. "Good fresh-run apple cider. And don't tell me those are old-fashioned cheese apples you're feeding into that hopper!"

intrusion: coming without invitation

"Yes," answered Mr. Junes, "the old orchard on the place is still bearing. They say nursery houses don't offer cheese apples any more."

"Haven't seen a juicy old cheese since I was knee-high to a grasshopper," he said, sinking his teeth into one picked from the hopper. "For a good drink of that cider, I'd just about swap my buckle and boots!"

There was considerable bustling about as Mrs. Junes funneled the plums from apron to basket, and Mr. Junes, flushed from the pleasant exertion of turning the mill, found a glass and filled it to the brim from the still-flowing wooden trough. From the last sweating turns of the press it had come, the tangiest of the run, the part the yellow jackets* hang around to get ranked up on before the hard "pummings" are fisted out of the wooden tubs. Glass after glass the tall boy zestfully downed.

yellow jackets: wild bees

"Since I've made such a glutton of myself, let me turn the next tubful," he said, shaking off his coat.

Noting the missing arm, Mr. Junes wanted to protest, but didn't know how.

"It's okay. Got to build up the old triceps!" the boy said, making the cleated rollers hum and rock as the fresh-washed apples splattered into the hopper.

Then Mr. Junes shoved the tub of dripping pulp under the press, and just as bubbling rivulets began to cascade* from the slatted wooden tub Mrs. Junes was back with a tray of food for the guest. "Since you had a long drive, I thought maybe—" she said, blushing and uncovering the tray. Mrs. Junes often left sentences unfinished for fear of being thanked.

cascade: flow

An enraptured* grin overspread the boy's features as he inventoried the big tray: crisp potato-yeast rolls melting with butter, a slab of seasoned souse*, a breast of young guinea, a saucer of damson preserves and another of quince marmalade, a bowl of black raspberries already purpling under the rich cream, and a silver pitcher of chilled clabber.

enraptured: delighted
souse: pickled meat

The boy ate with what Mrs. Junes would have described as a "growing appetite," savoring every morsel, letting it linger in his mouth as if it were too good to swallow. "Not since I used to visit my grandmother's have I tasted such food. 'Clabber' was my nickname, and I always hoped it would thunder so the milk would sour. . . ." He stood up and patted his stomach. "If I stayed with you folks long, I'd have a bay window* like a politician!"

bay window: large belly

"How tall are you?" asked Mr. Junes, looking up.

"Six-two, but they say infantrymen get shorter!" he laughed.

"Jim was six-two," said Mr. Junes.

"Six-two and a half," gently corrected Mrs. Junes.

"Jim?"

"Our boy. He was on the *Bunker Hill.*"*

Bunker Hill: an aircraft carrier

"A great crew, the *Bunker Hill*'s," he said soberly. "I'm sure he left you proud memories." And his own mind jerked involuntarily back to a shellhole in New Guinea. But it was not a thing to be dwelled on, and the pensiveness* of his mood soon passed. "Now that I've

about eaten you folks out of house and home, I'll explain why I'm here. The dog. The dog you advertised," he said, withdrawing a clipping from a pocket a bit awkwardly, as if he hadn't yet learned to do two-handed things with one hand.

pensiveness: sad thoughtfulness

"Yes, the dog," repeated Mr. Junes, sinking limply to an upthrust root of the old mulberry. "Of course, the dog."

"Four weeks ago," resumed the boy, "while driving through this county I had a flat tire, and while I was gone for help someone broke into my car and removed my suitcase and my dog. The case I didn't mind, but the dog—That happened about twenty miles away from here, and I spent three days looking for him but without a clue. Then when I saw your ad I hoped, but I admit it was only a hope."

"What kind of a dog was he?" Mr. Junes found himself saying in a leaden* voice, a terrible foreboding in his heart.

leaden: dull

"A big male setter, white and tan, with a tan saddle and a very handsome tan tail. And when he lay down, he had a way of crossing his front feet. I would know him instantly, and of course he would know me."

It was then that hope died in the heart of Mr. Junes. Weakly he got to his feet, his drooping carriage* and gaunt* features for the first time reflecting his sixty-six years. Even when you know a thing is going to happen, you hope it won't.

drooping carriage: posture
gaunt: thin and worn

But he was an honest man and he said: "I wouldn't think of charging you for keeping him. His companionship has more than repaid us. He is your dog, I'm sure, but I wonder if you'd mind calling him by his name and letting him recognize you. He went with a neighbor's boy for the cow and will be coming up through the field about now."

At the edge of the field, near a patch of beggar's-lice, the two men stepped into a bevy* of quail that went whirring away to the alder thicket on the branch.

---

bevy: group

"Did you see that? Did you see that?" said Mr. Junes excitedly. "This is where he found them the other day. At this very spot. There are a good many coveys around, but I don't think I could ever learn to hit them. They scare me so bad. You see, I haven't had a chance to hunt since I was fourteen, and now—"

"Wait," said the boy. "You say the dog found them here a few days ago. How did he behave? Tell me that."

"It was a thing to see!" said Mr. Junes, reliving the drama of the moment. "For the longest time he stood there with head high and tail aloft like a flag. He was a tan-and-white statue in the setting sun, with a soft breeze rippling his coat. It was something, I can tell you. But I'm afraid I couldn't ever learn to hit them. Do you think I could?" he asked eagerly, the words tumbling out. "Reckon I'm too—old?"

"Sure you could learn," answered the boy. "With a good dog and a little practice you could handle them just fine. Sure you could."

Carried away by the intimacy* of the moment and the ineffable* thrill of a big covey rise, the boy was impelled to ask a question of his own. "Do you think I could learn—" But quickly he reconsidered his rashness and turned away, half-ashamed.

---

intimacy: familiarity
ineffable: indescribable

"Here he comes now," announced Mr. Junes as the big setter strode forward. "I'm just about sure he is yours and that he will be glad to see you."

The dog started quickly toward the boy, then stopped and looked indecisively* over his shoulder at Mr. Junes. Standing halfway between the two, he looked from one to the other, a baffled* expression on his face. Then, having resolved whatever problem lay in his mind, he strode unwaveringly to Mr. Junes and licked his hand.

---

indecisively: hesitantly
baffled: confused

"There is a resemblance," said the boy. "A remarkable resemblance. But dogs often look alike. The name alone will tell. Here, Chief! Here, Chief!" he called softly.

The dog's only response was to whimper and jam his big muzzle against the out-stretched hand of Mr. Junes.

"That is not my dog," said the boy. "I hope you will find his right name. Bad luck to change a dog's name."

Back at the house, the boy hurriedly thanked them for their hospitality and was gone. Mr. and Mrs. Junes heard the big car roaring away. "Fine young fellow," said Mr. Junes. "Wonder why he was in such a hurry. When he described the dog, I was sure it was his. Scared me out of six months' growth," he grinned, remembering an expression from his boyhood.

When, after a week, no other claimants had appeared, Mr. Junes' fears were allayed. "Trouble now," he said, "is to find out his name. Just can't name a dog any old thing. I'll make up another list—"

But there was a telegram in his mailbox. It had come from a distant city, he noted, and was unsigned. Half-fearfully his eyes dropped to the body of the message, which was quite short. It said: "TRY TENNESSEE."

About the Story

1. Can you think of any Bible verses that are referred to in this story?
2. Why does Mr. Junes experience a "vague consciousness of guilt" even after he places the ad?
3. Why is the boy interested in the dog's behavior when the covey of quail is flushed?
4. What does the boy want to know if he can learn to do?
5. The author sets up a contrast between the boy and Mr. Junes. Which one of the characters does the author want the reader to approve of?

. . . About the Author

Havilah Babcock (1898-1964) had an outstanding career in education serving as a high school principal, a university professor, and the head of the University of South Carolina English department as well as being well known as a writer of outdoor tales such as this one. In fact, Babcock published at least one hundred seventy-five of these tales and even had one collection published in Braille by the Library of Congress. His stories have found worldwide appeal, being translated into several foreign languages—Dutch, Japanese, and Spanish. As might be expected, Babcock was also active in wildlife societies and the Izaak Walton League of America, named for an outdoorsman of the seventeenth century.

Most Valuable Player

W. H. Heath

On successful teams the players put the team first and themselves second. What does it cost Pete Stallings to put his team first? Does he receive anything in return?

The coach was talking. We were all dressed and ready, sitting around the locker room. Through the window above Billy Foxx's head I could see a square of blue sky, and I could hear the crowd noises and the sound of punting, which meant the Baxter team was already on the field.

"Remember," the coach was saying, "football is only a game. It's not a life-and-death matter, and I don't expect anybody to go out there and kill himself for Morgan High School. All I expect is for each of you to play the best you can, and keep it clean. You've heard me say before that it's not the game—it's the way you play it. That still goes."

"Now, these fellows from Baxter are big and they're fast. They haven't dropped a game this season. But remember this: when they're hit hard—and hit clean—they go down just the same as anybody else. We can take them if you boys play the kind of ball I know you can play."

Our coach's name is Chip Stallings. He's a gray-haired man of forty-five, but in his day he was quite a football player. He was an All-America halfback at Virginia—the first of

the climax runners, they called him. If you follow football you know what a climax runner is: he's the guy they feed the ball to in the clutch; he's the guy that can do magic when the biggest fullback on earth can't make a nickel. Breakaway runners, they sometimes call them.

But while I was sitting there in the locker room listening to him talk, I was thinking of how one November afternoon twenty-seven years ago he sat in this same dressing room and heard another coach say the same things he was saying now. You see, Chip Stallings wasn't only an All-American at Virginia; he was also the greatest player Morgan High ever had. This was his own team. He played his last high school game against Baxter—just as I was about to do—and after that game they voted him Most Valuable Player. They gave him a gold cup, which still stands on the mantel in his living room. I know, because Chip Stallings is my father.

The noises coming through the open window got louder. Somebody was thumping on a drum, cowbells were clanking, and now and then there'd be a ragged* cheer—girls' voices mostly, it seemed.

ragged: uneven

I thought of Patsy Lloyd out there, leading cheers, and I felt awful. But Patsy was just *one* of the things that had gone wrong for me in the past month and a half. My luck had turned sour in a big way; and now, at game time, troubles seemed to be piled up to where I couldn't see over them. "Stay relaxed," Dad told us. I was about as relaxed as a steel trap.*

relaxed as a steel trap: very tense

"Pete!" It was Dad talking straight at me this time. "Pay attention to what I'm saying."

"Yes, sir," I said. "Sorry, Coach." Where football was concerned he was the coach, not my father.

He had dragged a blackboard out in front of us, and now in big thick letters he wrote: PASS 22—PITCHOUT 22. I knew what he was going to say.

"This is our ace in the hole, fellows. This is the combo that will beat Baxter, if we can hold them till the fourth. We'll save it for late in the game because it probably will work only once, and it's got to pay off in points when we do use it. As you all should know by now, this one is an option. Both ways it begins the same: Marx going shallow, Jones deep, and Foxx in motion. Pete, when you take the ball from center you can either throw to Jones or pitchout to Foxx, whichever looks best. That will depend on how their defense shapes up. It's my opinion that the pitchout to Foxx is your best bet, but you're the quarterback, so it'll be up to you. Just use your head." He looked square at me when he said that, because he knew what I was thinking—about Foxx.

"Remember," he went on, "you don't have to decide what to do with the ball until the play is actually in motion. I want you to look,

decide what's best, and then do it, quick. That clear?"

"Yes, sir," I said.

He pushed the blackboard away, dusted the chalk off his hands, and grinned at us. "All right, gang. Let's go get 'em."

We trotted out through the doorway, cleats clattering on the concrete. As we went through the gate and onto the field a tremendous roar went up from the bleachers, everyone yelling for Billy Foxx.

Sure, I thought, cheer for Foxx, you nit-wits. Forget about the rest of the team. Cheer for the great glamour boy.

I don't mind saying that Billy Foxx stood pretty near the bottom of my list, and for more reasons than one. And it all went back to Dad and the gold cup on our mantel.

Dad loves football the way some men love horses or airplanes or playing golf. It's been an obsession* with him all his life. And so it was only natural, when I was born, that he started right in to make me the same kind of player he'd been. As things turned out, I'm an only child; and I've heard Mom say that if I'd been a girl, she believed Dad would have jumped right out of the hospital window the day I arrived. As a baby, the first toy I ever had to play with was the little gold football on Dad's watch chain.

obsession: irresistible desire

Maybe you're wondering why Dad was just a high school coach, instead of with some big college. I asked him about it myself one time. "What I like most about football is the spirit of it, Pete," he said. "High school ball has ten times the spirit college ball has. Why, I'm prouder of that gold cup they gave me at Morgan than I am of making All-American." And that was a fact.

Anyway, Dad started right in to make me a great player like himself. All through grade school he worked with me. He taught me to pass, to kick, and to run; year after year he kept working with me, but never pushing me too hard, just easing me along, polishing the rough spots. Many a time, after we had worked out in the back yard, we'd go into the house and Dad would point to the gold cup on the mantel and say, "Pete, one of these days you'll get a cup of your own to set up there beside mine. It'll say: *Peter Stallings—Most Valuable Player.* And I'll be mighty proud."

My sophomore year in high school, I went out for the varsity, and I made the team at quarter. I was pretty light that year, and pretty young, but Dad had begun to use the T a lot, and he said I was just the ball handler he needed. To tell the truth, I don't think I was much good, though I did manage to throw a couple of touchdown passes before the season was over. But I'll never forget the first game that year. We played Fairbanks High, and they beat us—on a fumble that was my fault. But when that game was over, Dad acted like I was a hero. "You played fine, Pete," he told me. "Everybody fumbles now and then, so don't let that worry you. You played hard and clean, and that's the main thing."

The next year I had gained twelve pounds. Dad shifted me to left half so I would have the ball more, and for three games I was the hottest thing you ever saw. I couldn't do anything wrong, and if I threw a pass with my eyes shut it fell right in somebody's face for a score. I was lucky. For a while it looked as though I was going to set that gold cup on the mantel a year ahead of schedule.

But then a bad break came. I turned my ankle in dummy* scrimmage and I was out for the rest of the season. A fellow named Steve Wallace won the cup that year, with Dad casting the deciding vote.

---

dummy: imitation

That brings us to this year. And, brother, if I thought my luck went rotten last year, I had a book to learn.

To begin with, I was still gaining weight. The ankle was all right, but I was up to 170. That isn't too much weight for some fellows to carry, but for me it was; it had slowed me down plenty. And I couldn't seem to shed a pound no matter how hard I worked.

But my real headache wasn't the added weight. It was a fellow named Billy Foxx, who had moved to town that summer. Foxx was a tall, slender, blond-haired guy who had never played football in his life, and he took a liking to me. "Lend me a hand, Pete," he said. "I think I'd like to play too. You could teach me enough so I could go out for the squad."

I taught him. Good old bighearted Pete Stallings. I taught him way too much. He not only made the squad; he made the line-up at right half.

Billy Foxx had a talent—I won't deny that. He wasn't too hot on defense, because he was a soft tackler; but he was shifty and he was fast, and he had the best instinctive judgment of any broken-field runner* I ever saw. Most of all, the crowd loved him—he had flash. If I made seven yards, the crowd cheered; if Billy Foxx made seven, they went wild. He made it *look* good, don't ask me how. . . .

---

broken-field runner: one who has broken through the
  defensive line

We lost our first game 28 to 21. Billy Foxx made all three of our touchdowns, and he made them from *beyond* the thirty-yard stripe. I piled up more yardage than he did during the game, but his paid off. He made a sixty-yard punt return (he went over standing up); a forty-five-yard pass interception (he ran through the entire team); and a forty-two-yard off-tackle waltz that sent the crowd into hysterics.*

---

hysterics: uncontrollable emotion

We won our next three games without any trouble, and at the end of the fourth, Billy Foxx had piled up more points than yards, I'll bet. He was stealing my thunder, but good, and that gold cup was getting harder and harder to see on my mantel.

How was Dad taking all this? He was taking it hard. But Dad was above all a square shooter, and when Foxx started showing up good, Dad gave him the breaks. He was going to do the right thing by the team no matter what. Pretty soon he was hatching new plays that featured Foxx. And he had stopped talking to me about the Most Valuable Player award.

Then, after the Bridgeport game, the real crusher came. Dad and I were walking home from practice one afternoon and he said to me, "Pete, I'm going to shift you back to quarter and give the left-half spot to Billy Foxx. He's faster than you, and I think he ought to be there."

It was like getting a blow on the head, but somehow I felt sorrier for Dad than for myself. *I* knew that *he* knew what this meant: I was out of the running for the gold cup now. Billy Foxx was in. But that was Dad for you—he was determined to be fair.

Well, we won two more games before this one with Baxter High—me at quarter now, like the fourth horse in a three-horse race. I worked hard on my passing—that's about all a lead-footed T quarterback can do—and I was connecting occasionally for some nice yardage. But judging from the crowd, Morgan fielded only one player a game: Billy Foxx. "Foxx the Fox," the newspapers called him. I got to where I could hear that in my sleep. Oh, he was quite the boy all right, and you could tell he was plenty proud of himself. I began to despise* the guy. When I thought of how I'd helped him along, and how he'd elbowed me out, I went green around the gills.

---

despise: dislike intensely

And then there was the business about Patsy Lloyd. This may seem silly, but I was crazy about Pat, and until Billy Foxx came along she and I went steady. But one afternoon—just four days before this Baxter game, in fact—I caught her walking home from school with Foxx. I got mad clear through, and that night I dropped around to her house and picked a fight.

"How are things with you and Foxx?" I said, as if I was asking about the weather.

"What do you mean?" she said.

"I mean, I see him walking home with you practically every afternoon, and I figured maybe you two had got up a hot case together."

She looked at me for a long time before she said anything. We were sitting in the swing on her front porch, and her mother was sitting by the parlor window, probably trying to hear what we said. "Well," Pat said finally, "I guess it's true after all."

"What's true after all?"

"What everyone's saying about you. How you're so jealous of Billy Foxx you can't see straight any more."

"The prima donna,"* I said. "The All-American of Morgan High."

---

prima donna: lit. first lady (of an opera)

"Billy's a good player, and you know it. He's one of the best players Morgan ever had, and there's no reason for you to act the way you're acting."

"Look," I said—I had completely lost my temper by now—"if you love this guy so much, why don't you wear his class ring instead of mine?"

She looked at me a minute longer, and then she said, "Maybe I will." She took the ring off and gave it to me and went into the house.

And that was where things stood when we lined up for the kickoff against Baxter High— the biggest game of the year and my last game for Morgan. I'd lost my girl, lost my chance at the gold cup, and, worst of all, I'd let my dad down. That was the part that hurt more than anything else: Dad had so wanted me to take that cup.

Baxter High won the toss and elected to kick. They had a big tackle that did their

kickoffs for them, and he put the ball in the end zone. Chuck Simmons, our right half, took it and managed to get back to the twenty, though I don't know how. Dad had told us these boys were big and fast, but that was an understatement. They got down there before the ball, practically, and when they hemmed old Chuck in and started to nail him down, you could have heard the pads popping in the next county. He was lucky to get up.

First play from scrimmage, I gave the ball to Foxx on a split buck and he lost a yard. Then I gave it to Horton, our fullback, and he lost two yards. I dropped back and punted on third down.

Exactly four plays later, Baxter High had scored seven points. It was so fast I don't even remember how they did it.

A big hush fell over the crowd. When we lined up for the second kickoff, I took a look toward the bench. Dad was sitting there as cool as a cucumber.

This time the kick fell to me, and I was none too anxious to get it. I ran it out to the twenty-four. Then, first play from scrimmage, I passed to Jones, connected, and we moved up to the thirty-three. Then I carried it myself on a quarterback sneak for two, which gave us a first down on the thirty-five. The crowd gave a cautious cheer.

Horton again failed to gain, and on second down I called for an end run, with Foxx carrying.

Foxx lost seven yards and came within an ace of fumbling.

I called another pass, throwing to Marx this time, and connecting, and that brought us back to where we had started the series. But it was fourth down and I had to punt again.

This time we managed to stop them, but not before they had worked it down to the ten. They had an end run, these boys, that was pure murder. It started like an off-tackle, then suddenly they'd all break wide and come thundering around poor old Jones like a herd of elephants. The halfbacks were having to make every tackle.

But we did stop them at the ten. I tried Simmons and Foxx, and they both failed to gain. So I punted again. I was kicking the socks off that ball.

On the next play Sam Barnes, our left guard and team captain, went out of the game with a broken rib. But he had got it in a nice way: he had recovered a Baxter fumble on their thirty-five. This looked like a break. I called for Foxx to carry over right tackle.

Foxx lost two yards.

By now a little idea had sneaked into my head. Billy Foxx, the great star, the great glamour boy, had yet to make his first yard. This Baxter crew had his number. They were laying for him, watching him like a hawk. They were playing every down for Billy Foxx. So what did I do? I called a fake spinner and threw a long one down the side to Bert Jones. He went over standing up.

We lined up as if to kick the point, but instead of kicking I passed to Jones again and the point was good. The score: 7 and 7. I had thrown four passes so far and hit my receiver every time. I had scored a touchdown and an extra point with nothing but my good right arm.

At the end of the quarter a big cheer went up. "Stallings!" they yelled. "Hurrah for Pete Stallings!" It sounded mighty good. The second quarter didn't amount to much. We slugged it out around the fifty, and I held off on the passing—didn't want to push my luck. At half time Dad was beginning to look nervous. "You boys are playing a whale of a game," was about all he said. Billy Foxx sat in the corner with his head down.

But in the third quarter they got away from us again. They camped inside our twenty and finally, just before the horn, their fullback punched it over from about the four. They kicked the point and went out front, 14 to 7. It looked like a mighty big lead, because we'd crossed their thirty only once all afternoon.

The third quarter ended 14 to 7.

The fourth quarter went slow for a while, and I decided if I was going to pass any more I'd better get started. I threw one to Simmons on the first down, and he got past their left half and down to the thirty-two. That was five completions for me without a miss.

On the next play I gave to Foxx and he got loose for the first time that afternoon. He went over with two men hanging on his belt. Naturally, the crowd went wild.

And that's where I made my first mistake. Instead of kicking, I decided to pass for the point—and it was batted down. A tremendous groan went up from the stands, as if I had tossed the game away all by myself. We wouldn't even have been in that game if it hadn't been for my passing, but did the crowd see it that way? Not on your life. I even heard a few people yelling, "Take him out." I was sick and mad and more disappointed than I have ever been in my life.

The game rocked on toward the last two or three minutes with us trailing, 13 to 14. Then the Baxter team got its steam roller working again and went down to our five. But we stopped them there—stopped them with plain old guts, because that was about all we had left. I thought it over and decided there was no sense in kicking out, because the game was already as good as lost. I called for an old forgotten play, with Horton carrying around right end, and . . . old Horton [shook] loose and stagger[ed] all the way out to the fifty. He'd have gone all the way if he'd had the strength to put one foot in front of the other. But he didn't. The Baxter safety man came over and blew his breath on him, and old

Horton folded like somebody had hit him with a broadax.* He was just plain worn out.

---

broadax: battle-ax

Well, this was the break. We still had time to score, if there was anybody left with the strength to run that last fifty, and that late in the game a single tally—whether we made the point or not—would probably put the game on ice. Baxter was just as sore and tired as we were.

I knew that now was the time for the option play Dad had mentioned, that ace in the hole that we hadn't yet had a chance to use. I took a look toward the bench and saw Dad walking back and forth like a caged lion, his overcoat flapping behind him. "The pitchout to Foxx is your best bet," he'd said. But was it? I wondered. Foxx had got loose only once all afternoon, whereas I'd completed every pass I'd thrown but one. If I could toss in the winning score, I felt pretty sure I'd win the cup Dad wanted me to have. It was a decision I hated to make, and I hoped Dad would send in a sub with orders on how to play it, but he didn't. He was leaving it up to me.

In the huddle I looked around at the gang, and they were a sorry sight: beat, bruised, dirty, and sweaty. Jones had a bloody nose and Oscar Sims had one eye swollen nearly shut. "You want to go out, Sims?" I said. He shook his head; this was his last one for Morgan High too.

Then I looked at Foxx. I knew what he was thinking. He wanted that ball worse than anything else in the world. He wanted just one more crack at it, and it was written all over his face. But he didn't ask. If he had, I'd have turned him down. But that was the trouble: he didn't ask. He just stood there, stooping over with his hands on his knees, staring at the ground.

"Pass twenty-two—pitchout twenty-two," I said. "And let's hustle, fellows. This may be the last play of the game."

When we lined up, I honestly didn't know whether I was going to risk another pass to Jones or pitchout to Foxx. As I called off the signals, Foxx stepped out and trotted toward the right end. It was so quiet in the stadium you could have heard an empty popcorn bag fall. I had the feeling that everyone was on his feet, watching me.

". . . thirty-three, twenty-seven, twenty-two, *hike*!"

The instant the ball touched my hands I knew what I was going to do. Foxx dug in and whirled, coming behind me like a shot out of a gun. I faked to Horton, then stood straight up and spotted Jones, way down there, running for all he was worth. I cocked my arm and threw. But I didn't let go the ball. Instead I brought it on around and fired it underhand to Foxx. I'd had a hunch he could do it, and he did.

I didn't actually see him cross the goal line, because by that time I was lying flat on my back with a two hundred-pound Baxter guard on top of me. The last thing I saw was Jones mowing down their safety while Foxx did a little magic through the secondary. Then the thunder broke loose in the stands, and I craned* my neck around to see Patsy Lloyd out there in front of the rooting section, jumping up and down.

---

craned: stretched

The game ended 19 to 14, our favor. "Foxx!" they screamed. "Hurrah for Billy Foxx!"

I showered and got dressed as fast as I could, keeping out of sight of Dad. When I went out through the gym I stopped at the table where the team manager was passing out little strips of paper. I voted for Billy Foxx— Most Valuable Player—and dropped my ballot in the slot. The banquet was to be held that night.

Somehow I got home before Mom and Dad did, so I went on up to my room and sat down in the dark. I don't really know how I felt. I didn't feel good, that's for sure—but I didn't exactly feel bad, either. I guess I just didn't feel anything. I was tired, numb.

After a while I heard them come in, and pretty soon Mom came up to my room. She switched on the light and smiled at me. "You played a fine game, Peter," she said. "We're proud of you."

"Thanks, Mom."

"Say," she said, "you should be getting dressed for the banquet. Mustn't keep Patsy waiting."

"Patsy isn't going with me," I said.

"Really?" She tried to act surprised. "Her mother said she was going with you—that is, her mother said if she went at all, she was going with you."

I looked up and I couldn't keep from grinning. "Is that some sort of message, sent by way of women?"

Mom smiled. "I think so. You'd better run down and call her right away. I understand she's pretty upset."

I ran downstairs to call Pat, but when I got to the foot of the stairs I saw Dad sitting at his desk, counting the ballots for the award they were going to give Billy Foxx that night.

When he saw me he got up and put out his hand. "Fine game, Pete," he said, grinning from ear to ear. "Best game you ever played, Son. I'm proud of you."

"Thanks, Dad," I said, trying to smile. "By the way, who—who wins the cup?"

"Billy Foxx," he said.

I was expecting that, but still it came hard. Suddenly I was sore about it. "Tell me something, Dad," I said. "Do you really think he played better than I did today? Do you really think he's a better man out there than I am?"

Dad frowned a little. . . . "Let's put it this way," he said. "Billy is a more stylish player than you are, Pete. He has a great love of the game and a terrific ability to come through when it counts most. *Someday* he'll be a much finer player than you. Someday Billy Foxx will be great. Another thing you've got to realize, Pete: Billy's the kind of player the crowd loves to watch. He's a climax runner; he gives them thrills, and after all, that's what they pay their money for."

"I see," I said. "I really don't care so much—it's just you, Dad. I know how you wanted for me to win the cup, and that's what hurts most, disappointing you."

"I'm not disappointed, Pete," he said. "As a matter of fact, I couldn't be prouder of you or I'd bust. You played the very best game you could, and when the time came, you made an unselfish decision. That was the main thing that worried me. For a while, after Billy came along, I thought you were going to be a poor loser. Now I know you're not."

Suddenly I felt a lot better. I felt like somebody had lifted a ten-ton load off my back. "Tell me something, Dad," I said. "Just how many votes did I get?"

"You got only two votes, Pete. Two out of twenty-nine. You got Billy Foxx's vote—and you got mine."

When I left the house that night to pick up Pat, I felt better than if I *had* won that cup.

About the Story

1. Who other than Pete puts the team first and himself last?
2. Whom do you think the title refers to?
3. Does Coach really believe that it is the way the game is played that is most important?
4. What, if anything, does Pete get instead of the trophy?

. . . About the Author

William Heath was born in Arkansas and grew up in Alabama. His literary endeavors began during his senior year of college, when he wrote stories for his school magazine and sold his first story to *Collier's*. Mr. Heath enjoys sports and music and has traveled a great deal. In his writing he has "tried to avoid the flashy, . . . writing that seems . . . to spoil so many books" and has worked for "an aura of honesty," believing that the author's primary responsibility is to tell the truth.

The Last Leaf

O. Henry

Generosity requires a willingness to give what you have. Are there different types of generosity portrayed in this O. Henry story? Does Behrman ever achieve his goal of painting a great work of art?

In a little district west of Washington Square* the streets have run crazy and broken themselves into small strips called "places." The "places" make strange angles and curves. One street crosses itself a time or two. An artist once discovered a valuable possibility in this street. Suppose a collector with a bill for paints, paper, and canvas should in traversing* this route suddenly meet himself coming back, without a cent having been paid on account!

Washington Square: a famous park in New York City
traversing: covering

So, to quaint* old Greenwich Village the art people soon came prowling, hunting for north windows and eighteenth-century gables and Dutch attics and low rents. Then they imported some pewter mugs and a chafing dish* or two from Sixth Avenue, and became a "colony."

quaint: old-fashioned
chafing dish: a dish set above a heating device

At the top of a squatty, three-story brick Sue and Johnsy had their studio. "Johnsy" was familiar for Joanna. One was from Maine; the other from California. They had met at the table d'hôte of an Eighth Street "Delmonico's,"* and found their tastes in art, chicory salad, and bishop sleeves* so congenial that the joint studio resulted.

table d'hôte . . . Delmonico's: a meal offered at a fixed price at a lower-priced version of the famous restaurant in New York
bishop sleeves: full, gathered sleeves of a woman's dress

That was in May. In November a cold, unseen stranger, whom the doctors called Pneumonia, stalked about the colony, touching one here and there with his icy fingers. Over on the east side this ravager* strode boldly, smiting his victims by scores,* but his feet trod slowly through the maze* of the narrow and moss-grown "places."

ravager: destroyer
scores: large numbers
maze: confused tangle

Mr. Pneumonia was not what you would call a chivalric* old gentleman. A mite of a little woman with blood thinned by California zephyrs* was hardly fair game for the red-fisted, short-breathed old duffer.* But Johnsy he smote; and she lay, scarcely moving, on her painted iron bedstead looking through the small Dutch windowpanes at the blank side of the next brick house.

chivalric: courteous
zephyrs: winds
duffer: slang: peddler

One morning the busy doctor invited Sue into the hallway with a shaggy, gray eyebrow.

"She has one chance in—let us say, ten," he said, as he shook down the mercury in his clinical thermometer. "And that chance is for her to want to live. This way people have of lining-up on the side of the undertaker makes the entire pharmacopoeia* look silly. Your little lady has made up her mind that she's not going to get well. Has she anything on her mind?"

pharmacopoeia: supply of medicine

"She—she wanted to paint the Bay of Naples someday," said Sue.

"Paint?—bosh! Has she anything on her mind worth thinking about twice—a man, for instance?"

"A man?" said Sue, with a jew's harp twang* in her voice. "Is a man worth—but, no, doctor; there is nothing of the kind."

jew's harp twang: the vibrating sound of this small
  musical instrument

"Well, it is the weakness, then," said the doctor. "I will do all that science, so far as it may filter through my efforts, can accomplish.

But whenever my patient begins to count the carriages in her funeral procession I subtract fifty per cent from the curative* power of medicines. If you will get her to ask one question about the new winter styles in cloak sleeves I will promise you a one-in-five chance for her, instead of one in ten."

curative: curing

After the doctor had gone Sue went into the workroom and cried a Japanese napkin* to a pulp. Then she swaggered* into Johnsy's room with her drawing board, whistling ragtime.*

napkin: handkerchief
swaggered: strutted
ragtime: a style of popular music

Johnsy lay, scarcely making a ripple under the bedclothes, with her face toward the window. Sue stopped whistling, thinking she was asleep.

She arranged her board and began a pen-and-ink drawing to illustrate a magazine story. Young artists must pave their way to Art by drawing pictures for magazine stories that

young authors write to pave their way to Literature.

As Sue was sketching a pair of elegant horseshow riding trousers and a monocle* on the figure of the hero, an Idaho cowboy, she heard a low sound, several times repeated. She went quickly to the bedside.

---

monocle: eyeglass for one eye

Johnsy's eyes were open wide. She was looking out the window and counting—counting backward.

"Twelve," she said, and a little later "eleven"; and then "ten," and "nine"; and then "eight" and "seven," almost together.

Sue looked solicitously* out of the window. What was there to count? There was only a bare, dreary yard to be seen, and the blank side of the brick house twenty feet away. An old, old ivy vine, gnarled and decayed at the roots, climbed half way up the brick wall. The cold breath of autumn had stricken its leaves from the vine until its skeleton branches clung, almost bare, to the crumbling bricks.

---

solicitously: anxiously

"What is it, dear?" asked Sue.

"Six," said Johnsy, in almost a whisper. "They're falling faster now. Three days ago there were almost a hundred. It made my head ache to count them. But now it's easy. There goes another one. There are only five left now."

"Five what, dear? Tell your Sudie."

"Leaves. On the ivy vine. When the last one falls I must go, too. I've known that for three days. Didn't the doctor tell you?"

"Oh, I never heard of such nonsense," complained Sue, with magnificent scorn. "What have old ivy leaves to do with your getting well? And you used to love that vine, so, you naughty girl. Don't be a goosey.* Why, the doctor told me this morning that your chances for getting well real soon were—let's see exactly what he said—he said the chances were ten to one! Why, that's almost as good a chance as we have in New York when we ride on the streetcars or walk past a new building. Try to take some broth now, and let Sudie go back to her drawing, so she can sell the editor man with it, and buy port wine for her sick child, and pork chops for her greedy self."

---

goosey: foolish person

"You needn't get any more wine," said Johnsy, keeping her eyes fixed out the window. "There goes another. No, I don't want any broth. That leaves just four. I want to see the last one fall before it gets dark. Then I'll go, too."

"Johnsy, dear," said Sue, bending over her, "will you promise me to keep your eyes closed, and not look out the window until I am done working? I must hand those drawings in by tomorrow. I need the light, or I would draw the shade down."

"Couldn't you draw in the other room?" asked Johnsy, coldly.

"I'd rather be here by you," said Sue. "Besides, I don't want you to keep looking at those silly ivy leaves."

"Tell me as soon as you have finished," said Johnsy, closing her eyes, and lying white and still as a fallen statue, "because I want to see the last one fall. I'm tired of waiting. I'm tired of thinking. I want to turn loose my hold on everything, and go sailing down, down, just like one of those poor, tired leaves."

"Try to sleep," said Sue. "I must call Behrman up to be model for the old hermit miner. I'll not be gone a minute. Don't try to move 'til I come back."

Old Behrman was a painter who lived on the ground floor beneath them. He was past sixty and had a Michelangelo's Moses beard curling down from the head of a satyr* along

the body of an imp.* Behrman was a failure in art. Forty years he had wielded the brush without getting near enough to touch the hem of his Mistress's* robe.* He had been always about to paint a masterpiece, but had never yet begun it. For several years he had painted nothing except now and then a daub in the line of commerce or advertising. He earned a little by serving as a model to those young artists in the colony who could not pay the price of a professional. He still talked of his coming masterpiece. For the rest he was a fierce little old man, who scoffed* terribly at softness in anyone, and who regarded himself as especial mastiff-in-waiting* to protect the two young artists in the studio above.

satyr: mythological creature of half man and half goat
imp: a small demon (devil)
Mistress's: Art's
robe: cf. Mark 5:24-34
scoffed: mocked
mastiff-in-waiting: watchdog

Sue found Behrman in his dimly lighted den below. In one corner was a blank canvas on an easel that had been waiting there for twenty-five years to receive the first line of the masterpiece. She told him of Johnsy's fancy,

and how she feared she would, indeed, light and fragile as a leaf herself, float away, when her slight hold upon the world grew weaker.

Old Behrman, with his red eyes plainly streaming* shouted his contempt* and derision* for such idiotic* imaginings.

streaming: crying
contempt: scorn
derision: ridicule
idiotic: stupid

"Vass!" he cried. "Is dere people in de world mit der foolishness to die because leafs dey drop off from a . . . vine? I haf not heard of such a thing. No, I will not bose as a model for your fool hermit-dunderhead. Vy do you allow dot silly pusiness to come in der brain of her? Ach, dot poor leetle Miss Yohnsy."

"She is very ill and weak," said Sue, "and the fever has left her mind morbid* and full of strange fancies.* Very well, Mr. Behrman, if you do not care to pose for me, you needn't. But I think you are a horrid old—old flibbertigibbet.*

morbid: psychologically unhealthy
fancies: images; thoughts
flibbertigibbet: silly person

"You are just like a woman!" yelled Behrman. "Who said I will not bose? Go on, I come mit you. For half an hour I haf peen trying to say dot I am ready to bose. Dis is not any blace in which one so goot as Miss Yohnsy shall lie sick. Someday I vill baint a masterpiece, and ye shall all go away. Yes."

Johnsy was sleeping when they went upstairs. Sue pulled the shade down to the window-sill, and motioned Behrman into the other room. In there they peered out the window fearfully at the ivy vine. Then they looked at each other for a moment without speaking. A persistent, cold rain was falling, mingled with snow. Behrman, in his old blue shirt, took his seat as the hermit miner on an upturned kettle for a rock.

When Sue awoke from an hour's sleep the next morning she found Johnsy with dull, wide-open eyes staring at the drawn green shade.

"Put it up; I want to see," she ordered, in a whisper.

Wearily Sue obeyed.

But, lo! after the beating rain and fierce gusts of wind that had endured through the livelong night, there yet stood out against the brick wall one ivy leaf. It was the last on the vine. Still dark green near its stem, but with its serrated* edges tinted with the yellow of dissolution* and decay, it hung bravely from a branch some twenty feet above the ground.

---

serrated: saw-toothed
dissolution: death

"It is the last one," said Johnsy. "I thought it would surely fall during the night. I heard the wind. It will fall today, and I shall die at the same time."

"Dear, dear!" said Sue, leaning her worn face down to the pillow, "think of me, if you won't think of yourself. What would I do?"

But Johnsy did not answer. The lonesomest thing in all the world is a soul when it is making ready to go on its mysterious, far journey. The fancy seemed to possess her more strongly as one by one the ties that bound her to friendship and to earth were loosed.

The day wore away, and even through the twilight they could see the lone ivy leaf clinging to its stem against the wall. And then, with the coming of the night the north wind was again loosed,

while the rain still beat against the windows and pattered down from the low Dutch eaves.

When it was light enough Johnsy, the merciless, commanded that the shade be raised.

The ivy leaf was still there.

Johnsy lay for a long time looking at it. And then she called to Sue, who was stirring her chicken broth over the gas stove.

"I've been a bad girl, Sudie," said Johnsy. "Something has made that last leaf stay there to show me how wicked I was. It is a sin to want to die. You may bring me a little broth now, and some milk with a little port in it, and—no; bring me a hand-mirror first, and then pack some pillows about me, and I will sit up and watch you cook."

An hour later she said:

"Sudie, someday I hope to paint the Bay of Naples."

The doctor came in the afternoon, and Sue had an excuse to go into the hallway as he left.

"Even chances," said the doctor, taking Sue's thin, shaking hand in his. "With good nursing you'll win. And now I must see another case I have downstairs. Behrman, his name is—some kind of artist, I believe. Pneumonia, too. He is an old, weak man, and the attack is acute.* There is no hope for him; but he goes to the hospital today to be made more comfortable."

acute: severe

The next day the doctor said to Sue: "She's out of danger. You've won. Nutrition and care now—that's all."

And that afternoon Sue came to the bed where Johnsy lay, contentedly knitting a very blue and very useless woolen shoulder scarf, and put one arm around her, pillows and all.

"I have something to tell you, white mouse," she said. "Mr. Behrman died of pneumonia today in the hospital. He was ill only two days. The janitor found him on the morning of the first day in his room downstairs helpless with pain. His shoes and clothing were wet through and icy cold. They couldn't imagine where he had been on such a dreadful night. And then they found a lantern, still lighted, and a ladder that had been dragged from its place, and some scattered brushes, and a palette* with green and yellow colors mixed on it, and—look out the window, dear, at the last ivy leaf on the wall. Didn't you wonder why it never fluttered or moved when the wind blew? Ah, darling, it's Behrman's masterpiece—he painted it there the night that the last leaf fell."

palette: board on which an artist mixes his colors

About the Story

1. Does Sue ever change her mind about her question "Is a man worth [thinking about]?"
2. Why is O. Henry's description of pneumonia effective?
3. Why is Mr. Behrman such a likable character?
4. How does the reader know that Johnsy is going to get well?

About the Author

O. Henry, otherwise known as William Sydney Porter (1862-1910), was born in Greensboro, North Carolina; lived in Austin, Texas; fled to Honduras; served time in Columbus, Ohio; and became known as the "prose laureate of Manhattan Island." During his time in Texas as a bank teller for his uncle, Porter was suspected of embezzling funds and skipped town, running all the way to Central America. Returning to the United States because of the severe illness of his wife, Porter was arrested, tried, and convicted. Of flight he was certainly guilty; of embezzlement there is still doubt today. He served three years of his five-year sentence and began writing magazine stories to earn money while in prison. He was deeply ashamed of his prison experience and chose to write under the pseudonym O. Henry.

After his release, Porter continued his productive career, moving to New York and writing about one hundred stories a year. His collection *The Four Million* established his fame and introduced his trademark: the surprise ending or "twist" that makes an O. Henry story such a pleasure to read. Other outstanding O. Henry stories are "The Gift of the Magi" and "The Ransom of Red Chief." Porter's stories, which find valuable lessons in everyday events, have admirable, even heroic, characters who demonstrate his understanding of human nature. Porter's emphasis on plot keeps the reader interested and entertained.

Mary

Katherine Mansfield

What does Kass give her sister besides a "green-plush bracket with a yellow china frog"? Why does she have second thoughts about her generosity? Which is her most generous act?

On poetry afternoons Grandmother let Mary and me wear Mrs. Gardner's white hemstitched pinafores because we had nothing to do with ink or pencil.

Triumphant and feeling unspeakably beautiful, we would fly along the road, swinging our kits* and half chanting, half singing our new piece. I always knew my poetry, but Mary, who was a year and a half older, never knew hers. In fact, lessons of any sort worried her soul and body. She could never distinguish between "m" and "n."

---

kits: bags

"Now, Kass—turmip," she would say, wrinkling her nose, 't-o-u-r-*m*-i-p, isn't it?"

Also in words like "celery" or "gallery" she invariably* said "cerely" and "garrely."

---

invariably: constantly

I was a strong, fat little child who burst my buttons and shot out of my skirts to Grandmother's entire satisfaction, but Mary was a "weed." She had a continual little cough. "Poor old Mary's bark," as Father called it.

Every spare moment of her time seemed to be occupied in journeying with Mother to the pantry and being forced to take something out of a spoon—cod-liver oil, Easton's syrup, malt extract. And though she had her nose held and a piece of barley sugar* after, these sorties,* I am sure, told on her spirits.

---

barley sugar: hard candy
sorties: trips

"I can't bear lessons," she would say woefully. "I'm all tired in my elbows and my feet."

And yet, when she was well she was elfishly* gay and bright—danced like a fairy and sang like a bird. And heroic! She would hold a rooster by the legs while Pat chopped his head off. She loved boys, and played with a fine sense of honor and purity. In fact, I think she loved everybody; and I, who did not, worshiped her. I suffered untold agonies when the girls laughed at her in class, and when she answered wrongly I put up my hand and cried, "Please, Teacher, she means something quite different." Then I would turn to Mary and say, "You meant 'island' and not 'peninsula,' didn't you, dear?"

---

elfishly: mischievously

"Of course," she would say—"how very silly!"

But on poetry afternoons I could be of no help at all. The class was divided into two and ranged on both sides of the room. Two of us drew lots as to which side must begin, and when the first half had each in turn said their piece, they left the room while Teacher and the remaining ones voted for the best reciter. Time and again I was top of my side, and time and again Mary was bottom. To stand before all

those girls and Teacher, knowing my piece, loving it so much that I . . . shivered all over, was joy; but she would stand twisting "Mrs. Gardner's white linen stitched," blundering and finally breaking down ignominiously.* There came a day when we had learned the whole of Thomas Hood's "I remember, I remember," and Teacher offered a prize for the best girl on each side. The prize for our side was a green-plush bracket* with a yellow china frog stuck on it. All the morning these treasures had stood on Teacher's table; all through playtime and the dinner hour we had talked of nothing else. It was agreed that it was bound to fall to me. I saw pictures of myself carrying it home to Grandmother—I saw it hanging on her wall—never doubting for one moment that she would think it the most desirable ornament in life. But as we ran to afternoon school, Mary's memory seemed weaker than ever before, and suddenly she stopped on the road.

ignominiously: shamefully
green-plush bracket: a velvet L-shaped wall fixture

"Kass," she said, "think what a s'rise if I got it after all; I believe Mother would go mad with joy. I know I should. But then—I'm so stupid, I know."

She sighed, and we ran on. Oh, from that moment I longed that the prize might fall to Mary. I said the "piece" to her three times over as we ran up the last hill and across the playground. Sides were chosen. She and I, as our names began with "B," were the first to begin. And alas! that she was older, her turn was before mine.

The first verse went splendidly. I prayed viciously for another miracle.

"Oh please, God, dear, do be nice!—If you won't—"

. . . Mary broke down. I saw her standing there all alone, her pale little freckled face flushed, her mouth quivering, and the thin fingers twisting and twisting at the unfortunate pinafore frill.* She was helped, in a critical condition, to the very end. I saw Teacher's face smiling at me suddenly—the cold, shivering feeling came over me—and then I saw the house and "the little window where the sun came peeping in at morn."

frill: ruffle

When it was over the girls clapped, and the look of pride and love on Mary's face decided me.

"Kass has got it; there's no good trying now," was the spirit on the rest of my side. Finally they left the room. I waited until the moment the door was shut. Then I went over to Teacher and whispered:

"If I've got it, put Mary's name. Don't tell anybody, and don't let the others tell her—oh, *please.*"

I shot out the last word at her, and Teacher looked astounded.

She shook her head at me in a way I could not understand. I ran out and joined the others. They were gathered in the passage, twittering like birds. Only Mary stood apart, clearing her throat and trying to hum a little tune. I knew she would cry if I talked to her, so I paid no attention. I felt I would like to run out of school and never come back again. Trying not to be sorry for what I had done—trying not to think of that heavenly green bracket, which seemed big and beautiful enough now to give Queen Victoria*—and longing for the voting to be over kept me busy. At last the door opened, and we trooped in. Teacher stood by the table. The girls were radiant. I shut my mouth hard and looked down at my slippers.

Queen Victoria: English queen, 1837-1901

"The first prize," said Teacher, "is awarded to Mary Beetham." A great burst of clapping; but above it all I heard Mary's little cry of joy. For a moment I could not look up; but when I did, and saw her walking to the desk, so happy, so confident, so utterly unsuspecting, when I saw her going back to her place with that green-plush bracket in her hands, it needed all my wildest expostulations with* the Deity to keep back my tears. The rest of the afternoon passed like a dream; but when school broke up, Mary was the heroine of the hour. Boys and girls followed her—held the prize in their "own hands"—and all looked at me with pitying contempt, especially those who were in on the secret and knew what I had done.

---

expostulations with: prayers to

On the way home we passed the Karori* bus going home from town full of businessmen. The driver gave us a lift, and we bundled in. We knew all the people.

Karori: city in New Zealand

"I've won a prize for po'try!" cried Mary, in a high, excited voice.

"Good old Mary!" they chorused.

Again she was the center of admiring popularity.

"Well, Kass, you needn't look so doleful,"* said Mr. England, laughing at me, "you aren't clever enough to win everything."

---

doleful: cheerless

"I know," I answered, wishing I were dead and buried.

I did not go into the house when we reached home, but wandered down to the loft and watched Pat mixing the chicken food.

But the bell rang at last, and with slow steps I crept up to the nursery.

Mother and Grandmother were there with two callers. Alice had come up from the kitchen; Vera was sitting with her arms around Mary's neck.

"Well, that's wonderful, Mary," Mother was saying. "Such a lovely prize, too. Now, you see what you really can do, darling."

"That will be nice for you to show your little girls when you grow up," said Grandmother.

Slowly I slipped into my chair.

"Well, Kass, you don't look very pleased," cried one of the tactful* callers.

tactful: tactless

Mother looked at me severely.

"Don't say you are going to be a sulky* child about your sister," she said.

sulky: pouting

Even Mary's bright little face clouded.

"You are glad, aren't you?" she questioned.

"I'm frightfully glad," I said, holding on to the handle of my mug, and seeing all too plainly the glance of understanding that passed between the grownups.

We had the yellow frog for tea, we had the green-plush bracket for the entire evening when Father came home, and even when Mary and I had been sent to bed she sang a little song made out of her own head:

I got a yellow frog for a prize,
An' it had china eyes.

But she tried to fit this to the tune of "Sun of My Soul," which Grandmother thought a little irreverent,* and stopped.

irreverent: disrespectful

Mary's bed was in the opposite corner of the room. I lay with my head pressed into the pillow. Then the tears came. I pulled the clothes over my head. The sacrifice was too great. I stuffed a corner of the sheet into my mouth to stop me from shouting out the truth. Nobody loved me, nobody understood me, and they loved Mary without the frog, and now that she had it I decided they loved me less.

A long time seemed to pass. I got hot and stuffy, and came up to breathe. And the Devil entered my soul. I decided to tell Mary the truth. From that moment I was happy and light again, but I felt savage. I sat up—then got out of bed. The linoleum was very cold. I crossed over to the other corner.

The moon shone through the window straight on to Mary's bed. She lay on her side, one hand against her cheek, soundly sleeping. Her little plait* of hair stood straight up from her head; it was tied with a piece of pink wool. Very white was her small face, and the funny freckles I could see even in this light; she had thrown off half the bedclothes; one button of her nightdress was undone, showing her flannel chest protector.

plait: braid

I stood there for one moment, on one leg, watching her sleep. I looked at the green-plush bracket already hung on the wall above her head, at that perfect yellow frog with china eyes, and then again at Mary, who stirred and flung out one arm across the bed.

Suddenly I stooped and kissed her.

About the Story

1. What does Kass give Mary other than the prize?
2. Why does Kass almost come to regret her generosity?

3. What are Kass's two acts of generosity?
4. Does the fact that Kass struggles with regret about her sacrifice make her less of an admirable character? Why or why not?

. . . About the Author . . . .

The works of Katherine Mansfield (1888-1923) are almost all autobiographical in a way. Growing up near Wellington, New Zealand, she attended the local school, in much the same circumstances as the children of this story. She was a published short story writer by age nine and at age thirteen was sent to London's Queen's College, where she became an accomplished cellist. Although she eventually became a successful writer, her literary career was hampered by her poor health. She often went for months or years without publishing anything.

Mansfield, whose New Zealand stories are considered her best, believed that serious literature is an "imitation into truth." In her stories, which are more concerned with leading the reader into flashes of insight into truth than with plot, Mansfield relies on symbols and atmosphere to communicate the emotions of her characters. Her characters often experience deep disappointment as she did in life and as do all men who seek truth and satisfaction from any source other than God.

Gold-Mounted Guns

F. R. Buckley

"How much better is it to get wisdom than gold!" writes Solomon in Proverbs 16:16. How is "Pecos Tommy's" generosity worth more than money to Will Arblaster?

Evening had fallen on Longhorn City, and already, to the south, an eager star was twinkling in the velvet sky, when a spare, hard-faced man slouched down the main street and selected a pony from the dozen hitched beside Tim Geogehan's general store. The town, which in the daytime suffered from an excess* of eye-searing* light in its open spaces, confined its efforts at artificial lighting to the one store, the one saloon, and its neighbor, the Temple of Chance; so it was from a dusky void* that the hard-faced man heard himself called by name.

excess: overabundance
eye-searing: burning
void: empty space

"Tommy!" a subdued voice accosted* him.

accosted: greeted

The hard-faced man made, it seemed, a very slight movement—a mere flick of the hand at his low-slung belt; but it was a movement perfectly appraised* by the man in the shadows.

appraised: expertly judged

"Wait a minute!" the voice pleaded.

A moment later, his hands upraised, his pony's bridle-reins caught in the crook of one arm, a young man moved into the zone of light that shone bravely out through Tim Geogehan's back window.

"Don't shoot," he said, trying to control his nervousness before the weapon unwaveringly trained upon him. "I'm—a friend."

For perhaps fifteen seconds the newcomer and the hard-faced man examined each other with the unwinking scrutiny* of those who take chances of life and death. The younger, with that lightning draw fresh in his mind, noted the sinister* droop of a gray moustache over a hidden mouth, and shivered a little as his gaze met that of a pair of steel-blue eyes. The man with the gun saw before him a rather handsome face, marred, even in this moment of submission, by a certain desperation.

scrutiny: study
sinister: suggesting trouble

"What do you want?" he asked, tersely.*

tersely: without unnecessary words

"Can I put my hands down?" countered the other.

The lean man considered.

"All things bein' equal," he said, "I think I'd rather you'd first tell me how you got round to callin' me Tommy. Been askin' people in the street?"

"No," said the boy. "I only got into town this afternoon, an' I ain't a fool anyway. I seen you ride in this afternoon, an' of course I knew. Nobody ever had guns like them but Pecos Tommy. I could ha' shot you while you was gettin' your horse, if I'd been that way inclined."

The lean man bit his moustache.

"Put 'em down. What do you want?"

"I want to join you."

"You want to *what*?"

"Yeah, I know it sounds foolish to you, mebbe," said the young man. "But, listen—your side-kicker's* in jail down in Rosewell. I figured I could take his place—anyway, till he got out. I know I ain't got any record, but I can ride, an' I can shoot the pips* out of a tenspot* at ten paces, an'—I got a little job to bring into the firm, to start with."

side-kicker: close friend
pips: spots
tenspot: playing card

The lean man's gaze narrowed.

"Have, eh?" he asked, softly.

"It ain't anythin' like you go in for as a rule," said the boy, apologetically, "but it's a roll of cash an'—I guess it'll show you I'm straight. I only got on to it this afternoon. Kind of providential* I should meet you right now."

providential: fitting

The lean man chewed his moustache. His eyes did not shift.

"Yeah," he said slowly. "What you quittin' punchin'* for?"

punchin': cow punching, i.e., taking care of cattle

"Sick of it."

"Figurin' robbin' trains is easier money?"

"No," said the young man, "I ain't. But I like a little spice in life. They ain't none in punchin'."

"Got a girl?" asked the lean man.

The boy shook his head. The hard-faced man nodded reflectively.

"Well, what's the job?" he asked.

The light from Geogehan's window was cut off by the body of a man who, cupping his hands about his eyes, stared out into the night, as if to locate the buzz of voices at the back of the store.

"If you're goin' to take me on," said the young man, "I can tell you while we're ridin' toward it. If you ain't—why, there's no need to go no further."

The elder slipped back into its holster the gold-mounted gun he had drawn, glanced once at the obscured window and again, piercingly, at the boy whose face now showed white in the light of the rising moon. Then he turned his pony and mounted.

"Come on," he commanded.

Five minutes later the two had passed the limits of the town, heading for the low range of hills which encircled it to the south—and Will Arblaster had given the details of his job to the unemotional man at his side.

"How do you know the old guy's got the money?" came a level question.

"I saw him come out of the bank this afternoon, grinnin' all over his face an' stuffin' it into his pants-pocket," said the boy. "An' when he was gone, I kind of inquired who he was. His name's Sanderson, an' he lives in this yer cabin right ahead a mile. Looked kind of a soft old geezer—kind that'd give up without any trouble. Must ha' been quite some cash there, judgin' by the size of the roll. But I guess when *you* ask him for it, he won't mind lettin' it go."

"I ain't goin' to ask him," said the lean man. "This is your job."

The boy hesitated.

"Well, if I do it right," he asked, with a trace of tremor in his voice, "will you take me along with you sure?"

"Yeah—I'll take you along."

The two ponies rounded a shoulder of the hill: before the riders there loomed, in the moonlight, the dark shape of a cabin, its windows unlighted. The lean man chuckled.

"He's out."

Will Arblaster swung off his horse.

"Maybe," he said, "but likely the money ain't. He started off home, an' if he's had to go out again, likely he's hid the money some

place. Folks know *you're* about. I'm goin' to see."

Stealthily he crept toward the house. The moon went behind a cloud-bank, and the darkness swallowed him. The lean man, sitting his horse, motionless, heard the rap of knuckles on the door—then a pause, and the rattle of the latch. A moment later came the heavy thud of a shoulder against wood—a cracking sound, and a crash as the door went down. The lean man's lips tightened. From within the cabin came the noise of one stumbling over furniture, then the fitful fire of a match illuminated the windows. In the quiet, out there in the night, the man on the horse, twenty yards away, could hear the clumping of the other's boots on the rough board floor, and every rustle of the papers that he fumbled in his search. Another match scratched and sputtered, and then, with a hoarse cry of triumph,

was flung down. Running feet padded across the short grass and Will Arblaster drew up, panting.

"Got it!" he gasped. "The old fool! Put it in a tea-canister right on the mantelshelf. Enough to choke a horse! Feel it!"

The lean man, unemotional as ever, reached down and took the roll of money.

"Got another match?" he asked.

Willie struck one, and, panting, watched while his companion, moistening a thumb, ruffled through the bills.

"Fifty tens," said the lean man. "Five hundred dollars. Guess I'll carry it."

His cold blue eyes turned downward, and focused again with piercing attention on the younger man's upturned face. The bills were stowed in a pocket of the belt right next to one of those gold-mounted guns which, earlier in the evening, had covered Willie Arblaster's heart. For a moment, the lean man's hand seemed to hesitate over its butt; then, as Willie smiled and nodded, it moved away. The match burned out.

"Let's get out of here," the younger urged; whereupon the hand which had hovered over the gun-butt grasped Will Arblaster's shoulder.

"No, not yet," he said quietly, "not just yet. Get on your hawss, an' set still awhile."

The young man mounted. "What's the idea?"

"Why!" said the level voice at his right. "This is a kind of novelty* to me. Robbin' trains, you ain't got any chance to see results, like: this here's different. Figure this old guy'll be back pretty soon. I'd like to see what he does when he finds his wad's gone. Ought to be amusin'!"

---

novelty: new thing

Arblaster chuckled uncertainly.

"Ain't he liable to—"

"He can't see us," said the lean man with a certain new cheerfulness in his tone. "An' besides, he'll think we'd naturally be miles away; an' besides that, we're mounted, all ready."

"What's that?" whispered the young man, laying a hand on his companion's arm.

The other listened.

"Probably him," he said. "Now stay still."

There were two riders—by their voices, a man and a girl: they were laughing as they approached the rear of the house, where, roughly made of old boards, stood Pa Sanderson's substitute for a stable. They put up the horses; then their words came clearer to the ears of the listeners, as they turned the corner of the building, walking toward the front door.

"I feel mean about it, anyhow," said the girl's voice. "You going on living here, Daddy, while—"

"Tut-tut-tut!" said the old man. "What's five hundred to me? I ain't never had that much in a lump, an' shouldn't know what to do with it if I had. 'Sides, your Aunt Elviry didn't give it you for nothin'. 'If she wants to go to college,' says she, 'let her prove it by workin'. I'll pay half, but she's got to pay t'other half.' Well, you worked, an'—Where on earth did I put that key?"

There was a silence, broken by the grunts of the old man as he contorted himself in the search of his pockets: and then the girl spoke: the tone of her voice was the more terrible for the restraint she was putting on it.

"Daddy—the—the—did you leave the money in the house?"

"Yes. What is it?" cried the old man.

"Daddy—the door's broken down, and—"

There was a hoarse cry: boot-heels stumbled across the boards, and again a match flared. Its pale light showed a girl standing in the doorway of the cabin, her hands clasped on her bosom—while beyond the wreckage of

the door a bent figure with silver hair tottered away from the mantelshelf. In one hand Pa Sanderson held the flickering match, in the other a tin box.

"Gone!" he cried in his cracked voice. "Gone!"

Willie Arblaster drew a breath through his teeth and moved uneasily in his saddle. Instantly a lean, strong hand, with a grip like steel, fell on his wrist and grasped it. The man behind the hand chuckled.

"Listen!" he said.

"Daddy—Daddy—don't take on so—please don't," came the girl's voice, itself trembling with repressed* tears. There was a scrape of chair-legs on the floor as she forced the old man into his seat by the fireplace. He hunched there, his face in his hands, while she struck a match and laid the flame to the wick of the lamp on the table. As it burned up she went back to her father, knelt by him, and threw her arms about his neck.

repressed: held in

"Now, now, now!" she pleaded. "Now, Daddy, it's all right. Don't take on so. It's all right."

But he would not be comforted.

"I can't replace it!" cried Pa Sanderson, dropping trembling hands from his face. "It's gone! Two years you've been away from me; two years you've slaved in a store; and now I've—"

"Hush, hush!" the girl begged. "Now, Daddy it's all right. I can go on working, and—"

With a convulsive* effort, the old man got to his feet. "Two years more slavery, while some skunk drinks your money, gambles it—throws it away!" he cried. "Curse him! Whoever it is, curse him! Where's God's justice? What's a man goin' to believe when years of scrapin' like your aunt done, an' years of slavin' like yours in Laredo there, an' all our happiness today can be wiped out by a thief in a minute?"

convulsive: violent and involuntary

The girl put her little hand over her father's mouth.

"Don't, Daddy," she choked. "It only makes it worse. Come and lie down on your bed, and I'll make you some coffee. Don't cry, Daddy darling. Please."

Gently, like a mother with a little child, she led the heartbroken old man out of the watchers' line of vision, out of the circle of lamplight. More faintly, but still with heartrending distinctness, the listeners could hear the sounds of weeping.

The lean man sniffed, chuckled, and pulled his bridle.

"Some circus!" he said appreciatively. "C'mon, boy."

His horse moved a few paces, but Will Arblaster's did not. The lean man turned in his saddle.

"Ain't you comin?" he asked.

For ten seconds, perhaps, the boy made no answer. Then he urged his pony forward until it stood side by side with his companion's.

"No," he said. "An'—an' I ain't goin' to take that money, neither."

"Huh?"

The voice was slow and meditative.

"Don't know as ever I figured what this game meant," he said. "Always seemed to me that all the hardships was on the stick-up man's side—gettin' shot at an' chased and so on. Kind of fun, at that. Never thought 'bout old men cryin'."

"That ain't my fault," said the lean man.

"No," said Will Arblaster, still very slowly. "But I'm goin' to take that money back. You didn't have no trouble gettin' it, so you don't lose nothin'."

"Suppose I say I won't let go of it?" suggested the lean man with a sneer.

"Then," snarled Arblaster, "I'll blow your . . . head off an' take it! Don't you move, you! I've got you covered. I'll take the money out myself."

His revolver muzzle under his companion's nose, he snapped open the pocket of the belt and extracted the roll of bills. Then, regardless of a possible shot in the back, he swung off his horse and shambled,* with the mincing gait* of the born horseman, into the lighted doorway of the cabin. The lean man, unemotional as ever, sat perfectly still, looking alternately at the cloud-dappled* sky and at the cabin, from which now came a murmur of voices harmonizing with a strange effect of joy, to the half-heard bass of the night-wind.

shambled: shuffled
mincing gait: short steps
cloud-dappled: spotted

It was a full ten minutes before Will Arblaster reappeared in the doorway alone, and made, while silhouetted* against the light, a quick movement of his hand across his eyes, then stumbled forward through the darkness toward his horse. Still the lean man did not move.

silhouetted: outlined

"I'm sorry," said the boy as he mounted. "But—"

"I ain't," said the lean man quietly. "What do you think I made you stay an' watch for, you young fool?"

The boy made no reply. Suddenly the hair prickled* on the back of his neck and his jaw fell.

prickled: tingled

"Say," he demanded hoarsely at last. "Ain't you Pecos Tommy?"

The lean man's answer was a short laugh.

"But you got his guns, an' the people in Longhorn all kind of fell back!" the boy cried. "If you ain't him, who are you?"

The moon had drifted from behind a cloud and flung a ray of light across the face of the lean man as he turned it, narrow-eyed, toward Arblaster. The pallid* light picked out with terrible distinctiveness the grim lines of that face—emphasized the cluster of sun-wrinkles about the corners of the piercing eyes and marked as if with underscoring black lines the long sweep of the fighting jaw.

pallid: pale

"Why," said the lean man dryly, "I'm the sheriff that killed him yesterday. Let's be ridin' back."

About the Story

1. What indications are there that Will Arblaster may not be cut out for the life of an outlaw?
2. Why does "Pecos Tommy's" hand hesitate over his gun?

3. How is "Pecos Tommy's" generosity more valuable than gold?
4. What does "Pecos Tommy" mean when he says, "Yeah—I'll take you along"?

About the Author

One might expect Fergus Reid Buckley (b. 1930) to hail from Ireland, and one would be right. However, one might not expect him to have been born in France and educated in England and to have lived much of his life in Spain, working in export, travel, and real estate. One would also not expect him to write so convincingly of the American West. And yet all of these facts are true. After coming to America, he served in the United States Air Force from 1952-54 and became a first lieutenant. He has also written novels, and others of his short stories have been anthologized.

The following three poems present three different views toward giving.

Country Doctor

Robert P. Tristram Coffin

Through rain, through sleet, through ice, through snow,
He went where only God could go,
He drove his old mare out of breath
Between a baby and a death.

He left an old man in the dark   5
And blew up a tiny spark
In a young man two-feet long
To carry on the dead man's song.

Under the midnight thunderheads
When lesser men were in their beds   10
He drove his mare by lantern light
Of chain-lightning splitting night.

When the heat waves troubled eyes
And the locust tuned his thighs,
When the snow erased stonewalls,   15
He was going on his calls.

When the scythe slipped, he was there,
He came in ahead of prayer,
He wrestled death as Jacob strove
With the angel in the grove.   20

He went to the county's ends,
Not for fees, but for friends,
Came like an angel fierce and fast,
He saw men first and saw them last.

He saw men when they were their best,   25
Most merciful and strange, undressed,
When they had monstrous peaks to climb,
When they were having the hardest time.

Our farms so lonely and spaced far
Could never have grown the nation we are   30
But for this man, come sun, come snow,
Who went where God alone could go.

About the Author

Growing up in rural Maine, Robert Coffin (1892-1955) knew well the area of a country doctor's activity. He earned several honors and awards for his work: he was a Rhodes scholar at Oxford and in 1935 won the Pulitzer Prize for poetry. He also ran several farms himself as well as writing and illustrating many of his own works. His writings celebrate the history and attitude that permeated American life in the first half of the twentieth century.

How to Avoid Contact

Lewis Gardner

If you keep your eyes straight ahead
and your forehead tense
and your mouth straight, not frowning, not smiling,
then no one will try to talk to you.

Beware. If you let your eye stray   5
even one quarter of an inch
to watch another walker,
he may smile back—

unless he too knows
and carefully observes these rules.   10

To bums who prepare with appealing looks
to ask for money, turn a brusque* shoulder.   brusque: abrupt and
If someone bumps into you,   ungracious
never say excuse me—nod, with a smirk.*   smirk: all-knowing smile

Above all, avoid the tapping approach   15
of the blind man
and the slump and shuffle* of the old.   shuffle: foot-dragging
They may ask you to help them.   walk

A Poison Tree

William Blake

I was angry with my friend:
I told my wrath, my wrath did end.
I was angry with my foe:
I told it not, my wrath did grow.

And I watered it in fears,　　　　5
Night and morning with my tears;
And I sunned it with smiles,
And with soft deceitful wiles.

And it grew both day and night
Till it bore an apple bright;　　　　10
And my foe beheld it shine,
And he knew that it was mine,

And into my garden stole
When the night had veiled the pole:
In the morning glad I see　　　　15
My foe outstretched beneath the tree.

...Åbout the Author.........

William Blake (1757-1827) was an English poet and painter born in London. His paintings and poems are highly symbolic and often difficult to understand. According to Blake, the trials of life such as war and sorrow are brought about by our faulty and incomplete knowledge of truth. He deplored excessive reliance on scientific inquiry and materialism and urged others to explore realms outside their five senses. Rather than accept God's truth, however, Blake believed that man should learn to trust his imagination and instincts in order to understand reality. Claiming visionary powers, he invented his own system of mythology to explain the universe.

About the Poems

1. What motivates the doctor to continue his job? What details in the poem emphasize the sacrifice of the doctor and the hardships he endures?
2. What is the poet's attitude toward the doctor?
3. What is the meaning of line 2 in Coffin's poem?
4. According to Gardner how should a person who wants to avoid contact pass others he meets on the street? How should he treat the poor and the elderly?
5. Does the poet believe the advice he gives? What point is he trying to make?
6. How is the speaker's anger toward his friend handled in Blake's poem, and what is the outcome? How is the speaker's anger toward his foe handled differently? What is the result?
7. What lesson about anger does this teach us? Look up Matthew 18:15, 21-22. Compare what this passage says to the message of the poem. Do they agree?

The Strangers That Came to Town

Ambrose Flack

What is the Duvitch family able to give their neighbors on Syringa Street? What makes it possible for the Duvitches to offer their gift? Who else in the story performs a generous action?

The first of April was dark and stormy. Silver whips of lightning were cracking open low-hanging clouds. My brother Tom and I were recovering from chest colds. Tired of listening to the radio, we turned to the big living-room window of our house on Syringa Street.

"Here they come, Mother," yelled Tom when a truck drove up in the rain and stopped at the empty cottage across the street.

Mother hurried in from the kitchen, and we three looked out. That truck, we knew, contained the Duvitch family and all their earthly possessions.

All afternoon Mother, Tom, and I had been watching for them with mixed emotions. For the Duvitches had just come over from Europe, and they were the first of the nationality to settle in our town.

A stream of children, accompanied by a big brown dog, poured out of the back of the truck and stood in a huddle in the rain. Mr. Duvitch and the biggest boy carefully helped Mrs. Duvitch from the seat and walked her into the house.

"I wonder if Mrs. Duvitch is ill," murmured Mother.

"She must be," said Tom. "I wonder if it would be all right for Andy and me to help them move in their stuff."

Mother shook her head. It was a strict family rule that any illness which kept us out of school also kept us indoors.

Yet the Duvitches got along very well without help from us. Every child pitched in and helped carry all the boxes and bundles into the house. In no time at all, it seemed, the truck was empty, and the Duvitches were settled in their new home.

That was the signal for Mother to step into the kitchen. She returned carrying a basket containing a roast chicken, steaming hot, a loaf of homemade bread, and a pie. These she took to the house across the street and gave to the boy who answered her knock.

The next day when Mother was fixing lunch, we heard a faint tap at the back door. I answered it, and there, holding Mother's basket, stood a pale, dark-eyed boy in a faded shirt and patched overalls.

In the basket were the empty dishes, all of which shone, and a tiny, very shapely, potted rose tree covered with delicate pinktipped buds. It was a beautiful plant—the first of its kind to be seen in our neighborhood.

"I send them a basket of food," Mother said slowly, deeply touched, "and get this queenly gift."

She stopped to visit the Duvitches a week later. But the boy who opened the door said, "Mamma sick. She stay in bed today."

Mrs. Duvitch never came to visit us, so Mother made no further attempts to see the family. But Father disagreed when she said that she thought the Duvitches wanted their Syringa Street neighbors to leave them alone.

Syringa Street seemed to be a friendly street, but from the start the Duvitches were marked* people. They were the one poor, struggling family in the midst of a prosperous* community. It didn't take people long to start talking about how different they were.

---

marked: noticeably different
prosperous: well-to-do

At school everyone made fun of the thick black-bread sandwiches the Duvitch boys ate for lunch. And the girls stared and pointed at their boiled-out, ragpickers'* clothes, obviously salvaged* from the dump on the outskirts of town.

---

ragpickers: men who sell rags
salvaged: saved

Mr. Duvitch's job in the local meatpacking plant made his walk home an odoriferous* one. The Syringa Street youngsters, meeting him on the street, would hold their noses as he walked by.

---

odoriferous: smelly

The Duvitches' dog Kasimar behaved just like the family to which he belonged. He seemed to be afraid of his own shadow, and nobody had ever heard him bark or growl.

But Mother, remembering the potted rose tree, always had a friendly word and a smile for the young Duvitches. And she always managed to find a bone for Kasimar when he scraped up the courage to venture across Syringa Street.

One fine Saturday in July, two years after the Duvitches had moved in, Father took Tom and me on a camping trip to Durston's Pond. The pond was only four miles north of town and was an excellent place for swimming and fishing.

We often had the quiet little pond all to ourselves. But on our arrival that afternoon we found the Duvitches in possession. Mr. Duvitch and the younger boys were casting from shore. The older sons were fishing for bass from a flat-bottomed rowboat.

Tom and I ignored the Duvitch boys. But Father went up to Mr. Duvitch and put out his hand.

"Hello, Mr. Duvitch. It's nice to see you and the boys here."

Mr. Duvitch was a lean little man with watery blue eyes and a kicked-about look. Gratitude for being agreeably noticed showed in his face as he shook Father's hand.

"I know the mosquitoes are biting," Father went on pleasantly. "But are the fish?"

Proudly, oh so proudly, Mr. Duvitch exhibited the catch that would probably feed his family for a week. He had a fine catch of bass,

perch, and sunfish, all of them alive, swimming around in the oaken washtub into which they'd been dropped.

Father told Mr. Duvitch that we couldn't hope to do as well but we'd try.

We three pitched our tent on a little hill beside the pond and rented a rowboat for the afternoon. Then Father, with a happy sigh, lay down on the blanket for a nap.

Tom and I got into our bathing suits, and for a while we stayed out in the boat, fishing. Feeling hot and sweaty later on, we rowed to shore to fetch towels and soap from the tent so we could wash.

On our way back to the water, we stopped to look at the fish still swimming around in the oaken tub. The Duvitches had moved on and were now fishing in a small arm of the pond

just below us. They had their backs to us and were almost out of sight.

Tom and I, our glances meeting over the big cake of soap in my hand, were similarly and wickedly tempted. We held a brief, whispered conversation. Then, egged on by Tom and quite willing on my own, I played a shameful trick on the Duvitches. Without considering further, I dropped the cake of soap into the tub of fish.

"Let's go," whispered Tom after we had watched the soap sink.

We raced back to the tent, had some sandwiches, and played ball for a while. Later on, we swam out to the deep water. Tom scrambled up on a floating log and dived off. I tried to climb on, too, but kept tumbling back into the water.

While we were splashing around, the Duvitches returned to the spot on shore where they had left their tub of fish. Soon Tom and I heard their muffled cries of disbelief and dismay.

Then we saw Father get up, walk over to them, and look down at the tub of fish near his feet. In a moment he motioned to Tom and me to come ashore at once.

Looking as guilty as we felt, we swam in and joined the group around the tub. In the midst of our stricken neighbors stood Father, holding the half-melted cake of soap in his palm.

The fish had perished miserably in the soapy water and were unfit to eat. Not only had Tom and I snatched precious food from the Duvitches' mouths, but we had also revealed the scorn we felt for them.

Father's eyes were narrow slits of blue fire in his white face. I had never seen him so angry. One look at Tom and me told him everything.

"You will begin," Father said in a voice I didn't recognize, "by saying you're sorry."

Tom and I stumbled through our apologies, trying to avoid looking at the Duvitches.

"Do you realize," Father went on coldly, "that in certain primitive communities the sort of stunt you've pulled would be punishable by death?"

"Turn over the tub," Father said sharply.

We turned it over. The gray soapy water ran away in bubbly streams, disappearing into the ground. And the poisoned fish lay exposed on the grass—quiet, strangled, openmouthed.

"Count the fish," Father ordered, his voice like steel.

Tom and I got down on our knees.

"How many are there?" demanded Father.

"Sixty-one," I said.

"How many bass?"

"Twelve."

"Get into that rowboat," Father said in the same steely tones. "You are not to come back until you've caught sixty-one fish to repay Mr. Duvitch. See to it that among them you bring in at least a dozen bass."

Father stepped up to the tent to fetch our shirts and blue jeans. Rolling them into a tight ball, he threw them angrily into the rowboat. He then turned his back on us and stalked away.

Tom and I lost no time in rowing out on the pond. We dropped anchor, threaded our steel

rods, and, baiting our hooks, began to fish. I knew that if it took us all summer to catch them, we dared not set foot ashore without sixty-one fish. Almost at once Tom pulled in a good-sized bass, and ten minutes later two yellow perch were added to our string.

The crestfallen* Duvitches went home. Father threw himself down on the blanket. That was about four in the afternoon.

---

crestfallen: dejected

Oh, the mosquitoes! They were bad enough while the light held. But as evening came on, millions of them swarmed out of the swampland surrounding the pond.

After an hour of it we wanted to leap overboard. They got in our ears, our noses, even our mouths. Nestling in our hair, they bit through to our scalps. Several times we slipped over the side of the boat, ducking under the water to escape the bloodthirsty swarms.

The night dragged on while the whining clouds of mosquitoes grew thicker.

"Andy, what time is it?"

"Ten o'clock, Tom."

"Is that all?" Tom groaned. He pulled in another bass and then killed six or eight mosquitoes with one slap. Two hours passed, and midnight was ghostly on the pond.

The moon sailed high in the purple sky, casting a great white shaft of quivering radiance on the water. But sitting on a hard rowboat seat, aching with tiredness, it all seemed like a nightmare.

"Andy, what *time* is it?"

"Two o'clock, Tom."

The treetops whispered in the breeze. Owls hooted—mockingly, we thought—and bats circled over our heads. Our only comfort was the campfire Father kept burning near the tent. The bright flame flared like a beacon light in the dark. We went on fishing as our tormentors bit and sang.

Each hour took forever to pass, and I fairly panted* for the light of dawn to come.

---

panted: eagerly longed

"Andy—"

"It's four o'clock, Tom, and we've got sixteen fish."

Dawn finally came. But a long stretch on Durston's Pond in the blistering July heat still faced us.

The rising sun cast glistening circles of rose-colored light on the windless surface of the pond. The mosquitoes thinned. The fish continued to bite, but as we fished, the sun mounted steadily. And by eleven o'clock it had become a ball of fire in the cloudless sky. Tom and I began to bake in the heat waves that shimmered over the pond.

"I wish it were night again, Andy," groaned Tom after sweating out an hour of it. "This is worse than the mosquitoes."

I tore a piece of cloth from my shirt and made it into a cap. "Take this, and cover your head, Tom," I said, handing it to him. "We might get sunstrokes and faint."

"I don't care if I do," Tom said feebly. "I'd rather be unconscious."

No breeze stirred. No cloud shadowed the pond. Even the bird life of the swamp, usually bursting with melody, was silent and motionless. Tom was drooping visibly in the glare, and I tried hard not to look at his scorched face.

Between three and four o'clock we dropped lines in a school of yellow perch and pulled up no fewer than twenty. The bass continued to bite in the deep black holes off the swamp, which bristled with tree trunks. Aching, blistered, moving like machines, Tom and I geared ourselves for the home stretch.

When the sun, dropping low, had lost its fury, and the sky began to pale, I pulled up the thirteenth bass. That bass was our sixty-first fish.

Drooping from lack of food and sleep, Tom and I rowed to shore where Father was waiting.

He received us coolly, making no comment on our condition. At once he asked to see the fish, and we held them up by the string.

"Count them," he said.

Obviously we would receive permission to land only when we had produced the required number.

"Sixty-one," said Tom, "including thirteen bass."

"Very good," said Father in businesslike tones. "We will now restore to Mr. Duvitch his rightful property."

I stumbled out of the boat, aching all over. But somehow something inside me was rejoicing. I guess that Father was secretly proud of Tom and me. And I realized, too, that all through the night he had suffered with us.

We drove in silence to the Duvitch cottage. There we found Mr. Duvitch sitting alone on the front porch.

When he saw Tom and me and we silently handed him the strings of fish, he gulped and swallowed hard. Then in a voice raw with emotion he protested that he had not wished us to suffer so.

"Will you shake hands with the boys?" asked Father.

Instead Mr. Duvitch broke down. Tom and I did not know where to look. During those moments we suffered more intensely than we had suffered in the clouds of mosquitoes and under the blazing sun. After our neighbor had composed* himself, he seized our hands and bowed his head over them. Tom and I swallowed hard.

composed: calmed

Then we went home to Mother, who had heard about our ordeal* on the pond from one of the neighbors. When she saw Tom and me she burst into tears. She tried to embrace us, but we drew back painfully. Soon she had us plastered* with a thick coating of soothing sunburn cream.

ordeal: painful experience
plastered: covered

In bed our skin stuck to the sheets and pillowcases, but we slept as if we had been drugged.

We woke up around noon the next day. "It is high time," I heard Father say calmly to Mother, "for this senseless feeling against the Duvitches to stop. And I'm willing to do my part.

"Tonight we're having supper with them. Mr. Duvitch said that since Andy and Tom caught the fish, he'd feel better if we all shared them. After a few hints from me, he invited us over. It may be a trial, but we ought to be able to bear it."

We walked across the street at six o'clock, not knowing what to expect. The Duvitches, dressed in their Sunday best, bright and shining as we had never seen them, received us as if we were royalty. They looked at Tom and me—and then delicately looked away.

I shuddered when I thought of what we would have had to endure had this been any other family.

The young Duvitches, thrilled by their first party and by the family's first acceptance in this country, kept showing their pleasure in wide, delighted smiles. I couldn't believe they were the same timid, downcast* youngsters I had known at school.

downcast: dejected

We ate fried fish at a long plank table in the back yard. Father kept the conversation going. As he told stories and jokes, we discovered that the Duvitches had a gift for gaiety. And how they loved to laugh.

After supper David played folk songs on his accordion. Mr. Duvitch turned out to be something of a ventriloquist.* He made the dog Kasimar talk in Polish and the cat Jan talk in German.

ventriloquist: one who can produce sound that seems to come from someone or something else

I could tell that the Duvitch family was a great surprise to Father and that he had enjoyed the evening tremendously.

"To think," he murmured as we crossed the street, "that they should turn out to be people of courtesy and accomplishment." Father sighed and shook his head. "They're being looked down on and ignored by their inferiors."

After that evening things began to improve for the Duvitches. Our neighbors looked up to Father and often followed his lead since he was the only college graduate on Syringa Street. They decided that if the Duvitches were good enough for a highly educated man like Father, they were good enough for them. So they started inviting Mr. and Mrs. Duvitch to the community parties.

It wasn't long before the Duvitch boys and girls started making friends in the community. David was invited to play his accordion at a country dance, and he ended up being one of the town's most popular musicians.

The other Duvitch youngsters taught their folk dances to the boys and girls at school. Even Kasimar began to take on the ways of an American dog, daring to bark and growl on occasion.

Syringa Street presently had reason to be grateful to Mrs. Duvitch, who turned out to have a great gift for nursing. In times of severe illness, the doctor invariably* suggested that she be sent for. When Mrs. Duvitch slipped into a sickroom, she never failed to bring along an air of peace. After an hour or two, the patient was calmed and the family reassured.

invariably: constantly

Soon people began to turn to the Duvitches with all kinds of problems. The elder Duvitches, with their Old World wisdom, would sit by the hour and talk gently and convincingly against fear, false pride, disgrace and grief.

One winter day, Mr. Duvitch gave Father a pair of handsome, fur-lined mittens—just the right size for Father's enormous hands. After our neighbor had left, Father drew on the mittens, which had a slight ashy odor.

"Probably one of the boys found them in an ash heap at the dump," Father remarked. "But why should I value them any the less? Who would have dreamed that the Duvitches would have so much more to offer us than we have to offer them?"

About the Story

1. What does the family give the Duvitches?
2. What makes it possible for the Duvitches to offer the gift of their friendship?
3. Who else besides the Duvitches performs a generous act?
4. What do the Duvitches give their neighbors?
5. What truth about prejudice is taught through this selection?
6. What Bible verse about friendship is illustrated through this story?

About the Author

Though unmarried, Ambrose Flack loved children and lived with his sister and her family. Having children running in and out of his study all the time let him "sit right at his typewriter and do research." He also used experiences from his own life to inspire the stories he wrote. One story, about a pair of shoes worn by Theodore Roosevelt while hunting in Africa, began with the personal experience of going to his father's job at a shoe factory and seeing those very same shoes. He also had another "Teddy Roosevelt" experience: finding the president's bird-watching notebook and getting complete stage fright at the moment of returning it at a banquet. He never did get the courage to speak to his hero, and someone later stole the notebook from his school desk. So, in a way, Flack writes from personal experience when discussing the way the strangers feel ill at ease in their new neighborhood and even the lack of pluck shown by the dog!

from

Preacher's Kids

Grace Nies Fletcher

A forty-dollar suit for the daughter created a near disaster in this family. What does the mother do that makes the problem so great? Are all the problems solved at the end of the story?

This story raises other issues as well. Is it ever right to do wrong in order to get a chance to do right? Is not telling the whole truth the same thing as lying?

Money may be the root of all evil* but it never stayed long enough in our family to put forth either roots or leaves. During the years we children were growing up, Dad's salary seldom averaged over three thousand dollars (his first church paid him ten dollars a week), but even this modest sum was misleading, for he promptly gave back to the church 10 per cent of his gross income. The "Tithe for the Lord" was taken out of Dad's monthly pay check first; then the remainder was divided equally between Dad and Mother, her portion for food and household running expenses, Dad's to pay for clothes, carfare, books, medicine, and all the rest. By the end of the first week neither of them would have much left in their pockets. Conversation at the breakfast table would run cautiously.

Money . . . evil: cf. I Tim 6:10

"Lee, could you lend me a dollar? The Ladies' Aid are meeting here this afternoon and I need a pound of butter and some tea."

"But, Sweet, I just gave you. . . ."

"I know, I know. But I met Sister 'Iggins at the grocery store. Lee, she's 'expecting' again! She looked like someone had drawn her

through a knothole. I simply couldn't go on buying pounds and pounds of food for us and not. . . ."

"Of course you couldn't, Darling," Dad would agree. . . .

"I got her duplicates of everything I bought us and that's little enough for eight people," Mother explained half-defiantly, to Dad. "It's her seventh baby in nine years and heaven knows she's entitled to her 'cuppa.' You know what she said? I asked if she was going to have her baby at home and she said, shocked, "Aow, no, Mrs. Nies! In the 'orspittel. Them two weeks is the honly 'oliday I 'as!" Mother, smiling, held out her hand to Dad, urging, "Give."

Dad put his hand into his pants pocket, drew out four dollars and sixty-five cents, admitting it was all he had left for the rest of the month. He'd been calling on Jed Steel yesterday in the hospital, he explained. "He's almost over his pneumonia bout," Dad explained, "but he's worried sick over his big doctor's bill, so I made him a little loan. You ought to see how much better he looked right off!"

"I'll bet," Mother said coldly. "Well, that's that." She reached over, filched* a dollar from Dad's little hoard. "I'll simply have to get that tea for this afternoon. And a loaf of bread. Someone always forgets what she's supposed to bring. Remember the time Mrs. Hanson forgot the bread for the missionary society and I had to cut my one loaf into sandwiches about as big as ten-cent pieces? Talk about the miracle of the loaves and little fishes!" . . .

---

filched: casually took

The only thing that could save us at this time of the month was when Mr. Hunter at the wedding license bureau sent Dad over a "stray couple." A prospective bride and groom who had no home church would often ask him to recommend a minister to marry them; and since Mr. Hunter went to our church, he would send them to Dad. . . .

The wedding fees all belonged to Mother; Dad always handed them over to her the moment the front door closed behind the happy couple and he never asked her how she spent the money. In all her forty years of married life, this was the only money Mother ever had of which she did not have to account for every penny. It meant far more than cash to her; it was the very breath of independence, her chance to play Lady Bountiful.* For usually she spent the money for little luxuries for the family, a new dressing gown for Dad to lounge in when he studied so he wouldn't wrinkle his good clothes lying on the bumpy couch, a party dress for me, once a secondhand policeman's hat bought from Johnny Guptile's father because a thief had shot a hole through it. Ike told Mother passionately that if she bought him that bullet-hole hat, he'd never ask for another thing as long as he lived! Naturally, the whole family could hardly wait till the wedding couple got out the front door, to see how much of a fee Mother got this time.

Bountiful: generous

Dad never asked anyone to pay him for a wedding, especially not our own parishioners,* but usually the groom handed Dad either two one-dollar bills or a single five. "Just a little remembrance, Pastor!" the happy groom would say and thrust a small sealed envelope into Dad's hand; or perhaps, if he was flustered, the groom would just gasp, "Here!" and rush out the door. Only wealthy parishioners who'd asked Dad to come to their home to perform the ceremony or had a big church wedding gave a fee as large as ten dollars; but when Aunt Laura's only daughter was married, Dad received twenty-five dollars!

parishioners: church members

"Oh!" Mother gasped when Dad (rather reluctantly but magnanimously*) handed the check over to her. "You can have that . . . book on prayer you want, Lee!" Her eyes grew wide and soft with happiness. "And I can have a new dress for the bishop's wife's reception!" Her face clouded; it was terribly selfish to spend so much on herself, but she hadn't had a new dress for . . . "Lee, do you think I'm an awful pig?"

magnanimously: generously

Dad looked down at his small pink-gingham wife. He couldn't ever remember her spending any of her wedding money on herself before. "A flower needs its petals and a bird its plumage,"* he said. He laid his cheek against her soft curls. "My Sweet, did I ever happen to mention that I love you?"

plumage: feathers

Seeing there were to be no dividends for us in this wedding check, Ike and I tiptoed out of the room and left them to what Ike called, "That gooey stuff." It had never occurred to us that all husbands and wives weren't as much in love as our Dad and Mother. So the gold of experience slips through your fingers without your ever knowing what riches you hold. . . .

The bridal couple who really burned us up, however, were the middle-aged man and woman who woke us up at two A.M. for the ceremony. We were all sound asleep when the pounding began on the parsonage front door and Mother shook Dad, urging, "Get up, Lee. Someone's in trouble!" Dad groggily* put on his dressing gown over his nightshirt, went to the door. The couple who stood there were gray-haired, well dressed, and very nervous. If they'd been teenagers Dad might have suspected they were eloping, but this middle-aged man and woman. . . . "Please marry us right now," they insisted. "We have a license."

groggily: unsteadily

When the groom thrust it at Dad he saw by the hall light that the groom was sixty-seven and the bride fifty-eight—certainly old enough to know their own minds, but too old to be breaking into other people's sleep. Dad yawned, "Couldn't you come back later this morning? I'm not dressed and I'd have to wake up the family to get two witnesses. . . ."

"No, we have to be married right now," the groom said, flatly. "I know it's an imposition*

but there isn't any other way. If you won't help us, we're sunk."

"Well, come in," Dad gave in.

"What's the big idea?" Mother asked Dad indignantly* when he told her she and I had to get dressed. We didn't get the answer until Dad pronounced the gray-haired couple husband and wife, and the groom sighed with relief as he turned to give his plump bride a loud smack.

"Well, we did it, Sally!" he exulted. He explained, "We had to elope from our children. She's got two and I have four. They didn't want us to marry for fear they'd miss a nickel when I die. So we crept out while they were in bed. Sorry to put you folks out this way, but it sure was worth it!"

He handed Dad a bill and went out with his Sally. Dad gasped and handed it over to Mother who cried triumphantly, "I'd wake up any night for a ten-dollar bill!"

This was the bill Mother paid down for the green suit I wanted so badly that I literally ached with longing. I was sixteen; up to now I had worn Mother's old skirts cut down to my size with a shirtwaist and sweater. We saw the suit first in the window of a Boston store so expensive we usually just looked through the plate-glass window and walked on. But today . . . "That is *my* suit!" I cried impulsively.* "Look, Mother!" The suit was a soft deep green, the color of the smooth leaves that cradle the lily of the valley; and I knew without trying it on how becoming it would be. It was the sort of suit Sylvia Meadows might wear, Sylvia expensive and silken like her name, who sat beside me in high school, who had everything she wanted, new clothes, an English bicycle, money to buy her lunch noons at school, instead of carrying sandwiches in a greasy paper bag. In this soft green suit, I would look like other girls who didn't live in a parsonage, well dressed, sure of myself, maybe even pretty. Mother saw these thoughts chasing themselves across my thin yearning face and said abruptly, "Let's go inside, see how much it costs."

The price was forty dollars. Not even Mother had ever paid that much for a suit; for a winter coat, maybe, but not for a suit warm enough to wear only a little while, spring and fall. I knew I couldn't possibly have the lovely thing but I made the mistake of trying it on. I looked in the mirror and gasped. There was something about the color that brought out the faint pink in my cheeks, the gold in my hair. For once in my life I was *beautiful*.

I didn't beg for the suit, there was no use. But I saw in the mirror Mother's eyes and I knew she thought, as I did, that this was the

most becoming suit I'd ever had on. The svelte salesgirl patted her hair back and drawled, "You'll never find anything anywhere that looks half as good, Miss." But she'd seen our shoes, Mother's worn handbag. I don't think even the salesgirl expected us to buy the suit, but suddenly. . . .

"We'll take it," Mother said too loudly. Her cheeks were blazing red and her eyes were flashing. She dug the precious ten-dollar wedding bill out of her bag and handed it to the salesgirl. "I'll pay ten dollars down and charge the rest till the first of the month."

But Dad didn't approve at all of her charging things. He said if you couldn't pay cash for what you wanted, the honest thing was to go without till you could. The salesgirl asked doubtfully, "Do you have an account here?" My mother lifted her head. "No, but I soon will. Where do I go to start one?" One good

thing about Dad's old-fashioned ideas, since he owed nothing, was that his credit was good.

I wore the green suit home on the streetcar, surreptitiously* smoothing its soft folds every now and then with my proud hand. I told Mother, fiercely happy, "I never can pay you back for this, never."

surreptitiously: secretly

"Every girl needs to feel beautiful at least once in her life," Mother said. "You'll never want *things* as much as you do right now, I reckon." Her eyes grew dreamy as she remembered, "When I was thirteen, Mother bought me a red dress. . . ."

Mother looked at me uneasily and said slowly, "I don't think there's any need to tell your father how much this suit cost. It'd just upset him. Oh, I don't mean for you to lie to him if he asks you, but there's no need to *volunteer* all you know."

"But if he asks me, what'll I say?"

"Just refer him to me," Mother said grimly. "Besides, I'm sure to get some more wedding fees before the first of the month. Then it's nobody's business but mine how much it cost."

This spoiled the fun of the new suit a little for I'd been planning to rush up to Dad's study, to pirouette,* demand, "Notice anything?" Then he'd say, "Well, if it isn't my beautiful daughter! How did you ever get that way with such a homely Dad? You must take after your mother." It was an old joke between us, how beautiful I was and how homely he was, neither of which was true; but it was a comfortable family illusion. But fortunately Dad was too busy thinking of his sermon even to ask how much the new suit cost. When I said, "Mother bought it for me," all he said was, "Oh? It's very becoming. Was it worth being waked up for, Susie, at two A.M.?" So he thought the suit cost ten dollars; well, it did, plus. . . .

---

pirouette: turn fully around

"Oh, yes," I managed. When I dared look at Mother, her face was flushed a bright pink but her lips were tightly closed, stubbornly silent. She would never have deceived Dad for herself, but her children had claims on her, too. As soon as she collected enough wedding fees, she'd tell Dad all about it.

But March didn't seem to be a month when a young man's fancy turned to love and marriage. Every time the front bell would ring, Mother would rush hopefully to open the door, but Mr. Hunter didn't send over a single "stray," for two weeks. When finally one couple did arrive, one of Lim's kittens, a sport who'd turned out to be completely black, got into the front parlor and ran up the bride's skirt to her shoulder. She had hysterics, yelling, "A black cat! Bad luck! Bad luck!" and refused to go on with the

ceremony. So there was no wedding fee out of that. Mother began to grow cross and tense. Usually she was relaxed and smiling, but all of a sudden even Ike's slamming the back door as he always did made her angry; she scolded me for coming to the table with wind-tossed hair; and once when Dad ventured to joke that the crust of the apple pie was soggy, Mother burst into tears and ran up to her room. Dad stared after her, really worried.

"Your Mother needs a vacation," Dad said anxiously to Ike and me. "I wish I could afford to send her home to Texas for a month, but I don't know where I'd get the money. . . ."

There was an accident that Sunday in front of our church. The March night had turned icy and very cold. Dad shook hands with the departing congregation inside the vestibule* instead of at the open door as he usually did, and while we were waiting for him to finish, a little old lady in black stood shivering next to the radiator in the vestibule. Mother went over to say "Good evening," and to see if she needed a ride home in this icy weather.

---

vestibule: small entranceway

"Oh no, my son's coming for me," the little old lady who wore an expensive black fur coat and a pretty feather hat explained. "I'm Mrs. Sims. My son told me to wait where it was warm till he drove up to the door. Oh, what's that?" There was a terrible crash outside and when Dad ran out to see what had happened, a big Packard car had crashed into the maple tree in front of the church and the driver was lying across the steering wheel, unconscious. It was Mrs. Sims's son whose car had skidded on the ice; and by the time the ambulance had carried him away and the tow truck had collected what was left of the Packard, his poor little mother was a jelly of apprehension.* "Would someone please call a taxi?" she quavered.* "To take me to Brookline? My son's got the house key. I hope the maid won't be asleep."

apprehension: dread
quavered: trembled

"You're coming right home with us," my mother said warmly, putting her arm around the shivering old lady. "Lee will go to the hospital to see how your son is. Of course, you'll stay with us tonight at the parsonage." Mother made fresh coffee, kept up cheerful conversation until Dad phoned that the son was going to be all right but the doctor thought he'd better spend the night in the hospital. When little Mrs. Sims dissolved in relieved tears, Mother insisted upon lending her a nightgown about four sizes too big for her and tucking her into bed in her and Dad's room. Mother would sleep with me, and Dad on the study couch. The Simses must have had an ample income, for the next afternoon the son turned up in a new car, thanked us profusely,* and drove his little expensive-looking mother away.

profusely: plentifully

. . . Mother went right to bed without waiting for Dad as she usually did; but next morning she looked as if she hadn't slept at all, so pale and drawn that Dad urged anxiously, "I wish you'd drop by Dr. Phillips' office today and get him to check you over."

"I'm perfectly all right," Mother snapped. "I just have one of my headaches. I'll go up and lie down."

My own throat went dry as I stared after her, for if Mother got really sick it'd be my fault. If I hadn't wanted the green suit so badly. . . . After Dad had gone off to make a call, I crept up to Mother's darkened room where she lay on the bed, to make the supreme sacrifice. I offered, my voice trembling, "I'll send the suit back, if you want." Mother said, exasperated,* "How can you send it back when you've worn it? It isn't your fault; it's mine. I should have told your father right off how much the suit cost. Now when the bill comes in, he'll know I've been deceiving him for weeks." She burst into tears and all I could think of to do

was to smooth back her soft curly hair from her forehead; it felt silky like a little girl's and it came to me for the first time that Mother wasn't so terribly much older than I was.

exasperated: irritated

On the morning of the first of the month when the bills usually arrived, Mother came down to breakfast looking ten years older, with her mouth a thin, determined slit. When we knelt for morning prayers as usual she put her hands over her face and prayed out loud.

"Oh, Lord," she said miserably, "I've prayed and prayed for help to make things right, but You didn't send it to me. I don't blame You at all. If You'll just give me strength to do what I have to, I'll never, never be so wicked again. Amen."

Dad shot her a worried glance as we got up from our knees but he didn't ask what her wickedness had been; that was between her and her Lord. Also he knew she would tell him anyway when she got ready, for Mother was normally as transparent as a piece of clear ice. No, he wouldn't force her confidence. Just then it happened, what Mother had been dreading. The mailman, who came early to our

end of the street, dropped the letters through the slot in our front door, and the flutter to my frightened ears was like heavy stones dropping onto the polished floor. As Dad started to get up to pick up the mail, Mother spoke.

"Wait, Lee," she said. "There's something I have to tell you first." The two little red spots into her cheeks spread to a deep flush all down her neck as she told him about the green suit, how I'd wanted it to look like other girls, how she'd paid forty dollars for it, almost a week's salary. She'd known perfectly well she shouldn't have done it, she admitted, but that wasn't the worst she'd done: she'd told me not to tell how much the suit cost and that was just the same as teaching me to lie. Mother's voice trembled, faded away, and then grew desperately louder. She wanted to apologize right here and now, not only to Dad but to us children for being a wicked, lying, deceitful woman. Would we ever forgive her?

For a moment we all three sat stunned to silence. She made us feel terrible because we knew this wasn't true; our mother was everything fine and sweet and loving, only this once she'd been tempted, not for herself but for her child. When Ike and I both burst out into sympathetic tears, Dad took command of the situation. He went over and put his arm around Mother.

"Stop that caterwauling,* you two!" Dad ordered. "There's nothing to feel badly about. Darling, you only acted like a mother!" He told Ike and me sternly, "If you two grow up to be half as fine as your mother is, you'll do all right." He kissed Mother and then ordered, "Now, let's all forget it." He walked out into the hall, picked up the letters, handed one to Mother. "It's for you, Sugar."

---

caterwauling: harsh crying

Mother opened her letter listlessly,* announced, "It's from that little Mrs. Sims." Her eyes began to grow bigger as she read and her hands shook so that a blue slip of paper fell out of the letter onto the breakfast table. Mother read aloud, "This is just a little something for you to spend as you like, for something you really want, for some frippery* maybe. Don't you dare send this back. It's not payment for a night's lodging at all. The Lord sent you this with His love." Dad picked up the blue slip, stared at it as Ike demanded, "What is it, Dad?"

---

listlessly: without enthusiasm
frippery: finery

"It's a check for twenty-five dollars," Dad told him slowly.

Mother's eyes lifted to Dad were awed pools of light. "Oh Lee, do you think. . . . No, she must have mailed this *before* I prayed!"

Dad smiled down at her and his eyes were a gentle hand caressing* his beloved as he said, " 'O ye of little faith. . . . Before ye call, I will answer.' "

---

caressing: lightly touching

About the Story

1. What is the "gold of experience" that the children do not treasure?
2. What is Mother's worst sin in this story?
3. The Bible teaches that the pleasures of sin are for a season; how are the pleasures of the suit limited?
4. What does this story teach us about God?
5. What does the story teach us about the correct way to handle sin?

. . . About the Author

Grace Nies Fletcher (b. 1895) won the "New England Women's Press Club award for best magazine story by a Massachusetts author" in 1953 and continued publishing well-received fiction after that. Since she was reared in a minister's household, it is not surprising that she used her literary talents for the benefit of her church. She also found enough material in her own life as a "preacher's kid" to make up the book from which this selection is taken. She traveled extensively to research material for her other books, and it is her attention to realism that accounts for much of the enjoyment readers find in her work.

We Give Thee But Thine Own

William W. How

We give Thee but Thine own,
Whate'er the gift may be:
All that we have is Thine alone,
A trust, O Lord, from Thee.

May we Thy bounties thus
As stewards true receive,
And gladly, as Thou blessest us,
To Thee our first-fruits give.

To comfort and to bless,
To find a balm for woe,
To tend the lone and fatherless,
Is angels' work below.

The captive to relieve,
To God the lost to bring,
To teach the way of life and peace—
It is a Christ-like thing.

And we believe Thy word,
Though dim our faith may be:
Whate'er for Thine we do, O Lord,
We do it unto Thee.

The Bible and Generosity

And Jesus answering said, A certain man went down from Jerusalem to Jericho, and fell among thieves, which stripped him of his raiment, and wounded him, and departed, leaving him half dead.

And by chance there came down a certain priest that way: and when he saw him, he passed by on the other side. And likewise a Levite, when he was at the place, came and looked on him, and passed by on the other side.

But a certain Samaritan, as he journeyed, came where he was: and when he saw him, he had compassion on him, And went to him, and bound up his wounds, pouring in oil and wine, and set him on his own beast, and brought him to an inn, and took care of him.

And on the morrow when he departed, he took out two pence, and gave them to the host, and said unto him, Take care of him; and whatsoever thou spendest more, when I come again, I will repay thee.

Which now of these three, thinkest thou, was neighbour unto him that fell among the thieves?

And he said, He that shewed mercy on him. Then said Jesus unto him, Go, and do thou likewise. (Luke 10:30-37)

4

Our Land

If we today neglect what we possess, all that Americans in the past have fought for and died for may become meaningless.

Our Land

Sometimes another country looks as though it might be a wonderful place to live. Rugged mountains, tumbling rivers, quaint storybook palaces, or colorful ethnic costumes may all conspire to make a foreign land seem very appealing.

But what if that land's government does not allow you to safely worship God? What if it does not give you the chance to become what you want to be? What if it permits you no freedom of speech or of movement within its borders or across them? Life on these terms would be very unappealing.

As citizens of the United States, we can rejoice at God's giving us the privilege of living in this land. The words of Rudyard Kipling, although written about his own homeland, England, take on special meaning for us:

> God gave all men all earth to love,
> But, since our hearts are small,
> Ordained for each one spot should prove
> Beloved over all. . . . I rejoice
> The lot has fallen to me
> In a fair ground—in a fair ground.

Like most people we seldom take time to reflect on the blessings of our "lot." The nation's laws and social stability, for example, protect our individual rights. The land's vast natural resources have brought wealth and comfort to the American people. The geographical separation from Europe and Asia along with the nation's military power has kept us relatively free of war. Until this century the country's pulpits gave sound, biblical guidance to the majority of Americans.

Along with these blessings, though, we need to remember certain truths about our land. First, peoples, nations, and governments are not historical accidents. God establishes them for His purpose. Second, our country's foundation was strongly religious. The first Virginia settlers arrived with a goal, among others, of evangelizing the Indians. The first New England settlers sailed here because they wanted the freedom to worship God according to their interpretation of the Bible. Both then and later our forefathers sacrificed their lives to lay, then to protect, the foundation for what we today enjoy.

Most of our writers have at some time written about our land. Some, it is true, have mocked its values and history. They have attacked the nation's faults and ignored its virtues. Others, as the result of their intense love for the nation, have believed that it can do no wrong. For some their patriotism has even become a substitute religion.

As Christians we need to remember that we have dual citizenship. Because God has put us in this nation, we ought to be good citizens. We are to obey those placed in authority over us (Rom. 13:1-7). By our behavior toward our political leaders, we are to give the ungodly around us an example of good citizenship (I Pet. 2:13-16).

But we must be good citizens of God's kingdom too (Phil. 3:20). At no time are we to let our earthly citizenship become more important than our heavenly. In Christ's words, we are to "render . . . unto Caesar the things which are Caesar's; and unto God the things that are God's" (Matt. 22:21). If a conflict arises in our citizenship responsibilities, we are to obey God first rather than man (Acts 5:29). We must take God's view, looking at our nation in the light of the Scriptures. We should neither distrustfully condemn all our country's actions nor unthinkingly accept all of them. Instead, we should live in spiritual wisdom toward it, walking "circumspectly [lit. looking around, taking heed], not as fools, but as wise" (Eph. 5:15).

As you might expect, the selections that follow reveal various attitudes toward the United States and life here. Some, like "Paul Revere's Ride" and "Molly Pitcher," recount oft-told events. Others, though, may not seem to fit the theme of this unit. "The Great Cherokee Bill," for instance, tells of a unique high school assembly speaker who makes more than one mark on his audience. "Monty Takes Charge of the Barter Store" reveals the early career of a man who founded one of the country's most successful mail-order houses. "Our Blessed Land," the last selection in the unit, reminds us of the blessings available to us Americans.

Although our land has enjoyed unprecedented success among the countries of the world, no nation can be genuinely successful unless it is properly related to God. "Righteousness exalteth a nation: but sin is a reproach to any people" (Prov. 14:34). "Blessed is the nation whose God is the Lord" (Ps. 33:12). The words of II Chronicles 7:14 bring comfort yet somber warning for the future. In spite of appearances to the contrary, God's judgment for sin will come as surely to our nation as it has to other nations in the past. As we look at our citizens' moral indifference, we cannot help remembering these solemn words: "Fools make a mock at sin" (Prov. 14:9).

No one knows what will happen to our nation if her people do not change their ways. The country's most cherished beliefs may slowly fade from the memory of new generations. Or the inherited beliefs may be quickly erased by some cataclysmic event. If we today neglect what we possess, all that Americans in the past have fought for and died for may become meaningless. As we begin a new unit, we need to utter special thanks as well as a special plea to God for the nation that we claim—because of His grace—as *our land*.

The Great Cherokee Bill

Jesse Stuart

If Cherokee Bill spoke at your school, would he have to overcome the same resistance he had at Maxwell High? Is he "great"?

Author's Introduction

I never really planned to write about the Great Cherokee Bill. But as the years passed, and I was no longer principal of Maxwell High School, and had returned to W-Hollow to help my father farm his land and mine, I couldn't forget him and the show he put on in an assembly program at my school. It was the most remarkable program we ever had.

I couldn't forget the way he walked into my office one day and told me that he was the Great Cherokee Bill. When he said that he was great, I doubted him. But he was right.

Five years after that day he had fascinated us all at Maxwell High School, I wrote an article about him. I sent it to a magazine which bought only factual articles. The editor didn't buy it because he thought it was a short story. He wouldn't believe it was true. The next magazine I sent it to turned it down for the same reason. Finally I sent it to a short-story magazine, and it was accepted immediately.

One night years later, I was at the movies one evening with my wife Naomi. Between the comedy and the feature an extra picture flashed on the screen. The Great Cherokee Bill. *"That's him,"* I shouted suddenly. Everybody started looking toward me.

"That's who?" Naomi whispered.

"That Indian," I said. *"That's the Great Cherokee Bill."*

"You mean there was a real Cherokee Bill?" she asked.

"Sure, there was a real one," I whispered softly, since everybody around us was getting curious. Several people gave me hard looks to keep quiet. *"There he is right up there on the screen. And that is part of the program he gave in Maxwell High School assembly. Somebody in Hollywood realized that he was 'The Great' Cherokee Bill and that he was no fake Indian."*

Naomi had read the story, but I had failed to tell her it was real. She, like the editor who had accepted the story for publication, had thought this was a product of my imagination when actually I had merely recorded in words what had transpired* in our most delightful assembly program.

---

transpired: happened

Now we listened to the enthusiastic reception of that movie audience, young and old, as the Great Cherokee Bill performed on the screen. I sat back and relaxed and enjoyed again the Great Cherokee Bill's delightful show. It hadn't changed much for the Great Cherokee Bill was a very determined man. He knew what he could do and he had to do what he did his own way. As I watched happily I could not help thinking what if all the people in this theater could have had the privilege to have seen "The Great" Cherokee Bill in per-

son as we had seen him years ago in our Maxwell High School assembly.

I believe this story catches some of the spirit of this great performer and individualist. I believe you will find the Great Cherokee Bill a most colorful character.

He walked into my office, a tall, olive-complexioned man of about thirty-five. His moist jet-black hair didn't reach his shoulders. His teeth were white, strong-looking and far apart. The green and black checked loose-fitting lumber jacket gave his shoulders a broad appearance, the rattlesnake-skin belt girdled* tightly made his waist look small. His riding pants encasing* his hips and legs made them look small. His boots were deeply scarred. My office secretary ran from the office before the man spoke; she was afraid of him.

---
girdled: drawn
encasing: enclosing

"Mr. Stringer," the stranger said without the slightest accent in his voice, "I'm the Great Cherokee Bill. I'm three parts Indian and one part white man. I've come to see you about putting on a show for your high school."

"Nothing doing, Cherokee Bill," I said, looking him over. "I wouldn't have another Indian program here under any consideration!"

"What's the matter?" he asked, gesturing with his hands as he spoke. "Don't you like Indians?"

"I like Indians all right. But we've had two Indian programs here this year and they've both been fakes."

"I'll tell you I'm no fake," he yelled. "I'm the Great Cherokee Bill." His black eyes looked straight into my eyes and his lips quivered.

"Look at this!" he said, reaching me a sheaf* of recommendations.

---
sheaf: bundle

There were two hundred at least. Many were written by teachers in Tennessee, men and women I'd gone to the University with; I knew it didn't pay to question one of their

recommendations. There was a fine recommendation from Willis Abernathy, Superintendent of Maitland High School, Maitland, Tennessee. In my four years in the University with Willis, I'd never heard him say a good word for anybody; yet he'd warmly recommended Cherokee Bill as the greatest entertainer that had ever given a program at the Maitland High School since he had been Superintendent. I read Willis Abernathy's letter carefully.

"Day before yesterday, we had an Indian here," I said. "The students went to sleep in chapel."

"They'll never go to sleep on the Great Cherokee Bill," the Indian said. "I'll keep 'em awake!"

"We're having chapel in just a few minutes," I told him. "Would you mind going to chapel with me and entertain them for a minute or two to show them you are a real Indian? If you can hold them we'll give you tomorrow's chapel program!"

"I want to show them what I can do," he said angrily. "The Great Cherokee Bill has never been treated like this!"

"Sorry, Cherokee Bill," I said, "but we're not having any more fake Indian shows."

When the bell rang, Cherokee Bill and I followed the students into the auditorium. When they saw the strange-looking man, a great laugh went up from the students. They were more interested in the personal appearance of Cherokee Bill than they had been in White Cloud's.*

White Cloud: the previous Indian speaker

"Our regular program, students, will be temporarily postponed," I said. "We have a man with us today who says he's three parts Indian and one part pale face. He doesn't claim to be full-blooded Indian as did our White Cloud."

"Old faker, White Cloud," some student said in an undertone* so everybody could hear. Everybody laughed.

undertone: a low voice

"I want to introduce to you, Cherokee Bill," I said, "and he will entertain you for a few minutes!"

Many of the students sighed.

"Some bad boys out there, Mr. Stringer," Cherokee Bill said. "I need my whip. Excuse me till I run to the car and get it!"

Like a flash the Indian shot out from the auditorium, his oily black hair floating on the wind behind him while the students roared. Each boy kidded the boy beside him saying, "You're Cherokee Bill's bad boy!" I wondered if he could pick the boys who had given the teachers trouble.

Cherokee Bill ran into the auditorium full speed and stopped suddenly like a car locking four wheels. Over his shoulder he carried a long whip.

"You back there," he pointed to Tim Sparks.

Everybody in chapel roared. Cherokee Bill hadn't missed his guess on Tim Sparks. Students called him "Sparkie."

"Come up here, young man!" Cherokee Bill commanded.

"I ain't comin'," Sparkie said twisting in his seat.

"But you will come," Cherokee Bill said. "I'll give you ten seconds and if you don't come, I'll bring you up here."

There was silence while Cherokee Bill looked at his wristwatch.

"Are you coming?"

"No."

Cherokee Bill threw his arm back across his shoulder; gripping the giant whipstalk, he brought the whip over his shoulder, over the rows of students in front of him. The approxi-

mately sixteen-foot long whip cracked like a rifle above Sparkie's head, its long cracker* wrapping around his neck. Then Cherokee Bill drew on the whip like one drawing a bucket of water from a well with a rope line. Everybody roared as Cherokee Bill drew Sparkie to the front. When Sparkie walked, the whip around his neck didn't choke him; when he balked,* the whip drew closer around his neck and pushed his tongue out. Everybody wondered how he had lassoed Sparkie with a whip without hitting one of the boys around him. But he had.

cracker: snapping end of the whip
balked: stopped

"Poor Sparkie," Bill Hilton said, laughing.

"Sparkie, you stand right here," Cherokee Bill said. "Two more boys I've got spotted. They're not good boys in school. I'm picking out three bad boys!"

"Come up here," Cherokee Bill commanded, pointing to James "Pewee" Fox. "You are a bad boy. You won't get your lessons!"

James Fox hadn't passed a single course in three months of high-school work. Every student and teacher laughed when Cherokee Bill threw his whip over the heads of the students and lassoed Pewee. When Pewee balked his tongue came out. The students screamed with laughter.

"You don't fool the Great Cherokee Bill when you're a bad boy," the Indian said as he drew Pewee up front.

Mrs. Burton, Pewee's home-room teacher, laughed hysterically* when Pewee stood beside Sparkie and Cherokee Bill and faced the laughing students.

hysterically: uncontrollably

"Why don't you fetch* one of the girls up here, Cherokee Bill?" Sparkie asked.

fetch: bring

"Girls are never bad," he answered him looking over the chapel for the third boy.

"Come," Cherokee Bill said, pointing to Henry "Custardpie" Jordan.

"He's found all three of the bad boys," Lucy Bowling spoke from the front row. There was a thunderclap of laughter as Cherokee Bill raised his whip and Custardpie started ducking down but the boys sitting beside him pushed him up straight. Cherokee Bill had picked the third boy all right. Custardpie had spent seven years in high school and hadn't finished yet. He had often left a cafeteria window unlocked, slipped back into the cafeteria at night and made away with the pies. The only way he had ever been caught was, a pie was doped and he got it. He was out of school a couple of weeks. Thereafter, he was "Custardpie" Jordan.

When Cherokee Bill drew Custardpie up front the students arose from their seats and laughed. Never had they seen such entertainment.

"Did I get your bad boys?" Cherokee Bill turned to me and said.

I didn't say anything but a voice in unison went up from the student body.

"Y-E-S!"

"I'm no fake Indian," Cherokee Bill told the student body. "I am the Great Cherokee

Bill. Now if you want me to come tomorrow for chapel, tell me!"

"WE WANT YOU CHEROKEE BILL!" the students' voices applauded!

"Then you can have our chapel period tomorrow, Cherokee Bill," I said.

"Tomorrow, I'll show you what I can do with my whip," he said. "I'll show you how I can shoot chalk from the students' mouths! Tell your parents to come for chapel tomorrow. Tell them I'm the Great Cherokee Bill!"

"We'll tell 'em, Cherokee Bill!" a student yelled.

"And bring your rifles," he said, "so I can show you that I'm not a fake!"

Cherokee Bill had taken all of our chapel time with his free entertainment. Now that he had proven himself not to be a fake but a real entertainer, the students talked the rest of the day about Cherokee Bill. They could hardly wait for the chapel program next day. The boys he had pulled from the audience with his whip were a little peeved* at him but he asked my permission to talk with them awhile. I told him to talk with them long as he wanted to. He took a walk over the school yard with them.

peeved: irritated with

Next day school busses were loaded almost beyond capacity. It seemed to me the whole county had turned out to see the Great Cherokee Bill after the students had gone home and advertised him. Hill men with lean beardy faces and long rifles came to the high school. My office was packed with their rifles until it looked like an arsenal.* Men that bark a squirrel* with every shot, with long lantern jaws* bulging with home-grown quids* of burley* tobacco came—first time many had ever been inside a high school. Men who had preached that education was a fake and that it was ruining the country came to watch the Indian shoot. Men who secretly believed that they were better shots than any Indian came. Women, young girls who had never gone to school, mothers of students and mothers carrying young . . . babies, came. I had never seen such crowds at the high school not even for commencement exercises as had packed the schoolhouse and the yard. I knew we couldn't have school that day if we waited for the chapel period. I called the teachers together and we made arrangements for chapel the first period since Cherokee Bill was already there.

arsenal: a place for the storage of guns
bark a squirrel: to shoot at the bark of a tree directly below the squirrel so that the reverberations kill the squirrel without mutilating its body
lantern jaws: protruding lower jaws
quids: cuts
burley: light colored

Then we called the special first period chapel. And our chapel receipts* set a record! Money for Cherokee Bill and money for Maxwell High School! Even Cherokee Bill was pleasantly surprised when I told him his part would be over two hundred dollars!

receipts: money received for admission

"I'll show 'em what the Great Cherokee Bill can do," he said seriously.

Every seat in the auditorium was taken. The bleachers were filled; there wasn't standing room in the aisles. Only the stage was free for Cherokee Bill to show the audience he was the Great Cherokee Bill. When he walked onto the stage, Custardpie, Sparkie and Pewee were with him. There was a great cry went up from the student body; but the lean hill men with the beardy jaws stood in the aisles unmoved. And the hill women didn't show any signs of emotion. They remained true to their hill blood; they had to be shown.

"I'll show you mothers how to use a whip on your bad boys," Cherokee Bill said.

A smile spread over their sun-tanned broken faces.

Custardpie stood on one side of the stage holding a sheet of notebook paper stretched between his hands. He held it about eighteen inches in front of him. Cherokee Bill stood back at the far side of the stage, pulled the long whip over his shoulder and struck at the paper. The cracker split the paper as near the center as if one had measured and cut it with a knife. The audience was so still when he slashed with the whip, they could hear it cut the paper. Custardpie turned to the audience and showed them the paper split in halves. A great roar of voices then came from the audience.

"Hold that half up, Custardpie," Cherokee Bill said.

Cherokee Bill split the half into equal quarters. Custardpie held the quarter piece between his hands and Cherokee Bill split it into eighths. An eighth of the sheet was very small. The audience sat spellbound.

"Hold that piece for me," Cherokee Bill commanded Custardpie.

"I'm afraid," he said, his hands trembling.

"Hold it, Pewee!"

"All right, Cherokee Bill!"

Pewee stood holding the narrow piece of paper before the audience, his hands were steady as steel. Cherokee Bill drew back with his great whip, his black eyes engulfing* the paper as if he were aiming with a rifle. He came over, the whip made a ripping noise between Pewee's hands. Pewee turned to the audience with the paper split into sixteenths. A great applause went up from the audience.

---

engulfing: figuratively swallowing

"He could shore whop* a youngin," one hill woman said to another.

---

shore whop: surely whip

"Hold it again," he commanded.

"Not me," Pewee said. "That whip was too close to my fingers!"

"I'll hold it," Sparkie said.

Sparkie held the paper while Cherokee Bill measured the strip with the width of his whip cracker.

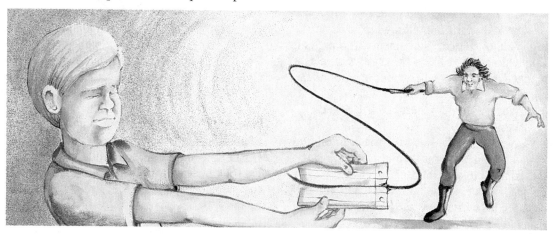

"Mighty close but I can do it," he said.

The audience waited breathlessly while he aimed and came over with the whip. There was a rip between Sparkie's hands. Sparkie turned with strips of paper almost razor-blade thinness. His hands were quivering. Cherokee Bill had done it.

"Did I hit your hands, Sparkie?"

"No, but it was awful close."

Great cheers came from the audience.

While Cherokee Bill rested from his whipping act, he asked the boys on the stage if they had money in their pockets. They told him they had. He told them it wasn't good money and they said it was. He asked to see a nickel. Pewee gave him a nickel. He put it between two of his front teeth, bent it double and gave it back to Pewee. "I told you it was no good," he said. Custardpie let him have a dime. He not only bent it but almost put a hole through it with his teeth. He bent a penny double. Then he took a quarter from his pocket, bent it double, and threw it back among the gawking beardy-jawed men in the aisle. Each examined it; then passed it to the next man.

"Wuz thar a trick to that whip stuff?" a long lean hill man pushed his way up front and asked. "Didn't the boys jerk the paper apart?"

"What do you think?" Cherokee Bill asked.

"I think thar wuz," he said.

Cherokee Bill drew his whip back as the high school students screamed with laughter. The whip cracked like a twenty-two rifle as it reached out—the cracker wrapping around the man's long unshaven neck.

"Was it a fake?" Cherokee Bill asked.

"Yes, I believe—"

Cherokee Bill drew the whip until the man's tongue shot out from his mouth as he pulled him close to the stage.

He shook his head "no" and Cherokee Bill released his whip. The man took back through the audience while the rest of the hill men laughed more than the students had ever laughed.

Then Cherokee Bill stepped off the stage. Pewee came with him. There was a long ladder, approximately fifteen feet, leaned against the wall. Pewee climbed up the ladder to the last rung. He locked his legs around the rung and held with his hands for dear life as Cherokee Bill lifted the ladder with one hand toward the high auditorium ceiling. A great applause went up and the beardy hill men craned* their long leather necks as Cherokee Bill's face, flushed red as a sliced beet, held the ladder trembling in the air—up, up, he lifted it—placing the bottom rung on his chin—walking beneath it—swaying back and forward—holding it balanced on his chin while Pewee reached up and touched the ceiling. There was a great applause as Cherokee Bill brought Pewee back safely to the floor.

---

craned: stretched

"Injuns must be a powerful lot," an old snaggled-tooth* squirrel hunter said.

---

snaggled-tooth: with irregular, broken teeth

Cherokee Bill leaped upon the high stage, Pewee climbed up the steps.

"Men, women, boys and girls," Cherokee Bill said, his breath a little short, "I will show you now how the Great Cherokee Bill can shoot!"

There was silence in the auditorium while Cherokee Bill placed a lead dish upon the stage wall to catch the cartridge balls. He arranged it to suit himself; then he placed Custardpie within four feet of it with a piece of chalk in his mouth. He put a blindfold over Custardpie's eyes and told him to stand still. He took his own rifle, stood at the far side of the stage, aimed the rifle, fired. "Ting" the battered bullet hit the lead dish and dropped on the floor approximately the same time half the stick of chalk fell. Half of the stick was in Custardpie's mouth. Custardpie trembled.

"Stand still, Custardpie," Cherokee Bill said, "I'm not goin' to hit you. I could cut that off with my whip and never touch your nose!"

He stood still while Cherokee Bill turned his rifle upside down and clipped the chalk even with his mouth. A great applause went up but Custardpie jerked the blindfold from over his eye and said someone else could have it since he felt the wind from the bullet. Then everybody laughed. The old squirrel hunters laughed, slapped each other on the shoulders and jabbed each other in the ribs with their bony hands. This was what they had come to see and this was what they liked. Two boys carried the rifles from the office to the stage floor. There was a tag on each rifle with the owner's name on it to keep from getting the rifles mixed.

"Men, the Great Cherokee Bill will try your rifles," the Indian said.

When he took a rifle from the stack, he shot it first at the lead plate on the wall; then he looked through the barrel. If the rifle suited him, he shot a piece of chalk from Sparkie's mouth. Many of the rifles he wouldn't use. He told the owners they weren't good—that the rifles* in the barrel were too well worn or that he didn't like the sight adjustments. Many of the rifles he bragged on* and this pleased the owners—men who loved the feel of a rifle— men attached to their rifles more than anything they possessed.

---

rifles: spiral grooves that give accuracy to the bullet
bragged on: praised

Just before he closed his program, he put a wheel rigged* so a boy could stand at the side and turn it. It had twenty-one pieces of chalk placed around it. With a rifle that shot twenty-one times, he got ready for his last, most difficult feat.* He arranged the wheel in front of the lead plate, so when he shot, the plate would catch the bullets. He showed Pewee how fast to turn the wheel. While he got himself in position, there was silence again. The men stood with their mouths open when the rifle began barking and the pieces of chalk, one by one, started falling as the wheel revolved past the lead plate. The bullets hit the lead plate, dropping to the stage floor like heavy grains of corn shelled from a cob. He broke the entire twenty-one. Everybody went wild with applause. The program was over. Men rushed up front to get their rifles. The chapel had lasted almost all morning. Cherokee Bill was a hero at Maxwell High School and more than a hero with the men from the hills. They wanted to shake his hand, invite him to their homes to squirrel hunt with them. And the high school students wanted him back for another program.

---

rigged: arranged
feat: act

"The Great Cherokee Bill must go on to new places," he told them.

While I penned a letter of recommendation to the principals of neighboring high schools for the Great Cherokee Bill, one of our teachers gave him his share of the chapel receipts. I tried to make it a letter of recommendation better than any I had read among the great sheaf of recommendations he was carrying. I tried to make it even better than the letter Willis Abernathy had written for him.

About the Story

1. Why were the students especially interested in Cherokee Bill's dress?
2. What is significant about Cherokee Bill's name?
3. Is Cherokee Bill just an entertainer?

4. What are the "tricks" Cherokee Bill performs?
5. Cherokee Bill is quite emphatic about his not being a fake, but are his skills traditional Indian ones?

About the Author

Jesse Stuart (1907-84) was born and reared in the hills of Kentucky and spent his childhood as most Kentucky boys did: plowing, harvesting, fishing, and rarely finishing a school year. He also spent quite a bit of time "coon hunting with a lantern and a volume of Robert Burns." He'd read poetry until the dogs had a coon treed. At the age of eighteen he ran away and joined a carnival but soon realized that he wanted an education. Eventually he finished college and returned to Kentucky where he taught and was principal in his old school. He wrote between ten and thirty thousand words a day, depending on whether school was in session. He loved the country and wanted to communicate that love to his readers. As one critic says, "All [his stories] have a heart."

The Landing of the Pilgrim Fathers

Felicia D. Hemans

The breaking waves dashed high
  On a stern and rock-bound coast,
And the woods against a stormy sky
  Their giant branches tossed;

And the heavy night hung dark   5
  The hills and waters o'er,
When a band of exiles* moored* their bark*
  On the wild New England shore.

Not as the conqueror comes,
  They, the true-hearted, came;
Not with the roll of the stirring drums,
  And the trumpet that sings of fame:

exiles: persons
  separated from their
  homeland
moored: anchored
10 bark: small ship

Not as the flying* come,
    In silence and in fear;
They shook the depths of the desert* gloom
    With their hymns of lofty cheer.

Amidst the storm they sang,
    And the stars heard, and the sea;
And the sounding* aisles of the dim woods rang
    To the anthem* of the free.

The ocean eagle soared
    From his nest by the white wave's foam,
And the rocking pines of the forest roared,—
    This was their welcome home.

. . . .

What sought they thus afar?
    Bright jewels of the mine?
The wealth of seas, the spoils* of war?—
    They sought a faith's pure shrine!*

Ay, call it holy ground,
    The soil where first they trod;
They have left unstained what there they found,—
    Freedom to worship God.

Glossary (margin notes):

flying: fleeing

15   desert: wilderness

20   sounding: resounding: i.e., reverberating, ringing

anthem: hymn

25

spoils: loot

shrine: sanctuary: They looked for a place to worship God truly.

30

About the Author

    Felicia D. Hemans (1793-1835) was born in Liverpool, England, and had her first volume of poetry published when she was fifteen. She later lived in Wales and Ireland, where she was a well-known figure. She was popular with both the public and with literary figures such as William Wordsworth, Lord Byron, and Sir Walter Scott. She wrote plays as well as sentimental verse, often with heroic subjects such as in this selection.

Crossing the Plains

Joaquin Miller

What great yoked brutes with briskets* low,
With wrinkled necks like buffalo,
With round, brown, liquid, pleasing eyes,
That turned so slow and sad to you,
That shone like love's eyes soft with tears,   5
That seemed to plead and make replies,
The while they bowed their necks and drew
The creaking load; and looked at you.
Their sable* briskets swept the ground,
Their cloven feet* kept solemn sound.   10

Two sullen* bullocks* led the line,
Their great eyes shining bright like wine;
Two sullen* captive kings were they,
That had in time held herds at bay,*
And even now they crushed the sod   15
With stolid* sense of majesty,
And stately* stepped and stately trod,
As if 't were something still to be
Kings even in captivity.

briskets: chests

sable: black
cloven feet: hoofs divided into two parts
sullen: moving slowly
bullocks: steers (cattle)
sullen: gloomy
held herds at bay: stopped or held herds at a safe distance
stolid: unemotional
stately: marked by imposing dignity

About the Poems

1. How does Hemans communicate the difficulties of the endeavor in her poem "The Landing of the Pilgrim Fathers"?
2. What is the attitude of the settlers and how does the poet communicate it?
3. Why did the settlers come to America?
4. Why does the poet say to "call [America] holy ground"?
5. How does Miller describe the oxen in "Crossing the Plains"?
6. What is the atmosphere created by the descriptions of the oxen?
7. How do the sounds in lines 16-18 help communicate the meaning of line 10?

Slurvian Self-Taught

John Davenport

Do you already speak Slurvian, or do you have a substitute language?

Listening to a well-known Hollywood commentator some time back, I heard her say that she had just returned from a Yerpeen trip and had had a lovely time nittly. I at once recognized her as an accomplished Slurvian linguist,* and, being a student of Slurvian, readily understood that she had just returned from a European trip and while there (in Yerp) had had a lovely time in Italy.

---

linguist: person accomplished in languages

Slurvian is coming into common use in the United States, but I am, so far as I know, the only scholar to have made a start toward recording it. There is no official written Slurvian language, but it is possible, by means of phonetic spelling,* for me to offer a brief course of instruction in it. In a short time the student can learn enough to add immeasurably to his understanding and enjoyment of conversation wherever he travels in the country.

---

phonetic spelling: spelling by sound

I first heard pure Slurvian fluently spoken by a co-worker of mine who told me that his closest friend was a man named Hard (Howard). Hard was once in an automobile accident, his car, unfortunately, cliding with another, causing Hard's wife Dorothy, who was with him, to claps. Dorothy didn't have much stamina but was a sweet woman—sweet as surp.

I soon discovered I had an ear for Slurvian, and since I began to recognize the language, I have encountered many Slurvians. At ballparks they keep track of hits, runs, and airs. On farms they plow furs. In florist shops they buy flars. When hard up, they bar money from banks, and spend it for everything from fewl for the furnace to gram crackers for the children.

When Slurvians travel abroad, they go to visit farn (or forn) countries to see what the farners do that's different from the way we Murcans do things. While in farn countries, they refer to themselves as Murcan tersts and usually say they will be mighty glad to get back to Murca. A Slurvian I once met on a train told me that he had just returned from a visit to Mexico. He deplored the lack of automobiles down there and said that the natives ride around on little burrs.

A linguistic authority of my acquaintance, much interested in my work in Slurvian, has suggested to me the possibility that the language may be related to, or a variation of, the one still spoken in England of which such a contraction as *Chumley,* for Cholmondeley, is a familiar example. However, I think the evidence insufficient for drawing such a conclusion. Surnames* cannot be considered subject to the ordinary rules of pronunciation. In fact, the only one I have positively identified in Slurvian is Faggot,* the name of the American admiral who won the Battle of Mobile Bay.

Surnames: last or family names
Faggot: Farragut

The name Faggot brings me to a discussion of what I designate as "pure" Slurvian. This includes those Slurvian words that when spelled exactly as pronounced also make good English words (such as *Faggot, burr,* and *claps*). The day I can add to the lexicon* such a word, hitherto unrecorded, is a happy day for me. Here are some examples of pure Slurvian, alphabetically listed:

---

lexicon: dictionary

---

bean, *n.* A living creature, as in *human bean.*

cactus, *n. pl.* The people in a play or story.

course, *n.* A group of singers.

fiscal, *adj.* Pertaining to the body, as opposed to the spurt.

form, *n.* Gathering place of the ancient Romans.

gnome, *n.* Contraction for *no, Ma'am, Colloq.*

line, *n.* The king of beasts.

lore, *n.* The more desirable of the two berths in a Pullman section.

myrrh, *n.* A looking glass.

par, *n.* An attribute of strength, as in *the par and the glory.*

plight, *adj.* Courteous.

sears, *adj.* Grave, intent.

sport, *v.t.* To hold up, to bear the weight of.

wreckers, *n. pl.* Discs on which music is recorded for phonographs.

I am presently engaged in compiling a dictionary of Slurvian words, which I hope will prove to be the definitive* work on the subject. The help of any interested students is welcomed, but I must caution such students to be certain the words are genuine Slurvian and not merely regional speech, such as that of Alabama, Texas, or New England.

---

definitive: authoritative

Let me close with a final example to make my meaning clear. Wherever you may be in the United States, if you hear the word "tare," the speaker probably is not referring to a biblical weed growing in the wheat.* More likely, he is describing the sensation of extreme fear experienced by a movie fan watching Borse Karloff in a harr picture.

---

biblical weed growing in the wheat: Matt. 13:25

About the Essay

1. Why does the author call this new language "Slurvian"?
2. Why is Slurvian not a written language?
3. Is the author as admiring of Slurvian as he says he is? Why or why not?

About the Author

John Davenport makes no claims to being a professional writer. Instead, he is a businessman who is, in his own words, "desperately fighting a losing battle against business English." His word game Slurvian grew out of his own enjoyment of listening to "the peculiarities of people's speech."

Billy, He's in Trouble

James Barton Adams

In this poem a father confesses that his son has failed him. Do you share the father's attitude?

I've got a letter, parson, from my son away out West,
An' my ol' heart's as heavy as an anvil* in my breast,
To think the boy whose futur' I had once so proudly
   planned
Should wander from the path o' right an' come to such
   an end!
I told him when he left us, only three short years ago,   5
He'd find himself a-plowin' in a mighty crooked row—

anvil: heavy iron block upon which metal is hammered

He'd miss his father's counsels, and his mother's prayers, too;
But he said the farm was hateful, an' he guessed he'd have to go.

I know thar's big temptation for a youngster in the West,
But I believed our Billy had the courage to resist;   10
An' when he left I warned him o' the ever-waitin' snares*   snares: traps
That lie like hidden sarpints* in life's pathway every-   sarpints: serpents
   wheres.
Our Bill, he promised faithful to be keerful,* an' allowed   keerful: careful
He'd build a reputation that'd make us mighty proud;
But it seems as how my counsel sort o' faded from his mind, 15
An' now the boy's in trouble of the very wustest* kind!   wustest: worst

His letters come so seldom that I somehow sort o' knowed
That Billy was a-trampin' on a mighty rocky road;
But I never once imagined he would bow my head in shame
An' in the dust would waller* his ol' daddy's honored   20   waller: wallow: disgrace
   name.
He writes from out in Denver, an' the story's mighty short;
I just can't tell his mother; it'd crush her poor ol' heart!
An' so I reckoned, parson, you might break the news to her—
Bill's in the Legislatur', but he doesn't say what fur.

. . . About the Author

Writing popular western stories and poems came naturally as a result of James Barton Adams's (b. 1843) lifetime spent in the West. He grew up in Ohio and Iowa and then spent time in the infantry during the Civil War. After the war he served as part of Captain North's famous Pawnee scouts, a unit using Indians to fight the Sioux and Cheyenne who attacked those building the Union Pacific Railroad. After the scouts were disbanded, Adams served as a courier, cowboy, rancher, prospector, and peace officer, or lawman, in the West. He was also a journalist for the *Denver Post*.

About the Poem

1. How remarkable is Billy's accomplishment?
2. Why did Billy go west?
3. Why does Billy's father go to the parson?

4. What does Billy's father obviously think the legislature is?

To Save the Golden State

Ralph Moody

The men and boys of the pony express galloped out of the American West into their own special place in American history. In Chapter 1 of Riders of the Pony Express, *Ralph Moody shows what brought the pony express into being. In Chapter 14 he shows how riders like Bart Riles dedicated their lives to the success of the venture. What do you think made them willing to risk their lives? Did anything good come from their efforts?*

When gold was discovered at Sutter's mill, the news had barely stirred a ripple in San Francisco, but April 3, 1860, was a day of wild excitement, joy, and celebration. A shouting crowd jammed Montgomery Street from gutter to gutter. Frightened horses bolted away, upsetting carriages and unseating riders.

The people of San Francisco had reason to celebrate. Their fastest means of communication with the East had been letters carried by stagecoach on the Butterfield Overland Mail route, and the trip took nearly a month. Now a rider, mounted on a swift horse, was ready to race away on the 1966-mile run to St. Joseph, Missouri, with the first Pony Express mail. If, as promised, the run could be made in ten days, Californians would for the first time be in close touch with news of the nation and their friends and relatives in the East. But the Pony Express had been established for a far greater reason than to furnish the Californians this convenience.

The embers of civil war were smoldering,* and slaveholding states were threatening to secede* from the Union. Although California had been admitted to the Union as a free state, its loyalty was very doubtful. Many of its citizens and government officials were from the South and were determined to swing the Golden State to the Confederacy. There was a great possibility of their success. Less than five hundred miles separated California from the slaveholding state of Texas, but nearly two thousand miles of wilderness and high mountains cut it off from the closest free state to the east. In addition, the Butterfield Overland Mail route lay entirely through the South, where Union communications to California could be cut at any time.

---

smoldering: burning slowly
secede: withdraw

The President and supporters of the Union were deeply worried. In case of war, the loss of California with its fabulous* wealth might be a staggering blow to the Union cause. If the state were to be saved, a faster and safer means of communication with loyal California Unionists must be established immediately.

fabulous: hardly believable

One of America's greatest strengths is her ability to produce men capable of meeting every national emergency. The man who rose to meet this one was William Russell. He was the senior partner of Russell, Majors & Waddell, overland freighters* between St. Joseph, Missouri, and Salt Lake City, Utah. He believed that by a central route light riders on relays* of fast horses could carry the mail between St. Joseph and San Francisco in ten days. From St. Joseph it could be speeded east by the newly built railroad.

freighters: cargo carriers
relays: fresh teams

At first everyone laughed at Mr. Russell's idea. Mountain men argued that the Rockies and Sierra Nevadas could never be successfully crossed in winter. Plainsmen argued that the Sioux and Paiute Indians would kill any lone rider trying to cross their homelands.

Mr. Russell still remained firm in his belief. He knew the western country thoroughly, and he knew the type of lightweight, hard-riding young horsemen it was producing. He was sure that eighty of the best among them, with four hundred fast horses, could overcome every obstacle with speed, courage, and determination.

To do the job, eighty well-supplied relay stations would have to be built along the most direct route—across the prairies and up the Platte and Sweetwater Rivers to South Pass, through rugged Utah, around Great Salt Lake, across the Nevada deserts and over the high Sierra Nevada Mountains of California. To guard the stations from Indian attack, and to provide food and shelter for riders and horses,

two hundred keepers and stablemen would be needed.

Mr. Russell knew the cost would be tremendous, but he offered to furnish the United States Government semiweekly,* ten-day Pony Express mail service between St. Joseph and San Francisco for $500 a round trip.

semiweekly: twice a week

When in January, 1860, Mr. Russell made his offer, the Senate was sharply divided between pro-slavery and anti-slavery forces. Southern senators were determined that Northern communications with California should not be improved. They were successful in blocking passage of a bill to pay for the carrying of Pony Express mail.

When the Senate refused to pay for their services, Mr. Russell and his partners decided that they had an obligation to their country, and would discharge* it regardless of cost to themselves. They immediately set to work, making careful plans for speeding and safeguarding the Pony Mail. They believed that both depended on the swiftness and endurance of relay ponies, since a single rider could not fight off Indian attacks and would have to escape them by running away. For this reason, a pony's load must be no more than 165 pounds. Only riders weighing 120 pounds or less would be hired, equipment must weigh no more than twenty-five pounds, and each rider's mail load would be limited to twenty pounds.

discharge: perform

To reduce weight, protect the mail, and speed up relays, Mr. Russell had special Pony Express saddles and *mochilas* made. The saddle was only a light wooden frame, with horn, cantle,* stirrups, and bellyband. The *mochila* (pronounced "mo CHEE la"), or mantle, was an easily removable leather cover that fitted

over the saddle, with openings to let the horn and cantle stick through. At each corner of the *mochila* there was a cantina, or pouch, for carrying mail. These were fitted with locks, and the keys would be kept only at Salt Lake City, San Francisco, and St. Joseph.

cantle: the rear part of a saddle, curved to form a seat

Each *mochila* would be carried the full length of the line, being moved from pony to pony as relays were made. Since the rider would be sitting on it, it could not be lost or stolen while he was mounted. If he were to be thrown or killed during his run, the *mochila* would remain on the saddle and, no doubt, be carried on to the next relay station by the riderless pony.

Mr. Russell knew every foot of the 1966-mile Pony Express trail, and divided it carefully into relays for the ponies and routes for the riders. Where the going would not be too hard for a pony, relay stations were spaced twenty-five to thirty miles apart. Where the country was rugged they were spaced nearer

together. Each rider was given from three to five relays in his route. At both ends he would have a "home station" where he would live between runs.

Every trip made with the Pony Express mail would be a race against time. In addition, Mr. Russell made them* races between the California and Mormon riders west of the Rockies and the prairie riders on the eastern side. Keen rivalry already existed, and he took full advantage of it in setting schedules and buying horses, doing his best to make the race an even one.

them: i.e., all pony express runs

For the rugged mountains and deserts west of the Rockies, he had tough mustangs* bought, and set the schedule at 165 miles a day. For the prairie riders he had many fast race horses purchased, and set the schedule at 220 miles a day. The prairie boys must ride considerably faster than the Westerners, but they would be following the Oregon Trail most of the way, and would have no high mountains to cross. Of course, there could be no finish line, for the race would start at both ends of the route. But whichever team was first to reach Bear River, on the Utah-Wyoming boundary, would be the winner.

mustangs: wild horses broken for riding

With their plans made, the partners wasted no time. They announced that Pony Express mail service would start from both San Francisco and St. Joseph at five o'clock on the afternoon of April 3. Then they sent the best men in their employ out to build relay stations, purchase hay and grain, buy the finest horses that could be secured at any price—and to find young men who were worthy of carrying their country's mail.

The West was full of rough, daring, and reckless gunmen who were afraid of nothing and could be hired for $80 a month: Russell, Majors & Waddell would have none of them. They would pay their Pony Express riders $100 to $150 a month, but no man would be entrusted to carry the mail until he had signed this pledge:

> I do hereby swear, before the Great and Living God, that during my engagement, and while I am an employe of Russell, Majors & Waddell, I will, under no circumstances, use profane language; that I will drink no intoxicating liquors; that I will not quarrel or fight with any other employe of the firm, and that in every respect I will conduct myself honestly, be faithful to my duties, and so direct all my acts as to win the confidence of my employers. So help me God.

As each rider was hired, he was given a light-weight rifle, a Colt revolver, a bright red flannel shirt, blue trousers, a horn, and a Bible. Each man was assigned to the part of the long trail that he knew best, and was given a few simple instructions.

In spite of weather, lack of rest, or personal danger to himself, the mail must go through. Whenever a *mochila* was brought in, he must immediately carry it over his route at the fastest speed his mounts could endure. Two minutes would be allowed for changing ponies at relay stops. To carry mail on schedule was his duty; to carry it safely was his trust. Whenever possible, he must avoid Indian fights, depending on his pony's speed to make an escape. The uniform might be worn or not, as the rider chose. If he wished, he might carry an extra revolver instead of a rifle.

Although the task seemed impossible, everything was in readiness by the afternoon of April 3. Twilight was just falling in San Francisco when the Pony Express agent locked the first St. Joseph mail into the cantinas. As the crowd whistled and shrieked, Jim Randall tossed the *mochila* over his saddle, swung aboard, and raced away on a beautiful Palomino pony.

Actually, Jim and the Palomino were no more than showpieces. Their run would be only to the wharf, where they would go aboard the steamer *Antelope* and ride quietly up the river to Sacramento. From there, the actual race was scheduled to start at midnight, and rough, tough Sam Hamilton would be the first real Pony Rider eastward.

Guard It with Your Life

At the height of the Paiute uprising, soldiers from Camp Floyd were sent into Nevada to punish the Indians. Being unfamiliar with the deserts, the officers often called upon Bart Riles to guide them.

At noon on May 15, 1860, Bart had just returned to Smith's Creek from an eighty-five mile guiding trip when a rider brought in the westbound mail. Stopping only to saddle his favorite Appaloosa pony, Bart took the *mo-chila* and cantered* away on the 117-mile Ambush Trail to Fort Churchill.

---

canter: a gait between galloping and trotting

He quit the trail soon after leaving Smith's Creek, circled far to the north, and began climbing the Shoshone mountain range cautiously. He planned to save enough of his pony's strength for a fast drive through Quaking Aspen Bottom, but the Indians had ambushed* every pass in the Shoshones. Three

San Francisco, California

times Bart was forced to out-race a band of well-armed warriors, and by the time he reached the thicket his pony was too leg-weary for a fast run.

---

ambushed: hidden in the bushes

Bart had barely entered the aspen thicket when an arrow whistled past his face. Ahead he could see no more than fifteen yards down the winding trail. But there, two warriors stood blocking his way with drawn bows. Dropping flat on his pony's neck, Bart charged them fiercely, hurrying their shots and making them miss. Spurring desperately, he drove his tired pony on at the very limit of its speed. From both sides of the trail arrows whizzed past them, and rifles blasted from no more than two or three yards away.

Halfway through the thicket the pony staggered, nearly fell, then regained its feet and plunged on heavily. Glancing back, Bart saw that the white patch on its rump was streaming blood. A bullet had ripped across it, laying the hide open as if cut by a knife. Bart stopped spurring and urged the pony on with his voice. It was doing its best and there was no sense in punishing it with the spurs. With every sharp

twist in the trail, the pony staggered, faltered, and drove on at a slower pace.

The trees were thinning and the end of the thicket was only yards away when Bart was nearly knocked from the saddle. There was no sharp pain, but he felt as if he had been hit in the side with a sledge hammer. He grabbed for the saddle horn with both hands as a bright light flashed before his eyes. Blackness closed in around the brightness, squeezing it down until only a speck remained. Then the speck flickered out.

When Bart came to, his hands were locked to the saddle horn, and his pony was struggling up the steep trail toward the pass through the Desatoya Mountains. It was only then that Bart realized he had been shot. A burning, aching pain dragged at his stomach. From above each hip blood oozed down the legs of his buckskins and dripped onto the *mochila*.

Dimly Bart realized that a bullet, fired from close range, had passed clear through him. He knew he was dying, but tried to shake the dizziness from his head, took off his neckerchief, tore it in half, and plugged the holes in his sides. Then, slowly and fumblingly, he ripped the hem from his jacket, tied it around

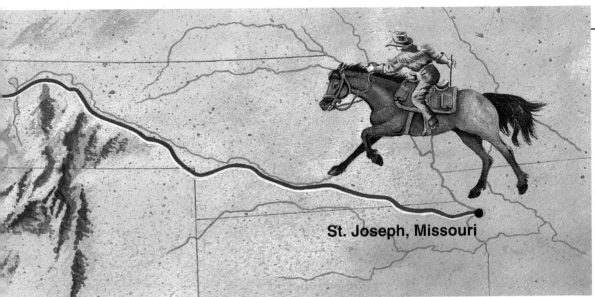

St. Joseph, Missouri

his waist and knotted himself tightly to the saddle horn. It was still ten miles to Cold Spring, and he knew he could never stay conscious to get there. If he fell from his pony it would stop or leave the trail and the mail would be destroyed by the Indians. If he could keep his body in the saddle, whether unconscious or dead, the pony would stick to the trail and keep going until it reached the station.

From the Cold Spring station, keeper Jim McNaughton and Jay Kelley saw an Appaloosa pony limping slowly down the mountain trail in the gathering twilight. It looked like a pack horse with the pack slipped far over to one side, but they knew the pony to be Bart's. And they knew only too well what the sagging pack would be. Mounting, they raced up the trail to meet the staggering pony and its burden. Bart's body hung from the saddle horn like a bloodsoaked bag of grain, his head resting on his knee. At first they could not be sure that he was breathing, but there was a weak murmur of pulse in his wrist.

The men who made the Pony Express successful were too strong to be deterred* by tragedy. As Jim McNaughton lifted Bart gently from the saddle, he told Kelley, "I'll get him back to the station and do what I can for him, Jay. You run that mail on through to Churchill. With night a-fallin' you can prob'ly make it all right."

deterred: stopped

Jay stripped the blood-streaked *mochila* from Bart's saddle and tossed it across his own. Jim McNaughton had barely turned down the trail with Bart in his arms before Jay raced past them, heading out on the 87-mile night ride to Fort Churchill.

All through the night Jim McNaughton sat at Bart's side, tending his wounds and trying to rouse him enough to swallow stimulants.* Toward morning semiconsciousness returned, but only long enough for Bart to whisper a few words about the ambush. At dawn he roused again and mumbled, *"Diga al Señor Bob que guardé con mi vida."* (Tell Mr. Bob that I guarded it with my life.) Then the light flickered out for one of the bravest Mexican boys this country has ever known.

stimulants: coffee or liquor

About the Author

Ralph Moody (b. 1898) began his writing career after his fiftieth birthday. His teenage daughter needed help with a writing assignment, and he volunteered to take a night class in writing to see if he could learn something that would help with her homework. The short story he turned in for the class was so well done that the teacher encouraged him to turn it into a book, and so he did. *Little Britches* became a beloved book for children of all ages, and Ralph Moody became a writer.

Moody grew up on a farm. After his father died and his family moved to the city, he was "banished to [his] grandfather's farm . . . because [he] just couldn't learn to be a city boy." As a result, his works give a picture of country life and the values that often result from a life spent in the outdoors in hard work. These values of courage, determination, and loyalty are clear in this selection about the founding of the pony express.

About the Story

1. What event made the pony express necessary?
2. What did the pony express save California from?
3. Why might a rider choose not to wear the uniform he was given?
4. The pony express rider was told that "to carry mail on schedule was his duty; to carry it safely was his trust"; what is the difference between "trust" and "duty" and which one accounts for Bart Riles's action?

Paul Revere's Ride

Henry Wadsworth Longfellow

In the last selection you read about an unknown American hero. In "Paul Revere's Ride" Longfellow retells a story that almost everyone knows. Which account of heroism do you find more inspiring?

Listen, my children, and you shall hear
Of the midnight ride of Paul Revere,
On the eighteenth of April, in Seventy-five;*   Seventy-five: 1775
Hardly a man is now alive
Who remembers that famous day and year.   5

He said to his friend, "If the British march
By land or sea from the town to-night,
Hang a lantern aloft in the belfry arch
Of the North Church tower as a signal light,—
One, if by land, and two, if by sea;   10
And I on the opposite shore will be,
Ready to ride and spread the alarm
Through every Middlesex village and farm,
For the country folk to be up and to arm."

Then he said, "Good night!" and with muffled* oar   15   muffled: quieted
Silently rowed to the Charlestown shore,
Just as the moon rose over the bay,
Where swinging wide at her moorings* lay   moorings: anchors or
The Somerset, British man-of-war;   ropes holding the ship
                                                 in place
A phantom* ship, with each mast and spar*   20   phantom: ghostlike
Across the moon like a prison bar,   mast and spar: poles
And a huge black hulk, that was magnified   supporting the sails
By its own reflection in the tide.   and lines

Meanwhile, his friend, through alley and street,
Wanders and watches with eager ears,   25
Till in the silence around him he hears
The muster of men at the barrack* door   barrack: building to
The sound of arms, and the tramp of feet,   house soldiers
And the measured tread of the grenadiers,*   grenadiers: British
Marching down to their boats on the shore.   30   soldiers

Then he climbed the tower of the Old North Church,
By the wooden stairs, with stealthy tread,
To the belfry-chamber overhead,
And startled the pigeons from their perch
On the sombre* rafters, that round him made   35   sombre: dark and gloomy
Masses and moving shapes of shade,—
By the trembling ladder, steep and tall,
To the highest window in the wall,
Where he paused to listen and look down
A moment on the roofs of the town,   40
And the moonlight flowing over all.

Beneath, in the churchyard, lay the dead,
In their night-encampment on the hill,
Wrapped in silence so deep and still
That he could hear, like a sentinel's* tread,   45   sentinel's: sentry's
The watchful night-wind, as it went
Creeping along from tent to tent,
And seeming to whisper, "All is well!"
A moment only he feels the spell
Of the place and the hour, and the secret dread   50
Of the lonely belfry and the dead;
For suddenly all his thoughts are bent
On a shadowy something far away,
Where the river widens to meet the bay,—
A line of black that bends and floats   55
On the rising tide, like a bridge of boats.

Meanwhile, impatient to mount and ride,
Booted and spurred, with a heavy stride
On the opposite shore walked Paul Revere.
Now he patted his horse's side,   60
Now gazed at the landscape far and near,
Then, impetuous,* stamped the earth,   impetuous: impulsive
And turned and tightened his saddle-girth;*   and forceful
But mostly he watched with eager search   saddle-girth: strap
The belfry-tower of the Old North Church,   65
As it rose above the graves on the hill,
Lonely and spectral* and sombre and still.   spectral: ghostly

And lo! as he looks, on the belfry's height
A glimmer, and then a gleam of light!
He springs to the saddle, the bridle he turns,   70
But lingers and gazes, till full on his sight
A second lamp in the belfry burns!

A hurry of hoofs in a village street,
A shape in the moonlight, a bulk in the dark,
And beneath, from the pebbles, in passing, a spark   75
Struck out by a steed flying fearless and fleet:
That was all! And yet, through the gloom and the light,
The fate of a nation was riding that night;
And the spark struck out by that steed, in his flight,
Kindled the land into flame with its heat.   80

He has left the village and mounted the steep,
And beneath him, tranquil and broad and deep,
Is the Mystic,* meeting the ocean tides;
And under the alders* that skirt its edge,
Now soft on the sand, now loud on the ledge,   85
Is heard the tramp of his steed as he rides.
It was twelve by the village clock,
When he crossed the bridge into Medford town.
He heard the crowing of the cock,
And the barking of the farmer's dog,   90
And felt the damp of the river fog,
That rises after the sun goes down.

It was one by the village clock,
When he galloped into Lexington.
He saw the gilded* weathercock*   95
Swim in the moonlight as he passed,
And the meeting-house windows, blank and bare,
Gaze at him with a spectral glare,
As if they already stood aghast
At the bloody work they would look upon.   100

It was two by the village clock,
When he came to the bridge in Concord town.
He heard the bleating of the flock,
And the twitter of birds among the trees,
And felt the breath of the morning breeze   105
Blowing over the meadows brown.

Mystic: a river flowing
into Boston harbor

alders: trees or shrubs
of the birch family

gilded: covered with a
thin layer of gold

weathercock:
weathervane

And one was safe and asleep in his bed
Who at the bridge would be first to fall,
Who that day would be lying dead,
Pierced by a British musket-ball.   110

You know the rest. In the books you have read,
How the British Regulars fired and fled,—
How the farmers gave them ball for ball,
From behind each fence and farm-yard wall,
Chasing the red-coats down the lane,   115
Then crossing the fields to emerge again
Under the trees at the turn of the road,
And only pausing to fire and load.

So through the night rode Paul Revere;
And so through the night went his cry of alarm   120
To every Middlesex village and farm,—
A cry of defiance and not of fear,
A voice in the darkness, a knock at the door,
And a word that shall echo forevermore!
For, borne on the night-wind of the Past,   125
Through all our history, to the last,
In the hour of darkness and peril and need,
The people will waken and listen to hear
The hurrying hoof-beats of that steed,
And the midnight message of Paul Revere.   130

About the Author

One of the most popular nineteenth-century writers, Henry Wadsworth Longfellow (1807-82) wrote stirring poetry that was familiar to almost every schoolchild of his day. He chose to write about American subjects, as he does in this selection about the American Revolution. He himself came from a long line of distinguished Americans. His father's people were outstanding New England colonists, and his mother's were of Puritan stock and included a Revolutionary War general. Longfellow was the first American to be honored in Poet's Corner in Westminster Abbey in London, England, in recognition not only of his skill but also his popularity among the readers of his age and of today as well.

Molly Pitcher

Kate Brownlee Sherwood

Molly Pitcher was a heroine of the War for Independence. She earned her nickname by carrying water to her husband and other American soldiers. Historians, however, believe that the following incident is legendary. Does that fact harm the poem?

'Twas hurry and scurry at Monmouth town,
  For Lee* was beating a wild retreat;
The British were riding the Yankees down,
  And panic was pressing on flying feet.

> Lee: General Charles Lee (1731-82)

Galloping down like a hurricane   5
  Washington rode with his sword swung high,
Mighty as he* of the Trojan plain*
  Fired by a courage from the sky.

> he: Achilles, hero of the Greek epic *The Iliad*
> Trojan plain: the plain outside the walls of Troy

"Halt, and stand to your guns!" he cried.
  And a bombardier* made swift reply.   10
Wheeling his cannon into the tide,*
  He fell 'neath the shot of a foeman* nigh.

> bombardier: soldier who operates a cannon
> tide: battle
> foeman: enemy

Molly Pitcher sprang to his side,
  Fired as she saw her husband do.
Telling the king in his stubborn pride   15
  Women like men to their homes are true.

Washington rode from the bloody fray*
  Up to the gun that a woman manned.
"Molly Pitcher, you saved the day,"
  He said, as he gave her a hero's hand.   20

> fray: battle

He named her sergeant with manly praise,
  While her war-brown face was wet with tears—
A woman has ever a woman's ways,
  And the army was wild with cheers.

. . . . Αbout the Author

Kate Sherwood (1841-1914) spent most of her life in journalism. Raised in Ohio in a judge's family, she received an excellent education, then married a journalist. Through his profession she found an excellent outlet for her own talents. Learning every aspect of the trade from setting type to writing stood her in good stead when her husband enlisted to fight in the Civil War. Rather than have the newspaper go under, Kate Sherwood ran it herself and contributed articles to other papers as well. When her husband became a member of Congress, Mrs. Sherwood became a Washington correspondent for several newspapers and continued her writing. In addition to her journalistic writing and political satires, she also wrote patriotic plays for schoolchildren to perform. The best of her work relates to patriotic events, often set in the Civil War.

About the Poems

1. In Longfellow's poem, what signals how the British move, by land or sea?
2. What kind of atmosphere does the author create in the poem?
3. What does line 78 mean in the context of the poem? What is the relationship of line 124 to the rest of the poem?
4. To what "king in his stubborn pride" does Molly demonstrate her love of home

in Sherwood's poem? Why is the bombardier's action so important?
5. What does the poet mean by "a woman has ever a woman's ways"?
6. A commonly accepted part of the Molly Pitcher story is that the gunner who was killed by the British shot was her husband; what effect does this have on your evaluation of Molly's action?

Monty Takes Charge of the Barter Store

Nina Brown Baker

Even as a teenager, Monty was a merchandising genius. What qualities of character, though, make him successful?

St. Joseph, Michigan, was a flourishing lake port, considerably larger than Monty's home town of Niles. Its twin village, Benton Harbor, was a woodworking center, but St. Joseph lived on shipping.

From its harbor the long ships plied* across the lake to Chicago and Milwaukee loaded with Michigan lumber and grain—and, at this time of the year, with Michigan peaches.

---
plied: sailed

Peaches were nothing new to young Ward. All the farmers around Niles relied upon fruit as their principal crop. Most of the barrels turned out at Mr. Johnny's factory were peach barrels. But Monty had never seen peaches in such quantities as came to the St. Joe docks. Day and night, in this summer weather, the air was heavy with the rich, tantalizing smell.

There was no refrigeration, and the shippers had to work fast before the precious cargo spoiled. Flares burned on the dock all night long. Captain Boughton was everywhere, urging the loaders to greater speed. While the peach season lasted, he had no time to spare for his store.

The store, Monty discovered, was rather an odd one. It was a big, shabby warehouse near the river. No attempt was made to attract town trade. Captain Boughton's customers were farmers who brought their products to town. The business done there was one of barter. So many bushels of peaches for a suit of clothes; so much corn for shoes or a dress length of flannel.

This business of barter was common enough in all country villages. Larger towns, such as St. Joseph, rather looked down upon it. Farmers with produce to trade found themselves more comfortable in Captain Boughton's place than in the more citified shops on Main Street.

The Captain dropped Monty off at the dock on a bright July morning. The big steamer was waiting for the load his smaller boat had brought.

"There she is." Captain Boughton gestured toward the store. "Won't have time to take you over. Just go along and tell Carver I sent you. He'll put you to work."

Monty picked up his carpetbag and made his way to the store. Several loaded wagons stood at the hitching rail. Inside, the single big room was already filling up with farmers and their families.

To the boy in the doorway, the scene was one of complete confusion. There were no counters, no shelves. Big wooden packing boxes spilled their contents onto the floor. Side by side with the store's goods were the barrels and crates of produce the farmers had brought in. The floor was littered with excelsior packing,* with overripe peaches trampled underfoot, with stray cabbage leaves and corn husks. A coop* full of live chickens squawked furiously above the din* of human voices.

---

excelsior packing: wood shavings
coop: cage
din: noise

Monty waited a minute, trying to sort it all out. Near him a calico-clad farm woman was trying on shoes. There was no place for her to sit down. She stood on one foot, balancing herself with the aid of a woman clerk, while a little girl tugged at her skirts. Further along, an old man was unrolling a length of oilcloth for two women. Farm families were milling* about, picking up articles and laying them down, waiting for someone to attend to them.

---

milling: moving

Monty picked his way toward the back, where a young man was arguing violently with a farmer and his half-grown son. The young man would be Mr. Carver, the manager, he decided. He drew close and listened.

It was all about a load of green corn the farmer had in his wagon outside. Mr. Carver had inspected the corn. He had agreed that it was worth a suit of clothes for the boy. Here was the suit. All right, maybe it wasn't the finest quality cloth. What could you expect for one measly* load of roasting ears? So the boy wasn't satisfied with the fit or color, was he? Now that was just too bad. It was news to Mr. Carver that a farm kid had to dress like a gentleman going to the governor's ball. This was plenty good enough for country wear. No,

he couldn't offer any other suit. Not for that corn. Take it or leave it.

measly: small

Grumbling, the farmer took it. As soon as they left, Monty approached the manager.

"I'm the new boy," he said awkwardly. "Captain Boughton said you'd put me to work."

"I'll do that, all right," Mr. Carver snapped. "No loafing around here, as you'll find out. What's your name? Ward? Come along, Ward."

He led the way to a door in the rear. Beyond it was a storeroom cluttered with packing boxes.

"Open these up," the manager ordered. "Get the stock out and fill up the boxes inside. Shoes with the shoes, yard goods on top of yard goods. You understand? Don't let 'em get low. As soon as one of these boxes is empty, split it up for kindling and pile it in the woodshed outside."

"You'll bunk there." Carver pointed to a cot in the corner. A packing box beside it held a tin washbasin and pail. "Miss Mattie will show you where to put the stuff inside. Step lively, now."

Miss Mattie was the clerk who had been selling shoes. She smiled at Monty as he approached her with an armload of rubbers and gum boots.

"Women's and children's in this box; men's in that one. Here, I'll help you. I like to keep 'em sorted out, though Mr. Carver thinks that's just my fussiness. Well, so you're our new mealer.* Didn't Captain tell you? He wants you to sleep in the store, sort of a guard against thieves. But you're to have your meals at my house. Hope we can fill you up—I know you boys all have hollow legs."

mealer: one who eats his meals with a family as part of his pay

She chattered on while they worked, demanding to know his name, how many brothers and sisters he had, and whether he smoked or drank or chewed tobacco.

"Because I might as well tell you now," she said severely, "Mother won't have any of that around her house. She's mighty strict."

Monty grinned. "So's my ma. I've never touched liquor or tobacco, ma'am. She'd make Pa lick me if I did. She only lets him smoke his pipe out in the woodshed."

Miss Mattie nodded approval. "I knew you came from a good home, minute I set eyes on you. But I had to ask. There. Now you better look around and see what else is getting low and fill up where it's needed."

The store, which had opened at daybreak, closed for an hour at noon. Monty went home with Miss Mattie Diefendorf for midday dinner.

Mr. Carver kept Monty busy until the store closed at sundown. He unloaded peaches and garden produce taken in trade and trundled* them down to the pier for shipment. He carried heavy bundles to the wagons and fed and watered the customers' horses. When the store closed, he swept out and covered the stock for the night. Then he went home with Miss Mattie for another lordly* meal.

trundled: rolled
lordly: large

"Carver's satisfied with you," Miss Mattie told him as they walked along. "He don't say much, but you could see. He likes the way you hop to it the first time he speaks. Looks like you got yourself a steady job, sonny."

"I hope so," Monty answered. "I like the work. But Miss Mattie, does the store have to be such a mess? I mean—well, wouldn't it be better if there was some sort of system to it—like the stock all on one side, where it wouldn't get mixed up with the farm stuff? I don't mean to find fault," he added hastily.

The little woman nodded. "That's exactly what I've told the Captain myself. He just laughs, and says he leaves the store to Carver. And Carver don't care. All he's interested in is to bargain the farmers down as low as he can. He says that's what he's there for."

"Yes, but—" Monty hesitated, and then plunged ahead. "He's so hateful to the farmers! Talks to 'em like they were the dirt under his feet. You'd think he could be a little polite."

It was less than six months later that young Mr. Carver departed to open his own store. As his successor, Captain Boughton named Mr. Brown. This was the old gentleman who had been Miss Mattie's fellow clerk.

"I know he's deaf and not very spry,"* the Captain told Miss Mattie and Monty. "But he's been with me a long time, and I hate to pass him over. You two will have to help him out. Monty, I'm hiring a new boy and moving you up to clerk in Brown's place. Just make out the best you can."

---

spry: active

They made out very well. Old Man Brown, proud of his new title, was quite content to leave his new duties to his staff. Between them, Miss Mattie and Monty ran the store. They ran it with an efficiency unknown up to now.

Their first move was to separate the two departments. One side of the store was left free for the farmers' produce. On the opposite side, Monty put up shelves and counters, made from the packing-box lumber. Miss Mattie proudly arranged her stock in orderly array.* And, for the first time, each article carried a price tag.

---

array: display

This was Monty's idea. Miss Mattie listened sympathetically while he explained it. Old Man Brown listened too.

"It'll make it easier for us, and it'll please the farmers," Monty argued. "They never see cash money for what they raise. But it's *worth* money. So why don't we put a cash price on it? Instead of saying we'll give a suit of clothes for a load of corn, we could say we'd give four dollars. Then let him pick out a four-dollar suit, or four dollars' worth of anything he wants."

"We've never done it that way," Miss Mattie observed. "It was always a case of what we wanted to sell most. If we were overstocked on shoes, we'd offer him shoes; or maybe a suit, if we'd got lots of suits. We didn't give him a free choice."

"I know, and that's just what I want to change. Why shouldn't he have a free choice? He would if he had the cash in hand, and his stuff is as good as cash. And about being overstocked—well, it doesn't seem to me that being overstocked is good business. Why can't we do some figuring before we make out our orders? Keep track of what we have the most call for, and buy more of that and less of the things they don't need so much."

Mr. Brown put in an unexpected word. "Reckon we got enough collar buttons on hand

to last till Judgment Day. Don't seem to be no call for collar buttons no more."

"Well, of course not," Monty said eagerly. "All our customers have *got* collar buttons. You don't wear a collar button out. Unless you lose one, you never have to buy another. It's not right to force things they don't need on people."

"I think you're right, Monty," Miss Mattie said. "And I like your notion* of putting cash prices on everything—their stuff and ours. Only I don't quite see how you'd handle it. You can't really give them cash. They might go out and spend it somewhere else. Captain Boughton would never stand for that."

---

notion: idea

"No, I'm afraid not. We'd have to keep it so no real money changes hands. What I'd do, I'd give them a due bill, good for so much in dollars. They'd take it across the store, look at the prices there, and spend it any way they wanted to. It'd be awful handy for the little things that make so much trouble now— thread and pins and such. Give a farmer's wife a dollar due bill, and I bet you she'd enjoy herself all morning. We might even get rid of a few collar buttons that way." He laughed.

"It looks like a grand scheme to me, Monty," Miss Mattie said warmly. "I'm in favor of trying it."

There was a little pause, while they waited for Old Man Brown to speak. After all, he *was* the manager.

At last he nodded. "It sounds all right to me. Captain don't like to be bothered. You young folks just go ahead and fix it up to suit yourselves."

As Monty had foreseen, the new system appealed strongly to the farmers. Even though they never saw the money, it was gratifying*

to have a cash figure placed on the fruits of their labors.

---

gratifying: pleasing

The women customers liked the new plan. Even better, they liked the attractive new displays of merchandise. Miss Mattie managed a sit-down bench for shoe fitting and a mirror for trying on hats. The place no longer looked like a cluttered jungle. It was a real store now.

As the months went by, Monty took on more and more of the manager's duties. Miss Mattie liked selling best. It was Monty who bargained with the farmers, and Monty who kept track of the stock and made out new orders for the wholesalers' salesmen. When Mr. Brown's failing eyesight made the bookkeeping difficult, Monty offered to take over the accounts.

"I don't know the first thing about it," he said frankly. "But I can learn if you'll show me, Mr. Brown."

The old man was glad to agree. His lessons were not very helpful, but Captain Boughton loaned Monty an up-to-date textbook on business accounting. The new boy was sleeping in the store now, and Monty had a room in the Diefendorf cottage. There, night after night, he studied until he turned himself into a first-class bookkeeper.

His interest did not end there. The whole field of merchandising fascinated him. In storekeeping he had found his life work, the "something a man can put his heart into." He bought or borrowed every business book he could lay hands on. Among them was a little volume on business letter writing. With it as a guide, he worked earnestly to bring correctness into his everyday speech. A big merchant, as he meant to be some day, must not talk like a day laborer.

Monty Takes Charge of the Barter Store   293

About the Story

1. What character qualities does Monty have that make him a success in business?
2. What is perhaps the primary quality that makes Monty change business practices and become a success?
3. Why does Mr. Carver not succeed?
4. List the changes that Monty makes to improve the barter store.
5. What is the name of the chain of stores that Monty established?

About the Author

In spite of the sale of her first story, Nina Baker (1888-1957) decided after her second story was rejected that she could not be a short story writer and went to school to become a teacher. Taking a school in the rural area of Colorado, she found she had many things to learn about the country. She and her students rode horses to school from many miles away. At least she rode *to* school. The first day of school she rode her horse to school but walked the seven miles home because she didn't know how to get on the horse by herself! She soon learned and eventually enjoyed her time teaching in the West. Her desire to write resurfaced, and she tried again with more success, but she found that she enjoyed writing books more than short stories. And she found that she enjoyed working on biographies more than any other kind of story. In addition to this story about an early merchandising magnate, she also wrote about F. W. Woolworth.

The Wright Brothers

Joseph Cottler and Haym Jaffe

Today we think nothing of an airplane flight across the country or even across an ocean. But only for the last few decades has flight been a possibility for mankind. This essay gives the European background for the Wright brothers' famous flight at Kitty Hawk. It also reminds us of our debt to those who have gone before us.

The story is told that in ancient Greece lived Daedalus, a famous mechanic, and his son Icarus. Once, when the two were far from home, visiting Crete, King Minos clapped them in prison. Seeking a means of escape over the vast sea, Daedalus fashioned wax wings for himself and Icarus, and away they flew to Sicily. Daedalus fared safely, but unhappily Icarus soared too near the sun. The wax melted, and down he plunged into the sea. . . .

Every age has told a story like this, because there have always been men wistful to fly. Some dreamed of floating lazily on a cloud, while others envied the wings of the bird. Both dreams have come true—although both came strangely disguised. He who wishes to float through the air may do so today in a balloon or in an airship, and the wings of an aeroplane will take man anywhere faster than the wings of the strongest bird.

We must thank the Montgolfier brothers for making the dream of floating in the air come true. In the little town of Annonay, France, there still stands the paper mill that was theirs. But life held for them many more interesting things than paper mills—chimney smoke, for instance.

"Stephen, just see how eagerly the smoke ascends," said Joseph to his brother, as they sat before the fireplace, watching the smoldering logs. "I was thinking," he continued, "that since the smoke rises with so much force, perhaps we can get it to carry something up with it. Up above it, it would float like a cloud."

Stephen was silent for a moment. "If we could capture a cloud, and put it in a bag, the bag would float. The bag would defy the pull of the earth."

"We can't do that. How could we reach the cloud? But I'll tell you what we can do. Let's catch the smoke of the chimney in a bag."

For the next six months, at odd moments, they made their bag "to catch smoke." Wisely they kept the idea secret, knowing well that the villagers would laugh if they heard of such a foolish plan. The bag was made of fine silk and blown up. The bottom of the silk bag they purposely left open.

In the middle of November, 1782, they were ready for their great test. Under the opening of the bag, Joseph Montgolfier put some burning paper. Smoke entered the bag. And as the bag filled with the smoke, it rose to the ceiling of the room.

"Smoke does carry the bag up," cried Stephen. "Let's try it again, under the open sky."

There, to their delight, the silken bag rose seventy feet high. And when it finally fell, it was by a very gentle decline.

People heard the strange news, and scoffed. The brothers therefore decided to make larger bags, and with these convince the world of their discovery. They invited all to see their new balloon. The crowd that came to laugh at the brothers who could make things float in the air stood in amazement when the balloon shot six thousand feet into the air.

When the great news reached Paris, the scientists there invited the brothers to repeat their experiment in the French capital. These learned men—among whom was Benjamin Franklin—stood with bated breath* as they watched the balloon rise.

bated breath: hardly breathing

The greatest triumph for the Montgolfier brothers came when the King of France wished them to repeat their experiment before the entire court of France. On this occasion the balloon carried the first passengers of the air—a sheep, a rooster, and a duck.

The Montgolfier brothers, however, might find it hard to believe that the mighty dirigible of today is the descendant of the bag they made to catch and hold chimney smoke.

II

"If a bird can master the air, why can't we?" thought other dreamers. But the daring ones who tried were usually killed and cited* as warnings to other rash* souls.

cited: mentioned
rash: reckless

To Otto Lilienthal in Pomerania, Germany, the fate of other men was not a warning. "No wonder we failed," he said. "We know too little about the laws of flying. First we must watch the birds."

For a long time he watched these creatures which glide about in the air so easily. "How does the wind lift a bird's wings?" was the question he studied. No one before had ever watched birds as thoroughly as Lilienthal did. He made hundreds of sketches of a bird's wings in various positions—when the bird begins to fly, when it rises, when it soars, and when it lands. For twenty years he continued his bird study. At the end of that time he was ready to build a machine which would make man a rival of the bird. There was no need for guesswork; he knew exactly how he ought to build it.

In 1891 the world had a shock. With its own eyes it saw a man gliding through the air on tremendous wings. He looked like a gigantic bat hovering aloft. The legend of Daedalus had come true.

"Man can fly. All he needs is practice," said Lilienthal, as he thrust his arms through padded tubes and held fast to a crossbar. Once the gliding machine was firmly attached, he was ready to leap from a hill into the air.

He could glide as much as a hundred yards, and learned to soar as well. To steer himself, he tried moving his body about—forward, backward, or from side to side. "I need more practice," he thought. "When I can balance myself as well as a cyclist who controls his wheel, I shall have won."

After a fashion, Lilienthal did win, for he learned to turn a complete circle and to stay poised in the air like a gull. Five years of practice and more than two thousand flights in his glider made Lilienthal an expert.

"I am now ready to try a motor in my glider," he said to his friends.

He built a new flying machine, into which he put a small motor. Then, one summer day, he took off, a large crowd watching him. For a few moments he soared. Then came a sudden lull in the wind. Something went wrong with the motor. Like Icarus, Lilienthal fell.

III

The newsboy had left a paper, as usual, at the Wright Cycle Company in Dayton, Ohio.

Wilbur Wright, a large man with gray eyes and a long aquiline* nose, glanced through the paper. "What's this!" he exclaimed, as he turned to his brother Orville. "The flying man killed!"

---

aquiline: curved like an eagle's beak

Orville looked up from his work. Wilbur continued: "Berlin, August 12—Herr Otto Lilienthal, an engineer, who for many years experimented with the building of flying machines, met with an accident that resulted in his death. . . ."

As he prolonged the reading about Lilienthal, both brothers became greatly interested. Deeply impressed by Lilienthal's work, they sent to Berlin for a copy of his book.

The book came. "It's in German," they said disappointingly. They could only look at the pictures. But within a short time they had learned enough German to understand the book thoroughly.

They liked the way Lilienthal emphasized the idea of constant practice. "Every bird is an acrobat," he wrote. "Whoever would master the air must learn to imitate the birds. We must fly and fall, and fall and fly, until we can fly without falling."

From the time of Lilienthal's fall, Orville and Wilbur thought less and less of their bicycle business. The lure of flying had seized them. They read all they could about flying, and they began to watch the birds on the wing. If, when they were in their shop, one of the brothers spied a flock of birds flying by, "Birds!" he would shout. Both would drop their work, and rush to the window, gazing until the birds were out of sight.

For the rest of the day, during their spare time, they would argue about what they had seen—about how the bird soars, how its wings are shaped when outstretched, how it balances. For days on end they talked about these matters.

"I'm right," Orville would say. "It's like this . . ."

"No, I'm right," Wilbur would insist. "It's like that . . ."

"Well," Orville would hesitate, "I guess you are right."

Wilbur would be silent for some moments. "No, Orville. I see that you have the better idea," he would finally admit. And they would laugh and go on happily.

They could hardly wait till Sunday afternoon. Then, for hours and hours, they would lie on their backs on a hill outside of Dayton, watching buzzards soar on the rising currents of air.

For five years they studied and argued about flying. They made tiny machines which they flew in the air like kites.

"I've figured it out," reflected one of the brothers. "Lilienthal, in five years, spent about five hours of actual gliding in the air."

"The wonder," returned his brother, "is not that he accomplished so little, but that he accomplished so much."

"Imagine a bicycle rider attempting to ride through crowded city streets after five hours of practice, spread out in bits of ten seconds over five years! Yet even with this brief practice, wasn't Lilienthal remarkably successful in overcoming the eddies* in the gusts of wind? If we could only find some way by which we could practice by the hour instead of by the second, we could solve the problem. . . ."

---

eddies: crosscurrents or circular movements

To this dangerous of hobbies, they began to devote all their time and energy, for Wilbur and Orville were thorough mechanics and, in addition, were captivated by aeronautics.*

aeronautics: the design and construction of aircraft

IV

From the time when Wilbur was eleven years old and Orville seven, they had shown an interest in flying. It began in this way. Their father, Bishop Milton Wright, once walked into the room in which they were playing. His hand playfully concealed some object.

"It flies," cried the boys, as they watched it spin across the room, and strike the ceiling. There it fluttered about for a few moments before it fell. The boys jumped for the toy, now lying on the floor. They picked it up, and eagerly examined it.

"What is it?" asked Orville.

"A toy bat," suggested Wilbur.

"It's a helicopter," explained their father.

"How does it work?" they asked.

Bishop Wright therefore showed them that the "bat" was only a cork and bamboo frame, covered with paper; that it rose in the air by means of some twisted rubber bands.

"Where did you get it, Father?" asked Wilbur.

"I bought it when I was in New York. Not long ago there lived a certain Frenchman, who fell sick and became a cripple. Since the poor fellow could not walk, he began to dream of flying. That is how he came to invent this flying toy. Once he tried to make a real flying machine, but he failed. Finally every one laughed at his ambitions, and he died of a broken heart."

The boys were silent for a moment. Then one exclaimed, "Perhaps some day a great man will succeed."

"Perhaps," replied their father.

Again and again they flew the toy. "I wonder if we can make it fly higher," said Wilbur.

"Let's make a bigger 'bat,'" replied his brother. They did make another flying toy, somewhat larger, but this one did not fly as well as the one which their father had brought them.

"Perhaps we did not make our 'bat' right," they said. "We must try again." What puzzled them was that, although their toys would fly, the larger the toy, the less time would it stay up in the air. And beyond a certain size their "bat" would not fly at all.

Defeated, they turned their interest to kites, which would stay up in the air. But the helicopter always remained a vivid memory to the Wright brothers.

Several years later, young Orville, in company with a friend, decided to publish a newspaper. It was to consist of four pages. They called it *The Midget,* but the first issue was even smaller than its name implied. For, alas, they ran short of news. They solved the difficulty in a very novel way: they left page 3 blank.

Orville's father was given a copy of *The Midget.* "It is imperfect work," he commented, and he suppressed* the entire edition.

suppressed: kept from being circulated

Not at all abashed by the failure of *The Midget,* both brothers decided to publish another paper. Not having enough money to buy a press, they made one themselves. And one Saturday night *The West Side News* was delivered to as many as four hundred subscribers.

From printing, however, they soon turned to the craze of the day, bicycles. They set up a little shop for repairing and making wheels. They made their own tools, even such complicated ones as lathes.

Before long people began to know and like these quiet, pleasant brothers. Not only were their wheels well-made, but on them they installed a splendid safety brake which they had invented.

One day they thought of having a bit of fun. They rode all over town on a huge tandem bicycle they built. It was made of two old high wheels, connected by a long gas pipe. "It's a better sight than seeing a circus," was the town's comment.

And then came the death of Lilienthal. The torch, which his helpless fingers let go, the brothers grasped to blaze the way to higher glories.

"Lilienthal was not on the right track when he shifted his body at every gust of wind to balance himself. It's both too difficult and too exhausting," said one brother.

"Yes, the wind often veers several times a second, much quicker than a man can think," agreed the other.

"But how can we get control? If I let a piece of paper fall, it doesn't swoop down straight. It turns over. The air resists it. How can we ride such an uncertain steed as an aeroplane and keep our balance?"

After much study, they concluded that if you could lie flat in the aeroplane instead of standing upright, as in Lilienthal's machine, the wind resistance could be reduced. And instead of the rider's shifting in the machine when he wanted to balance and to steer about, they decided that the machine should do this work. They put a rudder in front, and soon were able to control the aeroplane.

One day an elderly man appeared on the field. He watched them leap and soar, grasshopper fashion, from spot to spot on their wings of wood and canvas. He began to ask questions, as he carefully studied the gliding machine.

"Do you young men know," he finally said, "that you have come nearer to the art of flying than any other man who ever lived?"

It was Octave Chanute speaking, the greatest authority in America on the history of the flying machine. He, too, had been experimenting with flying machines. Chanute was most encouraging, and the brothers worked with a harder will than ever.

On December 17, 1903, they were ready. A general invitation was sent to the people of Kitty Hawk, North Carolina, to come and watch the fliers. Only five people were willing to face the cold December wind to see a flying machine that would not fly, as they thought.

The machine was made ready. The engine which the brothers had to build themselves, for no company would undertake to construct one for them, was started. Orville Wright got in.

And then a miracle! The aeroplane rose and stayed in the air twelve seconds! For the first time in history, a machine carrying a man raised itself into the air *by its own power* and landed without being wrecked.

Twelve seconds! From such beginnings, we have seen man fly across the ocean and by airplane circumnavigate the earth. At last man has nothing for which to envy the birds. He can fly faster than any living bird.

About the Story

1. Who were the predecessors of the Wright brothers and what were their contributions to the science of flying?
2. What are the key character qualities of these scientists that enabled them to accomplish what they did?
3. How did their childhood experiences prepare the Wright brothers for flying?
4. What character quality not possessed by Icarus contributed to the success of the Wright brothers?

About the Author

Joseph Cottler (1899-1981) collaborated on several works with his friend Haym Jaffe. The two men observed the First World War and its revelation of heroic action and attitudes and agreed that something should be created to bring out the best in mankind without the sacrifice of life. They then decided to write about the courageous acts of people who were fighting against obstacles other than wartime enemies in hopes that their example might inspire others to greater heights of moral excellence. Among their *Heroes of Civilization* are the Wright brothers and those interested in flight who came before the inventors at Kitty Hawk. In fact Cottler continued to write, when he was not playing the violin professionally, with this goal in mind. As history has shown, war is still part of life, but man has still other avenues open to him to spur him to greater excellence.

Nancy Hanks

Rosemary and Stephen Vincent Benét

How would you answer these questions by Nancy Hanks?

If Nancy Hanks
Came back as a ghost,
Seeking news
Of what she loved most,
She'd ask first   5
"Where's my son?
What's happened to Abe?
What's he done?"

"Poor little Abe,
Left all alone   10
Except for Tom,
Who's a rolling stone;*   rolling stone: wanderer
He was only nine
The year I died.
I remember still   15
How hard he cried.

"Scraping along
In a little shack
With hardly a shirt
To cover his back,   20
And a prairie wind
To blow him down,
Or pinching* times   pinching: difficult
If he went to town.

"You wouldn't know   25
About my son?
Did he grow tall?
Did he have fun?
Did he learn to read?
Did he get to town?   30
Do you know his name?
Did he get on?"

About the Author

Rosemary Benét assisted her husband in composing a collection of historical verse entitled *A Book for Americans,* published in 1933, in which "Nancy Hanks" was included.

Stephen Benét was born in Bethlehem, Pennsylvania, on July 22, 1898. First recognized for his writing at the age of twelve, the young poet went on to develop his talents in writing stories, plays, operas, and movie scripts. His fascination with American history and folklore, combined with his humor and imagination, gives original vitality to his historical writings. After receiving numerous honors, awards, and credits throughout his lifetime, Benét died in New York City on March 13, 1943.

The Day's Demand

Josiah Gilbert Holland

Is this poem relevant today? How does it compare with "Billy, He's in Trouble"?

God give us men! A time like this demands
Strong minds, great hearts, true faith, and ready hands;
Men whom the lust* of office does not kill;
   Men whom the spoils* of office cannot buy;
Men who possess opinions and a will;
   Men who have honor,—men who will not lie;
Men who can stand before a demagogue,*
   And damn* his treacherous flatteries without winking!
Tall men, sun-crowned, who live above the fog
   In public duty, and in private thinking:
For while the rabble,* with their thumb-worn creeds,*
Their large professions* and their little deeds,—
Mingle* in selfish strife, lo! Freedom weeps,
Wrong rules the land, and waiting Justice sleeps.

lust: intense desire
spoils: benefits

5

demagogue: a leader
  who gains control by
  appealing to the
  emotions of the people
damn: condemn

10

rabble: mob
thumb-worn creeds:
  well-worn statements
  of belief
professions: claims
Mingle: mix

Josiah Gilbert Holland (1819-81), or Timothy Titcomb as some of his readers knew him, led a varied life as a schoolteacher, doctor, school superintendent, journalist, lecturer, magazine founder, and editor. His superintendent days saw him lobbying for the right to use corporal punishment in his schools and caused him "to say during the civil war, that he had 'whipped more rebels' than any other man in America.'" His verse, often sentimental in nature, caused his readers to assume he was a minister. In addition to his poetry, he wrote one of the first important biographies of Abraham Lincoln, published in 1865. His writing abilities gave him the opportunity to cofound the prestigious *Scribner's Magazine*. Unfortunately, as one critic has said, "Few men have been so popular in their lifetime and so completely forgotten immediately after their death."

About the Poems

1. Who is the poem "Nancy Hanks" really about? What do you think is the major point of the poem?
2. What do the poets assume about the reader?
3. Based on Holland's poem "The Day's Demand," what character qualities should men possess?

4. What might "the fog" in line 9 represent? Which line(s) of the poem state the main idea?
5. Josiah Holland lived in the 1800s; is his poem relevant today, and if so, how does the poet make it relevant?

Charlie Coulson: Drummer Boy

Dick Larson

> *This radio script tells the true story of the doctor who found Charlie Coulson severely wounded on the battlefield of Gettysburg. The account was dramatized as part of the "Miracles" series produced by radio station WMUU, Greenville, South Carolina. How does this radio script differ from the short stories you have been reading? Does this script have a clear theme?*

Characters

the doctor
Private Smith
Charlie Coulson, the drummer boy
Miss Graham
a nurse

Music:	[*Sweep into something with measured beat—minor.*]
Doctor:	I think that hell must be a little like a battlefield after the rage and fury of the fighting has left it and there's nothing but the suffering moan of dying men that falls on the deaf ears of the dead. The terrible scream when some poor beggar regains consciousness in a red world of agony. . . . Yes, a battlefield is a hundred-fold more terrible when the fighting's over. If you're a doctor, like I am, you have to pick your way through the human ruins lying in strange, twisted heaps. You choose the ones most likely to live. You have them carried to the field hospital where a few of them pull through. You don't dare let the horror of it get inside you. You harden yourself. Either that or you run away from it. I hardened. Clear down to my soul I turned as hard as stone. I didn't feel love, or hate, or even fear. I was rather proud of my reputation for steel nerves and no heart. I didn't believe in God or the devil.
	That's the way I was the day we found Charlie on the field of Gettysburg. They'd sent me a new orderly from headquarters. I could tell he'd heard about me from the way he "sirred" me respectfully every time I gave an order. We'd been on the field for quite a long time and I could see it was beginning to get to him. He was still pretty green.
Sound:	[*Restless horses*]
Smith:	The wagon's full now, Doctor sir.

Doctor:	We can put one more in the stretcher rack. Come on, Smith. I saw a boy back there.
Smith:	No! This is enough!
Doctor:	[*Pause*] What was that, Smith?
Smith:	I'm . . . I'm sorry, sir. But isn't this enough, sir?
Doctor:	I wasn't asking your opinion, Smith. I gave an order. Now, let's go get that boy.
Smith:	No! I'm not going!
Doctor:	This means a court-martial, Smith. You're disobeying a direct order.
Smith:	I don't care! I've taken all I can take! Just because you're made of stone, doesn't mean we all are. I can't stand any more, I tell you! [*Exit*]
Music:	[*Sting and to background.*]
Doctor:	I was disgusted with headquarters for sending me a greenhorn to do a man's work. I went out on the field where I'd seen the boy. I'd bring him in alone. He was lying quietly beside his shattered drum. His left side was drenched with blood. There wasn't much use taking him in. It didn't take a doctor to see that. But I wouldn't come back empty handed. I knelt beside the boy. He was slight . . . [and] couldn't have been much more than seventeen. Then he opened his eyes. [*Music out*]

Charlie Coulson: Drummer Boy   307

Charlie:	Can't . . . can't beat the charge . . . can't beat the charge . . . my drum's broken, sir. . . .
Doctor:	All right, son. Save your strength. I'm going to have to put a tourniquet on that leg before I move you.
Charlie:	You . . . you're . . . a doctor, aren't you?
Doctor:	Yes, son.
Charlie:	Then it's all over?
Doctor:	That's right. Now don't talk, son. You're going to need all that energy to pull through.
Charlie:	Yes, sir. Is it bad, sir?
Doctor:	It's plenty bad. I'm afraid you're going to lose this leg.
Charlie:	Are you going to do it now, sir?
Doctor:	No, I'm taking you to the field hospital. [*Groan*] There! The tourniquet's on. Now, put your arms around my neck.
Charlie:	I'm all bloody, sir. Get dirty—
Doctor:	Do what I tell you . . . quickly.
Charlie:	Yes, sir.
Doctor:	All right. I'll have to get my hands under you. This is going to hurt pretty badly. Don't let go.
Charlie:	I won't, sir!
Doctor:	All right. Now. [*Effort of lifting*]
Charlie:	[*Gasp of pain*]
Doctor:	Steady, son, steady.
Charlie:	[*Through teeth*] I'm all right, sir. I'm all right.
Doctor:	Sure you are. We'll have you right as rain as soon as we get you to the hospital.
Sound:	[*Wagon and horses*]
Doctor:	Is this the best speed you can get out of these mules?
Smith:	We've got a lot of men on this wagon. It ain't so easy to pull.
Doctor:	There'd probably be a little more pulling if you did a little more driving. Don't you have a whip?
Smith:	I generally just slap the reins on their backs, sir.
Doctor:	Then do it now!
Smith:	Yes, sir!
Doctor:	Don't you know army mules won't go without a whip? That's standard equipment for these wagons.
Smith:	Yes, sir. There was one but I never used it and it got lost.
Doctor:	Smith, I'm afraid you're too dumb to court-martial.

Smith:	Yes, sir.
Doctor:	Here! Give me those reins. Maybe I can get something out of these mules.
Smith:	Yes, sir!
Doctor:	And listen, Smith, pay very close attention because I don't want any blunders on this.
Smith:	I'm listening, sir.
Doctor:	When we get to the hospital, you are to find Miss Graham, the head nurse. Do you understand that?

Smith:	Yes, sir. Miss Graham, sir.
Doctor:	You're to find Miss Graham and tell her I want these cases put in ward "C." Do you have that?
Smith:	I think so, sir.
Doctor:	Well make sure! Now, most important! Tell Miss Graham she's to prepare the last case I picked up, the drummer boy. She's to prepare him for surgery and take him into the operating room. Is that clear?
Smith:	Yes, sir!
Doctor:	All right! That takes care of everything. Now if these mules will just get us to the hospital!
Music:	[*Dramatic motion*]

Smith: . . . and Miss Graham, ma'am, he went back for the boy by himself. He was real angry with me for not helpin' him. He said he was going to court-martial me. But I couldn't help it, ma'am. I couldn't stand going out there, ma'am.

Graham: I understand, Smith. It's all right. But what did he say about the wounded? Where are we supposed to put them?

Smith: He said to put them in ward "C," ma'am.

Graham: But that ward's full now. Practically every bed is taken. They've been coming in here in a steady stream since the battle.

Smith: Yes, ma'am. But I'd get 'em in there somehow if I was you. He don't seem to take reasoning.

Graham: Yes, Smith, I know. You'd better get one of the other orderlies to help you set up some extra cots in ward "C." We'll have to use those. Where's the doctor now?

Smith: He said he was going to wash up for an operation.

Graham: Did he say which case was to be first?

Smith: Oh yes, ma'am! That's right! He said you was to get a boy ready for surgery and take him to the operating room.

Graham: Oh, Smith! You have to try harder to remember things. Are you sure that was all the doctor said, now?

Smith: I think so, ma'am. It's a drummer boy, ma'am. The one he went back to pick up by himself. I'll show you which one.

Graham:	Hurry, Smith!
Music:	[*Fast motion down to.*]
Doctor:	Oh, Miss Graham.
Graham:	Yes, Doctor.
Doctor:	Did Smith see you?
Graham:	Yes, sir. We're setting up cots in ward "C" for the overflow. And I'm getting the boy ready for the operating room as quickly as possible.
Doctor:	Good. I want to take him first. We'll have to amputate the left leg. You'll administer the anesthetic, please. [*Pause*] Well?
Graham:	I don't think there's any chloroform left.
Doctor:	What?
Graham:	Dr. Braynard used the last of it this afternoon.
Doctor:	But that's impossible! What about that requisition I placed two weeks ago?
Graham:	It evidently hasn't come through, sir.
Doctor:	But the boy's too weak to be operated on without chloroform.

Graham:	I'm sorry, Doctor.
Doctor:	Have the field kits checked. I have to have that anesthetic.
Music:	[*Sting (and hold).*]
Smith:	I'm sorry, Miss Graham. There wasn't any chloroform in the field kits.
Graham:	Well, check the storage room again. That shipment might have been put away without our knowing it.
Smith:	I'll check, ma'am.
Music:	[*Sting (and hold).*]
Smith:	No, Miss Graham. I looked through every inch of the storage room. There isn't any chloroform.
Graham:	Thank you, Smith. I guess the doctor is going to have to operate without it.
Music:	[*Sting and into dramatic bridge (down and out).*]

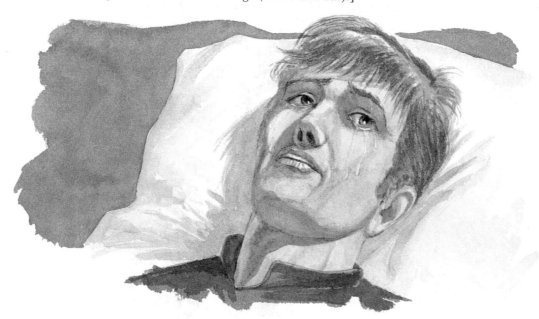

Graham:	I'm sorry, Doctor. There just isn't any chloroform. We've checked absolutely everything!
Doctor:	[*Deep breath*] Well, is the boy ready for surgery?
Graham:	I've sterilized the wound, Doctor.
Doctor:	All right. Maybe we had better put it up to him. Come on.
Music:	[*Short bridge. Tense.*]
Doctor:	Hello, son.
Charlie:	Hello, Doctor!

Doctor:	Listen, boy, we have a real problem. I'm going to put it to you straight. We've got to amputate your leg if we're going to save you from gangrene. But, well, you see, a requisition we put in a long time ago hasn't come through. We don't have any anesthetic.
Charlie:	Oh . . . I see . . . You mean, you want to try it without any anesthetic.
Doctor:	If you think you can take it.
Charlie:	Yes, Doctor . . . I'm game.
Doctor:	It will probably be a good deal worse than you can imagine, son.
Charlie:	Yes, sir. But I have a Friend who'll stand by me and help me through it.
Doctor:	Oh . . . you're religious, are you, son?
Charlie:	I believe in Jesus, if that's what you mean.
Doctor:	Well, if religion can help you, son, then believe anything you want to.
Charlie:	My Lord won't let me down, Doctor.
Doctor:	[*To nurses*] Tell Smith and one of the other orderlies to come and help hold the boy, Nurse.
Charlie:	No, Doctor! You won't need anybody to hold me. I won't jerk, sir. I won't even make a sound, sir. I promise.
Doctor:	That's a mighty big order, boy.
Charlie:	My Lord will stand by me, sir. I won't make a sound, I promise.
Doctor:	All right, son. For your sake, I hope your Lord is a good deal more powerful than I expect Him to be. [*To nurse—step back*] Are the instruments ready?
Graham:	[*Off*] All sterile, Doctor.
Doctor:	Are there plenty of clamps?
Graham:	Yes, sir.
Doctor:	Well, if you know a prayer, say it for the boy, now. All right, son. We're ready to start. Still game?
Charlie:	Yes, Doctor. I'm ready!
Doctor:	[*Off*] Scalpel.
Graham:	[*Off*] Scalpel.
Music:	[*High pitched note without vibrato increasing in intensity under next speech.*]
Charlie:	[*Tight*] Lord Jesus. . . . Stand by me now. . . . Stand by me now. . . . Lord Jesus. . . . Stand by me now. . . . Stand by me now.
Music:	[*Note crashes into full chord and to background.*]
Doctor:	It took me fifteen minutes. As fast as I could work, it still took me fifteen minutes. They must have been endless torture for the boy. He didn't whimper once. I heard him whisper one phrase over and over. "Lord Jesus,

stand by me now." That was the only sound he made. I thought I was hard. I thought there weren't any feelings left in me. But when I finished the operation, I was drenched in sweat. I had a hard time keeping the instruments steady. When it was over, I left the nurse to take care of the instruments. Somehow I got through the other cases I had to attend to. Then I went to my room and tried to sleep.

Music:	[*Up slightly and then hold.*]
Charlie:	[*On filter*] Lord Jesus, stand by me now. Stand by me now, Lord Jesus. . . . Stand by me now. . . . Stand by me now. . . .
Doctor:	[*Groan*] Oh . . . I couldn't sleep. That boy's voice kept echoing in my mind. It wouldn't let me rest! What was the matter with me? Was I finally losing my nerve? Was I going to let a boy break me down? I'd done operations like that before. What was it? Something kept gnawing at my mind. Those words. . . . Finally, I did something I'd never done before! I went to the hospital at night, without being called! [*Music out*]
Sound:	[*Door opening. Steps in staccato.*]
Nurse:	Why, why there must be some mistake. There was no call for you, Doctor.
Doctor:	Does there always have to be a call for me before I can come into my own hospital?
Nurse:	No, no. Of course not, sir.
Doctor:	I'm just checking up on the cases that came in today. How are they?
Nurse:	Five fatalities so far, Doctor.
Doctor:	Oh. The boy . . . the drummer boy, amputation case . . . What about him?
Nurse:	He wasn't one of the five. The last time I saw him he seemed to be sleeping quietly.
Doctor:	I see. . . . I think I'll stop in there and check on him anyway. It's a very critical case.
Nurse:	All right, Doctor.
Sound:	[*Steps staccato*]
Doctor:	Oh, and Nurse . . .
Nurse:	[*Off mike*] Yes, Doctor?
Doctor:	You won't need to sign me into the log. This is just an unofficial call.
Nurse:	[*Odd*] Yes, Doctor.
Sound:	[*Steps on again staccato.*]
Doctor:	I knew I was making a fool of myself. But something made me go in and take a look at that boy. It was something I couldn't lay my finger on. It was as though he had the answer for something that was burning inside of me. I couldn't find that hardness I had been relying on.
Sound:	[*Door opens. Steps. Door closes. Steps of different quality to bed.*]

Doctor:	When I got to the boy's bedside, he was awake.
Charlie:	Doctor? Hello, Doctor.
Doctor:	How are you feeling, son?
Charlie:	I'm all right now, sir. I want to thank you, sir, very much.
Doctor:	That's all right, son. I just wanted to see how you were getting along. Wanted to see if there was anything I could do for you.
Charlie:	If it . . . isn't too much trouble, could you do something for me?
Doctor:	Yes, son. What is it?
Charlie:	Under my pillow. There's a Bible there. I've had it with me ever since I enlisted. My mother's address is inside the front cover. Would you send it to her please?
Doctor:	Of course I will, son. But aren't you going to want it?
Charlie:	[*Smiling*] No, sir. I won't need it where I'm going.
Doctor:	That's foolish talk, lad. You're going to get well.
Charlie:	No, sir, my Lord's told me He's going to take me home.
Doctor:	Don't talk like that.
Charlie:	Oh, it's all right, sir. I'm happy about it. I'll be seeing my Lord, face to face. There . . . isn't any sadness . . . when . . . you're looking forward . . . to seeing . . . the one you . . . love more than . . . anything in the world.
Doctor:	You're going to be all right, lad. You're going to be all right.
Charlie:	Doctor?
Doctor:	Yes, lad.
Charlie:	You don't know Him, do you?
Doctor:	You mean—your Lord?
Charlie:	Yes, sir.
Doctor:	Oh, I heard about him in Sunday School. But that was a long time ago. I'm afraid I've forgotten.
Charlie:	Doctor . . . you remember, when you were cutting off my leg?
Doctor:	Yes, son, I remember.
Charlie:	I was praying . . . for you, Doctor.
Doctor:	Praying for me?
Charlie:	Yes, sir. I was praying . . . that the Lord would . . . save your soul, sir.
Doctor:	Oh . . . I see. I'm afraid it's a little late for that, son.
Charlie:	No, sir. He told me . . . I'd see you . . . in heaven.
Doctor:	That's enough, boy. I don't think you'd better talk any more. It isn't good for you to tire yourself.

Charlie: I'm not . . . tired, Doctor . . . just can't breathe too good. . . . When . . . when . . . you do . . . accept the . . . Lord . . . I'm going to be . . . very happy. . . . I'm going to be very happy.

Doctor: [*Waits a moment*] Son? Son! [*Long pause*]

Music: [*Steal in organ theme sad-happy. (Down to background.)*]

Doctor: Hundreds of soldiers died in my hospital during the war. I followed only one to the grave. That was the drummer boy. Charlie Coulson, his name was. I found it on the inside of his Bible. I had him dressed in a new uniform and placed in an officer's coffin with a United States flag over it. I rode three miles to see him buried.

Music: [*Taps steals into the theme. Up slightly and down. Ends out.*]

Sound: [*Wind in slightly.*]

Doctor: Then, everyone had gone and I was alone at the grave. We had buried him on a little rise overlooking the battlefield of Gettysburg where he had been wounded. I stood looking down over the field, remembering how I had been when I found him there. . . . And then for the first time in my life, I prayed.

Music: [*Sneak in sweet beautiful.*]

Doctor:	Dear God, . . . It took a boy to show me what a fool I've been. . . . I thought I was self-sufficient. I thought I could stand alone against any odds. But I've seen myself, as You see me. I am utterly ashamed. I have a yearning in my soul to know You, . . . Lord. Charlie spoke to You as though . . . as though you were friends. I humbly beg that friendship too. I know I'm not fit for it, Lord. But if it please You, cleanse my heart . . . cleanse my heart. . . . I'm not sufficient to myself. I need Your salvation. As Charlie prayed, Lord, save my soul.
Music:	[*Up slightly and hold.*]
Charlie:	[*On filter*] When . . . when . . . you do . . . accept the Lord . . . I'm going to be . . . very happy . . . very happy.
Music:	[*Up full.*]
Doctor:	They have made a national shrine of Gettysburg now. There are great spreading trees with deep spaces of cool shade beneath. There are more than two thousand marble monuments there now, but the most important one for me is the little marker that I placed at Charlie's grave. There isn't any sadness in my heart when I go there, only joy. That small shrine marks the spot where I began a new life. A life of living for my Lord, the one that Charlie introduced me to. In a way I feel I'm somehow carrying on the work that Charlie might have done if he had lived.
	Mr. Lincoln said it well, the day he came to dedicate the cemetery, Charlie's grave with all the rest. It seemed as though he spoke my thoughts. "It is for us the living, rather, to be dedicated here to the unfinished work which they who fought here have thus far so nobly advanced. It is rather for us to be here dedicated to the great task remaining before us that from these honored dead we take increased devotion to that cause for which they gave the last full measure of devotion!"
Music:	[*Majestic up to climax.*]
Announcer:	You have been listening to the true story of Charlie Coulson, a drummer boy in the American Civil War, as told by the doctor who was the last one to see him alive. Although the dialogue is fictitious, the essential facts are accurate. It will interest you to know that the doctor contacted Charlie's mother and told her of her dying son's ministry.
Music:	[*Theme martial (in and under).*]

About the Drama

1. How is this radio script different from a short story?
2. Why is the doctor concerned that the nurse not record his "unofficial call" on Charlie?
3. How does the reader know about the change in the doctor's attitude?
4. How does Lincoln's speech have a different meaning for the doctor?

All Yankees Are Liars

Eric Knight

People often refuse the truth because it sounds unbelievable. Some even declare, "Don't confuse me by telling me the facts." How does Mr. Smith in this story finally get his audience to believe him? Do you think that this story is as funny to an Englishman as it is to us? Does it say anything about how the rest of the world views our land?

You can always tell the Irish,
  You can always tell the Dutch.
You can always tell a Yankee;
  But you cannot tell him much.

Mr. Smith was pleased with The Spread Eagle. He was pleased with Polkingthorpe Brig. The village was off the beaten track—the

truly rural sort of English village the American always wants to see.

The inn was low and rambling, with great sloping roofs. Over the door swung the sign—a darksome bird in a weatherbeaten setting.

Everything justified his decision to take this bicycle trip up into the north—the mullioned* windows, the roaring fire, the Yorkshire accents of the men who shuffled over the sanded stone floor of the low-ceilinged room as they played darts. Mr. Smith was almost beginning to understand what they were talking about. During his excellent high tea* he had sorted out the four men playing darts. One was Saw Cooper, a farmer; a small old man was referred to as Sam; a young, bright-faced lad who played darts left-handed was Gollicker Pearson; and the fourth, a huge man, was just called Ian.

mullioned: having panes divided by vertical wooden
  strips
high tea: a late-afternoon meal

Mr. Smith watched them play, listening to the endless thwock of the darts in the cork board as he finished his meal. The barmaid, plump, cornhaired, came toward him, her apron rustling stiffly.

"Would there be owt* else?"

owt: aught: anything whatever

"No. It was a very good meal." Mr. Smith smiled. He wanted to make the girl talk some more. "Er—what do they do for fun in this place of an evening?"

"Foon?" she repeated. "Well, they sit here—or o' Sat'day neights lots o' fowk goa ovver to Wuxley to t'pictures." She waited. "They gate Boock D'Arcy i' T' Singing Cowboy," she added suggestively.

Mr. Smith had already become acquainted with British cinemas in small towns. Also, he was a Southern Californian, and had that familiarity with movies that belongs to all Southern Californians. He had no inclination to go four miles to see a last year's Class B Western. "No. I think I'll have another ale and sit here," he said.

"If tha'll sit ovver by t' fire, Ah'll bring it to thee theer. Then Ah can clean oop here."

Mr. Smith sat on the bench by the generous fire and nursed* his ale. The dart game came to an end with Saw Cooper losing and paying for the round. The men brought their mugs to the fire. Mr. Smith shifted politely. The men,

Sam

in the presence of a stranger, grew quiet. Mr. Smith decided to put them at ease.

---

nursed: drank slowly

"Pretty chilly for an October evening, isn't it?"

The men considered the remark, as if looking at both sides of it. Finally Saw Cooper spoke.

"Aye," he said.

The others nodded. There was silence, and the five regarded the fire. Then, suddenly, young Gollicker smiled.

"Tha shouldn't heed t' cowd, being a Yankee," he said.

"Ah, but I'm not a Yankee," Mr. Smith said.

They stared at him in disbelief.

"Yankees," explained Mr. Smith, "come from New England."

They looked from Mr. Smith to one another. The big man named Ian took a deep breath.

"Yankees," he said, "coom fro' t' United States."

"Well, yes. New England is a part of the United States," Mr. Smith said. "But it's thousands of miles away from where I live. In fact, believe it or not, I should think you're closer to the Yankees than I am. You see, the United States is a big country. In the part where the Yankees come from, it gets very cold in the winter. Where I am—in Southern California—it never snows. Why, I've never known it to snow there in all my life."

"No snow?" Gollicker breathed.

Mr. Smith smiled. For, after all, he was a Southern Californian—and they were discussing climate. "No snow," he said. "In wintertime we have a bit of a rainy season, but after February it clears, and then it doesn't even rain for nine months—not a drop."

"Noa rain for a nine month—noan at all?" Saw Cooper asked.

"Not a drop. Day after day, the sun comes out, clear skies, never a drop of rain for nine months. Never!"

"Whet do ye graw theer, lad?" Saw asked, slyly.

"Lots of things. Truck,* vegetables, oranges—all kinds of things."

Truck: garden produce for market

There was a silence again. Big Ian took a breath.

"Orinjis," he said, and then took another breath, "graw i' Spain."

He looked at Mr. Smith so emphatically that Mr. Smith nodded.

"Oh, yes," he said. "They grow in Spain, too, I understand."

"Orinjis," Ian repeated, "graw i' Spain."

That seemed to settle the question. They all looked in the fire in silence. Saw Cooper sniffed.

"Whet else graws theer?"

"Well, I have a ranch there; we grow alfalfa."

"Whet's that off to be?"

"Alfalfa? We use it for hay. It's a desert plant originally, but it thrives in California. We get eight cuttings a year."

"Eight cuttings o' hay a year?"

"Eight cuttings a year."

The little man, Sam, spoke for the first time: "Mister, if it doan't rain for a nine month, how can ye get eight cuttings o' hay a year?"

"Oh, that's easy," Mr. Smith said. "We irrigate the land." He went into a short but conclusive* description of irrigating.

---

conclusive: expressed without doubt

"Heh," Saw Cooper said. "Wheer's this here watter coom fro'?"

Saw Cooper

"In the San Fernando Valley we buy it from the water company, just like you do in your homes."

"Wheer do they get it?"

"From reservoirs."

"If it doan't rain, where's t' reservoys get t' watter?"

"Oh, we pipe it down from five hundred miles north. It rains a lot up there."

"And ye sprinkle t' farming land out o' t' watter tap. How mony acres hesta?"

"It isn't like sprinkling from the tap, of course. I used that to illustrate. The pipes are large—we have fourteen-inch valves on our pipes. We flood the land—cover it right over with water."

Saw looked in the fire. "Does corn grow theer?"

"Well, generally our land is too valuable to put into corn. But it will grow corn fourteen feet high."

They made noises in their throats and shifted their feet.

"Fohteen foot," Saw breathed. "Eigh, ba gum!"

"Mister," Saw said, "once Ah were oop to see t' Firth o' Forth brig. Ah suppose they hey bigger brigs i' Yankeeland?"

Mr. Smith should have touched on the new Oakland bridge, but then, he was a *Southern* Californian.

"We have bridges, but they're building vehicular tunnels under the rivers now."

"Whet for?"

"Well, there's so much motor traffic."

"How mony moatorcars goa through 'em?"

Mr. Smith lit his pipe happily. They seemed quite interested in America.

"I couldn't say. The way they turn 'em out, I should say there's hundreds of thousands."

"How fast do they turn 'em out?" Gollicker asked.

"I don't know. I think they roll out finished at the rate of one every couple of minutes."

"And they goa i' tunnels, not i' brigs?" Sam commented.

"Oh, we have some bridges."

"Big uns, Ah suppose."

"Well," Mr. Smith said modestly, thinking of the Pulaski Skyway coming into New York, "we have some that go right over entire towns. You're practically on one bridge for miles."

Saw Cooper spat in the fire. "How mony fowk is there in all America?"

Mr. Smith didn't know, but he felt expansive.* And after all, there was South America too.

---
expansive: generous

"A quarter of a billion, I should say," he hazarded.*

---
hazarded: ventured as a guess

"A quarter of a billion," they repeated. Then they stared at Mr. Smith, and he became aware of their disbelief.

"Wait a moment," he said. "I think a billion is different in America from here. It's a thousand million in America and a million million here, isn't it?"

"A billion," said Ian slowly, "is a billion."

The others nodded, and then Ian stood. The others rose too.

"Oh—er—wait a minute. Won't you all have a drink with me?" Mr. Smith invited.

"Us is off to play darts for a round—us four," Ian said, meaningly.

The other three laughed.

"Ah knew them theer brigs o' thine'd hev to be big," Saw Cooper said as a parting shot as he swung over the bench. "That's so's they'd be able to goa ovver wheat what grows fohteen foot high when ye sprinkle it fro' t' watter tap."

He grinned at the others in victory.

"I didn't say wheat; I said corn," Mr. Smith protested.

"Same thing," Saw snapped.

"It isn't. Wheat grows in an ear. Corn grows on a cob; it has broad long leaves."

"Heh! That's maize," Saw said.

Big Ian stepped between Saw Cooper and Mr. Smith.

"Now, lad," he said flatly, "tha said corn, and Ah heerd thee. Thee and thy orinjis, and farming out o' t' watter tap, and brigs ovver cities, and it nivver rains, and denying th' art a Yankee, and a billion is a billion and yet it ain't. Tha's tripped thysen oop a dozen times, it seems to me. Now, hesta owt to say?"

Mr. Smith looked at Big Ian, standing belligerently* with legs widespread and his thumbs in the waistband of his corduroy trousers. He looked round and saw everyone in the inn waiting, silent.

---
belligerently: ready to fight

Then a curious thing happened. In that minute the smell of soft-coal smoke and pig-twist tobacco and ale was gone, and instead Mr. Smith was smelling the mixed odor of sun-baked land and citrus blossom and jasmine and eucalyptus trees, just as you smell it in the cool darkness coming across the San Fernando Valley. And he was homesick. Suddenly it felt unreal that he should be so far from home, sitting in an English inn with these men about him. He looked up at the faces, forbidding in their expression of disapproval. And he began to laugh.

It was all so unreal that he laughed until he cried. Every time he looked up he saw the faces, now even more comical in their bewilderment than they had been in their disapproval. They stared at him, and then Big Ian began to laugh.

"Eigh, Ahj'll be jiggered!" he roared. "Drat ma buttons if Ah won't!"

It was Mr. Smith's turn to be puzzled now.

Big Ian roared, and suddenly slapped Mr. Smith on the back so heartily that his chin flew up in the air and then banged back on his chest. The others looked on in amazement.

"Why, whet's oop, Ian?" Saw asked.

"Why, ye gowks!" Ian roared. "He's laughing at ye! He's been heving us on! Sitting theer for an hour, keeping his mug straight and telling us the tale! And us swallering it, thinking he was serious!"

"But," Mr. Smith said—"but you don't—"

"Nay, now no moar on it!" Ian roared. "Ye've codded* us for fair, and done it champion! Lewk at owd Sam's face!"

---

codded: fooled

The others regarded Ian and scratched their heads and grinned sheepishly,* and finally looked at Mr. Smith in admiration.

---

sheepishly: with embarrassment

"But—" Mr. Smith began again.

"Nay, now, ye copped us napping," Ian said, "and here's ma hand on it. Soa we'll hev noa moar—onless ye'd like to tell us whet Yankeeland's rightly like."

Mr. Smith drew a deep breath. "Well, what would you like to hear about?"

"About cowboys," young Gollicker breathed. "Werta ivver a cowboy?"

For a moment Mr. Smith stood on a brink, and then an imp* pushed him over.

---

imp: a mischievous spirit

"Of course I've been a cowboy—naturally," Mr. Smith said. "What would you like to hear about it?"

"Wait a minute," Gollicker said. They all adjusted themselves on the bench. "Now," he went on, "tell us about a roundup—the knaws, 'Ah'm yeading for t' last roundup,' like Bing Crosby sings."

Mr. Smith held his mental breath and plunged.

"Ah," he said. "A roundup and the life of a cowboy. Up at the crack of dawn, mates, and down to the corral. There you rope your horse—"

"A mustang?" Gollicker asked.

"A mustang," Mr. Smith agreed.

"A wild one off'n the prairies, happen?"

"Indeed a wild one from off the prairies," Mr. Smith agreed. "I see you know America yourself."

Gollicker grinned modestly.* "Doan't let me interrupt, measter," he apologized.

---

modestly: humbly

Mr. Smith drew another breath. He saw he was up against at least one expert, so he made it very good. Inwardly he thanked fate* for what he had hitherto* regarded as two entirely misspent weeks on a Nevada dude ranch.* He gave them, in more senses than one, a moving picture of the cowboy's life.

---

fate: the power supposedly predetermining events
hitherto: before
dude ranch: a resort ranch

When he was done, Gollicker sighed and Big Ian nodded.

"Now," Sam said, "how about them . . . buffalo?"

"Ah, the buffalo," Mr. Smith said. "The thundering herd! The bison! For a while there was danger—or thought to be—that the herds were dying out. But now, I am glad to say—and no doubt you are just as glad to hear—the herds are increasing, and ere* long, again the crack of a rifle will bring down a bull in full gallop."

---

ere: before

"But how about them . . . Indians?" Saw put in.

Mr. Smith considered the Indians at the station in Santa Fe. They didn't seem at all satisfactory. But he was inspired. He drew himself up.

"You will pardon me if I do not speak of that," he said. "We have not too much love for the paleface who stole our lands. I say 'we,' for my mother was Yellow Blanket, a princess of the Blackfoot tribe. Therefore, let us not speak of the white man and the red man."

He stared into the fire—majestically, he hoped.

"Now, see what tha's done?" Ian said to Saw. "Happen it'll learn thee to keep thy yapper shut once in a while. . . . Tha maun* excuse him, measter. Tell us about gangsters instead. Didta ivver run into any gangsters?"

---

maun: must

"Run into them? Why, how could you help it?" Mr. Smith asked.

Swiftly and graphically he painted for them an America in which here was the town where the bullets of the gangs cracked day and

night. Here was the last street, and on it the last house, and beyond that was the trackless prairie where the buffalo thundered, the cowboy rode, and the Indian ever lurked.

As he finished, he looked up. Everyone in the inn was listening. Men had gathered behind him silently. At the bar, the maid leaned on her elbows, entranced.*

---

entranced: filled with wonder

"Ah, I talk too much," Mr. Smith said.

"Nay, goa on, lad," they said. "Goa on."

"Well, it's dry work. How about a drink?"

"Champion," said Saw.

"Owd on," Big Ian said. "Us'll play darts for a round."

"Now, Ian, if the lad wants to buy—"

"Ah said," Ian repeated, "us'll play darts—onybody that wishes to be in on t' round. And t' loser will pay."

Mr. Smith paid anyhow, for the dart game was trickier than he had thought, and they all seemed to be experts.

He was getting very much better when the barmaid called, "Time, gentlemen, please."

Mr. Smith was sorry. It had been a good evening. They all said good night cheerfully. Big Ian shook him by the hand.

"Well, soa long, lad. We had a champion time. But Ah just want to say, tha didn't fool me when tha were kidding us at first. Tha sees, for one thing, us goas to t' pictures and so us knows whet America's really like. And then Ah'd allus heeard tell that all Yankees were liars."

"Yes," Mr. Smith said, regarding his conscience, "I did tell some lies."

"Aye, but Ah suppose it's a way ye Yankees hev," Ian said. "But it's all right as long as tha told us t' trewth finally."

About the Story

1. What is The Spread Eagle, and why is Mr. Smith there?
2. Why do the Englishmen consider Mr. Smith to be a Yankee? Why does he disagree with them?
3. When Mr. Smith tells the truth, what happens?
4. How does he finally satisfy these men?

About the Author

Eric Knight was born in England in 1897. Before he came to the United States at the age of fifteen, he worked in the steel mills, textile mills, and sawmills of his native land. In this country he first worked as a newspaperman and then enlisted in Canada when World War I began. After the war was over (his two brothers were killed on the same day in France while fighting with the American army), Knight became a journalist, novelist, cartoonist, author of books for children, and Hollywood scriptwriter. In 1943, the year in which he won a literary award for *Lassie, Come Home,* Major Eric Knight died in the crash of a U.S. military transport plane en route to Cairo, Egypt.

Lift Ev'ry Voice and Sing

James Weldon Johnson

What wisdom does this poem teach Americans? Is the nation heeding it?

Lift ev'ry voice and sing
Till earth and heaven ring,
Ring with the harmonies of Liberty;
Let our rejoicing rise
High as the listening skies,   5
Let it resound* loud as the rolling sea,   resound: sound loudly
Sing a song full of the faith that the dark past has
    taught us,
Sing a song full of the hope that the present has
    brought us,
Facing the rising sun of our new day begun,
Let us march on till victory is won.   10

Stony the road we trod,
Bitter the chastening* rod,   chastening: correcting
Felt in the days when hope unborn had died;   by punishing
Yet with a steady beat,
Have not our weary feet   15
Come to the place for which our fathers sighed?
We have come over a way that with tears has
    been watered,
We have come, treading our path through the blood
    of the slaughtered,
Out from the gloomy past,
Till now we stand at last   20
Where the white gleam of our bright star is cast.

God of our weary years,
God of our silent tears,
Thou who hast brought us thus far on the way;
Thou who hast by Thy might   25
Led us into the light,
Keep us forever in the path, we pray.
Lest* our feet stray from the places, our God,   Lest: for fear that
    where we met Thee,
Lest our hearts drunk with the wine of the world,
    we forget Thee;
Shadowed beneath Thy hand,   30
May we forever stand.
True to our God, true to our native land.

About the Poem

1. What wisdom does the poem teach and what Bible verses reflect this truth?
2. What indications are there in the poem that Johnson is a black writer?
3. Why is it significant that Johnson ends the poem with an address to God?
4. What does Johnson consider the Negroes' native land?

About the Author

James Weldon Johnson (1871-1938) was instrumental in contributing new artistry to black literature. His work was a predecessor to the efforts of the Harlem Renaissance writers who wanted to call attention to their skill, not their color. Johnson led a varied life: he was a teacher, principal, songwriter (two of his songs were used in Theodore Roosevelt's successful 1904 presidential campaign), poet, U.S. consul to Venezuela and Nicaragua, lawyer, newspaper editor, and field representative for the NAACP, where he held a conservative position on race. This selection from his works was selected by the NAACP and is now commonly known as the "Negro National Hymn." Johnson is also well known for his work *God's Trombones,* a collection of sermon-poems in which the attentive listener can note the eloquence of the preacher and the responses of the audience. His work uses rich, musical language without relying on the stereotypes of the Negro tradition. As an indication of his popularity and influence, over "two thousand mourners attended his Harlem funeral" in 1938.

Our Blessed Land

James J. Kilpatrick

Noted newspaper columnist James J. Kilpatrick here brings much of our nation's past into perspective. What wisdom does he teach us about viewing our nation?

I am a newspaperman, and autumn usually takes me abroad, to Europe or Africa or South America. I come back to my country home in Virginia in November, my mind overloaded with impressions that cannot be contained— man's pettiness,* self-deceit, mulish stubbornness, the blindness of his mind to the needs of others. We all of us have our blue and broody* days, and the spirit flags.*

---

pettiness: concern for trivial matters
broody: sulking
flags: droops

But I pick up my car at the airport and head west toward the Blue Ridge Mountains. The highway that leads me home has nothing much to offer for the first fifty miles. Then, just west of Amissville, an engineer with the soul of a poet has laid out a great climbing curve. At its crest the whole world opens. In one glorious burst of trumpets, the mountains fill the sky. And the bruised and weary heart gives grateful thanks.

Do we Americans ever truly reflect upon our blessings? Not often, I suspect. Do we understand—deeply understand—how fortunate we are? I doubt it. As a people, we are the biggest bellyachers on the face of the earth. We complain of racism, of discrimination, of rights unfulfilled; we complain of traffic jams, of perfidy* in public office, of poverty, of ill-housing. Well, I have seen Soweto in South

Africa, and smelled the stinks* of Rio, and looked in the faces of Leningrad; and I have come home to my mountains and wept.

---

perfidy: cheating; deceit
stinks: stench

We, too, have wretched slums, and there is hunger and suffering here. But in the general quality of our lives, Americans are incredibly* better off than most of the people a reporter sees around the world.

---

incredibly: unbelievably

I coast in exultation* down the long hill past the engineer's curve. Up ahead is Washington, Va., and off to the right the white steeple of Trinity Church catches the sun's last shaft* of light. There is the courthouse, where lives the rule of law. And there is the sheriff's office; he will not come at midnight pounding on my door. There is a polling* place. There is the office of the Rappahannock *News,* there the library, there the public school.

---

exultation: triumph
shaft: ray
polling: voting

The roads that have led around the world lead now to a graveled country lane, a bridge across White Walnut Run, a lamp in the window, a fire in the kitchen hearth. Home.

Once I returned from the road on a bleak and sullen day, the mountains shawled* in mist. All the way home the radio had chattered of bad news: the cost of living was edging up, a crisis was promised in natural gas. This was only months after a President had resigned, and the stain of those sickening events had barely begun to fade. If some saccharine* minister had urged us, on such an afternoon, to count our blessings, a sardonic* voice would have asked: *What* blessings? I was close to despair.

shawled: covered
saccharine: sickishly sweet
sardonic: mocking

I went to the office to check the mail and turned on the lamps. After a while the bitterness slipped away. The office walls are lined with books. Here are the law books, row on row, red and khaki;* they stand as straight as Leathernecks* on review. Here are the Annals of America, eagle-crested, bound in blue and gold. Here are the shelves on history and government, here the lives of famous men.

khaki: beige
Leathernecks: marines

At such a time, in such a mood, one listens; and there is more to be heard than the wind piercing the storm windows, more than the bark of a dog outside. If one listens, the room fills with voices. These are the voices of Jamestown in the bitter winter of 1607; voices of Valley Forge and of Yorktown; voices that ring like great bronze bells. One has only to listen to hear young Tom Jefferson and old Ben Franklin, John Marshall laughing, Abe Lincoln lifting his high-pitched voice above a crowd in Illinois: "Our reliance is in the love of liberty which God has planted in us. . . ."

The imagination stirs. The books are clamoring* to be heard. Here is the letter of a young soldier in the Revolution: "We seem always hungry, and most always wet, and by night chilled to the bone." The voices speak across regions and generations, soft voices from the South, hard voices from the West, Lee and

Douglass side by side, soldier and slave together on a shelf, freed of the past. "I am as strong as a bull moose," cries Teddy Roosevelt from a top shelf. "You can use me to the limit!"

clamoring: shouting

One listens, and rubs the worn volumes of history, coaxing them to speak out; and they speak of war, of depression, of the human struggle that won the West. They speak of slavery, dust bowls, soup lines, sweatshops, floods and earthquakes, of Presidents who lied. Look, they cry! America has known all this. And America has survived!

Do we hear these voices in winter? Or do we hear only the ticking of a clock, the wind in the eaves, the creaking of a rafter? Is the American dream no more than that—a dream? We know better. It has all happened; it is there to build on—the successes, the failures, the trials and errors, the good men and bad, the blood and tears and laughter.

Perhaps it is banal* to say it, but it needs to be said. Politically, economically and spiritually, for all its manifest* shortcomings, our blessed land is the freest and strongest on earth. Wherever Americans bow their heads, the prayer should rise—not only from our lips but from our hearts—a prayer of thanks for what has been, and knowing that, for what will be.

banal: ordinary; common
manifest: obvious

About the Essay

1. How does Kilpatrick use the road in the essay?
2. How does Kilpatrick address the complaints of Americans?
3. What do the books represent for Kilpatrick?
4. What does Kilpatrick say ensures the continued greatness of America? Is he right?

About the Author

James Kilpatrick (b. 1920) is one of America's most widely read political columnists. His opinions on current events and political positions also make him one of the most controversial. He is thoroughly American, as you can see from this selection. By age seven he knew that he wanted to be a journalist and set out to become one, editing the high school paper and then majoring in journalism at the University of Missouri. He is a humorous man as well as an opinionated one. He includes in his column an annual birthday letter to his oldest grandchild and has even founded the Black Eyed Pea Society of America. It is unclear whether he likes or dislikes that particular vegetable! He also likes "sedentary gardening," which he describes as "watching his wife" do the work. He is interested in vexillology, or the study of flags, and flies not only the American flag but also "a Revolutionary War banner depicting a black snake and captioned 'Don't Tread on Me' " over his house in Virginia.

America

Samuel F. Smith

My country, 'tis of thee,
Sweet land of liberty,
Of thee I sing:
Land where my fathers died,
Land of the pilgrim's pride,
From every mountain side
Let freedom ring!

My native country, thee,
Land of the noble, free,
Thy name I love:
I love thy rocks and rills,*
Thy woods and templed* hills;
My heart with rapture* thrills,
Like that above.

Let music swell the breeze,
And ring from all the trees
Sweet freedom's song:
Let mortal tongues awake;
Let all that breathe partake;*
Let rocks their silence break,
The sound prolong.

Our fathers' God, to Thee,
Author of liberty,
To Thee we sing:
Long may our land be bright
With freedom's holy light;
Protect us by Thy might,
Great God, our King!

rills: brooks

templed: shaped like a
  temple

rapture: a state of
  overwhelming emotion

partake: take part in

About the Poem

1. Read the first three lines of each stanza of this song. What aspect of America is emphasized in these lines in every stanza?
2. In each of the first three stanzas, a different person or group of people is shown enjoying the freedom of America. Identify the person or people in each.
3. Who is credited as being the "author of liberty"?

About the Author

Samuel Francis Smith (1808-95) was born in Boston. He attended Boston Latin School and later graduated from Harvard and Andover Theological Seminary. It was while he was studying at Andover that he wrote the words to what has sometimes been called our "unofficial national anthem." The story is brief but interesting.

In 1831 a New York educator named William Woodbridge traveled to Germany to examine the public schools there and to take note of any methods that might be used in the American system. During his visit he learned that the German schools stressed the teaching of music to children. Interested in this addition to the curriculum, Mr. Woodbridge acquired several German music books, brought them back to America, and showed them to his friend Mr. Lowell Mason, a skilled American musician. Though interested in the books, Mr. Mason knew no German. He did know a young man, however, who was fluent in several languages, and he took the books to him. Samuel Smith, only twenty-four years old at the time, began looking through the books to provide translations for Mr. Mason. While leafing through one of them, he was attracted by a German patriotic song. He liked the simple melody and the stirring words, which began "God bless our native land; / Firm may she ever stand, / In storm and night." Instantly Mr. Smith was strongly prompted to write a patriotic hymn for his own country to fit the same melody. "Seizing a scrap of waste paper," he later recorded, "I began to write, and in half an hour, I think, the words stood upon it substantially as they are sung today."

During his long life Samuel Smith was a Baptist pastor and a language teacher. Having written poetry from his childhood, he composed many other hymns besides "America," though none became as popular as his early patriotic piece. Samuel Smith died at the age of eighty-seven while he was on his way to a preaching engagement in Boston.

The Bible and Our Land

All the commandments which I command thee this day shall ye observe to do, that ye may live. . . . And thou shalt remember all the way which the Lord thy God led thee. . . .

For the Lord thy God bringeth thee into a good land, a land of brooks of water, of fountains and depths that spring out of valleys and hills; A land of wheat, and barley, and vines, and fig trees, and pomegranates; a land of oil olive, and honey; A land wherein thou shall eat bread without scarceness, thou shalt not lack any thing in it; a land whose stones are iron, and out of whose hills thou mayest dig brass.

When thou hast eaten and art full, then thou shalt bless the Lord thy God for the good land which he hath given thee.

Beware that thou forget not the Lord thy God, in not keeping his commandments, and his judgments, and his statutes, which I command thee this day: Lest when thou hast eaten and art full, and hast built goodly houses, and dwelt therein; And when thy herds and thy flocks multiply, and thy silver and thy gold is multiplied, and all that thou hast is multiplied; Then thine heart be lifted up, and thou forget the Lord thy God . . . And thou say in thine heart, My power and the might of mine hand hath gotten me this wealth.

But thou shalt remember the Lord thy God: for it is he that giveth thee power to get wealth, that he may establish his covenant which he swore unto thy fathers, as it is this day.

And it shall be, if thou do at all forget the Lord thy God, and walk after other gods, and serve them, and worship them, I testify against you this day that ye shall surely perish. As the nations which the Lord destroyeth before your face, so shall ye perish; because ye would not be obedient unto the voice of the Lord your God. (Deuteronomy 8:1-2, 7-14, 17-20)

Let every soul be subject unto the higher powers. For there is no power but of God: the powers that be are ordained of God.

Whosoever therefore resisteth the power, resisteth the ordinance of God: and they that resist shall receive to themselves damnation.

For rulers are not a terror to good works, but to the evil. Wilt thou then not be afraid of the power? do that which is good, and thou shalt have praise of the same:

For he is the minister of God to thee for good. But if thou do that which is evil, be afraid; for he beareth not the sword in vain: for he is the minister of God, a revenger to execute wrath upon him that doeth evil.

Wherefore ye must needs be subject, not only for wrath, but also for conscience sake. For this cause pay ye tribute also: for they are God's ministers, attending continually upon this very thing.

Render therefore to all their dues: tribute to whom tribute is due; custom to whom custom; fear to whom fear; honour to whom honour. (Romans 13:1-7)

5

Humility

The more a person tries to get others to see his humility, the less of true humility they are able to see in him.

Humility

The larger I get,
The harder to see;
And when I am found,
I'll no longer be.
      What am I?

Riddles can be fun and frustrating at the same time. Here are some riddles that you can pass on to either friend or foe (your teacher has the answers):

What has eighteen legs and catches flies?
What is the world's largest operation?
What is the most stirring book you can read?

Actually riddles have an ancient and honorable heritage. For thousands of years they were used in actual contests, in friendly jests, even in literature. Do you remember Samson's riddle "Out of the eater came forth meat, and out of the strong came forth sweetness" (Judg. 14:14)? Samson challenged the Philistines to solve the riddle in seven days. Without the help of his Philistine wife, though, they never would have been successful.

Have you solved the riddle that opens this essay yet? It describes a puzzle that existed long before Samson. The answer, of course, is humility, the lack of which helped bring about Samson's downfall.

Humility puzzles most people. Can you see how the opening riddle works? The more a person tries to get others to see his humility, the less of true humility they are able to see in him. And if someone ever believes that he has finally become humble, humility vanishes like air in a punctured balloon.

Even though humility is hard to attain, the Bible commands us to strive for it. Paul tells us to "put on . . . humbleness of mind" (Col. 3:12), and Peter encourages us to be "clothed with humility: for God resisteth the proud, and giveth grace to the humble" (I Pet. 5:5). The Bible not only tells us to be humble but also gives guidelines for attaining humility.

The first step toward humility is to fear God. Solomon says, "By humility and the fear of the Lord are riches, and honour, and life" (Prov. 22:4). The basis for God's being able to use us lies in our allowing Him to control our lives and in recognizing Him as the source of wisdom. In the selection from *Dr. Ida,* a teenage girl finally realizes, like Samuel in the Bible, that it is God's call she hears. God can use her if she listens to His voice and obeys Him.

Recognizing our proper role as God's servant is another important part of humility. Christ taught, "Whosoever will be chief among you, let him be your servant" (Matt. 20:27). Many a company asks its future executives to work in all divisions of the company. As a result, the trainees become valuable to the whole company. First they learn all parts of the company's operations. Second, they show in their willingness to do even the lowliest jobs that they can earn the respect of those they will someday lead. A poem like "Godolphin Horne" helps show the importance of a servant's heart.

Another important part of this trait is a truth expressed by Solomon in Proverbs 15:33: "Before honour is humility." If we exalt ourselves, not preferring others to ourselves, we run the risk of being humiliated (Luke 14:7-11). In "Alas! Poor Annabelle!" (a chapter from *Caddie Woodlawn*), Annabelle brags to her relatives about the superiority of her clothes, her customs, and her hometown, Boston. She exalts herself before her cousins, whose practical jokes in retaliation effectively humble her.

Other selections in this unit also illustrate some aspect of humility or the lack of it. A thirty-four-year-old woman tells of her humiliation over not being able to read. In "The Soloist," a high school tuba player plays a solo before a hostile audience even though he thinks he will be laughed off the platform. "The Split Cherry Tree," a story you should read with discernment, gives a picture of the overemphasis sometimes placed on education with the resulting sense of false humility.

The Bible gives models of humility for our understanding. Mary, for instance, anointed the feet of Jesus, wiping them with her hair. Her humble action indicated her desire to place herself under God's leadership. Also, Moses humbly chose "to suffer affliction with the people of God, [rather] than to enjoy the pleasures of sin for a season" (Heb. 11:25).

In Jesus, the central figure of all Scripture, we see the most complete portrait of humility. Paul tells us that Jesus "humbled himself, and became obedient unto death, even the death of the cross" (Phil. 2:8). Peter, describing the example Christ set for us, reports that Christ did not strike back at His accusers, but rather "committed himself to him that judgeth righteously" (I Pet. 2:23). After Jesus had washed the disciples' feet, He told them that His act was an example of humility for them to imitate.

The Bible thus lifts the curtain of mystery from humility. It is fearing God enough to put His will first, serving Him in obedience, and preferring others before ourselves. Where then is the riddle? The Bible certainly seems clear enough on this subject. Maybe the real puzzle is not what humility is but why so few practice it.

Primer Lesson

Carl Sandburg

Carl Sandburg talks here about pride, the opposite of humility. What are the characteristics of "proud words"?

Look out how you use proud words.
When you let proud words go, it is not easy to call them back.
They wear long boots; they walk off proud; they can't hear you calling—
Look out how you use proud words.

About the Poem

1. Why is the title an appropriate one for the selection?
2. What is the meaning of "long boots" in line three?
3. What does the poet mean by "they can't hear you calling—"?
4. What is the effect achieved by the repetition of the first and last lines?

About the Author

Carl Sandburg (1878-1967) is known as the "poet of industrial America." He knew that he wanted to be a writer by the time he was six years old. Yet his writing was enriched by the fact that he spent much of his youth working at odd jobs and then finally decided to pursue a traditional education to achieve a profession. After failing grammar and arithmetic at West Point, he returned to Lombard College in Illinois. He became an outstanding newspaper reporter as well as a successful poet. Sandburg is also well known for his children's stories and his collection of American folksongs. Perhaps Sandburg is most known for his complete biography of Abraham Lincoln, for which he won the Pulitzer Prize for history in 1939. In recognition of his contributions to the field of knowledge about Lincoln, Sandburg became the first private citizen to address a joint session of Congress on the one hundred fiftieth anniversary of Lincoln's birth. A memorial service for Sandburg was held at the Lincoln Memorial on September 17, 1967.

Casey at the Bat

Ernest Lawrence Thayer

Pick out the words and phrases that the poet uses to describe Casey. What kind of character is he? Are you surprised by the last line?

The outlook wasn't brilliant for the Mudville nine that day;
The score stood four to two, with but one inning more to play;
And so, when Cooney died at first, and Burrows did the same,
A sickly silence fell upon the patrons* of the game.

> patrons: supporters

A straggling few got up to go in deep despair. The rest   5
Clung to the hope which springs eternal in the human breast;
They thought, if only Casey could but get a whack, at that,
They'd put up even money now, with Casey at the bat.

But Flynn preceded Casey, as did also Jimmy Blake,
And the former was a pudding and the latter was a fake;   10
So upon that stricken* multitude grim melancholy* sat,
For there seemed but little chance of Casey's getting to the bat.

> stricken: afflicted by misfortune
>
> melancholy: dejection

But Flynn let drive a single, to the wonderment of all,
And Blake, the much-despised, tore the cover off the ball;
And when the dust had lifted, and they saw what had occurred,   15
There was Jimmy safe on second, and Flynn a-hugging third.

Then from the gladdened multitude went up a joyous yell;
It bounded from the mountaintop, and rattled in the dell;*
It struck upon the hillside, and recoiled upon the flat;
For Casey, mighty Casey, was advancing to the bat.   20

> dell: valley

There was ease in Casey's manner as he stepped into his place;
There was pride in Casey's bearing, and a smile on Casey's face;
And when, responding to the cheers, he lightly doffed* his hat,
No stranger in the crowd could doubt 'twas Casey at the bat.

> doffed: tipped

Ten thousand eyes were on him as he rubbed his hands with dirt;   25
Five thousand tongues applauded when he wiped them on his shirt;
Then while the writhing* pitcher ground the ball into his hip,
Defiance* gleamed in Casey's eye, a sneer curled Casey's lip.

writhing: twisting

Defiance: contempt of opposition

And now the leather-covered sphere came hurtling through the air,
And Casey stood a-watching it in haughty* grandeur* there;   30
Close by the sturdy batsman the ball unheeded sped.
"That ain't my style," said Casey. "Strike one," the umpire said.

haughty: proud

grandeur: splendor

From the benches, black with people, there went up a muffled roar,
Like the beating of the storm waves on a stern and distant shore;
"Kill him! Kill the umpire!" shouted someone on the stand;   35
And it's likely they'd have killed him had not Casey raised his hand.

With a smile of Christian charity great Casey's visage* shone;
He stilled the rising tumult;* he bade the game go on;
He signaled to the pitcher, and once more the spheroid flew;
But Casey still ignored it, and the umpire said, "Strike two."   40

visage: face

tumult: commotion

"Fraud!" cried the maddened thousands, and the echo answered, "Fraud!"
But a scornful look from Casey, and the audience was awed;
They saw his face grow stern and cold, they saw his muscles strain,
And they knew that Casey wouldn't let that ball go by again.

The sneer is gone from Casey's lips, his teeth are clenched in hate,   45
He pounds with cruel violence his bat upon the plate;
And now the pitcher holds the ball, and now he lets it go,
And now the air is shattered by the force of Casey's blow.

Oh! somewhere in this favored land the sun is shining bright;
The band is playing somewhere, and somewhere hearts are light;   50
And somewhere men are laughing, and somewhere children shout,
But there is no joy in Mudville—mighty Casey has struck out!

. . . About the Author

Ernest Thayer (1863-1940) developed an interest in baseball while at
Harvard because his friend was captain of one of the best teams that Harvard
ever had. In fact it was Harvard's best season ever that prompted Thayer to write
this poem. Thayer also wrote for the *San Francisco Examiner* for a friend from
his college days, William Randolph Hearst. After reading some of William S.
Gilbert's *Bab Ballads,* Thayer decided to try his hand at a Sunday humor column,
which he wrote under the name of "Phin." It was in this column that "Casey"
appeared, but the poem got little notice until De Wolf Hopper, an actor, recited
the poem at a gathering of baseball players. A friend, after reading "Casey" in
the newspaper, suggested that Hopper recite it between acts of his play, but since
Hopper's child was extremely ill, he replied that he couldn't concentrate enough
to memorize anything new. However, after a telegram arrived telling him that
his child was much improved, he managed to memorize "Casey" in an hour. He
estimated that he recited Thayer's poem about fifteen thousand times in his
career. It took Hopper four years to track down Thayer as the author since the
poem was published with only the initials E. L. T. The authorship controversy
haunted Thayer for the rest of his life as others tried to take the credit for his
work. Thayer was responsible for the writing, but it was really Hopper who made
the work famous, for if the recitation had been up to Thayer, Casey would
certainly never have been heard again.

Godolphin Horne

Hilaire Belloc

What prevents Godolphin from being hired as a page? Is the poet speaking only about six year olds?

Godolphin Horne was Nobly Born;
He held the Human Race in Scorn,
And lived with all his Sisters where
His Father lived, in Berkeley Square.*

And oh! the Lad was Deathly Proud!   5
He never shook your Hand or Bowed,
But merely smirked* and nodded thus:
How perfectly ridiculous!
Alas! That such affected* Tricks
Should flourish in a Child of Six!   10
(For such was Young Godolphin's age.)
Just then, the Court required a Page,*

Whereat the Lord High Chamberlain
(The Kindest and the Best of Men),
He went good-naturedly and took   15
A Perfectly Enormous Book
Called "People Qualified to Be
Attendant on* His Majesty,"
And murmured, as he scanned* the list
(To see that no one should be missed),   20
"There's William Coutts has got the Flu,
And Billy Higgs would Never do,
And Guy de Vere is far too young,
And . . . wasn't D'Alton's Father hung?
And as for Alexander Byng—! . . .   25
I think I know the kind of thing,
A Churchman, cleanly, nobly born,
Come, let us say Godolphin Horne."
But hardly had he said the word
When Murmurs of Dissents* were heard.   30

Berkeley Square: aristocratic section of London, including many notable homes

smirked: smiled in a self-satisfied way

affected: artificial, pretended

Page: boy employed by the royal court

Attendant on: to wait on
scanned: examined

Dissents: disagreements

The King of Iceland's Eldest Son
Said, "Thank you! I am taking none!"
The Aged Duchess of Athlone   sub-acid: sour
Remarked, in her sub-acid* tone,
"I doubt if He is what we need!"   35
With which the Bishops all agreed;
And even Lady Mary Flood
(So kind, and, oh, so *really* good)
Said, "No. He wouldn't do at all,
He'd make us feel a lot too small."   40

The Chamberlain said, "Well, well, well,
No doubt you're right . . . One cannot tell!"
He took his Gold and Diamond Pen
And Scratched Godolphin out again.

So Godolphin is the Boy   45
Who blacks the Boots at the Savoy.*   Savoy: a well-known
                                                     hotel in London

. . . **A**bout the Author . . . .

   Hilaire Belloc (1870-1953) was an outstanding British author of varied
skills. He was a poet, biographer, novelist, writer of travel books, and
essayist. He collaborated on satiric novels with G. K. Chesterton so successfully that George Bernard Shaw nicknamed them "Chesterbelloc."

Sir Joseph's Song

Sir W. S. Gilbert

How does this office boy rise to the top? What is strange about his appointment as the "Ruler of the Queen's Navee"?

When I was a lad I served a term
As office boy to an Attorney's firm.
I cleaned the windows and I swept the floor,
And I polished up the handle of the big front door.
   I polished up that handle so carefullee   5
   That now I am the Ruler of the Queen's Navee!

As office boy I made such a mark
That they gave me the post* of a junior clerk.   post: position
I served the writs* with a smile so bland,*   writs: written orders
And I copied all the letters in a big round hand.   10 bland: soothing
   I copied all the letters in a hand so free,
   That now I am the Ruler of the Queen's Navee!

In serving writs I made such a name
That an articled* clerk I soon became;   articled: apprenticed
I wore clean collars and a brand new suit   15
For the pass examination at the Institute,
   And that pass examination did so well for me,
   That now I am the Ruler of the Queen's Navee!

Of legal knowledge I acquired such a grip
That they took me into the partnership.   20
And that junior partnership, I ween,*   ween: suppose
Was the only ship that I ever had seen.
   But that kind of ship so suited me,
   That now I am the Ruler of the Queen's Navee!

I grew so rich that I was sent   25
By a pocket borough* into Parliament.   pocket borough: an
I always voted at my party's call,   English town whose
And I never thought of thinking for myself at all.   representation in
   I thought so little, they rewarded me   Parliament was
   By making me the Ruler of the Queen's Navee!   30 controlled by one
                                         person or family

Now Landsmen all, whoever you may be,
If you want to rise to the top of the tree,
If your soul isn't fettered* to an office stool,
Be careful to be guided by this golden rule—
  Stick close to your desks and never go to sea,   35
  And you all may be Rulers of the Queen's Navee!

fettered: tied

About the Author

William S. Gilbert's (1836-1911) career covered many areas; he was playwright, librettist, poet, humorist, lawyer, and author. He is perhaps best known as the librettist half of the musical team Gilbert and Sullivan, who were responsible for such musical successes as *The Pirates of Penzance* and *The Mikado.* He began writing humorous verses for *Punch* under the pseudonym Bab, his childhood nickname. He then became a clerk in the Privy Office, much like Sir Joseph, but he never rose as far as Sir Joseph did! After resigning, he started his law career but was not very successful at that either. He moved on to journalism and then on to stage work with Sir Arthur Sullivan. It was the musical *H.M.S. Pinafore* that made him famous and prompted Queen Victoria to make him a knight.

About the Poems

1. What kind of character is Casey? How do you know? What kind of players are Flynn and Jimmy Blake?
2. The phrase "a smile of Christian charity" in line 37 is ironic; what does the poet really mean? What Bible verse is reflected in the fact that Casey strikes out?
3. What is the author's attitude toward Godolphin?
4. What does the poet mean by saying that Lady Mary Flood is "so kind, and oh, so *really* good"?
5. What keeps Godolphin Horne from being hired as a page? Is this flaw restricted to children?
6. What relationships do Sir Joseph's qualifications have with each of his posts? How does he rise to being the "Ruler of the Queen's Navee"?
7. Line 34 refers to the "golden rule"; what "golden rule" does Sir Joseph mean?

Being a Public Character

Don Marquis

This story is told from a very unusual viewpoint. Who tells it? How do you respond to his saying, "And you have to act the way humans expect you to act, if you want to slide along through the world without too much trouble"? What does this story tell you about humility?

Ever since I bit a circus lion, believing him to be another dog like myself, only larger, I have been what is called a Public Character in our town.

Freckles, my boy, was a kind of Public Character, too. He went around bragging about my noble blood and bravery, and all the other boys and dogs in the town sort of looked up to him and thought how lucky he was to belong to a dog like me. And he deserved whatever glory he got out of it, Freckles did. For, if I do say it myself, there's not a dog in town got a better boy than my boy Freckles, take him all in all. I'll back him against any dog's boy that is anywhere near his size, for fighting, swimming, climbing, foot racing, or throwing stones farthest and straightest. Or I'll back him against any stray boy, either.

Well, some dogs may be born Public Characters, and like it. And some may be brought up to like it. I've seen dogs in those traveling *Uncle Tom's Cabin* shows that were so stuck on themselves they wouldn't hardly notice us town dogs. But with me, becoming a Public Character happened all in a flash, and it was sort of hard for me to get used to it. One day I was just a private kind of a dog, as you might say, eating my meals at the Watsons' back door, and pretending to hunt rats when requested, and standing out from underfoot when told, and other unremarkable things like that. And the next day I had bit that lion and was a Public Character, and fame came so sudden I scarcely knew how to act.

Even drummers* from big places like St. Louis and Chicago would come into the drugstore and look at my teeth and toenails, as if they must be different from other dogs' teeth and toenails. And people would come tooting up to the store in their little cars and get out and look me over and say:

"Well, Doc, what'll you take for him?"

drummers: traveling salesmen

And Doc would wink and say: "He's Harold's dog. You ask Harold."

Harold is Freckles's other name. But any boy that calls him Harold outside of the schoolhouse has got a fight on his hands, if that boy is anywhere near Freckles's size. Harry goes, or Hal goes, but Harold is a fighting word with Freckles.

Freckles would always say, "Spot ain't for sale."

And even Heinie Hassenyager, the butcher, got stuck on me after I got to be a Public Character. Heinie would come two blocks up Main Street with lumps of hamburg steak, and give them to me. Steak, mind you, not gristly scraps. And before I became a Public Character Heinie even grudged me the bones I would drag out of the box under his counter when he wasn't looking.

My daily hope was that I could live up to it all. I had always tried, before I happened to bite that lion, to be a friendly kind of a dog toward boys and humans and dogs, all three. I'd always been expected to do a certain amount of tail wagging and be friendly. But as soon as I got to be a Public Character, I saw right away I wasn't expected to be *too* friendly any more. So, every now and then, I'd growl a little, for no reason at all. A dog that has bit a lion is naturally expected to have fierce thoughts inside of him; I could see that. And you have to act the way humans expect you to act, if you want to slide along through the world without too much trouble.

So when Heinie would bring me the ready-chewed steak, I'd growl at him a little bit. And then I'd bolt and gobble the steak like I didn't think so . . . much of it, after all, and was doing Heinie a big personal favor to eat it. And now and then I'd pretend I wasn't going to eat a piece of it unless it was chewed finer for me and growl at him about that.

That way of acting made a big hit with Heinie, too. I could see that he was honored and flattered because I didn't go any further than just growl. It gave him a chance to say he knew how to manage animals. And the more I growled, the more steak he brought. Everybody in town fed me. I pretty near ate myself to death for a while there.

But my natural disposition* is to be friendly. I would rather be loved than feared. I had to growl and keep dignified and go on being a Public Character, but often I would say to myself it was losing me all my real friends, too.

---

disposition: temperament; urge

The worst of it was that people, after a week or so, began to expect me to pull something else remarkable. Freckles, he got up a circus, and I was the principal* part of that circus. I was in a cage, and the sign over me read:

---

principal: main

I didn't care for being caged and circused that way myself. And it was right at that circus that considerable trouble started.

Seeing me in a cage like that, all famoused up, with more meat poked through the slats than two dogs could eat, made Mutt Milligan and some of my old friends jealous.

Mutt, he nosed up by the cage and sniffed. I nosed a piece of meat out of the cage to him.

Mutt grabbed it and gobbled it down, but he didn't thank me any. Mutt, he says:

"There's a new dog downtown that says he blew in from Chicago. He says he used to be a Blind Man's Dog on a street corner there. He's a pretty wise dog, and he's a right ornery-looking dog, too. He's peeled considerably where he has been bit in fights."

"Well, Mutt," says I, "as far as that goes I'm peeled considerable myself where I've been bit in fights."

"I know you are, Spot," says Mutt. "You don't need to tell me that. I've peeled you some myself from time to time."

"Yes," I says, "you did peel me some, Mutt. And I've peeled you some, too. More'n that, I notice that right leg of yours is a little stiff yet where I got to it about three weeks ago."

"Well, then, Spot," says Mutt, "maybe you want to come down here and see what you can do to my other three legs. I never saw the day I wouldn't give you a free bite at one leg and still be able to lick you on the other three."

"You wouldn't talk that way if I was out of this cage," I says, getting riled.

"What did you ever let yourself be put into that fool cage for?" Mutt says. "You didn't have to. You got such a swell head on you the last week or so that you got to be licked. You can fool boys and humans all you want to about that accidental old lion, but us dogs got your number, all right. What that Blind Man's Dog from Chicago would do to you would be aplenty!"

"Well, then," I says, "I'll be out of this cage along about suppertime. Suppose you bring that Blind Man's Dog around here. And if he ain't got a spiked collar on him, I'll fight him. I won't fight a spike-collared dog to please anybody."

And I wouldn't, neither, without I had one on myself. If you can't get a dog by the throat or the back of his neck, what's the use of fighting him? You might just as well try to eat a blacksmith shop as fight one of those spike-collared dogs.

Well, that night after supper, along comes that Blind Man's Dog. Never did I see a Blind

348   *HUMILITY*

Man's Dog that was as tight-skinned. I ain't a dog that brags, myself, and I don't say I would have licked that heavy a dog right easy, even if he had been a loose-skinned dog. What I do say is that I had been used to fighting loose-skinned dogs that you can get some sort of a reasonable hold onto while you are working around for position. And running into a tight-skinned dog that way, all of a sudden and all unprepared for it, would make anybody nervous.

Lots of dogs wouldn't have fought him at all when they realized how they had been fooled about him and how tight-skinned he was. But I was a Public Character now, and I had to fight him. More than that, I ain't ready to say yet that that dog actually licked me. Freckles, he hit him in the ribs with a lump of soft coal, and he got off me and run away before I got my second wind. There's no telling what I would have done to that Blind Man's Dog, tight-skinned as he was, if he hadn't run away before I got my second wind.

Well, the word got around town, in spite of his running away like that before I got my second wind, that that Blind Man's Dog, so called, had actually licked me. Many pretended to believe it. Every time Freckles and me went down the street someone would say:

"The dog that licked the lion got licked himself, did he?"

If it was a girl that said it Freckles would rub a handful of sand into her hair. And if it was a boy anywhere near his size, there would be a fight.

For a week or so it looked like Freckles and I were fighting all the time. Three or four times a day, every day.

No matter how much you may like to fight, some of the time you would like to pick the fights yourself and not have other people picking them off you. Kids began to fight Freckles that wouldn't have dast to stand up to him a month before. I was still a Public Character, but I was getting to be the kind you josh about instead of the kind you are proud of. I didn't care so awful much for myself, but I hated it for Freckles. For when they got us pretty well hackled,* all the boys began to call him Harold again.

hackled: ready for a fight

And after they had called him Harold for a week, he must have begun to think of himself as Harold. For one Saturday afternoon when there wasn't any school, instead of going swimming with the other boys or playing baseball, or anything, he went and spent the afternoon with girls.

Right next to the side of our yard was the Wilkinses'. They had a bigger house and a bigger yard than ours. Freckles was sitting on the top of the fence, looking into their orchard one day, when the three Wilkins girls came out to play. There were only two boys in the Wilkins family, and they were twins; but they were only year-old babies and didn't amount to anything. The two eldest Wilkins girls, the taffy-colored-haired one and the squint-eyed one, each had one of the twins, taking care of it. And the other Wilkins girl, the pretty one, she had one of those big dolls made as big as a baby. They were rolling those babies and the doll around the grass in a wheelbarrow, and the wheel came off, and that's how Freckles happened to go over.

Freckles, he fell for it. After he got the wheel fixed, they got to playing charades and fool girl games like that up in the attic. The hired girl was off, and pretty soon Mrs. Wilkins hollered up the stairs that she was going to be gone for an hour, and to take good care of the twins, and then we were alone in the place.

Well, it wasn't much fun for me. They played and they played, and I stuck to Freckles, because a dog should stick to his boy, and a boy should stick to his dog, no matter what

the disgrace. But after a while I got pretty tired and lay down on a rug and went to sleep.

I must have slept pretty sound and pretty long. All of a sudden I waked up with a start, and almost choking, for the place was smoky. I barked and no one answered.

I ran out to the landing, and the whole house was full of smoke. The house was on fire, and it looked like I was alone in it. I went down the back stairway, which didn't seem so full of smoke, but the door that let out onto the first-floor landing was locked, and I had to go back up again.

By the time I got back up, the front stairway was a great deal fuller of smoke, and I could see glints of flame winking through it way down below. But it was my only way out of that place. On the top step I stumbled over a gray wool bunch of something or other, and I picked it up in my mouth. Thinks I, "That is Freckles's gray sweater, that he is so stuck on. I might as well take it down to him."

It wasn't so hard for a lively dog to get out of a place like that, I thought. But I got kind of confused and excited, too. And it struck me all of a sudden, by the time I was down to the second floor, that that sweater weighed an awful lot.

I dropped it on the second floor, and ran into one of the front bedrooms and looked out.

By jings, the whole town was in the front yard and in the street.

And in the midst of the crowd was Mrs. Wilkins, carrying on like mad.

"My baby!" she yelled. "Save my baby. Let me loose! I'm going after my baby!"

I stood up on my hind legs, with my head just out of that bedroom window, and the flame and smoke licking up all around me, and barked.

"My dog! My dog!" yells Freckles, who was in the crowd. "I must save my doggie!" And he made a run for the house, but someone grabbed him and slung him back.

And Mrs. Wilkins made a run, but they held her, too. The front of the house was one sheet of flame. Old Pop Wilkins, Mrs. Wilkins's husband, was jumping up and down in front of Mrs. Wilkins, yelling here was her baby. He had a real baby in one arm and that big doll in the other, and was so excited he thought he had both babies. Later I heard what had happened. The kids had thought they were getting out with both twins, but one of them had saved the doll and left a twin behind.

Well, I think that baby will likely turn up in the crowd somewhere, after all, and I'd better get out of there myself while the getting was good. I ran out of the bedroom and ran into that bunched-up gray bundle again.

I'm not saying that I knew it was the missing twin in a gray shawl when I picked it up the second time. And I'm not saying that I didn't know it. But the fact is that I did pick it up. I don't make any brag that I would have risked my life to save Freckles's sweater. It may be I was so rattled* I just picked it up because I had had it in my mouth before and didn't quite know what I was doing.

---

rattled: flustered

But the *record* is something you can't go behind, and the record is that I got out the back way and into the back yard with that bundle swinging from my mouth and walked round into the front yard and laid that bundle down— *and it was the twin!*

I don't make any claim that I *knew* it was the twin till I got into the front yard, mind you. But you can't prove I *didn't* know it was.

And nobody tried to prove it. The gray bundle let out a squall.*

---

squall: cry

"My baby!" yells Mrs. Wilkins. And she kissed me! I rubbed it off with my paw. And then the taffy-colored-haired one kissed me! And the first thing I knew the pretty one kissed me. But when I saw the squint-eyed one coming, I got behind Freckles and barked.

"Three cheers for Spot!" yelled the whole town. And they gave them.

And then I saw what the lay of the land was, so I wagged my tail.

It called for that hero stuff, and I throwed my head up and looked noble.

An hour before, Freckles and me had been outcasts. And now we were Public Characters again. We walked down Main Street, and we owned it. And we hadn't any more than got to Doc Watson's drugstore than in rushed Heinie Hassenyager with a lump of hamburg steak, and tears in his eyes.

About the Story

1. Who tells the story?
2. What is amusing about the dog's name for the boy?
3. Discuss the dog's philosophy that "you have to act the way humans expect you to act, if you want to slide along through the world without too much trouble."

4. This story gives two examples of being a Public Character; which one is a truly heroic action?
5. Does Spot learn anything from his experience as a Public Character?

About the Author

Don Marquis (1878-1937) led a varied life as a schoolteacher, worker in a sewing machine factory, clerk in a census office, journalist, poet, and playwright. He spent time as assistant editor of the *Uncle Remus Magazine,* working with Joel Chandler Harris. He used his skills in social satire and found that one of his characters was successful enough to make the transition from a newspaper column to the stage and take Marquis into the area of play writing, where he won the Mark Twain Medal for comedy.

Mr. K*A*P*L*A*N, the Comparative and Superlative

Leonard Q. Ross

Have you ever had to read your composition before a class? Were you embarrassed? What is Mr. Kaplan's reaction when it is his turn to read his writing? How is he able to survive the criticism from the class and the teacher?

For two weeks Mr. Parkhill had been delaying the inescapable:* Mr. Kaplan, like the other students in the beginners' grade of the American Night Preparatory School for Adults, would have to present a composition for class analysis. All the students had had their turn writing the assignment on the board, a composition of one hundred words, entitled "My Job." Now only Mr. Kaplan's rendition* remained.

---

inescapable: unavoidable
rendition: performance

It would be more accurate to say Mr. K*A*P*L*A*N's rendition of the assignment remained, for even in thinking of that distinguished student, Mr. Parkhill saw the image of his unmistakable signature, in all its red-blue-green glory. The multicolored characters were more than a trademark; they were an assertion of individuality, a symbol of singularity,* a proud expression of Mr. Kaplan's Inner Self. To Mr. Parkhill, the signature took on added meaning because it was associated with the man who had said his youthful ambition had been to become "a physician and sergeant," the Titan* who had declined* the verb "to fail" "fail, failed, bankrupt."

---

singularity: marking him as different from the others
Titan: one who stands out for greatness of achievement
declined: given the grammatical forms of

One night, after the two weeks' procrastination,* Mr. Parkhill decided to face the worst. "Mr. Kaplan, I think it's your turn to—er—write your composition on the board."

---

procrastination: postponement

Mr. Kaplan's great, buoyant* smile grew more great and more buoyant. "My!" he exclaimed. He rose, looked around at the class proudly as if surveying the blessed who were to witness a linguistic* *tour de force,* stumbled over Mrs. Moskowitz's feet with a polite "Vould you be so kindly?" and took his place at the blackboard. There he rejected several pieces of chalk critically, nodded to Mr. Parkhill—it was a nod of distinct reassurance— and then printed in firm letters:

buoyant: cheerful
linguistic: relating to language
tour de force: French: feat of strength

"You need not write your name on the board," interrupted Mr. Parkhill quickly. "Er—to save time . . ."

Mr. Kaplan's face expressed astonishment. "Podden me, Mr. Pockheel. But de name is by me *pot* of mine composition."

"Your name is *part* of the composition?" asked Mr. Parkhill in an anxious tone.

"Yas*sir!*" said Mr. Kaplan with dignity. He printed the rest of H*Y*M*A*N K*A*P*L*A*N for all to see and admire. You could tell it was a disappointment for him not to have colored chalk for this performance. In pale white the elegance of his work was dissipated.* The name, indeed, seemed unreal, the letters stark, anemic,* almost denuded.*

dissipated: lost
anemic: pale
denuded: bare

His brow wrinkled and perspiring, Mr. Kaplan wrote the saga* of A Cotter In Dress Faktory on the board, with much scratching of the chalk and an undertone of sound. Mr. Kaplan repeated each word to himself softly, as if trying to give to its spelling some of the flavor and originality of his pronunciation. The smile on the face of Mr. Kaplan had taken on something beatific* and imperishable:* it was his first experience at the blackboard; it was his moment of glory. He seemed to be writing more slowly than necessary as if to prolong the ecstasy* of his Hour. When he had finished he said "Hau Kay" with distinct regret in his voice, and sat down. Mr. Parkhill observed the composition in all its strange beauty:

My Job A Cotter In Dress Faktory
Comp. by
H*Y*M*A*N K*A*P*L*A*N

Shakspere is saying what fulls man is and I am feeling just the same way when I am thinking about mine job a cotter in Dress Faktory on 38 st. by 7 av. For why should we slafing in dark place by laktric lights and all kinds hot for $30 or maybe $36 with overtime, for Boss who is fat and driving in fency automobil? I ask! Because we are the deprassed workers of world. And are being exployted. By Bosses. In mine shop is no difference. Oh how bad is laktric light, oh how is all kinds hot. And when I am telling Foreman should be better conditions he hollers, Kaplan you redical!!

saga: long, detailed account
beatific: blissful
imperishable: not subject to decay
ecstasy: intense delight

At this point a glazed look came into Mr. Parkhill's eyes, but he read on.

So I keep still and work by bad light and always hot. But somday will the workers making Bosses to work! And then Kaplan will give to them bad laktric and positively no windows for the air should come in! So they can know what it means to slafe! Kaplan will make Foreman a cotter like he is. And give the most bad dezigns to cot out. Justice. Mine job is cotting Dress dezigns.

T-H-E E-N-D

Mr. Parkhill read the amazing document over again. His eyes, glazed but a moment before, were haunted now. It was true: spelling, diction, sentence structure, punctuation, capitalization, the use of the present perfect for the present—all true.

"Is planty mistakes, I s'pose," suggested Mr. Kaplan modestly.

"Y-yes . . . yes, there are many mistakes."

"Dat's because I'm tryink to give *dip ideas*," said Mr. Kaplan with a sigh of those who storm heaven.

Mr. Parkhill girded his mental loins.* "Mr. Kaplan—er—your composition doesn't really meet the assignment. You haven't described your *job*, what you *do*, what your work *is*."

---

girded his mental loins: prepared himself

"Vell, it's not soch a interastink jop," said Mr. Kaplan.

"Your composition is not a simple exposition. It's more of a—well, an *essay* on your *attitude*."

"Oh, fine!" cried Mr. Kaplan with enthusiasm.

"No, no," said Mr. Parkhill hastily. "The assignment was *meant* to be a composition. You see, we must begin with simple exercises

before we try—er—more philosophical essays."

Mr. Kaplan nodded with resignation. "So naxt time should be no ideas, like abot Shaksbeer? Should be only *fects?*"

"Y-yes. No ideas, only—er—facts."

You could see by Mr. Kaplan's martyred smile that his wings, like those of an eagle's, were being clipped.

"And Mr. Kaplan—er—why do you use 'Kaplan' in the body of your composition? Why don't you say '*I* will make the foreman a cutter' instead of '*Kaplan* will make the foreman a cutter?' "

Mr. Kaplan's response was instantaneous. "I'm so glad you eskink me dis! Ha! I'm usink 'Keplen' in de composition for plain and tsimple rizzon: becawss I didn't vant de reader should tink I am *prajudiced* aganst de foreman, so I said it more like abot a strenger: 'Keplen vill make de foreman a cotter!' "

In the face of this subtle passion for objectivity, Mr. Parkhill was silent. He called for corrections. A forest of hands went up. Miss Mitnick pointed out errors in spelling, the use of capital letters, punctuation; Mr. Norman Bloom corrected several more words, rearranged sentences, and said, "Woikers is exployted with an '*i,*' not '*y*' as Kaplan makes"; Miss Caravello changed "fulls" to "fools," and declared herself uncertain as to the validity of the word "Justice" standing by itself in "da smalla da sentence"; Mr. Sam Pinsky said he was sure Mr. Kaplan meant "*oppressed* voikers of de void, not *depressed*, aldough dey are deprassed *too*," to which Mr. Kaplan replied, "So ve bote got right, no? Don' *change* 'deprassed,' only *add* 'oppressed.' "

Then Mr. Parkhill went ahead with his own corrections, changing tenses, substituting prepositions, adding the definite article. Through the whole barrage* Mr. Kaplan kept

shaking his head, murmuring "Mine goot-
ness!" each time a correction was made. But
he smiled all the while. He seemed to be proud
of the very number of errors he had made; of
the labor to which the class was being forced
in his service; of the fact that his *ideas,* his
creation, could survive so concerted* an onslaught.* And as the composition took more
respectable form, Mr. Kaplan's smile grew
more expansive.

barrage: rapid outpouring
concerted: united
onslaught: fierce attack

"Now, class," said Mr. Parkhill, "I want
to spend a few minutes explaining something about adjectives. Mr. Kaplan uses the
phrase—er—'most bad.' That's wrong.
There is a word for 'most bad.' It is what we
call the superlative form of 'bad.'" Mr.
Parkhill explained the use of the positive,
comparative, and superlative forms of the
adjective. "'Tall, taller, tallest.' 'Rich,
richer, richest.' Is that clear? Well then, let
us try a few others."

The class took up the game with enthusiasm. Miss Mitnick submitted "dark, darker,
darkest"; Mr. Scymzak, "fat, fatter, fattest."

"But there are certain exceptions to this
general form," Mr. Parkhill went on. The class,
which had long ago learned to respect that
gamin,* The Exception to the Rule, nodded
solemnly. "For instance, we don't say 'good,
gooder, goodest,' do we?"

gamin: a boy who roams about the streets

"No, sir!" cried Mr. Kaplan impetuously.*
"'Good, gooder, good*est?*' Ha! It's to leff!"

impetuously: impulsively forceful

"We say that X, for example, is good. Y,
however, is—?" Mr. Parkhill arched an eyebrow interrogatively.*

interrogatively: questioningly

"Batter!" said Mr. Kaplan.
"Right! And Z is—?"
"High-cless!"
Mr. Parkhill's eyebrow dropped. "No," he
said sadly.
"*Not* high-cless?" asked Mr. Kaplan in-
credulously.* For him there was no word more
superlative.

incredulously: unbelievingly

"No, Mr. Kaplan, the word is 'best.' And
the word 'bad,' of which you tried to use the
superlative form . . . It isn't '*bad, badder,
baddest.*' It's 'bad' . . . and what's the comparative? Anyone?"
"Worse," volunteered Mr. Bloom.
"Correct! And the superlative? Z is the
—?"
"'Worse' also?" asked Mr. Bloom hesitantly. It was evident he had never distinguished the fine difference in sound between
the comparative and superlative forms of
"bad."
"No, Mr. Bloom. It's not the *same* word,
although it—er—sounds a good deal like it.
Anyone? Come, come. It isn't hard. X is *bad,*
Y is *worse,* and Z is the—?"
An embarrassed silence fell upon the class,
which, apparently, had been using "worse" for
both the comparative and superlative all
along. Miss Mitnick blushed and played with
her pencil. Mr. Bloom shrugged, conscious
that he had given his all. Mr. Kaplan stared at
the board, his mouth open, a desperate concentration in his eye.
"*Bad—worse.* What is the word you use
when you mean 'most bad'?"
"Aha!" cried Mr. Kaplan suddenly. When
Mr. Kaplan cried "Aha!" it signified that a
great light had fallen on him. "I know! De
exect void! So easy! *Ach!* I should know dat
ven I vas wridink! *Bad—voise—*"

"Yes, Mr. Kaplan!" Mr. Parkhill was definitely excited.

"Rotten!"

Mr. Parkhill's eyes glazed once more, unmistakably. He shook his head dolorously,* as if he had suffered a personal hurt. And as he wrote "W-O-R-S-T" on the blackboard there ran through his head, like a sad refrain, this latest manifestation* of Mr. Kaplan's peculiar genius: "bad—worse—rotten; bad—worse . . ."

---

dolorously: sorrowfully
manifestation: instance

About the Story

1. Why do you think Mr. Kaplan is so proud of his composition?
2. How would you describe Mr. Kaplan's response to the criticisms of the others?
3. Do Mr. Parkhill's criticisms hinder Mr. Kaplan's eagerness for success?

About the Author

Leonard Q. Ross (b. 1908), known as Leo C. Rosten to readers of this story, lives two rather distinct lives—one as a social sciences research expert who has written important books on the journalists of Washington, D.C., and the workings of Hollywood and the other as the author of the Hyman Kaplan stories, published in the *New Yorker*. They created such a loyal following that they were published in book form and inspired other books about Mr. Kaplan. Ross was born in Poland but came to the United States when he was two. His character who has been said to be a compilation of "all the minor humorous characters of Dickens and Shakespeare" survived and conquered all the language difficulties of the emigrant that Ross himself was spared.

How Beautiful with Mud

Hildegarde Dolson

Although Hildegarde's predicament is bizarre, she actually resembles many adolescents both female and male. What are her motives for buying Beauty Clay? What is her brother's response to her experiment? Is the author of this excerpt from We Shook the Family Tree *sympathetic to young people?*

Perhaps the surest way to tell when a female goes over the boundary from childhood into meaningful adolescence is to watch how long it takes her to get to bed at night. My own cross-over, which could be summed up in our family as "What on earth is Hildegarde *doing* in the bathroom?" must have occurred when I was a freshman in high school. Until then, I fell into bed dog-tired each night, after the briefest possible bout* with toothbrush and washcloth. But once I'd become aware of the Body Beautiful, as portrayed in advertisements in women's magazines, my absorption was complete and my attitude highly optimistic. I too would be beautiful. I would also be Flower-Fresh, Fastidious* and Dainty—a triple-threat virtue obviously prized above pearls by the entire male sex, as depicted* in the *Ladies' Home Journal.*

bout: session
Fastidious: difficult to please
depicted: represented

Somehow, out of my dollar-a-week allowance, I managed to buy Mum, Odorono, Listerine and something called Nipso, the latter guaranteed to remove excess hair from arms and legs, and make a man think, "Oooo, what a flawless surface." It's true that I had no men, nor was I a particularly hairy child, having only a light yellow down on my angular appendages.* Nevertheless, I applied the Nipso painstakingly in the bathroom one night, with Sally as my interested audience. I had noticed the stuff had a rather overpowering, sickish sweet scent, but this was a very minor drawback, considering the goal I had in mind. After Sally had been watching me for a few minutes, she began holding her nose. Finally she asked me to unlock the door and let her out. "Don't you want to see me wash it off?" I asked, rather hurt.

---
angular appendages: bony arms and legs

"No," Sally said. "It smells funny."

In the next hour, as my father, mother and brothers followed their noses to the upstairs hall, there were far more detailed descriptions of just how Nipso affected the olfactory senses.* Jimmy, being a simple child, merely said "Pugh" and went away. My father thought it was most like the odor of rotten eggs, but Bobby said No, it was more like a mouse that's been dead quite a while. Mother was more tactful, only remarking that Nipso obviously wasn't meant to be applied in a house people lived in. Since it certainly wasn't meant to be applied in a wooded dell,* either, I was prevailed upon to throw the rest of the tube away.

---
olfactory senses: sense of smell
dell: valley

I didn't mind too much, because I already had my eye on something that sounded far more fascinating than Nipso. This was a miraculous substance called Beauty Clay, and every time I read about it in a magazine advertisement, the words enveloped me in rapture.* Even the story of its discovery was a masterpiece in lyrical* prose. Seems this girl was traveling in an obscure European country (name on request) and ran out of those things ladies always run out of at the wrong time, such as powder and make-up lotion. The worst part was that the girl really *needed* such artifices* to cover up bumps. Through some intuitive* process which escapes me at the moment, she had the presence of mind to go to a near-by hamlet,* pick up a handful of mud, and plaster it on her face. Then she lay dozing in the sun, by a brook. When she came to, washed the claylike mud off her face, and looked at her reflection in the brook, she knew she had hit the jackpot. Boy, was she beautiful. Looking at the Before-and-After pictures, I could see that *this* beauty was more than skin-deep, having benefited even her nose, eyes and hair.

---
rapture: great delight
lyrical: poetic; elevated
artifices: devices
intuitive: instinctive
hamlet: village

After pondering* all this, I could well understand why a jar of the imported Beauty Clay cost $4.98. In fact, it was dirt cheap at the price, and my only problem was how to lay my hands on $4.98. Certainly I had no intention of enlisting financial support from my parents. For one

thing, it was too much money, and for another thing, parents ask too many questions. Far better, I thought, to let the transformation* of their oldest daughter come as a dazzling surprise.

---

pondering: considering
transformation: change

Due to the fact that I had such important things as Beauty Clay on my mind, it was understandable that my monthly marks in algebra should cause even more distress than usual in the bosom of my family. Each month, the high school Honor Roll, consisting of the names of the ten highest students in each class, was published in the *Franklin News Herald*. (The *Herald*, as I'd known it on Armistice Day, had been taken over by the *News*.) And each month, my own name was prominently absent. Appeals to my better nature, my pride, and the honor of the Dolsons did no good. I honestly meant well, and I even went so far as to carry books home from school and carry them back again the next morning. But freshman algebra, implying as it did that X equals Y, was simply beyond me. Finally my father said that if I got on the Honor Roll he'd give me five dollars. Wobbly as I was in mathematics, it took me only a flash to realize this sum was approximately equal to $4.98, or the piddling* price of the Beauty Clay. From there on in, I was straining every muscle. When I say that I got 89 in algebra and climbed to the bottom rung on the Honor Roll, I am stating a miracle simply. What is more important, I got the five bucks.

---

piddling: very small

My father said that if I liked, he'd put most of it in my savings account. Bobby said, with even more enthusiasm, that he knew where I could get a bargain in a second-hand pistol. I declined both offers, marveling at the things men could think of to do with money, and made my way, on foot, to Riesenman's drugstore. When Mr. Riesenman said he had no Beauty Clay, I was grieved. When he said he'd never even heard of the stuff, I was appalled.* It took three trips to convince him that he must order it immediately, money on the line.

appalled: shocked

Then I went home and waited. With admirable restraint, I waited five days. After that, I made daily inquiries on my way home from school. If I was with friends, I'd say I had to do an errand for Mother and would catch up to them later. They must often have wondered, in the next thirty days, at the number of unobtainable items my mother demanded of a drugstore. Finally came the wonderful afternoon when Mr. Riesenman said, "Here you are, Hildegarde." His jovial* air may have been due to the fact that he was rid of me at last. My own joy was primitive* and unconfined. At last I'd got hold of a rainbow.

jovial: jolly
primitive: simple

It took a week more before I could achieve the needed privacy for my quick-change act. Mother was taking Jimmy and Sally down town to get new shoes, Bobby was going skiing, and my father, as usual, would be at the office. I got home to the empty house at twenty minutes of four, and made a beeline for the Beauty Clay. According to the directions, I then washed off all make-up, which in my own case was a faint dash of powder on my nose, and wrapped myself in a sheet "To protect that pretty frock," or, more accurately, my blue-serge middy blouse. Then I took a small wooden spatula the manufacturer had thoughtfully provided, and dug into the jar.

The Beauty Clay was a rather peculiar shade of grayish-green, and I spread this all

over my face and neck—"even to the hairline where tell-tale wrinkles hide." The directions also urged me not to talk or smile during the twenty minutes it would take the clay to dry. The last thing in the world I wanted to do was talk or smile. That could come later. For now, a reverent* silence would suffice.* In fact as the thick green clay dried firmly in place, it had to suffice. Even though my face and neck felt as if they'd been cast in cement, the very sensation reassured me. Obviously, something was happening. I sat bolt upright in a chair and let it happen.

reverent: respectful
suffice: be sufficient

After fifteen minutes of this, the doorbell rang. I decided to ignore it. The doorbell rang again and again, jangling* at my conscience. Nobody at our house ever ignored doorbells, and I was relieved when it stopped. In my eagerness to see who had been calling on us, I ran to my window, opened it, and leaned out. The departing guest was only the man who brought us country butter each week, I was glad to note. Hearing the sound of the window opening above him, he looked up. When he saw me leaning out, his mouth dropped open and he let out a hoarse, awful sound. Then he turned and ran down the steep hill at incredible* speed. I couldn't imagine what had struck him, to act so foolish.

jangling: grating
incredible: unbelievable

It wasn't until I'd remembered the clay and went to look in a mirror that I understood. Swathed in a sheet, and with every visible millimeter of skin a sickly gray-green, I scared even myself.

According to the clock, the Beauty Clay had been on the required twenty minutes, and was now ready to be washed off. It occurred to me that if twenty minutes was enough to make me beautiful, thirty minutes or even forty minutes would make me twice as beautiful. Besides, it would give me more lovely moments of anticipation, and Mother wouldn't be home till after five.

By the time my face was so rigid that even my eyeballs felt yanked from their sockets, I knew I must be done, on both sides. As I started back to the bathroom, I heard Bobby's voice downstairs yelling "Mom!" With the haste born of horror I ran back and just managed to bolt myself inside the bathroom as Bobby leaped up the stairs and came down the hall toward his room. Then I turned on the faucet and set to work. The directions had particularly warned "Use only gentle splashes to remove the mask—No rubbing or washcloths." It took several minutes of gentle splashing to make me realize this was getting me nowhere fast. Indeed, it was like splashing playfully at the Rock of Gibraltar. I decided that maybe it wouldn't hurt if I rubbed the beauty mask just a little, with a nailbrush. This hurt only the nailbrush. I myself remained imbedded in Beauty Clay.

By this time, I was getting worried. Mother would be home very soon and I needed a face—even any old face. Suddenly it occurred to me that a silver knife would be a big help, although I wasn't sure just how. When I heard Bobby moving around in his room, I yelled at him to bring me a knife from the dining room sideboard. Rather, that's what I intended to yell, but my facial muscles were still cast in stone, and the most I could do was grunt. In desperation, I ran down to the sideboard, tripping over my sheet as I went, and got the knife. Unfortunately, just as I was coming back through the dusky upstairs hall, Bobby walked out of his room and met me, face to face. The mental impact, on Bobby, was terrific. To do him justice, he realized almost instantly that this was his own sister, and not, as he had at first imagined, a sea monster. But even this realization was not too reassuring.

I had often imagined how my family would look at me after the Beauty Clay had taken effect. Now it had taken effect—or even permanent possession of me—and Bobby was certainly reacting, but not quite as I'd pictured it.

"Wh—what?" he finally managed to croak,* pointing at my face.

---

croak: cry hoarsely

His concern was so obvious and even comforting that I tried to explain what had happened. The sounds that came out alarmed him even more.

Not having the time or the necessary freedom of speech to explain any further, I dashed into the bathroom and began hitting the handle of the knife against my rocky visage.* To my heavenly relief, it began to crack. After repeated blows, which made me a little groggy,* the stuff had broken up enough to allow me to wriggle my jaw. Meanwhile, Bobby stood at the door watching, completely bemused.*

---

visage: appearance
groggy: shaky
bemused: bewildered

Taking advantage of the cracks in my surface, I dug the blade of the knife in, and by scraping, gouging, digging and prying, I got part of my face clear. As soon as I could talk, I turned on Bobby. "If you tell anybody about this, I'll kill you," I said fiercely.

Whether it was the intensity of my threat or a latent* chivalry* aroused by seeing a lady tortured before his very eyes, I still don't know, but Bobby said, "Cross my heart and hope to die."

---

latent: hidden
chivalry: courtesy

He then pointed out that spots of the gray-green stuff were still very much with me. As I grabbed up the nailbrush again, to tackle these remnants, he asked in a hushed voice, "But what *is* it?"

"Beauty Clay," I said. "I sent away for it."

Bobby looked as though he couldn't understand why anyone would deliberately send away for such punishment, when there was already enough trouble in the world. However, for the first time in a long, hideous half hour, I remembered why I'd gone through this ordeal, and I now looked into the mirror expecting to see results that would wipe out all memory of suffering. The reflection that met my eye was certainly changed all right, varying as it did between an angry scarlet where the skin had been rubbed off, to the greenish splotches* still clinging.

---

splotches: spots

Maybe if I got it all off, I thought. When it was all off, except those portions wedded to my hair, I gazed at myself wearily, all hope abandoned. My face was my own—but raw. Instead of the Body Beautiful I looked like the Body Boiled. Even worse, my illusions* had

been cracked wide open, and not by a silver knife.

---

illusions: false dreams

"You look awfully red," Bobby said. I did indeed. To add to my troubles, we could now hear the family assembling downstairs, and mother's voice came up, "Hildegarde, will you come set the table right away, dear?"

I moved numbly.

"You'd better take off the sheet," Bobby said.

I took off the sheet.

Just as I reached the stairs, he whispered, "Why don't you say you were frostbitten and rubbed yourself with snow?"

I looked at him with limp gratitude.

When Mother saw my scarlet, splotched face, she exclaimed in concern. "Why, Hildegarde, are you feverish?" She made a move as if to feel my forehead, but I backed away. I was burning up, but not with fever.

"I'm all right," I said, applying myself to setting the table. With my face half in the china cupboard, I mumbled that I'd been frostbitten and had rubbed myself with snow.

"Oh, Cliff," Mother called. "Little Hildegarde was frostbitten."

My father immediately came out to the kitchen. "How could she be frostbitten?" he asked reasonably. "It's thirty-four above zero."

"But her ears still look white," Mother said.

They probably did, too, compared to the rest of my face. By some oversight, I had neglected to put Beauty Clay on my ears. "I'm all right," I insisted again. "I rubbed hard to get the circulation going."

This at least was true. Anyone could tell at a glance that my circulation was going full blast, from the neck up.

Bobby had followed me out to the kitchen to see how the frostbite story went over. As Mother kept exclaiming over my condition he now said staunchly,* "Sure she's all right. Let her alone."

---
staunchly: faithfully

My father and mother both stared at him, in this new role of Big Brother Galahad.* In fact, my father reacted rather cynically.* "Bobby, did you and your friends knock Hildegarde down and rub her face with snow?" he asked.

Galahad: famous knight known for being courteous
cynically: distrustfully

"Me?" Bobby squeaked. He gave me a dirty look, as if to say "You'd better talk fast."

I denied hotly that Bobby had done any such thing. In fact, I proceeded to build him up as my sole rescuer, a great big St. Bernard of a brother who had come bounding through the snowdrifts to bring me life and hope.

Bobby looked so gratified* at what he'd been through in my story that I knew my secret was safe.

---
gratified: pleased

Sally, always an affectionate child, began to sob. "She might have died. Bobby saved her from freezing."

My father and mother remained dry-eyed. Against this new set-up of Brother Loves Sister they were suspicious, but inclined to do nothing.

And in a way I *had* been frostbitten, to the quick.* Lying in bed that night, still smarting, I tried to think up ways to get even. It wasn't clear to me exactly whom or what I had to get even with. All I knew was that I was sore and unbeautiful, and mulcted* of five dollars. With the hot and cold fury of a woman stung, I suddenly conceived my plan for revenge. It was so simple and logical and yet brilliant that my mind relaxed at last. Some day I, too, would write advertisements.

---
quick: the very center
mulcted: swindled

About the Story

1. What are the motives of the main character for buying all the beauty aids and specifically the mud?
2. What is her brother's response?
3. Is the author sympathetic to the main character's predicament?
4. What does the speaker mean by her statement that she "*had* been frostbitten"?

About the Author

Hildegarde Dolson (1908-81), like many other writers we have read, had an early beginning to her writing career. She had her first sale, a magazine piece, when she was twenty-one years old. In addition to writing for young people, she began writing mysteries, after she met and then married her favorite mystery writer! She said that one of the best bits of advice she got was to write in a journal every day so that she would realize that people can and do write even if they aren't "inspired."

What It's Like When You Can't Read or Write

U.S. News and World Report

Have you ever been called illiterate? To students the term is a joke. But to millions of people illiteracy is no laughing matter. Many of these people, though, never learn to read, even when they want to, because they will not admit their problem to anyone else. What is Inetta Bush's attitude toward her predicament? What is her most serious problem?

People talk about illiteracy like it was a disease. Well, it's more like a handicap that hangs on you from the time you get up till you go to sleep. I trust my common sense to keep me out of trouble from not knowing how to read and write. But that doesn't work always.

When I look at a printed page, all I see is jumbled-up stuff that don't make any sense. I'll try to read my horoscope, but it sometimes takes me two minutes to get through a sentence and by the time I get to the end, I've forgotten the meaning.

I get notes and report cards sent home from my kids' schools, and there's not much I can do with them. I stay away from school meetings and teacher conferences because, you know, you can't hide something like that from your kids.

It was my children that forced me to seek help. I look at my seventeen-year-old son and my twelve-year-old daughter and I want to help them with their homework, but I can't. My son was supposed to repeat ninth grade for the third time this year, and he finally said he wanted to drop out of day school and take a night course to get his high school diploma. I see my handicap being passed on to my son, and I tell you, it scares me.

When I was growing up, my own mother didn't know I couldn't read and write, even though she could do *both*. People ask how I could hide something like that from her. Well, I have a good memory and I just memorized everything—telephone numbers, street signs, calendars, bus routes, textbooks, record albums. I'd go in the grocery store with my mother's shopping list and give it to the man. He would tell me where things were.

I was pretty much ignored in school. Nobody ever tried to find out what I needed. I wasn't a trouble-maker, so they kept pushing me from one grade to another, when I should have been moved back three or four grades. Once you find out nobody really cares, ain't nothin' to do but get away from it. You realize that you're not keeping up, and you get so disgusted. In junior high, I would get to school and then slip out. I found a job cleaning tables in a diner and quit going to school.

For years, I'd get on a bus and watch people read books and papers. I felt so out of place that I would get a paper and pretend to read. I would memorize words like *pizza* and

HUMILITY

hamburger and *steak* so that when I went to a restaurant I could look for these words on the menu.

It took me four years to pass the written test for my driver's license. I knew the answers, but I couldn't read the questions. Finally, I just memorized all seventy-two questions and answers.

Being illiterate means that I have to be on guard all the time. I listen to the radio news to keep up. I trust my instincts and use my street smarts, but you can't be prepared all the time. I still get cheated or fooled. Drugstores give me the wrong prescription, or I buy the wrong phonograph record, or I end up on the wrong bus because I can't read good enough to follow somebody's directions. My bank account gets overdrawn because of problems I have making out checks and sending them to the right places.

Illiteracy has made big trouble in my personal life, too. I was once married to an Air Force officer who was brilliant. He would say, "Here's a book you've just *got* to read," but I wasn't into books and we just couldn't communicate on that level. He was always so far ahead of me that our marriage just fell apart.

It's pathetic in this country how many people can't read or write. Half of them are women who are able to cover it up well. Society says if you can't read by the time you are eighteen, you aren't able to do it after that, no way. People tell you over and over that you can't do anything if you can't read, and you believe them.

I've always been able to work for a living, but I know a lot of illiterate people who end up on the welfare line. I have two sisters—my baby sisters who can't read either. One is on welfare, and the other has a job cleaning office buildings. They can't apply for a better job because they can't even fill out the application!

I was scared to death when I first went to the literacy center for help. The people were so understanding, but when they said they wanted to test my reading ability, the word *test* just freaked me out, and I turned around and went back home. You can't imagine the terror that gets hold of illiterate people when they have to face those books again. They are afraid of failing, of being ridiculed like when they were children.

I used to go out and buy novels. I got a whole bookshelf that I keep dusted off. I want to read them someday. I especially want to read the Bible through because if you can't read that book yourself, all you have is the opinions of others.

I earn my living operating machines that reproduce architectural drawings. I've been doing it for about fifteen years, but I've gone about as far as I can go with my present skills. I've still got a lot of dreams and fantasies. I want to write poetry, design clothes, get a better job, make a better life. But I won't be able to achieve any of those things if I don't learn to read.

About the Story

1. What is the speaker's attitude toward her inability to read and write?
2. What are the reasons Inetta gives for not being able to read?
3. How well does the speaker cope with her handicap?
4. What book does Inetta most want to read for herself and why?

Three Visitors in the Night

Dorothy Clarke Wilson

In this excerpt from the biography Dr. Ida, *the author shows us one eventful night in the life of a teenager. While visiting her missionary parents in India, Ida Scudder meets three men. Each wants her to come to his home to help his wife. But Ida refuses all three. She can do nothing else. What does the author mean by writing that "there had been only one Samuel lying on his bed. . . . But here there were two Idas"? To resolve the turmoil within her, she finally gains the humility to make the right choice.*

"Dear Annie," she wrote. "I am sitting in my room with your letter in front of me. It is late at night, and the compound is so quiet I can almost hear a *palli* (that's a lizard) darting up the wall to catch a bug. My father is working in his bedroom-study next door, and my mother, I hope, is asleep. She is much better and should be quite well by the time my short term is finished."

Ida glanced up sharply. She was always imagining things here in India, whispers of ghostly footsteps, disembodied eyes peering at her out of the darkness. Resolutely* she summoned a vision of Annie Hancock's eager, sensitive features.

Resolutely: with determination

"You say you wish you could be a missionary like me. *Don't say that.* I'm not a missionary and never will be. But you're not like me. You always were more—more spiritual, Annie darling. You might really like it here. I can see you going into the *zenanas* (women's quarters in Indian homes) and visiting the little wives and mothers. Some of them have to live all their lives within four walls, and they're so young, Annie, not near as old as you and I—"

Ida heard a discreet* cough from the verandah outside. She was not alarmed. A cough was a substantial thing, with a human body behind it. People were always coming to the bungalow, at any hour of the day or night, to ask help of her father. Lifting the lamp by its long spiraled stem, she went to the door and opened it.

HUMILITY

discreet: polite

A young Indian stood there, tall and grave and dignified. Even if she had not recognized him as one of the town's leading Brahmins, she would have known he belonged to this highest priestly caste by his dress. Above the spotless white vaishti* and beneath the finely pleated gold-bordered angavasthram* over his shoulders she could see the three-stranded white thread that was the badge of the Hindu "twice born."* The dark, clean-cut features beneath the neatly bound turban were tense with urgency.*

vaishti: shirt
angavasthram: long scarf worn by men
twice born: The men of the three highest castes of the
  Hindu religion receive a second birth at a religious
  initiation ceremony.
urgency: the need for immediate action

"What is it?" asked Ida. "Can I do anything for you?"

So agitated* was the young man that when he lifted his hands in a gesture of greeting she could see that they were trembling.

agitated: upset

"Oh, yes, ammal!"* The voice too, well modulated* and speaking in cultured English, was unsteady. "I desperately need your help. My wife, a young girl of only fourteen, is dying in childbirth. The barber woman* can do nothing for her and says she must die. And, *ammal,* she is such a lovely girl! I heard that you had come to India from America and thought you might help her."

ammal: young woman
modulated: regulated
barber woman: a midwife; a woman who assists
  women in childbirth

"Oh!" exclaimed Ida in swift sympathy. "I'm so sorry. But it's my father you want, not I. He's the doctor. He's right next door in his study. Come, I'll take you to him."

About to lead the way, she found passage to the verandah blocked by a shape as unyielding as one of its square white posts. The anxious young husband had vanished. In his place stood a haughty* and outraged* Brahmin.

haughty: proud
outraged: angry

"What! Take a man into my house to care for my wife? No man other than those of her own family have ever looked upon her. You don't know what you say!"

"B-but," stammered Ida, "surely, to—to save her life—"

"It is better that she should die," returned the young man, "than that another man should look on her face."

Ida stared at him. "You—you can't mean that." But she could see that he did. She tried again. "I'll go with my father," she promised. "He'll tell me just what to do, and I'll do it. He wouldn't even have to touch her."

The young man turned without answering and started away.

"Wait!" cried Ida. "Don't go yet—please!" She had to find some way to stop him. "You—you said she was young and beautiful. And she's suffering, maybe even dying. You said so yourself. Don't you— don't you care?"

The young Brahmin turned. He made no reply, and in the ring of lamplight his fine features looked hard as a stone mask. But—he had turned. The flame of the lamp streaming, Ida ran along the L-shaped verandah and around the corner to her father's bedroom-study. Hastily, but in a whisper so as not to awaken her mother, she poured out the story, brought him back with her to where the young man was waiting, and together they reasoned with him. But it was no use.

"Then—you will not come, *ammal*." His eyes looked out at her through the mask, tortured and, somehow, accusing.

She shook her head miserably. "It would do no good. I—don't know anything. I'd be no better than—than the barber's wife."

Nor as good, she added to herself silently. For, crude and unsanitary though they might be, the barber woman, traditional midwife, had her instruments and her techniques. She had nothing.

She watched him turn away and go down the steps, into the darkness. "Why?" she demanded fiercely, turning to her father. "*Why?*"

He patted her shoulder. "Because," he said gently, "it's the rule, the custom. It would violate his caste law."*

---

caste law: the law of his social class

"Custom—law—" She choked on the words.

"Why, yes." His tone revealed some surprise. "Surely you've known about these things before, my child."

It was true. Since her return to India Ida had become well acquainted with the caste system, that ancient institution separating Hindus by reason of birth into rigid social groups. Though once an undoubted aid to economic security, insuring to every person some occupation, however menial,* it had acquired grave evils through the centuries. The original four castes—priests, warriors, merchants, laborers—had been divided and subdivided ad infinitum,* each group maintaining its own rigid exclusiveness.* Then, below all the castes and subcastes, was the vast army of untouchables who, born to the so-called unclean occupations, like leather working, washing, sweeping, filth removal, were doomed to complete segregation.*

---

menial: lowly
ad infinitum: without end
exclusiveness: restrictiveness or separateness
segregation: separation

Members of castes or even subcastes were forbidden by their own laws to intermarry, hold social intercourse,* share food or water with those of lower groups. Especially was this true of the Brahmins, originally the priestly caste. And, while not directly responsible for the inferior position traditionally accorded to Hindu women, the caste system had contributed to its survival.

---
intercourse: communication

It was the women Ida had always pitied most, the Brahmins almost more than the untouchables. Visiting with her mother or a Bible woman in the *zenanas,* she had ached in sympathy for the sheltered wives and mothers and daughters, cringing* into subservience* behind their veils whenever a man of the household appeared, some of them never in a lifetime emerging from their courtyards except to change one set of high walls for another.

---
cringing: shrinking back
subservience: submissiveness

She had gone too with her father to more than one high-caste home, seen him take the pulse of a delicate female wrist thrust through a small hole in a curtain, heard him patiently diagnose and prescribe as best he could with nothing more to guide him than the fluttering of a pulse and the timid muffled answers to his insistent questions.

"Yes," she admitted to him now. "I—I suppose I have known. But—"

But always before, she understood suddenly, these had seemed quaint* and at times amusing customs, not—*not matters of life and death.*

---
quaint: unfamiliar

"Our friend," comforted her father, "is a deeply religious man. We must respect him for it."

"*Respect!*" She backed away from him, eyes flashing. "When he's letting her suffer, maybe die, a—a girl not much more than a child!"

"Perhaps," said Dr. John gently, "he's sacrificing more for his convictions than we are for ours. He looked to me as if he really loves his little wife. Go back to your room now, child, and forget it."

"*Forget—*"

"Yes. It's a lesson I learned long ago. If I hadn't, I couldn't have borne it to live in a country where there's so much suffering and despair. If there's nothing you can do to remedy a bad matter, it's the part of wisdom to forget it."

Ida went back to her room. She set the lamp down on the desk. Her father was right, of course. If there was nothing you could do, it was better to forget. The yellow light spread its warm comforting circle as she picked up her pen.

"... and they're so young, annie, not near so old as you and I."

She began writing furiously, telling Annie Hancock all the reasons she could think of for not wanting to live in India and not wanting to be a missionary. Her pen fairly flew over the pages.

When the sound of footsteps came again, she sprang up so quickly that the *palli,* poised motionless on the whitewashed wall above her desk, flashed away at lightning speed, not stopping until it reached the narrow shelf under the overhanging eaves of thatch.*

---
thatch: plant stalks used as roofing

Relief lent wings to her feet. The young Brahmin had changed his mind. He had come back for her father, and she would go with them. She had been foolish to feel upset. To save time, on her way to the door she snatched a light wrap from its hook, in case the night should turn cold. If the young man had brought no conveyance,* she would run and waken a

servant while her father was packing his bag, or, better yet, harness the pony herself.

conveyance: transportation

"I thought you'd come back," she began eagerly, before the figure in the shadows had a chance to speak. "I was sure you really cared—"

She stopped abruptly. Even without the lamp she could tell it was not the young Brahmin. Even before he spoke.

"Salaam, Madam. May Allah give you peace. If you could help me—"

The voice was hesitant, diffident,* the face a dark blur between the long tightly buttoned coat and the white brocaded* cap.

diffident: reserved
brocaded: with raised designs

"Of course," said Ida automatically. "What can I do for you, sir?"

"It's my wife," said the man gently. "She has had other children, but this time the little one does not come. There is no one to help her but an ignorant, untrained woman. I am afraid she is dying. Please forgive me for troubling you."

Ida could not believe her ears. It was just in stories that such coincidences occurred, not in real life. The man moved nearer the door,

into the lamplight. She could see his features now, thin and anxious above a gray triangle of beard.

"I have heard there is a doctor here," he continued hesitantly, "one not long since come from America."

"Oh, yes!" Ida's dismay evaporated. God was being good. He was giving them a chance to make up for failing the little fourteen-year-old girl. If one must die, another should live. This man was a Moslem. He would be bound by no laws of caste. "Wait!" she told him impetuously,* brushing past him and running along the verandah.

impetuously: impulsively

"Here's my father," she explained breathlessly, returning a moment later with Dr. John. "He's the doctor you're looking for. But if you like, I'll be glad to go with him and try to help."

"Madam,"—the voice was apologetic but firm—"you do not understand our ways. Only the men of her immediate family ever enter a Moslem woman's apartment. It is you, a woman, whose help I came seeking, not a man."

Ida stared at him incredulously. "But I can't help you," she replied. "It's you who don't understand. I'm not even a nurse. I know nothing about midwifery, absolutely nothing. I'd be glad to help you if I could."

"Then my wife must die," returned the Moslem with stolid* resignation.* "It is the will of Allah."

stolid: unemotional
resignation: acceptance

The girl watched him go down the steps and along the path until his white coat was lost in the blur of dust which marked the curving driveway. She heard the faint click of the metal as he passed through the gate and closed it carefully behind him. Then, without even

Three Visitors in the Night   371

glancing at her father, she fled into her room and shut the door.

Going straight to her desk, she dipped her pen so vigorously that its point jabbed the glass bottom of the inkwell.

"You can see now, Annie, why you wouldn't like being a missionary, especially in India. You'd simply hate it, and I ought to know. Believe me, I'm going to get back home just as quickly as I possibly can. Why, the people here don't even want you to help them. They'd rather let their wives and children die, even if they're beautiful and they say they love them and some of them are no more than fourteen. . . .

No use trying to write when you got so angry and homesick that the tears kept dropping on your paper and blurring the ink! But she had to do something. Jumping up, she ran across the room to the *almirah,** opened its doors, and began taking down her dresses, shaking them out, laying them on the bed, until the closet space was empty. Then, wringing a cloth in the wash basin of her cement bathing cubicle,* she wiped the closet vigorously from top to bottom, digging her nails into the corners. You couldn't be too careful about clothes in this country, especially if you wanted to keep them looking good for two years, until you could go back home and enjoy them again. She shook the dresses once more as she hung them up: the green silk she had worn to the New Year's party with the Taylor boys, her white graduation dress wrapped in an old sheet, the brown cashmere that was her favorite because her mother had chosen the cloth and made it for her away back when she was only fourteen. . . .

---

almirah: closet
bathing cubicle: small compartment

Fourteen. Suddenly she swept up all the remaining dresses and bundled them into the *almirah,* then stood very still trying to remember what it was like to be fourteen. She had been fourteen when her mother left her, when she had rushed upstairs and cried all night into her pillow. Things hurt so terribly when you were only fourteen, and life seemed so unbearably sweet!

It was then that the third call came.

"Ammal?" a diffident voice murmured.

She moved mechanically toward the door, not daring to hope. *But if it should be one of them, let it be the tall young Brahmin, with the tortured eyes and the little wife who was just fourteen and so very beautiful.* She lifted the lamp from the desk as she passed.

It was neither the tall young Brahmin nor the grave Moslem. She recognized this man as the father of one of her pupils in the Hindu Girls' School, a respected member of the Mudaliar caste. She had gone to his house one day with Mrs. Isaac to visit his wife, a lovely young woman no older than herself with a shy smile and big shining eyes.

"Kamla?" The child's name sprang to her lips in response to the urgency in the man's face. "Is she sick? Has anything happened?"

"Illai, no. Not Kamla, Missy *Ammal."* The man spoke in stilted,* halting English. "But I have trouble. Much trouble." He lifted his hands palm to palm as his eyes implored her. "I beg Missy, come to my house. I need much help."

---
stilted: stiff

Her eyes widened in horror. Her lips felt dry. "Not—not your wife—"

"Amma, yes." He returned her look with wonder. "How did Missy know? She is sick, much sick." Suddenly he was prostrating himself before her on the verandah floor, his hands touching her feet. "I beg Missy *Ammal* to come. If she come not, my wife dies."

"Please—don't kneel to me!" Ida drew back so swiftly that the lamp flared.

"The Missy *Ammal* will come?"

"But—it would do no good for me to come!" She repeated the words tonelessly. "I'm not a doctor. It's my father who is the doctor. Let me call him. He will go with you. He's a very good doctor. I'm sure he can do something for your wife. If—if you'll just let him—"

She knew the answer even before he lifted himself to his feet, revealing the outraged dignity, the bitterness of disappointment. No need even to listen to his words of shocked protest. She had heard them all twice before. But she did listen. There was no way to help it without covering her ears. And she couldn't do that, with the stem of the lamp clutched tightly in one hand.

"The Missy *Ammal* will come?" he pleaded again finally.

"I'm sorry." She heard her own voice, thin and remote, as if coming from a long distance. "I'd go with you if it would do any good. But it wouldn't. Can't you understand?" The voice rose to a higher pitch, held suddenly a hint of hysteria.* "There's nothing—nothing at all—that I could do!"

---
hysteria: uncontrollable emotion

This time she did not tell her father. After the man had turned and gone away, she shut the door tightly and bolted it, set the lamp down on the desk. Then with swift motions, not once pausing to give herself time to think, she made ready for bed. Brushed her hair a hundred times with long fierce strokes. Entered the little bathing cubicle, checking automatically to make sure the open drains had not invited a stray snake or scorpion.* Bathed. Pulled on her high-necked, long-sleeved, ruffled nightgown. Turned back the top sheet, lifting it high to make sure the tentlike space beneath was not occupied by an insect, caterpillar, or lizard. Blew out the lamp. Groped* her way back to the bed and lay down upon it. But not to sleep.

---
scorpion: small, eight-legged animal with a dangerous, poisonous sting in its tail
Groped: felt around uncertainly

"Forget," Dr. John had told her. "If there's nothing you can do to remedy a bad matter, it's the part of wisdom to forget it."

If there's nothing you can do. . . .

At first, as she lay tense and wakeful, nothing but darkness and silence. Then, slowly, the night became shape and scent and sound . . . the dim rectangle of a window, a sighing in the dusty thatch, the delicate fragrance of cork tree blossoms mingled with the faintly bitter tang* of tamarinds. Somewhere in the distance a nightjar began his restless hawking.

---
tang: flavor

Chuk-chuk-chuk-r-r-r! Chuk-chuk-chuk-r-r-r! Chuk-chuk-chuk-r-r-r!

Funny how often things seemed to come in threes, even the calls of birds! Temptations.

The crowing of cocks. A voice speaking to a young boy as he lay wakeful, like this, on his bed. Samuel had known just what to do when he heard his name called three times. The priest Eli had told him. And he had not only known just what to do. *He had wanted to do it.*

There had been only one Samuel lying on his bed, waiting, listening. But here there were two Idas, one tremulously* aware, the other rebelling with every fiber of her taut* body. As the night wore on they struggled, one with the other.

tremulously: fearfully
taut: stiff

"It's nonsense! God doesn't speak to people in these days."

No? You have eyes to see things, haven't you, like children lying by the roadside. Ears to hear people coming to your door?

"But—it's not my fault if they're foolish enough to let their wives die! It's nothing to me!"

Isn't it? Women like yourself loving life, one of them only fourteen—

"Stop! Didn't my father tell me it's better to forget a bad matter?"

If there is nothing you can do to remedy it.

"But there is nothing."

Nothing? With three women dying less than a mile away for want of a woman doctor? With millions more—

"No, no, I couldn't do that! Not if God himself were to ask me!"

Can't you understand, Ida Scudder? It's God himself who is asking.

When she heard a coppersmith bird begin his loud metallic "tuk . . . tuk" outside the window, she knew the night was over. Next came the crows, and, even before it began to get light, human sounds: creaking of cart wheels, the *"hinh, hinh"* of a bullock driver, the padding of bare feet, and the gentle slosh-ing of pails of water. Then, faint at first but growing steadily louder, the insistent beating of tom-toms.

Rising with sudden urgency, she slipped her feet into sandals, pulled a long wrapper over her nightgown, and, unbolting the door, stepped out on the verandah. The sound came from the left, where a road passed the compound beyond the thick clusters of tamarinds. Without hesitation she sped toward it.

Crouched behind the stone wall surrounding the compound, heart accelerating in pace with the insistent drumbeats, she watched the procession come. It was not an unusual sight, for Hindu funeral corteges* were always passing along this road on their way to the burning place beside the river. Yet she stared as if she had never seen one before. The white blur in front would be the drummers; the swath* of green just behind, another group carrying plantain trees. Her eyes clung to the single bright focus of color, a cloth of crimson wound about the wicker bier.* The groups following were blurs also, the chanting relatives and friends, the swaying, wailing women mourn-ers. Nothing remained after the procession's brief passing but the faint beat of drums, the echo of wailing cries, the memory of a bright bit of cloth, crimson like a bridal dress.

---

corteges: processions
swath: broad strip
bier: stand on which a corpse lies to be carried to the grave

---

When Ida went back through the tamarinds, she caught sight of a servant and called his name.

"Souri, I want you to do something for me."

He peered at her through the gray dawn, blinking a little at her appearance, but only a little, having learned long since that the ways of this youngest Scudder were unpredictable. As she gave him instructions, he wagged his head with that peculiar motion which to a Westerner looks like "no" but invariably means "yes." *Amma,* he knew the house she meant in the street of the Brahmins. *Amma,* he was acquainted with the dwelling place of the Sri Mudaliar who was father of the little Kamla. As for the other, *amma,* yes, there were ways of discovering. He would go. He would inquire. He understood.

She went back to her room. Soon, with the coming of sunrise, the compound was fully astir, schoolboys chattering and darting from one building to another, servants bustling. Ida dressed, combed her hair, waited. It was less than an hour before Souri returned, but it seemed an eternity. Hearing the shuffle of sandals, she ran to the door. The servant's face was, as usual, noncommittal.*

---

noncommittal: giving no hint of his feelings

"You did what I asked you, Souri?"

"*Amma.* I did so, Missy."

"You were able to find all the places?"

"I found them, Missy."

"And the three women who were sick?"

"Dead," replied Souri.

She gasped. "You—you don't mean—all three of them?"

"*Amma.* All three of them, Missy."

She shut the door and fled back into her room. Throwing herself on the bed, heedless of the carefully puffed and twisted hair, she buried her head deep in a pillow. Not since she was fourteen, crying into that other pillow, had she endured such torture of body and spirit.

A door opened. She heard whispers of footsteps, swift, light. Salomi, Souri's daughter. "Your chota,* Missy."

---

chota: small breakfast

"Put it down, Salomi. On the table. Anywhere."

"Missy not feel well?"

"It's—nothing. Just a headache. Please don't tell Mother."

"Can Salomi help?" The young voice was concerned.

"No. Just tell your father I—I won't be going to school this morning."

"Yes, Missy."

Minutes . . . hours . . . they meant nothing. It was a life she was living. It swept her up, clothed her in silks and velvets and bright colors. It poured music into her ears—a lover's endearments,* the voices of children; set her whirling to the tunes of gay polkas.

---

endearments: acts of affection

"See!" it called above the music. "Here they are—all the things you have dreamed about and wanted. Surely you wouldn't give them up for—"

"No, no!" she cried aloud into the pillow. "I wouldn't—couldn't!"

It wasn't fair. Life wasn't supposed to be like this. And death. She had thought it was necessary to die only once. But already today she had died three times. Must it be so every day to the end of life, not just three times but

Three Visitors in the Night 375

as many times as there were dying women within possible reach of one's hands?

"No, no!" This time the cry was too deep within her to be spoken aloud. "I—I *can't*, I tell You! How—how can You ask it of me?"

Minutes . . . hours . . . years. . . .

She rose finally from the bed, crossed the room to the mirror, straightened her hair. She went into the washroom, poured water, patted it into her burning face. Salomi had put the tray on the table. She stooped over it, felt the coffee cup and found it stone-cold, lifted the overturned bowl and inspected the soggy toast, waved the cloud of fruit flies from the stubby little plantain.

The letter to Annie Hancock still lay, unfinished, on her desk. She picked it up, read it, tore it slowly into small pieces, and watched them flutter where they would, to the top of the desk, to the chair, to the floor.

Like snow, she thought, *falling white and clean on Massachusetts hills.*

Then she heard again the sound of tom-toms, faint at first, growing insistently louder.

No, not like snow. Like white pollen. Torn that it might be scattered. Dying that it might bring new life into being.

Stooping, she gathered up the bits of paper, careful to retrieve every one, and dropped them in the wastebasket. Then she crossed the room, opened the door, leaving it flung wide to the sunshine, and walked briskly along the verandah. She found her father and mother together in the bedroom-study.

"I'm going to America and study to be a doctor," she announced steadily, "so I can come back here and help the women of India."

About the Story

1. What does the author mean by "there was only one Samuel"?
2. Ida's father tells her to forget the three calls in the night if there is nothing she can do. Is there nothing she can do?
3. The author uses a biblical reference to discuss the struggle in Ida's heart. What do the dresses represent?
4. What does Ida's father mean by saying that the young Brahmin is perhaps "sacrificing more for his convictions than we are"?

About the Author

Since she is the daughter of a minister as well as the wife of one, it comes as no surprise that Dorothy Clarke Wilson (b. 1904) desires "to inspire people with lessons from courageous and constructive Christian lives." In addition to biographies, she also writes Christian fiction based on biblical characters such as Moses, Amos, and James. She has toured extensively in such places as India, Palestine, Lebanon, and Egypt, doing research for her writing. She has conducted workshops as well for those interested in writing religious drama as she has also done, contributing over sixty plays for use in churches.

The Crucifixion

Alberta Hawse

Some people swallow their pride and, like Ida Scudder, accept in humility God's call for their lives. Others, like most of those present at Christ's crucifixion, stiffen their necks and reject His appeal. We see both reactions in this chapter from Vinegar Boy, *the story of an orphan's search for healing of a vivid birthmark on his face. We also see quite clearly here the suffering that Christ in His humility accepted for our sins.*

The plateau of the hill had turned into a place of confusion. Many of those who had come to enjoy the killing were like guests who moved about seeking a choice seat at a banquet. The boy compared them with vultures hovering and waiting, anxious to descend with beak and claw. . . .

As the boy's glance roamed about the hill seeking for [Marconius] the centurion, he saw the woman with the baby pushing for a front seat on the boulders which had been . . . formed into a rude amphitheater on two sides of the arena. Her friend, breathing hard from the climb, had eyes only for the condemned men.

These women were among the common people who always came to such executions. But as he looked about, he was amazed because today the crowd was different. There were Pharisees and Sadducees, stern-faced men with oiled locks from the Sanhedrin, which was the ruling court for the Jews in both religious and civil affairs. . . .

These men were among those who would shrink from eating off an unwashed platter, who would be defiled* if they touched pork. But they stood together in this place of horror, rubbing their hands in evident approval each

time a voice was raised in insults for the Nazarene.

---

defiled: made unclean

One could not expect the outlaws' friends and relatives to crowd the hill, but where were Jesus' friends? Where were those He had healed? His mourners were few. Three women huddled under the skimpy* branches of the old tree. Their mantles were about their heads, but the sound of the moaning could be heard.

---

skimpy: thin

Suddenly a cheer went up. The executioner had stepped from the shed. . . . The crowd roared in anticipation. Among the men of the common people, the usual wagers* were being laid. Which of the condemned men would be the first to feel the nails?

---

wagers: bets

Vinegar Boy saw Marconius step from the shed behind the executioner, and he pressed his way toward him. He lifted the vinegar bottle from his shoulder and started on a run around the inside edge of the arena. Another roar split the air.

Those who had laid their bets on the larger outlaw won. The four soldiers who had accompanied him in the march took their stations beside him. Their faces were grim; they were expecting trouble, and the crowd knew it. Tenseness gripped the hill. The boy let his eyes rise to the face of the doomed rebel. He was watching when the frustrated terror exploded into rebellious hatred. Each of the four soldiers made a swift grab for an arm or leg. The victim was lifted . . . and slung downward to the crossbeam so hard that the earth shook. The boy could hear the breath knocked out of him. Then as the air came back, the outlaw cursed and fought. He heaved and twisted, his muscles threatening to burst through the skin. . . .

The soldiers laid the full weight of their armored legs against his forearms to hold his hands in place. Other soldiers ran to help, and pressed his body against the beam. The executioner chose the spike. Silence fell.

Vinegar Boy rushed toward Marconius. "He hasn't had his vinegar!"

The executioner lifted his mallet. But Marconius spoke, and the hammer was lowered. A soldier reached for the vinegar. He snatched the wooden stopper out and thrust the bottle into the outlaw's mouth. He drank and choked. Vinegar ran out of his mouth and through his beard. The soldier tried to pull the bottle away, but the man's teeth had clamped about it. He took another mouthful. The executioner leaned over to place the nail, and the vinegar hit him full in the face.

The crowd roared in appreciation. The executioner would have smashed the man's skull, but one of the soldiers stopped him. . . .

The hands were prepared again. The mallet lifted. Again the hill went quiet and tense. Vinegar Boy turned away, trying to close his ears as tightly as he had closed his eyes. This was always the worst moment of all—this first nail. The sickness and fear on the faces of those who would follow the first man were always terrible to see. But the sound could not be shut out. The hammer thudded and thudded again. Through flesh and wood the spikes sank deep. The cheers of the crowd buried the groans of the man.

Vinegar Boy opened his eyes to find himself looking upward into the frightened face of the golden-haired Dysmas. . . .

The young one did not struggle. He knelt first, his lips moving and his face toward the sun. Vinegar Boy knelt too, offering the bottle. "Dysmas," he said, "here is your vinegar."

The outlaw . . . drank deeply and gratefully. Then he laid himself back and held his wrists close to the wood. The spikes thudded. He moaned once as his body was yanked upward. He spoke to Arno, the Syrian officer, and Arno hailed Marconius.

"Captain! This one wishes to be hung so he can see the setting sun."

A murmur of support ran about the hill. Marconius was quick to assent. "He gave no trouble. Do as he asks."

So the younger outlaw hung on the outer cross facing west, and the middle cross waited for Jesus.

The Nazarene stood with His head lowered; drops of blood and water stood on His forehead. His brown hair looked almost black where it was streaked with perspiration. His face was swollen and purple. Across His back and ribs the livid marks of the scourging* crossed and recrossed.

scourging: whipping

Vinegar Boy wanted to run to Jesus, to beg the favor of restoration for his face,* but he could not. How could he bother this suffering Man?

restoration for his face: removing the birthmark from his
  face

But deep inside the hope and the desire would not die quietly.

He would give Jesus the vinegar, and then—then maybe he would speak to Him as he had to Dysmas. Maybe if Jesus just looked at him, he would not need to ask, for Jesus would know.

The soldiers came forward, and the Nazarene went quietly. He spread His arms to the beam.

The boy fell beside Him and opened the bottle. Words struggled to come, but he could not utter them. The eyes of Jesus were closed.

Open them. Open them, the boy pleaded silently. Words filled his head, but he could not speak. Oh, surely, surely Jesus could feel his thoughts—such a little thing. Before the hands were nailed down, He could touch the stain and make it fair.

A soldier yanked the vinegar bottle from him. "We haven't got all day, Boy," he growled. . . .

The executioner stooped. . . . Jesus opened His hands and laid the wrists straight. The hammer sounded. Vinegar Boy could not turn his eyes away from the blood that filled the hollow of the Nazarene's hands. Two hands filled with blood as though they were Passover cups. Hands that had healed the lepers and restored the deaf. Hands that had plucked grain for the disciples and pulled the saw that helped to fill His mother's house with bread.

The beam was jerked upward. It fell into place. . . .

A wild cry arose above the other voices on the hill. It came from the path, and the centurion turned swiftly, alert. Arno stepped forward to block the rush of a young man who came screaming, "In the name of the Holy God of Israel, let Him down! Let Him down!"

The voice rose high and shrill as a trumpet. Vinegar Boy moved with the centurion. The other boy was larger and taller, but still a few years from being a man.

"Stand back!" Arno commanded.

"I won't let you kill Him! I won't!" He struck at the Syrian. Arno grabbed him about the shoulders and lifted him, kicking and screaming. He looked toward Marconius for orders.

The centurion hesitated, and Arno said, "We can't afford a riot, Captain."

Marconius nodded. "Shut him up!"

Arno dropped the boy, shoved him back with one hand, and slammed a fist into his chin with the other. The boy fell, sprawled with his arms flung wide, his face to the sky. No one came to his defense. Vinegar Boy hunched down beside him. The fallen youth was fine-boned but sturdy. . . . Blood trickled from the corner of his mouth. His fingers moved in the gravel as he struggled to sit up.

His thumb touched the tip of his tongue tenderly and came away with blood on it. "Cowards," he muttered, and Vinegar Boy did not know if he meant Arno and Marconius or someone else on the hill who should have come forward.

As the glazed look faded from the youth's eyes, Vinegar Boy saw that they were a gentle dusk gray. They were hard and angry now, but surely they could glow warm as hearth fire.

"Riot?" the boy said bitterly. "How could I start a riot? Where are those who would join me? Hiding like dumb sheep in my mother's feast room, that's where."

His face flushed. "What good am I? Twice they've mortified* me like an infant. Last night I ran into the olive grove to warn Him, and they caught me and sent me home, naked."

---

mortified: shamed

"Who did?"

"The mob that was after Him. The temple officers gathered up a bunch of riffraff to bring Him in. Are you His friend?"

"Yes—wanted to be."

"I am John Mark of Jerusalem. Everyone calls me Mark except my mother. She's a widow. What's your name? I never saw you before."

"Everyone calls me Vinegar Boy. I live at the fortress with the steward. His name is Nicolaus. He raised me."

"My father's dead too. Haven't you got any mother?"

"No."

"Where did you get your name, Vinegar Boy?"

"I bring the vinegar to the hill. But mostly it's because I—I used to sleep in a vinegar cask—when I was little, of course. Here, let me help you up."

Their hands met. They were warm in one another's. Mark scrambled to his feet as Vinegar Boy considered him with an ache of envy. This was the kind of son he would like to be. Mark was handsome, brave and good.

Brushing the dirt off his fine robes, Mark then raised his head. . . .

"They must be doing something—listen!"

There was nothing to hear. A strange quiet had fallen over the crowd. The hill had a feeling of oppressive stillness, such as foretells a storm.

A low muttering, like faraway thunder, ran through the edges of the rocky area.

The two boys pushed past the men and women who stood in front of them. A soldier was nailing a placard above the head of Jesus. This was the *titulus,* the title board which was always tacked over the head of the victim to inform the public of his criminal act.

The signs for the outlaws were simple and to the point. "Thief" and "murderer."

But the sign being nailed above Jesus was unlike the others. Words were scrawled in large letters, large enough to be read from afar off. Each line of writing was different, and yet the boy knew that the meaning must be the same. The signature of Pontius Pilate, procurator* of Judea, was written beneath.

---

procurator: a Roman administrator

The storm of protest did not come all at once. It took time for the meaning of the sign to break through. But when the understanding came, the hill shook with the varied furies.

Pharisees, who had been standing apart holding their fringed skirts against contamination, rushed forward. Their skirts were forgotten as their fists flailed the air.

Priests stooped and lifted what dust they could gather to pour over their oiled locks while they intoned* lamentations* and denials.

---

intoned: recited
lamentations: expressions of grief

What the rulers and the priests started, the common people swept to a hideous height.

Under the uproar of the crowd, the boy thought he caught the mournful but ecstatic* cries of the three women under the old yew tree. They were rocking themselves in a paroxysm* of worship.

ecstatic: intensely emotional
paroxysm: sudden outburst of emotion

"Amen! Amen!" they cried over and over, tears running down their cheeks.

Nicolaus and Marconius had taught the boy to read the common languages of both Aramaic and Greek, but some of the letters on the sign appeared to be written with an agitated* hand. Vinegar Boy was not certain of his reading. "What does it say?" he asked Mark. "Why is everyone so angry?"

agitated: shaking

Mark's gray eyes held a weird, hard light. "Pilate has written in three languages. He wants everyone to understand, and so they shall!"

Before he could be stopped, Mark had leaped beyond the line of boulders into the arena of fine stone. And beneath the cross of Jesus he began to yell. His arm lifted as he shouted the words in the language printed. He screamed into the faces of the Pharisees and the priests, the Sadducees and the soldiers. Into the faces of common laborers and tradesmen, he screamed,

"THIS IS JESUS OF NAZARETH, THE KING OF THE JEWS."

The scribes and the Pharisees forgot their dignity and screamed back, "If He be the King of Israel, let Him come down from the cross and we will believe Him."

"THIS IS JESUS OF NAZARETH, THE KING OF THE JEWS."

The priests screamed back, "He boasted that He would tear down our temple and raise it in three days. Let Him now restore Himself and we will believe Him."

"THIS IS JESUS OF NAZARETH, THE KING OF THE JEWS."

Even the common people joined in the tumult until the hill shook. "We have no king but Caesar. Hail Caesar!"

Men advanced toward Mark, their faces black with fury.

"Mark, stop it! Come away!" Vinegar Boy begged frantically.

The soldiers had moved forward too with angry faces, but they fell back as Marconius strode into the arena. His purpose was clear. He struck Mark twice against the cheeks. . . . Mark turned and stumbled through the crowd.

Vinegar Boy watched him go. They had been together only a few minutes but they were friends. Now he would never see him again. Not once had Mark's eyes fastened in embarrassment or curiosity on the ugly cheek.

Vinegar Boy looked up at Jesus. He was lonely too. He hung friendless and forsaken against the bosom of the sky. The drops from the cups of Passover lay on the stones—like dark petals drying in the sun.

About the Story

1. How is Christ's humility evident?
2. Which of the two thieves is more likely to repent and why?
3. What is the purpose of Vinegar Boy's job and why doesn't Jesus take advantage of it?

The Fool's Prayer

Edward R. Sill

Who is the fool in this poem? What biblical passages are echoed in this selection?

The royal feast was done; the king
    Sought some new sport to banish care,
And to his jester cried: "Sir Fool,
    Kneel now, and make for us a prayer!"

The jester doffed* his cap and bells,   5   doffed: tipped
    And stood the mocking court before;
They could not see the bitter smile
    Behind the painted grin he wore.

He bowed his head, and bent his knee
    Upon the monarch's silken stool;   10
His pleading voice arose: "O Lord,
    Be merciful to me, a fool!

"No pity, Lord, could change the heart
    From red with wrong to white as wool;
The rod must heal the sin: but, Lord,   15
    Be merciful to me, a fool!

" 'Tis not by guilt the onward sweep
    Of truth and right, O Lord, we stay;
'Tis by our follies that so long
    We hold the earth from heaven away.   20

"These clumsy feet, still in the mire,*   mire: mud
    Go crushing blossoms without end;
These hard, well-meaning hands we thrust
    Among the heart-strings of a friend.

"The ill-timed truth we might have kept—   25
    Who knows how sharp it pierced and stung?
The word we had not sense to say—
    Who knows how grandly it had rung?

"Our faults no tenderness should ask,
   The chastening* stripes must cleanse them all;
But for our blunders*—oh, in shame
   Before the eyes of heaven we fall.

"Earth bears no balsam* for mistakes;
   Men crown the knave,* and scourge* the tool
That did his will; but Thou, O Lord,
   Be merciful to me, a fool!"

The room was hushed; in silence rose
   The king, and sought his gardens cool,
And walked apart, and murmured low,
   "Be merciful to me, a fool!"

30 chastening: punishing
    blunders: mistakes

    balsam: soothing
      ointment
35 knave: crafty man
    scourge: whip

40

About the Author

. . . .

   Educator and poet, Edward Sill (1841-87) was "poet of his class at Yale"
and has gone down in the history of that school as the writer of one of the
most remarkable class poems. After graduation he became a teacher and then
headmaster at several schools. One critic says that "he cared more about being
a genuine man than a recognized poet." His values are clearly seen in this
selection.

Two Went Up to the Temple to Pray

Richard Crashaw

Two went to pray? O, rather say,
One went to brag, the other to pray;

One stands up close and treads on high,
Where the other dares not lend his eye;

One nearer to God's altar trod,
The other to the altar's God.

About the Author

Richard Crashaw's father was a noted Puritan clergyman, and Crashaw grew up with a strong religious background. He usually wrote in George Herbert's style of devotional poetry although he was not as accessible to the common man as was Herbert. This poem by Crashaw is not his typical work; there are no elaborate symbols or parallelisms. He usually wrote in the emblematic school, a school of poetry that began each poem with a drawn picture, which the poem then explained. This poem strongly alludes to the biblical account of the Pharisee and the publican but has no actual emblem.

About the Poems

1. Who is the fool in Edward Sill's poem? What is the double meaning of the title?
2. What biblical passages are evident in the poem?
3. The fool differentiates between sin, faults, and blunders; which does he consider to be the one that needs God's mercy?
4. On what biblical episode does Crashaw base his poem?
5. What is the author's attitude toward the characters?
6. What does the title of the poem refer to?
7. Which of the two "prayers" was more effective?

The Soloist

Malcolm Wood

Homer starts this story as the school bully. What is he at the end? When does he show genuine courage? Does he show humility? What, if any, is the relationship between these two virtues? Why does he play his sousaphone solo before the whole school?

A quarter mile beyond our high school huddled a ramshackle* collection of squatters'* huts known as Tarville. A boy named Homer Curtis lived in one of those tarpaper shacks with his father and an older cousin. Homer was the only kid from Tarville who ever came to Garden Plain High School.

---

ramshackle: rickety
squatters: people settled on property they do not own
  or rent

His size alone would have set him apart from the rest of us. Although he said he was only sixteen, he weighed one hundred and sixty-five pounds of bone and muscle. His arms were heavy and brown, with blue veins across the biceps and the backs of his hands. He had a prominent Adam's apple and a heavy-boned, square face. His eyes were wide-set and gray.

The authorities placed Homer in the ninth grade. Ordinarily he would have remained unknown to a twelfth-grader like me, but within two weeks, Homer Curtis was notorious.* It started when he cornered Don Thomas and Fletcher Smith behind the gym and beat them up. "He got mad because we wouldn't invite him to play catch," Fletcher reported.

notorious: widely and unfavorably known

"He's just a big bully," Don added, and no one doubted him.

There were other reports, some of them probably exaggerated, of chasings and drubbings.* Soon the whole school was terrified of the stocky, handsome ninth-grader. I had no encounters with Homer Curtis myself until one afternoon when I had stayed at school late to help Mr. Roland arrange chairs and music stands for a band rehearsal. As I walked down the deserted hallway, I heard someone following me. The lights had been turned off, and in the dark corridor our footsteps echoed spookily.

drubbings: beatings

"Hey kid, wait up."

I recognized Homer Curtis' voice. I'd heard he liked to catch kids alone in the hall after school, and I quickened my pace toward the bright doorway at the end of the hall. There were running steps behind me. A hand spun me roughly against the lockers.

"You're the kid's been saying things about me, ain't you?" Homer Curtis, the collar of his blue shirt turned up around his jaws, glared at me. "Ain't your name Joe Tully?"

Before I could answer, he waved a fist in my face. I raised my hands; he prodded* me painfully in the stomach. I doubled up; he kicked me in the shin. Finally I babbled* out that I wasn't Joe Tully, and hadn't been talking about him. "I don't even know you," I said, to prove I couldn't have been talking about him.

prodded: poked
babbled: blurted

"You know me now. Next time I holler, stop and find out what I want." He stepped away from me and put one hand uncertainly on the brass pushrod of the door. "Tell Joe Tully, if he's saying things about me that ain't true, he'll be sorry." He glared at me reproachfully.* "Remember what I tole you, kid," he muttered. And he shouldered out through the doorway and walked lonesomely through the weeds toward Tarville.

reproachfully: in rebuke

Weak with relief, I suddenly liked Homer Curtis better. When he heard that I wasn't Joe Tully, he had left me alone. He didn't just go around beating kids up for nothing. He had his reasons.

This first flickering sympathy of mine for Homer was promptly dampened.* That same week, he got into an argument with Mr. Walker in shop. When Mr. Walker grabbed his arm to steer him away from the lathe, Homer snapped, "Lay offa' me," and shoved Mr. Walker against a bench, knocking off his glasses. Mrs. Murphy, my home room teacher, commented on the incident. "That boy will come to a bad end," she said, and added, "he's vicious."

dampened: deadened

For shoving Mr. Walker, Homer was suspended from school for two weeks, and we heard that he was nearly expelled. When he did come back, Mr. Hill, the principal, gave him some long talks. And there were conferences with Mr. Walker and a school psychologist from the administration building downtown. They must have talked powerfully to Homer, because right afterwards he seemed quieter and withdrawn. We kids noticed this, but our mistrust was deep. We still expected violence from the husky boy with the smoky, sometimes smouldering,* eyes.

smouldering: with suppressed anger

Mr. Hill and Mr. Walker and the school psychologist seemed to have influenced Homer, but it was Mr. Roland, the instrument music instructor, who made the most daring move.

That autumn, Mr. Roland had finally achieved something that he had been working on for years. He'd acquired a brand-new sousaphone for Garden Plain. The huge instrument caused a sensation. All of us in the band were fascinated by its size and weight, by its massive, plunging valves, and by the heavy smell of brass polish and valve oil, enough for twenty trumpets. We would touch it as it rested awkwardly on the floor, and when Mr. Roland wasn't looking, we would bend down and put our lips to the mouthpiece, trying to get a musical sound out of its ponderous* coils. We demanded to know who was going to play it.

ponderous: huge

Mr. Roland was exasperatingly* noncommittal.* But under constant badgering,* he finally disclosed, "I've got a boy learning tuba in Beginning Band who looks good." There was a gleam of mischief in his eye. "He's big enough anyway. After he's learned tuba, I'll let him play the sousaphone."

exasperatingly: irritatingly
noncommittal: giving no hint of his choice
badgering: pestering

During fifth period that day, I was in the hall on an errand for Mrs. Murphy. Hearing the inharmonious,* wheezing* efforts of the Beginners' Band and Orchestra, I dashed up the stairs two at a time and peered into the band room. There among scraping violins and squeaky flutes sat Homer Curtis. On his face was a frown of concentration and on his lap, a tuba.

inharmonious: not in harmony
wheezing: breathing with difficulty

I was startled, then amused. "He's big enough, all right," I thought to myself, and somehow I understood Mr. Roland's looks of secret pleasure.

Soon after Homer began learning the tuba, Mr. Hill gave him a job as assistant janitor. Sometimes when I was in the halls late in the afternoon I would see him, wearing overalls and pushing yellow sawdust down the hallway with a big broom, or bustling from one classroom to another, noisily moving chairs, emptying wastebaskets, and, on Fridays, washing the blackboards.

Most of the kids would pretend not to see Homer when he was working as janitor, and he seemed to understand this and collaborate* in it. But whenever I saw him, I would say, "Howdy," partly out of fearfulness, and partly because I was a big-shot on the French horn and I thought I should acknowledge a beginning school musician. Invariably* Homer would stop sweeping for just an instant and answer, "Howdy."

collaborate: cooperate
Invariably: at all times

We had heard, probably from Mr. Roland, that Homer Curtis was using his janitor pay for tuba lessons, and that he was practicing very hard.

At the beginning of the spring semester, we had band "tryouts." We stirred restlessly and then were silent as Alex, a veteran of several semesters, played a familiar score* expertly, and later fumbled through the sight-reading.

score: piece of music

"Homer?"

Homer opened the spit-valve of his instrument, blew through it casually, and then played the repertoire* number without an error, looking straight at Mr. Roland and not once at the music on the stand before him. His sight-reading, however, was as bad as Alex's. The room was hushed as we waited for Mr. Roland to name the winner.

repertoire: tryout

"Alex," he said, "you're first chair again." Before Homer could show any reaction, Mr. Roland added, "And next week, Homer, you'll start on sousaphone."

By the time the semester was well under way, Homer was playing the sousaphone exclusively, and expertly, too. Whenever Mr. Roland called on him to play his part alone, he would ignore the score in front of him, as he had in tryouts, and would look directly at Mr. Roland, following exactly the tempo of his baton.

In April, after the winter snow had gone, and I had begun staying late in the afternoons on the school tennis courts, I learned why Homer could disregard the sheets of music and look squarely at the director. He systematically memorized each new piece as Mr. Roland gave it out. The deep, unmelodic sounds of the "part for tuba and sousaphone" in the band selections would begin to drift across the weeds in the evening, played over and over, with loving regard for every marking of *ritardando** and attack, *legato,** and *crescendo.** When I would finally mount my bicycle in the near darkness, the windows of Tarville would be orange with lamplight, and Homer would still be practicing.

ritardando: gradually slowing
legato: smooth, even style
crescendo: gradually getting louder

Because of his janitorial duties, Homer didn't have time for other school activities. He did, however, take part in the spring boxing tournament. He was matched in the heavyweight finals with Lou Stark, a friendly, popular kid.

It was a four-round event, and both boys fought their hardest. Lou was the better boxer, and he was unquestionably inspired by the frenzied support of the crowd. Homer fought without a single voice to cheer him, but he appeared indifferent to this screaming evidence of his unpopularity, and his punches were solid and punishing.

The final round ended in an explosion of slugging, toe to toe. The crowd stamped feet and chanted "Stark, Stark, Stark, Stark, Stark ..." Mr. Larson, the referee, walked erratically around the ring for over a minute, trying to quiet the crowd for an announcement. Finally he raised Lou Stark's hand.

The students screamed with approval, banged on the chair arms, and threw books in the air. In the midst of the din, Homer strode across the ring and said something to Mr. Larson, beseechingly at first, and then argumentatively. When the gym teacher clamped his lips shut and turned his back, Homer shrugged once in disagreement and dejection, and walked back to his corner for his towel. There were hoots and catcalls from the crowd. Homer looked out numbly across the auditorium, his gray eyes flat and empty.

The unanimous antagonism* of the crowd must have hurt Homer far more than Lou Stark's punches. He didn't come to classes the following day, though he did report for work after school to Mr. Jensen, the regular janitor. When I saw Homer again in band, he declined to talk about the fight, other than to remark, "I thought it was a draw."

antagonism: hostility

I agreed with him, and I admired the restraint of his protest. I argued against Mr. Larson's decision with my friends but to no avail. In the eyes of the students, and of the teachers as well, Homer Curtis had received a humiliation that was coming to him. For the first time there was a quality of derision* in the attitude of the school toward Homer.

derision: ridicule

Three days later, my feelings about the fight, and about Homer, were still fresh as I sat in the auditorium with a thousand other students, teachers, and parents, listening to the spring recital concert. The glee club had just finished its part of the program, and Marcia Graham was setting up her music stand to play a violin solo when Mr. Roland appeared at the door that led backstage. He beckoned to me.

"Have you seen Homer Curtis?" he whispered as I came up to him.

"Not since third period," I answered. "Why?"

"I've got to find him," said Mr. Roland. "He's supposed to play a solo."

"A solo!" I exclaimed. "On the sousaphone? Are you kidding?"

"No, I'm not kidding," snapped Mr. Roland with some heat. "Go find Homer. Tell him he goes on two numbers after this one." He shoved me unceremoniously into the hall.

Homer was standing just inside the furnace room door. His hands were deep in his pockets and he was looking morosely* out across the prairie.

morosely: gloomily

"Hey, Homer," I said. "You'd better hurry. They're looking for you up in the auditorium."

"That so?" said Homer. I noticed that his hair had been slicked down with water and that he was wearing a white shirt.

"There were only three before you on the program," I said.

"I guess I ain't going to play," said Homer. "I smashed up my finger."

". . . That's too bad," I said. "I guess Mr. Roland was counting on you."

Homer said nothing. He frowned very hard.

"Well, I guess I better go tell him," I said.

"Wait a minute," said Homer quickly. "It ain't that. There ain't nuthin' wrong with my finger." He gave me a quick look. "It's just—well, it's just that I don't feel much like playing, that's all."

I noticed for the first time that his eyes seemed uncertain and frightened.

"Look," he said, "how would *you* feel, going out there and having 'em laugh at you?"

I looked away.

"Would you do it?" he asked insistently.

"Aw, I don't know, Homer," I said. "I'll admit a sousaphone's different than playing a trumpet or something."

"They'll laugh at me, won't they?" said Homer immediately, as if I'd confirmed his fear. "Won't they?"

"Maybe they will, maybe they won't," I said. There was a long silence. I thought I ought to say something else. "Thing is, Homer," I said finally, "they're expecting you."

"Yeah, yeah, I know," said Homer in a hopeless tone. He turned away from me into the furnace room. "I told old man Roland I'd do it, so I'll have to do it. Come on," he said. "We'll go up this way."

I followed Homer through the semidarkness of the furnace room past the huge boilers and up the steel stairway that led to the main floor.

At the top of the stairs, Homer turned toward me. "But you watch," he said. "They'll laugh. They'll laugh just because it's me."

I slipped back into my seat just as the clarinetist who preceded Homer on the program was finishing his solo. As he left the stage, the audience consulted their programs.

A murmur of amused whispering ran through the auditorium.

I half hoped that Homer wouldn't appear. But he came out promptly, the bulky sousaphone on his shoulders, and walked to the center of the stage, the same stage where he had fought Lou Stark. With his hair plastered down and the collar of his white shirt pressed flat across his chest, he looked strangely vulnerable.* He stood motionless, his eyes looking at no one, while Gertrude Cohen changed places with the preceding accompanist, scraping the piano bench noisily on the cement floor.

---

vulnerable: open to attack

Gertrude played a tuning note, and Homer blew a deep, comical sound on his instrument. Joe Tully laughed loudly. There was some tittering in the audience.

Homer adjusted his tuning slide and again blew a low and funny noise. In spite of the laughter, he was being careful to tune the sousaphone perfectly. There was more snickering* in the auditorium. Homer stood helplessly, fluttering the valves with his fingers. He nodded to Gertrude to begin. The audience stirred, restless and noisy.

snickering: partly suppressed laughter

Homer adjusted the big round mouthpiece to his lips and looked straight ahead, unseeingly, into the air above the audience. As Gertrude played the final chord of the introduction, I realized that no person could ever be more alone than Homer Curtis was at that moment.

The simplicity of the opening melody stunned me. The poignant* air, pitched far above the range of the average sousaphone player, seemed to come from a mellophone or French horn. By the time Homer reached the first ending, the entire audience was silent and attentive. He repeated the melody expressively and without an error, and passed on to the First Variation. It was faster, in triplets, and Homer glided through it easily, with Gertrude playing behind him perfectly. The Second Variation was faster yet, and suggested hunting horns and the chase. Then came a section that made use of the lowest notes of the sousaphone. By this time the audience was ready to enjoy those deep, moist pedal tones.

poignant: piercing

At last, though no one really expected it, came the cadenza.* Homer, as if he were playing a trumpet, leaped from the highest notes to deep, throbbing low ones; he paused and played slowly; he trilled;* he took off again like the wind with sudden impetuous* bursts of speed. Finally, after the last trill of the cadenza, Homer and Gertrude rushed into the finale,* which was victorious and warlike, full of double-tonguing and uninhibited* blasts on the tonic.*

cadenza: a difficult solo passage
trilled: rapidly alternated between two tones
impetuous: forcefully impulsive
finale: last section of the piece
uninhibited: unchecked, unrestrained
tonic: first tone of a scale

They landed together on the final chord, and before the sound had stopped echoing in the auditorium, applause broke from the crowd. There was no whistling or shouting, no stamping of feet; only handclapping, but handclapping so sincere, so steady, and so sustained, that its meaning could not be missed.

Homer, who had promptly left the stage, finally reappeared. When Gertrude curtsied quickly, Homer bowed, and the big brass bell of the sousaphone dipped awkwardly for a moment and then righted. There was a little shout of friendly laughter from the audience. Then Homer, the moment too important for smiling, walked with dignity into the wings.

About the Story

1. When does Homer show genuine courage?
2. What is the relationship between humility and courage?
3. Why does Homer play before the student body?
4. Homer progresses from school bully to what by the end of the story?

Both this selection and the next one are chapters from the novel Caddie Woodlawn. *In this chapter a pretty city cousin arrives, but she constantly rubs most of the Woodlawn children the wrong way. So they decide to get even with her. What pranks do they pull? Who resents Annabelle the most? Who has the least humility?*

Alas! Poor Annabelle!

Carol Ryrie Brink

There were rains after that and things grew green again. And presently it was time for Cousin Annabelle to arrive on the Little Steamer. Mrs. Hyman and Katie had come out to help make the girls' new summer dresses, and Clara and Mother had been in their element,* turning the pages of the *Godey's Lady's Book* and talking of muslin,* bodices,* buttons, and braids.

---
had been in their element: were doing what they were
  especially interested in
muslin: cotton fabric
bodices: lace garments worn like vests or blouses

"Of course," said Clara sadly, "anything we can make here will be sure to be six months behind the fashions in Boston, to say the least; and I do wish I might have hoops* for every day."

---
hoops: long, full skirts belled out with connecting hoops

"I don't!" cried Caddie. "Good gracious, every time I sit down in hoops they fly up and hit me in the nose!"

"That's because you don't know how to manage them," said Clara. "There's an art to wearing hoops, and I suppose you're too much of a tomboy ever to learn it."

"I suppose so," said Caddie cheerfully. But to herself she added: "I'm not really so much of a tomboy as they think. Perhaps I *shall* wear

hoops some day, but only when I get good and ready."

Then one day Cousin Annabelle came. The Little Steamer seemed full of her little round-topped trunks and boxes, and, after they had all been carried off, down the gangplank tripped* Annabelle Grey herself in her tiny buttoned shoes, with her tiny hat tilted over her nose and its velvet streamers floating out behind. Clara and Caddie had been allowed to come with Mother and Father to meet her, and Caddie suddenly felt all clumsy hands and feet when she saw this delicate apparition.*

---
tripped: skipped lightly
apparition: unusual sight

"Dearest Aunty Harriet, what a pleasure this is!" cried Annabelle in a voice as cultivated* as her penmanship. "And this is Uncle John? And these the little cousins? How quaint* and rustic* it is here! But, just a moment, let me count my boxes. There ought to be seven. Yes, that's right. They're all here. Now we can go."

cultivated: refined
quaint: unusual
rustic: rural

Father piled the seven boxes in the back of the wagon and Clara and Caddie climbed in on top of them, while Annabelle sat between Mother and Father, her full skirts billowing* over their knees. Above the rattle of the wagon wheels her cultivated voice ran on and on. Clara leaned forward to catch what they were saying and sometimes put in a word of her own, but Caddie sat tongue-tied and uncomfortable, conscious only of her own awkwardness and of a sharp lock on one of Annabelle's boxes which hurt her leg whenever they went over a bump.

billowing: swelling out

When they reached the farm Hetty, Minnie, and the boys ran out and stood in a smiling row beside the wagon. Tom held baby Joe in his arms.

"Dear me!" said Cousin Annabelle, "are these children all yours, Aunty Harriet?"

"There are only seven," said Mother, "and every one is precious."

"Of course! Mother told me there were seven. But they do look such a lot when one sees them all together, don't they?"

"I picked you a nosegay,"* said Hetty, holding out a rather wilted bunch of flowers which she had been clutching tightly in her warm hands for a long time.

nosegay: small bouquet of flowers

"How very thoughtful of you, little girl," said Annabelle. "But do hold it for me, won't you? I should hate to stain my mitts.* You've no idea what a dirty journey this has been, and what difficulty I have had in keeping clean."

mitts: gloves

"You look very sweet and fresh, my dear," said Mother, "but I'm sure that you must be tired. Come in and take a cup of tea."

Caddie stayed outside a moment to put a quick arm about Hetty's shoulders. "That was an awful pretty nosegay you made, anyway, Hetty," she said.

Hetty's downcast face suddenly shone bright again. "Yes, it was, wasn't it, Caddie? Would you like it?"

"Why yes, I would. I think it would look real nice here on my new dress, don't you?"

"Oh, it would be lovely, Caddie!"

That evening everyone listened to Annabelle telling about Boston. Mother's eyes shone and her cheeks were pinker than usual. It had been a good many years now since she had seen one of her own kin direct from home. Now she could find out whether Grandma Grey's rheumatism was really better or whether they only wrote that to reassure her. She could find out what pattern of silk Cousin Kitty had chosen for her wedding gown, who had been lecturing in Boston this winter, what new books had come out since the end of the war, why Aunt Phoebe had forgotten to write to her, and a hundred other things that she longed to know but could never get them to put into letters. From time to time Father glanced at her happy face, over the old newspapers which Annabelle had brought him. It was only at moments such as this that Father understood how much Mother had given up when she left Boston to come with him to Wisconsin.

But after an hour or so of Boston gossip, Tom grew restless. Both he and Caddie were well tired of Annabelle's city airs.

"Well, I guess Boston's a pretty good place all right, but how about Dunnville?" Tom said.

Cousin Annabelle's silvery laughter filled the room. "Why, Tom, Boston is one of the world's great cities—the only one *I'd* care to live in, I am sure; and Dunnville—well, it's just too quaint and rustic, but it isn't even on the maps yet."

"Why, Tom," echoed Hetty seriously, "you hadn't ought to have said that. I guess Boston is just like—like Heaven, Tom." Everyone burst out laughing at this, and Cousin Annabelle rose and shook out her flounces,* preparatory to going to bed.

---

flounces: ruffles

"But really, Tom," she said, "I want you to show me *everything* in your savage country. I want to be just as *uncivilized* as you are while I am here. I shall learn to ride horseback and milk the cows and—and salt the sheep, if that is what you do—and—and turn somersaults in the haymow—and—what else do you do?"

"Oh, lots of things," said Tom, and suddenly there was an impish* twinkle in his eyes.

---

impish: mischievous

"And you, Caroline," said Annabelle, turning to Caddie. "I suppose that you do all of those amusing things too?"

"Yes I'm afraid I do, Cousin Annabelle," replied Caddie. She tried to avoid Tom's eyes, but somehow it seemed impossible, and for just an instant an impish twinkle in her own met and danced with the impish twinkle in Tom's.

"You must begin to teach me tomorrow," said Annabelle sweetly. "I'm sure that it will be most interesting, and now, if you will excuse me, I am really quite fatigued."*

---

fatigued: tired

"Yes, of course, dear Annabelle, and you're to sleep with me," said Clara, linking her arm through Annabelle's and leading her upstairs.

The next morning Tom, Caddie, and Warren had a brief consultation behind the straw stack. They ran through the list of practical jokes which they were used to playing when Uncle Edmund was among them.

"We can make up better ones than most of those," said Tom confidently. "It'll do her good."

"Let's see," said Caddie dreamily. "She wants to ride horseback and salt the sheep and turn somersaults in the haymow. Yes, I think that we can manage."

"What fun!" chirped Warren, turning a handspring.

When they entered the house, Annabelle had just come bouncing down the stairs, resolved* upon being uncivilized for the day. She wore a beautiful new dress which was of such a novel* style and cut that Mother and Clara could not admire it enough. Up and down both front and back of the fitted bodice was a row of tiny black jet buttons that stood out and sparkled at you when you looked at them.

---

resolved: determined
novel: new

"You don't need all those buttons to fasten up your dress, do you?"

"Of course not," laughed Annabelle. "They are for decoration. All the girls in Boston are wearing them now, but none of them have as many buttons as I have. I have eight and eighty, and that's six more than Bessie Beasely and fourteen more than Mary Adams."

"You don't say!" said Tom, and once again he and Caddie exchanged a twinkling glance.

"When shall I have my riding lesson?" asked Annabelle after breakfast.

"Right away, if you like," said Caddie pleasantly.

Clara stayed to help Mother, and Minnie was playing with baby Joe, but Hetty came with the others.

"Hadn't you better stay with Mother, Hetty?" said Tom in his kindest voice.

But, no, Hetty wanted to see the riding lesson.

Annabelle chattered vivaciously* of how much better everything was done in Boston, while Tom went into the barn to bring out the horse.

vivaciously: lively

"Why, Tom," cried Hetty, when he returned, "that's not Betsy, that's Pete."

Pete was perfectly gentle in appearance, but he had one trick which had kept the children off his back for several years.

"Hetty," said Caddie firmly, "we must have perfect quiet while anyone is learning to ride. If you can't be perfectly quiet, we'll have to send you right back to the house."

"I suppose he bucks," said Cousin Annabelle. "All Western horses do, don't they? Shall I be hurt?"

"He's pretty gentle," said Tom. "You'd better get on and you'll find out."

"Bareback and astride?"* quavered Annabelle. "Dear me! How quaint and rustic!"

astride: one leg on each side of the horse's back

Caddie and Tom helped her on.

"He hasn't started bucking yet," said Annabelle proudly. "I *knew* that I should be a good rider!"

"Just touch him with the switch a little," advised Tom.

At the touch of the switch, Pete swung into a gentle canter,* but instead of following the road, he made for a particular shed at the back of the barn. It was Pete's one accomplishment.

canter: a gait of a horse, smoother and slower than a gallop

"How do I pull the rein to make him go the other way?" queried Annabelle, but already Pete was gathering momentum, and, before they could answer, he had swung in under the low shed, scraped Annabelle neatly off into the dust, and was standing peacefully at rest inside the shed, picking up wisps of hay.

Annabelle sat up in a daze. The little straw sun hat which she had insisted on wearing was

over one ear and she looked very comical indeed.

"I don't yet understand what happened," she said politely. "I thought that I was going along so well. In Boston, I'm sure the horses never behave like that."

"Would you like to try another horse?" said Tom.

"Oh no!" said Annabelle hastily. "Not today, at least. Couldn't we go and salt the sheep now, perhaps?"

"Do you think we could, Tom?" asked Caddie doubtfully.

"Why, yes, I believe we could," said Tom kindly. "Here let me help you up, Cousin Annabelle."

"I'll get the salt," shouted Warren, racing into the barn.

Hetty looked on in silence, her eyes round with surprise. Annabelle rose, a bit stiffly, and brushed the back of her beautiful dress.

"She's not a crybaby at any rate," thought Caddie to herself. "Maybe it's kind of mean to play another trick on her."

But Warren had already returned with the salt, and he and Tom, with Annabelle between them, were setting out for the woodland pasture where Father kept the sheep. Caddie hastened to catch up with them, and Hetty, still wondering, tagged along behind.

"Will they eat out of my hand if I hold it for them?" asked Annabelle, taking the chunk of salt from Warren.

"Sure," said Tom, "they're crazy about salt."

"But you mustn't *hold* it," said Hetty, coming up panting. "You must lay it down where the sheep can get it."

"Now, Hetty," said Caddie, "what did I tell you about keeping perfectly quiet?"

"You do just as you like, Annabelle," said Tom kindly.

"Well, of course," said Annabelle, "I should prefer to hold it and let the cunning* little lambs eat it right out of my hands."

---

cunning: clever

"All right," said Tom, "you go in alone then, and we'll stay outside the fence here where we can watch you."

"It's so nice of you to let me do it," said Cousin Annabelle. "How do you call them?"

Tom uttered a low persuasive call—the call to salt. He uttered it two or three times, and sheep began coming from all parts of the woods into the open pasture.

Annabelle stood there expectantly, holding out the salt, a bright smile on her face. "We don't have sheep in Boston," she said. But almost immediately the smile began to fade.

The sheep were crowding all around her, so close that she could hardly move; they were treading on her toes and climbing on each other's backs to get near her. Frightened, she held the salt up out of their reach, and then they began to try to climb up *her* as if she had been a ladder. There was a perfect pandemonium* of bleating and baaing, and above this noise rose Annabelle's despairing shriek.

---

pandemonium: wild uproar

"Drop the salt and run," called Tom, himself a little frightened at the success of his joke.

But running was not an easy matter with thirty or forty sheep around her, all still believing that she held the salt. At last poor Annabelle succeeded in breaking away, and they helped her over the fence. But, when she was safe on the other side, everybody stopped and looked at her in amazement. The eight and eighty sparkling jet buttons had disappeared from her beautiful frock. The sheep had eaten them!

"Oh! my buttons!" cried Annabelle. "There were eight and eighty of them—six more than Bessie Beasely had! And where is my sun hat?"

Across the fence in the milling crowd of sheep, the wicked Woodlawns beheld with glee Annabelle's beautiful sun hat rakishly* dangling from the left horn of a fat old ram.

rakishly: jauntily

Father Speaks

In this chapter Caddie takes the punishment for her pranks very poorly. She becomes resentful and plans to get even by running away from home to live among the Indians. What brings her to her senses? How is she different at the end of this selection from what she has been before?

If Annabelle had rushed home crying and told Mother, the Woodlawn children would not have been greatly surprised. But there seemed to be more in Annabelle than met the eye.

"What a quaint experience!" she said. "They'll hardly believe it when I tell them about it in Boston." Her voice was a trifle shaky, but just as polite as ever, and she went right upstairs, without speaking to Clara or Mother, and changed to another dress. That evening she was more quiet than she had been the night before and she had almost nothing to say about the superiority of her native city over the rest of the uncivilized world. Caddie noticed with remorse* that Annabelle walked a little stiffly, and she surmised* that the ground had not been very soft at the place where Pete had scraped her off.

remorse: guilt
surmised: guessed

"I wish I hadn't promised Tom to play that next trick on her," Caddie thought to herself. "Maybe he'll let me off."

But Tom said, no, it was a good trick and Annabelle had asked for it, and Caddie had promised to do her part, and she had better go through with it.

"All right," said Caddie.

After all, it was a good trick and Annabelle *had* asked for it.

"Let's see," said Tom the next day. "You wanted to turn somersaults in the haymow, didn't you, Cousin Annabelle?"

"Well, I suppose that's one of the things one always does on a farm, isn't it?" said Cousin Annabelle, a trifle less eagerly than she had welcomed their suggestions of the day before. The beautiful eight-and-eighty-button dress had not appeared today. Annabelle had on a loose blouse over a neat, full skirt. "Of course, I never turn somersaults in Boston, you understand. It's so very quaint and rustic."

"Of course, we understand that," said Caddie.

"But out here where you have lots of hay—"

"It's bully* fun!" yelled Warren.

bully: excellent

"Now, Hetty," directed Tom, "you better stay at home with Minnie. A little girl like you might fall down the ladder to the mow and hurt herself."

"Me fall down the haymow ladder?" demanded Hetty in amazement. "Why, Tom Woodlawn, you're just plumb crazy!"

"Well, run into the house then and fetch us some cookies," said Tom, anxious to be rid of Hetty's astonished eyes and tattling tongue. Hetty departed reluctantly with a deep conviction that she was missing out on something stupendous.*

stupendous: marvelous

When she returned a few moments later with her hands full of cookies, she could hear them all laughing and turning somersaults in the loft above. She made haste to climb the ladder and peer into the loft. It was darkish there with dust motes* dancing in the rays of light that entered through the chinking. But

Hetty could see quite plainly, and what she saw was Caddie slipping an egg down the back of Annabelle's blouse, just as Annabelle was starting to turn a somersault.

motes: specks

"I can turn them every bit as well as you can already," said Annabelle triumphantly, and then she turned over, and then she sat up with a surprised and stricken* look upon her face, and then she began to cry!

stricken: wounded

"Oh, it's squishy!" she sobbed. "You're horrid and mean. I didn't mind falling off the horse or salting the sheep, but oh, this—this—this is squishy!"

Hetty climbed down from the haymow and ran to the house as fast as she could go.

"Mother, if you want to see something, you just come here with me as fast as you can," she cried.

On the way to the barn she gave Mrs. Woodlawn a brief but graphic* account of the riding lesson and the sheep salting. When they reached the haymow, Annabelle was still sobbing.

graphic: vivid

"Oh, Aunty Harriet!" she cried. "I don't know what it is, but it's squishy. I can't—oh dear! I can't bear squishy things!"

"You poor child!" said Mrs. Woodlawn, examining the back of Annabelle's blouse, and then, in an ominous voice, she announced: "It's egg." With a good deal of tenderness Mother got Annabelle to the house and put her into Clara's capable hands. Then she turned with fury on the three culprits.* But it was Caddie whom she singled out for punishment.

culprits: guilty ones

"Caroline Woodlawn, stand forth!" she cried. Caddie obeyed.

"It was only a joke, Mother," she said in a quivering voice. Mrs. Woodlawn took a little riding whip which hung behind the kitchen door and struck Caddie three times across the legs.

"Now go to your bed and stay until morning. You shall have no supper."

"Ma, it was as much my fault as hers," cried Tom, his ruddy face gone white.

"No, Tom," said Mrs. Woodlawn. "I cannot blame *you* so much. But that a *daughter* of mine should so far forget herself in her hospitality to a guest—that she should be such a hoyden* as to neglect her proper duties as a lady! Shame to her! Shame! No punishment that I can invent would be sufficient for her."

hoyden: rude young woman

As Caddie went upstairs, she saw Father standing in the kitchen door and she knew that he had witnessed her disgrace. But she knew too that he would do nothing to soften the sentence which Mother had spoken, for it was an unwritten family law that one parent never interfered with the justice dealt out by the other.

For hours Caddie tossed about on her bed. The upper room was hot and close,* but an even hotter inner fire burned in Caddie. She had some of her mother's quick temper, and she was stung by injustice. She would have accepted punishment without question if it had been dealt out equally to the boys. But the boys had gone free! All the remorse and the resolves to do better, which had welled up in her as soon as she had seen Annabelle's tears, were dried up now at the injustice of her punishment. Hot and dry-eyed, she tossed about on the little bed where she had spent so many quiet hours. At last she got up and tied a few things which she most valued into a towel. She put them under the foot of her mattress and lay down again. Later she would slip down to the kitchen and get a loaf of bread and Father's old water bottle which she would fill at the spring. At least they could not begrudge her that much. They would soon cease to miss her. Perhaps they would adopt Annabelle in her place.

close: stuffy

Her anger cooled a little in the fever of making plans. It would have been much easier if she had known just where the Indians were. But at this season the woods were full of berries and there would soon be nuts. John's [the Indian chief's] dog would protect her and she could live a long time in the woods until she could join the Indians. She knew that they would take her in, and then she would never have to grow into that hateful thing which Mother was always talking about—a lady. A lady with fine airs* and mincing* walk who was afraid to go out into the sun without a hat or a sunshade! A lady who made samplers* and wore stays* and was falsely polite no matter how she felt!

airs: artificial manners
mincing: dainty
samplers: decorative pieces of needlework
stays: a corset stiffened with bones

A soft blue twilight fell, and still Caddie tossed, hot, resentful, and determined. There was the clatter of supper dishes down below, and no one relented* enough to send her a bite of bread. A velvet darkness followed the twilight and, through the window, summer stars began to twinkle. Presently Hetty and Minnie came up to bed. Hetty came and stood by Caddie's bed and looked at her. Caddie could feel the long wistful* look, but she did not stir or open her eyes. Hetty was a tattletale. It was torture to have to lie so still, but at last the little sisters were breathing the regular breath of sleep, and Caddie could toss and turn again as much as she pleased. She must keep awake now until the house was all still and the lights out, and then she would be free to run away.

Her heart beat fast, and with every beat something hot and painful seemed to throb in her head. A cooler breeze began to come in at the window. How long it took the house to grow quiet tonight! How tiresome they were! They wouldn't even go to bed and let her run away!

---

relented: softened
wistful: with unfulfilled longing

Then the door creaked a little on its hinges, there was a glimmer of candlelight, and Father came in. He went first and looked at Minnie and Hetty. He put a lock of hair back from Minnie's forehead and pulled the sheet up over Hetty's shoulder. Then he came and stood by Caddie's bed. She lay very still with tightly closed eyes so that Father should think her asleep. It had fooled Hetty, but Father knew more than most people did. He put the candle down and sat on the side of the bed and took one of Caddie's hot hands in his cool ones. Then he began to speak in his nice quiet voice, without asking her to wake up or open her eyes or look at him.

"Perhaps Mother was a little hasty today, Caddie," he said. "She really loves you very much, and, you see, she expects more of you than she would of someone she didn't care about. It's a strange thing, but somehow we expect more of girls than of boys. It is the sisters and wives and mothers, you know, Caddie, who keep the world sweet and beautiful. What a rough world it would be if there were only men and boys in it, doing things in their rough way. A woman's task is to teach them gentleness and courtesy and love and kindness. It's a big task too, Caddie—harder than cutting trees or building mills or damming rivers. It takes nerve and courage and patience, but good women have those things. They have them just as much as the men who build bridges and carve roads through the wilderness. A woman's work is something fine and noble to grow up to, and it is just as important as a man's. But no man could ever do it so well. I don't want you to be the silly, affected* person with fine clothes and manners whom folks sometimes call a lady. No, that is not what I want for you, my little girl. I want you to be a woman with a wise and understanding heart, healthy in body and honest in mind. Do you think you would like to be growing up into that woman now? How about it, Caddie, have we run with the colts long enough?"

---

affected: artificial

There was a little silence, and the hot tears which had not wanted to come all day were suddenly running down Caddie's cheeks unheeded into the pillow.

"You know, Caddie," added Father gently and half-apologetically, "you know I'm sort of responsible for you, honey. I was the one who urged Mother to let you run wild, because I thought it was the finest way to make a splendid woman of you. And I still believe that, Caddie."

Suddenly Caddie flung herself into Mr. Woodlawn's arms.

"Father! Father!"

It was all she could say, and really there was nothing more that needed saying. Mr. Woodlawn held her a long time, his rough beard pressed against her cheek. Then with his big hands, which were so delicate with clockwork, he helped her to undress and straighten the tumbled bed. Then he kissed her again and took his candle and went away. And now the room was cool and pleasant again, and even Caddie's tears were not unpleasant, but part of the cool relief she felt. In a few moments she was fast asleep.

But something strange had happened to Caddie in the night. When she awoke she knew that she need not be afraid of growing up. It was not just sewing and weaving and

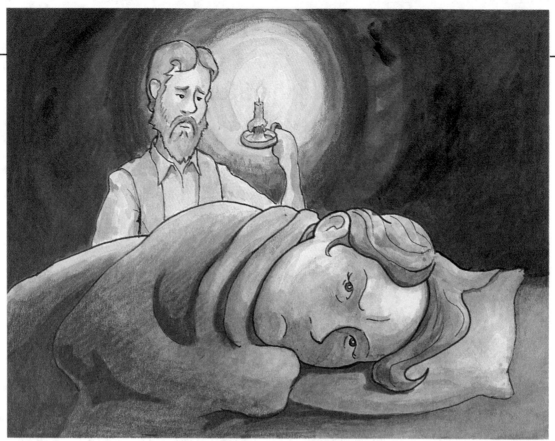

wearing stays. It was something more thrilling than that. It was a responsibility, but, as Father spoke of it, it was a beautiful and precious one, and Caddie was ready to go and meet it. She looked at the yellow sunshine on the floor and she knew that she had slept much longer than she usually did. Both Hetty's and Minnie's bed were empty, but as soon as Caddie began to stir around, Hetty came in as if she had been waiting outside the door.

"Oh, say, Caddie," she said, "I'm awful sorry I went and told on you yesterday. Honest, I am. I never thought you'd get it so hard, and I'll tell you what, I'm not going to be a tattler ever any more, I'm not. But, say, Caddie, I wanted to be the first to tell you Father took Tom and Warren out to the barn yesterday afternoon and he gave 'em both a thrashing.

He said it wasn't fair that you should have all the punishment when the same law had always governed you all, and Tom said so too, although he yelled good and plenty when he was being thrashed."

"It's all right, Hetty," said Caddie. "I guess we won't be playing any more silly jokes on people."

"What's this?" asked Hetty, pulling at the corner of a queer bundle that stuck out under the corner of Caddie's mattress. Out came a knotted towel with an odd assortment of Caddie's treasures rattling around inside.

"Oh, that!" said Caddie, untying the knots and putting things away. "Those are just some things I was looking at yesterday when I had to stay up here alone."

About the Story

1. What pranks do the children play on Annabelle?
2. Who resents Annabelle the most and why?
3. Who shows the least humility?
4. What are the results of Caddie's talk with her father?

About the Author

During her high school years, Carol Ryrie Brink (1895-1981) decided that she wanted to write and published her first children's fiction in Sunday school papers. She succeeded with *Caddie Woodlawn,* her second novel, from which this selection is taken. Living with her grandmother and aunt after her parents died, Carol Brink found enjoyment in reliving the Wisconsin pioneer life of her grandmother and later turned those stories into the novel *Caddie Woodlawn*, which won her a Newbery Award in 1936. Her grandmother approved of Brink's novel, and though Brink changed the names slightly (her grandmother was Caddie Woodhouse), the events and characterizations are accurate. Her grandmother told Carol, "There is only one thing that I do not understand. . . . You never knew my mother and father and brothers—how could you write about them exactly as they were?" It is Carol Ryrie Brink's realism that makes *Caddie Woodlawn* such a pleasure to read.

The Split Cherry Tree

Jesse Stuart

Professor Herbert says that since Dave helped break the cherry tree he would have to help pay for it. Wrong, says Dave's father. And he comes to school with his pistol to prove the teacher wrong. How does Professor Herbert respond to the father's anger and pride? What does the father come to accept? How does he reveal that he is a big man?

What Dave's father comes to believe, however, is not the same thing we should. What does the father place his faith in for the future? Why is this faith wrong?

"I don't mind staying after school," I says to Professor Herbert, "but I'd rather you'd whip me with a switch and let me go home early. Pa will whip me anyway for getting home two hours late."

"You are too big to whip," says Professor Herbert, "and I have to punish you for climbing up in that cherry tree. You boys knew better than that! The other five boys have paid their dollar each. You have been the only one who has not helped pay for the tree. Can't you borrow a dollar?"

"I can't," I says "I'll have to take the punishment. I wish it would be quicker punishment. I wouldn't mind."

Professor Herbert stood and looked at me. He was a big man. He wore a gray suit of clothes. The suit matched his gray hair.

"You don't know my father," I says to Professor Herbert. "He might be called a little old-fashioned. He makes us mind him until we're twenty-one years old. He believes: 'If you spare the rod you spoil the child.' I'll never be able to make him understand about the cherry tree. I'm the first of my people to go to high school."

"You must take the punishment," says Professor Herbert. "You must stay two hours after school today and two hours after school tomorrow. I am allowing you twenty-five cents an hour. That is good money for a high-school student. You can sweep the schoolhouse floor, wash the blackboards, and clean the windows. I'll pay the dollar for you."

I couldn't ask Professor Herbert to loan me a dollar. He never offered to loan it to me. I had to stay and help the janitor and work out my fine at a quarter an hour.

I thought as I swept the floor, "What will Pa do to me? What lie can I tell him when I go home? Why did we ever climb that cherry tree and break it down for anyway? Why did we run crazy over the hills away from the crowd? Why did we do all of this? Six of us climbed up in a little cherry tree after one little lizard! Why did the tree split and fall with us? It should have been a stronger tree! Why did Eif Crabtree just happen to be below us plowing and catch us in his cherry tree? Why wasn't he

a better man than to charge us six dollars for the tree?"

It was six o'clock when I left the schoolhouse. I had six miles to walk home. It would be after seven when I got home. I had all my work to do when I got home. It took Pa and me both to do the work. Seven cows to milk. Nineteen head of cattle to feed, four mules, twenty-five hogs, firewood and stovewood to cut, and water to draw from the well. He would be doing it when I got home. He would be mad and wondering what was keeping me!

I hurried home. I would run under the dark, leafless trees. I would walk fast uphill. I would run down the hill. The ground was freezing. I had to hurry. I had to run. I reached the long ridge that led to our cow pasture. I ran along this ridge. The wind dried the sweat on my face. I ran across the pasture to the house.

I threw down my books in the chipyard.* I ran to the barn to spread fodder* on the ground for the cattle. I didn't take time to change my clean school clothes for my old work clothes. I ran out to the barn. I saw Pa spreading fodder on the ground for the cattle. That was my job. I ran up to the fence. I says, "Leave that for me, Pa. I'll do it. I'm just a little late."

chipyard: place for cutting stovewood
fodder: feed for livestock

"I see you are," says Pa. He turned and looked at me. His eyes danced fire. "What in th' world has kept you so? Why ain't you been here to help me with this work? Make a gentleman out'n one boy in th' family and this is what you get! Send you to high school and you get too onery fer th' buzzards to smell!"

I never said anything. I didn't want to tell why I was late from school. Pa stopped scattering the bundles of fodder. He looked at me. He says, "Why are you gettin' in here this time o' night? You tell me or I'll take a hickory withe* to you right here on th' spot!"

withe: switch

I says, "I had to stay after school." I couldn't lie to Pa. He'd go to school and find out why I had to stay. If I lied to him it would be too bad for me.

"Why did you haf to stay atter school?" says Pa.

I says, "Our biology class went on a field trip today. Six of us boys broke down a cherry tree. We had to give a dollar apiece to pay for the tree. I didn't have the dollar. Professor Herbert is making me work out my dollar. He gives me twenty-five cents an hour. I had to stay in this afternoon. I'll have to stay in tomorrow afternoon!"

"Are you telling me th' truth?" says Pa.

"I'm telling you the truth," I says. "Go and see for yourself."

"That's jist what I'll do in th' mornin'," says Pa. "Jist whose cherry tree did you break down?"

"Eif Crabtree's cherry tree!"

"What was you doin' clear out in Eif Crabtree's place?" says Pa. "He lives four miles from th' county high school. Don't they teach you no books at that high school? Do they jist let you get out and gad* over th' hillsides? If that's all they do I'll keep you at home, Dave. I've got work here fer you to do!"

gad: roam

"Pa," I says, "spring is just getting here. We take a subject in school where we have to have bugs, snakes, flowers, lizards, frogs, and plants. It is biology. It was a pretty day today. We went out to find a few of these. Six of us boys saw a lizard at the same time sunning on a cherry tree. We all went up the tree to get it. We broke the tree down. It split at the forks. Eif Crabtree was plowing down below us. He ran up the hill and got our names. The other boys gave their dollar apiece. I didn't have mine. Professor Herbert put mine in for me. I have to work it out at school."

"Poor man's son, huh," says Pa. "I'll attend to that myself in th' mornin'. I'll take keer o' 'im. He ain't from this county nohow. I'll go down there in th' mornin' and see 'im. Lettin' you leave your books and galavant* all over th' hills. What kind of a school is it nohow! Didn't do that, my son, when I's a little shaver in school. All fared alike too."

galavant: wander

"Pa, please don't go down there," I says, "just let me have fifty cents and pay the rest of my fine! I don't want you to go down there! I don't want you to start anything with Professor Herbert!"

"Ashamed of your old Pap are you, Dave," says Pa "atter th' way I've worked to raise you! Tryin' to send you to school so you can make a better livin' than I've made.

"I'll straighten this thing out myself! I'll take keer o' Professor Herbert myself! He ain't got no right to keep you in and let the other boys off jist because they've got th' money! I'm a poor man. A bullet will go in a professor same as it will any man. It will go in a rich man same as it will a poor man. Now you get into this work before I take one o' these withes and cut the shirt off'n your back!"

I thought once I'd run through the woods above the barn just as hard as I could go. I thought I'd leave high school and home forever! Pa could not catch me! I'd get away! I couldn't go back to school with him. He'd have a gun and maybe he'd shoot Professor Herbert. It was hard to tell what he would do. I could tell Pa that school had changed in the hills from the way it was when he was a boy, but he wouldn't understand. I could tell him we studied frogs, birds, snakes, lizards, flowers, insects. But Pa wouldn't understand. If I did run away from home it wouldn't matter to Pa. He would see Professor Herbert anyway. He would think that high school and Professor Herbert had run me away from home. There was no need to run away. I'd just have to stay, finish foddering the cattle, and go to school with Pa the next morning.

I would take a bundle of fodder, remove the hickory-withe band from around it, and scatter it on rocks, clumps of green briers, and brush, so the cattle wouldn't tramp it under their feet. I would lean it up against the oak trees and the rocks in the pasture just above our pigpen on the hill. The fodder was cold and frosty where it had set out in the stacks. I would carry bundles of the fodder from the stack until I had spread out a bundle for each steer. Pa went to the barn to feed the mules and throw corn in the pen to the hogs.

The moon shone bright in the cold March sky. I finished my work by moonlight. Professor Herbert really didn't know how much work I had to do at home. If he had known he would not have kept me after school. He would have loaned me a dollar to have paid my part on the cherry tree. He had never lived in the hills. He didn't know the way the hill boys had to work so that they could go to school. Now he was teaching in a county high school where all the boys who attended were from hill farms.

After I'd finished doing my work I went to the house and ate my supper. Pa and Mom had eaten. My supper was getting cold. I heard Pa and Mom talking in the front room. Pa was telling Mom about me staying in after school.

"I had to do all th' milkin' tonight, chop th' wood myself. It's too hard on me atter I've turned ground all day. I'm goin' to take a day off tomorrow and see if I can't remedy things a little. I'll go down to that high school tomorrow. I won't be a very good scholar fer Professor Herbert nohow. He won't keep me in atter school. I'll take a different kind of lesson down there and make 'im acquainted with it."

"Now, Luster," says Mom, "you jist stay away from there. Don't cause a lot o' trouble. You can be jailed fer a trick like that. You'll get th' Law atter you. You'll jist go down there and show off and plague* your own boy Dave to death in front o' all th' scholars!"

plague: embarrass

"Plague or no plague," says Pa, "he don't take into consideration what all I haf to do here, does he? I'll show 'im it ain't right to keep one boy in and let the rest go scot free. My boy is good as th' rest, ain't he? A bullet will make a hole in a schoolteacher same as it will anybody else. He can't do me that way and get by with it. I'll plug 'im first. I aim to go down there bright and early in the mornin' and get all this straight! I aim to see about bug larnin' and this runnin' all over God's creation huntin' snakes, lizards, and frogs. Ransackin' th' country and goin' through cherry orchards and breakin' th' trees down atter lizards! Old Eif Crabtree ought to a-poured the' hot lead to 'em instead o' chargin' six dollars fer th' tree! He ought to a-got old Herbert th' first one!"

I ate my supper. I slipped upstairs and lit the lamp. I tried to forget the whole thing. I studied plane geometry. Then I studied my biology lesson. I could hardly study for thinking about Pa. "He'll go to school with me in the morning. He'll take a gun for Professor Herbert! What will Professor Herbert think of me! I'll tell him when Pa leaves that I couldn't help it. But Pa might shoot him. I hate to go with Pa. Maybe he'll cool off about it tonight and not go in the morning."

Pa got up at four o'clock. He built a fire in the stove. Then he built a fire in the fireplace. He got Mom up to get breakfast. Then he got me up to help feed and milk. By the time we had our work down at the barn, Mom had breakfast ready for us. We ate our breakfast. Daylight came and we could see the bare oak trees covered white with frost. The hills were white with frost. A cold wind was blowing. The sky was clear. The sun would soon come out and melt the frost. The afternoon would be warm with sunshine and the frozen ground with thaw. There would be mud on the hills again. Muddy water would then run down the little ditches on the hills.

"Now, Dave," says Pa, "let's get ready fer school. I aim to go with you this mornin' and look into bug larnin', frog larnin', lizard and snake larnin' and breakin' down cherry trees! I don't like no sicha foolish way o' larnin' myself!"

Pa hadn't forgot. I'd have to take him to school with me. He would take me to school with him. We were going early. I was glad we were going early. If Pa pulled a gun on Professor Herbert there wouldn't be so many of my classmates there to see him.

I knew that Pa wouldn't be at home in the high school. He wore overalls, big boots, a blue shirt and a sheepskin coat and slouched black hat gone to seed* at the top. He put his gun in its holster. We started trudging toward the high school across the hill.

---

seed: worn out

It was early when we got to the county high school. Professor Herbert had just got there. I just thought as we walked up the steps into the schoolhouse, "Maybe Pa will find out Professor Herbert is a good man. He just doesn't know him. Just like I felt toward the Lambert boys across the hill. I didn't like them until I'd seen them and talked to them. After I went to school with them and talked to them, I liked them and we were friends. It's a lot in knowing the other fellow."

"You're th' Professor here, ain't you?" says Pa.

"Yes," says Professor Herbert, "and you are Dave's father."

"Yes," says Pa, pulling out his gun and laying it on the seat in Professor Herbert's office. Professor Herbert's eyes got big behind his black-rimmed glasses when he saw Pa's gun. Color came into his pale cheeks.

"Jist a few things about this school I want to know," says Pa. "I'm tryin' to make a scholar out'n Dave. He's the only one out'n eleven youngins I've sent to high school. Here he comes in late and leaves me all th' work to do! He said you's all out bug huntin' yesterday and broke a cherry tree down. He had to stay two hours atter school yesterday and work out money to pay on that cherry tree! Is that right?"

"Wwwwy," says Professor Herbert, "I guess it is."

He looked at Pa's gun.

"Well," says Pa "this ain't no high school. It's a bug school, a lizard school, a snake school! It ain't no school nohow!"

"Why did you bring that gun?" says Professor Herbert to Pa.

"You see that little hole," says Pa as he picked up the long blue forty-four and put his finger on the end of the barrel, "a bullet can come out'n that hole that will kill a schoolteacher same as it will any other man. It will kill a rich man same as a poor man. It will kill a man. But atter I come in and saw you, I know'd I wouldn't need it. This maul* o' mine could do you up in a few minutes."

maul: his fist

Pa stood there, big, hard, brown-skinned, and mighty beside of Professor Herbert. I didn't know Pa was so much bigger and harder. I'd never seen Pa in a schoolhouse before. I'd seen Professor Herbert. He'd always looked big before to me. He didn't look big standing beside of Pa.

"I was only doing my duty, Mr. Sexton," says Professor Herbert, "and following the course of study the state provided us with."

"Course o' study," says Pa "what study, bug study? Varmint study? Takin' youngins to th' woods and their poor old Ma's and Pa's at home a-slavin' to keep 'em in school and give 'em a education! You know that's dangerous, too, puttin' a lot o' boys and girls out together like that!"

Students were coming into the schoolhouse now.

Professor Herbert says, "Close the door, Dave, so others won't hear."

I walked over and closed the door. I was shaking like a leaf in the wind. I thought Pa was going to hit Professor Herbert every minute. He was doing all the talking. His face was getting red. The red color was coming through the brown, weather-beaten skin on Pa's face.

"I was right with these students," says Professor Herbert. "I know what they got into and what they didn't. I didn't send one of the other teachers with them on this field trip. I went myself. Yes, I took the boys and girls together. Why not?"

"It jist don't look good to me," says Pa, "a-takin' all this swarm of youngins out to pillage* th' whole deestrict. Breakin' down cherry trees. Keepin' boys in atter school."

pillage: loot

"What else could I have done with Dave, Mr. Sexton?" says Professor Herbert. "The boys didn't have any business all climbing that cherry tree after one lizard. One boy could have gone up in the tree and got it. The farmer charged us six dollars. It was a little steep* I think, but we had it to pay. Must I make five boys pay and let your boy off? He said he didn't have the dollar and couldn't get it. So I put it in for him. I'm letting him work it out.

He's not working for me. He's working for the school!"

"I just don't know what you could a-done with 'im," says Pa, "only a-laruped* 'im with a withe! That's what he needed!"

"He's too big to whip," says Professor Herbert, pointing at me. "He's a man in size."

"He's not too big fer me to whip," says Pa. "They ain't too big until they're over twenty-one! It jist didn't look fair to me! Work one and let th' rest out because they got th' money. I don't see what bugs has got to do with a high school? It don't look good to me nohow!"

Pa picked up his gun and put it back in its holster. The red color left Professor Herbert's face. He talked more to Pa. Pa softened a little. It looked funny to see Pa in the high-school building. It was the first time he'd ever been there.

"We were not only hunting snakes, toads, flowers, butterflies, lizards," says Professor Herbert, "but, Mr. Sexton, I was hunting dry timothy grass to put in an incubator and raise some protozoa."*

"I don't know what that is," says Pa. "Th' inclubator is th' new-fangled way o' cheatin' th' hens and raisin' chickens. I ain't so sure about th' breed o' chickens you mentioned."

"You've heard of germs, Mr. Sexton, haven't you?" says Professor Herbert.

"Jist call me Luster, if you don't mind," says Pa, very casual-like.

"All right, Luster, you've heard of germs, haven't you?"

"Yes," says Pa, "but I don't believe in germs. I'm sixty-five years old and I ain't seen one yet!"

"You can't see them with your naked eye," says Professor Herbert. "Just keep that gun in the holster and stay with me in the high school today. I have a few things I want to show you. That scum on your teeth has germs in it."

"What," says Pa "you mean to tell me I've got germs on my teeth!"

"Yes," says Professor Herbert. "The same kind as we might be able to find in a living black snake if we dissect it!"

"I don't mean to dispute your word," says Pa, "but I don't believe it. I don't believe I have germs on my teeth!"

"Stay with me today and I'll show you. I want to take you through the school anyway! School has changed a lot in the hills since you went to school. I don't guess we had high schools in this county when you went to school!"

"No," says Pa, "jist readin', writin', and cipherin'.* We didn't have all this bug larnin', frog larnin', and findin' germs on your teeth and in the middle o' black snakes! Th' world's changin'."

"It is," says Professor Herbert, "and we hope all for the better. Boys like your own there are going to help change it. He's your boy. He knows all of what I've told you. You stay with me today."

"I'll shore stay with you," says Pa. "I want to see th' germs off'n my teeth. I jist want to see a germ. I've never seen one in my life. 'Seein' is believin',' Pap allus told me."

Pa walks out of the office with Professor Herbert. I just hoped Professor Herbert didn't have Pa arrested for pulling his gun. Pa's gun has always been a friend to him when he goes to settle disputes.

The bell rang. School took up. I saw the students when they marched in the schoolhouse look at Pa. They would grin and punch each other. Pa just stood and watched them pass in at the schoolhouse door. Two long lines marched in the house. The boys and girls were clean and well dressed. Pa stood over in the schoolyard under a leafless elm, in his sheepskin coat, his big boots laced in front with buckskin, and his heavy socks stuck above his boot tops. Pa's overalls legs were baggy and wrinkled between his coat and boot tops. His blue work shirt showed at the collar. His big black hat showed his gray-streaked black hair. His face was hard and weather-tanned to the color of a ripe fodder blade.* His hands were big and gnarled* like the roots of the elm tree he stood beside.

fodder blade: leaf of the plant used for animal fodder
gnarled: twisted

When I went to my first class I saw Pa and Professor Herbert going around over the schoolhouse. I was in my geometry class when Pa and Professor Herbert came in the room. We were explaining our propositions* on the blackboard. Professor Herbert and Pa just quietly came in and sat down for awhile. I heard Fred Wurts whisper to Glenn Armstrong, "Who is that old man? . . . he's a roughlooking scamp." Glenn whispered back, "I think he's Dave's Pap." The students in geometry looked at Pa. They must have wondered what he was doing in school. Before the class was over, Pa and Professor Herbert got up and went out. I saw them together down on the playground. Professor Herbert was explaining to Pa. I could see the prints of Pa's gun under his coat when he'd walk around.

propositions: theorems to be proved

At noon in the high school cafeteria Pa and Professor Herbert sat together at the little table where Professor Herbert always ate by himself. They ate together. The students watched the way Pa ate. He ate with his knife instead of his fork. A lot of the students felt sorry for me after they found out he was my father. They didn't have to feel sorry for me. I wasn't ashamed of Pa after I found out he wasn't going to shoot Professor Herbert. I was glad they had made friends. I wasn't ashamed of Pa. I wouldn't be as long as he behaved. He would find out about the high school as I had found out about the Lambert boys across the hill.

In the afternoon when we went to biology Pa was in the class. He was sitting on one of the high stools beside the microscope. We went ahead with our work just as if Pa wasn't in the class. I saw Pa take his knife and scrape tartar* from one of his teeth. Professor Herbert put it on the lens and adjusted the microscope for Pa. He adjusted it and worked awhile. Then he says: "Now Luster, look! Put your eye right down to the light. Squint the other eye!"

tartar: hard, yellowish deposit on the teeth

Pa put his head down and did as Professor Herbert said. "I see 'im," says Pa. "Who'd a ever thought that? Right on a body's teeth! Right in a body's mouth. You're right certain they ain't no fake to this, Professer Herbert?"

"No, Luster," says Professor Herbert. "It's there. That's the germ. Germs live in a world we cannot see with the naked eye. We must use the microscope. There are millions of them in our bodies. Some are harmful. Others are helpful."

Pa holds his face down and looks through the microscope. We stop and watch Pa. He sits upon the tall stool. His knees are against the table. His legs are long. His coat slips up behind when he bends over. The handle of his gun shows. Professor Herbert pulls his coat down quickly.

"Oh, yes," says Pa. He gets up and pulls his coat down. Pa's face gets a little red. He knows about his gun and he knows he doesn't have any use for it in high school.

"We have a big black snake over here we caught yesterday," says Professor Herbert. "We'll chloroform* him and dissect him and show you he has germs in his body, too."

---

chloroform: kill

"Don't do it," says Pa. "I believe you. I jist don't want to see you kill the black snake. I never kill one. They are good mousers and a lot o' help to us on the farm. I like black snakes. I jist hate to see people kill 'em. I don't allow 'em killed on my place.

The students look at Pa. They seem to like him better after he said that. Pa with a gun in his pocket but a tender heart beneath his ribs for snakes, but not for man! Pa won't whip a mule at home. He won't whip his cattle.

"Man can defend hisself," says Pa, "but cattle and mules can't. We have the drop on 'em. Ain't nothin' to a man that'll beat a good pullin' mule. He ain't got th' right kind o' a heart!"

Professor Herbert took Pa through the laboratory. He showed him the different kinds of work we were doing. He showed him our equipment. They stood and talked while we worked. Then they walked out together. They talked louder when they got out in the hall.

When our biology class was over I walked out of the room. It was our last class for the day. I would have to take my broom and sweep two hours to finish paying for the split cherry tree. I just wondered if Pa would want me to stay. He was standing in the hallway watching the students march out. He looked lost among us. He looked like a leaf turned brown on the tree among the treetop filled with growing leaves.

I got my broom and started to sweep. Professor Herbert walked up and says, "I'm going to let you do that some other time. You can go home with your father. He is waiting out there."

I laid my broom down, got my books, and went down the steps.

Pa says, "Ain't you got two hours o' sweepin' yet to do?"

I says, "Professor Herbert said I could do it some other time. He said for me to go home with you."

"No," says Pa. "You are goin' to do as he says. He's a good man. School has changed from my day and time. I'm a dead leaf, Dave. I'm behind. I don't belong here. If he'll let me I'll get a broom and we'll both sweep one hour. That pays your debt. I'll hep you pay it. I'll ast 'im and see if he won't let me hep you."

"I'm going to cancel the debt," says Professor Herbert. "I just wanted you to understand, Luster."

"I understand," says Pa, "and since I understand, he must pay his debt fer th' tree and I'm goin' to hep 'im."

"Don't do that," says Professor Herbert. "It's all on me."

"We don't do things like that," says Pa, "we're just and honest people. We don't want somethin' fer nothin'. Professor Herbert, you're wrong now and I'm right. You'll haf to listen to me. I've larned a lot from you. My boy must go on. Th' world has left me. It changed while I've raised my family and plowed th' hills. I'm a just and honest man. I don't skip debts. I ain't larned 'em to do that. I ain't got much larnin' myself but I do know right from wrong atter I see through a thing."

Professor Herbert went home. Pa and I stayed and swept one hour. It looked funny to see Pa use a broom. He never used one at home. Mom used the broom. Pa used the plow. Pa did hard work. Pa says, "I can't sweep. Darned if I can. Look at th' streaks o' dirt I leave on th' floor! Seems like no work a-tall fer me. Brooms is too light 'r somethin'. I'll jist do th' best I can, Dave. I've been wrong about th' school."

I says, "Did you know Professor Herbert can get a warrant* out for you for bringing

your pistol to school and showing it in his office! They can railroad* you for that!"

warrant: authorization for arrest
railroad: send to prison without a fair trial

"That's all made right," says Pa. "I've made that right. Professor Herbert ain't goin' to take it to court. He likes me. I like 'im. We just had to get together. He had the remedies. He showed me. You must go on to school. I am as strong a man as ever come out'n th' hills fer my years and th' hard work I've done. But I'm behind, Dave. I'm a little man. Your hands will be softer than mine. Your clothes will be better. You'll allus look cleaner than your old Pap. Jist remember, Dave, to pay your debts and be honest. Jist be kind to animals and don't bother th' snakes. That's all I got agin' th' school. Puttin' black snakes to sleep and cuttin' 'em open."

It was late when we got home. Stars were in the sky. The moon was up. The ground was frozen. Pa took his time going home. I couldn't run like I did the night before. It was ten o'clock before we got the work finished, our suppers eaten. Pa sat before the fire and told Mom he was going to take her and show her a germ sometime.

Mom hadn't seen one either. Pa told her about the strange school across the hill and how different it was from the school in their day and time.

About the Story

1. For what action is Dave being punished?
2. How does Pa react to this?
3. How does Professor Herbert respond to Pa's threatening words and actions?
4. How does Pa's attitude change throughout the day, and why?

5. How might the story have concluded differently if Professor Herbert had responded differently to Pa's threats?
6. Which characters in this story exhibit humility?

When I Survey the Wondrous Cross

Isaac Watts

When I survey the wondrous cross,
On which the Prince of glory died,
My richest gain I count but loss,
And pour contempt on all my pride.

Forbid it, Lord, that I should boast,
Save in the death of Christ, my God;
All the vain things that charm me most,
I sacrifice them to His blood.

See, from His head, His hands, His feet,
Sorrow and love flow mingled down;
Did e'er such love and sorrow meet,
Or thorns compose so rich a crown?

Were the whole realm of nature mine,
That were a present far too small;
Love so amazing, so divine,
Demands my soul, my life, my all.

Carlo Portelli, *Christ Crucified*, The Bob Jones University Collection

The Bible and Humility

Servants, be subject to your masters with all fear; not only to the good and gentle, but also to the froward. For this is thankworthy, if a man for conscience toward God endure grief, suffering wrongfully.

For what glory is it, if, when ye be buffeted for your faults, ye shall take it patiently? but if, when ye do well, and suffer for it, ye take it patiently, this is acceptable with God.

For even hereunto were ye called: because Christ also suffered for us, leaving us an example, that ye should follow his steps: Who did no sin, neither was guile found in his mouth: Who, when he was reviled, reviled not again; when he suffered, he threatened not, but committed himself to him that judgeth righteously: Who his own self bare our sins in his own body on the tree, that we, being dead to sins, should live unto righteousness: by whose stripes ye were healed. For ye were as sheep going astray; but are now returned unto the Shepherd and Bishop of your souls.

Likewise, ye younger, submit yourselves unto the elder. Yea, all of you be subject one to another, and be clothed with humility: for God resisteth the proud, and giveth grace to the humble.

Humble yourselves therefore under the mighty hand of God, that he may exalt you in due time: Casting all your care upon him; for he careth for you. (I Peter 2:18-25; 5:5-7)

6

Family

Your family is one of God's special tools in helping shape you for a lifetime of service.

Family

The family is unquestionably the most important unit in human society. History shows that strong families generally produce strong nations. When a nation allows or encourages a decline in the family unit, that nation's fall is inevitable.

According to a popular saying, "The family that prays together stays together." Thousands of Christian families have proved this statement true. It is also important, however, for families to work and play and laugh together. Someday your fondest memories will most likely include the special times you shared with your family.

Today many American families are headed for disaster. Lured by false values, they are worshiping the god of materialism. A full-time job for Mother and a second one for Father seem necessary because their first priority is a fashionable house, a new boat, another new car, a resort cottage, or a trip to the Bahamas. Some families evidently believe that their financial condition is more important than their emotional and spiritual health. Their love for money and their desire for things lead them to ignore their most important responsibilities.

Divorce is tearing more and more families apart because parents are worshiping at the shrine of personal happiness. According to recent statistics, half or more of the marriages made this year will fail. As a result of divorce, many children are growing up without necessary parental influence.

Indifference to what the Bible teaches about the family is undermining the strength of even many Christian homes. Some parents ignore their duty to supply spiritual guidance to their children (Eph. 6:4). Some children refuse to submit to their parents' authority (Prov. 13:1; 15:20). Both these parents and these children are in rebellion against God.

The current trends within our nation are not part of God's plan for the family. He wants parents to love their children (Titus 2:4), regard them as God's special gift (Ps. 127:3), discipline them (Prov. 29:15; Heb. 12:7), and teach them important lessons for life (Deut. 6:6-7; Josh. 4:21-24; Prov. 31:1). At the same time children should obey as well as honor their parents (Eph. 6:1-2) and should pay attention to what their parents say (Prov. 4:1; 15:5). According to God's plan, parents and children serve Him together. They follow principles of Christian living (Josh. 24:15; II Tim. 1:5) and spread the gospel among those around them (Acts 21:8-9).

The Bible reveals God's high regard for families. It describes with family terms the special bond between believers and God. Christians, for instance, belong to the "household of God" (Eph. 2:19). God is our Father and we are

His children (II Cor. 6:18). Christ, to believers, is both bridegroom (John 3:29) and elder brother (Rom. 8:29). On the other hand, the Bible shows God's hatred of sins that destroy the family, such as adultery, divorce, and rebellion.

Because the family is a universal institution, writers frequently portray it in their works. Sometimes their treatment explores the humorous and the unexpected. In "Mister Chairman," an excerpt from the biography *Cheaper by the Dozen,* the Gilbreths show the surprising results of their family council. Some writers inspire us to examine our own families and attitudes more closely. In "Sioux Trouble" a rebellious teenager learns that he needs not only his family but also the God of his mother and stepfather. In an episode from *Old Yeller,* Fred Gipson gives a stirring account of a family's united response when danger threatens one of the children.

Writers may also lead us to wisdom. Stephen Leacock slyly questions how we celebrate our special family days as he recounts his family's celebration of Mother's Day. Don Wickenden in "Uncle Randolph's Buried Treasure" shows an uncle's special, loving sacrifice for a young nephew bored by his stay at his grandmother's house. The poems "Those Winter Sundays" and "The Secret Heart" open our eyes to truths about the nature of life itself. Floyd Dell's story, "The Blanket," must be read with discernment; it tells of an adult son's intended treatment of his aged father.

Those who believe everything that literature, television, and other modern forms of communication tell them will develop a grossly distorted view of the family. Only the Word of God gives us the truthful view. Just as each person is unique in God's eyes (Ps. 139:14; Jer. 1:5), so each family is unique as well. Your family, in fact, is one of God's special tools in helping shape you for a lifetime of Christian service.

Both of the following poems describe the father's role in the family but from different perspectives. Although humorous, the works reveal some real fears and problems.

Speed Adjustments

John Ciardi

A man stopped by and he wanted to know
Why my son John had become so slow.

I looked out the window and there was John
Running so fast he had been and gone
Before I saw him. "Look at him go!"   5
I said to the man. "Do you call *that* slow?"

"He seems to be fast when he wants to be,"
The man said. "He appears to be
One of those two-speed boys. You know—
Sometimes fast, and sometimes slow,   10
He can run a mile in nothing flat.
He can run right out from under his hat
When there's nowhere, really, to go. And yet
That very same boy that's as fast as a jet
Will take all day—and sometimes two—   15
To get to school. I'm sure that you
Send him to school. But yesterday
He didn't arrive. And all he would say
Was, yes, he started at half-past eight
But it took him so long he got there late."   20

"How late?" said I.
          Said the man, "A day."

"I see," said I, "and I think I can say
He won't be late again. He needs
A little adjustment in his speeds,
And I'm sure I know the place to adjust."   25

"Well, then," said he, "that's that, and I must
Be on my way."
                    "Thank you," said I.
"If you see John as you go by
Would you be so good as to send him in?
There is never a better time to begin   30
A speed adjustment than right away."
"Agreed, and I will," said the man. "Good day."

And just a few minutes after that
In came John and down he sat:
"You wanted to see me, I understand?"   35

"I did and I do. But you'll have to stand—
At least at first—for what I need.
I'm going to have to adjust your speed.
And when I'm through adjusting it,
I think you won't much care to sit.   40
Do you know what I mean?"
                    "Oh, oh," said he,
"I'm afraid I do. Is it going to be
Terribly long before you're through?"

"Why, not at all," said I. "Like you,
I can be speedy sometimes, too."   45

And soon after that his speed was adjusted.
And also the seat of his pants was dusted.
It was busy work, but it didn't take long,
Though I double-checked as I went along
Just to make sure there was nothing wrong.   50

And whatever *was* wrong, I set it straight,
For since that time he hasn't been late.

. . . About the Author

. . . .

   John Ciardi (1916-86) is known as a writer both for children and for
adults. Several of his books came about as a result of his contact with children.
For example, his first book of poems resulted from games that he would play
with his nephews when they were young. Another book was inspired by his
daughter's list of new reading words sent home by her teacher. He wanted to
write the first book that she would ever read all the way through; as a result,

he wrote *I Met a Man*. Much of his writing for children is based on nonsense-type humor. Ciardi's writing, however, extends beyond the realm of children's literature. Among other things, he has translated scholarly poetical works such as Dante's *Divine Comedy*, written textbooks, and conducted studies in word origins. He published forty books of poetry and criticism alone.

Ciardi's life is an example of the fact that hardship does not have to prevent a person from accomplishing much in his lifetime. Ciardi, the son of Italian immigrants, lost his father in an auto accident when Ciardi was only three years old. In spite of a tempestuous start to life, Ciardi became well educated and carved a sizable niche for himself in the literary world. In addition to being a writer, he also was an educator, lecturer, magazine editor, and father of three children. He died on March 30, 1986, in his home in New Jersey, following a heart attack.

First Lesson

Phyllis McGinley

The thing to remember about fathers is, they're men.
A girl has to keep it in mind.
They are dragon-seekers, bent on improbable* rescues.
Scratch any father,* you find
Someone chock-full of* qualms* and romantic terrors,   5
Believing change is a threat—
Like your first shoes with heels on, like your first bicycle
It took such months to get.

Walk in strange woods, they warn you about the snakes there.
Climb, and they fear you'll fall.   10
Books, angular* boys, or swimming in deep water—
Fathers mistrust them all.
Men are the worriers. It is difficult for them
To learn what they must learn:
How you have a journey to take and very likely,   15
For a while, will not return.

improbable: unlikely

Scratch any father: just under the surface of any father

chock-full of: stuffed with

qualms: misgivings, doubts

angular: bony and lean

...**A**bout the Author

Phyllis McGinley was born in Ontario, Oregon, in 1905, but spent her childhood on a ranch in eastern Colorado. After teaching for some time, she began her writing career as a poet, winning in May of 1961 the first Pulitzer Prize for Poetry awarded to a writer of light verse. Later she concentrated on prose works for both children and adults.

About the Poems

1. In Ciardi's poem, what has John done to cause the man to come to talk with his father? What does he say is John's problem?
2. How is John's speed adjusted?
3. What is really John's problem?
4. According to Phyllis McGinley, how do fathers and daughters disagree in their views of what daughters want to do?
5. What is the journey the poet refers to in line 15?

Hit and Run

John D. MacDonald

"Hit and Run" is the account of a detective's dogged search for a killer. It is also the story of how family members respond when they learn that their car has been a murder weapon. Does their discovery draw them apart or together? What other two families appear briefly in the story?

Twenty-eight days after the woman died, Walter Post, special investigator for the Traffic Division, squatted on his heels in a big parking lot and ran his fingertips lightly along the front right fender of the car which had killed her. It was a blue and gray four-door sedan, three years old, in the lower price range.

The repair job had probably been done in haste and panic. But it had been competently done. The blue paint was an almost perfect match. Some of it had got on the chrome stripping and had been wiped off but not perfectly. The chrome headlight ring was a replacement, with none of the minute* pits* and rust flecks of the ring on the left headlight. He reached up into the fender well and brushed his fingers along the area where the undercoating had been flattened when the fender had been hammered out.

minute: tiny
pits: indentations

He stood up and looked toward the big insurance company office building, large windows and aluminum panels glinting in the morning sun, and wondered where Mr. Wade Addams was, which window was his. A vice-president, high up, looking down upon the world.

It had been a long hunt. Walter Post had examined many automobiles. The killing had occurred on a rainy Tuesday morning in September at nine-thirty, in the 1200 block of Harding Avenue. It was an old street of big elms and frame houses. It ran north and south. Residents in the new suburban areas south of the city used Harding Avenue in preference to Wright Boulevard when they drove to the center of the city. Harding Avenue had been resurfaced a year ago. There were few traffic lights. The people who lived on Harding Avenue had complained about fast traffic before Mary Berris was killed.

Mr. and Mrs. Steve Berris and their two small children had lived at 1237 Harding Avenue. He was the assistant manager of a supermarket. On that rainy morning she had put on her plastic rain cape to hurry across the street, apparently to see a neighbor on some errand. It was evident she had not intended to be gone long, as her two small children were left unattended. The only witness was a thirteen-year-old girl, walking from her home to the bus stop.

Through careful and repeated interrogations* of that girl after she had quieted down, authorities were able to determine that the street had been momentarily empty of traffic, that the death car had been proceeding toward the center of town at a high rate of speed, that Mary Berris had started to cross from right to left in front of the hurrying car. Apparently, when she realized she had misjudged the speed and distance of the car, she had turned and tried to scamper* back to the protection of the curb.

---

interrogations: questionings
scamper: move quickly

Walter Post guessed that the driver, assuming the young woman would continue across, had swerved to the right to go behind her. When she had turned back, the driver had hit the brakes. There were wet leaves on the smooth asphalt. The car had skidded. Mary Berris was struck and thrown an estimated twenty feet through the air, landing close to the curb. The car had swayed out of its skid and then accelerated.

The child had not seen the driver of the car. She said it was a pale blue car, a gray or blue, not a big car and not shiny new. Almost too late she realized she should have looked at the license number. But by then it was so far away that she could only tell that it was not an out-of-state license and that it ended, in her words, "in two fat numbers. Not sharp numbers like ones, sevens and fours. Fat ones, like sixes, eights, and nines."

Mary Berris lived for nearly seventy hours with serious brain injuries, ugly contusions and abrasions,* and a fractured* hip. She lived long enough for significant bruises to form, indicating from their shape and placement that the vehicle had struck her a glancing blow on the right hip and thigh, the curve of the bumper striking her right leg just below the knee. The fragments of glass from the lens of the shattered sealed-beam headlamp indicated three possible makes of automobile. No shellac or enamel was recovered from her clothing. It was believed that, owing to the glancing impact, the vehicle had not been seriously damaged. She did not regain consciousness before death.

---

contusions and abrasions: bruises and scrapes
fractured: broken

For the first two weeks of the investigation Walter Post had the assistance of sufficient manpower to cover all the places where repairs could have been made. The newspapers cooperated. Everyone in the metropolitan area was urged to look for the death car. But, as in so many other instances, the car seemed to disappear without a trace. Walter Post was finally left alone to continue the investigation, in addition to his other duties. And, this time, he devoted more time to it than he planned. It seemed more personal. This was not a case of one walking drunk lurching* into the night path of a driving drunk. This was a case of a young, pretty housewife—very pretty, according to the picture of her he had seen—mortally injured on a rainy Tuesday by somebody who had been in a hurry, somebody too callous* to stop and clever enough to hide. He had talked to the broken husband and seen the small, puzzled kids, and heard the child witness say, "It made a terrible noise. A kind of—thick noise. And then she just went flying in the air, all loose in the air. And the car tried to go away so fast the wheels were spinning."

---

lurching: staggering
callous: feeling no sympathy for others

Walter Post would awaken in the night and think about Mary Berris and feel a familiar anger. This was his work, and he knew the cost of it and realized his own emotional involvement made him better at what he did. But this was a very small comfort in the bitter mood of the wakeful night. . . .

His wife Carolyn endured this time of his involvement as she had those which had gone before, knowing the cause of his remoteness,* his brutal* schedule of self-assigned work hours. Until this time of compulsion* was ended, she and the children would live with—and rarely see—a weary man who kept pushing himself to the limit of his energy, who returned and ate and slept and went out again.

---

remoteness: emotional separation
brutal: harsh
compulsion: irresistible drive

Operating on the assumption that the killer was a resident of the suburban areas south of the city, he had driven the area until he was able to block off one large section where, if you wanted to drive down into the center of the city, Harding Avenue was the most effi-

cient route to take. With the cooperation of the clerks at the State Bureau of Motor Vehicle Registration, he compiled a discouragingly long list of all medium- and low-priced sedans from one to four years old registered in the name of persons living in his chosen area, where the license numbers ended in 99, 98, 89, 88, 96, 69, 86, 68, and 66. He hoped he would not have to expand it to include threes and fives, which could also have given that impression of "fatness," in spite of the child witness's belief that the numbers were not threes or fives.

With his list of addresses he continued the slow process of elimination. He could not eliminate the darker or brighter colors until he was certain the entire car had not been repainted. He worked with a feeling of weary urgency, suspecting the killer would feel more at ease once the death car was traded in. He lost weight. He accomplished his other duties in an acceptable manner.

At nine on this bright October tenth, a Friday, just twenty-eight days and a few hours after Mary Berris had died, he had checked the residence of a Mr. Wade Addams. It was a long

and impressive house on a wide curve of Saylor Lane. A slim, dark woman of about forty answered the door. She wore slacks and a sweater. Her features were too strong for prettiness, and her manner and expression were pleasant and confident.

"Yes?"

He smiled and said, "I just want to take up a few moments of your time. Are you Mrs. Addams?"

"Yes, but really if you're selling something, I just—"

He took out his notebook. "This is a survey financed by the automotive industry. People think we're trying to sell cars, but we're not. This is a survey about how cars are used."

She laughed. "I can tell you one thing. There aren't enough cars in this family. My husband drives to work. We have a son, eighteen, in his last year of high school, and a daughter, fourteen, who needs a lot of taxi service. The big car is in for repairs, and today my husband took the little car to work. So you can see how empty the garage is. If Gary's marks are good at midyear, Wade is going to get him a car of his own."

"Could I have the make and year and model and color of your two cars, Mrs. Addams?"

She gave him the information on the big car first. And then she told him the make of the smaller car and said, "It's three years old. A four-door sedan. Blue and gray."

"Who usually drives it, Mrs. Addams?"

"It's supposed to be mine, but my husband and Gary and I all drive it. So I'm always the one who has it when it runs out of gas. I *never* can remember to take a look at the gauge."

"What does your husband do, Mrs. Addams?"

"He's a vice-president at Surety Insurance."

"How long has your boy been driving?"

"Since it was legal. Don't they all? A junior license when he was sixteen, and his senior license last July when he turned eighteen. It makes me nervous, but what can you do? Gary is really quite a reliable boy. I shudder to think of what will happen when Nancy can drive. She's a scatterbrain. All you can do is depend on those young reflexes, I guess."

He closed his notebook. "Thanks a lot, Mrs. Addams. Beautiful place you have here."

"Thank you." She smiled at him. "I guess the automobile people are in a tizzy, trying to decide whether to make big cars or little cars."

"It's a problem," he said. "Thanks for your cooperation."

He had planned to check two more registrations in that immediate area. But he had a hunch about the Addams' car. Obviously Mrs. Addams hadn't been driving. He had seen too many of the guilty ones react. They had been living in terror. When questioned, they broke quickly and completely. Any questions always brought on the unmistakable guilt reactions of the amateur criminal.

So he had driven back into the city, shown his credentials to the guard at the gate of the executive parking area of the Surety Insurance Company and inspected the blue-gray car with the license that ended in 89.

He walked slowly back to his own car and stood beside it, thinking, a tall man in his thirties, dark, big-boned, a man with a thoughtful, slow-moving manner. The damage to the Addams' car could be coincidence. But he was certain he had located the car. The old man or the boy had done it. Probably the boy. The public schools hadn't opened until the fifteenth.

He thought of the big job and the fine home and the pleasant, attractive woman. It was going to blow up that family as if you stuck a bomb under it. . . .

He went over his facts and assumptions. The Addamses lived in the right area to use Harding Avenue as the fast route to town. The car had been damaged not long ago in precisely the way he had guessed it would be. It fitted the limited description given.

He went into the big building. The information center in the lobby sent him up to the twelfth-floor receptionist. He told her his name, said he did not have an appointment but did not care to state his business. She raised a skeptical eyebrow, phoned Addams' secretary and asked him to wait a few minutes. He sat in a deep chair amid an efficient hush. Sometimes, when a door opened, he could hear a chattering drone of tabulating equipment.

Twenty minutes later a man walked quickly into the reception room. He was in his middle forties, a trim balding man with heavy glasses, a nervous manner, and a weathered golfing tan. Walter stood as he approached.

"Mr. Post? I'm Wade Addams. I can spare a few minutes."

"You might want to make it more than a few minutes, Mr. Addams."

"I don't follow you."

"When and how did you bash in the front right fender of your car down there in the lot?"

Addams stared at him. "If that fender is bashed in, Mr. Post, it happened since I parked it there this morning."

"It has been bashed in and repaired."

"That's nonsense!"

"Why don't we go down and take a look at it?" He kept his voice low.

Wade Addams was visibly irritated. "You'd better state your business in a—a less cryptic* way, Mr. Post. I certainly have more to do than go down and stare at the fender on my own car."

---

cryptic: mysterious

"Do you happen to remember that hit-and-run on Harding Avenue? Mary Berris?"

"Of course I remem—" Wade Addams suddenly stopped talking. He stared beyond Post, frowning into the distance. "Surely you can't have any idea that—" He paused again, and Post saw his throat work as he swallowed. "This is some mistake."

"Let's go down and look at the fender."

Addams told the receptionist to tell his secretary he was leaving the building for a few moments. They went down to the lot. Post pointed out the unmistakable clues. There was a gleam of perspiration on Addams' forehead and upper lip. "I never noticed this. Not at all. . . . you don't look this carefully at a car."

"You have no knowledge of this fender's being bashed since you've owned the car?"

"Let's go back to my office, Mr. Post."

Addams had a big corner office, impressively furnished. Once they were alone, and Addams was seated behind his desk, he seemed better able to bring himself under control.

"Why have you—picked that car?"

Post explained the logic of his search and told of the subterfuge* he had used with Mrs. Addams.

---

subterfuge: deception

"Janet would know nothing about—"

"I know that, from talking to her."

"My wife is incapable of deceit. She considers it her great social handicap,"* he said, trying to smile.

---

handicap: disadvantage

"You didn't kill that woman either."

"No, I—"

"We're thinking of the same thing, Mr. Addams."

Addams got up quickly and walked restlessly over to the window. He turned suddenly with a wide, confident smile. ". . . I remember now. Completely slipped my mind. I drove that car over to Mercer last July. I—uh—skidded on a gravel road and had it fixed in a little country garage . . . hit it against a fence post when I went in the ditch."

Walter Post looked at him and shook his head slowly. "It won't work."

"I swear it's—"

"Mr. Addams, this is not a misdemeanor.* In this state a hit-and-run killing is a mandatory* murder charge. Second degree. The only way out of it is a valid insanity plea. In either case the criminal has to spend plenty of time locked up. You'd have to prove the date of the trip, show police officers exactly where you skidded, take them to the country garage, find people to back up the story. No, Mr. Addams. Not even a good try."

---

misdemeanor: crime of little seriousness
mandatory: required

Addams went behind his desk and sat down heavily. "I don't know what to do. Get hold of a lawyer, I guess. All of a sudden I'm a hundred years old. I want to make myself believe that Gary bashed a fender and had it repaired on his own so he wouldn't lose his driving privilege."

"Why can't you believe that?"

"He has—changed, Mr. Post. In the last month. The teenage years are strange, murky* years, if what I remember of my own is any clue. He's a huge youngster, Mr. Post. They all seem to grow so big lately. I've had trouble with him. The normal amount. . . . Gary has been a sunny type, usually. Reliable. Honest. He's traveled with a nice pack of kids. He's a pretty fair athlete and a B student. His contemporaries* seem to like and respect him. Here's his picture. Taken last June."

---

murky: clouded; confused
contemporaries: those of his own age

Crew cut and a broad, smiling face, a pleasant, rugged-looking boy, a good-looking kid.

"He's changed. Janet and I have discussed it and we've tried to talk to him, but he won't talk. He's sour and moody and gloomy. Off his feed. He doesn't seem interested in dates or athletics or his studies. He spends a lot of time in his room with the door closed. He grunts at us and barks at his sister. We thought it was a phase and have hoped it would end soon. We've wondered if he's in some kind of trouble that he can't or won't tell us about."

"I appreciate your being so frank, Mr. Addams."

"I can't, in my heart, believe him capable of this. But I've read about all the polite, decent, popular kids from good homes who have got into unspeakable trouble. You know—you can live with them and not understand them at all."

"Were you here in the office on the ninth?"

"Yes, if it was a weekday."

"What time did you get in?"

Addams looked back in his appointment calendar. "A Tuesday, I'd called a section meeting for nine. I was in at eight-thirty, earlier than usual. I can't believe Gary—"

"A kid can panic, Mr. Addams. A good kid can panic just as quick as a bad kid. And once you run, it's too late to go back. Maybe he loaned the car to some other kid. Maybe your wife loaned it."

Addams looked across the desk at Walter Post, a gleam of hope apparent. "It's against orders for him to let any of his friends drive it. But it could have happened that way."

"That's what we have to find out, Mr. Addams."

"Can we—talk to my boy? Can we go together and talk to Gary?"

"Of course."

Wade Addams phoned the high school. He said he would be out in twenty minutes to speak to his son on a matter of importance, and he would appreciate their informing him and providing a place where they could talk privately.

When they arrived at the high school, they went to the administration office and were directed to a small conference room. Gary Addams was waiting for them and stood up when they came in and closed the door. He was big. He had a completely closed expression, watchful eyes.

"What's up, Dad? I phoned the house to find out but Mom didn't know a thing. I guess I just got her worried."

Wade Addams said, "I was going to let Mr. Post here ask you some questions, Gary, but with his permission I think I would like to ask you myself."

Walter Post had to admire the man. The answers he would get would very probably shatter a good life and, unless the kid was one in ten thousand, his future would be ruined beyond repair. Yet Wade Addams was under control.

"Go ahead," Post said.

"You have acted strange for a month, Gary. You know that. Your mother and I have spoken to you. Now I'm desperately afraid I know what has been wrong."

"Do you?" the boy said with an almost insolent* indifference.

---

insolent: insulting

"Will you sit down?"

"I'd just as soon stand, thanks."

Wade Addams sighed. "You'd better tell us about the front right fender on the small car, Gary. You'd better tell us the whole thing."

Post saw the flicker of alarm in the boy's light-colored eyes as he glanced sideways at Post. He had hunted a killer, and now he felt sick at heart, as in all the times that had gone before.

"You better clue me, Dad. That question is far out."

"Did you repair it yourself? Were you driving or was one of your friends driving when you hit that woman? Does that—clue you enough?" he asked bitterly.

The boy stiffened and stared at his father with a wild, naked astonishment. "No!" the boy said in an almost inaudible* voice. "You couldn't possibly—you couldn't be trying to—"

---

inaudible: cannot be heard

"To what? I'm ordering you to tell me about that fender."

The boy changed visibly in a way Walter Post had seen once before and would always remember. It takes a curious variety of shock to induce* that look of boneless lethargy.* Once, at a major fire, he had seen a man who believed his whole family had perished, had seen that man confronted by his family. There was the same look of heavy, brooding* wonder.

---

induce: produce
lethargy: indifference
brooding: gloomy

Gary Addams slid heavily into one of the wooden armchairs at the small conference table. He looked at the scarred table and said in a dull voice, "I'll tell you about that fender. The fourteenth of September was a Sunday. You can look it up. You and Mom had gone to the club. Nancy was off some place. School started the next day. I played tennis. I got back about four in the afternoon, Dad. I decided to wash the car. I hadn't washed it in two weeks, and I figured you'd start to give me a hard time about it any day. That was when I found out somebody had bashed the right fender and had it fixed since the last time I'd washed it. You wash a car, and you can spot something like that right away."

"But, Gary, you didn't say anything."

"If anybody'd been home, I'd have gone right in and asked who clobbered* the fender.

You know, like a joke. But there wasn't anybody home. And it—it kept coming into my mind. About that woman." Wade Addams had moved to stand beside his son. The boy looked up at him with a dull agony. "Dad, I just couldn't stop thinking about it. We always go down Harding Avenue. Our car matches the description. And if—if you or Mom had bashed a fender in some kind of harmless way, you wouldn't have kept it a secret. I couldn't imagine you or Mom doing such a terrible thing, but I kept thinking about it, and it got worse and worse. I thought I was going to throw up. And ever since then, I haven't known what to—"

---

clobbered: smashed

"Where were you on the day that woman was hit, son?" Walter Post asked.

The boy frowned at him. "Where was I? Oh, a guy picked me up real early, about dawn, and a bunch of us went up to his folks' place at the lake and swam and skied all day and got back late."

Wade Addams spoke to his son in a strange voice. "Let me get this straight. For the last month, Gary, you've been living with the idea that either your mother or I could have killed that woman and driven away?" Walter Post could see how strongly the man's hand was grasping the boy's shoulder.

"But nobody else ever drives the car!" the boy cried. "Nobody else."

Walter Post watched Wade Addams' face and saw the fierce indignation of the falsely accused change to a sudden understanding of what the boy had been enduring. In a trembling voice Wade Addams said, "We didn't do it, boy. Neither of us. Not one of the three of us. Believe me, son. You can come out of your nightmare. You can come home again."

When the boy began to cry, to sob in the hoarse clumsy way of the manchild years, Walter Post stepped quietly out into the corridor and closed the door and leaned against the wall. . . , tasting his own gladness, a depth of satisfaction he had never before experienced in this deadly occupation. It made him yearn for* some kind of work where this could happen more often. And he now knew the prob-

able answer to the killing.

When Addams and his son came out of the room, they had an identical look of pride and exhaustion. The boy shook hands with Post and went back to class.

"Now we go to your house and talk to your wife," Walter Post said. "We were too quick to think it was the boy. We should have talked to her first."

"I'm glad we did it just this way, Mr. Post. Very glad. About the car. I think now I can guess what—"

"Let's let your wife confirm it."

At three-thirty that afternoon Walter Post sat in the small office of Stewart Partchman, owner of Partchman Motors. With him were Partchman and a redheaded service manager named Finnigan and a mechanic named Dawes.

Finnigan was saying, "The reason I didn't let Thompson go, Mr. Partchman, is that he's always been a reliable little guy, and this is the first time he goofed. Dawes drove him out there to bring back the Addams job, around nine o'clock, and figured Thompson was following him right on back into town, and Thompson doesn't show up with the car until after lunch. He had some story about his wife being sick and stopping by his house to see how she was."

Partchman said angrily, "So it gave him time to take it someplace and hammer that fender out, then come back here and sneak the headlamp and chrome ring out of stock and get some paint onto it."

"It was in for a tune-up," Finnigan said, looking at the service sheet on the job, "new muffler, lube, and oil change. It got in so late we couldn't deliver it back out there until the next day. I remember apologizing to Mrs. Ad-dams over the phone. I didn't tell her why it was late. She was pretty decent about it."

The mechanic said, "Tommy has been jumpy lately. He's been making mistakes."

"How do you want to handle it?" Partchman asked Walter Post.

"Bring him in here right now, and everybody stay here and keep quiet and let me do the talking," Post said wearily.

Thompson was brought in, small, pallid,* worried. His restless eyes kept glancing quickly at Post. Post let the silence become long and heavy after Thompson asked what was wanted of him. At last he said, "How did you feel during those three days, while you were wondering whether she was going to die?"

Thompson stared at him and moistened his lips. He started twice to speak. The tears began to run down his smudged* cheeks. "I felt terrible," he whispered. "I felt just plain terrible." And he ground his fists into his eyes like a guilty child.

Walter Post took him in and turned him over to the experts from the Homicide Section and accomplished his share of the paperwork. He was home by six o'clock. He told Carolyn about it that evening, when he was lethargic* with emotional reaction to the case. He talked to her about trying to get into some other line of investigatory work and tried to explain his reasons to her.

But they woke him up at three in the morning and told him to go out to River Road. He got there before the lab truck. He squatted in a floodlighted ditch and looked at the broken old body of a bearded vagrant* and at the smear of green automotive enamel ground into the fabric of a shabby coat. He straightened up slowly, bemused* by his own ready acceptance of the fact it was not yet time to leave this work. Somebody was driving in a personal terror through the misty night, in a car so significantly damaged it would wear—for Walter Post—the signs and stains of a sudden murder.

---

vagrant: one with no established home
bemused: lost in thought

About the Story

1. What evidence does Walter Post have that points to the Addams' car as the homicide vehicle?
2. What convinces the inspector of Mrs. Addams' innocence?
3. What alibis do Wade and Gary Addams have?

4. How has Gary changed during the past month? Why?
5. Whom do you consider to be the story's main character? Why?
6. State two lessons that can be learned from this story.

. . . About the Author

Born on July 24, 1916, in Sharon, Pennsylvania, John D. MacDonald is an American detective-story writer who has authored over sixty books (mostly novels) in addition to numerous short stories. His first short story was written for his wife in lieu of a letter while he was serving in the army overseas. The fact that *Story* magazine bought it for twenty-five dollars was enough encouragement for him to try writing as a career. He works hard, often spending up to fourteen hours a day at writing, revising, and editing, usually with at least three books in the works at the same time.

Old Yeller and the Bear

Fred Gipson

Brothers, as well as sisters, all too often quarrel with one another. But when danger threatens, they usually forget their quarrels. In this chapter from Old Yeller, *the older brother, Travis, reveals that he has a quarrel with the younger brother, Little Arliss. When trouble comes to Little Arliss, how does the family react?*

That Little Arliss! If he wasn't a mess! From the time he'd grown up big enough to get out of the cabin, he'd made a practice of trying to catch and keep every living thing that ran, flew, jumped, or crawled.

Every night before Mama let him go to bed, she'd make Arliss empty his pockets of whatever he'd captured during the day. Generally, it would be a tangled-up mess of grasshoppers and worms and praying bugs and little rusty tree lizards. One time he brought in a horned toad that got so mad he swelled out round and flat as a Mexican *tortilla** and bled at the eyes. Sometimes it was stuff like a young bird that had fallen out of its nest before it could fly, or a green-speckled spring frog or a striped water snake. And once he turned out of his pocket a wadded-up baby copperhead that nearly threw Mama into spasms. We never did figure out why the snake hadn't bitten him, but Mama took no more chances on snakes. She switched Arliss hard for catching that snake. Then she made me spend better than a week, taking him out and teaching him how to throw rocks and kill snakes.

tortilla: thin pancakelike bread

That was all right with Little Arliss. If Mama wanted him to kill his snakes first, he'd kill them. But that didn't keep him from sticking them in his pockets along with everything else he'd captured that day. The snakes might be stinking by the time Mama called on him to empty his pockets, but they'd be dead.

Then, after the yeller dog came, Little Arliss started catching even bigger game. Like cottontail rabbits and chaparral birds and a baby possum that sulked and lay like dead for the first several hours until he finally decided that Arliss wasn't going to hurt him.

Of course, it was Old Yeller that was doing the catching. He'd run the game down and turn it over to Little Arliss. Then Little Arliss could come in and tell Mama a big fib about how he caught it himself.

I watched them one day when they caught a blue catfish out of Birdsong Creek. The fish had fed out into water so shallow that his top fin was sticking out. About the time I saw it, Old Yeller and Little Arliss did, too. They made a run at it. The fish went scooting away toward deeper water, only Yeller was too fast for him. He pounced on the fish and shut his big mouth down over it and went romping to the bank, where he dropped it down on the grass and let it flop. And here came Little Arliss to fall on it like I guess he'd been doing everything else. The minute he got his hands on it, the fish finned him and he went to crying.

But he wouldn't turn the fish loose. He just grabbed it up and went running and squawling toward the house, where he gave the fish to Mama. His hands were all bloody by then, where the fish had finned him. They swelled up and got mighty sore; not even a mesquite thorn hurts as bad as a sharp fish fin when it's run deep into your hand.

But as soon as Mama had wrapped his hands in a poultice of mashed-up prickly-pear root to draw out the poison, Little Arliss forgot all about his hurt. And that night when we ate the fish for supper, he told the biggest windy* I ever heard about how he'd dived way down into a deep hole under the rocks and dragged that fish out and nearly got drowned before he could swim to the bank with it.

---

windy: lie

But when I tried to tell Mama what really happened, she wouldn't let me.

"Now, this is Arliss's story," she said. "You let him tell it the way he wants to."

I told Mama then, I said: "Mama, that old yeller dog is going to make the biggest liar in Texas out of Little Arliss."

But Mama just laughed at me, like she always laughed at Little Arliss's big windies after she'd gotten off where he couldn't hear her. She said for me to let Little Arliss alone. She said that if he ever told a bigger whopper than the ones I used to tell, she had yet to hear it.

Well, I hushed then. If Mama wanted Little Arliss to grow up to be the biggest liar in Texas, I guessed it wasn't any of my business.

All of which, I figure, is what led up to Little Arliss's catching the bear. I think Mama had let him tell so many big yarns about his catching live game that he'd begun to believe them himself.

When it happened, I was down the creek a ways, splitting rails to fix up the yard fence where the bulls had torn it down. I'd been down there since dinner, working in a stand of tall slim post oaks. I'd chop down a tree, trim off the branches as far up as I wanted, then cut away the rest of the top. After that I'd start splitting the log.

I'd split the log by driving steel wedges into the wood. I'd start at the big end and hammer in a wedge with the back side of my axe. This would start a little split running lengthways of the log. Then I'd take a second wedge and drive it into this split. This would split the log further along and, at the same time, loosen the first wedge. I'd then knock the first wedge loose and move it up in front of the second one.

Driving one wedge ahead of the other like that, I could finally split a log in two halves. Then I'd go to work on the halves, splitting them apart. That way, from each log, I'd come out with four rails.

Swinging that chopping axe was sure hard work. The sweat poured off me. My back muscles ached. The axe got so heavy I could hardly swing it. My breath got harder and harder to breathe.

An hour before sundown, I was worn down to a nub.* It seemed like I couldn't hit another lick. Papa could have lasted till past sundown, but I didn't see how I could. I shouldered my axe and started toward the cabin, trying to think up some excuse to tell Mama to keep her from knowing I was played clear out.*

---

worn down to a nub: worn out
played clear out: tired

That's when I heard Little Arliss scream.

Well, Little Arliss was a screamer by nature. He'd scream when he was happy and scream when he was mad and a lot of times he'd scream just to hear himself make a noise. Generally, we paid no more mind to his screaming than we did to the gobble of a wild turkey.

But this time was different. The second I heard his screaming, I felt my heart flop clear over. This time I knew Little Arliss was in real trouble.

I tore out up the trail leading toward the cabin. A minute before, I'd been so tired out with my rail splitting that I couldn't have struck a trot.* But now I raced through the tall trees in that creek bottom, covering ground like a scared wolf.

---

struck a trot: walked quickly

Little Arliss's second scream, when it came, was louder and shriller and more frantic-sounding than the first. Mixed with it was a whimpering crying sound that I knew didn't come from him. It was a sound I'd heard before and seemed like I ought to know what it was, but right then I couldn't place it.

Then, from way off to one side came a sound that I would have recognized anywhere. It was the coughing roar of a charging bear. I'd just heard it once in my life. That was the time Mama had shot and wounded a hog-killing bear and Papa had had to finish it off with a knife to keep it from getting her.

My heart went to pushing up into my throat, nearly choking off my wind. I strained for every lick of speed I could get out of my running legs. I didn't know what sort of fix Little Arliss had got himself into, but I knew that it had to do with a mad bear, which was enough.

The way the late sun slanted through the trees had the trail all cross-banded with streaks of bright light and dark shade. I ran through these bright and dark patches so fast that the changing light nearly blinded me. Then suddenly, I raced out into the open where I could see ahead. And what I saw sent a chill clear through to the marrow of my bones.

There was Little Arliss, down in that spring hole again. He was lying half in and half out of the water, holding onto the hind leg of a little black bear cub no bigger than a small coon. The bear cub was out on the bank, whimpering and crying and clawing the rocks with all three of his other feet, trying to pull away. But Little Arliss was holding on for all he was worth, scared now and screaming his head off. Too scared to let go.

How come the bear cub ever to prowl close enough for Little Arliss to grab him, I don't know. And why he didn't turn on him and bite loose, I couldn't figure out, either. Unless he was like Little Arliss, too scared to think.

But all of that didn't matter now. What mattered was the bear cub's mama. She'd heard the cries of her baby and was coming to save him. She was coming so fast that she had the brush popping and breaking as she crashed through and over it. I could see her black heavy figure piling off down the slant* on the far side of Birdsong Creek. She was roaring mad and ready to kill.

---

slant: slope

And worst of all, I could see that I'd never get there in time!

Mama couldn't either. She'd heard Arliss, too, and here she came from the cabin, running down the slant toward the spring, screaming at Arliss, telling him to turn the bear cub loose. But Little Arliss wouldn't do it. All he'd do was hang with that hind leg and let out one shrill shriek after another as fast as he could suck in a breath.

Now the she bear was charging across the shallows in the creek. She was knocking sheets of water high in the bright sun, charging with her fur up and her long teeth bared, filling the canyon with that awful coughing roar. And no matter how fast Mama ran or how fast I ran, the she bear was going to get there first!

I think I nearly went blind then, picturing what was going to happen to Little Arliss. I know that I opened my mouth to scream and not any sound came out.

Then, just as the bear went lunging up the creek bank toward Little Arliss and her cub, a flash of yellow came streaking out of the brush.

It was that big yeller dog. He was roaring like a mad bull. He wasn't one third as big and heavy as the she bear, but when he piled into her from one side, he rolled her clear off her feet. They went down in a wild, roaring tangle of twisting bodies and scrambling feet and slashing fangs.

As I raced past them, I saw the bear lunge up to stand on her hind feet like a man while she clawed at the body of the yeller dog hanging to her throat. I didn't wait to see more.

Without ever checking my stride, I ran in and jerked Little Arliss loose from the cub. I grabbed him by the wrist and yanked him up out of that water and slung him toward Mama like he was a half-empty sack of corn. I screamed at Mama. "Grab him, Mama! Grab him and run!" Then I swung my chopping axe high and wheeled, aiming to cave in the she bear's head with the first lick. But I never did strike. I didn't need to. Old Yeller hadn't let the bear get close enough. He couldn't handle her; she was too big and strong for that. She'd stand there on her hind feet, hunched over, and take a roaring swing at him with one of those big front claws. She'd slap him head over heels. She'd knock him so far that it didn't look like he could possibly get back there before she charged again, but he always did. He'd hit the ground rolling, yelling his head off with the pain of the blow; but somehow he'd always roll to his feet. And here he'd come again, ready to tie into her for another round.

I stood there with my axe raised, watching them for a long moment. Then from up toward the house, I heard Mama calling: "Come away from there, Travis. Hurry, son! Run!"

That spooked* me. Up till then, I'd been ready to tie into that bear myself. Now, suddenly, I was scared out of my wits again. I ran toward the cabin.

spooked: scared

But like it was, Old Yeller nearly beat me there. I didn't see it, of course; but Mama said that the minute Old Yeller saw we were all in the clear and out of danger, he threw the fight to that she bear and lit out for the house. The bear chased him for a little piece, but at the rate Old Yeller was leaving her behind, Mama said it looked like the bear was backing up.

But if the big yeller dog was scared or hurt in any way when he came dashing into the house, he didn't show it. He sure didn't show it like we all did. Little Arliss had hushed his screaming, but he was trembling all over and clinging to Mama like he'd never let her go. And Mama was sitting in the middle of the floor, holding him up close and crying like she'd never stop. And me, I was close to crying, myself.

Old Yeller, though, all he did was come bounding in to jump on us and lick us in the face and bark so loud that there, inside the cabin, the noise nearly made us deaf.

The way he acted, you might have thought that bear fight hadn't been anything more than a rowdy romp* that we'd all taken part in for the fun of it.

rowdy romp: rough frolic

About the Story

1. What habit of Little Arliss's finally gets him into trouble?
2. How does Travis feel about Little Arliss? How do you know?
3. What characteristics does Travis show?
4. What similar characteristics are shown by Old Yeller?

About the Author

Born on a farm in Mason, Texas, on February 7, 1908, Fred Gipson grew up roaming the Texas woods, hunting and fishing—experiences he drew heavily from in writing his distinctively Western stories with endearing human and animal characters. Although his first year of free-lance writing earned him only $150, his first book, *Hound-dog Man,* brought not only financial rewards but the praise of critics as well. His best-known book, the award-winning *Old Yeller,* has been made into a film and translated into several foreign languages.

Mister Chairman

Frank B. Gilbreth Jr. and
Ernestine Gilbreth Carey

> *A dozen children can make family life quite complicated. In this chapter from* Cheaper by the Dozen, *the Gilbreth family establishes a family council. The purpose, according to the father, is to help matters run more smoothly. But what actually happens in this episode is that the children outmaneuver him and put through their own "pet" project.*

Mother came from a well-to-do family in Oakland, California. She had met Dad in Boston while she was en route to Europe on one of those well-chaperoned tours for fashionable young ladies of the 'nineties.*

'nineties: 1890s

Mother was a Phi Beta Kappa* and a psychology graduate at the University of California. In those days women who were scholars were viewed with some suspicion. When Mother and Dad were married, the Oakland paper said:

"Although a graduate of the University of California, the bride is nonetheless an extremely attractive young woman."

Phi Beta Kappa: a member of a national fraternity for honor students

Indeed she was.

So it was Mother the psychologist and Dad the motion study man and general contractor, who decided to look into the new field of the psychology of management, and the old field of psychologically managing a houseful of children. They believed that what would work in the home would work in the factory, and what would work in the factory would work in the home.

Dad put the theory to a test shortly after we moved to Montclair [N.J.]. The house was too big for Tom Grieves, the handyman, and Mrs. Cunningham, the cook, to keep in order. Dad decided we were going to have to help them, and he wanted us to offer the help of our own accord.* He had found that the best way to get cooperation out of employees in a factory was to set up a joint employer-employee board, which would make work assignments on a basis of personal choice and aptitude.* He and Mother set up a Family Council, patterned after an employer- employee board. The council met every Sunday afternoon, immediately after dinner.

of our own accord: voluntarily
aptitude: ability

At the first session, Dad got to his feet formally, poured a glass of ice water, and began a speech.

"You will notice," he said, "that I am installed here as your chairman. I assume there are no objections. The chair, hearing no objections, will . . ."

"Mr. Chairman," Anne interrupted. Being in high school, she knew something of parliamentary procedure, and thought it might be a good idea to have the chairman represent the common people.

"Out of order," said Dad. "Very much out of order when the chair has the floor."

"But you said you heard no objections, and I want to object."

"Out of order means sit down, and you're out of order," Dad shouted. He took a swallow of ice water, and resumed his speech. "The first job of the Council is to apportion* necessary work in the house and yard. Does the chair hear any suggestions?"

apportion: assign

There were no suggestions. Dad forced a smile and attempted to radiate* good humor.

radiate: send out

"Come, come, fellow members of the Council," he said. "This is a democracy.* Everybody has an equal voice. How do you want to divide the work?"

democracy: government by the people

No one wanted to divide the work or otherwise be associated with it in any way, shape, or form. No one said anything.

"In a democracy everybody speaks," said Dad, "so, by jingo, start speaking." The Good Humor Man was gone now. "Jack, I recognize you. What do you think about dividing the work? I warn you, you'd better think something."

"I think," Jack said slowly, "that Mrs. Cunningham and Tom should do the work. They get paid for it."

"Sit down," Dad hollered. "You are no longer recognized."

Jack sat down amid general approval, except that of Dad and Mother.

"Hush, Jackie," Mother whispered. "They may hear you and leave. It's so hard to get servants when there are so many children in the house."

"I wish they would leave," said Jack. "They're too bossy."

Don was next recognized by the chair.

"I think Tom and Mrs. Cunningham have enough to do," he said, as Dad and Mother beamed and nodded agreement. "I think we should hire more people to work for us."

"Out of order," Dad shouted. "Sit down and be quiet!"

Dad saw things weren't going right. Mother was the psychologist. Let her work them out.

"Your chairman recognizes the assistant chairman," he said, nodding to Mother to let her know he had just conferred* that title upon her person.

conferred: granted

"We could hire additional help," Mother said, "and that might be the answer."

We grinned and nudged each other.

"But," she continued, "that would mean cutting the budget somewhere else. If we cut out all desserts and allowances, we could afford a maid. And if we cut out moving pictures, ice cream sodas, and new clothes for a whole year, we could afford a gardener, too."

"Do I hear a motion to that effect?" Dad beamed. "Does anybody want to stop allowances?"

No one did. After some prodding by Dad, the motion on allotting work finally was introduced and passed. The boys would cut the grass and rake the leaves. The girls would sweep, dust and do the supper dishes. Everyone except Dad would make his own bed and keep his room neat. When it came to apportioning work on an aptitude basis, the smaller girls were assigned to dust the legs and lower shelves of furniture; the older girls to dust table tops and upper shelves. The older boys would push the lawnmowers and carry leaves. The younger ones would do the raking and weeding.

The next Sunday, when Dad convened* the second meeting of the Council, we sat self-consciously around the table, biding* our time. The chairman knew something was in the air, and it tickled him. He had trouble keeping a straight face when he called for new business.

---

convened: assembled
biding: waiting for

Martha, who had been carefully coached in private caucus,* arose.

---

caucus: a meeting

"It has come to the attention of the membership," she began, "that the assistant chairman intends to buy a new rug for the dining room. Since the entire membership will be required to look upon, and sit in chairs resting

upon, the rug, I move that the Council be consulted before any rug is purchased."

"Second the motion," said Anne.

Dad didn't know what to make of this one. "Any discussion?" he asked, in a move designed to kill time while he planned his counter attack.

"Mr. Chairman," said Lillian. "We have to sweep it. We should be able to choose it."

"We want one with flowers on it," Martha put in. "When you have flowers, the crumbs don't show so easily, and you save motions by not having to sweep so often."

"We want to know what sort of a rug the assistant chairman intends to buy," said Ernestine.

"We want to make sure the budget can afford it," Fred announced.

"I recognize the assistant chairman," said Dad. "This whole Council business was your idea anyway, Lillie. What do we do now?"

"Well," Mother said doubtfully, "I had planned to get a plain violet-colored rug, and I had planned to spend a hundred dollars. But if the children think that's too much, and if they want flowers, I'm willing to let the majority rule."

"I move," said Frank, "that not more than ninety-five dollars be spent."

Dad shrugged his shoulder. If Mother didn't care, he certainly didn't.

"So many as favor the motion to spend only ninety-five dollars, signify by saying aye."

The motion carried unanimously.

"Any more new business?"

"I move," said Bill, "that we spend the five dollars we have saved to buy a collie puppy."

"Hey, wait a minute," said Dad. The rug had been somewhat of a joke, but the dog question was serious. We had wanted a dog for years. Dad thought that any pet which didn't lay eggs was an extravagance that a man with

twelve children could ill afford. He felt that if he surrendered on the dog question, there was no telling what the council might vote next. He had a sickening mental picture of a barn full of ponies, a roadster for Anne, motorcycles, a swimming pool, and, ultimately,* the poor house or a debtors' prison, if they still had such things.

---

ultimately: in the end

"Second the motion," said Lillian, yanking Dad out of his reverie.*

---

reverie: daydreaming

"A dog," said Jack, "would be a pet. Everyone in the family could pat him, and I would be his master."

"A dog," said Don, "would be a friend. He could eat scraps of food. He would save us

waste and would save motions for the garbage man."

"A dog," said Fred, "would keep burglars away. He would sleep on the foot of my bed, and I would wash him whenever he was dirty."

"A dog," Dad mimicked, "would be an accursed nuisance. He would be our master. He would eat me out of house and home. He would spread fleas from the garret* to the portecochere.* He would be positive to sleep on the foot of *my* bed. Nobody would wash his filthy, dirty, flea-bitten carcass."

---

garret: attic
portecochere: a covered entranceway

He looked pleadingly at Mother.

"Lillie, Lillie, open your eyes," he implored. "Don't you see where this is leading us? Ponies, roadsters, trips to Hawaii, silk stockings, rouge, and bobbed hair."

"I think, dear," said Mother, "that we must rely on the good sense of the children. A five-dollar dog is not a trip to Hawaii."

We voted, and there was only one negative ballot—Dad's. Mother abstained.* In after years, as the collie grew older, shed hair on the furniture, bit the mailman, and did in fact try to appropriate* the foot of Dad's bed, the chairman was heard to remark on occasion to the assistant chairman:

"I give nightly praise to my Maker that I never cast a ballot to bring that lazy, disreputable,* ill-tempered beast into what was once my home. I'm glad I had the courage to go on record as opposing that illegitimate, shameless flea-bag that now shares my bed and board. You abstainer, you!"

---

abstained: did not vote
appropriate: to take over for one's own use
disreputable: not respectable in character, action, or appearance

---

About the Story

1. What are Mother's and Dad's fields of expertise?
2. What system do the Gilbreths establish for making family decisions?
3. How does the decision to operate the family like a business backfire on Dad?
4. Does the Gilbreth family sound like a family you would enjoy being a part of? Why or why not?

About the Author

Frank Gilbreth (b. 1911) and his older sister Ernestine (b. 1908) collaborated in the writing of two books about their famous family: *Cheaper by the Dozen* and *Belles on Their Toes*. Both of these books became nonfiction bestsellers, and both were made into films. After working as a reporter in New York City and serving in the U.S. Navy during World War II, in 1947 Frank joined the staff of a Charleston (South Carolina) newspaper, where he has continued his journalistic career. After working as a buyer for the famous Macy's in New York City, in 1949 Ernestine became a professional lecturer and writer.

Sioux Trouble

Bernard Palmer

Donald has grown so angry with his stepfather that he is at the breaking point. This man has stepped into the place Donald reserved for his real father. Moreover, the man keeps talking to him about "Jesus and sin and becoming a Christian." The next morning Donald is going to run away from the family he does not want or even need anymore. But that night . . . the Sioux come.

Donald Kennan stood in the doorway of the crude little two-room cabin, his rifle in his hands and his jaw set stubbornly. He was a tall, thin wisp of a boy with flashing brown eyes and the first soft fuzz of manhood on his cheeks.

"I reckon I'm a-stayin' here," he said.

"There ain't no time to lose, Don," the man on horseback exclaimed impatiently. "That band of renegade* Sioux killed two families over acrost the river last night and they was seen a-headin' this way."

---

renegade: outlaw

The boy shook his head determinedly. "I ain't a-goin'."

How could he leave? His Paw had cut down the logs and built the cabin long before he had died. He had trudged through the un-tracked forest all the way to St. Paul to get the oxen they were using and had taken the only cow they had now into the house as a new-born calf and nursed it to health. Killed himself caring for his family. That's what he did.

Don had been going to leave home, though. He had everything packed and hid out in the haymow. An extra pair of buckskin pants and two boxes of rifle shells he'd filched* from Scotty, his step-paw, a couple of chunks of jerked venison* and a quart of his own

Paw's whisky Maw had told him to pour out. But he couldn't leave now, he reasoned.

filched: secretly stolen
jerked venison: smoked or dried deer meat

"I ain't a-going over to your place, Clem," he repeated. "I reckon Scotty and Maw and the young 'un'll be along any time."

"Like as not the Major won't even let 'em out of the Fort until this mess is cleaned up," Clem Taylor said, fidgeting in the saddle. "You get them oxen and your cow put up and get over to my place!"

The color drained from Don's cheeks and his hand quivered on the rifle but he shook his head decisively.*

decisively: firmly

"If ye don't I'll tell the preacher and your Maw when they get home and he'll thrash* ye good."

thrash: whip

"Him and who else," Don demanded hotly.

"You get over to my place. I ain't a-tellin' you no more!" With that the buckskin-clad rider went galloping away.

Don had been going to leave, all right. He had taken all he was going to take from Scotty MacFarland, bossing him around like he was his own Paw, making him throw away his chewing tobacco and sit there in the cabin as pious as a guinea bird* every morning whilst Scotty read out of the Bible and gave a little talk about sin and stuff, and prayed.

guinea bird: pheasantlike fowl

It was bad enough having to put up with that, but to see him kissing Maw, too, and cooing to that young 'un, that had come along a couple of months ago was more than Don could stand. He had everything set. He was sneaking out first chance he had and heading west. Maw didn't need him around any more.

Not after tonight and she and Scotty got home from the Fort, she didn't.

Don listened a moment until the clatter of hoofs died away. He had seen the smoking ruins of cabins that the renegade Sioux, crazed on the white man's firewater,* had burned, and had heard the agonizing sobs of women whose husbands would come back no more.

firewater: whisky

There was no sound in the still forest save for the wind moaning softly in the tops of the trees. He was alone.

But that silence didn't mean he was safe. They could be lurking anywhere—everywhere—waiting for the moment to attack.

He shuddered and took a quick look at the sun that was already dropping behind the forest. In a short while it would be dark. He had to get out and get the stock* in.

stock: farm animals

Don sucked in his breath sharply and started to walk out towards the log shed that served as a barn. He carried his gun in the crook of his arm and his gaze raced nervously along on either side of the path.

If Maw hadn't married that preacher, Scotty MacFarland, everything would be all right. He and Maw could have taken the oxen and cow over to Clem's with them. They could have handled things.

But no, it wasn't more than a year after Paw had died that she had started letting the preacher come to see her. And the first thing he knew they were married and Scotty moved into the house his own Paw had built.

He still recollected the night she told him. "It ain't that I'm not happy here with just you, Donald," she had said, her soft gray eyes pleading for understanding. "But it's just that a body gets so lonesome and—and we do need a man around the place."

"I reckon I could take care of things," he had bristled.*

---

bristled: replied angrily

"I know," she answered. He had never seen that look on her face before, even when Paw was alive. It was soft and sweet and beautiful. "But I love Scotty so much," she said.

Then the young 'un came, a weak, spindling* little thing that kept Maw worried half silly over him until she and Scotty set out for the Fort to have the Army doctor see what was wrong. And now he was all alone with renegade Indians on the prowl.

---

spindling: frail

He heard a twig crack in the brush and turned quickly, his rifle ready. Panic seized him. But it had only been a half grown fawn peering at him through the leaves.

Hurriedly he put the cow into the shed and milked her, and fed the oxen. Back in the cabin he bolted the door and fixed himself a bowl of bread and milk. He dare not build a fire. The thin spiral of smoke in the clear air would shout the location of the cabin.

Don looked uneasily across the table at the big Bible Scotty had placed there just before he left.

"If ye want to read, Laddie," he had said with that soft, smiling voice of his, "I'd be much obliged if ye'd turn to the book o'John. 'Tis wonderful company on a lonely night."

Always thinking about that Bible. Always talking to him about Jesus and sin and becoming a Christian until he got to feeling that he was the wickedest person in the world.

His Maw had been the preacher's first convert, as Scotty called it. She got down on her knees by the kitchen chair and prayed out loud, right in front of everybody.

She wouldn't have done it if his Paw had lived. He'd have thrown Scotty MacFarland out of there on his ear. Then he'd have knocked some sense into Maw. That's what he'd have done.

There was a sound outside the cabin and Don sprang to the window. Dusk was dragging the shadows out of the trees and shrouding* familiar things with weird, unnatural shapes that set his blood to racing and a fine line of sweat to beading his forehead. Was that a man crouched in the clump of blackberry bushes? Did someone move across the clearing just then, running silently, or had that quick blur been a bird soaring up from a low-hanging limb to silhouette* for a heart-beat against the darkening sky? He waited tensely, his rifle in his hand.

shrouding: concealing
silhouette: outline

The wind toyed with the window pane and grated a long, heavy branch against the eave of the cabin roof. Don started at the sound and whirled quickly, grinning at himself when he realized what it was.

Getting jumpy as a cat and those Indians were probably a hundred miles from there.

He stared into the shadows outside but there was nothing there. There couldn't be! He moved back to the chair and sat down, laying the rifle across his lap. Maw and Scotty would be home before long and they'd laugh at him and tell him to scoot up to bed.

Scotty smiled easy and he had a handy way about him with a rifle and an ax. He was a big man, towering a head and a half above Don. He had a pleasant face and a serious set to that jaw of his. And when he talked about the Lord he fairly bored two holes into a fellow, deep down into his heart. It made Don cringe* just to think of it.

cringe: shrink in fear

But for all of that Don would probably have liked the big Scotsman if he hadn't come sparking around* Maw with all that pretty talk about the Bible and Jesus and being "born into the Kingdom."

sparking around: courting

The slender-faced youth crossed his legs and ran his hand through his thick black hair. It was getting dark. He could scarcely make out the Bible verse Scotty had painted on a board and hung on the opposite wall. Oh well, come morning and he'd be rid of Scotty and all his preaching.

Sitting in the dark that way he must have dozed a few minutes. There was a sound outside, a flat, muffled sound that scarcely woke him. He straightened slowly, shaking the sleep from his head. For an instant he didn't realize where he was or what was happening. And then it came again almost at the very door! The soft, measured step of one who walks silently by nature!

Instantly a spasm of fear seized him. They were there! Just outside the door. He leaped to his feet and fumbled a bullet into the rifle chamber. He had heard the one at the door, but there would be others—out at the barn, at the windows, on top of the low-roofed cabin, silently awaiting the high-pitched scream of battle.

He took a deep breath and cocked the rifle. Scotty would be praying if he were here. He'd be standing alongside of him, his rifle ready, talking to God in that soft, musical voice of his.

Suddenly there was a loud, demanding knock at the door. "Open!" a rasping, guttural* voice thundered. "Open, or we knock it in!"

guttural: produced in the throat

Don didn't answer. He could not. Carefully he raised the rifle to his shoulder and took aim in the darkness for the middle of the door. Then, with his finger squeezing the trigger, he stopped. That door was of oak, two inches thick. His Paw had cut down the tree and hewed out* the planks for it by hand. No bullet could go through a door like that and kill a man. And besides, what of the rest of them? They would come swarming through the window before the black powder smoke had cleared the air, before he could re-load and fire again.

hewed out: shaped with an ax

"Oh God," he began between trembling lips, only to stop pitifully. *How did Scotty go about praying?*

"Open! Open up! We hungry."

He could hear the voices of the others, jabbering in Sioux.

"Wait a minute!" he called to them, taking the gun and hiding it under a loose board in the cabin floor.

They hammered again.

"Let me get the bolt down."

He lighted the lamp and let the Indians in. There were seven or eight of them, dirty, pock-marked* fellows carrying rifles and knives.

pock-marked: covered with pitlike scars

"We hungry," the self-appointed leader announced, shoving past Don into the end of the room that served as a kitchen.

The others had gone into the bedroom and up into the loft where Don slept, jerking the covers off the bed and peering into the corners. They were looking for rifles and ammunition and whisky. The Indian spokesman tore things out of the cupboard, spilling corn across the floor and grunting with satisfaction when he found the last of the jerked venison.

"We hungry," he announced again.

"I—I'll fix you something to eat," Don said hurriedly.

While the rest were snooping through the house and prowling around outside the tall Indian who had done the talking stood over Don while he built a fire and put a kettle of water on to boil. It would finish the last of the venison and most of their precious potatoes and corn.

When he had the meal ready they dropped around the table like pigs at a trough and began to gulp the food. Don didn't notice that one was missing until he came staggering in from the barn with a bottle of whisky in his hand.

Paw's whisky! The bottle Maw had told him to pour out and he'd hid instead. The bottle he'd sneaked a drink or two out of just to see what it tasted like. The bottle he had been going to take with him when he skinned out.*

---

skinned out: ran away

The instant they saw it their eyes lit up fiendishly* and they began to fight for it, clawing desperately for the right to take a pull at the bottle.

---

fiendishly: wickedly

Their tongues began to loosen and their faces flushed as the liquor began to do its work. They looked at Don and whispered tensely in low, guttural tones.

Then the leader turned to him. "More whisky," he demanded. "Whisky!"

Don shook his head. "No more," he said. "T-t-there isn't any more on the place."

The Indian got to his feet and advanced unsteadily until he was towering over him. "More whisky!" His voice was tense and ominous.

"But there isn't any!" Don cried desperately. "Scotty, he—" he reached over and picked up the Bible, pointing to it expressively.

The angered Indian jerked the Book out of his hands and threw it across the floor. "More whisky," he shouted.

And then Don heard the squeak of Scotty's light wagon coming up the lane. His Maw and the young 'un were out there!

His heart began to hammer wildly and his hands and arms began to tremble. He knew what happened to women as pretty and young as Maw who came in the path of Indians like that! He knew about how long the young 'un'd last if he chanced to cry! *And there wasn't anything he could do!*

"Oh God!" he tried to pray again, but the words stuck in his throat.

The wagon was coming closer now, that squeaking wheel sounding above the drunken babble* of the Indians. And then *they* heard it. Two or three of the renegades staggered to the window and looked out, chortling* in drunken lust.

babble: confused talk
chortling: chuckling

At that instant he leaped for the table, grabbed the kerosene lamp and hurled it across the room. The kerosene exploded with a roar, bathing the cabin wall in flame.

With an oath the Indian nearest Don grabbed up a stool and slammed it against the side of his head. His knees sagged and he crumpled to the floor.

It was later, much later, that he came to, his head in his mother's lap.

"W-w-what happened, Maw?" he asked hesitantly. "I remember a-gettin' hit on the head and the fire, but how . . ." his voice trailed away.

"Scotty," she said, explaining. "He drove the Indians away a-a-and then went into the cabin after you."

"A-a-after me?" he asked, scarcely believing his ears.

"Ay, Laddie," the Scotsman said, coming up with a pail of cold water. Don saw that the preacher's hands were swollen and blistered and that his face was black with soot. "Ye did a bonnie* job on that cabin, though. 'Tis a heap of re-buildin' she's a-goin' to be needing. From the ground up." He chuckled. "But ye're a good boy, Donnie," he went on softly. "It was a big thing ye did."

bonnie: Scottish: pretty

The boy on the ground felt his throat choke. Scotty had gone into the fire after him. He had sassed him and hated him and had fixed to run away because his Maw had married him. Still Scotty had fought the Indians and the flames to save him. He could hardly stand to think of it, after what he had done.

"It was the whisky, Scotty," he murmured between clenched teeth. "I saved Paw's whisky instead of pourin' it out like you and Maw told me to. They—they'd have eaten, maybe, and gone away if it hadn't been for the whisky."

"Don't you be a-frettin' your head about that now," Scotty said. "I reckon we all make mistakes now and then. We ought to be a-thankin' God that we're all alive and well."

Donnie opened his eyes and looked up at the tall, serious faced man his mother had married. Suddenly he saw him in a new light, in the way she saw him. He closed his eyes again and a smile came across his face. In the morning, when his head didn't ache so much, he was going into that "being born into the Kingdom" business. He saw now that he had to have the strength and peace his Maw and the preacher had.

In a moment or two he opened his eyes and looked up into Scotty's face. "I'm much obliged for you a-carryin' me out of the burnin' cabin, *Paw*," he said softly.

Scotty's eyes narrowed for an instant. "Get along wi' ye," he scolded pleasantly. "What else is a man expected to do for his *son*?"

They looked at one another and smiled.

About the Story

1. List at least three reasons that Don resents Scotty MacFarland.
2. What danger is Don facing? Why is he facing it alone?
3. What does Don attempt in vain to do once he realizes that his gun will be of no help?
4. What causes the Indians to become belligerent?
5. How does Don escape from the Sioux?
6. Compare Scotty to Travis from "Old Yeller and the Bear." What similar characteristics do they exhibit?

About the Author

The popular Christian author Bernard Palmer (b. 1914) began writing stories in junior high school. About those stories he says, "I had a sort of traveling library in my homeroom. I would write a page and pass it to the boy behind me, who read it and gave it to someone else." However, it was not until 1942 that he published his first book, *Parson John*. Since then he has authored more than two hundred volumes, the best known being his youth fiction including the popular Danny Orlis series. Although his home is in Nebraska, many of Palmer's stories are set in the northern United States and Canada, where he spent much time as a child and vacations as an adult.

Love Story, Sort Of

Phyllis Reynolds Naylor

Paul seldom visits his grandmother, but in this story he brings her three gifts. What are they? What does he plan to bring her next time? Does he learn anything from his visit? Do you believe that this title is appropriate for the story?

You've got to get the picture. Here I am— . . . wrinkled shirt, dirty jeans, Army boots—standing in Walgreen's looking over the heart-shaped boxes of candy. Even the salesgirl thought it was funny.

"Going soft, huh?" she said, smiling. "Your girl?"

"Naw. My grandmother."

"I'll bet."

I paid five ninety-eight plus tax for a large box and asked her to put it in a sack so people wouldn't stare at me on the bus. Then I clomped out, waded through the snow to the curb, and got on the bus to Tilden Heights.

I just had to do it. Every Christmas since I was twelve, Grandma had sent me a check for five dollars because she'd broken her hip and couldn't get out to shop like she used to. And she always sent a note along with it. This year it said:

Dear Paul,

Don't you dare spend this for socks or underwear. Buy one of those new kind of shirts that lace down the front, or maybe some guitar music. Have a good Christmas. I'm wishing you lots of snow so you can ski over the holidays.

Love, Grandma

That's why I wanted to go see her. Nobody said I had to. I just knew I should. And I spent half the money in my wallet for that box of candy.

The bus rumbled under the railroad bridge and on up the hill past the cemetery. I looked at the gravestones, sticking up through the snow, and wondered what Grandma thought when she looked at them. In fact, what did it feel like to be old?

I'll have to admit I didn't come to Grandma's often. It had been over a year already. Not that I didn't like her—as a grandmother, she was great. It's just that her age scared me, I guess, like maybe it was contagious or something.

She didn't have much hair left, and what there was hung in white wisps* around her face like spider webs. She sometimes drooled as she spoke, and had to keep dabbing her mouth with a handkerchief. Part of Grandma, in fact, wasn't even her at all. One eye was glass, her teeth were false, there was a hearing aid in her ear and a steel pin in her hip. Sometimes I had the weird feeling that if I reached out and touched her, part of her would come right off in my hands.

---

wisps: strands

I looked down where my own hands lay in my lap and imagined how they'd look all wrinkled. Everybody was getting older all the time—even me. Some day I'd be sitting in a wheelchair and drooling, and I wondered how I'd feel about myself then. I was glad when the bus rounded the hill on King Street and headed for the row houses in Tilden Heights.

I hadn't told her I was coming, but I knew she was there. I could tell by the squeak of her wheelchair when she heard the doorbell. Grandma was always in except on Thursday afternoons when a neighbor took her to the doctor. What was it like to be a prisoner in your own house? The thought depressed me.

The door opened and there she was in a lavender house dress, her swollen feet crammed in a pair of gray felt slippers. Her thin lips stretched in a joyous smile, and she flung open the door with such force I was afraid she'd fall out of the chair.

"Paul! You come right in, and don't tell me you can only stay a few minutes!"

She took the words right out of my mouth, so I had to change my story.

"Well, I can stay a little longer than that," I grinned. "How you doing, Grandma?" I bent over and kissed her on the cheek. It smelled of camphorated oil.* Then I handed her the sack. "Brought you a Valentine present."

---

camphorated oil: oil containing camphor, used as medicine

I sat on the sofa and watched while she fumbled excitedly with the paper. The big red heart fell out in her lap and she gasped, beating her gums together. "Paul Larkins!" she said finally. "What did you pay for this?"

"Oh, couple dollars."

Her good eye fell on the price tag which the girl hadn't removed. I winced.

"Five dollars and ninety-eight cents! You spent your whole Christmas check on me and then some!" Suddenly she laughed gaily and lifted the lid. "All right, young man, you just take a fistful and eat 'em while you sit here and talk to me."

I obliged, and enjoyed watching Grandma poke around to find one with coconut filling, her favorite.

"How've you been feeling?" I asked again.

She waved my question aside with a fling of her hand. "I've time enough to think about myself," she said. "Tell me about Christmas and skiing and school. And how do you think the President's doing?"

I talked about everything I could think of. I described a stem turn, a snowplow, and a christie.* I told her about the college board exams and my term paper and how I was learning to type. I told how the dog knocked over the Christmas tree and about the candlelight service at church and how great the sanc-

tuary looked with poinsettias all over the place.

---
stem turn, a snowplow, and a christie: snow-skiing movements

Grandma caught me looking at my watch and said, "Now that we've absolutely ruined your appetite, you've got to stay for lunch." Without waiting for an answer, she whirled her chair around and headed for the kitchen.

If there was one thing I didn't want to do, it was eat lunch at Grandma's. For one thing, she can't see too well, and her dishes have little pieces of egg and orange pulp sticking to the sides. For another, she saves absolutely everything. When I saw her lifting little dabs of this and that from the refrigerator—a saucer of broccoli, half a pork chop—I knew I just couldn't do it.

"Nope, Grandma," I said. "I've got it all planned. You set the table and I'll be back in ten minutes with our lunch."

She turned around. "You've brought a sack lunch?"

I laughed. "No, it's special. Put on some plates and I'll be right back."

It wasn't planned at all, but when I reached the street, I remembered the Chinese carry-out on the corner. Grandma had never had sweet and sour pork in her life, much less a fried wonton.* I spent the remaining money in my wallet, with only bus fare left, and headed back up the street with three small containers in a bag.

---
wonton: Chinese dumpling

"Well, I never!" Grandma exclaimed, spooning some of it onto her plate. "Always did wonder what they ate, and it smells right good, doesn't it?"

The little kitchen seemed to take on a warm glow as we sat there stuffing our faces. I made some hot tea and we laughed at our fortune cookies.

"A full stomach makes better conversation," Grandma's read.

"Wisdom never comes from a big mouth," said mine.

I had planned to stay about twenty minutes. It was now an hour and a half, and I poured us each another cup of tea.

"Such good food!" Grandma exclaimed. "You know what I always wanted to try, Paul?"

"What's that, Grandma?"

She leaned forward and whispered the awful secret. "Pizza with anchovies!"

We burst out laughing. "Best in the world!" I said.

I helped her wash the dishes and asked if there was anything I could do for her. She asked me to take down some curtains and lift a box off the shelf in the closet. She was glad I'd asked, and so was I.

Finally it was time to go. She was cheerful right up to the last, but didn't ask me to come back. She was afraid it would make me feel obliged. She wanted people to come because they liked to.

I could see her watching me from the window as I went down the hill to the bus stop. When I reached the corner, I leaned against a store front and thought about Grandma back there in her lavender dress.

What was it about the visit she had enjoyed so much? It wasn't just me. And it wasn't the candy. It was the chance to escape herself, to keep in touch with youth, shake her mind from the confines of her four walls, and be once more a part of the world outside.

It wouldn't be a year before I saw her again, I knew. I promised myself that sometime during spring vacation, I'd be back. I'd bring my guitar and sing the songs I'd heard in the coffee house on Saturday nights. I'd tell her about the colleges I'd visited and why I was choosing a Christian college over State. Next time I'd bring Grandma a big flat box without any wrapping on it at all. She'd open it up right there on her lap and find a big pizza with anchovies. And we'd sit around the kitchen, stuffing our faces, talking about how the Italians ate and the books I was reading and how I thought the President was doing.

About the Story

1. What two tangible things does Paul give to his grandmother on this visit?
2. What makes these things special to her?
3. In addition to these items, Paul also gives his grandmother something else that money cannot buy. What?
4. What can we learn about giving through this story?
5. How is Paul changed through this visit to his grandmother?

About the Author

Phyllis Naylor's (b. 1933) love of reading was instilled in her at an early age through her parents' practice of reading to the family nightly. She was born in Indiana, but by the time she had reached high school age, she had lived in eight different homes throughout Indiana, Illinois, and Iowa. Between frequent moves and summers spent in the country with her grandparents, Phyllis's background supplied her with much material for the many books and stories she has written. She sold her first story to a children's Sunday school paper for $4.67 when she was sixteen years old. When she learned that she could earn money doing something so enjoyable, she was very excited! Since that first story, she has written more than sixty books for children and young adults and has also won numerous literary awards.

Although many writers specialize in one type of writing, Naylor says that she enjoys the variety of audiences for whom she writes and will often finish a children's book only to turn around and write a book directed toward parents. One piece of memorable advice that has guided her writing throughout her career is a suggestion given by the well-known author Willa Cather to "let your writing grow out of the land beneath your feet." Naylor has done so, writing of and for children, parenting, and other things that she herself has experienced. She lives with her husband Rex and her two cats, Ulysses and Marco, in Bethesda, Maryland.

How We Kept Mother's Day

Stephen Leacock

Have you ever planned a special celebration for your mother? Was your celebration at all like this family's?

Of all the different ideas that have been started lately, I think that the very best is the notion of celebrating once a year "Mother's Day."* I don't wonder that May the eleventh is becoming such a popular date all over America and I am sure the idea will spread to England too.

It is especially in a big family like ours that such an idea takes hold. So we decided to have a special celebration of Mother's Day. We thought it a fine idea. It made us all realize how much Mother had done for us for years, and all the efforts and sacrifice that she had made for our sake.

So we decided that we'd make it a great day, a holiday for all the family, and do everything we could to make Mother happy. Father decided to take a holiday from his office, so as to help in celebrating the day, and my sister Anne and I stayed home from college classes, and Mary and my brother Will stayed home from high school.

It was our plan to make it a day just like Christmas or any big holiday, and so we decided to decorate the house with flowers and with mottoes over the mantelpieces, and all that kind of thing. We got Mother to make mottoes and arrange the decorations, because she always does it at Christmas.

The two girls thought it would be a nice thing to dress in our very best for such a big occasion, and so they both got new hats. Mother trimmed both the hats, and they looked fine, and Father had bought four-in-hand silk ties* for himself and us boys as a souvenir of the day to remember Mother by. We were going to get Mother a new hat too, but it turned out that she seemed to really like her old grey bonnet better than a new one, and both the girls said that it was awfully becoming to her.

four-in-hand silk ties: neckties tied in a knot with the ends left hanging and overlapping

Well, after breakfast we had it arranged as a surprise for Mother that we would hire a

motor car and take her for a beautiful drive away into the country. Mother is hardly ever able to have a treat like that, because we can only afford to keep one maid, and so Mother is busy in the house nearly all the time. And of course the country is so lovely now that it would be just grand* for her to have a lovely morning, driving for miles and miles.

grand: wonderful

But on the very morning of the day we changed the plan a little bit, because it occurred to Father that a thing it would be better to do even than to take Mother for a motor drive would be to take her fishing. Father said that as the car was hired and paid for, we might just as well use it for a drive up into hills where the streams are. As Father said, if you just go out driving without any object, you have a sense of aimlessness, but if you are going to fish, there is a definite purpose in front of you to heighten the enjoyment.

So we all felt that it would be nicer for Mother to have a definite purpose; and anyway, it turned out that Father had just got a new rod the day before, which made the idea of fishing all the more appropriate, and he said that Mother could use it if she wanted to; in fact, he said it was practically for her, only Mother said she would much rather watch him fish and not try to fish herself.

So we got everything arranged for the trip, and we got Mother to cut up some sandwiches and make up a sort of lunch in case we got hungry, though of course we were to come back home again to a big dinner in the middle of the day, just like Christmas or New Year's Day. Mother packed it all up in a basket for us ready to go in the motor.*

motor: car

Well, when the car came to the door, it turned out that there hardly seemed as much

room in it as we had supposed, because we hadn't reckoned on Father's fishing basket and the rods and the lunch, and it was plain enough that we couldn't all get in.

Father said not to mind him, he said that he could just as well stay home, and that he was sure that he could put in the time working in the garden; he said that there was a lot of rough dirty work that he could do, like digging a trench for the garbage, that would save hiring a man, and so he said that he'd stay home; he said that we were not to let the fact of his not having had a real holiday for three years stand in our way; he wanted us to go right ahead and be happy and have a big day, and not to mind him. He said that he could plug away all day, and in fact he said he'd been a fool to think there'd be any holiday for him.

But of course we all felt that it would never do to let Father stay home, especially as we knew he would make trouble if he did. The two girls, Anne and Mary, would gladly have stayed and helped the maid get dinner, only it seemed such a pity to, on a lovely day like this, having their new hats. But they both said that Mother had only to say the word, and they'd gladly stay home and work. Will and I would have dropped out, but unfortunately we wouldn't have been any use in getting the dinner.

So in the end it was decided that Mother would stay home and just have a lovely restful day round the house, and get the dinner. It turned out anyway that Mother doesn't care for fishing, and also it was just a little bit cold and fresh out of doors, though it was lovely and sunny, and Father was rather afraid that Mother might take cold if she came.

He said he would never forgive himself if he dragged Mother round the country and let her take a severe cold at a time when she might be having a beautiful rest. He said it was our duty to try and let Mother get all the rest and quiet that she could, after all that she had done for all of us, and he said that that was principally* why he had fallen in with this idea of a fishing trip, so as to give Mother a little quiet. He said that young people seldom realize how much quiet means to people who are getting old. As to himself, he could still stand the racket,* but he was glad to shelter Mother from it.

principally: most importantly
racket: noise

So we all drove away with three cheers for Mother, and Mother stood and watched us from the verandah* for as long as she could see us, and Father waved his hand back to her every few minutes till he hit his hand on the back edge of the car, and then said that he didn't think that Mother could see us any longer.

verandah: balcony

Well, we had the loveliest day up among the hills that you could possibly imagine, and Father caught such big specimens that he felt sure that Mother couldn't have landed them anyway, if she had been fishing for them, and Will and I fished too, though we didn't get so many as Father, and the two girls met quite a lot of people that they knew as we drove along, and there were some young men friends of theirs that they met along the stream and talked to, and so we all had a splendid time.

It was quite late when we got back, nearly seven o'clock in the evening, but Mother had guessed that we would be late, so she had kept back the dinner so as to have it just nicely ready and hot for us. Only first she had to get towels and soap for Father and clean things for him to put on, because he always gets so messed up with fishing, and that kept Mother busy for a little while, that and helping the girls get ready.

But at last everything was ready, and we sat down to the grandest kind of dinner—roast turkey and all sorts of things like on Christmas Day. Mother had to get up and down a good bit during the meal fetching things back and forward, but at the end Father noticed it and said she simply mustn't do it, that he wanted her to spare herself, and he got up and fetched the walnuts over from the sideboard himself.

The dinner lasted a long while, and was great fun, and when it was over all of us wanted to help clear the things up and wash the dishes, only Mother said that she would really much rather do it, and so we let her, because we wanted just for once to humor* her.

humor: pamper

It was quite late when it was all over, and when we all kissed Mother before going to bed, she said it had been the most wonderful day in her life, and I think there were tears in her eyes. So we all felt awfully repaid for all that we had done.

About the Story

1. List at least five things that the family does or plans in order to make Mother's Day special.

2. How does Mother end up fitting into each of these plans?
3. At the end of the day, how do you think Mother feels about her "special day"?

About the Author

Although Stephen Leacock (1869-1944) was born in Hampshire, England, he is considered a Canadian author because his family moved to Canada when he was seven years old. With his typical humor he writes of this event: "My parents migrated to Canada in 1876, and I decided to go with them." Leacock spent eleven years on his father's farm in Ontario before going to Upper Canada College, and then on to the University of Toronto from which he graduated in 1891. He writes of the ignorance he felt when he graduated, saying that he was at that point "intellectually bankrupt."

After having taught for eight years, Leacock attended the University of Chicago where he studied economics and political science. In 1903 he completed his doctor of philosophy degree, of which he says: "The meaning of this degree is that the recipient of instruction is examined for the last time in his life, and is pronounced completely full."

Leacock spent a number of years as a professor of economics at McGill University in Montreal. It is, however, for his gentle humorous prose, such as that seen in "How We Kept Mother's Day," that he is best known. *Sunshine Sketches of a Little Town*, which is considered to be his best book, offended many of the residents of one small Ontario town. Apparently many of them found themselves too accurately described in Leacock's witty fashion, although he insists that the book is written about not one but many such small towns he visited.

One of Us

Margaret Curtis McKay

Families sometimes open their arms and hearts to let others less fortunate share their bounty. In "One of Us" the Matthews family takes in an orphaned English girl. But before she can become genuinely one of the family, both she and the Matthewses must make some adjustments. What is the secret Melissa learns that makes it possible for the title to become true for Elizabeth Maltby?

I was out by the lily pond, that July day, throwing peanuts to Flick when Billy came running up, calling, "Daddy is home and wants a conclave!"*

---
conclave: a family council

I jumped up at once. Flick, who is a chipmunk, vanished behind the old stump. It must be important if Daddy was home as early as this and calling a conclave before dinner.

My parents have queer ideas about many things. And one of the queerest—according to Aunt Melissa, for whom, alas, I was named—is their notion that their children should be consulted about anything that affects the family as a whole.

For instance, we had a conclave—which is what we call these consultations—before my parents decided to move from the city to where we live now in Brookside, a suburb of Washington. Mother pointed out that we would all have to get up earlier to be at school on time. . . . Billy, who was then only eight, was the only one who didn't want to move. The rest of us, Ralph, Frances and Louise, who are twins, and I, all thought the lovely yard with a lily pond and a tennis court more than made up for being so far from school. . . . That was two years ago, and now even Billy is glad that we came here.

Another important conclave was about Selassie, our black cat. Last year he got an infected foot. The veterinary said that Selassie must either be chloroformed* at once, or have his leg amputated. The amputation would cost twenty-five dollars. Daddy said we would all have to help pay for it, which meant giving up half our allowance for eight weeks. It meant no . . . ice-cream sodas after school. But, of course, we voted to have it done and Selassie got well. Having only three legs keeps him from catching birds. That makes us happy as well as the birds. And we pet him a lot to make it up to him, so perhaps the amputation was a blessing all around.

---

chloroformed: killed

I know I am too long getting to the main story, but I thought I had better explain these things so you will have an idea of the Matthews household at the time of the most important conclave we ever had. Just to give a "complete picture," as Miss Arner tells us in English composition, my brother Ralph is eighteen, my twin sisters, Fran and Lou, are sixteen, I am fourteen, and Billy is ten. Truth compels me to state that I am the ugly duckling of the family, though I'm afraid I shall never turn out to be a swan. I am small and colorless alongside Fran and Lou, who are pretty and sparkling.

Now I am really coming to that all-important conclave. As I went in through the kitchen, Donie, the maid we've had for years, was putting on a clean apron. If even Donie was to be in on this, it must be important indeed.

The long and the short of it was that my parents were thinking of taking a war refugee, a fifteen-year-old English girl who had recently landed at Halifax and was already on her way to Washington. A friend of Father's

had been going to take her, but his brother died suddenly and he thought he ought to help his nephews and nieces instead. So Father said he would consider taking her, but he would consult his family first.

We all shouted, "Let's take her! What fun!"

But my father raised his hand and said, "Wait, now. We must look at this proposition from every side." Then he told us that it would mean some sacrifice for each one of us. For one thing, the girl was penniless. Her parents had been killed. An aunt had got her out of England, along with her own children, who were to live in Canada with relatives. But these relatives had little money and less room. If we took the girl, we should each have to give up part of our allowance so she could have some spending money. She would have to share my bedroom. And we should have to consider her in all we did.

"Like another sister," exclaimed Billy and made a face. To Billy, sisters were not always an asset.* "I wish she was a boy," he added.

---

asset: a valuable item

It would mean more work for Donie and we couldn't afford to raise her wages. But I knew Donie would like to have another outlet in the family for the molasses cookies and apple dumplings that she so loves to make.

We had until the next day to think it over, and the next evening found us all firmly decided to take her. Mother passed us slips of paper for the voting.

"Before you write *yes* or *no*," she warned us, "each of you must be very sure. Remember, we know nothing whatever about the girl except that her name is Elizabeth Maltby, that she is fifteen years old, of good family, and hasn't a cent in the world."

I tried to think of a single reason why I wouldn't want the girl to come, and I couldn't find one. Neither could any of the others, so

the conclave broke up in considerable excitement.

Ralph said, "I'll give her my new tennis racket and teach her to play tennis. That will be a lot of fun for her."

"Maybe she knows how already—maybe she can beat you," retorted Billy. Ralph made a dive at him to chastise* him for such impudence;* Nippy, the fox terrier, started to bark; and there was a small riot, which Mother had to quell.*

---

chastise: punish
impudence: disrespect
quell: quiet

Billy went off shouting, "I'll teach her mumbly-peg! I'll bet no English girl ever heard of *that* game."

Fran and Lou said they would give a party for her. I went upstairs to look over my room. I began to clean out my bureau drawers and to plan which ones I would turn over to my new roommate.

That was on Tuesday. Elizabeth was to arrive in time for dinner Thursday evening. Thursday is Donie's day off, but she insisted on staying to cook what she called a "real welcome dinner" for the newcomer.

Even Mother was excited. I could tell by the way she kept picking up, then laying aside the sweater she is knitting for the Red Cross. We all wanted to go to the station to meet Elizabeth, but Mother said, no, Father was to go alone. It would be too overpowering to be met in a public place by such a bunch of wild Indians.

The only living creature not excited in our house that afternoon was Selassie. He hobbled to his favorite chair and, after giving himself a good washing, went to sleep.

It was hot and we had on our coolest clothing. Fran and Lou looked pretty in their white sharkskin, sunback dresses. Ralph had on his best white trousers. I knew he wanted to make an impression on Elizabeth because, instead of a sport shirt, he had put on a shirt with a stiff collar and tie, his best tie. Billy never can look anything but grubby, but he had tried to comb his hair, so that only half of it stood on end instead of all of it as usual. He kept racing with Nippy across the front lawn, peering down the road to see if they were coming.

"Shall we kiss her, Mother?" asked Fran.

"I shall kiss her," put in Lou. "She's to be our sister, isn't she? Well, we should make her feel right away that we love her."

"Well, dears," said Mother, "do what seems natural at the time, but remember, everything will be strange to her. I shall have to turn her over to you children for the next two weeks or so, as I've promised to go every day to the Red Cross. I know you will try to make Elizabeth happy."

"We will, Mother. Don't worry," we all chimed in.

A sudden shout came from Billy. "Here they come now!"

The car turned into the driveway. I shut my eyes and whispered to myself, When you open your eyes, Melissa Matthews, you will see—actually see—a refugee from war-torn England. I heard the car door bang and Father's voice. "Well, children, here she is—Elizabeth Maltby!"

Into my head at that minute flashed the images of Jane Eyre and Cathy and Elizabeth Bennett and little Nell and Florence Dombey. From the time I was six years old, Mother has read to us nearly every evening. She sometimes says I am the only one of her children who has the "gleam"—whatever that is. Perhaps she means that I never find those English stories long-winded and tiresome, as Fran and Lou and Ralph often do.

I love you, Elizabeth Maltby, no matter what, I said to myself. If for no other reason, just on account of all those girls in the books. I felt sort of solemn as if I had taken an oath. Then I opened my eyes.

I saw a thin, dark girl in a black dress and black straw hat. The dress was too long and the hat was queer. She wasn't pretty and she looked white and tired. Just as Fran and Lou and Ralph were crowding about her, Nippy suddenly leaped at her. It was his joyous way of welcoming her, but it startled her. She pushed him off, and for an instant I thought she was going to burst into tears. Instead, she drew herself up and said, "How do you do," stiffly, holding out her hand.

Lou did not kiss her. Something about her forbade it. We all shook hands, feeling suddenly awkward and tongue-tied.

Mother drew her gently toward the house, saying, "You must be awfully tired. Dinner won't be ready for half an hour, so you can have a little rest."

I wanted to go up with her to my room, but Mother waved me back.

Things would go better at dinner, I thought, but they didn't. Elizabeth talked very little,

and she hardly touched Donie's good fried chicken.

Billy burst out, "Don't you like it?"

She answered, "I'm not hungry."

After dinner, when Lou passed some fudge she had made, Elizabeth said, "No, thank you. I don't eat sweets."

The way she pronounced her words and the inflection she gave them sounded queer to us. For instance, *don't* sounded like *daon't,* and *no* like *nay-o.*

After dinner, the twins dragged her off to show her around the yard and I tagged along. We went past the tennis court and along the path above the brook to the deep place where the neighborhood children go swimming.

"We'll go swimming tomorrow morning," said Lou. "I'll lend you a bathing suit if you haven't one."

"Thank you," replied Elizabeth coolly, "but I don't like the water."

Fran put her arm around her. "OK, old dear, you don't have to. Say, do we have to call you Elizabeth? I like Betty as a nickname. May we call you that?"

"I think not. Only my best friends call me Betty."

It was almost as if she had slapped Fran, who took her arm from around Elizabeth's waist and began to talk to Lou about the tennis tournament. After that we sat out by the lily pond watching the fireflies as it grew dark, until I suggested to Elizabeth that we go to bed.

When she was ready for bed she picked up an armful of clothing she had unpacked and said, "Where shall I put these so the laundress will do them tomorrow?"

"Donie doesn't wash until Monday," I told her. "Tomorrow's Friday, and she will be off after breakfast. She stayed in today because you were coming."

"Well, maybe the cook will do them for me," she answered, not seeming to comprehend that Donie is all the cook we have.

I stared. "The cook? But Donie's it! She is our only maid and she does everything—except my father's shirts."

Elizabeth's mouth opened in astonishment. I hurried on, "If we want things done betweentimes, we do them ourselves. Fran and Lou and I always do our own underwear and stockings, anyway."

She said nothing, only dropped the clothes in the middle of the floor and got into bed. As I was already in bed, on the studio couch—I had given her my bed—I thought she might have turned off the light. However, I didn't say anything, but got up and switched it off myself. I was a long time getting to sleep that night. Just as I was dozing off, I thought I heard a smothered sob.

It was that sound which made me get up early next morning, gather up that pile of clothes, and slip down to the basement to wash them. I hung them out to dry just as the sun began to turn the drops of dew on the shrubbery into diamonds.

Elizabeth never inquired about the clothes, even when late in the day they appeared folded in a neat pile on her dressing table.

As we girls got dinner that evening, we tried to draw her into the fun. On Donie's day off, one of us always tries a new dish. It was my turn to act as chef this evening.

"Don't you want to help me?" I asked Elizabeth. "You could beat the eggs."

"I'll help you, of course," she replied with a kind of stiff politeness.

"Oh, never mind," I said hastily. "You'd better go out to the porch—it's cooler there."

"Very well, if you don't mind," she answered.

Well, that was that. I fought back angry tears of disappointment. How differently things were turning out from the way we had expected! And they went from bad to worse. She refused to come down to meet Fran's and Lou's friends on Saturday night. The twins were good and mad about that. They had talked about our refugee and everyone was dying to meet her. Ralph, too, had counted on showing her off to *his* friends, and she wouldn't even play tennis with him in our own yard.

Mother might have helped, if she hadn't been up to her ears in Red Cross work. As it was, we children struggled on, trying to be friendly and to get Elizabeth to do the things we did. Billy voiced our secret feelings one afternoon at the swimming pool when he said openly, "I don't like her. She is mean to Nippy and she acts as if I weren't there."

I remembered the solemn promise I had made to myself just before I saw her—to love her, no matter what, on account of the girls in England's books. And I tried my best. I gave her my bubble beads and my charm bracelet, but she never wore them. I ignored her silences and talked away, pretending she was interested. But she just walked off, leaving me to talk to the rose bushes, or the reading lamp, or whatever it was we happened to be near.

The only member of the family Elizabeth seemed not to dislike was Selassie. It was seeing her with him that made me think she did, after all, have an affectionate nature. Selassie had hobbled out to the lily pond and was sitting, gazing majestically down at the gold-fish darting about among the lily pads. I was stretched out with a book behind a clump of butterfly bushes, and Elizabeth didn't know I was there. She sat down beside Selassie and caught him up in her arms.

"Nice old pussy cat," she crooned. "Nice, poor, poor black pussy!" I could hardly believe my ears or my eyes, and then and there I made up my mind to win her. I knew she would never be happy unless she learned to like us.

Already, all of us had done everything we knew to make her happy. Ralph had taken her to the movies, tried to take her to a dance, tried to get her to play tennis; Fran and Lou had their friends in, and they had showered her with invitations to parties and badminton and what not; I had washed her stockings and underwear for her every day, and had given her my books and jewelry and tried to get her to go over to my best friend's house. (Sheila Evans is my best friend.) But she resisted every one of us. She seemed to prefer to mope about* alone. The consequence was, of course, that everyone began to dislike her and to show it, too. They couldn't help it. And Elizabeth grew whiter and thinner and more and more unhappy.

mope about: to be gloomy

One night, when she had been with us about three weeks, I woke up suddenly. I didn't know what woke me. I sat up in bed, feeling confused and frightened. The room was very still. I listened intently, wide awake now. Then I heard from downstairs the soft closing of a door.

I scrambled out of bed and crossed the room. Elizabeth's bed was empty. I ran to the window that looks out on the back yard.

It was one of those lovely, soft moonlit nights, the kind Shakespeare must have been thinking of when he wrote those lines we had to learn in school, beginning, "On such a night as this . . ." And then I saw Elizabeth glide across the yard like a ghost, and limping after her went Selassie, a small, misshapen shadow on the silvery brightness of the lawn.

I put on my slippers, grabbed my kimono,* and crept downstairs. Tiptoe, I followed Elizabeth into the garden. She was huddled on the bench under the big oak. Selassie was clutched tightly against her breast and she was sobbing—long, shuddering sobs.

kimono: a loose robe

I stood still behind her in the shadow, not knowing what to do. I had never seen anyone cry like that before and I felt frightened.

"I can't bear it, I can't bear it," she said over and over, and I knew she had no idea I was there.

As I watched her, "scales fell from my eyes" as the fairy books say, and I saw myself in Elizabeth's place, in a foreign country among strange people. I felt the loneliness, the strangeness. Forgetting everything else, I came and sat down beside her. "Elizabeth—oh Elizabeth, I know how you must feel," I said. Then I began to cry, too.

She gave a start. Selassie wriggled free and jumped down from her lap. I put my arms around Elizabeth and for a long time we cried together. Then, without saying a word, we got up and walked back to the house, holding hands. Before going upstairs we had some bread and milk. Still neither of us said a word, but before she got into bed she gave my hand a squeeze. She went to sleep before I did.

The next morning Elizabeth seemed so tired that Mother persuaded her to stay in bed. About the middle of the morning, I went out to my favorite seat by the lily pond. Ralph and the twins had gone on a picnic, and Billy and Nippy were off somewhere, so Selassie and I had the yard to ourselves.

The lily pond was very still under the oak trees. Even the goldfish were resting. Presently a frog leaped on a lily pad and gave a hollow *ga-lumph.* I did not move. Only part of my mind saw the frog and the pool and the trees. The rest of it was taken up with Elizabeth and the problem of making her happier. There must be some way. Flick, the chipmunk, frisked into sight from behind his stump. I had forgotten to bring peanuts and he seemed indignant. As I did not move, he grew bolder and came almost within reach of my hand. A nuthatch crept, upside down, on the trunk of a tree not three feet away.

Suddenly I saw what the trouble was. All the pieces of the puzzle I was trying to solve fell into a pattern. Of course. Of course. We had gone about it all wrong. In Elizabeth's loneliness, after the shock of losing her parents and leaving her own country, we must have been as terrifying to her as we were to Flick when he first came to our garden.

(Even now, when I want Flick to come out of his stump, I pay no attention to him, or if I call him I keep my distance and stay very still, tossing out the peanuts quietly and unobtrusively.* It's the same way with the frogs and the birds and the squirrels.)

unobtrusively: not readily noticeable

Then I had another idea, one that proved our way, well-meaning though it was, was all wrong. Which one of the family did Elizabeth seem to like the best—or, rather, dislike the least? Why, Selassie, the old cat. Selassie never forces himself on anyone. He keeps his distance and his dignity.

All that day I kept away from Elizabeth. She needed to sleep and to be left alone for a change. When Mother and Daddy came home, I took them out in the yard so Elizabeth couldn't hear me and there I told them my new idea.

"I believe you are right," Father exclaimed. "Tell the others when they come in and decide on a program among yourselves."

Mother patted my hand. "I think I'll let you young folks work out something alone. After all, I seem to be doing my part by keeping out of it—as I have been."

"But you'll call a conclave," I asked anxiously, "so the others will realize the importance of changing the—the treatment?"

"Yes, of course," agreed my parents.

The others were stunned at first at the idea that they could have been too friendly.

"What must we be," exclaimed Ralph "—little diplomats as if it was an international question?"

"Exactly," replied Father. "That is just what it is. We assumed it would be easy—that sheer friendliness was enough—and we expected gratitude. Well, just put yourselves in the place of these youngsters deprived suddenly of* everything they had always been used to, shoved into a totally strange environment. Melissa is right—we must stop overpowering the poor girl with attentions. How near could you get to Flick here, for instance, if you pummeled* him with peanuts?"

deprived suddenly of: taken suddenly away from
pummeled: beat

"We'd better drown Nippy then," muttered Ralph darkly. "No one can keep that dog from being overfriendly."

This made us laugh and we felt better. Then we began to plan our campaign. Fran suggested that if any member of the family thought another of us was making a blunder before Elizabeth, we would exclaim, "T.M.E.H." (I mean we would say the initials out loud—they stood for *To Make Elizabeth Happy.*) Billy pointed out that when you said them fast, they sounded something like "tummy ache." We had just about decided to adopt "tummy ache" as our slogan, when Ralph said that such a word would surely arouse Elizabeth's curiosity. So we finally decided just to rub our stomachs, as if we had a tummy ache. The program was to start immediately.

Next day Elizabeth was up and around, but I made no overtures, such as "Let's go here," or "Let's do this." I simply said "Good morning" pleasantly and went about my own affairs. The others did the same. Ralph played tennis with Bob Overton, with never a suggestion to Elizabeth to join them. Fran and Lou went off on some excursion of their own with a cheerful "See you all later." Ordinarily they would have begged Elizabeth to go along, and then acted mad when she refused.

By the end of the week the atmosphere seemed better. The sense of strain was gone. I thought Elizabeth looked happier. Often, instead of moping by herself, she would get a book and come of her own accord to the porch where some of us would be sitting. Ralph stopped leaping to his feet and offering her a chair. He began to treat her the way he does his sisters—which, if it isn't too polite, still isn't too bad. We even made Donie stop giving her an extra large glass of orange juice for breakfast. In short, we behaved as if she were one of us, instead of a guest to be petted, or a refugee to be pitied. She must have wondered about it. Sometimes I caught a puzzled look on her face.

One evening, toward the end of August, Father announced at dinner that he had an invitation from Mr. Newberry to bring his whole family on an all-day trip down the Potomac. Mr. Newberry has a forty-foot cabin cruiser, and we are always tickled to death when he asks us to take a trip with him.

"All in favor raise the right hand," went on Father.

Of course our hands shot up, all except Elizabeth's. Father noticed this and began, "Elizabeth, wouldn't you . . . ," when I started rubbing my stomach and groaning loudly.

Ralph burst out laughing. "Your youngest daughter seems to have a bad tummy ache," he said.

Daddy looked puzzled a moment, then he caught on. "Too bad," he murmured. "Hope it won't keep you home tomorrow, daughter. Raise the hands again, please," he repeated. "Everybody in the house is invited."

Suddenly I felt as if this were a test, and that it would show whether or not our new plan was working. If Elizabeth consented to go, I would know that the experiment was succeeding. But she did not raise her hand. She just sat there, a troubled frown between her dark eyebrows. It was as if she had scarcely heard

Father. She stared at me, but she didn't seem to see me.

Suddenly I felt a lump in my throat. I knew I was going to burst into tears. Nothing was of any use, we had failed. There was simply no bridging the gap between her life and ours. She did not like us and she never would. I jumped up from the table so suddenly that my chair overturned, but I didn't care. I rushed upstairs, threw myself on my bed, and buried my face in my pillow.

Presently I felt a soft, jarring movement at the foot of my bed. Selassie, I thought, must have been in the room and had jumped up to be near me, in that quiet way he has. I kept right on sobbing until I had cried all the tears I had. Then I opened my eyes and raised myself on one elbow. On the foot of my bed sat, not Selassie, but Elizabeth. She had been there all the time.

I stared at her and she stared back at me, clasping and unclasping her hands. "Is the pain very bad?" she asked.

"The pain?" I repeated.

"Your stomach ache. It must be dreadful. Oh, how I wish I could help you." She came closer and timidly patted my hand.

Finally I managed to say, "I haven't any pain. I was crying because you didn't want to go with us tomorrow."

Elizabeth gave a little gasp. "But I did want to go. I waited a minute to be sure your father meant to include me—and then you got that pain. And I wouldn't think of going without you, especially if you were sick. If ever you get sick, I am going to take care of you."

I sprang up from the bed. "Glory be!" I cried. Then I began. "Why, Elizabeth . . ."

She caught my hand, interrupting me. "Won't you call me Betty?" she said, taking my hand in both her own. "Please do!"

About the Story

1. Why has Elizabeth come to live with the Matthews family?
2. How do the Matthews children's lives change after Elizabeth comes?
3. Is Elizabeth's response to the family satisfying? Explain.
4. What do the Matthewses finally do that helps Elizabeth feel like one of the family?
5. What lesson about hospitality can be learned from this story?

The following three poems show a child's awakening to a new under-standing of a parent. What wisdom does each poem reveal?

Those Winter Sundays

Robert Hayden

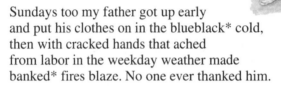

Sundays too my father got up early
and put his clothes on in the blueblack* cold,
then with cracked hands that ached
from labor in the weekday weather made
banked* fires blaze. No one ever thanked him.   5

blueblack: darkest part
   of the night

I'd wake and hear the cold splintering, breaking.
When the rooms were warm, he'd call,
and slowly I would rise and dress,
fearing the chronic* angers of that house,

banked: ash-covered

Speaking indifferently to him,   10
who had driven out the cold
and polished my good shoes as well.
What did I know, what did I know
of love's austere* and lonely offices?

chronic: always present

austere: simple;
   self-denying

About the Author

Born on August 4, 1913, in Detroit, Michigan, the black poet Robert E. Hayden is a university professor of English. He has edited several anthologies of black literature in addition to collections of his own poetry. Among his credits are several awards for his poetry, including the grand prize from the World Festival of Negro Arts in 1966 for *A Ballad of Remembrance*.

The Secret Heart

Robert P. Tristram Coffin

Across the years he could recall
His father one way best of all.

In the stillest hour of night
The boy awakened to a light.

Half in dreams, he saw his sire*　　　　5
With his great hands full of fire.

The man had struck a match to see
If his son slept peacefully.

He held his palms each side the spark
His love had kindled in the dark.　　　10

His two hands were curved apart
In the semblance* of a heart.

He wore, it seemed to his small son
A bare* heart on his hidden one.

A heart that gave out such a glow
No son awake could bear to know.

It showed a look upon a face
Too tender for the day to trace.

One instant, it lit all about,
And then the secret heart was out.

But it shone long enough for one
To know that hands held up the sun.

sire: father
semblance: shape
bare: exposed

The Courage That My Mother Had

Edna St. Vincent Millay

The courage that my mother had
Went with her, and is with her still:
Rock from New England quarried;
Now granite in a granite hill.

The golden brooch my mother wore   5
She left behind for me to wear;
I have no thing I treasure more:
Yet, it is something I could spare.

Oh, if instead she'd left to me
The thing she took into the grave!—   10
That courage like a rock, which she
Has no more need of, and I have.

About the Author

Known to her friends as "Vincent Millay," this writer began her career as a five-year-old child, encouraged by her mother. After winning a major poetry contest when she was nineteen, she had a volume of poetry published by the time she graduated from college. Leaving her childhood home of Maine, she made her way to New York to experience the theater world. Writing, acting, and living in Greenwich Village, she still continued her writing and won the Pulitzer Prize for poetry in 1923. Her lyric poetry is especially beautiful though affected by her recognition of the universal truth of death.

About the Poems

1. In the first two poems, each son is recounting some quiet action on the part of his father. What is the action in each?

2. Why do these fathers make the sacrifices that they make?

3. How is this action on the part of the father in "Those Winter Sundays" "austere and lonely"?
4. In Millay's poem, what qualities make the poet's comparison of courage to granite appropriate? What is the granite hill that the poet refers to in line 4?

5. How does the daughter feel about her mother's pin?
6. What is the reason that the speaker values her mother's courage more than the brooch?

Uncle Randolph's Buried Treasure

Dan Wickenden

> *Uncle Randolph is the kind of uncle any bored boy or girl would like to have. What buried treasure does the boy find on the island? What buried treasure lies within the uncle?*

One summer Charles went back to Seawater to put his grandmother's house in order before it was sold. He expected to feel depressed: the air smelled ancient and sterile,* the furniture looked ghostly under sheets furred* thick with dust, and the garden had fallen into a desolation* of weeds; but in the end he stayed an extra week, until the memory of his only other visit, and the brief sojourn* of Uncle Randolph, had become complete in his mind once more.

---

sterile: barren
furred: covered as though with fur
desolation: wasteland
sojourn: stay

It began with the picture of a small boy, himself at seven or eight, kneeling in the window of the upstairs hall with his nose pressed

to the glass. Rain fell outside; rain had been falling for days and the small boy was bored and unhappy. His grandmother was so very old that she found it difficult to believe he existed, except when he made a noise; his parents were thousands of miles away in a place called Europe, and it seemed improbable to him that they would ever return.

The small boy kneeled in the window for a long time, watching the rain, until at last he was diverted* by the appearance of a man who walked briskly under the wet trees across the road. He was a short stout man, carrying an umbrella and a suitcase, and he bounced a little as he walked: there was so much gaiety in his movement that Charles was irritated and made a face at him through the window.

---

diverted: distracted

Immediately the stout man halted and gazed across the street, angrily, Charles thought, drawing back from the window. He stood with his fists clenched in fear, and watched as the umbrella waved about uncertainly, made up its mind, and floated across the street with the stout man trotting beneath. The gate clicked, footsteps sounded on the flagged walk, in the depths of the house a bell jingled. Then there was a long silence, until Charles became more curious than frightened. He crept to the window, inched it up, and leaned out to discover what had happened.

At first he could see nothing but the rain and the dripping shrubbery, but suddenly the umbrella bobbed out backward and there the stout man was, staring up, with raindrops hitting his spectacles and draggling the long black ribbon attached to them. Charles clutched the curtain tight and almost pitched head foremost on top of him; at last, because he could think of nothing else to do, he made another face.

This gave the stout man pause; he continued to gaze up through the falling rain at Charles. Then he made a face at Charles.

Charles smiled, and the man smiled. He swept off his hat and bowed very low, with the umbrella wilting over his shoulder like a monstrous black flower.

That was Charles' first memory of his Uncle Randolph.

The next time he was sitting on the beach in the sun, building a sand castle and thinking even that wasn't much fun when there was no one around to admire it.

Presently his Uncle Randolph appeared, coming along jauntily* in his shiny black suit with the sun flashing on his glasses and the ribbon streaming in the breeze. Charles felt distrustful: his uncle had mostly ignored him since the first afternoon, but had talked incessantly* to the old lady, Charles' grandmother, and at intervals had uttered a high shrill laugh, snatching the glasses from his nose and waving them in the air, for no reason at all, so far as Charles could see.

---

jauntily: briskly
incessantly: unceasingly

Now he opened his eyes wide in admiration. "Well!" he said. "What a wonderful castle!"

Charles merely grunted.

"Would you mind very much if I helped?" Uncle Randolph asked.

Charles dug his fists into the sand. "All right," he said. "I guess you can if you want to."

The castle became enormous. It extended over the beach in all directions and the central tower was almost as tall as Charles. When it was finished they both sat back and looked at it dreamily, uttering sighs of pride and satisfaction. There had never been a sand castle like that before, and Charles thought a little sadly there would never be one like it again.

"I suppose you wonder why I've come here," Uncle Randolph said after a while, but he continued to gaze fondly at his handiwork.

Charles shook his head.

"To see your grandmother, of course. That's one reason. *But*," said Uncle Randolph explosively, with a noise like a cork popping from a bottle, "it isn't the only reason. Oh, dear me, no!" He chuckled; he took off his glasses and tapped with them on Charles' knee. "You're bored, aren't you?" he said.

Charles nodded.

"You shouldn't be," said Uncle Randolph, and beamed at him. "And do you know why? Because," he said, lowering his voice, "there's a buried treasure in the neighborhood. What do you think of that?"

Charles stared at him solemnly. "Where?" he whispered.

"Ah!" said Uncle Randolph, and set the glasses back on his nose. "That I don't know yet. But I mean to find out, Charles—with your assistance." He nodded his head rapidly.

"You mustn't tell your grandmother I said so, but one of your ancestors was a pirate, and he was the one who buried the treasure . . . Have you looked in the attic for anything like an old map? He must have left a map behind him. One day when your grandmother isn't around, we'll have to find it."

Charles wanted to start looking right away. He jumped up, but his uncle stretched out one hand warningly. "I must tell you," he said, "there is a certain amount of danger. Because, my dear Charles, some one else knows about this treasure. A thin, squinty-eyed individual by the name of Ginsberg, Emmanuel Ginsberg. Somehow he has come into possession of a duplicate map, and once let the news leak out that we're hunting for the treasure and he'll be there like a shot, with his squinting eyes, Charles, and a limp, a very slight limp, and, of course, the duplicate map. So you mustn't talk about it to anybody. If we're careful, Emmanuel Ginsberg will never know."

Uncle Randolph's Buried Treasure   477

Charles nodded.

"Emmanuel Ginsberg," said Uncle Randolph, as impressively as he could in his high voice, "is a villain of the deepest dye."*

of the deepest dye: of the worst kind

Charles was sure of it.

He could remember several days after that when he was afraid his uncle was never going to say anything more about the treasure; but Emmanuel Ginsberg, with his squinty eyes and the slight limp, walked through Charles' dreams, carting off the treasure while Uncle Randolph stood by, impotently* waving his glasses.

impotently: powerlessly

At last, however, on a still, hot afternoon when Charles' grandmother was visiting in the village and Lulu the cook was busy in the kitchen, Uncle Randolph plucked at his sleeve and drew him upstairs into the attic, locking the door behind him. They searched a long time in the thick warmth that smelled of shingles and camphor* and old clothes, until Charles was sure they would never find the map: there were so many trunks, and all the trunks were so large. But just as he was growing tired Uncle Randolph leaned past him, plunging his arm deep into a hatbox stuffed full of old letters, and said, "Look! Look, Charles! What's that?" From under the letters he pulled a piece of parchment and waved it in Charles' face. "Here we are!" he cried, and beamed at Charles in the twilight. Dust streaked his face and clung to the knees of his trousers; he looked hot and distracted,* but very happy. "Parchment," he said, gazing down at the map, "parchment, Charles, the real stuff." He jammed the glasses back on his nose and rolled the map into a tight wad. "I'll keep it in a safe place, and as soon as I've deciphered* it, we'll set out."

camphor: chemical used for protection from insects
distracted: bewildered
deciphered: interpreted

Charles did not sleep well that night; in the morning he woke much earlier than usual. When Uncle Randolph did not appear at the breakfast table and Lulu said he had gone out in a rowboat before the sun was up, Charles was really angry, and ran out of the house, down to the beach, to see where his uncle was. Obviously he must be looking for the treasure by himself.

He appeared presently, rowing hard, but Charles stood silent and accusing until he had beached the boat and jumped out. He was carrying a shovel, and when he saw Charles he looked guilty.

"You've been looking for the treasure," Charles said.

"Well," said Uncle Randolph, and tried to hide the shovel behind him, "yes and no, Charles, yes and no. I've hired a boat, you see, because I *suspect* that the treasure is buried on the island out there." He waved a hand at the small island that floated half a mile offshore; Charles gazed at it with a new appreciation. "I've been doing a little—a little preliminary* prospecting. I wanted to verify* a few points that came up last night when I was studying the map. But see for yourself!" He dropped the shovel, reached into his pocket, and unrolled the map on the sand. "See," he said, "here's a cove, here's a boulder, and *here* is the stump of an old pine tree. And fifty paces to the east, then twenty-five paces to the north, and you'll find yourself precisely above the spot where the treasure is." He put the map away again. "Doesn't it excite you, Charles? It's almost within our grasp."

preliminary: preparatory
verify: test the accuracy of

"And then we'll all be rich?" Charles asked.

His uncle stooped to pick up the shovel.

"Well—not *rich,* exactly. No, your ancestor was a pirate in a rather modest way. But!" he said explosively, "a buried treasure is a buried treasure, after all." He beamed at Charles. "His name, incidentally, was Roderick the Ruthless.* In his modest way he was a terror, my dear Charles, a terror. The Scourge* of Seawater, they sometimes called him."

Ruthless: merciless
Scourge: something causing great suffering

Charles expressed a wish to set out for the island immediately, but his uncle persuaded him to wait until the next morning. "We'll start early," he said, "and take a picnic lunch. Tomorrow morning, Charles, *if* the weather is fine."

They stole across the lawn under a sky that looked remote and pure; trees stood motionless and silence lay implacably* on the world as though nothing could break it. The scrunch* of their feet in wet sand was no disturbance in that enormous quiet; the bay stretched to the horizon without a ripple. Charles, in a state of

ecstasy* and terror, scrambled into the rowboat, where two shovels and a rusty pickaxe lay waiting. He had never been up so early before and he felt as though he must be still asleep and dreaming. The creak of rowlocks* and the faint lapping of water against the boat were comforting noises, but it was a long time before he dared to look back at the shore, and saw that nowhere on the wide expanse of sand was there a sign of Emmanuel Ginsberg.

implacably: not capable of being changed
scrunch: crunch
ecstasy: delight
rowlocks: device to hold the oars in place

By the time they reached the island the sun was well above the trees, but no sound came to them from the mainland, and the light remained clear and innocent: on such a day no squinting villain would dare limp forth, and Charles, while gazing at the island, began to forget Emmanuel Ginsberg.

They rowed on slowly, ten yards offshore, searching for the cove indicated on the map. But there were many coves and many boulders; from all aspects the island looked the same, a disappointing mound of sand and rocks, grown over thickly with scrub pine, beach plum, and bayberry bushes.

After they had been all the way round once, Uncle Randolph slipped the oars and mopped his face with a dirty handkerchief. "Would you like to row for a change, Charles?" he suggested. "Then I can keep a sharper lookout. We seem to have missed it the first time. But never mind," he said, patting Charles on the knee, "we'll find the right cove sooner or later."

Charles pulled hard on the oars; he was so pleased with his skill at rowing that he was almost disappointed when his uncle stood up suddenly and shouted out, "There it is, Charles! That's the one!"

They dragged the boat well up on the beach and hid the lunch basket under a bayberry bush,

Uncle Randolph's Buried Treasure 479

and then squatted side by side over the map. At last Uncle Randolph reached a decision; he walked straight back from the boulder with Charles trotting after him, pushing away the stiff-twigged branches, until, among the sand and pine needles and drifted leaves, he discovered the stump of what must have been a larger tree than any now growing on the island.

"This is it, this is it!" Uncle Randolph squeaked, and in his excitement stamped a heel down hard on the sand. He removed his glasses and wiped them, blinking his eyes solemnly at Charles. The sun was very hot, the pines were fragrant all about them, and the astonishing silence went on and on, so that it seemed necessary to talk in whispers. "Fifty paces due east from this spot," said Uncle Randolph, gazing about rather wildly, "and twenty-five paces to the north—" He stared at the sun, he consulted his watch. "A compass," he muttered, "now why didn't I think of a compass? . . . But it doesn't matter."

He swung about and thrust his way between the bushes, counting aloud and mopping his brow. Branches snapped into place behind him; the shiny black suit vanished, but Charles could hear the crashings and the rustlings still, and his uncle's voice counting breathlessly aloud: ". . . forty-eight, forty-nine, fifty! All right, Charles, come on . . . Now you stand *here,*" he said when Charles had found him, "and I'll pace off the rest." He seemed actually to be quivering; the glasses vibrated on his nose and he stared at the small boy with his eyes wide open and his brows raised. "Midnight," he called back over his shoulder, "it was midnight, Charles, when they buried the treasure, and his men stood in a ring with flaring pine knots held high over their heads; and within a year they were dead, every one of them. Dead! Only half of them left this island alive, that night, and the rest were murdered within the year. Oh, he was a cruel one, a ruthless one, but he's dust these hundred years, Charles, and he can't harm us now, or keep his treasure from us. Twenty-four, twenty-five," said Uncle Randolph. "Here's the spot, Charles. Run and get the shovels, will you, while I mark off a circle?"

Charles went quickly and in terror back to the place where they had left the boat. He did not like being alone in the hot silence; even under such a bright sun the ghosts of murdered pirates might rise and bar his way, and he could not be sure there was nothing malicious* in the way branches snapped in his face and scratched his knees.

---

malicious: desiring to cause pain

It was a great relief to see his uncle again. He had cleared the pine needles and the dead leaves and twigs away from a large circular patch of open ground, in the middle of which he now sat panting; for he had not removed his coat.

"Ah, here you are!" he said, and reached his hand for a shovel.

They began to dig immediately.

They dug for hours while the sunlight fell hotter and the pines smelled stronger; sand slid back into their excavation,* it seemed, as fast as they dug it out.

---

excavation: hole

In the end it was Charles' shovel that struck the chest first. At the sound of metal on wood he began to dig in a frenzy* and created a landslide which half filled the hole again. After that they both dug more carefully and at last the chest was uncovered completely, and they hauled it up.

---

frenzy: wild excitement

It was quite small but Charles hardly noticed that. He banged away at a padlock thick with rust and was glad that Uncle Randolph was now so exhausted by his labors that he could only stand, leaning on his shovel and watching through the glittering spectacles. Charles wanted all the final glory for himself.

The padlock broke off and the curved cover of the chest lifted easily. When he saw what was inside he could not speak for a moment. He turned around; he stared at his uncle.

"There's nothing in it!" he said. "It's just full of a lot of old sand." His voice shook; he discovered how hot he was, and how his arms and shoulders ached.

"Are you sure?" Uncle Randolph bent forward. "Dig down, Charles, dig down. That probably just drifted in through those cracks."

Charles thrust his hands into the sand and weariness was lifted from him; for they encountered several smaller boxes of copper or brass, and when he got them out into the sun they were as bright as they must have looked when Roderick the Ruthless stowed them away.

They were filled with jewels: ropes of pearls, rubies, diamonds, emeralds cascaded* flashing into the sunlight, and in one box were ancient coins, black with the years. And down at the bottom of the chest he found two daggers and a small scimitar,* also black, but covered with delicately-chased* designs.

---

cascaded: poured out
scimitar: Oriental saber with a curved blade
delicately-chased: finely engraved

He sat back, feeling quite numb. And then his joy grew too large and he began to cry.

That was almost the end of the episode; the rest was a little confused in his memory.

He was lying in his bedroom, many hours later, listening to the sound of angry voices: his grandmother and his uncle were quarreling about something, but his head ached so much he could not feel worried.

Then he wondered if the whole thing had not been a dream; perhaps Uncle Randolph himself had been only a dream. But when he sat up he saw the scimitar and the daggers, lying at the foot of his bed. He reached out and touched them: they felt cold and hard, as nothing in a dream could feel. Perched on the edge of the bed he laid these ancient weapons across his knees and tried to hear what the angry voices were saying. His head did not ache quite so much any more, and presently he became really curious.

But he had to go all the way downstairs into the lower hall, carrying the scimitar with him, before he could understand a word.

"What *harm* has been done, what *harm* has been done?" Uncle Randolph was squeaking. "A little sunburn, a little headache; he'll be all over that in the morning."

Uncle Randolph's Buried Treasure   481

Charles could hear his grandmother sniff, in the way she did when he made too much noise. "Filling the boy's head with a lot of nonsense about pirates and villains," she said. "No wonder he's been looking pale lately. If you'd ever had any children of your own, you'd have known how bad it was for him."

"Not as bad," cried Uncle Randolph, "as letting him die of boredom."

"And all this trash," said Charles' grandmother, "this ten-cent-store jewelry. What are we going to do with it, I'd like to know, how are we going to explain to him—"

Here Charles became enraged and burst into the room, clutching the scimitar against his chest. "It is *not* trash!" He glared at his grandmother, who tapped with her hand on the chair arm, and then stood up.

"Now, Charles," she said severely, "you must understand—"

"Don't listen to her!" Uncle Randolph piped, and waved his glasses in a frenzy. "You know just as well as I do that it was a real treasure, buried hundreds of years ago by Roderick the Ruthless. You believe that, don't you, Charles?"

Charles blinked; as he closed his eyes he had a vision of Emmanuel Ginsberg, who was certainly real.

"Yes," he said.

Uncle Randolph almost danced in his triumph.

"There!" he cried. "Look at that scimitar. There's nothing fake about that, I can tell you, *or* about those coins. He believes it was a real treasure, and so do I!" cried Uncle Randolph. "And so of course it was!"

In a trunk in the attic Charles found the scimitar; and among the papers in his grandmother's desk was a receipted* bill, yellow with age, from Emmanuel Ginsberg, dealer in

antiques. He smiled and put it away in his wallet, for it occurred to him that all those years ago Uncle Randolph, in his own curious way, had been telling the truth.

receipted: paid

About the Story

1. Why does Uncle Randolph help Charles with his sand castle?
2. What "secret" does Uncle Randolph tell Charles?
3. How does the thought of this buried treasure and the mission of finding it affect Charles?
4. What is the significance of the receipt Charles finds from Emmanuel Ginsberg's antique shop?
5. What clues throughout the story tell the reader that Uncle Randolph has made up the story for Charles's enjoyment?
6. What is the real treasure that is "found" during Uncle Randolph's stay?

About the Author

Born on March 24, 1913, in Tyrone, Pennsylvania, Dan Wickenden is an author who says he has always wanted to write. Successful with both short stories and novels, he has won many awards for his various works but calls "Uncle Randolph's Buried Treasure" his favorite story. In addition to freelance writing, he has worked as a newspaper reporter and publicity writer for CBS.

The Blanket

Floyd Dell

This story forces readers to consider two problems. The first is the way that society tends to treat old people. What attitudes are presented in this story? The second is the way in which the story ends. Who sets matters right? Or has nothing changed?

Petey hadn't really believed that Dad would be doing it—sending Granddad away. "Away" was what they were calling it. Not until now could he believe it of Dad.

But here was the blanket that Dad had that day bought for him, and in the morning he'd be going away. And this was the last evening they'd be having together. Dad was off seeing that girl he was to marry. He'd not be back till late, and they could sit up and talk.

It was a fine September night, with a silver moon riding high over the gully. They washed up the supper dishes and then took their chairs out onto the porch. "I'll get my fiddle," said the old man, "and play you some of the old tunes." But instead of the fiddle he brought out the blanket. It was a big, double blanket; red, with black stripes.

"Now, isn't that a fine blanket!" said the old man, smoothing it over his knees. "And isn't your father a kind man to be giving the old fellow a blanket like that to go away with? It cost something, it did—look at the wool of it! And warm it will be on cold winter nights. There'll be few blankets there the equal of this one!"

It was like Granddad to be saying that. He was trying to make it easier. He'd pretended all along that he wanted to go away to the great brick building—the government place. There he'd be with so many other old fellows having the best of everything. . . . But Petey hadn't believed Dad would really do it, until this night when he brought home the blanket.

"Oh, yes, it's a fine blanket," said Petey, and got up and went into the house. He wasn't the kind to cry, and besides, he was too old for that. He'd just come in to fetch Granddad's fiddle.

The blanket slid to the floor as the old man took the fiddle and stood up. It was the last night they'd be having together. There wasn't any need to say, "Play all the old tunes." Granddad tuned up for a minute, and then said, "This is one you'll like to remember."

The silver moon was high overhead, and there was a gentle breeze playing down the gully. He'd never be hearing Granddad play like this again. It was just as well Dad was moving into that new house, away from here. He'd not want to sit here on the old porch of a fine evening, with Granddad gone.

The tune changed. "Here's something gayer." Petey sat and stared out over the gully. Dad would marry that girl. Yes, that girl who'd kissed him and fussed over him, saying she'd try to be a good mother to him, and all. . . . His chair creaked as he gave his body a painful twist.

The tune stopped suddenly. Granddad said: "It's a poor tune, except to be dancing to." And then: "It's a fine girl your father's going to marry. He'll be feeling young again, with a pretty wife like that. And what would an old fellow like me be doing around their house, getting in the way? An old nuisance, what with my talk of aches and pains! And then there'll be babies coming, and I don't want to be there to hear them crying at all hours. It's best that I take myself off, like I'm doing. One more tune or two, and then we'll be going to sleep. I'll pack up my fine blanket in the morning, and take my leave. Listen to this, will you? It's a bit sad, but a fine tune for a night like this."

They didn't hear the two people coming down the gully path. Dad had one arm around the girl with the hard, bright face like a doll's. But they heard her when she laughed, right close by the porch. The tune stopped on a wrong note. Dad didn't say anything, but the girl came forward and spoke to Granddad prettily: "I won't be here when you leave in the morning, so I came over to say good-by."

"It's kind of you," said Granddad, with his eyes cast down. Then, seeing the blanket at his feet, he stooped to pick it up. "And will you look at this," he said in embarrassment, "the fine blanket my son has given me to go away with!"

"Yes," she said, "it's a fine blanket." She felt of the wool, and repeated in surprise, "A fine blanket—I'll say it is!" She turned to Dad and said to him coldly, "That blanket really cost something."

He cleared his throat and defended himself: "I wanted him to have the best. . . ."

The girl stood here, still intent on the blanket. "It's double, too," she said, as if accusing Dad.

"Yes," said Granddad, "it's double—a fine blanket for an old fellow to be going away with."

The boy went suddenly into the house. He was looking for something. He could hear that girl scolding Dad, and Dad becoming angry in his slow way. And now she was suddenly going away in a huff. . . . As Petey came out, she turned and called back, "All the same, he doesn't need a double blanket!" And she ran off up the gully path.

Dad was looking after her as if he weren't sure what he ought to do.

"Oh, she's right," said the boy coldly. "Here, Dad"—and he held out a pair of scissors. "Cut the blanket in two."

Both of them stared at the boy, startled. "Cut it in two, I tell you, Dad!" He cried out. "And keep the other half."

"That's not a bad idea," said Granddad gently. "I don't need so much of a blanket."

"Yes," said the boy harshly, "a single blanket's enough for an old man when he's sent away. We'll save the other half, Dad; it will come in handy later."

"Now, what do you mean by that?" asked Dad.

"I mean," said the boy slowly, "that I'll give it to you, Dad—when you're old and I'm sending you—away."

There was a silence. Then Dad went over to Granddad and stood before him, not speaking. But Granddad understood, for he put out a hand and laid it on Dad's shoulder. And he heard Granddad whisper, "It's all right, son—I knew you didn't mean it. . . ." And then Petey cried.

But it didn't matter—because they were all crying together.

About the Story

1. How does Petey feel about having Granddad leave?
2. How does his attitude about this differ from his father's attitude and the attitude of his father's girlfriend?
3. Over what do Petey's father and his girlfriend quarrel?
4. Is this the main conflict in the story? Explain.
5. How is the situation resolved?

About the Author

Floyd Dell (1887-1969) was born in Barry, Illinois. Poverty forced Dell to drop out of high school and go to work in a factory. In his adult years he lived in Greenwich Village, a section of New York known for its artists and writers. Unfortunately, most of the people who live there have adopted an unconventional lifestyle referred to as "bohemian." Along with joining others of this lifestyle, Dell also converted to socialism. In the midst of this, he wrote many one-act plays, short stories, and novels. In fact, he eventually became well known enough to become one of a prestigious group of poets called the "Chicago School." Among these authors was Carl Sandburg, one of the best loved of all American poets. In spite of his worldly lifestyle and misguided values, Dell did produce some worthwhile literature, among which is his story "The Blanket."

Mother's Hallowe'en Trick

Sherwood Anderson

In his autobiography, A Story-Teller's Story, *Sherwood Anderson relates this episode from his poverty-stricken boyhood in Ohio. Only the imaginative actions of his mother kept food on the family's table during the long winters. But is her resourcefulness a problem?*

During the fall of that year, after father had set out on his adventures as an actor, mother did something she had often done before. By a stroke of strategy she succeeded in getting a winter's supply of cabbages for her family, without the expenditure* of any monies.

---

expenditure: expense

The fall advanced, father had gone, and the annual village cut-up time, called among us "Hallowe'en," came on.

It was the custom among the lads of our town, particularly among those who lived on the farms near town, to make cabbages part of their celebration of the occasion. Such lads, living as they did in the country, had the use of horses and buggies, and on Hallowe'en they hitched up and drove off to town.

The country lads, giggling with anticipated pleasure, drove into one of the quieter residence streets of our town and, leaving the horse standing in the road, one of them got out of the buggy and took one of the cabbages in his hand. The cabbage had been pulled out of the ground with the great stalklike root still clinging to it and the lad now grasped this firmly. He crept toward one of the houses, preferably one that was dark—an indication that the people of the house, having spent a hard day at labor had already gone to bed. Approaching the house cautiously, he swung

the cabbage above his head, holding it by the long stalk, and then he let it go. The thing was to just hurl the cabbage full against the closed door of the house. It struck with a thunderous sound and the supposition* was that the people of the house would be startled and fairly lifted out of their beds by the hollow booming noise, produced when the head of cabbage landed against the door and, as a matter of fact, when a stout* country boy had hurled the cabbage the sound produced was something quite tremendous.

---

supposition: assumption
stout: strong

The cabbage having been thrown the country boy ran quickly into the road, leaped into his buggy and, striking his horse with the whip, drove triumphantly away. He was not likely to return unless pursued, and there it was that mother's strategy came into play.

On the great night she made us all sit quietly in the house. As soon as the evening meal was finished the lights were put out and we waited while mother stood just at the door, the knob in her hand. No doubt it must have seemed strange to the boys of our town that one so gentle and quiet as mother could be so infuriated* by the hurling of a cabbage at the door of our house.

---

infuriated: enraged

But there was the simple fact of the situation to tempt and darkness had no sooner settled down upon our quiet street than one of the lads appeared. It was worthwhile throwing cabbages at such a house. One was pursued, one was scolded, threats were hurled: "Don't you dare come back to this house! I'll have the town marshal after you, that's what I'll do! If I get my hands on one of you I'll give you a drubbing!" There was something of the actor in mother also.

What a night for the lads! Here was something worthwhile and all evening the game went on and on. The buggies were not driven to our house, but were stopped at the head of the street, and town boys went on pilgrimages to cabbage fields to get ammunition and join in the siege. Mother stormed, scolded and ran out into the darkness waving a broom while we children stayed indoors, enjoying the battle—and when the evening's sport was at an end, we all fell to and gathered in the spoils. As she returned from each sally* from the fort mother had brought into the house the last cabbage thrown—if she could find it; and now, late in the evening when our provident* tormentors were all gone, we children went forth with a lantern and got in the rest of our crop. Often as many as two or three hundred cabbages came our way and these were all care-

fully gathered in. They had been pulled from the ground, with all the heavy outer leaves still clinging to them, so that they were comparatively uninjured and, as there was also still attached to them the heavy stalklike root, they were in fine shape to be kept. A long trench was dug in our back yard and the cabbages buried, lying closely side by side, as I am told the dead are usually buried after a siege.

---

sally: assault
provident: providing for future needs

Perhaps indeed we were somewhat more careful with them than soldiers are with their dead after a battle. Were not the cabbages to be, for us, the givers of life? They were put into the trench carefully and tenderly with the heads downward and the stalks sticking up, mother supervising, and about each head straw was carefully packed—winding sheets.* One could get straw from a strawstack in a near-by field at night, any amount of it, and one did not pay or even bother to ask.

---

winding sheets: sheets for wrapping dead bodies

When winter came quickly, as it did after Hallowe'en, mother got small white beans from the grocery and salt pork from the butcher, and a thick soup, of which we never tired, was concocted.* The cabbages were something at our backs. They made us feel safe.

---

concocted: prepared

And there was also a sense of something achieved. In the land in which we lived one did not need to have a large income. There was food all about, plenty of it, and we who lived so precariously* in the land of plenty had, by our "mother's wit," achieved this store of food without working for it. A common sense of pride in our cleverness held us together.

---

precariously: insecurely

About the Story

1. What trick do the country boys typically play on the families in town each Hallowe'en?
2. Why is the storyteller's house a particularly favorite target for these tricksters?
3. What does the family do with the cabbages once the boys have thrown them?
4. Why is the title appropriate?

....About the Author

At the age of fourteen, Sherwood Anderson (1876-1941) began developing an interest in writing as he drifted from job to job and served in the Spanish-American War. Although he did settle down in Ohio for a while, marry, and become manager of a paint factory, he left everything to go to Chicago to pursue his writing career. Encouraged by such writers as Carl Sandburg and Floyd Dell (author of "The Blanket"), he published his first book in 1916. *A Story-Teller's Story,* published in 1924, is an autobiographical narrative describing Anderson's impoverished childhood and other experiences that influenced his creative pursuits to finally make him a "teller of tales."

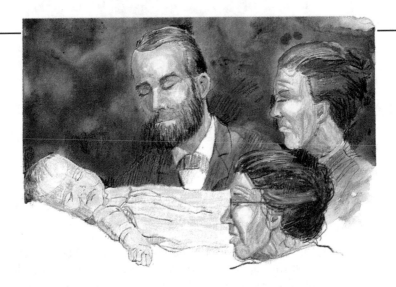

In the following selections, two families face a crisis involving the death of loved ones. The first selection is an incident from Rosalind Goforth's biography of her husband, Goforth of China. *The second selection, a poem, is like Goforth's biographical excerpt in its Christian perspective. Apart from this common perspective, however, each selection teaches several other significant truths. What are some of these truths?*

The Safest Place

Rosalind Goforth

A few days after my husband arrived, we were all once again on a houseboat with everything ready for the three weeks' return journey upstream. I could see Jonathan was just waiting for the opportunity to lay something important before me. Indeed he was simply bubbling over with eagerness. Then it came out. In brief it was as follows:

The personnel of our old Changte station was entirely changed. Two married couples and two single women from Chuwang (a station not to be reopened), had been added to the staff. The whole Changte region had been divided into three distinct fields, the part allot-ted to Mr. Goforth being the great region northeast to northwest of the city, with its many towns and almost countless villages. With great enthusiasm my husband laid bare his plans for the evangelization of this field.

"My plan," he said, "is to have one of my helpers rent a suitable place in a large centre for us to live in, and that we, as a family, stay a month in the centre, during which time we will carry on intensive evangelism. I will go with my men to villages or on the street in the daytime, while you receive and preach to the women in the courtyard. The evenings will be given to a joint meeting with you at the organ and with plenty of gospel hymns. Then at the end of the month, we will leave an evangelist behind to teach the new believers while we go on to another place to open it in the same way. When a number of places are opened, we will return once or twice a year."

Yes, it was a very wonderfully thought-out plan and should be carried out *if there were no children in the question!*

As I listened, my heart went like lead! The vision of those women with their smallpox children at Hopei, crowding about me and the baby, the constant danger to the children from all kinds of infectious diseases that life would mean, (for the Chinese cared nothing of bringing infection to others), and the thought of our four little graves—all combined to make me set my face as adamant* against the plan. My one and only reason, however, in opposing and refusing to go with my children, as my husband suggested, was because it seemed a risking of the children's lives.

---

adamant: stubbornly unyielding

Oh, how my husband pleaded! Day by day in the quiet stillness of that long river journey, he assured me that the Lord would keep my children from harm. He was *sure* the Lord would keep them. He was *sure* God was calling me to take this step of faith. Then as we drew near the journey's end, he went further. He said:

"Rose, I am so sure this plan is of God, that I fear for the children if you refuse to obey His call. *The safest place for you and the children is the path of duty.* You think you can keep your children safe in your comfortable home at Changte, but God may have to show you you cannot. But He can and will keep the children if you trust Him and step out in faith!"

Time proved he was right, but, as yet, I had not the faith nor the vision nor the courage to regard it in that light. . . .

We reached our Changte home on a Saturday evening. Sunday morning I left the children with the faithful nurse, Mrs. Cheng, who had saved little Ruth from the Boxers' blows. They all seemed perfectly well. Two hours later I returned to be met by Mrs. Cheng saying, "Wallace is ill." The doctor was called who pronounced it "one of the worst cases of Asiatic dysentery he had come across."

For two weeks we literally fought for the child's life during which time my husband whispered to me gently, "O Rose, give in, before it is too late!" But I only thought him hard and cruel, and refused. Then, when Wallace began to recover, my husband packed up and left on a tour *alone*.

The day after he left, my precious baby Constance, almost one year old, was taken ill suddenly, as Wallace had been, only much worse. From the first, the doctors gave practically no hope. The father was sent for. Constance was dying when he arrived. We had laid her on a cot in the middle of my husband's study. Our faithful friend, Miss Pyke, knelt on one side. My husband knelt next to Constance and I beside him. The little one was quietly passing, all was still, when suddenly I seemed to apprehend in a strange and utterly new way the *love* of God—as a *Father*. I seemed to see all at once, as in a flash, that *my Heavenly Father could be trusted to keep my children!* This all came so overwhelmingly upon me, I could only bow my head and say, "O God, it is too late for Constance, but I will trust you. I will go where you want me to go. But keep my children!"

Oh, the joy that came and peace—so when my husband turned to me saying, "Constance is gone"—I was ready and comforted, knowing that her life had not been in vain. Our little

Constance's remains were laid beside her two sister's graves on her birthday October 13, 1902.

The evening our little one passed away I sent for a Mrs. Wang, whom I had come to love and honour for her fine Christian character and her outstanding gifts. When she came I said, "Mrs. Wang, I cannot tell you all now but I have decided to join forces with my husband and am going with him in opening up work outside. Will you come with me?"

The tears sprang to her eyes as she replied, "Oh, I cannot. I have a child and to take her

into all kinds of conditions outside would be too risky."

Thinking it best not to urge her I said, "Go home and pray about it and tomorrow after the funeral come and tell me what you decide."

The next evening as she entered, though her eyes were overflowing, she said with a joyous smile, "I'm coming with you." For years while carrying on the work, . . . we two worked, prayed, and wept together for our Chinese sisters in the region north of Changte. From this time on, the following lines by Whittier had new significance:

And as the path of duty is made plain
May grace be given that I may walk therein.
Not like the hireling for his selfish gain,
Making a merit of his coward dread,
With backward glances and reluctant tread,
But cheerful in the Light around me thrown
Walking as if to pleasant pastures Led
Doing God's will as if it were my own,
Yet trusting not in mine, but in His strength alone.

Death

Verna K. Peterson

each morning
as I fixed our family's breakfast
I would see them
(our kitchen windows met across
the way)
a woman, gentle-faced and sweet
laying out the morning things
and he, sitting at the table,
would take the family Bible out
smoothing its pages—
for forty years, or more
they plied this self-same ritual
starting the day
together
and with God

and then one night
quickly
death called
and she was gone

the next morning
I watched
as tears stood in my eyes
an old man
his shoulders hunched against the years
take down his cup and saucer
smooth the family Bible out
sitting at the table
alone . . .
and with God

About the Story and Poem

1. Why is Mrs. Goforth reluctant to go along with her husband's plan for evangelizing Changte?
2. What reveals God's graciousness to Mrs. Goforth?
3. What does the author mean when she says "[Constance's] life had not been in vain"? What Bible verses are taught through this selection?
4. What practice of the couple was observed by the speaker of the poem?
5. What does the old man do the next morning after the death of his wife? What does this reveal about him?

Happy the Home
When God Is There

Henry Ware, the Younger

Happy the home when God is there,
And love fills every breast;
When one their wish, and one their prayer,
And one their heav'nly rest.

Happy the home where Jesus' name
Is sweet to every ear;
Where children early lisp His fame,
And parents hold Him dear.

Happy the home where prayer is heard,
And praise is wont to rise;
Where parents love the sacred Word,
And all its wisdom prize.

Lord, let us in our homes agree
This blessed peace to gain;
Unite our hearts in love to Thee,
And love to all will reign.

The Bible and Family

Now these are the commandments, the statutes, and the judgments, which the Lord your God commanded to teach you, that ye might do them in the land whither ye go to possess it: That thou mightest fear the Lord thy God, to keep all his statutes and his commandments, which I command thee, thou, and thy son, and thy son's son, all the days of thy life; and that thy days may be prolonged.

And thou shalt love the Lord thy God with all thine heart, and with all thy soul, and with all thy might. And these words, which I command thee this day, shall be in thine heart: And thou shalt teach them diligently unto thy children, and shalt talk of them when thou sittest in thine house, and when thou walkest by the way, and when thou liest down, and when thou risest up.

And thou shalt bind them for a sign upon thine hand, and they shall be as frontlets between thine eyes. And thou shalt write them upon the posts of thy house, and on thy gates.

The fear of the Lord is the beginning of knowledge: but fools despise wisdom and instruction.

My son, hear the instruction of thy father, and forsake not the law of thy mother: For they shall be an ornament of grace unto thy head, and chains about thy neck. Train up a child in the way he should go: and when he is old, he will not depart from it.

Children, obey your parents in the Lord: for this is right. Honour thy father and mother; which is the first commandment with promise; That it may be well with thee, and thou mayest live long on the earth.

And, ye fathers, provoke not your children to wrath: but bring them up in the nurture and admonition of the Lord. (Deuteronomy 6:1-2; 5-9; Proverbs 1:7-9; 22:6; Ephesians 6:1-4)

Glossary of Literary Terms

allusion: A reference within a work of literature to something outside it. When an author uses an allusion, he assumes that the reader has knowledge of the thing, person, or event of which he is writing.

analogy: An extended comparison that is used to explain or to persuade.

autobiography: A work written by an author about himself.

character: Representations of persons in literature. The chief or main character is known as the **protagonist,** whereas his opponent is the **antagonist.**

cinquain: A stanza with five lines.

climax/crisis: A point of suspense in the story at which the main character makes a decision that changes the course of the remainder of the story.

conflict: The heart of plot; conflict may be external (between characters or between a character and his environment, whether society or nature) or internal (between a character's emotions or duties or both).

couplet: A pair of rhymed lines.

dialogue: A conversation between characters.

dynamic character: A character who changes as the story progresses.

episode: A single incident in a work of fiction.

falling action: The element of the plot immediately following the climax; it unfolds the results of the decision made at the climax.

figurative language: An artful deviation from the usual way of saying things.

flashback: Going back in time to an incident that occurred earlier in order to shed light on a character's words, actions, or situation.

foil: A contrasting character used to emphasize another character's attitude or appearance (e.g., Cinderella and her stepsisters).

foreshadowing: The technique of doling out significant bits of information that will prepare the reader for future events.

frame story: A story within a story; a preliminary narrative within which one or more of the characters proceed to tell a story.

genre: A type or category of literature; examples of genre include novel, short story, poetry, historical fiction, and essay.

haiku: A seventeen-syllable poem about nature, composed of three lines of five, seven, and five syllables.

historical fiction: A story set in an authentic historical setting but in which the main characters are fictitious.

imagery: The use of words or phrases that convey an impression appealing to one or more of the five senses (hearing, sight, smell, touch, and taste).

imaginative comparison: A broad term that encompasses such figures of thought as metaphor, simile, and personification.

inciting moment: The point at which the conflict is introduced into a story or novel.

irony: The use of language to convey meaning other than what is stated. The reader usually knows more than the characters in the story. An example is our knowledge that Delilah had allied herself with the Philistines and had set a snare for Samson.

legend: A narrative that is handed down from the past and is generally believed to have at least some historical validity.

metaphor: The stated or implied equivalence of two things (e.g., "I am the bread of life").

meter: The regular arrangement of stressed and unstressed syllables in a poem.

narrative poem: A poem that tells a story.

onomatopoeia: The use of words that sound like what they mean (e.g., *hiss, buzz*).

parable: An extended illustration of a spiritual truth using everyday experiences and characters.

persona: The speaker or voice in a literary work.

personification: Giving human characteristics to something that is not human.

plot: A series of events arranged to produce a definite sense of movement toward a specific goal.

resolution: The final outcome of a story.

rising action: The events that follow the inciting moment and lead up to the crisis in a story.

rhyme scheme: The pattern of rhyme sounds in a poem or in a stanza of poetry.

setting: The time and place in which a narrative takes place.

simile: A stated comparison of two things using a linking word or phrase (e.g., *like, as, as if*: "My love is like a red, red rose").

static character: Describes one who remains essentially the same throughout the story.

style: The manner of expression in prose or verse, in written or oral discourse.

surprise: The violation of the reader's expectations.

suspense: The anticipation created in the reader because of the author's withholding information about the nature or outcome of a situation while raising the reader's curiosity or anxiety.

symbol: An object that stands for something else as well as for itself.

theme: A recurring or emerging idea in a work of literature. A theme may be **explicit** (a moral stated by a character or by the author in his own voice) or **implicit** (a conception that must be inferred).

tone: The attitude of a work toward its subject.

viewpoint: The point of view from which an author tells his story. In the **omniscient viewpoint,** the author tells his story in the third person, and as the storyteller, he "knows all." In the **limited omniscient viewpoint,** the author also tells the story in the third person but "gets inside" only one of his characters. In the **first-person viewpoint,** the author *becomes* one of the characters, sometimes a minor character but most often a major character.

Index

Illustrators

'Twas a Dark and Dreary Night Vince Barnhart

Run, Boy, Run! Jim Harris, Tim Banks

The Most Important Day John Bjerk

Betsy Dowdy's Ride Del Thompson, Tim Banks

The Friend Inside Del Thompson, Tim Banks

Yes, Your Honesty Jim Harris, John Bjerk

Rikki-Tikki-Tavi Tim Davis, Vince Barnhart

A Kind of Murder Stephanie True, Tim Banks

Edith Cavell Johanna Berg

Whether By Life or By Death Del Thompson, Vince Barnhart

Spikenard Very Precious Del Thompson, Vince Barnhart

Catalogue Vince Barnhart

The Mahogany Fox Stephanie True, Vince Barnhart

Wild Blackberries Roger Bruckner

The Life and Death of a Western Gladiator Tim Davis, Vince Barnhart

The King's Provider Vince Barnhart

Snapshot of a Dog Bob Martin

The Attack John Roberts

Castaways John Roberts

Old Sly Eye Tim Banks

The Windmill Tim Banks

A Hillside Thaw John Bjerk

The Raven and the Swan Tim Banks

The Swallow's Advice Scotty Pruitt

The Farmer and the Stork Tim Banks

Koyo, the Singer Tim Davis, John Bjerk

Mr. Payne's Investment Stephanie True, John Nolan

Stopover in Querétaro Johanna Berg

Martin and Abraham Lincoln Tim Banks

The Buffalo Dance Del Thompson, John Bjerk

The Two Strangers Stephanie True, Steve Christopher, John Bjerk

Most Valuable Player Tim Davis, John Bjerk

The Last Leaf Johanna Berg

Mary Johanna Berg

Gold-Mounted Guns Kathy Pflug

A Poison Tree Jim Hargis, John Nolan

The Strangers That Came to Town Del Thompson, John Bjerk

Preacher's Kids Del Thompson, John Bjerk

We Give Thee But Thine Own Jim Hargis, John Bjerk

The Great Cherokee Bill Tim Davis, Tim Banks

Billy, He's in Trouble Mary Ann Lumm

To Save the Golden State Kathy Pflug

Guard It with Your Life Kathy Pflug

Monty Takes Charge of the Barter Store Stephanie True, John Bjerk

The Wright Brothers Vince Barnhart

The Day's Demand Del Thompson, John Bjerk

Charlie Coulson: Drummer Boy John Roberts

All Yankees Are Liars Stephanie True, John Bjerk

Casey at the Bat John Bjerk

Being a Public Character Dana Thompson, John Bjerk

Mr. K*A*P*L*A*N Del Thompson, John Bjerk

How Beautiful with Mud Paula Cheadle

Three Visitors in the Night Tim Davis, John Bjerk

The Crucifixion Johanna Berg

The Fool's Prayer John Bjerk

The Soloist Johanna Berg

Alas! Poor Annabelle! Tim Davis, John Bjerk

Father Speaks Tim Davis, John Bjerk

The Split Cherry Tree Bob Reynolds

Speed Adjustments Tim Davis, John Nolan

Hit and Run Jim Harris, Tim Banks

Old Yeller and the Bear Del Thompson, Vince Barnhart

Mister Chairman Paula Cheadle

Sioux Trouble Stephanie True, John Bjerk

Love Story, Sort Of Del Thompson, John Bjerk

How We Kept Mother's Day Stephanie True, Paula Cheadle

One of Us Mike Kuechenmeister

Those Winter Sundays Jim Hargis, John Bjerk
The Secret Heart Mary Ann Lumm
The Courage That My Mother Had Tim Banks
Uncle Randolph's Buried Treasure
　　Stephanie True, Johanna Berg
The Blanket John Bjerk

Mother's Hallowe'en Trick Johanna Berg
The Safest Place Dick Sheets
Death Mary Ann Lumm
Happy the Home When God Is There
　　Mary Ann Lumm

Photograph Credits